W9-BIH-706

Essentials of
Children's Literature

Essentials of Children's Literature

Carol Lynch-Brown
Florida State University

Carl M. Tomlinson
Northern Illinois University

Allyn and Bacon
Boston • London • Toronto • Sydney • Tokyo • Singapore

Series Editor: Virginia C. Lanigan
Series Editorial Assistant: Nicole DePalma
Production Administrator: Annette Joseph
Production Coordinator: Holly Crawford
Editorial-Production Service: Lynda Griffiths, TKM Productions
Cover Administrator: Linda K. Dickinson
Cover Designer: Suzanne Harbison
Manufacturing Buyer: Mary Beth Lynch

Copyright © 1993 by Allyn and Bacon
A Division of Simon & Schuster, Inc.
160 Gould Street
Needham Heights, MA 02194

This book is printed on
recycled, acid-free paper.

Library of Congress Cataloging-in-Publication Data

Lynch-Brown, Carol
    Essentials of children's literature / by Carol
Lynch-Brown and Carl M. Tomlinson.
      p.   cm.
    Includes bibliographical references and index.
    ISBN 0–205–13937–X
    1. Children's literature--Study and teaching (Higher)
2. Children's literature--History and criticism.   3. Children and
literature.   4. Children's literature--Bibliography.   I. Tomlinson,
Carl M. II. Title.
PN1009.A1L96   1992
809'.89282'0711--dc20   92–28378
                                      CIP

Printed in the United States of America
10 9 8 7 6 5 4 3 2 1   97 96 95 94 93 92

Acknowledgments are listed on page 332, which constitutes a continuation of the copyright page.

To my sons, Matthew, Alexander, and Garth Brown (C. L.-B.)

To the students in my children's literature
and language arts classes (C. M. T.)

Brief Contents

PART ONE   *Children and Literature*

1   **Learning about Children and Their Literature**   1

2   **Learning about Books**   20

PART TWO   *Categories of Literature*

3   **Poetry**   36

4   **Picture Books**   54

5   **Traditional Literature**   87

6   **Modern Fantasy**   103

7   **Realistic Fiction**   120

8   **Historical Fiction**   137

9   **Nonfiction**   151

10   **Multicultural and International Literature**   171

PART THREE   *Literature in the School*

11   **Planning the Literature Curriculum**   205

12   **Developing Teaching Strategies**   232

Contents

Preface   **xv**

PART ONE   *Children and Literature*

1   **Learning about Children and Their Literature**   **1**
Definition of Children's Literature   *1*
   Content   2
   Quality   2
The Personal Value of Literature to Children   *3*
The Academic Value of Literature to Children   *4*
   Reading   4
   Writing   6
   Content Area Subjects   6
   Art Appreciation   6
The Transactional View of Reading and Response to
   Literature   *7*
Choosing Books for Children   *7*
   Know the Child   8
   Know the Books   8
   Consider the Level of Difficulty   8
Reliable Sources for Book Titles   *9*
Research in Children's Literature   *11*
Children's Reading Preferences   *11*
Children's Reading Interests   *12*
Child Development   *14*
   Physical Development   14
   Mental Development   15
Books for Different Age Levels   *15*
   Ages 0 to 2   15
   Ages 2 to 4   16
   Ages 4 to 7   16
   Ages 7 to 9   17
   Ages 9 to 12   17
References   *18*

2   **Learning about Books**   **20**
Elements of Fiction   *21*
   Plot   21
   Characters   23
   Setting   25

Theme   25
Style   26
Visual Elements   *27*
Line   28
Color   28
Shape   28
Texture   29
Composition   29
Artistic Styles   *29*
Artistic Media   *30*
Book Format   *31*
Balance and Variety in Book Selections   *33*
Categories of Literature   *34*
Reference   *35*

PART TWO   *Categories of Literature*

3   Poetry   36
Definition and Description   *36*
Elements of Poetry   *38*
Values of Poetry for Children   *40*
Evaluation and Selection of Poetry   *41*
Historical Overview of Poetry   *41*
Poetry Types and Forms   *43*
Children's Poetry Preferences   *48*
References   *48*
Notable Poets   *49*
Recommended Poetry Books   *50*

4   Picture Books   54
Definition and Description   *54*
Values of Picture Books   *55*
Evaluation and Selection of Picture Books   *56*
Historical Overview of Picture Books   *57*
Types of Picture Books   *58*
Baby Books   60
Interactive Books   60
Toy Books   61
Mother Goose and Nursery Rhyme Books   61
Nursery and Folk Song Books   61
Alphabet Books   62

Counting Books   62
Concept Books   62
Wordless Books   63
Picture Storybooks   63
Easy-to-Read Books   64
Picture Books for Older Readers   64
Transitional Books   64
Notable Authors and Illustrators of Picture Books   *65*
Recommended Picture Books   *67*

5   Traditional Literature   87
Definition and Description   *87*
Values of Traditional Literature for Children   *88*
Evaluation and Selection of Traditional Literature   *90*
Historical Overview of Traditional Literature   *91*
Types of Traditional Literature   *92*
Myths   93
Epics and Ballads   93
Legends and Tall Tales   93
Folktales   94
Fables   95
Religious Stories   95
Modern Folktales   96
Notable Retellers, Collectors, and Illustrators of Traditional
   Literature   *96*
Recommended Traditional Literature   *97*

6   Modern Fantasy   103
Definition and Description   *103*
Values of Modern Fantasy for Children   *104*
Evaluation and Selection of Modern Fantasy   *105*
Historical Overview of Modern Fantasy   *105*
Types of Modern Fantasy   *108*
Modern Folktales   109
Animal Fantasy   109
Personified Toys and Objects   110
Unusual Characters and Strange Situations   110
Worlds of Little People   111
Supernatural Events and Mystery Fantasy   111
Historical Fantasy   111
Quest Stories   112
Science Fiction and Science Fantasy   112
References   *113*

Notable Authors of Modern Fantasy   *113*
Recommended Modern Fantasy Books   *114*

7   **Realistic Fiction**   **120**
Definition and Description   *121*
Values of Realistic Fiction for Children   *122*
Evaluation and Selection of Realistic Fiction   *123*
Historical Overview of Realistic Fiction   *124*
Types of Realistic Fiction   *127*
   Family Situations   127
   Peer Relationships   128
   Growth and Maturity   128
   Acceptance of Cultural Differences   129
   Popular Topics in Realistic Fiction   129
References   *130*
Notable Authors of Realistic Fiction   *131*
Recommended Realistic Fiction Books   *132*

8   **Historical Fiction**   **137**
Definition and Description   *137*
Values of Historical Fiction for Children   *138*
Evaluation and Selection of Historical Fiction   *139*
Early Books and Trends in Historical Fiction   *140*
Topics in Historical Fiction   *141*
   Themes in Historical Fiction   141
   Periods of History in Fiction   143
Reference   *145*
Notable Authors of Historical Fiction   *146*
Recommended Historical Fiction Books   *146*

9   **Nonfiction**   **151**
Definition and Description   *152*
Values of Nonfiction for Children   *153*
Evaluation and Selection of Nonfiction   *154*
Historical Overview of Nonfiction   *157*
Topics of Nonfiction   *159*
   The Biological Sciences   160
   The Physical Sciences   160
   The Social Sciences   160
   The Applied Sciences   160
   The Humanities   161
   Biography   161
References   *163*

Notable Authors of Nonfiction   *163*
Recommended Nonfiction Books   *164*

10 Multicultural and International Literature   171
SECTION ONE: MULTICULTURAL LITERATURE   172
Definition and Description   172
Values of Multicultural Literature for Children   172
Evaluation and Selection of Multicultural Literature   173
Historical Overview of Multicultural Literature   175
Types of Multicultural Literature   178
    African-American Literature   178
    Asian-American Literature   179
    Hispanic-American Literature   180
    Jewish-American Literature   180
    Native-American Literature   181
SECTION TWO: INTERNATIONAL LITERATURE   181
Definition and Description   181
Values of International Literature for Children   182
Evaluation and Selection of International Literature   182
Historical Overview of International Literature   185
International Books by World Regions   188
References   189
*Notable Authors and Illustrators of Multicultural
    Literature   189*
*Notable Authors, Illustrators, and Translators of International
    Literature   191*
Recommended Multicultural Books   192
Recommended International Books   198

PART THREE   *Literature in the School*

11 Planning the Literature Curriculum   205
Curriculum Models in Literacy   205
    Literature-Based Reading   206
    Basal Reading Program Supplemented by Children's
        Literature   207
    Integrated Day and Thematic Learning   209
Organization of Curriculum   211
    Theme or Topic   211
    Author or Illustrator   212
    Genre   212
    Literary Element   213

Developing the Literature Curriculum *213*
  Designing a Classroom Reading Environment 213
  Building a Classroom Library Collection 216
  Outlining a Year-Long Curriculum 217
  Fleshing Out the Units of Study 220
  Implementing a Schoolwide Curriculum in
    Literature 223
Evaluating the Literature Program *227*
References *231*

12 Developing Teaching Strategies **232**
Experiencing Literature *232*
  Reading Aloud by Teachers 233
  Silent Reading by Students 238
  Booktalks 239
  Shared Reading 240
  Storytelling 242
  Choral Poetry 243
  Audiotapes and Videotapes 244
Responding to Literature *244*
  Oral Response 245
  Written Response 251
  Graphic Arts Response 253
References *257*

Appendix A **Children's Book Awards** **259**

Appendix B **Holiday Books** **289**

Appendix C **Predictable Books** **293**

Appendix D **Transitional Books** **295**

Appendix E **Short Read-Alouds for Intermediate and
Middle-Level Grades** **299**

Appendix F **Children's Magazines** **303**

Appendix G **Professional Resources** **307**

Index **325**

Preface

Essentials of Children's Literature is a straightforward presentation on literature and sharing literature with children. In planning for and teaching our undergraduate children's literature courses, we have become aware of the need for a concise, paperback text written especially for the undergraduate audience and tailored to the purposes of beginning survey courses.

This book is the product of a full collaboration between the two authors—we have shared in all decisions and written and rewritten all chapters together. Although one author is listed first, we both have contributed equally. Being conscious of gender perspectives, we have decided to alternate *he* and *she* by chapter rather than to use the traditional generic *he* or *she* for teachers, both of which have sexist overtones. This collaboration in developing *Essentials of Children's Literature* extends beyond the authors to include university colleagues and students, many public school teachers, and school and public librarians who have advised and encouraged us.

Overview

Part One: Children and Literature

The two chapters in Part One cover the introductory material students need in order to begin selecting, reading, and evaluating children's trade books. Chapter 1 defines children's literature, discusses its values, and provides research evidence supporting its use with children. Concepts about literature, elements of fiction, visual elements, and aspects of book format are treated extensively in Chapter 2. We mention well-known books as examples, when needed, but avoid lengthy book reviews. We believe that instructors and their students can conduct in-depth booktalks within the context of their college courses. A facts-only approach is taken in all chapters.

Part Two: Categories of Literature

Each of the eight chapters in Part Two defines and describes a specific category and discusses the types of books that fall within that category. Following the narrative is a list of notable authors (poets, illustrators, compilers, etc.) of books in the category. At the end of each chapter is a list of recommended books for students' use in selecting books to read within the category. These eight chapters include more than 2,000 recommended titles in the end-of-chapter lists.

Most chapters in Part Two discuss a particular literary genre. In addition, Chapter 4 focuses on picture books of all types and genres, and Chapter 10 treats the important topics of multicultural literature and international literature. It should be noted that multicultural and international books are also included in the lists of recommended books in the other chapters. Chapter 10 features the history and current status of multicultural and international literature in the children's book field and highlights notable writers and artists of this body of literature.

In our courses we promote reading as many works of children's literature as practical. For this reason we have included extensive lists of recommended books at the end of each chapter. These lists are comprehensive—the best of the older books and many carefully selected, well-reviewed, recent books.

This text does not contain a separate chapter on the history of children's literature. Each genre chapter notes certain historic milestones—landmark books and events that contributed to the development of the genre. This approach will allow instructors to highlight historical facts as they directly relate to a category of literature. By studying history in the context of each book category, students and their instructors will find it easier to incorporate this facet of children's literature into their courses. The redundancy that results from this history-by-genres approach can lead students to the understanding that societal trends and literary trends parallel one another and spread across genres.

The lists of notable authors in each chapter of Part Two may be used in various ways: subjects for author/illustrator papers or for literature webs written by students, names for students to become acquainted with in acquiring knowledge of the field, and sources for book selection, among others. We are aware of the subjective nature of the choices on these lists. And, of course, an author listed under one category may write books of other genres as well. We expect instructors to guide their students to the authors they consider most important and to add their own favorites to these lists.

Part Three: Literature in the School

The last two chapters concern curriculum and teaching strategies. For example, step-by-step instructions are given for building and setting up a classroom library collection and reading center, producing a creative drama based on a book, conducting booktalks, and selecting and directing choral poetry. Some controversial literature-related topics, such as "basalization" of literature, the literary canon, censorship, and the efficacy of written book reports, are treated in these chapters.

Appendices

Award lists, professional resources, as well as topical lists of trade books can be found in the appendices. We indicate genre, type, or topic of the books in the Newbery and Caldecott Award lists to assist students who may be seeking books of a particular type, topic, or genre for their free-choice readings or for their projects and term papers. Many of the book lists have been especially designed with the undergraduate education major in mind. Lists for particular age groups (e.g., the transitional reader) and for particular situations (e.g., predictable books for shared reading) will help the preservice teacher meet the demands of classroom field experiences. Professional sources for the study of literature and pedagogy are included in Appendix G, which was compiled and fully annotated by Marie Sorensen. Histories of children's literature that served as references for the development of the historical overview sections are also included in that appendix.

Pedagogy

In considering the students, we believe that the primary focus of an undergraduate course should be *reading children's trade books,* not reading an exhaustive textbook *about* children's books. Students need direct experience with these trade books— reading them, reading them aloud to others, writing about them, comparing them, criticizing them, evaluating them, applying them to their own lives, and thinking about using them with their future students. At the same time, the body of knowledge about literature and about teaching literature to children can be conveyed most efficiently through a textbook, freeing class time for involvement with literature. *Essentials of Children's Literature* presents this body of knowledge in a concise, direct narrative using brief lists, examples, figures, and tables in combination with prose.

Outstanding Features

- This book is comprehensive yet concise.
- It is geared to the undergraduate and initial graduate survey course.
- The genre approach to literature is supplemented by chapters on curriculum and teaching.
- Half of the book is narrative, and half consists of lists of recommended books, award winners, and books for particular situations.
- Extensive, handy, reading lists include more than 2,000 recommended book titles for students.
- There is a thorough integration of multicultural and international children's literature as well as a separate chapter on these topics.
- Each genre chapter contains a section on notable authors.
- A nonintrusive approach permits instructors flexibility in course design.
- Each chapter opens with a poem to highlight the importance of introducing and sharing poetry across the curriculum throughout the school year.
- Emphasis is placed on the importance of cooperation between teachers and school and public librarians in fostering children's love of books.

Acknowledgments

We chose to write and publish a children's literature text in order to have the book we always wanted, yet we found the project a daunting one that could not have been accomplished without the advice and encouragement of many people. We wish to express our appreciation

To Marie Sorensen for writing the excellent bibliography of resource materials found in Appendix G

To friends and colleagues from our universities: Michael Tunnell and Donald Richgels (Northern Illinois University) and Barbara Tobin, Diana Scott, Judith

L. Irvin, Kathryn P. Scott, Charles Wolfgang, and Jeryl R. Matlock (Florida State University)

To colleagues at other institutions: Phyllis Van Orden (Wayne State University), Carol J. Fisher (University of Georgia), Priscilla Griffith and Janell Klesius (University of South Florida), E. Maureen White (University of Houston), Barbara Elleman (American Library Association), Ann Trousdale (Louisiana State University), Sara Lundsteen (University of North Texas), and Gerry Bohning (Barry College)

To the external reviewers who diligently read, critiqued, and improved immeasurably our various drafts: Joanne E. Bernstein (Brooklyn College), Carol J. Fox (Illinois State Library), M. Jean Greenlaw (University of North Texas), Judith Hakes (Angelo State University), John Hemphill (Elon College), Julie M. Jensen (University of Texas at Austin), Barbara Kiefer (Columbia University), Sam Perez (Western Washington University), Masha Rudman (University of Massachusetts at Amherst), Rosemary Salesi (University of Maine, Orono), and Donna Wiseman (Texas A&M University)

To our graduate students: Johanna Frese, Marsha Gontarski, Lisa Jenkins, Margaret Benson, Nancy Fichtman Dana, Pamela Kahlich, Kay Bishop, Susan Higgins, Joy McGregor, Judy Pitts, Lyn Forrest, Cheryl Hudson, Janet Griffith, Sally Morrison, and Vinitha Joyappa, and to Richard Casey for his help in creating the graphics for Chapters 2 and 11

To secretaries: Tanya Makarell and Debbie Holderness for computer help and Lucy Knox for help with tables

To the many wonderful librarians and children's literature consultants who helped us locate information, lent us books, and assisted in a myriad of other ways: Marva Carter, Katherine Blackmon, and Connie Morris (Florida State University libraries), Ann Spady (Leon County Public Library, Tallahassee, Florida), Carole Fiore (State of Florida Children's Services Librarian), Jean Getzel (Children's Literature Consultant, Naperville, Illinois), and Teresa Winterbauer and Joyce Lothson (DeKalb Public Library, Illinois)

The cover artwork was created by Patricia Polacco. We also wish to acknowledge and thank the American Library Association for permission to use this work. In her picture storybooks, Polacco imbues her characters with all of the best traits we want to associate with children the world over—curiosity, joy, and the capacity to love and learn. The cover captures these traits and projects the overall message that reading and sharing good books is a joyous, rewarding enterprise.

Essentials of
Children's Literature

Chapter *1*

Learning about Children and Their Literature

My Book Holds Many Stories

My book holds many stories, wrapped tightly in itself,
And yet it never makes a noise but waits upon my shelf
Until I come and take it; then soon my book and I
Are sailing on a fairy sea or floating in the sky.
　　　　　　　　　　　　　　　—Annette Wynne

A child leans forward, head cupped in hands, eyes wide with anticipation, raptly concentrating on hearing a story—this is an image for all time. Whether that child was seated beside an open fire in the Stone Ages, on a rough bench in a medieval fairground, or in a modern-day classroom, the message of that image is the same: Children love a good story.

Definition of Children's Literature

This book is written about literature for children from infancy to adolescence, for you who will be meeting and working with these children as teachers, librarians, and parents. In these roles, your opportunities to lead children to literature will be unparalleled, if you have the prerequisite knowledge.

A definition of children's literature is a logical way to begin an investigation into the world of children's books. *Children's literature* is good-quality trade books for children from birth to adolescence, covering topics of relevance and interest to children of those ages, through prose and poetry, fiction and nonfiction. This definition contains several key concepts that will be explained in the following sections. Understanding these concepts will help you find your way around the over 50,000 children's

1

titles currently in print, the 4,000 or more new children's titles being published annually in the United States, as well as the additional thousands of children's books published worldwide each year in English.

Content

Children's books are about the experiences of childhood, both good and bad. Although these experiences may be set in the past, present, or future, they should be relevant to the child of today. Birthday parties, losing a tooth for the first time, anticipating adulthood, the risks and thrills of adventure, getting a new pet, sibling rivalries, and family problems are representative of experiences common to children today. The content of children's books also includes the amazingly diverse topics that are not a part of childhood but are of interest to children, such as dinosaurs, Egyptian mummies, world records, and fighter planes.

The manner in which content is treated also helps to define children's books. Childhood stories told in a forthright, humorous, or suspenseful manner are appropriate for young readers, whereas stories *about* childhood told in nostalgic or overly sentimental terms are inappropriate. Likewise, when stories show children as victims of natural and human-made disasters, the stories should emphasize the hope for a better future rather than the hopelessness and utter despair of the moment.

The subject matter of children's literature can be expressed in prose or poetry. If the literary work is prose, it must be presented as fiction (a product of the imagination, an invented story), nonfiction (factual), or a combination of the two.

Teachers and librarians distinguish between the terms *textbook* and *trade book*. A *textbook*, by design and content, is for the purpose of instruction. School systems buy textbooks in volume, and each child in a classroom or instructional group typically has the same textbook for a subject. The textbook for elementary-grade reading instruction, the basal reader, is typically marketed as part of a series through which each student progresses from year to year. In contrast, a *trade book*, by design and content, is primarily for the purposes of entertainment and information. Currently, many teachers use trade books in place of basal readers for reading instruction, and in this situation, it is not uncommon for each child in a classroom to have a different book. Trade books are often referred to as *library books* and *storybooks*. The term *trade books* comes from the fact that they are published for the general public, or trade, rather than for a specific consumer group. The books that we will be discussing in this text will be trade books, not textbooks.

Quality

Not all trade books aimed at young readers are worth attention. Books ranging in quality from excellent to poor are now readily available to parents, teachers, and children in the United States and Canada. Look around and you will see racks of children's books in department stores, drugstores, and even grocery stores. But the question is: Are they *good* children's books?

Quality in writing is never easy to define, but it has to do with originality and importance of ideas, imaginative use of language, and beauty of literary and artistic style that enable a work to remain fresh, interesting, and meaningful for years and years. These books have permanent value.

This is not to say that books of good-but-not-great quality have no value. Children have enjoyed fast-moving, adventure-filled, easily predictable stories from the so-called penny-dreadfuls of the seventeenth and eighteenth centuries to the serial adventures of the Hardy Boys, Nancy Drew, and the Babysitters Club of the twentieth century. These works have won no literary prizes but many young readers enjoy them; and because books such as these encourage newly independent readers to read more, they have worth. However, you will probably not want to select books of this calibre to read aloud to your students. Why deprive them of the pleasure of reading such easy and enjoyable books independently? If a child's entire literary experience was limited to serial adventures and other books of trendy but passing interest, he would miss much of the wonder of the natural world and the human experience. The best children's books offer readers enjoyment as well as memorable characters and situations and valuable insights into the human condition.

Many of the so-called children's books today are actually nothing more than advertisements for television cartoon characters and their associated products, such as candy, clothing, and toys. These books represent the low end of the quality spectrum.

The Personal Value of Literature to Children

The most important personal gain that good books offer to children is the most obvious one—enjoyment. Those of you who read widely as children will never forget stories so funny that you laughed out loud, or mysteries so scary that your heart thumped with apprehension. Good books open the doors of our imaginations, and that in itself is valuable.

• When a story is so convincingly written that the reader feels as though he has lived through an experience or has actually been in the place and time where the story is set, the book has given him a vicarious experience. Experiences such as these are broadening for children because they, as readers, are taken to places and times that they could never actually visit—and might not want to! A vicarious experience can also be a good mental exercise for children, since they are asked to view situations from perspectives other than their own.

• When this happens, children often develop a greater capacity to empathize with others. Children around the world can benefit from stories that explain what life is like for people whose lives are restricted by handicaps, politics, religion, or circumstance, or whose lives are different from theirs because of culture or geography.

• Another valuable result of children interacting with literature is that they quickly come to recognize the literary and artistic styles of many authors and illustrators. This is an important first step to literary awareness—that is, recognizing that the style of one writer or illustrator differs from another and that a piece of writing or an illustration has personal appeal. Children who read regularly from a wide variety of children's books soon develop their own personal preferences for types of books and select favorite authors and illustrators. Good teachers and librarians have long recognized the motivation potential of personal preference and interest as expressed through self-selection of reading materials. They also know that the more children read and the greater variety of literature they read, the more discerning readers they become.

The more children know about their world, the more they discover about themselves—who they are, what they value, and what they stand for. Children's literature holds a world of knowledge and experience that can provide the reader with valuable personal insights and, as we will discuss in the following section, academic benefits.

The Academic Value of Literature to Children

In addition to the personal benefits of literature for young readers, there are several important academic benefits.

Reading

Many of you already may have reached the common-sense deduction that reading ability, as with any other skill, improves with practice. As educators, you should also know some of the landmark research studies that have confirmed this belief and have revealed other important findings about the worth of literature in teaching reading. Table 1–1 summarizes these studies and their findings.

A glance at Table 1–1 clearly shows that literature can be invaluable in teaching children to read. Two procedures seem especially important: reading aloud to children and silent independent reading by children, both on a daily basis, if possible. To discover another truth, you must read between the lines of the table. Who makes the books available? Who decides to read aloud to the children? Who makes the first decisions about what to read aloud? Who makes a child's first experiences with literature enjoyable? Who makes the experiences interactive by asking thought-provoking questions? The truth is that there must first be someone, more than likely an adult, who has the knowledge, willingness, and patience to guide children to books. Who will this be? For some children, it will be their parents; for many others, it will be you—their teacher or librarian.

Several recent publications have much of importance to say to parents and teachers about the role of literature (among other things) in learning to read and reading instruction. *Becoming a Nation of Readers: The Report of the Commission on Reading* (Anderson, Hiebert, Scott, & Wilkinson, 1985) and *Counterpoint and Beyond: A Response to Becoming a Nation of Readers* (Davidson, 1988) present an excellent over-

TABLE 1–1 Important Studies on Literature and Reading

Study	Subjects	Findings
Butler (1975)	Cushla, from ages 4 months to 3 years	Reading aloud from children's books to a severely handicapped child from age 4 months enabled the child to learn to read.
Durkin (1966)	Children who learned to read before attending school	Children who learned to read before attending school were read to regularly from the age of 3. Early reading and early writing are often linked.
Cohen (1968)	7-year-olds	Reading to children who have not been previously exposed to literature can help them learn to read.
Cullinan, Jaggar, and Strickland (1974)	500 black children, grades K to 3	Listening to literature combined with oral language extension activities helps children make larger language gains than listening to literature alone. The earlier the literature experiences, the better.
Eldredge and Butterfield (1986)	1,149 beginning readers in 50 classrooms	Use of children's literature to teach reading has a much greater positive effect on students' achievement and attitudes toward reading than does use of basals with traditional homogeneous grouping.
Cosgrove (1987)	4th- and 6th-graders	A read-aloud program resulted in significant gains in reading comprehension scores and positive shift in attitude toward reading.
Leinhardt, Zigmond, and Cooley (1981)	Elementary-grade children	The amount of time children spend reading silently in school is associated with their year-to-year gains in reading achievement. Children improve their reading ability by reading a lot.
Fielding, Wilson, and Anderson (1986)	Middle-graders	Students who read a lot at home show larger gains on reading achievement tests.
Fader, Duggins, Finn, and McNeil (1976)	Boys, ages 12 to 17	Classrooms "saturated" with high-interest books and print for self-selected reading significantly improve low-achieving students' attitudes toward school, learning, and reading as well as their verbal proficiency and language comprehension.
Applebee (1978)	Children ages 2 to 17	Children's sense of story grows as they mature. Literature has a positive effect on children's language development.
Carlsen and Sherrill (1988)	Thousands of college students who were committed readers	Conditions that promote a love of reading include: Availability of books and magazines Family members who read aloud Adults and peers who model reading Role models who value reading Sharing and discussing books Owning books Availability of libraries and librarians Freedom of choice in reading material

view of reading and what works in reading instruction as based on research findings. The U.S. Department of Education's 65-page monograph, *What Works: Research about Teaching and Learning* (1986) is a distillation of years of research findings organized into terse (sometimes single-sentence) statements of effective teaching and learning practices in the home, classroom, and school. Since reading instruction in U.S. class-rooms is currently dominated by basal reading series, you should also be aware of the *Report Card on Basal Readers* (Goodman, Shannon, Freeman, & Murphy, 1988) in which the shortcomings of basal readers and alternatives to them are discussed. Two summary statements of the *Report Card on Basal Readers* are available from the National Council of Teachers of English. They are entitled *Report on Basal Readers* (Weaver & Watson, 1988) and *Basal Readers and the State of American Reading Instruction: A Call for Action*. These documents are well worth the short time it takes to read them.

Writing

Since people tend to assimilate or adopt what they like of what they read and hear, children may, by listening to and reading literature, begin to develop their own writing "voice," or unique, personal writing style. By listening to and reading quality literature, children are exposed to rich vocabulary and excellent writing styles, which serve as good models for their own speaking and writing voices.

Content Area Subjects

In reading about and discussing children's literature, you will often hear the phrase *literature across the curriculum*. This means using works of literature as teaching materials in the content areas of reading, social studies and history, science, health, and, possibly, math. Good teachers have always used literature across the curriculum. Today, the practice is particularly appropriate given the abundance of masterfully written, information-relevant children's trade books available to teachers and librarians. Few resources are available to the teacher that will help as much to make learning interesting and memorable to children as good trade fiction and nonfiction.

Art Appreciation

Illustration in children's picture books can be appreciated both for its ability to help tell the story (cognitive value) and for its value as art (aesthetic value). The cognitive value of illustration in picture books will be dealt with in more detail in Chapter 4, but the point to be emphasized here is that if you appreciate this art for its own sake, there is much that you can do in your classroom to instill in your students a similar appreciation for art. It takes only a moment to call to your students' attention particularly striking and unusual illustrations. By doing so, you show them that you value art. You can also discuss the artist's style, the medium used (watercolor, oils, pastels, etc.), the palette (range of colors), and how the artist's style compares to others. In addition, picture book art serves well as a model for applied art lessons. By suggesting to your students that they use media, techniques, and topics suggested by picture book illustrations in their own artwork, you make good use of a handy, valuable resource and in yet another way show that you value this art.

From the foregoing discussion, it should be clear that students are not the only ones in schools who can benefit from children's literature. As a teacher or librarian, you will find that excellent literature is rich in social, historical, and scientific information about the world and its people and that it has great potential for developing the entire elementary school curriculum.

The Transactional View of Reading and Response to Literature

In 1938, Louise Rosenblatt introduced the transactional view of reading in which she asserted that what the reader brings to the reading act—his world of experience, personality, and current frame of mind—is just as important in making meaning of the text as what the author writes. According to this view, reading is a fusion of text and reader. Consequently, any text's meaning will vary from reader to reader and, indeed, from reading to reading of the same text by the same reader. Almost everyone has experienced reading a book only to discover that a friend has reacted to or interpreted the same book quite differently.

Rosenblatt's theory was not readily accepted. Until the 1960s, most teachers who used literature in their classes took the view that there is only one correct interpretation of any work of literature. According to this view, reading is a process of taking from the text only what was put there by the author. Young readers' success with any work of literature was determined by how closely their interpretations matched the "authorized" interpretation found, for example, in a teacher's edition of their basal reader. Children's responses to literature were thus limited to naming (or guessing) the "right" answers to teachers' questions. Although Rosenblatt (1978) points out that the text of any book guides and constrains the interpretation that is made, an important corollary to her view of reading is that personal interpretations, within reason, are valid, permissible, and, in fact, to be encouraged.

Another interesting aspect of Rosenblatt's theory is that reading is done for two distinct purposes: to take knowledge from the text (efferent reading) and to live through a literary experience, in the sense of assuming the identity of a book character (aesthetic reading). Whether we read efferently or aesthetically depends on what we are reading (e.g., a want-ad versus a mystery novel) and why we are reading it (e.g., information versus escape). Rosenblatt's view of reading is in tune with teaching practices today and has important implications for the way you will encourage your students to respond to the literature you share with them.

Choosing Books for Children

If given a choice in housing, child care, education, food, or clothing, parents usually choose what they consider to be the best for their children. Why should it be any different with the literature adults choose to share with children? The points made about quality and content of literature at the beginning of this chapter definitely play a part in any book selection for children. In addition, you will also want to consider the following suggestions.

Know the Child

The best teachers tend to know their students well. For instance, you will find it helpful to know your students' long-term and short-term interests, their home environment (family makeup, siblings, pets), their friends and social activities, their hobbies, their skills (athletic, academic, artistic), and their hopes or plans for the future. Children's interests have been shown to be one of the most powerful motivating forces available to teachers. Since there are now books on almost every topic conceivable and written at varying degrees of difficulty, you should be able to match the right children with the right books.

Know the Books

Teachers and librarians who read children's books regularly, who are familiar with a wide variety of genres, and who are informed about recently published books are likely to be able to interest children in books. Of course, it is advantageous to have read widely and to be able to share and compare your reactions to a book with children. However, it is not necessary to read every book that your students read in order to be well versed in children's literature or to be an effective promoter of good books. Aside from reading the books, there are a number of other ways to become familiar with them. You can ask librarians for information about the most current titles, share information about books with your colleagues, and read book reviews (see the following section for specific review journals). Your own reading program can be made more effective by focusing on award-winning and notable books, as well as those selected for their appeal to individual children under your care. Knowledge of children's classics (works whose excellent quality and enduring appeal to children through several generations are generally recognized) is also an advantage. After you have read a number of books from a genre, particularly classic examples, you will develop a framework for thinking about books of that kind, whether or not you have read an individual title.

Consider the Level of Difficulty

Level of difficulty refers to reading level, listening level, and conceptual level of a work of literature. Reading level has to do with difficulty of vocabulary and sentence structure and is more important when evaluating a book for a beginning reader than for a fluent reader. Conceptual level pertains to the complexity of ideas treated in the work and how these ideas are presented. For example, ideas in one work might be presented in a simple, straightforward narrative with one event following another in chronological order, whereas another work might depend heavily on symbolism for its meaning or present a disrupted chronology through the use of flashback. The former would probably be successful with primary-grade readers or listeners; the latter would require readers or listeners capable of understanding symbols and of thinking through operations in reverse order—abilities that often do not develop until about third grade.

Whether the book is intended for independent reading by children or for reading aloud by an adult is another important consideration in choosing a book for children. Children can listen with good comprehension to a book that is too difficult for them to read independently. In fact, good teachers often select books that challenge their students intellectually so that they can guide them in their appreciation of deeper works of literature.

Reliable Sources for Book Titles

Several awards have been established in this century for the purposes of elevating and maintaining the literary standards of children's books and for honoring the authors and illustrators whose work is judged by experts in the field to be the best. These awards lists provide the teacher with one means for selecting quality works to share with children. Table 1–2 itemizes what are considered to be the major awards for children's books in the United States, Canada, and Great Britain. Complete lists of the books that won these awards can be found in Appendix A.

Many states have their own awards for children's books, often generated from school children who nominate and vote on books based on their appeal or popularity. You will want to check the listings of these state awards in Appendix A, and familiarize yourself with your own state's children's choice award. Teachers and librarians across the country report that children enjoy participating in the selection process and give these award programs high marks for reading motivation.

Because journals are published several times yearly, they are helpful in keeping current with children's book publishing. *The Horn Book Magazine, School Library Journal, Booklist,* and *Bulletin of the Center for Children's Books* are review journals that evaluate, annotate, and discuss the most recently published trade books on a monthly or semimonthly basis. Two language-related teacher journals often subscribed to by elementary teachers, *Language Arts* and *The Reading Teacher,* have columns devoted to reviewing new children's books in each monthly issue. *The New Advocate,* a quarterly journal dedicated entirely to children's literature and those involved in it, also has extensive reviews of newly published children's books. *Book Links,* an American Library Association bimonthly publication, helps teachers and librarians to integrate the best children's books into their curriculum by presenting annotated lists of books selected around themes and topics. These journals are readily available in school libraries and the children's section of most public libraries.

In cooperation with various national teaching associations, The Children's Book Council (CBC) publishes annual, annotated lists of the best trade books to supplement content area subjects in grades K–8. Two excellent lists of this kind are Out-

TABLE 1–2   Major U.S., Canadian, and British Children's Book Awards

Award/Country	Period	For/Year Established
Newbery Award/USA	Annual	The most distinguished contribution to children's literature published in the previous year. Given to a U.S. author. Established 1922.
Caldecott Award/USA	Annual	The most distinguished picture book for children published in the previous year. Given to a U.S. illustrator. Established 1938.
Laura Ingalls Wilder Award/USA	Every 3 years	Lifetime work that has made a substantial and lasting contribution to children's literature. Given to a U.S. author or illustrator. Established 1954.
Mildred Batchelder Award/USA	Annual	The most distinguished translated work for children published in the previous year. Given to a U.S. publisher. Established 1968.
Canadian Library Awards/Canada	Annual	The most distinguished contribution to children's literature by a Canadian published in the previous year. Established 1947. Also the most distinguished children's book published in French. Established 1954.
Amelia Frances Howard-Gibbon Award/Canada	Annual	The most distinguished picture book for children published in the previous year. Given to a Canadian illustrator. Established 1971.
Carnegie Medal/Great Britain	Annual	The most distinguished contribution to children's literature first published in the United Kingdom in the previous year. Given to an author. Established 1936.
Kate Greenaway Award/Great Britain	Annual	The most distinguished picture book for children first published in the United Kingdom in the previous year. Given to an illustrator. Established 1956.
Hans Christian Andersen Award/International	Biannual	Recognition of an entire body of work. Given to an author and an illustrator. Established 1956.

standing Science Trade Books for Children (published in cooperation with the National Science Teachers Association) and Notable Children's Trade Books in the Field of Social Studies (published in cooperation with the National Council for the Social Studies).

Extensive lists or bibliographies, often annotated, of both older and newer books are valuable aids in book selection. These are usually organized around subject headings and can be remarkably helpful and efficient when developing units of study and topical reading lists for students or when seeking read-aloud literature about a specific subject. Some of the most helpful bibliographic sources are the following:

A to Zoo: Subject Access to Children's Picture Books, 3rd ed., 1989.
The Best in Children's Books: The University of Chicago Guide to Children's Literature, vol. 1, 1966–1972; vol. 2, 1973–1978; vol. 3, 1979–1984.

The Bookfinder: A Guide to Children's Literature about the Needs and Problems of Youth Aged 2 and Up, vol. 3, 1985.

The Elementary School Library Collection: A Guide to Books and Other Media, 17th ed., 1990.

Reading Ladders for Human Relations, 6th ed., 1981.

Research in Children's Literature

As in any field of study, the field of children's literature naturally gives rise to many and varied questions: Does reading literature aloud to young children help them learn to read? How do children's reading preferences differ by age and sex? What are the common features in recent children's books about World War II? What factors help to ensure success in public library summer reading programs? At some point you will read and review books or articles in which some aspect of children's literature has been investigated in an effort to answer such questions. Sometimes the findings of a single research study are enlightening. More importantly, over time, research can provide a body of evidence that either proves or disproves a claim, theory, generalization, or assumption.

The field of children's literature has attracted the interest of three major groups—educators, children's librarians, and specialists in literature, including literary critics. Generally speaking, researchers in the fields of education and library and information science are primarily interested in children and how literature affects their lives and learning. Literature specialists, on the other hand, are primarily interested in the literature itself, especially the literary characteristics of children's literature in terms of how they affect a work's quality or how the work compares to other works.

Both approaches to research in children's literature have resulted in valuable knowledge that helps us serve children better in our various roles. One of the most rewarding practices that you can develop as an educator or librarian is to read professional journals and notable new children's trade books regularly. In this way you will benefit from a constant renewal of information and ideas.

Children's Reading Preferences

A *reading preference* is a stated or implied choice between several reading options. For example, in response to the question, Which would you rather read: a romance, a mystery, or a science fiction adventure? if you chose the mystery option, you would have stated a reading preference for mystery.

Many studies of children's reading preferences have been conducted during this century. Differences in the choices offered to children and in the ways data were gathered from study to study make extensive generalization difficult, but a few patterns have emerged from these studies (Haynes, 1988).

- There are no significant differences between the preferences of boys and girls before age 9.
- The greatest differences in reading preferences of boys and girls occur between ages 10 and 13.
- Boys and girls in the middle grades (ages 10 to 13) share a pronounced preference for mystery and, to a lesser degree, humor, adventure, and animals.
- Preferences of boys in the middle grades include action and adventure stories and sports stories.
- Preferences of girls in the middle grades include fantasy stories, animal stories, and stories about people.

A teacher or librarian might use the foregoing information to make general predictions about what types of books boys or girls of a certain age might enjoy.

Reading preferences should not be depended on as the sole guide in making specific book recommendations to individuals. The reason for this should be clear when you consider the hypothetical question involving romance, mystery, and science fiction books posed earlier. Even though you had to choose one or the other of the options offered to you, it is quite possible that you rarely, if ever, read any of these types of books; mystery may have been just the least uninteresting to you of the three. Knowing this so-called preference would not benefit, and could possibly hinder, a teacher or librarian who was seeking to help you find a book that you would enjoy. General reading preferences do not capture individual reading interests.

Children's Reading Interests

Reading interests and reading preferences are not the same. A *preference*, as noted above, implies a forced choice between options selected by someone other than oneself. An *interest*, on the other hand, comes from within oneself, can encompass whatever can be imagined, and implies freedom of choice. Knowledge of children's reading preferences provides information about children in general, but knowledge of children's reading interests is personal and individual. Since most teachers and school librarians work with particular groups of children over an extended time, they can learn the interests of each child within the group. In doing this, they gain powerful, effective knowledge to use in successfully matching children and books.

Common sense tells us that children will apply themselves more vigorously to read or learn something that they are interested in than they will to read or learn something that they find uninteresting or boring. Interest generates motivation, and good teachers and librarians put that motivation to work by guiding students to good books on topics that satisfy their individual interests.

Learning your students' interests can be accomplished in several ways. The best way is to get to know your students by talking to them in whole-class sharing and in one-to-one conferences. All people like to talk about themselves and what interests them, and children are no different. You can also learn about children's interests through their free-choice writing. Journal writing is particularly helpful in this regard. A perfectly valid and more direct approach is to ask children to list their interests. Many teachers keep such lists in their students' writing folders to use during individual conferences. Because children's interests change often, data of this sort must be updated regularly.

Yet another way for teachers and librarians to keep current on students' interests is to conduct their own interest inventories several times a year to assure that the reading selections available in their classroom or school libraries reflect the general interests of their students. The following steps show one way to conduct a classroom interest inventory.

1. Collect 30 to 40 appropriate books that are new to your students and represent a wide variety of genres and topics.
2. Number the books by inserting paper markers with numbers at the top.
3. Note on a Master List the number and genre of each book.
4. Design a response form for students, such as the one shown in Figure 1–1.
5. Hold each book up and tell your students the title, the type, and a one-sentence summary of the book. You might use the Library of Congress summary that is printed with the cataloguing information on the copyright page of each book.
6. Place the books in order on tables and shelves around the classroom or media center.
7. Give the students 20 to 30 minutes to make the circuit, peruse the books, and mark their response forms.
8. Collect and tally the students' responses and compare to your Master List to arrive at the types of books in which your students are currently most interested.

Would You Like to Read This Book?

As you look at each book, answer this question by circling either YES or NO next to the appropriate book number. Be sure to match the book number and the item number before circling your answer.

1.	YES	NO	16.	YES	NO
2.	YES	NO	17.	YES	NO
3.	YES	NO	18.	YES	NO
4.	YES	NO	19.	YES	NO
5.	YES	NO	20.	YES	NO

etc.

FIGURE 1–1   Sample Student Response Form for Interest Inventory

Classroom interest inventories not only provide teachers and librarians with helpful information about their students' current interests but also introduce children to new genres, topics, and titles. In this way, teachers and librarians can help accomplish their fundamental task of expanding students' fields of interest and knowledge bases.

Teachers and librarians are often surprised at how extensive and varied their students' interests are. Rockets and space travel? Lizards? Semitrailer trucks? When your students come to you with interests as diverse as these, expecting you to help them find books on these topics, you can, of course, send them to the card catalog or its computerized equivalent. In addition, however, you need to know about such general subject guide indexes as *Children's Catalog* (15th edition, 1986) and the annually updated *Subject Guide to Children's Books in Print*, which is a cross-referenced subject guide to all children's books listed in *Children's Books in Print*. (For more information on these resource books, see Appendix G.) There are few reference tools as helpful as a subject guide index for finding books on specific topics.

Child Development

Just as children's interests change and develop rapidly, so do their minds and bodies. This phenomenon of rapid growth and change in children is one of the primary determinants of a child's response to literature. We are most often aware of a child's physical development because we can see it. But in its larger sense, development includes mental growth and change as well. Certainly, both aspects of child development are pertinent to the decisions we make about the books we use with children at different ages and stages in their lives.

Physical Development

From infancy, children exhibit a delight—and sometimes a determination—in doing things for themselves. Their physical growth and abilities are constant sources of both frustration and pride for them as they struggle to learn to walk, dress, ride a bicycle, whistle, and construct things like kites or clubhouses.

For each general stage in a child's physical development, there are characteristic experiences and behaviors. For example, at age 5 or 6, children begin to lose teeth; at 8 or 9, they assert their growing abilities to meet their own needs by doing such things as camping out or going to the mall without Mom and Dad; at about age 13, they see and feel the first physical signs of adulthood in themselves and may even have a first romance. For many children, a book can help to approach, endure, or see the significance of a momentous physical change. As someone who serves children's needs, you will want to be aware of physical development and know the good books that mirror the skills and abilities that children work for and the experiences they undergo during their growth toward independence and maturity.

Mental Development

From your day-to-day observations of children, you know that they are not born with what we would consider an accurate concept of the world. We are charmed by their assertions that all four-legged creatures are *doggie,* or that their toys talk to them, and dismayed at their inability to understand that they cannot take all of their friend's toys home with them. You also know that, over time, children learn to distinguish fantasy from reality, sort the world out, and begin to behave accordingly.

Most educators currently agree with the findings of the Swiss psychologist, Jean Piaget, that all children who reach intellectual maturity go through the same four stages of mental development. These stages include the sensorimotor (children learn through their senses and motor activity), preoperational (children are egocentric, are focused on the present, and make little distinction between reality and fantasy), concrete operational (children are capable of flexible and reversible thought, can understand past and future time, and can recognize points of view other than their own), and formal operational (children are capable of abstract thought such as the meaning of symbols).

Piaget's studies showed that although all children do not reach and leave these stages at precisely the same age, the progression of the stages is always the same. As a teacher or librarian, you must be particularly mindful of the intellectual development and characteristic behaviors within each stage that might influence your choice of a book for a child and a child's response to the book.

In addition to physical and mental development, children appear to go through developmental stages in social and emotional development, language development, and moral development. All of these facets of children's growth are observable in the classroom setting and help us to determine what types of stories and story topics will be most appropriate for children within a given age range.

Books for Different Age Levels

In this section we will discuss types of books and general topics most likely to be appreciated by children of different age levels. By overlaying this general information with the specific interests of any child, you can begin to match titles to children successfully.

Ages 0 to 2

Even infants can enjoy and benefit from good literature. In choosing books for them, we must consider such practical aspects of physical development as how well they can see the illustrations and how long they will sit still for a book experience. For instance, books chosen for babies to hold and look at themselves should feature clearly defined, brightly colored pictures, usually placed on a plain background. Most often, these books will be the brief, plotless, idea books called *concept books*, and they will concern the everyday routines and familiar objects that fill the infants' lives. These books are often constructed of heavy, nontoxic cardboard and are called *board books*. Examples are *Dressing* by Helen Oxenbury and *What Is It?* by Tana Hoban.

Since babies have a strong, positive reaction to any exaggerated patterns in sound or movement, the natural music created by strong rhymes and rhythms in *nursery rhymes,* as well as the brevity and humor of these verses, make this appropriate read-aloud material for children of this age level. For example, see *The Little Dog Laughed and Other Nursery Rhymes* illustrated by Lucy Cousins.

To take advantage of the primacy of the senses and muscular coordination in early learning, you will want to use *interactive books* with children aged 0 to 2. In these books, participation (clapping, moving) or manipulation of the book (touching, opening little doors) is encouraged. Examples include *Pat the Bunny* by Dorothy Kunhardt and *Where's Spot?* by Eric Hill.

All of the best baby books, whether wordless or with brief text, invite the reader or readers to "talk the book through." In this way, the books promote oral language development, which is the child's first step toward literacy.

Ages 2 to 4

Many aspects of the recommended books for babies apply as well to books for toddlers. Daily routines and objects familiar to the child remain good topics. For this audience, such topics can be incorporated into *picture storybooks* featuring simple plots, beautiful illustrations that tell part of the story, and interesting, humorous characters, which are often animals. These books are meant to be read aloud to the child. *Concept books* are excellent for children who are beginning to make sense of their world, and these concepts can now include numbers (*counting books*), letters (*ABC books*), and more complex concepts like opposites. The *illustrated dictionary* or *word book* is another variety of concept book that promotes the naming and labeling of objects, actions, and people, which is so important to children who are rapidly developing their language skills. Examples are *Push-Pull, Empty-Full: A Book of Opposites* by Tana Hoban and *Richard Scarry's Biggest Word Book Ever!* by Richard Scarry.

Children aged 2 to 4 will enjoy nursery rhymes even more than they did as infants and will easily commit these verses to memory. *Folktales*, an important part of our literary heritage, work well with children at this age level, particularly the repetitive ones. For example, see *Henny Penny* and *The Gingerbread Boy*, both illustrated by Paul Galdone.

Ages 4 to 7

Picture storybooks will still be the heart of the literature experience for children during these years. Most of these books are meant to be read aloud to children by a fluent reader, but it is common for children at this stage to choose a favorite picture storybook, memorize the text over repeated hearings, and enjoy the book on their own through "play-reading." Folktales are still a favorite for storytelling and read-aloud experiences, as are humorous poems with strong rhyme and rhythm.

During these years many children will acquire the fundamentals of reading: the notion that stories and the words within them carry meaning, the letter-sound relationship, left-to-right and top-to-bottom progression of print on the page, and a sight vocabulary (certain words that children can recognize and say on sight). *Easy-to-read books* support children's enthusiasm for learning to read by using familiar words, word patterns, informative illustrations, and, in some cases, rhyme to make the text predictable. Examples are *Rosie's Walk* by Pat Hutchins and *Noisy Nora* by Rosemary Wells.

Children at this age level exhibit great enthusiasm for finding out about the world and how it works. This interest can be fed and stimulated through *informational books* for the beginning reader. Examples include *Milk Makers and Farming,* both by Gail Gibbons.

Ages 7 to 9

During these years most children who have had the benefit of a rich literature experience will become fluent and willing readers. This skill, combined with their increased flexibility in thinking, makes many new story types appropriate for them. Now that they can understand and accept others' perspectives, they can enjoy reading about the lives of other children of the past, present, or future in *transitional readers* and later in *novels.*

Transitional readers are chapter books with simple, straightforward plots and writing styles for children who are ready to move from short picture books to slightly longer chapter books. A helpful guide to books of this type is *Beyond Picture Books: A Guide to First Readers* (Barstow & Riggle, 1989). Examples include the "Ramona" and "Henry Huggins" books by Beverly Cleary and the "Julian" books by Ann Cameron.

Chapter books with more sophisticated writing styles or more complicated plots can be greatly enjoyed as read-alouds in the classroom and as independent reading by the better readers. Also, many picture storybooks are appropriate for independent reading by children of this age level. For example, see William Steig's *Sylvester and the Magic Pebble* and *The Amazing Bone.*

A common phenomenon among children who are learning to read is the penchant for rereading the same book many times. Often misconstrued by adults as somehow wrong, the act of rereading the same text many times is, in fact, good reading practice made palatable to the child by the security of a familiar, or "friendly," text.

Although folktales continue to be popular with many 7-year-olds, studies have shown that interest in this genre generally peaks and falls off by age 8. Children then begin to show more interest in the here and now and begin to shift toward a preference for realism in their stories and poems.

Ages 9 to 12

With their rapidly developing physical and mental skills and abilities, 9- to 12-year-olds are ready for the great variety of literature that awaits them. Plots in novels can now be more complicated, including such devices as flashback and symbolism. Both historical fiction and science fiction, which are set in the distant past and distant future, respectively, can be understood and enjoyed. Examples are *Julie of the Wolves* by Jean George and *Tuck Everlasting* by Natalie Babbitt.

These children are particularly interested in reading about young people who, like them, are growing up, asserting and using their new-found skills, moving toward independence, and experiencing growth through meeting challenges. Survival stories, peer stories, and realistic animal stories intrigue these children. Examples include *Hatchet* by Gary Paulsen, *The Great Gilly Hopkins* by Katherine Paterson, and *King of the Wind* by Marguerite Henry.

An interesting parallel to the 7- to 9-year-olds' tendency to reread books occurs at this age level. Many 9- to 12-year-olds discover series books such as the Sweet Valley Twins, the Hardy Boys, or the Three Investigators adventures and read every book in the series one after the other. This is rereading of a sort, since all books within such a series are written to a formula and vary only slightly one from the other. Reading these books is beneficial to many children, simply due to the hours of reading practice they willingly gain.

Although most 9- to 12-year-olds will be competent readers, there is no valid reason for librarians or teachers to discontinue their read-aloud programs for these children. More challenging novels as well as sophisticated picture books for older children sometimes can be more fully appreciated by children when read aloud by an excellent reader. Examples include *My Brother Sam Is Dead* by James and Christopher Collier, *The Garden of Abdul Gasazi* by Chris Van Allsburg, and *Rabbit Island* by Jörg Steiner and illustrated by Jörg Müller.

Teachers and librarians who are consistently successful in helping children find books they like rapidly narrow the field of choices by first considering general factors such as age level and types of books appropriate for children of that general age level. Then they consider more personal factors such as the child's current reading interests and reading ability in order to select specific titles. Knowing children's general reading preferences provides some guidance in book selection, but there is no substitute for knowing the child.

Thoughtful book selection should also include serious consideration of literary and artistic quality. If children are to develop an appreciation for writing and art of depth and originality, then they must be exposed regularly to books that have these traits. Chapter 2 investigates those features of a book that determine its quality.

References

Anderson, R. C., Hiebert, E. H., Scott, J. A., & Wilkinson, I. A. G. (1985). *Becoming a nation of readers: The report of the commission on reading.* Washington, DC: National Institute of Education.

Applebee, A. N. (1978). *The child's concept of story.* Chicago: University of Chicago.

Barstow, B., & Riggle, J. (1989). *Beyond picture books: A guide to first readers.* New York: R. R. Bowker.

Butler, D. (1975). *Cushla and her books.* Boston: Horn Book.

Carlsen, G. R., & Sherrill, A. (1988). *Voices of readers: How we come to love books.* Urbana, IL: National Council of Teachers of English.

Cohen, D. (1968). The effect of literature on vocabulary and reading achievement. *Elementary English, 45,* 209–213, 217.

Cosgrove, M. S. (1987). *Reading aloud to children: The effects of listening on the reading comprehension and attitudes of fourth and sixth graders in six communities in Connecticut.* Unpublished doctoral dissertation, University of Connecticut, Storrs.

Cullinan, B., Jaggar, A., & Strickland, D. (1974). Language expansion for black children in the primary grades: A research report. *Young Children, 29,* 98–112.

Davidson, J. L. (Ed.). (1988). *Counterpoint and beyond: A response to Becoming a Nation of Readers.* Urbana, IL: National Council of Teachers of English.

Dreyer, S. S. (Ed.). (1977–1989). *The bookfinder: A guide to children's literature about the needs and problems of youth aged 2–15* (Vols. 1–4). Circle Pines, MN: American Guidance Service.

Durkin, D. (1966). *Children who read early.* New York: Columbia Teachers College Press.

Eldredge, J. L., & Butterfield, D. (1986). Alternatives to traditional reading instruction. *The Reading Teacher, 40*(1), 32–37.

Fader, D., Duggins, J., Finn, T., & McNeil, E. (1976). *The new hooked on books.* New York: Berkley Books.

Fielding, L. G., Wilson, P. T., & Anderson, R. C. (1986). A new focus on free reading: The role of trade books in reading instruction. In T. Raphael (Ed.), *The contexts of school-based literacy* (pp. 149–160). New York: Random House.

Goodman, K. S., Shannon, P., Freeman, Y., & Murphy, S. (1988). *Report card on basal readers.* New York: Richard C. Owen.

Haynes, C. (1988). Explanatory power of content for identifying children's literature preferences. *Dissertation Abstracts International, 49-12A,* p. 3617. (University Microfilms No. DEW8900468)

Isaacson, R., Hillegas, F., & Yaakov, J. (1986). *Children's catalog* (15th ed.). New York: H. W. Wilson.

Leinhardt, G., Zigmond, N., & Cooley, W. W. (1981). Reading instruction and its effects. *American Educational Research Journal, 18,* 343–361.

Lima, C. W., & Lima, J. A. (1989). *A to zoo: Subject access to children's picture books* (3rd ed.). New York: R. R. Bowker.

National Council of Teachers of English. (1988). *Basal readers and the state of American reading instruction: A call for action.* Urbana, IL: Commission on Reading.

Rosenblatt, L. (1978). *The reader, the text, the poem.* Carbondale, IL: Southern Illinois University.

Subject guide to children's books in print. (1989). New York: R. R. Bowker.

Sutherland, Z. (1973–1986). *The best in children's books: The University of Chicago guide to children's literature* (Vols. 1–3). Chicago: University of Chicago Press.

Tway, E. (Ed.). (1981). *Reading ladders for human relations* (6th ed.). Washington, DC: American Council on Education.

Weaver, C., & Watson, D. (1988). *Report on basal readers.* Urbana, IL: National Council of Teachers of English.

What works: Research about teaching and learning. (1986). Washington, DC: U.S. Department of Education.

Winkel, L. (Ed.). (1990). *The elementary school library collection: A guide to books and other media* (17th ed.). Williamsport, PA: Bro-Dart Foundation.

Chapter 2

Learning about Books

A Book

I'm a strange contradiction; I'm new and I'm old,
I'm often in tatters, and oft deck'd in gold;
Though I never could read, yet letter'd I'm found;
Though blind, I enlighten; though loose, I am bound—
I am always in black, and I'm always in white;
I am grave and I'm gay, I am heavy and light.
In form too I differ—I'm thick and I'm thin,
I've no flesh, and no bones, yet I'm covered with skin;
I've more points than the compass, more stops than the flute—
I sing without voice, without speaking confute;
I'm English, I'm German, I'm French and I'm Dutch;
Some love me too fondly; some slight me too much;
I often die soon, though I sometimes live ages,
And no monarch alive has so many pages.

—Hannah More

In Chapter 1 it was stated that reading is a fusion of text and reader and that each reading of a particular literary work results in a different transaction. Even rereadings by the same reader will result in a different experience. But if each time a book is read the transaction is different, how, then, can general assessments of literary merit be made? Rosenblatt answers that, although the notion of a single, correct reading of a literary work is rejected, "*given agreed-upon criteria,* it is possible to decide that some readings are more defensible than others" (1985, p. 36). Although each reading of a given literary work will be different, there are certain generally agreed-upon interpretations of that work by a community of educated readers. In this chapter, traditional literary elements are reviewed in order to heighten your awareness of literary criticism and to enable you to express more precisely your responses to children's books.

Elements of Fiction

Learning to evaluate children's books can best be accomplished by reading as many excellent books as possible. Gradually your judgment on the merits of individual books will improve. Discussing your responses to these books with children, teachers, and other students and listening to their responses will also assist you in becoming a more appreciative critic. Understanding the different parts, or elements, of a piece of fiction and how they work together can help you to become more analytical about literary works; and this, too, can improve your judgment of literature. The elements of fiction are discussed separately in the following sections, but it is the unity of all these elements that produces the story.

Plot

The events of the story and the sequence in which they are told constitute the plot of the story. In other words, the plot is what happens in the story. Plot is the most important element of fiction to the child reader. Often adults believe that a story for children needs only to present familiar, everyday activities—the daily routines of life. Perhaps 2- and 3-year-olds will enjoy hearing narratives such as this, but by age 4, children want to find more excitement in books. A good plot produces conflict in order to build the excitement and suspense that are needed to keep the reader involved.

The nature of the *conflict* within the plot can arise from different sources. The basic conflict may be one that occurs within the main character, called *person-against-self*. In this type of story, the main character is struggling against inner drives and personal tendencies in order to achieve some goal. Stories about adolescence will frequently have this conflict as the basis of the story problem. For example, in *Language of Goldfish* by Zibby O'Neal, 13-year-old Carrie struggles to find herself and to accept herself and others. A conflict usually found in survival stories is the struggle the character has with the forces of nature. This conflict is called *person-against-nature*. Worthy examples are *Island of the Blue Dolphins* by Scott O'Dell and *Hatchet* by Gary Paulsen. In other children's stories, the source of the conflict is found between two characters. Conflicts with peers, sibling rivalries, and children rebelling against an adult are *person-against-person* conflicts. For example, the young badger, Frances, in *A Bargain for Frances* by Russell Hoban, struggles to get a fair deal from her friend, Thelma, who sells Frances a tea set. Occasionally a story for children presents the main character in conflict with society. This conflict in children's stories is most often either about the environment being destroyed by new technology or changing times, or about children caught up in a political upheaval such as war. The conflict is then called *person-against-society*. *My Brother Sam Is Dead* by James Lincoln Collier and Christopher Collier and *Across Five Aprils* by Irene Hunt, both war stories, pose this type of conflict.

Plots are constructed in many different ways. The most usual plot structures found in children's stories are *chronological plots,* which cover a particular period of time

FIGURE 2–1   Diagram of a Progressive Plot

and relate the events in order within the time period. For example, if a book relates the events of one week, then Monday's events will precede Tuesday's, and so on. An example of a story with a chronological plot is *Charlotte's Web* by E. B. White. There are two distinct types of chronological plots, progressive and episodic. In books with *progressive plots,* the first few chapters are the exposition, in which the characters, setting, and basic conflict are established. Following the expository chapters, the story builds through rising action to a climax. The climax occurs, a satisfactory conclusion (or denouement) is reached, and the story ends. Figure 2–1 suggests how a progressive, chronological, plot might be visualized.

An *episodic plot* ties together separate short stories or episodes, each an entity in itself with its own conflict and resolution. These episodes are typically unified by the same cast of characters and the same setting. Often, each episode comprises a chapter. Although the episodes are usually chronological, time relationships among the episodes may be nonexistent or loosely connected by "during that same year" or "later that month." An example of a short chapter book with an episodic plot structure is *Beezus and Ramona* by Beverly Cleary. Because episodic plots are less complex, they tend to be easier to read. Thus, the reader who is just making the transition from picture books to chapter books may find these plots particularly appealing. Many easy-to-read books for the beginning reader are also structured in this way. *Frog and Toad Are Friends* by Arnold Lobel is a good example of an episodic plot in an easy-to-read book. Figure 2–2 suggests how a chronological, episodic plot might be visualized.

A *flashback* is used by authors to convey information about events that occurred earlier in the story, for example, prior to the beginning of the story. In this case, the

FIGURE 2–2   Diagram of an Episodic Plot

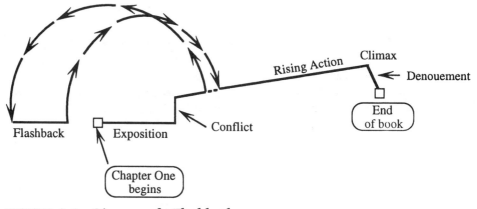

FIGURE 2–3   Diagram of a Flashback

chronology of events is disrupted and the reader is taken back to an earlier time. Flashbacks can occur more than once and in different parts of a story. The use of a flashback permits authors to begin the story in the midst of the action but later fill in the background for full understanding of the present events. Flashbacks in children's books are mostly found in chapter books for older readers, since such plots can confuse children younger than age 8 or 9. Teachers can help students understand this plot structure by reading aloud good examples of this type of story, such as Jean Craighead George's *My Side of the Mountain*. Class discussion can then focus on the sequence of events and why the author may have chosen to relate the events in this manner. Figure 2–3 illustrates the structure of a flashback in a book.

A stylistic plot device used to prepare readers for coming events in a story is *foreshadowing*. This device gives clues to a later event, possibly even the climax of the story. For example, in *Tuck Everlasting* by Natalie Babbitt the detailed description of the long yellow road in the first chapter foreshadows the long journey the Tuck family members must travel in their lives. You can alert young readers to one of the subtle ways authors prepare them for the outcomes of stories by discussing foreshadowing.

Plot is an important element to all readers, but especially to young readers who enjoy fast-moving, exciting stories. A well-constructed plot contributes substantially to children's acceptance and enjoyment of stories.

Characters

Memorable characters populate the world of children's literature. Ferdinand, the bull; Charlotte, the spider; Frances, the badger; Little Toot, the young tugboat; Karana, the Indian girl; and Peter, the African-American child in New York City with his dog Willie, are all remembered fondly by generations of readers.

Story characters, then, are another element of fiction vital to the enjoyment of a story. A well-portrayed character can become a friend, a role model, or a temporary parent to a child reader. Although exciting events are enjoyed by young readers, the characters involved in those events must matter to the reader or the events no longer seem important. How characters are depicted and how they develop in the course of the story are important to the reader. Two aspects to consider in studying a character are characterization and character development.

Characterization refers to the way an author helps the reader know a character. The most obvious way an author can do this is to describe the character's physical appearance and personality. Portraying the character's emotional and moral traits or revealing her relationships with other characters are more subtle and effective techniques. In the most convincing characterizations, we see the character through a combination of her own actions and dialogue, the responses of other characters to her, and the narrator's descriptions.

Character development refers to the changes, good or bad, the character undergoes during the course of events in the story. If a character experiences significant, life-altering events, we, as readers, expect that the character will somehow be different as a result of those events. For example, Matt, a boy of age 11 who was left alone for months in the Maine territory to take care of his family's new cabin, becomes a stronger, more independent young man by the end of *The Sign of the Beaver* by Elizabeth George Speare.

In a work of fiction for children there are usually one or two main characters and some minor characters. Ideally each main character, sometimes called the *protagonist,* will be a fully described, complex individual who possesses both good and bad traits, like a real person. Such a character is called a *round character.*

Minor, or secondary, characters may be described in a less complete or partial manner. The extent of description depends on what the reader needs to know about the character for a full understanding of the story. Some of the minor character's traits are described fully, whereas other facets of the character's personality may remain obscure. The purpose is to build the story and make it comprehensible, thus fragmentary knowledge of a minor character may suffice. Occasionally, an author will insert a *flat character*—that is, a character described in a one-sided or underdeveloped manner. Although such persons do not exist in real life, they may be justified within the story to propel the plot. Sometimes the character is shown as an all-evil or all-frivolous person; for instance, folktales present flat characters as symbols of good and evil. In some stories a flat character plays the role of *character foil,* a person who is in direct juxtaposition to another character (usually the protagonist) and serves to highlight the characteristics of the other individual. A character foil may occur as a flat or as a round character.

The main characters in an excellent work of fiction for children are rounded, fully developed characters who undergo change in response to life-altering events. Because children generally prefer personified animals or children of their own age, or slightly older, as the main characters of their stories, authors of children's books often face a dilemma. Although in real life children usually have restricted freedom of action and decision making within the confines of a family, the author can develop a more vivid and exciting story if the main characters are "on their own." Thus, in many children's stories parents are absent, no longer living, or no longer functioning. Furthermore, by making up situations, authors are able to focus on just one aspect of life, thereby enabling young readers to see and understand this one facet of life more clearly.

Setting

The time when the story occurs and the place(s) where it occurs constitute the setting of a story. The setting has a more or less important function depending on the story. For example, in historical fiction the authentic re-creation of the period is essential to the comprehension of the story events. In this situation, the setting, fully described both in time and place, is called an *integral setting*. The story could not be the same if placed in another setting.

On the other hand, the setting in folktales is often vague and general. For example, "long ago in a cottage in the deep woods" is meant to convey a universal, timeless tale, one that could have happened anywhere and almost anytime except the present or very recent past. This type of setting is called a *backdrop setting*. It simply sets the stage and the mood.

Theme

The theme of a story is its underlying meaning or significance. Although we sometimes think of the theme as the message or moral of the story, it can just as likely be an aesthetic understanding, such as appreciation for nature, or a viewpoint on a current societal issue. Sometimes in order to identify the theme, you may want to ask yourself what the author's purpose was in writing the story, or what the author is saying through this story.

A theme is better expressed by means of a complete sentence than by a single word. For example, students often suggest that a theme found in *Charlotte's Web* by E. B. White is friendship. A better statement of the theme is "Friendship is one of the most satisfying things in the world," as Wilbur the pig tells us in the story. The single word *friendship* may be a topic found in the story, but it is not an expression of the theme.

Themes in children's books should be worthy of children's attention and should convey truth to children. Furthermore, the themes should be based on high moral and ethical standards. A theme, however, must not overpower the plot and characters of the story; children read fiction for enjoyment, not for enlightenment. If the theme is expressed in a heavy-handed, obvious fashion, then the reader feels "preached at" and the pleasure of the reading experience is diminished. Certainly, a well-written book may convey a moral message, but it should also tell a good story from which the message evolves. In this way, the theme is subtly conveyed to the reader.

Often adults write stories not for children's pleasure but to teach morality lessons. Although we think of stories of this sort as the thinly disguised religious tracts found in the early history of children's literature, we must be alert to a tendency for some current authors to use children's literature as a platform to preach about drug abuse, animal rights, and other issues of contemporary interest. Inevitably, the literary quality of these so-called problem novels is weakened, and the story and characters become secondary to the issue or problem.

Style

Style is the way an author tells the story; it can be viewed as the writing itself, as opposed to the content of the book. However, the style must suit the content of the particular book; they are intertwined.

Different aspects of style are considered in evaluating a work of fiction. Most obviously, you can look at the *words* chosen to tell the story. Are they long or short, common or uncommon, rhyming or melodic, boring and hackneyed or rich and challenging, unemotional or emotional, standard dialect or regional/minority dialect? The words should be appropriate to the story being told. As an evaluator of books for children, you will want to ask yourself as you read: Why did the author choose these words? What effect was the author trying to achieve?

The *sentences* may also be considered. Do the sentences read easily? Do they flow without the reader needing to reread to gain the meaning of the text? Sometimes an author chooses to limit the word choices in order to write a book that can be read by a beginning reader. Yet in the hands of a gifted writer, the sentences will remain no less melodic, varied in length and structure, and enjoyable to read and hear than sentences in the best books for the more advanced reader. A good example of a well-written book for beginning readers is Arnold Lobel's *Frog and Toad Are Friends*.

The *organization* of the book may be considered by noting the paragraphs and transitions, length of chapters, headings and chapter titles, preface, endnotes, prologue, epilogue, and length of the book. For the beginning reader it is important whether a story is divided into chapters. After years of looking at, listening to, and reading books without chapters, it is quite an accomplishment for a 6-year-old to move up to so-called chapter books, even if each chapter is only three pages long.

Chapter titles can provoke interest in what will follow, as well as provide the reader with clues to predict story events. Some books provide the readers with a prologue, an introductory statement telling events that precede the start of the story. Some authors include an epilogue, a concluding statement telling events that occur after the story. Gary Paulsen, in speaking to readers about what they bring to the reading act in his prologue to *The Winter Room,* heightens their sensitivity to the story that is to follow. In the epilogue of *Tuck Everlasting,* Natalie Babbitt allows the readers to revisit the scene of the story some years later and resolve at least one of the questions they inevitably have at the story's end. Occasionally an author presents information on the sources or historical facts used in the story. In *Friedrich,* for example, Hans Peter Richter adds a chronology of historical events in the endnotes.

Point of view is another aspect of an author's style. If the story is told through the eyes and voice of a *third-person narrator* (the use of *he, she, it*), then the reader can know whatever the narrator knows about the events of the story. In many stories the narrator is *omniscient* and can see into the minds of all characters and be at many places at the same time. Other stories are narrated from the perspective of only one character in the story. In this case, the story is still told in the third person but the reader knows only what that particular character can see and understand. This latter technique is called *limited omniscient* point of view.

Other times authors choose to tell the story through a *first-person narrator* (the use of *I*), generally the main character of the story. In this case, the reader gains a sense of closeness to the main character but is not privy to any information unavailable to this character. As you read, you will note that some authors have accomplished a first-person point of view by writing as though their main character were writing a diary or letters, as in *A Gathering of Days: A New England Girl's Journal, 1830–1832* by Joan Blos. Occasionally, a story is told in first person through the eyes of a minor character. For example, *Ben and Me,* by Robert Lawson, is the story of Benjamin Franklin told through the eyes of a mouse in his house. *A shifting point of view* permits the reader to see events from different characters' points of view. This technique is demanding on young readers' skill. When the point of view shifts, the author must carefully cue readers to the changing point of view, as in *A Hero Ain't Nothin' But a Sandwich* by Alice Childress.

Symbolism is an artistic invention used by authors to suggest invisible or intangible meanings by analogy to something else through association, resemblance, or convention. Often a symbol—a person, an object, or a situation—represents an abstract or figurative meaning in the story in addition to its literal meaning. Some symbols are universal and can be found repeatedly in literary works; others may be particular to the story. For example, a farm often stands for love and security in works of literature. Children often read only on a literal level but they can be helped by teachers to note more obvious symbols existing in the books they are reading.

A story for children must be more than a plot and a character study; a story is the integration of all the elements of fiction into a pleasing whole. In drawing together these elements, authors create new worlds for young readers.

Visual Elements

In many children's books the story is told through both text and pictures. This is particularly true of picture books but also true of other books for children in which pictures serve an important function. Many different purposes can be accomplished by book illustrations. They convey meaning and feeling by helping the reader visualize the physical settings and the characters' appearance and actions. They also provide an aesthetic dimension to books by offering the readers additional pleasure and insights beyond the message within the text. Thus, the role of pictures in children's books is both to reflect the text and to extend and enrich the text without contradicting its message.

When you read many illustrated books and carefully observe the illustrations and their relationships to the texts, you begin to increase your appreciation of this aspect of children's literature. You may consider the different parts of illustrations as one aspect of your evaluation of illustrations. These parts, or *visual elements,* are line, color, shape, texture, and composition and can help you become more observant of illustrations in order to select well-illustrated books.

Line

The stroke marks that form part of a picture and often define its outline are the lines. The line of a picture generally defines the objects within the picture. Artists may choose to use lines that are dark or pale, heavy or light, solid or broken, wide or thin, straight or curved, or combinations of these. The lines may be mostly vertical, horizontal, or on a diagonal. In pictures of the ocean and open prairies, the lines are predominantly horizontal; the impression is one of calm and tranquility. If the ocean is in a storm, then the lines are more likely diagonal and upward moving, suggesting action or emotion or both. Each of these choices results in a different visual effect and can help set a different mood. In evaluating the element of line within a picture, you may ask yourself whether the lines of the picture help to create and convey both the meaning and the feeling of the story.

Color

Color, another visual element of a book, may be observed for its hue, lightness, and saturation. Colors may be considered for the actual part of the color spectrum they represent or their hue. The predominant colors may be from the cool end of the spectrum, the blues, greens, and gray-violets, or from the warm end of the color chart, the reds, oranges, and yellows. The colors may be intense or pale (that is, more or less saturated). The lightness of the colors may range from diaphanous to opaque. The colors used must first complement the text. For example, if the mood of the story is that of calm and contentment, the illustrator may choose soft, warm tones that strengthen the emotional warmth of the story. If the events and mood of the text change during the course of the story, then the colors will change to reflect and signal the shift occurring in the story. In Margaret Wise Brown's *Goodnight Moon* (1947), the colors gradually darken from page to page, as the sun sets and night falls. Sometimes an illustrated book will be noteworthy for its lack of color, which can be very appropriate and effective, as in *Hildilid's Night* by Cheli Durán Ryan and illustrated by Arnold Lobel.

Shape

Shape, or the spatial forms of a picture, is produced by areas of color and by lines joining and intersecting to suggest outlines of forms. Shapes can be evaluated for their simplicity or complexity, their definition or lack of definition, their rigidity (as in geometric shapes) or suppleness (as in organic shapes), and their size. It is easy to see how this visual element can help to create a mood or carry a message. In looking at shapes in a picture, the proportion of one object to another and the spaces surrounding the shapes are noteworthy for the nonverbal messages they carry (the bigger, the more important). The use of negative space or blank space may also be observed for its ability to highlight an object or to show isolation or loneliness.

Texture

The tactile surface characteristics of pictured objects comprise the texture of a picture or, more simply, the impression of how a pictured object feels is its texture. Textures may be rough or slick, firm or spongy, hard or soft, jagged or smooth. Textural effects generally offer a greater sense of reality to a picture, as happens in Leo Lionni's *Frederick,* where the torn edges of paper collage lend a convincing furriness to the little mice's bodies. Texture also permits the artist to provide contrasts within the picture.

Composition

Composition includes the arrangement of the visual elements within a picture and the way in which these visual elements relate one to the other and combine to make the picture. Many artists arrange each illustration around a single focal point, which is often a key to understanding composition. The artist decides on proportion, balance, harmony, and disharmony within the various elements to produce the desired visual impact. The total effect should not overpower the story but rather extend and enrich the meaning and mood of the text.

Obviously the details in the illustrations must not conflict with those in the text. Surprisingly, many examples can be cited where the illustrator was not true to the text in all details. Children are keenly observant of these contradictions and find them distracting. Although children are open to illustrations that are varied in all visual elements and artistic styles, they have little tolerance for inaccuracies.

Artistic Styles

Children come to note the distinctive features that identify the work of their favorite illustrators. Although the style of a picture is individual by artist, artwork in general can be grouped by style similarities. Five broad categories of artistic styles are realistic, impressionistic, expressionistic, abstract, and surrealistic. Although an artist's works seldom fit neatly into one single art style, facets of these styles may be merged into the artist's personal expression of the world.

Realistic art represents natural forms and provides accurate representations without idealization. Susan Jeffer's illustrations in *Black Beauty* by Anna Sewell are examples of realistic art, as is Christopher G. Knight's photographic rendering of the story *Sugaring Time* by Kathryn Lasky.

Impressionistic art depicts natural appearances of objects by rendering fleeting visual impressions with an emphasis on light. The illustrations in *Anno's Journey* by Mitsumasa Anno emphasize the play of light in nature.

Expressionistic art communicates an inner feeling or vision by distorting external reality. An example can be found in *A Chair for My Mother* by Vera B. Williams. Graphic art, used heavily in advertising and billboards, can be considered a form of expressionistic art. The intent of the artist is to draw attention to the central message by eliminating competing details. Donald Crews has successfully developed this art style into concept books for the very young child in *Truck* and *Freight Train*.

Abstract art emphasizes intrinsic form and surface qualities with little or no direct representation of objects but rather an emphasis on mood and feeling. The illustrations by Leo and Diane Dillon in *Why Mosquitoes Buzz in People's Ears* by Verna Aardema distort reality and thus convey the feelings evoked by the African tale.

In emphasizing the unconscious, *surrealistic art* often presents incongruous dream and fantasy images, sometimes juxtaposing unlikely objects. Molly Bang's illustrations in *The Grey Lady and the Strawberry Snatcher* present a semirealistic creature, the Grey Lady, in a nightmarish adventure. The unusual use of color and unlikely happenings reassure the reader that this wordless book is an imaginary story.

In addition, *primitive art* and *folk art* styles are seen in books about a particular culture in which a type of art depicted the time of the story's origin. In illustrating *Ox-Cart Man* by Donald Hall, Barbara Cooney used features of Early American art in order to express the culture of early nineteenth-century New England. Folktales from tribal societies also present occasions for artists to choose a folk art style reminiscent of the art from earlier cultures.

Because *cartoons* are popular with children, some artists select this style for their children's books. In this type of art, exaggerated figures with little or no background are the focal point of the illustrations. Dr. Seuss's many books, such as *Horton Hatches the Egg* and *The Cat in the Hat,* as well as many of William Steig's popular stories, including *The Amazing Bone* and *Caleb and Kate,* have illustrations representative of the cartoon style.

Artistic Media

The artistic media refer to the materials and technical means used by artists to create pictures. Although the variety of techniques and materials used by book illustrators is virtually unlimited, some of the more common media found in children's books are listed here.

Drawing: Pen and ink, colored pencils, pastels (colored chalk), charcoal pencils

Collage: Real objects of assorted textures and designs such as lace, birchbark, buttons, torn paper, and cotton used to construct an illustration

Print making: Woodcuts, linoleum prints, block prints, lithography

Photography: Black and white, color

Painting: Oils, acrylics, watercolors, gouache, tempera

Of course, the tools with which the artist applies the paint will affect its look. Tools as varied as brushes, air brushes, and sponges are used to apply paint.

Artists will generally design a picture in one predominant medium, drawing from other media for special effects. Occasionally an artist will choose to combine media more liberally to achieve the desired effect. Brief explanations of the artist's techniques and materials have recently begun to be included on the publishing history page of children's picture books and other times at the end of illustrated books.

Book Format

Children's books are more than text, or text and pictures combined. Other parts of a book contribute to the final product we call a book. The *dust jacket* is a removable paper cover wrapped around the book, which serves as protection against soiling. It also attracts purchasers and readers as well as informs them about the book, its author, and its illustrator. The *covers* of a book are usually made of two boards, which make the book more durable and allow the book to stand on a shelf. When no dust jacket is on a book, the front cover provides the reader with a first impression of the story. The *title,* an important part of the text, usually first seen by the reader on the dust jacket or front cover, combines with the illustrations of the dust jacket or cover to communicate the nature of the story to young readers who choose books primarily by title and cover. Many titles suggest the topic of the story and can assist readers in deciding whether to read the book. Other titles and covers may not offer as much information about the story. In such cases, some explanation by a teacher or librarian in the form of a booktalk may prove invaluable to young readers seeking just such a book.

The *endpapers* are the pages glued to the inside front and back boards of the cover, and the *flyleaf* is the page facing each endpaper. In many fine, well-illustrated books, the endpaper and flyleaf are utilized to provoke curiosity in the reader for what follows, to set a mood, or to evoke an affective response in preparation for the story. Often those first colors and first decorative touches are the visual introduction to the story. When readers turn the flyleaf, they are further prepared by the artist for the story by viewing the title page. The *title page* tells the book's full title and subtitle, if there is one, the names of the author(s) and illustrator(s), and the name and location of the publisher. Occasionally a book will include a *frontispiece,* an illustration facing the title page, which is intended to establish the tone and to entice the reader to begin the story.

On the reverse side of the title page, often referred to as the *verso* of the title page, is the *publishing history* of the book. On this page is the copyright notice, a legal right giving only the the holder permission to produce and sell the work. Others who wish to reproduce the work in any way must request permission of the copyright holder. The copyright is indicated by the international symbol ©. This symbol is followed by the name of the person(s) holding the copyright and the date it takes effect, which is the year the book is first published. Later publications are also listed. The country in which the book was printed, the number assigned to the book by the Library of Congress, the International Standard Book Number (ISBN), and the edition of the book are also included on this page. Many publishers now include on this page cataloguing information for libraries, a very brief annotation of the story, and a statement on the media and techniques used in the illustrations.

The title page typically presents the *typeface,* the style of print to be used throughout the book. The size and legibility of the typeface must be suited to the book's intended audience. In children's books this can be extremely important. Books for the young child just learning to read should have large, well-spaced print for easy eye scanning. The print style for an easy-to-read book should be a somewhat larger-than-average standard block print with easily distinguishable and recognizable upper- and lowercase letters. Many children's trade books are now being produced in "big book" size for beginning reading activities with a whole class or group of children. In this case, the print needs to be large enough to be readily seen from a distance of 10 to 12 feet minimum. Legibility is diminished when background colors are used behind the text, leaving insufficient contrast for easy reading.

The size, shape, and darkness of the print type may vary from book to book. The lines may be heavy and strong, or light and willowy. The choice of print type should enhance the overall visual message of the illustrations and fit with the illustrations in style and mood. Note also that the placement of the print on the pages in relation to the illustrations can subtly guide the reader and become a functional part of the story.

Unusual print styles are sometimes selected for a children's book. In a book with a diary format, the use of script print gives the impression of handwriting. In this case, the amount of script print is usually brief, and standard block print is used throughout most of the book for greater ease of reading. In place of print some illustrators choose to hand-letter the text. Classic examples of lettering as part of the illustrative component of a book are found in *Millions of Cats* by Wanda Gág and *The Story of Babar* by Jean De Brunhoff.

The *page layout* is also worth observing. You will notice that illustrations are variously placed one on a page, on facing pages, on alternating pages, or on parts of pages. When the picture extends across the two facing pages, it is called a *doublespread*. A doublespread gives the effect of motion, since the eye is drawn to the next page. It can also give a feeling of grandeur, openness, and expansiveness. Sometimes a picture will begin on a right-hand page and spill over to the following page, the reverse side. This offers a strong sense of continuity from one part of the story to the next. Some pictures have a *frame*. Framing of a picture can work to distance the reader from the action, lend a sense of order to the story, or make the mood more formal. The frame itself may be anything from a simple line to a broad, ornately decorated ribbon of information. Decorations on a frame may repeat certain images or symbols to reinforce the meaning of the story.

Pages are another part of the book makeup. In evaluating the pages, you should ask yourself: What is the quality of the paper? Is it thick, high quality? Is it glossy or textured, white or colored? Are the pages square, rectangular, or shaped in the form of a concrete object? Are they in keeping with the rest of the book? Are unique or unusual page formats, such as half pages, see-through pages, or partial pages, appropriate and logical?

The *size* of the book is also worth noting. Large picture books are well suited for reading aloud to a class. Smaller picture books are usually not satisfactory choices for read-alouds, unless, of course, you are reading to only one child or a small group of children.

Next, consider the *book binding*. Books may be bound in hard cover, paperback, or in some special-purpose material. For example, books for babies are frequently bound in sturdy cardboard or vinyl to withstand the dual role of toy and book. If buying a hardcover book, determine whether the binding is glued or sewn. Look for the stitching. Sewn bindings last much longer than glued ones. Durability relative to cost are the usual trade-offs you must weigh in selecting paper or hardcover bindings for classroom or school libraries. Generally speaking, the cost of hardcover books is justified when you expect fairly heavy use.

Balance and Variety in Book Selections

In addition to evaluating the various textual and visual elements that are central to the issue of quality, the child's age and development and the balance and variety among books are also important considerations. In Chapter 1, the age and development of children relative to their reading materials were discussed. Because the children in any elementary-grade class have a wide range of reading abilities and reading interests, you need to provide books of many different types, including picture books, easy-to-read books, short chapter books and longer books, and books of prose and poetry, fiction and nonfiction on many different topics. Selecting outstanding biographies for an entire year of reading aloud to a class would hardly offer students a range of literary experiences. Thus, balance among the *genres of literature* as well as *variety in topic* are essential. Classroom libraries are usually limited in scope, therefore school libraries are necessary to provide adequate balance and variety of books for students' research needs and independent reading. Frequent visits to the library by the class and by individual students need to be arranged by the teacher and librarian.

A balance between *male and female main characters* over the course of a year is necessary to meet the needs of children of both sexes and to help members of each sex to understand more fully the perspectives, problems, and feelings of members of the opposite sex. Classroom and school library collections need to have a wide range of topics with a balance of male and female main characters.

The representation of minorities as main characters in choices of literature for the classroom and school library is also essential to present a realistic view of society and the world. Through well-written *multicultural literature,* children can see that someone from a different race, ethnic group, or religion has many of the same basic needs and feelings that they themselves have. Literature by and about people different from oneself can help to develop an understanding and appreciation for all peoples. Minority children will enjoy reading books in which children from backgrounds similar to theirs play the leading, and sometimes, heroic roles. Characters with whom one can identify permit a deeper involvement in literature and at the same time help children to understand situations in their own lives.

International literature—that is, literature from other nations and regions of the world—needs to be included in read-aloud choices and in classroom and library collections in order to guide students toward global understanding. Through reading or listening to the favorite books of children from other nations, your children will experience cultural literacy on a worldwide basis.

Categories of Literature

In Chapters 3 to 10 of this book, the various categories of children's books will be defined and explained, followed by book titles recommended for reading in each of the categories. Most of the chapters focus on the literary genres, as presented in Table 2–1. However, Chapter 4, Picture Books, diverges from this pattern in that it discusses a book format, and Chapter 10, Multicultural and International Literature, presents books organized by topic. Although multicultural and international books have been placed in a separate chapter for special focus, many multicultural and international titles are also recommended in the genre chapters.

TABLE 2–1   Genres of Children's Literature

PROSE				*POETRY (3)*
Fiction			*Nonfiction (9)*	
Realistic (7)	*Fantasy*			
	Traditional Literaure (5)	*Modern Fantasy (6)*		

Family Situations
Peer Relationships
Growth and Maturity
Cultural Differences
Sports
Mysteries
Humorous Stories
Animal
	Myths
	Epics
	Ballads
	Legends/Tall
	   Tales
	Folktales
	Fables
	Religious Stories
		Modern Folktales
		Animal Fantasy
		Personified Toys
		   and Objects
		Unusual Characters/
		   Situations
		Little People
		Supernatural
		   Events/Mystery
		Historical Fantasy
		Quest Stories
		Science Fiction/
			Biological Science
			Physical Science
			Social Science
			Applied Science
			Humanities
			Biography
				Nursery Rhymes
				Lyric Poems
				Narrative Poems

Historical (8)		Fantasy		

An overview of the genres and their relationships to one another is displayed in Table 2–1. These genres can be used in making balanced choices for library and classroom reading collections and for choosing books to read aloud. The number of the chapter in which each genre of literature is discussed is noted next to the genre.

Reference

Rosenblatt, L. M. (1985). The transactional theory of the literary work: Implications for research. In C. R. Cooper (Ed.), *Researching response to lit-* *erature and the teaching of literature: Points of departure* (pp. 33–53). Norwood, NJ: Ablex.

C h a p t e r 3

Poetry

A Word

A word is dead
When it is said,
Some say.
I say it just
Begins to live
That day.
—Emily Dickinson

Poetry is a natural beginning to literature for young children and an enjoyable literary form for all ages. In their earliest years, children acquire language and knowledge of the world around them through listening and observing. Poetry, primarily an oral form of literature that draws heavily on the auditory perceptions of the listeners, is ideally suited to children at this stage. Throughout the elementary and middle school years, poetry that relates to any and every subject can be found and shared orally throughout the school day, providing a flash of humor or a new perspective on the subject. Too often in the classroom poetry is neglected or ignored. For this reason, we have chosen to discuss poetry before other types of literature. We hope you will read and reread favorite poems to your students each day.

Definition and Description

Poetry is the expression of ideas and feelings through a rhythmical composition of imaginative and beautiful words selected for their sonorous effects. In its origin, poetry was oral, and as various minstrels traversed the countryside, they recited poetry and sang songs to groups of listeners of all ages. This musicality of poetry makes it an especially suitable literary form for teachers to read aloud and, at times, put to music.

Children often believe that rhyme is an essential ingredient of poetry, yet some types of poetry do not rhyme. What, then, distinguishes poetry from prose? The concentration of thought and feeling expressed in succinct, exact, and beautiful language, as well as an underlying pulse or rhythm are the traits that most strongly set poetry apart from prose.

Not all rhyming, rhythmical language merits the label of poetry. *Verse* is a language form in which simple thoughts or stories are told in rhyme with a distinct beat or meter. Nursery rhymes are a good example of well-known, simple verses for children. And, of course, we are all too aware of the *jingle*, a catchy repetition of sounds heard so often in commercials. The most important feature of verses and jingles is their strong rhyme and rhythm. Content is light or even silly. Although verses and jingles can be enjoyable and have a place in the classroom, poetry can enrich children's lives by giving them new insights and fresh views on life's experiences and by bringing forth strong emotional responses.

The term *poetry* is used in this chapter both to refer to a higher quality of language—a form of language that can evoke great depth of feeling and provoke new insights through imaginative and beautiful language—and to refer to favorite verses of childhood.

A wide variety of poetry books is available for use in classrooms by teachers and students. A large, comprehensive *anthology* of poetry for children is a must in every classroom. Anthologies should be organized by subjects for easy retrieval of poems appropriate for almost any occasion. In addition, indices of poets and titles, or first lines, are usually provided. Contemporary and traditional poets' work can be found in most of these anthologies with appeal to a wide age range—from nursery rhymes for toddlers to longer, narrative poems for the middle grade student. An example is *A New Treasury of Children's Poetry: Old Favorites and New Discoveries* selected by Joanna Cole.

Specialized poetry books are also readily available in which the poems are all by one poet, on one topic, for one age group, or of one poetic form. These specialized collections become necessary adjuncts for a teacher and class who come to love certain kinds of poetry or specific poets. Beautifully illustrated collections are also available and seem to be especially enjoyed by children for independent reading of poetry. Examples include *Words with Wrinkled Knees: Animal Poems* by Barbara Juster Esbensen and *Doodle Soup* by John Ciardi.

Single narrative poems of medium length are being presented more frequently in picture book formats. These editions make poetry more appealing and accessible to many children, but in some cases, the illustrations may remove the opportunity for children to form their own mental images from the language created by poets. The poetry section of your school library is worth perusing for interesting poetry books to use in the classroom.

Elements of Poetry

Just as with a work of fiction, the elements of a poem should be considered in order to understand and evaluate the poem. Each of these parts—meaning, rhythm, sound patterns, figurative language, and sense imagery—is discussed below.

- *Meaning.*   Meaning is the underlying idea, feeling, or mood expressed through the poem. As with other literary forms, poetry is a form of communication, the way a poet chooses to express emotions and thoughts. Thus, the meaning of the poem is the expressed or implied message the poet is conveying.
- *Rhythm.*   Rhythm is the beat or regular cadence of the poem. Poetry, usually an oral form of literature, relies on rhythm to help communicate the meaning of the poem. A fast rhythm is effected through short lines, clipped syllables, sharp, high vowel sounds such as the sounds represented by the letters *a, e,* and *i,* and abrupt consonant sounds, such as the sounds represented by the letters *k, t, w,* and *p.* A fast rhythm can provide the listener with a feeling of happiness, excitement, drama, and even tension and suspense. A slow rhythm is effected by longer lines, multisyllabic words, full or low vowel sounds such as the sounds represented by the letters *o* and *u,* and resonating consonant sounds such as the sounds represented by the letters *m, n,* and *r.* A slow rhythm can evoke languor, tranquility, inevitability, and harmony among other feelings. A change in rhythm during a poem signals the listener to a change in meaning. In the poems that follow, "Song of the Train" exhibits a fast rhythm evoking the rapid speed of a train; "A Summer Morning" proceeds more slowly in communicating the calm and quiet of summer.

Song of the Train

Clickety-clack,
Wheels on the track,
This is the way
They begin the attack:
Click-ety-clack,
Clickety-clack,
Click-ety-clack-ety,
Click-ety
Clack.

Clickety-clack,
Over the crack,
Faster and faster
The song of the track:
Clickety-clack,
Clickety-clack,
Clickety, clackety,
Clackety
Clack.

Riding in front,
Riding in back,
Everyone hears
The song of the track:
Clickety-clack,
Clickety, clack,
Clickety, clickety,
Clackety
Clack.
—David McCord

A Summer Morning

I saw dawn creep across the sky,
And all the gulls go flying by.
I saw the sea put on its dress
Of blue mid-summer loveliness,
And heard the trees begin to stir
Green arms of pine and juniper.
I heard the wind call out and say:
"Get up, my dear, it is to-day!"
—Rachel Field

• *Sound Patterns.* Sound patterns are made by repeated sounds and combinations of sounds in the words. Words, phrases, or lines are sometimes repeated in their entirety. Also, parts of words may be repeated as, for example, with rhyme, the sound device children most recognize and enjoy. *Rhyme* occurs when the ends of words (the last vowel sound and any consonant sound that may follow it) have the same sounds. Examples of rhyming words are: *vat, rat, that, brat,* and *flat,* as well as *hay, they, flay, stray,* and *obey. Assonance* is another pattern poets use for effects. In this case, the same vowel sound is heard repeatedly within a line or a few lines of poetry. Assonance is exemplified in these words: *hoop, gloom, moon, moot,* and *boots. Alliteration* is a pattern in which initial consonant sounds are heard frequently within a few lines of poetry. Examples are *ship, shy,* and *shape. Consonance* is similar to alliteration but usually refers to a close juxtaposition of final consonant sounds, as in fla*ke*, chu*ck*, and stro*ke. Onomatopoeia* is the device in which the sound of the word imitates the real-world sound. Examples are *buzz* for the sound of a bee and *hiss* for the sound a snake makes.

• *Figurative Language.* Figurative language takes many different forms, but it involves comparing or contrasting one object, idea, or feeling with another one. A *simile* is a direct comparison, typically using *like* or *as* to point out the similarities. A *metaphor* is an implied comparison without a signal word to evoke the similarities. *Personification* is the attribution of human qualities to animate, nonhuman beings or to inanimate objects for the purpose of drawing a comparison between the animal or object and human beings. *Hyperbole* is an exaggeration to highlight reality or point out ridiculousness. Children often delight in hyperbole in that it appeals to their strong sense of the absurd.

　　• *Sense Imagery.*　A poet will play on one or more of the five senses in descriptive and narrative language. *Sight* may be awakened through the depiction of beauty; *hearing* may be evoked by the sounds of a city street; *smell* and *taste* may be recalled through the description of a fish, left too long in the sun; and finally, *touch* can be sensitized through describing the gritty discomfort of a wet swimsuit caked with sand from the beach. After listening to a poem, children can be asked to think about which of the senses the poet is eliciting.

　　These elements of poetry may be considered in order to select varied types of poems and to group them for presentation. However, little is gained by teaching each of these elements as a separate item to be memorized and/or analyzed. Poetic analysis has caused many students to dislike poetry. On the other hand, students who have teachers who love poetry, who select it wisely, who read it aloud well, and who provide students with many opportunities to enjoy it will come to appreciate poetry.

Values of Poetry for Children

Poetry touches our minds and our hearts through drawing on our five senses. Children, too, are reached by poetry, even though the subjects that move them may differ from those that move us. The values of poetry for children are as far reaching and wide ranging as the topics one can find in children's poems.

- The most important value of poetry and verse is that they are fun and enjoyable for children. Poetry lends itself to word play; tongue twisters as well as zany rhymes and puns are frequently found in collections of poetry.
- Poetry can help children see and hear unusual things or usual things in a new way. The images and music of poetry have the power to give children wonderment and understanding.
- Poems are excellent to use as bridges between classroom activities, or for livening and lightening up the day, or for accenting the events in the class. (In Chapter 12, ideas for having students model different poetic forms for writing poetry are proposed.)
- Some poetry and verse are part of a child's literary heritage. Starting with Mother Goose and other nursery rhymes, children can become acquainted with the characters who are in these favorite childhood rhymes and who have become a part of our cultural heritage.
- The rhythm and sound elements of poetry make it an especially useful vehicle for the teaching strategy of shared reading used with beginning readers. (Chapter 12 has sections on shared reading techniques and on choral reading of poetry.)

Evaluation and Selection of Poetry

The criteria to keep in mind in evaluating a poem for use with children are:

- The ideas and feelings expressed are worthy, fresh, and imaginative.
- The expression of the ideas and feelings is unique, often causing the reader to perceive ordinary things in new ways.
- The poem is appropriate to the experiences of children and does not preach to them.
- The poem presents the world through a child's perspective and focuses on child life and activities as well as on activities to which people of all ages can relate.
- A poem that panders to children's base instincts is probably best avoided and replaced by other enjoyable, worthy choices.
- Poetry collections should be judged on the quality of the poetry choices. If you decide the poetry is well selected, consider the illustrations and the appearance of the book. Beautiful illustrations do not ensure a good collection of poems within the covers.
- Children report a preference for narrative poems. You will want to include some narrative poems along with other types of poetry.
- Although certain poets may be favored by your students, they will also enjoy the poetry of many other poets. Thus, be sure to share with your students poems by a variety of authors.

In selecting poems to read to students, the list of notable poets at the end of this chapter, the Golden Age poets mentioned later in Table 3–1, and the list of poets who have won the National Council of Teachers of English (NCTE) Award (see Appendix A) would be good starting points for your selections. The NCTE Award was established in 1977 in the United States to honor poets whose poetry has contributed substantially to the lives of children. This award is given to a poet for the entire body of poetry produced, not for a particular poem or book of poems.

Historical Overview of Poetry

Poetry for children began centuries ago in the form of nursery rhymes that were recited to babies and toddlers by caregivers and passed along via the oral tradition. The earliest published collection of these nursery rhymes that survives today is *Tommy Thumb's Pretty Song Book* (1744) and is housed in the British Museum (Gillespie, 1970). This songbook contains familiar rhymes such as "Hickory Dickory Dock" and "Mary Mary Quite Contrary." These rhymes and others like them came to be called *Mother Goose rhymes*, but the term *Mother Goose* was first used in France by Charles Perrault in his *Stories and Tales of Past Times with Morals; or, Tales of Mother Goose* (1697) to refer to his collection of fairy tales. Later editions contained nursery rhymes, which became so popular that Mother Goose became a general name for nursery rhymes. The rhymes are light, rhythmical, often nonsensical verses shared with young children. The rhymes are recited by parents, and children soon become familiar with them and join in the fun. For many, nursery rhymes and other poems were their first forms of literature and symbolize the reassuring sounds of childhood.

Another early type of poetry was quite different from nursery rhymes in nature and was intended for a somewhat older audience of children. Poems of a moral and religious bent were shared with obvious didactic intent, reflecting the strict attitude toward the rearing of children that held sway in the Western world from the Middle Ages to the late nineteenth century. Fear of death and punishment was instilled as a means of gaining obedience to authority. Ann and Jane Taylor's *Original Poems, for Infant Minds, by Several Young Persons* (1804) provided verse of this kind. Some titles of poems from this early collection are "The Idle Boy," "Greedy Richard," "Meddlesome Matty," and "The Church-Yard." A few purely descriptive, nondidactic poems from this same collection are still remembered today, especially "Twinkle, Twinkle Little Star." Clement Moore's "A Visit from St. Nicholas" (1823), another nondidactic, narrative poem, is still enjoyed and known today as "Twas the Night Before Christmas."

TABLE 3–1   Milestones in Poetry during the Golden Age

Date	Poet	Landmark Work	Country	Characteristics
1846	Edward Lear	*A Book of Nonsense*	England	Father of nonsense poetry, limericks
1864	Lewis Carroll	"Jabberwocky"	England	Nonsense verses, mostly in *Alice's Adventures in Wonderland*
1872	Christina Rossetti	*Sing Song*	England	Poems on children and the small things around them
1885	Robert Louis Stevenson	*A Child's Garden of Verses*	England	Descriptive poems of childhood memories
1888	Ernest Thayer	"Casey at the Bat"	U.S.A.	Famous ballad on baseball
1890	Laura E. Richards	*In My Nursery*	U.S.A.	Poems with hilarious situations, wordplay, and strong rhythm
1896	Eugene Field	*Poems of Childhood*	U.S.A.	Retrospective poems of children and child life
1902	Walter de la Mare	*Songs of Childhood*	England	Musical and imaginative poetry
1920	Rose Fyleman	*Fairies and Chimneys*	England	Imaginative poems about fairies
1922	A. A. Milne	*When We Were Very Young*	England	Poems of fun in which the child's world is observed
1926	Rachel Field	*Taxis and Toadstools*	U.S.A.	Poems about city and country through the child's eyes

Poetry for children flourished from the middle of the nineteenth century through the 1920s, a period that can be considered the Golden Age of Poetry for Children. In Table 3–1, the poets, countries, landmark works and dates, and characteristics are listed. The Golden Age of Poetry moved away from moralistic poetry, instead providing children with poems describing the beauty of life and nature, with poems of humor, nonsense, and word fun, and with imaginative poems that interpreted life from the child's perspective. Much of the Golden Age poetry retains its appeal for today's children; for example, *A Child's Garden of Verses* (1885) by Robert Louis Stevenson remains a favorite collection of poems among parents and children. This positive shift in poetry for children set the standard for poetry created during the remainder of the twentieth century.

In the 1960s and 1970s, the general trend toward realism in children's literature was also reflected in poetry. More topics considered suitable for the child audience resulted in protest poetry, poems about girls in nontraditional roles, and irreverent poems. For example, parents, teachers, and other adults became fair game for ridicule and mockery. Minority poets were more frequently published and their poetry gained in popularity. Most of the early poetry for children prior to the 1950s was by English poets, but during the last half of the century many U.S., Canadian, and Australian poets have gained favor with children. Poems by John Ciardi, Myra Cohn Livingston, Jack Prelutsky, Shel Silverstein, Dennis Lee, and Max Fatchen have engendered popular interest in this genre. An award for excellence in poetry, established in 1977 by the National Council of Teachers of English, has conferred a new importance on poetry for children.

Poetry Types and Forms

Poetry can be classified many ways; one way is to consider two main types that generally differ in purpose: lyric and narrative poetry. *Lyric poetry* captures a moment, a feeling, or a scene, and is descriptive in nature, whereas *narrative poetry* tells a story or includes a sequence of events. From this definition, you will recognize the following to be a lyric poem.

Long Trip

The sea is a wilderness of waves,
A desert of water.
We dip and dive,
Rise and roll,
Hide and are hidden
On the sea.
Day, night,
Night, day,
The sea is a desert of waves,
A wilderness of water.
> —Langston Hughes

The following is an example of a narrative poem:

The Broken-Legg'd Man

I saw the other day when I went shopping in the store
A man I hadn't ever ever seen in there before,
A man whose leg was broken and who leaned upon a crutch—
I asked him very kindly if it hurt him very much.
"Not at all!" said the broken-legg'd man.

I ran around behind him for I thought that I would see
The broken leg all bandaged up and bent back at the knee;
But I didn't see the leg at all, there wasn't any there,
So I asked him very kindly if he had it hid somewhere.
"Not at all!" said the broken-legg'd man.

"Then where," I asked him, "is it? Did a tiger bite it off?
Or did you get your foot wet when you had a nasty cough?
Did someone jump down on your leg when it was very new?
Or did you simply cut it off because you wanted to?"
"Not at all!" said the broken-legg'd man.

"What was it then?" I asked the man, and this is what he said:
"I crossed a busy crossing when the traffic light was red;
A big black car came whizzing by and knocked me off my feet."
"Of course you looked both ways," I said, "before you crossed the street."
"Not at all!" said the broken-legg'd man.

"They rushed me to a hospital right quickly," he went on,
"And when I woke in nice white sheets I saw my leg was gone;
That's why you see me walking now on nothing but a crutch."
"I'm glad," said I, "you told me, and I thank you very much!"
"Not at all!" said the broken-legg'd man.

—John Mackey Shaw

Poetry can also be categorized by its *poetic form,* which refers to the way the poem is structured or put together. *Couplets, tercets, quatrains* and *cinquains* refer to the number (two, three, four, and five) of lines of poetry in a stanza—a set of lines of poetry grouped together. Couplets, tercets, quatrains, and cinquains usually rhyme, though the rhyme scheme may vary; these poetic forms may constitute an entire poem, or a poem may be comprised of a few stanzas of couplets, tercets, and so on.

Other specific poetic forms frequently found in children's poetry are limericks, ballads, haiku, free verse, and concrete poetry.

A *limerick* is a humorous, one-stanza, five-line verse form, usually a narrative, in which lines 1, 2, and 5 rhyme and are of the same length and lines 3 and 4 rhyme and are of the same length but shorter than the other lines. The following is an example of a limerick by Edward Lear, the poet who popularized this poetic form in the nineteenth century.

> *There was a young lady of Firle,*
> *Whose hair was addicted to curl;*
> *It curled up a tree,*
> *And all over the sea,*
> *That expansive young lady of Firle.*
> —Edward Lear

A *ballad* is a fairly long narrative poem of popular origin usually adapted to singing. These traditional story poems are often romantic or heroic. "The Outlandish Knight," a 13-stanza ballad, tells the tale of the clever young woman who tricks the man who deceived her.

The Outlandish Knight

An outlandish knight came out of the North
  To woo a maiden fair,
He promised to take her to the North lands,
  Her father's only heir.

"Come, fetch me some of your father's gold,
  And some of her mother's fee;
And two of the best nags out of the stable,
  Where they stand thirty and three."

She fetched him some of her father's gold
  And some of her mother's fee;
And two of the best nags out of the stable,
  Where they stood thirty and three.

He mounted her on her milk-white steed,
  He on the dapple grey;
They rode till they came unto the sea-side,
  Three hours before it was day.

"Light off, light off thy milk-white steed,
  And deliver it unto me;
Six pretty maids have I drowned here,
  And thou the seventh shall be."

"Pull off, pull off thy silken gown,
  And deliver it unto me;
Methinks it looks too rich and too gay
  To rot in the salt sea."

"Pull off, pull off thy silken stays,
    And deliver them unto me;
Methinks they are too fine and gay
    To rot in the salt sea."

"Pull off, pull off the Holland smock
    And deliver it unto me;
Methinks it looks too rich and gay
    To rot in the salt sea."

"If I must pull off my Holland smock,
    Pray turn thy back unto me;
For it is not fitting that such a ruffian
    A woman unclad should see."

He turned his back towards her,
    And viewed the leaves so green;
She caught him round the middle so small,
    And tumbled him into the stream.

He dropped high, and he dropped low,
    Until he came to the tide—
"Catch hold of my hand, my pretty maiden,
    And I will make you my bride."

"Lie there, lie there, you false-hearted man,
    Lie there instead of me;
Six pretty maidens have you drowned here,
    And the seventh has drowned thee."

She mounted on her milk-white steed,
    And led the dapple grey.
She rode til she came to her father's hall,
    Three hours before it was day.
                    —Traditional

Haiku is a lyric, unrhymed poem of Japanese origin with three lines of 17 sylla-bles, arranged line by line with syllables of 5, 7, and 5. Haiku is highly evocative poetry frequently espousing harmony with and appreciation of nature.

Small bird, forgive me.
I'll hear the end of your song
    in some other world.
                    —Anonymous
        (translated by Harry Behn)

Free verse is unrhymed poetry with little or light rhythm. Sometimes words within a line will rhyme. The subjects of free verse are often abstract and philosophical, but always reflective.

> *An evenly balanced*
> *word   W H A L E*
> *it floats*
> *lazily on the page*
> *or dives straight down*
> *to the bottom and beyond*
> *all breath held   held*
> *held   then whoooosh!*
> *The A blows its top*
> *into the sun!   W H A L E*
> *serene*
> *sings to us   wet*
> *green sounds from the deepest*
> *part of the alphabet*
>   —Barbara Juster Esbensen

Concrete poetry is written and printed in a shape signifying the subject of the poem. Concrete poems are a form of poetry that must be seen as well as heard in order to be fully appreciated. These poems do not usually have rhyme or definite rhythm, but mostly rely on the words, their meanings and shapes, and the way they are arranged on the page to evoke images. In "Concrete Cat" you will note through the position of the word that the mouse appears to have met with an accident.

Concrete Cat

—Dorthi Charles

Children's Poetry Preferences

Findings from two studies in which children's poetry preferences were surveyed can be helpful to teachers in selecting poems for a new group of students. Fisher and Natarella (1982) surveyed primary-grade children and their teachers, whereas Terry (1974) studied intermediate-grade children. The two age groups were similar, although not identical, in their preferences.

- Both age groups preferred narrative poems over lyric poems.
- Limericks were the favored poetic form of both age groups.
- Free verse and haiku were not well liked by either age group.
- Children of both age groups preferred poems that had pronounced sound patterns of all kinds, but especially enjoyed poems that rhymed.
- Rhythm was also an important element to students of both age groups; they preferred poems with regular, distinctive beats.
- Imagery and figurative language were not as well received by students of both age groups, who reported that they did not always understand poems with considerable figurative language.
- Children of both age groups liked humorous poems, poems about animals, and poems about well-liked familiar experiences.
- The subjects most preferred by primary-grade children were strange and fantastic events, animals, and other children; the older children preferred the realistic content of humor, well-liked familiar experiences, and animals.

Although children's appreciation of poetry can be broadened and deepened by a good teacher, you may be wise to proceed with caution on less-liked aspects of poetry until your students become fans of poetry. Thus, a good selection of rhyming, narrative poems with distinct rhythms about humorous events, well-liked familiar experiences, and animals is a good starting point with a new class of students.

References

Ciardi, J. (1985). *Doodle soup.* Illus. by Merle Nacht. Boston: Houghton Mifflin.

Cole, J. (1984). *A new treasury of children's poetry: Old favorites and new discoveries.* Illus. by Judith Gwyn Brown. Garden City, NY: Doubleday.

Esbensen, B. J. (1986). *Words with wrinkled knees: Animal poems.* Illus. by John Stadler. New York: Crowell.

Fisher, C. J., & Natarella, M. A. (1982). Young children's preferences in poetry: A national survey of first, second and third graders. *Research in the Teaching of English, 16*(4), 339-354.

Gillespie, M. C. (1970). *Literature for children: History and trends.* Dubuque, IA: Wm. C. Brown.

Terry, A. C. (1974). *Children's poetry preferences: A national survey of upper elementary grades.* Urbana, IL: National Council of Teachers of English.

Notable Poets

Arnold Adoff, recipient of the National Council of Teachers of English (NCTE) Award for Excellence in Poetry for Children. Many poems about relating to people across racial groups. *All the Colors of the Race.*

Dorothy Aldis, a poet known for her narrative poems about everyday activities and emotions. *All Together: A Child's Treasury of Verse.*

Byrd Baylor, a poet whose themes are the desert and harmony with nature. *Hawk, I'm Your Brother.*

Gwendolyn Brooks, an African-American poet known for poems about the lives of urban children. *Bronzeville Boys and Girls.*

John Ciardi, an NCTE award-winning poet known for his humor and, at times, satire in poems for children. *The Man Who Sang the Sillies.*

Walter de la Mare, British poet who gave new importance to early childhood experiences. *Songs for Childhood.*

Barbara Juster Esbensen, contemporary poet who writes free verse for children. *Cold Stars and Fireflies.*

Eleanor Farjeon, first recipient of the Hans Christian Andersen Medal in 1956. British poet known for well-written poems. *Poems for Children.*

Max Fatchen, Australian poet noted for his poems about children's thoughts and activities. *The Country Mail Is Coming: Poems from Down Under.*

Rachel Field, a Golden Age poet known for her city and country poems. *Taxis and Toadstools.*

Aileen Fisher, an NCTE award-winning poet whose poems express a closeness to nature and all its inhabitants. *Going Barefoot.*

Paul Fleischman, winner of the Newbery Award for his *Joyful Noise: Poems for Two Voices* in which the poems are composed and printed for two readers to read lines in unison and solo.

Nikki Giovanni, an African-American poet known for her free verse (using mostly lowercase letters) about growing up African-American. *Spin a Soft Black Song: Poems for Children.*

Eloise Greenfield, an African-American poet noted for poems of courage and love. *Under the Sunday Tree.*

Langston Hughes, African-American poet whose protest poems speak of racial pride. *Selected Poems of Langston Hughes.*

X. J. Kennedy, a favorite creator of nonsense and humorous verse about contemporary themes. *One Wonderful Night in August and Other Nonsense Jingles.*

Karla Kuskin, an NCTE award-winning poet known for sometimes serious, sometimes funny poems, including many narrative poems. *Dogs & Dragons, Trees & Dreams: A Collection of Poems.*

Edward Lear, classic Golden Age poet whose nonsense verse and limericks remain favorites today. *The Book of Nonsense.*

Dennis Lee, popular Canadian poet known for humorous poetry. *Alligator Pie.*

Myra Cohn Livingston, an NCTE award-winning poet and an anthologist whose poetry exhibits a balance of perspective and form. *Whispers and Other Poems.*

David McCord, the first winner of the NCTE Award for Excellence in Poetry for Children, known for regular rhythms, agile language, and the use of shape in his poems. *One at a Time.*

Eve Merriam, an NCTE award-winning poet whose poems, often humorous, display an inventive use of language. *A Poem for a Pickle: Funnybone Verses.*

A. A. Milne, English poet whose two collections of poems from the 1920s, *When We Were Very Young* and *Now We Are Six,* remain enjoyable today.

Lilian Moore, an NCTE award-winning poet known for her brief, pithy poems for young children. *See My Lovely Poison Ivy: And Other Verses About Witches, Ghosts, and Things.*

Jack Prelutsky, a popular contemporary poet known for his nonsense poems and poems with humorous characters. *Nightmares: Poems to Trouble Your Sleep.*

Laura E. Richards, a Golden Age poet known for the musical wordplay in her poems. *Tirra Lirra: Rhymes Old and New.*

Annie M. G. Schmidt, poet and author from the Netherlands and winner of the Hans Christian

Andersen Medal. Known for her humorous, narrative poems. *Pink Lemonade.*

Shel Silverstein, popular contemporary children's poet who creates nonsense and humorous poetry. *Where the Sidewalk Ends.*

Kaye Starbird, a poet whose poems often feature a dialogue between a child and the reader. *A Snail's a Failure Socially.*

Robert Louis Stevenson, Golden Age poet whose *A Child's Garden of Verses* remains a classic.

Valerie Worth, an NCTE award-winning poet known for free verse poetry. *Small Poems.*

Recommended Poetry Books

General Anthologies

Bedrick, Peter, editor. *The Book of a Thousand Poems.* Harper, 1986.

Blishen, Edward, compiler. *Oxford Book of Poetry for Children.* Illustrated by Brian Wildsmith. Watts, 1963.

Booth, David, editor. *'Til All the Stars Have Fallen.* Illustrated by Kady Denton. Viking, 1989.

Cole, Joanna, compiler. *A New Treasury of Children's Poetry; Old Favorites and New Discoveries.* Illustrated by Judith Gwyn Brown. Doubleday, 1984.

Corrin, Sara and Stephen, editors. *Once Upon a Rhyme.* Illustrated by Jill Bennett. Faber, 1982.

de Regniers, Beatrice Schenk, Eva Moore, Mary Michaels White, and Jean Carr. *Sing a Song of Popcorn: Every Child's Book of Poems.* Scholastic, 1988.

Downie, Mary, and Barbara Robertson, compilers. *The New Wind Has Wings.* Oxford/Merrimack, 1985.

————, compilers. *The Wind Has Wings: Poems from Canada.* Illustrated by Elizabeth Cleaver. Walck, 1968.

Dunning, Stephen, Edward Lueders, and Hugh Smith, compilers. *Reflections on a Gift of Watermelon Pickle.* Scott, Foresman, 1967.

Elledge, Scott, editor. *Wider than the Sky: Poems to Grow Up With.* HarperCollins, 1990.

Ferris, Helen, compiler. *Favorite Poems Old and New.* Illustrated by Leonard Weisgard. Doubleday, 1957.

Hall, Donald, compiler. *The Oxford Book of Children's Verse in America.* Oxford, 1985.

Harrison, Michael, and Christopher Stuart-Clark, editors. *The Oxford Treasury of Children's Poems.* Oxford, 1988.

Janeczko, Paul, editor. *Preposterous: Poems of Youth.* Watts, 1991.

Kennedy, X. J., and Dorothy Kennedy, compilers. *Knock at a Star; A Child's Introduction to Poetry.* Little, Brown, 1982.

Moore, Lilian, compiler. *Go with the Poem.* McGraw, 1979.

Philip, Neil, editor. *A New Treasury of Poetry.* Illustrated by John Lawrence. Stewart, Tabori & Chang, 1990.

Prelutsky, Jack, editor. *The Random House Book of Poetry for Children.* Illustrated by Arnold Lobel. Random House, 1983.

————, editor. *Read-Aloud Rhymes for the Very Young.* Illustrated by Marc Brown. Knopf, 1986.

Wilner, Isabel. *The Poetry Troupe; An Anthology of Poems to Read Aloud.* Scribner's, 1977.

Untermeyer, Louis, editor. *Rainbow in the Sky.* Illustrated by Reginald Birch. Harcourt, 1985.

Specialized Books— By Poet or Topic

Adoff, Arnold. *All the Colors of the Race.* Illustrated by John Steptoe. Lothrop, 1982.

————. *Chocolate Dreams.* Illustrated by Turi MacCombie. Lothrop, 1989.

————. *Eats.* Illustrated by Susan Russo. Lothrop, 1979.

————. *I Am the Darker Brother.* Illustrated by Benny Andrews. Macmillan, 1968.

————. *I Am the Running Girl.* Illustrated by Ronald Himler. Harper, 1979.

————, editor. *My Black Me: A Beginning Book on Black Poetry.* Dutton, 1974.

————. *Sports Pages.* Illustrated by Steve Kuzma. Lippincott, 1986.

Baylor, Byrd. *Desert Voices*. Scribner's, 1981.

Bierhorst, John, editor. *The Sacred Path: Spells, Prayers & Power Songs of the American Indians*. Morrow, 1983.

Blake, William. *Songs of Innocence*. Illustrated by Harold Jones. Barnes, 1961.

Bodecker, N. M. *Hurry, Hurry, Mary Dear! And Other Nonsense Poems*. Illustrated by author. Atheneum, 1976.

———. *Let's Marry Said the Cherry and Other Nonsense Poems*. Illustrated by author. Atheneum, 1974.

Booth, David, editor. *Voices on the Wind: Poems for All Seasons*. Illustrated by Michèle Lemieux. Morrow, 1990.

Brooks, Gwendolyn. *Bronzeville Boys and Girls*. Illustrated by Ronni Solbert. Harper, 1956.

Browning, Robert. *The Pied Piper of Hamelin*. Illustrated by Kate Greenaway. Warne, 1888.

Carter, Anne, compiler. *Birds, Beasts, and Fishes: A Selection of Animal Poems*. Illustrated by Reg Cartwright. Macmillan, 1991.

Ciardi, John. *Doodle Soup*. Illustrated by Merle Nacht. Houghton, 1985.

———. *Fast and Slow: Poems for Advanced Children of Beginning Parents*. Illustrated by Becky Garver. Houghton Mifflin, 1975.

———. *The Hopeful Trout and Other Limericks*. Illustrated by Susan Meddaugh. Houghton, 1989.

———. *I Met a Man*. Illustrated by Robert Osborn. Houghton, 1961.

———. *The Man Who Sang the Sillies*. Illustrated by Edward Gorey. Lippincott, 1961.

———. *You Read to Me, I'll Read to You*. Illustrated by Edward Gorey. Lippincott, 1962.

Cole, Joanna. *Anna Banana: 101 Jump-rope Rhymes*. Illustrated by Alan Tiegreen. Morrow, 1989.

Cole, William, editor. *Oh, What Nonsense!* Illustrated by Tomi Ungerer. Viking, 1966.

Esbensen, Barbara Juster. *Cold Stars and Fireflies; Poems of the Four Seasons*. Illustrated by Susan Bonners. Crowell, 1984.

———. *Words with Wrinkled Knees: Animal Poems*. Illustrated by John Stadler. Crowell, 1986.

Fatchen, Max. *The Country Mail Is Coming: Poems from Down Under*. Little, Brown, 1990.

Fields, Julia. *The Green Lion of Zion Street*. Illustrated by Jerry Pinkney. Macmillan, 1988.

Fisher, Aileen. *Feathered Ones and Furry*. Illustrated by Eric Carle. Crowell, 1971.

———. *Out in the Dark and the Daylight*. Harper, 1980.

Fleischman, Paul. *I Am Phoenix: Poems for Two Voices*. Illustrated by Eric Beddows. Harper, 1985.

———. *Joyful Noise: Poems for Two Voices*. Illustrated by Eric Beddows. Harper, 1988.

Froman, Robert. *Seeing Things: A Book of Poems*. Illustrated by Ray Barber. Crowell, 1974.

Frost, Robert. *Stopping by Woods on a Snowy Evening*. Illustrated by Susan Jeffers. Dutton, 1978.

Gerrard, Roy. *Sir Cedric*. Farrar, 1984.

Gordon, Ruth, compiler. *Time Is the Longest Distance: An Anthology of Poems*. HarperCollins, 1991.

Greenfield, Eloise. *Honey, I Love, and Other Love Poems*. Illustrated by Diane and Leo Dillon. Crowell, 1978.

———. *Under the Sunday Tree*. Illustrated by Amos Ferguson. Harper, 1988.

Holman, Felice. *The Song in My Head*. Illustrated by Jim Spanfeller. Scribner's, 1985.

Hopkins, Lee Bennett, compiler. *Side by Side: Poems to Read Together*. Illustrated by Hilary Knight. Simon & Schuster, 1988.

———. *Surprises*. Illustrated by Megan Lloyd. Harper, 1984.

Hughes, Langston. *The Dream Keeper, and Other Poems*. Illustrated by Helen Sewell. Knopf, 1932.

Hughes, Shirley. *Out and About*. Lothrop, 1988.

Janeczko, Paul B., editor. *The Music of What Happens: Poems That Tell Stories*. Watts, 1988.

Kennedy, X. J. *Brats*. Illustrated by James Watts. Atheneum, 1986.

———. *The Forgetful Wishing Well: Poems for Young People*. Illustrated by Monica Incisa. Atheneum, 1915.

Knudson, R. R., and May Swenson, editors. *American Sports Poems*. Watts, 1988.

Kuskin, Karla. *Dogs & Dragons, Trees & Dreams: A Collection of Poems*. Harper, 1980.

Larrick, Nancy, compiler. *Mice Are Nice*. Illustrated by Ed Young. Philomel, 1990.

———. *To the Moon and Back: A Collection of Poems*. Illustrated by Catharine O'Neill. Delacorte, 1991.

————. compiler. *When the Dark Comes Dancing: A Bedtime Poetry Book*. Illustrated by John Wallner. Philomel, 1983.

Lear, Edward. *The Complete Nonsense Book*. Dodd, 1946.

————. *The Scroobious Pip*. Completed by Ogden Nash. Illustrated by Nancy Ekholm Burkert. Harper, 1968.

Lee, Dennis. *Garbage Delight*. Illustrated by Frank Newfeld. Houghton, 1978.

Lewis, Richard, editor. *In a Spring Garden*. Illustrated by Ezra Jack Keats. Dial, 1965.

Livingston, Myra Cohn. *A Circle of Seasons*. Illustrated by Leonard Everett Fisher. Holiday, 1982.

————. *O Sliver of Liver and Other Poems*. Illustrated by Iris Van Rynbach. Atheneum, 1979.

————. *Sky Songs*. Illustrated by Leonard Everett Fisher. Holiday, 1983.

————, editor. *Thanksgiving Poems*. Illustrated by Stephen Gammell. Holiday, 1985.

————, editor. *Why Am I Grown So Cold? Poems of the Unknowable*. Atheneum, 1982.

McCord, David. *Far and Few: Rhymes of the Never Was and Always Is*. Illustrated by Henry B. Kane. Little, 1952.

————. *One at at Time: His Collected Poems for the Young*. Illustrated by Henry B. Kane. Little, 1977.

Merriam, Eve. *Blackberry Ink*. Illustrated by Hans Wilhelm. Morrow, 1985.

————. *Finding a Poem*. Illustrated by Seymour Chwast. Atheneum, 1970.

————. *Halloween ABC*. Illustrated by Lane Smith. Macmillan, 1987.

————. *Out Loud*. Atheneum, 1973.

Milne, A. A. *The World of Christopher Robin*. Illustrated by Ernest Shepard. Dutton, 1958.

Moore, Lilian. *Something New Begins: New and Selected Poems*. Illustrated by Mary Jane Dunton. Atheneum, 1982.

Moore, Clement Clarke. *The Night Before Christmas*. Illustrated by Tomie dePaola. Holiday House, 1980.

Morrison, Lillian, compiler. *Rhythm Road: Poems to Move To*. Lothrop, 1988.

————, compiler. *The Sidewalk Racer and Other Poems of Sports and Motion*. Lothrop, 1977.

Nash, Ogden. *Custard and Company: Poems by Ogden Nash*. Illustrated by Quentin Blake. Little, 1980.

————, compiler. *The Moon Is Shining Bright as Day*. Illustrated by Rose Shirvanian. Lippincott, 1953.

O'Neill, Mary. *Hailstones and Halibut Bones*. Illustrated by Leonard Weisgard. Doubleday, 1961.

Pomerantz, Charlotte. *If I Had a Paka: Poems in Eleven Languages*. Illustrated by Nancy Tafuri. Greenwillow, 1982.

Prelutsky, Jack. *The Baby Uggs Are Hatching*. Illustrated by James Stevenson. Greenwillow, 1982.

————, editor. *For Laughing Out Loud: Poems to Tickle Your Funnybone*. Illustrated by Marjorie Priceman. Knopf, 1991.

————. *The New Kid on the Block*. Illustrated by James Stevenson. Greenwillow, 1984.

————. *Nightmares: Poems to Trouble Your Sleep*. Illustrated by Arnold Lobel. Greenwillow, 1976.

————. *Rolling Harvey Down the Hill*. Illustrated by Victoria Chess. Greenwillow, 1980.

————. *Something Big Has Been Here*. Illustrated by James Stevenson. Greenwillow, 1990.

Rylant, Cynthia. *Waiting to Waltz: A Childhood*. Illustrated by Stephen Gammell. Bradbury, 1984.

Service, Robert W. *The Cremation of Sam McGee*. Illustrated by Ted Harrison. Greenwillow, 1987.

————. *The Shooting of Dan McGrew*. Illustrated by Ted Harrison. Godine, 1988.

Silverstein, Shel. *A Light in the Attic*. Illustrated by author. Harper, 1981.

————. *Where the Sidewalk Ends: The Poems and Drawings of Shel Silverstein*. Harper, 1974.

Smith, William Jay. *Laughing Time*. Illustrated by Juliet Kepes. Little, 1955.

Sneve, Virginia Driving Hawk, selector. *Dancing Teepees: Poems of American Indian Youth*. Illustrated by Stephen Gammell. Holiday, 1989.

Starbird, Kaye. *The Covered Bridge House*. Illustrated by Jim Arnosky. Four Winds, 1979.

Thayer, Ernest Lawrence. *Casey at the Bat*. Illustrated by Patricia Polacco. Putnam, 1888.

Viorst, Judith. *If I Were in Charge of the World and Other Worries: Poems for Children and Their Parents*. Illustrated by Lynne Cherry. Atheneum, 1982.

Wallace, Daisy, editor. *Fairy Poems*. Illustrated by Trina Schart Hyman. Holiday, 1980.

————. *Witch Poems.* Illustrated by Trina Schart Hyman. Holiday, 1976.

Whipple, Laura, compiler. *Eric Carle's Dragons Dragons and Other Creatures that Never Were.* Illustrated by Eric Carle. Philomel, 1991.

Willard, Nancy. *A Visit to William Blake's Inn: Poems for Innocent and Experienced Travelers.* Illustrated by Alice and Martin Provensen. Harcourt, 1981.

————. *The Voyage of the Ludgate Hill: Travels with Robert Louis Stevenson.* Illustrated by Alice and Martin Provensen. Harcourt, 1987.

Woolger, David, editor. *Who Do You Think You Are? Poems About People.* Oxford, 1990.

Worth, Valerie. *More Small Poems.* Illustrated by Natalie Babbitt. Farrar, 1976.

————. *Small Poems.* Illustrated by Natalie Babbitt. Farrar, 1972.

————. *Still More Small Poems.* Illustrated by Natalie Babbitt. Farrar, 1978.

C h a p t e r **4**

Picture Books

Picture Books

In my playroom there are books,
*   Red and blue and gold,*
With pretty pictures in them
*   Of the stories that are told.*

I don't like reading much,
*   But the pictures that I see*
Are full of many meanings
*   The words don't have for me.*

If pictures tell me everything
*   The books can have to tell,*
There doesn't seem much sense to me
*   In learning how to spell.*
—Tom Robinson

In an era when picture books abound and provide many children with a delightful introduction to the world of books, it is difficult to imagine a time when books had no illustrations. Nonetheless, the picture book as we know it is a product of the twentieth century. The development of different types of picture books over the last half century can be seen as a response to our developing awareness of the importance of early learning.

Definition and Description

Picture books are profusely illustrated books in which the illustrations are, to varying degrees, essential to the enjoyment and understanding of the story. For this reason, illustrations in picture books are said to be *integral* to the story. The illustrations in picture books provide actual plot or concept information as well as clues to character traits, setting, and mood. Without the illustrations, these books would be diminished, and in some cases the story would make no sense or would be nonexistent.

Many children's books have illustrations but are not picture books. For example, novels and anthologies often have a few, scattered illustrations that depict what has already been described in the text or serve to decorate the text. These illustrations are said to be *incidental* to the story. When well done, illustrations of this kind are appreciated and enjoyed by readers, but they are not necessary for a complete understanding of the story.

Values of Picture Books

Picture books enable children to enjoy literature from their earliest years, since they can "read" the illustrations to follow the story or to name the objects or characters depicted. In most cases these books are first read aloud to children, and it is in the read-aloud context that the following important values of the picture book become apparent.

- Hearing good picture books read aloud regularly can help children learn to read and value reading. Reading and discussing picture books bring young children and adults together for a shared activity that is enjoyable to both and extremely valuable to children, since such experiences lay the foundation for a child's learning to read and for becoming a lifelong reader. Since the best picture books can be enjoyed at several different levels of understanding, adults can also sincerely look forward to reading and rereading these books.
- Sharing picture books with children fosters language development. The combination of intriguing text, art, and topics found in the best picture books feeds children ideas, stimulates their imagination and curiosity, and provides them with a rich vocabulary to use in book-related questions and discussions.
- Picture books can foster children's appreciation of art. Some of the best artists of today are illustrating children's picture books. Many parents, teachers, and librarians take the opportunity to comment on the artwork as they share picture books with children. Their comments range from what they like about an illustration to calling attention to how artistic styles in different picture books vary and which of the varying styles the children prefer and why.
- Visual clues enable nonreaders and beginning readers to enjoy picture books by themselves. After a picture book has been read to a child, she can return to the book and use picture clues to reproduce enough of the language of the text from memory for a satisfying independent reading.

Evaluation and Selection of Picture Books

The most important criterion for evaluating a picture book is whether children will enjoy it. Children's first experiences with books must be enjoyable or they will soon not want to be involved with books and, because of this, they may never learn to read or to enjoy reading. For this reason, children's own picture book choices must be included during read-aloud and independent reading times.

On the other hand, children can be led to love and appreciate books that they would not select on their own. One way to do this is to give a new book an introduction that explains new concepts and relates the book to the audience. A teacher's or librarian's sincere enthusiasm for a story or her skillful reading of it can also increase children's willingness to accept a new book.

Over a period of time, evaluation and selection of picture books become a matter of achieving a good balance between what children naturally enjoy and what you want to lead them to enjoy. Balance must also be achieved in terms of adequate representation in one's book collection of genres, topics and themes, male and female characters, majority and minority races and ethnic groups, and native and foreign settings.

The following criteria will help you in identifying the best of the picture books.

- The ideas in the best picture books are original or are presented in an original way and are appropriate in theme and complexity for children. Picture books on topics that children enjoy and find interesting are preferable to books about childhood, in the sense of nostalgia for or reminiscence of childhood. Books of the latter sort are for adults, not children.
- Picture books selected for use with children should avoid racial or sexual stereotyping in text and illustrations.
- Language and writing style should be rich and varied but not so complicated as to be incomprehensible to the child. New or unusual vocabulary presented within the context of interesting situations and complementary illustrations is a valuable criterion. Overly sentimental and trite language, as well as writing characterized by short, choppy sentences and lifeless vocabulary, should be avoided.
- When evaluating illustrations, look for inclusion of supporting details, accuracy, and style appropriate to the story. In picture books for infants, look for relatively uncomplicated pages showing outlined figures against a plain background. Elements of perspective (a distant building appearing smaller than a nearby person) or unusual page design (only parts of a figure being shown) may not be readily understood or appreciated by very young children. By age 3, most children can easily manage more complicated page designs. Colored illustrations are preferred by children but color is not essential for illustrations to work well in picture books. The more important point to consider is whether the illustrations are right for the story.
- Text and illustrations must be well integrated. This means more than the illustrations on a certain page "go along with" the accompanying text. It means that the

illustrations complement or add to the text either by presenting added information about plot, characters, or setting, or by projecting the mood of the story through the use of color and line. Furthermore, arranging text and illustrations in varying ways on pages can add to the reader's interest and may subtly aid in leading beginning readers' eyes from left to right across the page. Good integration of text and illustrations demands a balance; one must not overwhelm the other.

• Format, as it affects size of illustrations, is an important consideration when a book is chosen to be shared with a large group, since one must determine whether the illustrations are large enough to be seen from a distance. Teachers and librarians must also be concerned about the durability of the picture books they select, especially those selected for infants and toddlers. Durability is determined by type of cover, type of binding, and paper quality, as discussed in Chapter 3.

• The amount of time necessary to read a picture book must not exceed the audience's attention span. Picture books usually vary in length between 16 and 32 pages. The amount of text on a page is also important in determining how long it will take to read the book aloud to a group of students or for a child to read the book to herself. A picture book that has more text than usual can be read aloud over two or three sessions. Also, children's willingness to listen to stories grows with experience, which may result in a younger child who has been read to regularly having a much longer attention span than an older child with no story experience.

Many teachers and librarians rely on the professional judgment of committees that choose what they consider to be the most outstanding picture books published each year in this country and abroad. The most prestigious picture book award in the United States is the Caldecott Award. The equivalent award in Great Britain is the Kate Greenaway Award, and in Canada, the Amelia Frances Howard-Gibbon Award. (See Appendix A for lists of award winners.) Another reliable source of information about good quality picture books is the New York Times Best Illustrated Children's Books of the Year, which is published in early November as a part of the New York Times Book Review Supplement.

Historical Overview of Picture Books

Orbis Pictus (Visible World), an ABC book written and illustrated by John Amos Comenius in Czechoslovakia and published in 1657, is considered to be the first children's picture book. Comenius's emphasis on using pictures to explain and expand the meaning of the text in books for young people is an important first. But since early books were rare and prohibitively expensive, they were seen by very few children. Moreover, until well into the nineteenth century, Europeans and Americans believed that books were for the serious business of educating and soul saving, not enjoyment! Today's full-color, extravagantly illustrated, highly amusing picture book is the product of the following important developments.

• *Technological advances in color printing.*   Improved four-color printing presses and printing techniques made high-quality illustrations in books more affordable. These advances were a direct result of the Industrial Revolution.

• *A more understanding attitude toward childhood.*   As late as the eighteenth century, the Western world thought of children as miniature adults and expected them to behave and work accordingly. During the nineteenth century, society began to accept the notion of childhood as a time for playing and learning. At the same time, the general economy began to be able to afford the average child the leisure time these activities require.

• *Higher standards of excellence in picture book illustrations.*   The first great children's book illustrators lived and worked during the 1800s. The beauty, charm, and humor of the illustrations of Randolph Caldecott, Kate Greenaway, and Walter Crane brought children's book art to the attention of the general public. The establishment of national awards for excellence in children's book illustration in the twentieth century had the same effect and encouraged more artists to enter the children's book field.

• *A greater demand for books.*   Growth of public school systems and public and school library systems accounted for much of this increase. In addition, reading came to be recognized as one of the child's best tools for learning and an important and worthy source of entertainment.

As a result of these developments, an economic, social, and political infrastructure was in place in most of the Western world by the early twentieth century that would support the widespread publishing of children's books. With its superb children's book illustrators and color printers of the time, England led the world in publishing picture books from the 1860s until the 1930s. Milestones in the development of picture books are highlighted in Table 4–1.

Today, the picture book genre is well established. Current trends in the field are toward an ever-widening audience, more multicultural themes and realistic themes, greater diversity in formats, and more illustrated retellings of folktales. Another trend (which will be discussed in Chapter 9) is greater and more effective use of illustration in informational books. Quite recently, parents, as major consumers of books for their children, have pushed the demand for children's books in most developed nations to unprecedented heights.

Types of Picture Books

The first picture books were meant to be read aloud to children. In the latter half of this century, in response to new educational theories and new markets, new types of picture books were developed to be read and enjoyed independently by a wider range of children than just kindergartners and first-graders. Thus, today's picture books differ in intended audience, purpose, format, and relative amount of text and illustration. These differences are not absolute, however; quite often one will find a picture

TABLE 4–1   Milestones in the Development of the Picture Book

Date	Event	Significance
1427	Publication of *Aesop's Fables,* illustrated by William Caxton.	One of the first known illustrated books enjoyed by children.
1657	Publication of *Orbis Pictus,* written and illustrated by John Amos Comenius.	Considered to be the first picture book for children.
1850	Public Libraries Act in Great Britain. Similar acts in New Hampshire (1849), Massachusetts (1851), and Ontario (1882).	Began the move to create tax-supported public libraries, which helped to create a demand for children's books.
1860–1900	Golden Age of children's book illustration in Great Britain, led by Randolph Caldecott, Walter Crane, and Kate Greenaway.	Increased awareness, stature, popularity, and appreciation of children's picture books.
1860s	Edmund Evans worked as a printer in Great Britain.	Introduced the use of color in picture books.
1902	Publication of *The Tale of Peter Rabbit* by Beatrix Potter.	First modern picture storybook in English.
1924	Publication of *Horn Book Magazine.*	Signaled recognition of children's literature as worthy of analysis and criticism.
1928	Publication of *Millions of Cats* by Wanda Gág.	First modern American picture storybook.
1938	Establishment of the Caldecott Award for illustration in children's books in the United States.	Promoted excellence in illustrating for children and encouraged talented artists to illustrate children's books.
1940	Publication of *Pat the Bunny* by Dorothy Kunhardt.	One of the first books for babies. Began the move to supply different types of picture books for different child audiences.
1955	Establishment of the Kate Greenaway Award for illustration in children's books in Great Britain.	Promoted excellence in illustrating for children.
1957	Publication of *The Cat in the Hat,* written and illustrated by Dr. Seuss and *Little Bear* written by Else Minarik and illustrated by Maurice Sendak.	Introduced the easy-to-read genre of picture books.
1962	Publication of *A Snowy Day,* written and illustrated by Ezra Jack Keats.	First recognition of a minority character as the protagonist in a picture book for children.
1967	Publication of *A Boy, a Dog, and a Frog,* illustrated by Mercer Mayer.	Popularized the wordless book genre.
1971	Establishment of Amelia Frances Howard-Gibbon Award for illustration in children's books in Canada.	Promoted excellence in illustrating for children.
1972	Publication of *Push Pull, Empty Full* by Tana Hoban.	Signaled the growing popularity of the concept picture book.

Continued

TABLE 4–1   *Continued*

Date	Event	Significance
1974	Publication of *Arrow to the Sun: A Pueblo Indian Tale* by Gerald McDermott.	Signaled the emergence of picture books for older readers as a distinct type of picture book.
1970s	Picture books first published in paperback form; children's bookstores appear and grow.	Picture books become more affordable and more available to the general public.
1981	Publication of "The Baby Board Books" by Helen Oxenbury.	Baby books were established as a distinct and important type of picture book.
1990	*Color Zoo* by Lois Ehlert wins a Caldecott Honor Award.	Recognition of the engineered book genre.

book having characteristics of several specific types. With the understanding that overlap between types is inevitable, you will want to learn to recognize the following kinds of picture books (organized by the intended age of the primary audience from youngest to oldest). Informational picture books are covered in Chapter 9.

Baby Books

Baby books are simply designed, brightly illustrated, durable picture books intended for use with children aged 0 to 2. An example is *Dressing* by Helen Oxenbury. They gained popularity in the 1980s in response to the growing evidence of the remarkable learning capacity of very young children. The types of baby books actually denote the material used in their construction. *Board books* are constructed of heavy, laminated cardboard, either bound as a book with pages or made to fold out in an accordion fashion. *Vinyl books* and *cloth books* are also types of baby books. These books have little or no text. Their content, which deals with the objects and routines familiar to the infant and toddler, is presented mainly by the illustrations. The best baby books, such as those produced by Helen Oxenbury and Jan Ormerod, are intelligently designed to emphasize patterns and associations as well as to promote dialogue between the caregiver and the young child who will often look at these books together.

Interactive Books

Interactive books are picture books that stimulate a child's verbal or physical participation as the book is read. These books ask the child direct questions, invite unison recitation of chants or repeated lines, encourage clapping or moving to the rhythm of the words, or require the child to touch or manipulate the book. An example is *Hoot, Howl, Hiss* by Michelle Koch. The intended audience is usually children aged 2 to 6, and the books are seen as an extension of their world of play. One early example of this type of book that is still greatly enjoyed by toddlers today is Dorothy Kunhardt's *Pat the Bunny*.

Toy Books

Sometimes called *engineered* or *mechanical* books, toy books use paper that has been engineered (i.e., cut, folded, constructed) to provide pop-up, see-through, movable, changeable, or three-dimensional illustrations. Toy books can be found for all ages, but only the simpler types of engineering, such as split pages (as in John Goodall's *Paddy Pork* and *Naughty Nancy* books) or drilled holes for see-through effects (as in Eric Carle's *The Very Hungry Caterpillar*), would be appropriate for most young children. Toy books with fragile or elaborate pop-up features would not last in the hands of a very young child.

Mother Goose and Nursery Rhyme Books

Mother Goose and nursery rhyme picture books are heavily illustrated collections of traditional verse. *Tomie dePaola's Mother Goose*, collected and illustrated by Tomie dePaola, is a good example of this category. Often, a familiar illustration is all a child needs to begin reciting one of these well-loved verses. Collected nursery rhymes first appeared in editions of Charles Perrault's *Tales of Mother Goose* in France in the early eighteenth century. These verses are now part of our children's literary heritage. Also, they have proven to be a wonderful introduction to the world of literature for young children. In societies where countless allusions are made every day to the characters and situations found in nursery rhymes, knowledge of this literature is part of being culturally literate.

Because there are so many of these verses, the better collections include large numbers of them thoughtfully organized around themes or topics and indexed by titles or first lines. A favorite book of this kind is *The Book of Nursery and Mother Goose Rhymes*, collected and illustrated by Marguerite de Angeli. Some lesser-known traditional verses were collected and illustrated by Arnold Lobel in *The Random House Book of Mother Goose*.

Nursery and Folk Song Books

Nursery and folk song picture books are heavily illustrated collections of both traditional and modern verses and their musical notation. *Songs from Mother Goose*, compiled by Nancy Larrick and illustrated by Robin Spowart, is a good example. Melody further emphasizes the innate musicality of these verses and turns some into games ("Ring Around the Roses") and others into lullabies ("Rock-a-bye Baby"). In choosing a songbook, teachers, librarians, and parents should be certain that there is a good selection of songs and that the music is well arranged for young voices and playable. Those who plan to work with preschoolers and first- and second-graders will be wise to make these songs part of their repertoire.

Alphabet Books

The alphabet, or ABC, book presents the alphabet letter-by-letter in order to acquaint young children with the shapes, names, and, in some cases, the sounds of the 26 letters. For example, see *Eating the Alphabet: Fruits and Vegetables from A to Z* by Lois Ehlert. Almost all ABC book authors and illustrators choose a theme (animals, elves, fruit, etc.) or device (finding the many objects in the accompanying illustration beginning with the featured letter) to give their books cohesion. Literally hundreds of ABC picture books have been published during the last 20 years, and naturally some are better than others. When choosing an ABC book, consider the appropriateness of the theme or device for students, whether both upper- and lowercase letters are displayed, and the style of print used (Old Gothic print, for example, would be unnecessarily complicated).

Most ABC books are intended for the nonreader or beginning reader. Some authors and illustrators use the alphabet itself as a device for presenting information. In these cases, the intended audience already knows the alphabet. *Ashanti to Zulu* by Margaret Musgrove and illustrated by Leo and Diane Dillon, for example, presents facts and illustrations about 26 African tribes, each beginning with a different letter of the alphabet.

Counting Books

The counting book presents numbers, usually 1 through 10, in order to acquaint young children with the numerals and their shapes (1, 2, 3 . . .), the number names (one, two, three . . .), the concept of how many each numeral represents, and the counting sequence. *1, 2, 3* by Tana Hoban is a good example of this type of book. As in alphabet books, authors and illustrators of counting books employ themes or devices to make them more cohesive and interesting. Specific considerations in evaluating a counting book are the appeal to children of the theme and objects chosen to illustrate the number concepts, and the clarity with which the illustrator presents the concept of number.

Illustrators often fill their alphabet and counting books with unusual and intriguing objects for children to name and count, such as aardvarks, barracudas, and chameleons. Children pick up a great deal of interesting information and vocabulary in this way. You will be in the best position to decide whether the novelty of these objects will be motivating or confusing to your students.

Concept Books

A concept book is a picture book that explores or explains an idea or concept (e.g., opposites), an object (e.g., a train), or an activity (e.g., working) rather than tell a story. Many concept books have no plot but use repeated elements in the illustrations and text to tie the book together. A good example is *I Touch* by Rachel Isadora. Limited text and clearly understood illustrations in the best concept books stimulate children's exploratory talk about the concepts, objects, and activities presented.

Alphabet and counting books are considered types of concept books. Another variety of the concept book popular with 2- to 4-year-olds is the *naming book,* which presents simple, labeled pictures loosely organized around a theme for young children to name. *Macmillan Picture Wordbook* edited by Judith S. Levey is an example of a naming book.

Wordless Books

The wordless book is a picture book that depends entirely on carefully sequenced illustrations to present the story. There is no text or the text is limited to one or two pages in the book. *The Gift* by John Prater is a good example of this category. Wordless books are generally intended for prereaders, usually children aged 4 to 6. When children "read" these illustrations in their own words, they benefit from the book's visual story structure in several ways:

- They develop a concept of story as a cohesive narrative with a beginning and an end.
- They use language inventively, which promotes language development.
- They learn the front-to-back, left-to-right page progression in reading.
- They begin to understand that stories can be found not only in books but in themselves.

Publishers began to produce wordless picture books in noticeable quantities in the 1960s. Mercer Mayer, with his wordless book series about a boy, a dog, and a frog, helped to popularize this type of picture book. More sophisticated wordless books for older readers, such as David Weisner's *Tuesday,* are also available.

Picture Storybooks

The picture storybook is a picture book in which both illustrations and text are equally responsible for telling the story. Text and illustration occur with equal frequency in these books, and on most double spreads, both are in view. A good example is *Babushka's Doll* by Patricia Polacco. The first modern picture book was a picture storybook, *The Tale of Peter Rabbit,* written and illustrated by Beatrix Potter and published in England in 1902. The first modern American picture storybook, *Millions of Cats,* written and illustrated by Wanda Gág, was published in 1928. The picture storybook is the most common of the types of picture books.

The text of most picture storybooks is meant to be read aloud to the intended audience of 4- to 7-year-olds, at least for the first time or two, and often includes challenging vocabulary. Many of the best picture storybooks are also read and enjoyed independently by 8- to 10-year-olds.

Easy-to-Read Books

Easy-to-read books are created to help the beginning reader read more successfully. They use larger print, more space between lines, limited vocabulary, as well as such devices as word patterns, repeated text, rhyming text, and illustration clues. For example, see *The Josephina Story Quilt* by Eleanor Coerr, illustrated by Bruce Degen. Easy-to-read books that strongly emphasize word patterns are sometimes called *pattern books*. For example, see *Is This a House for Hermit Crab?* by Megan McDonald, illustrated by S. D. Schindler. Easy-to-read picture books were first developed in the 1950s by such authors as Dr. Seuss (*The Cat in the Hat, Fox in Sox*) and Else Holmelund Minarik, who, along with illustrator Maurice Sendak, created the *Little Bear* series. Easy-to-read books can be used with children whenever they want to learn to read, but the audience for this type of book is usually the 5- to 7-year-old.

The easy-to-read book differs in appearance from the picture storybook in several obvious ways: Because they are intended for independent reading, they do not have to be seen from a distance and are smaller; the text takes up a greater proportion of each page; and the text is often divided into short chapters. Especially in these "chapter" books, the illustrations are proportionately smaller and less profuse than in picture storybooks, occurring on approximately every other page.

Picture Books for Older Readers

Picture books for older readers, which are varied in degree of sophistication, abstraction, or complexity in themes, stories, and illustrations, are suitable for children aged 10 and older. A good example is *Black and White* by David Macaulay. This type of picture book began to appear in the 1970s, and now artists such as David Macaulay, Jörg Steiner, and David Weisner are known for their picture books for older readers. The types of picture books most commonly found for older readers are picture storybooks, wordless books, and toy books.

Transitional Books

Transitional books are a special type of book for the child who can read but who has not yet become a fluent reader. These books, less profusely illustrated and having lengthier text than the other types of books discussed in this chapter, are not considered picture books by some teachers and librarians; in truth, they lie somewhere between picture books and full-length novels. For this reason, we have not included transitional books in the annotated list of titles at the end of this chapter. These titles can be found in the end-of-chapter lists of the appropriate genre chapters and in Appendix D.

Characteristic of transitional books are an uncomplicated writing style and vocabulary, an illustration on about every third page, division of text into chapters, and slightly enlarged print. Children who read these books are typically between the ages of 8 and 11. Often, books for the transitional reader occur in series, as in Donald Sobol's

Encyclopedia Brown books, Ann Cameron's *Julian* books, and Robert Newton Peck's *Soup* books.

With easy-to-read and transitional books in mind, it is wise to remember that children by the age of 5 or 6 have become accustomed to hearing wonderful, richly descriptive stories read and told to them. They are fluent and often sophisticated users of oral language. For children to find themselves suddenly limited to simplistic, boring stories while learning to read would be disheartening, to say the least. To write well for the beginning reader is a real challenge, since these stories must treat interesting topics in vivid language while remaining relatively easy to read. Finding the best of these books for the beginning and transitional readers in your charge will be time well spent.

Within this century the picture book was begun and developed as a genre, diversified to meet the demands of an ever-expanding audience and market, and improved as a result of new and refined printing technology. As researchers came to realize the connections between positive early experiences with good literature, early learning, and future school success, new types of picture books were developed to serve both younger and older audiences. Today, high-quality picture books on nearly every imaginable topic can enrich the lives and imaginations of young children and the classrooms and libraries where they learn.

Notable Authors and Illustrators of Picture Books

Janet and Allan Ahlberg, author/illustrator. British. Interactive books. *Each Peach Pear Plum; The Jolly Postman.*

Mitsumasa Anno, author/illustrator. Japanese. Sophisticated wordless and concept books. *Anno's Journey; Anno's Counting Book.*

Molly Bang, author/illustrator. Wordless and concept books illustrated in a variety of styles and media. *The Grey Lady and the Strawberry Snatcher; Ten, Nine, Eight.*

Ludwig Bemelmans, author/illustrator. Creator of "Madeline" series of picture storybooks. *Madeline; Madeline's Rescue.*

Marcia Brown, author/illustrator. Reteller and illustrator of folktales from foreign lands. Three Caldecott Awards, six Caldecott Honor Book Awards. *Once a Mouse . . . ; Stone Soup.*

Anthony Browne, author/illustrator. British. Surreal illustrations in picture books for older readers. *Gorilla; The Tunnel.*

Nancy Ekholm Burkert, author/illustrator. Extensive research into the period gives her illustrations authenticity. *Valentine and Orson.*

John Burningham, author/illustrator. British. Concept books. *Grandpa; Time to Get Out of the Bath, Shirley.*

Eric Carle, author/illustrator. Unusually formatted picture storybooks and concept books about insects and animals. *The Grouchy Ladybug; The Very Busy Spider.*

Lucille Clifton, author. Creator of "Everett Anderson" series of rhyming picture storybooks about African-American family life. *Amifica; Everett Anderson's Goodbye.*

Barbara Cooney, author/illustrator. Picture storybooks reflect values of New England. *Miss Rumphius.*

Donald Crews, author/illustrator. Concept books about aspects of transportation. *Freight Train; Truck.*

Tomie dePaola, author/illustrator. Droll characters like Strega Nona and Big Anthony; uses formal, balanced artistic style. *The Legend of the Bluebonnet; Strega Nona: An Old Tale.*

Jean deBrunhoff, author/illustrator. Creator of "Babar, the Elephant" series of picture storybooks.

The Story of Babar, the Little Elephant; Babar the King.

Wanda Gág, author/illustrator. Wrote the first modern American picture book. *Millions of Cats; Nothing at All.*

Stephen Gammell, illustrator. Uses colored pencil in an informal, airy style. *The Relatives Came* (by Cynthia Rylant).

Paul Goble, author/illustrator. Reteller and illustrator of folktales of the North American Indian. *Beyond the Ridge.*

John Goodall, illustrator. Wordless books in split-page format. *Naughty Nancy; The Adventures of Paddy Pork.*

Diane Goode, illustrator. Rosy-cheeked children and color tones lend a sense of the past to her illustrations. *Watch the Stars Come Out* (by Riki Levinson).

Eric Hill, author/illustrator. Features "Spot," the dog, in toy and board books. *Where's Spot?*

Russell Hoban, author. Creator of "Frances," the badger, in easy-to-read books. *Bedtime for Frances.*

Tana Hoban, author/illustrator. Using photographs, created some of the first and best concept books. *Push Pull, Empty Full; Is It Rough? Is It Smooth? Is It Shiny?*

Margaret Hodges, author. Reteller of folktales for older children. *Saint George and the Dragon* (illustrated by Trina Schart Hyman).

Shirley Hughes, author/illustrator. British. Picture storybooks about family life. *Alfie Gets in First.*

Pat Hutchins, author/illustrator. British. Pattern books for beginning readers. *Rosie's Walk; Tidy Titch.*

Trina Schart Hyman, illustrator. Illustrator of retold folktales. *Little Red Riding Hood; Hershel and the Hanukkah Goblins.*

Roberto Innocenti, author/illustrator. Italian. Picture storybooks for older readers. *Rose Blanche.*

Susan Jeffers, illustrator. Representational style used to illustrate folktales, classic stories, and poems. *The Three Jovial Huntsmen* (Mother Goose).

Ezra Jack Keats, author/illustrator. One of the first to portray ethnic minorities in the United States as major characters in picture books. *A Snowy Day; Peter's Chair.*

Steven Kellogg, author/illustrator. Uses animals as characters in picture storybooks. *Island of the Skog.*

Leo Lionni, author/illustrator. Uses collage technique to illustrate modern fables. *Swimmy; Frederick.*

Arnold Lobel, author/illustrator. Creator of "Frog and Toad" easy-to-read series. *Days with Frog and Toad; Fables.*

David Macaulay, author/illustrator. Uses pen and ink to illustrate picture books for older readers. *Baaa; Cathedral.*

Robert McCloskey, author/illustrator. Realistic style used in several modern classic picture storybooks. *Make Way for Ducklings; Time of Wonder.*

Patricia McKissack, author. Picture storybooks with African-American characters and themes. *Nettie Jo's Friends* (illustrated by Scott Cook).

James Marshall, author/illustrator. Humorously retold and illustrated folktales. *Goldilocks and the Three Bears.*

Bill Martin, Jr., author. Pattern and rhyming stories for the beginning reader. *Brown Bear, Brown Bear, What Do You See?* (illustrated by Eric Carle).

Mercer Mayer, author/illustrator. One of the first to develop the wordless picture book. *A Boy, A Dog and a Frog.*

Else Holmelund Minarik, author. Her "Little Bear" books were some of the first easy-to-read books. *Little Bear's Visit* (illustrated by Maurice Sendak).

Jörg Müller, illustrator. Swiss. Picture books for older readers. *The Changing City; Rabbit Island* (by Jörg Steiner).

Jan Ormerod, author/illustrator. Baby books. *Messy Baby.*

Helen Oxenbury, author/illustrator. British. Board books for babies. *Dressing; Say Goodnight.*

Peter Parnall, author/illustrator. Illustrates nature in spare, open style. *Hawk, I'm Your Brother* (by Byrd Baylor).

Bill Peet, author/illustrator. Former Disney animator known for humorous picture storybooks about animals and his picture book autobiography. *Merle the High Flying Squirrel; Bill Peet: An Autobiography.*

Jerry Pinkney, illustrator. Represents the African-American experience in realistic, watercolor illustrations. *Mirandy and Brother Wind* (by Patricia McKissack).

Leo Politi, author/illustrator. Picture storybooks about ethnic groups in the United States, particularly Mexican Americans. *Song of the Swallows*.

Beatrix Potter, author/illustrator. British. Wrote the first modern, English picture storybook. *The Tale of Peter Rabbit*.

Alice and Martin Provensen, authors/illustrator. *The Glorious Flight: Across the Channel with Louis Blériot*.

H. A. Rey, author/illustrator. Created "Curious George" character in a series of humorous picture storybooks. *Curious George Gets a Medal*.

Cynthia Rylant, author. Picture storybooks set in Appalachia; "Henry and Mudge" easy-to-read series. *The Relatives Came* (illustrated by Stephen Gammell).

Richard Scarry, author/illustrator. Concept, or naming, books in large format. *Richard Scarry's Biggest Word Book Ever!*

John Schoenherr, illustrator. Crisp, representational style well suited to realistic stories. *Owl Moon* (by Jane Yolen).

Maurice Sendak, author/illustrator. Explores the dreams and imagination of children in complex picture storybooks. *Where the Wild Things Are; Outside Over There*.

Dr. Seuss, (pseudonym for Theodor Geisel), author/illustrator. One of the first to develop the easy-to-read genre. *The Cat in the Hat*.

Peter Spier, author/illustrator. Wordless and interactive books. *Peter Spier's Rain*.

William Steig, author/illustrator. Animal fantasy picture storybooks. *Dr. De Soto*.

Jörg Steiner, author. Swiss. Picture books for older children (with Jörg Müller). *Rabbit Island; The Bear Who Wanted to Be a Bear*.

John Steptoe, author/illustrator. One of the first successful African-American picture book illustrators. *Stevie; Mufaro's Beautiful Daughters*.

Chris Van Allsburg, author/illustrator. Uses shadow and unusual perspectives to create mysterious moods in picture storybooks for intermediate-grade readers. *Jumanji; The Garden of Abdul Gasazi*.

Julie Vivas, illustrator. Australian. Down-to-earth humor is evident in illustrations. *The Nativity*.

Rosemary Wells, author/illustrator. Creator of excellent board books and pattern books. *Hooray for Max, Noisy Nora*.

Brian Wildsmith, author/illustrator. British. Innovative, modernistic illustrations. *Brian Wildsmith's ABC*.

Vera B. Williams, author/illustrator. Expressive artistic style used to depict nontraditional families in picture storybooks. *A Chair for My Mother; Three Days on a River in a Red Canoe*.

Audrey and Don Wood, author/illustrator. Action-filled, humorous illustrations and excellent language characterize rich pattern books. *King Bidgood's in the Bathtub; Heckedy Peg*.

Paul O. Zelinsky, illustrator. Illustrates folktales with richly colored oil paintings. *Rumpelstilskin* (adapted by illustrator).

Harve and Margot Zemach, author/illustrator. Use humor in retelling and illustrating folktales. *Duffy and the Devil: A Cornish Tale*.

Charlotte Zolotow, author. Wrote many picture books about family life and emotions. *The Quarreling Book; William's Doll*.

Recommended Picture Books

Ages refer to approximate interest levels. YA = young adult.

Baby Books

These books are generally suitable for ages 0 to 3.

Duke, Kate. *What Bounces?* Dutton, 1986. (Others in the Guinea Pig Board Book series: *Clean-up Day; Bedtime; The Playground*.)

Hoban, Tana. *What Is It?* Greenwillow, 1985.

Kunhardt, Dorothy. *Pat the Bunny*. Golden, 1940.

Ormerod, Jan. *Bend and Stretch*. Lothrop, 1987. (Others in this series: *Making Friends,* 1987; *Mom's Home,* 1987; *This Little Nose,* 1987.)

Oxenbury, Helen. "Out and About Books." *The Birthday Party*. Dutton, 1983. (Others in the series: *The Car Trip; The Checkup; The Dancing Class;*

Eating Out; First Day of School; Grandma and Grandpa; Our Dog.)

———. *I Can.* (Baby Board Book) Random, 1986. (Others in the series: *I Hear; I See; I Touch.*)

———. "The Baby Board Books." *Dressing.* Simon and Schuster, 1981. (Others in the series: *Family; Friends; Playing; Working.*)

———. "Very First Books." *Mother's Helper.* Dial, 1982. (Others in the series: *Shopping Trip; Beach Day; Good Night, Good Morning; Monkey See, Monkey Do.*)

Tafuri, Nancy. *My Friends.* Greenwillow, 1987.

———. *Where We Sleep.* Greenwillow, 1987.

Wells, Rosemary. "Very First Books." *Max's Bath.* Dial, 1985. (Others in the series: *Max's Bedtime,* 1985; *Max's Birthday,* 1985; *Max's Breakfast,* 1985; *Max's First Word,* 1979; *Max's New Suit,* 1979; *Max's Ride,* 1979; *Max's Toys,* 1979.)

Interactive Books

Ahlberg, Janet, and Allen Ahlberg. *The Baby's Catalogue.* Little, Brown, 1982. Ages 2–4.

———. *Each Peach Pear Plum: An I-Spy Story.* Viking, 1978. Ages 2–4.

———. *Peek-a Boo!* Viking, 1981. Ages 3–5.

Burton, Marilee Robin. *Tail Toes Eyes Ears Nose.* Harper, 1988. Ages 2–4.

Carlstrom, Nancy White. *Jesse Bear, What Will You Wear?* Illustrated by Bruce Degan. Macmillan, 1986. Ages 2–4.

Christelow, Eileen, reteller. *Five Little Monkeys Jumping on the Bed.* Clarion, 1989. Ages 3–5.

Dodds, Dayle Ann. *Wheel Away!* Illustrated by Thacher Hurd. Harper, 1989. Ages 5–7.

Hennessy, B. G. *The Missing Tarts.* Illustrated by Tracey Campbell Pearson. Viking, 1989. Ages 3–5.

Hill, Eric. *Where's Spot?* Putnam, 1980. (Others in the series: *Spot's First Walk,* Putnam, 1981; *Spot's Birthday Party,* Putnam, 1982; *Spot's First Christmas,* Putnam, 1983.) Ages 3–5.

Koch, Michelle. *Hoot, Howl, Hiss.* Greenwillow, 1991. Ages 4–6.

Martin, Bill Jr., and John Archambault. *Barn Dance.* Illustrated by Ted Rand. Holt, 1986. Ages 4–6.

Noll, Sally. *Jiggle, Wiggle, Prance.* Greenwillow, 1987. Ages 3–5.

———. *Watch Where You Go.* Greenwillow, 1990. Ages 4–6.

Spier, Peter. *Crash! Bang! Boom!* Doubleday, 1972. Ages 5–7.

Tafuri, Nancy. *Have You Seen My Duckling?* Greenwillow, 1984. Ages 3–5.

Watanabe, Shigeo. "I Can Do It All By Myself." *How Do I Put It On?* Illustrated by Yasou Ohtomo. Philomel, 1980. (Also in series: *What a Good Lunch!,* 1980; *Get Set Go!,* 1981; I'm King of the Castle, 1982; *Where's My Daddy?,* 1982; *I Can Ride It!,* 1982.) Ages 4–6.

Wilkes, Angela. *My First Activity Book.* Knopf, 1990. Ages 3–5.

Williams, Vera B. *"More More More," Said the Baby.* Greenwillow, 1990. Ages 2–4.

Wolff, Ashley. *Only the Cat Saw.* Dodd, Mead, 1985. Ages 4–6.

Yoshi. *Who's Hiding Here?* Picture Book Studio, 1987. Ages 5–7.

Toy Books

Baker, Keith. *The Magic Fan.* Harcourt, 1989. Ages 7–9.

Carle, Eric. *The Honeybee and the Robber: A Moving/Picture Book.* Philomel, 1981. Ages 5–7.

———. *The Very Hungry Caterpillar.* World, 1968. Ages 4–6.

Goodall, John S. *The Adventures of Paddy Pork.* Harcourt, 1968. Ages 6–8.

———. *The Ballooning Adventures of Paddy Pork.* Harcourt, 1969. Ages 6–8.

———. *Naughty Nancy.* Atheneum, 1975. Ages 6–8.

———. *Paddy Pork's Holiday.* Atheneum, 1976. Ages 6–8.

———. *The Story of an English Village.* Atheneum, 1979. Ages 7–9.

———. *The Surprise Picnic.* Atheneum, 1977. Ages 6–8.

Hellen, Nancy. *The Bus Stop.* Orchard, 1988. Ages 5–7.

———. *Old MacDonald Had a Farm.* Orchard, 1990. Ages 5–7.

Hill, Eric. *Where's Spot?* Putnam, 1980. Ages 3–5.

Jonas, Ann. *Where Can It Be?* Greenwillow, 1986. Ages 5–7.

Schweninger, Ann. *Birthday Wishes*. Viking, 1986. Ages 6–8.

Mother Goose and Nursery Rhyme Books

These books are generally suitable for ages 2 to 7.

Alderson, Brian. *Cakes and Custard*. Illustrated by Helen Oxenbury. Morrow, 1975.

Arnold, Ted. *Mother Goose's Words of Wit and Wisdom: A Book of Months*. Dial, 1990.

Briggs, Raymond. *The Mother Goose Treasury*. Coward-McCann, 1966.

Cauley, Lorinda Bryan. *The Three Little Kittens*. Putnam, 1982.

Cousins, Lucy, illustrator. *The Little Dog Laughed and Other Nursery Rhymes*. Dutton, 1990.

DeAngeli, Marguerite. *Marguerite DeAngeli's Book of Nursery and Mother Goose Rhymes*. Doubleday, 1954.

DeForest, Charlotte B. *The Prancing Pony: Nursery Rhymes from Japan Adapted into English Verse for Children*. Illustrated by Keiko Hida. Walker/Weatherhill, 1968.

dePaola, Tomie, compiler. *Tomie dePaola's Mother Goose*. Putnam, 1985.

Emerson, Sally, selector. *The Nursery Treasury: A Collection of Baby Games, Rhymes and Lullabies*. Illustrated by Moira and Colin MacLean. Doubleday, 1988.

Greenaway, Kate. *Mother Goose, or The Old Nursery Rhymes*. Warne, 1881.

Griego, Margot C., Betsy L. Bucks, Sharon S. Gilbert, and Laurel H. Kimball. *Tortillitas Para Mama*. Illustrated by Barbara Cooney. Holt, 1981.

Hale, Sarah Josepha. *Mary Had a Little Lamb*. Photographs by Bruce McMillan. Scholastic, 1990.

Hoguet, Susan Ramsey. *Solomon Grundy*. Dutton, 1986.

Jeffers, Susan. *Three Jovial Huntsmen*. Bradbury, 1973.

Lines, Kathleen. *Lavender's Blue*. Illustrated by Harold Jones. Watts, 1964.

Lobel, Arnold. *Gregory Griggs and Other Nursery Rhyme People*. Greenwillow, 1978.

———. *Whiskers and Rhymes*. Greenwillow, 1985.

———, selector. *The Random House Book of Mother Goose*. Random, 1986.

Marshall, James. *James Marshall's Mother Goose*. Farrar, 1979.

Opie, Peter and Iona, compilers. *Tail Feathers from Mother Goose: The Opie Rhyme Book*. Little, Brown, 1988.

Provensen, Alice, and Martin Provensen. *The Mother Goose Book*. Random, 1976.

Reed, Philip. *Mother Goose and Nursery Rhymes*. Atheneum, 1963.

Rojankovsky, Feodor. *The Tall Book of Mother Goose*. Harper, 1942.

Spier, Peter. *London Bridge Is Falling Down*. Doubleday, 1967.

———. *To Market, To Market*. Doubleday, 1967.

Sutherland, Zena. *The Orchard Book of Nursery Rhymes*. Illustrated by Faith Jaques. Orchard, 1990.

Tripp, Wallace. *Granfa' Grig Had a Pig and Other Rhymes Without Reason*. Little, Brown, 1976.

Tudor, Tasha. *Mother Goose*. Walck, 1944.

Westcott, Nadine Bernard. *Peanut Butter and Jelly: A Play Rhyme*. Dutton, 1987.

———, adaptor. *The Lady with the Alligator Purse*. Little, Brown, 1988.

Wildsmith, Brian. *Brian Wildsmith's Mother Goose*. Watts, 1963.

Wright, Blanche Fisher. *The Real Mother Goose*. Rand McNally, 1916.

Wyndham, Robert. *Chinese Mother Goose Rhymes*. Illustrated by Ed Young. World, 1968.

Zuromskis, Diane, illustrator. *The Farmer in the Dell*. Little, Brown, 1978.

Nursery and Folk Song Books

Aliki, pseud. (Aliki Brandenberg). *Go Tell Aunt Rhody*. Macmillan, 1974. Ages 6–10.

Brett, Jan, illustrator. *The Twelve Days of Christmas*. Dodd, 1986. Ages 6–10.

Brown, Marc. *Finger Rhymes*. Dutton, 1980. Ages 5–7.

———. *Hand Rhymes*. Dutton, 1985. Ages 5–7.

dePaola, Tomie. *Tomie dePaola's Book of Christmas Carols*. Putnam, 1987. Ages 6–10.

Durell, Ann, selector. *The Diane Goode Book of American Folk Tales and Songs*. Illustrated by Diane Goode. Dutton, 1989. Ages 6–10.

Fowke, Edith, compiler. *Sally Go Round the Sun: Three Hundred Children's Songs, Rhymes, and*

Games. Illustrated by Carlos Marchiori. Doubleday, 1970. Ages 6–10.

Fox, Dan, editor. *Go In and Out the Window: An Illustrated Songbook for Young People*. Holt/Metropolitan Museum of Art, 1987. Ages 6–10.

Langstaff, John, editor. *What a Morning! The Christmas Story in Black Spirituals*. Illustrated by Ashley Bryan, arrangements for singing and piano by John Andrew Ross. Macmillan, 1987. Ages 6–10.

Larrick, Nancy, compiler. *Songs from Mother Goose: With the Traditional Melody for Each*. Illustrated by Robin Spowart. Harper, 1989. Ages 3–7.

Raffi. *Raffi's Christmas Treasury*. Illustrated by Nadine Bernard Westcott. Crown, 1988. Ages 6–10.

Spier, Peter. *The Fox Went Out on a Chilly Night*. Doubleday, 1961. Ages 6–8.

———. *The Star-Spangled Banner*. Doubleday, 1973. Ages 6–10.

Staines, Bill. *All God's Critters Got a Place in the Choir*. Illustrated by Margot Zemach. Dutton, 1989. Ages 6–10.

Yolen, Jane, editor. *The Lullaby Songbook*. Musical arrangements by Adam Stemple. Illustrated by Charles Mikolaycak. Harcourt, 1986. Ages 3–5.

Zemach, Harve. *Mommy, Buy Me a China Doll*. Illustrated by Margot Zemach. Follett, 1966. Ages 3–5.

Zemach, Margot. *Hush, Little Baby*. Dutton, 1976. Ages 4–6.

Alphabet Books

These books are generally suitable for ages 3 to 6. Ages will be provided only for those books intended for an older audience.

Anno, Mitsumasa. *Anno's Alphabet*. Crowell, 1975. Ages 7–9.

Azarian, Mary. *A Farmer's Alphabet*. Godine, 1981.

Baskin, Hosea, Tobias, and Lisa. *Hosie's Alphabet*. Illustrated by Leonard Baskin. Viking, 1972. Ages 7–9.

Berger, Terry, and Alice S. Kandell. *Ben's ABC Day*. Lothrop, 1982.

Brown, Marcia. *All Butterflies: An ABC*. Scribner's, 1974.

Burningham, John. *John Burningham's ABC*. Bobbs-Merrill, 1967.

Duke, Kate. *The Guinea Pig ABC*. Dutton, 1983.

Duvoisin, Roger. *A for the Ark*. Lothrop, 1952.

Ehlert, Lois. *Eating the Alphabet: Fruits and Vegetables from A to Z*. Harcourt, 1989.

Ellis, Veronica Freeman. *Afro-Bets First Book about Africa*. Illustrated by George Ford. Just Us Books, 1990.

Feelings, Muriel. *Jambo Means Hello: Swahili Alphabet Book*. Illustrated by Tom Feelings. Dial, 1974. Ages 6–8.

Gardner, Beau. *Have You Ever Seen...? An ABC Book*. Dodd, 1986.

Geisert, Arthur. *Pigs from A to Z*. Houghton, 1986. Ages 6–10.

Greenaway, Kate. *A-Apple Pie*. Warne, 1886.

Hoban, Tana. *A, B, See!* Greenwillow, 1982.

———. *26 Letters and 99 Cents*. Greenwillow, 1987.

Hughes, Shirley. *Lucy and Tom's A.B.C.* Viking, 1986.

Isadora, Rachel. *City Seen from A to Z*. Greenwillow, 1983.

Jonas, Ann. *Aardvarks, Disembark!* Greenwillow, 1990.

Kellogg, Steven. *Aster Aardvark's Alphabet Adventures*. Morrow, 1987.

Kightley, Rosalinda. *ABC*. Little, Brown, 1986.

Kitchen, Burt. *Animal Alphabet*. Dial, 1984.

Lobel, Anita. *Alison's Zinnia*. Greenwillow, 1990.

Lobel, Arnold. *On Market Street*. Illustrated by Anita Lobel. Greenwillow, 1981.

MacDonald, Suse. *Alphabatics*. Bradbury, 1986.

Martin, Bill, Jr., and John Archambault. *Chicka Chicka Boom Boom*. Illustrated by Lois Ehlert. Simon and Schuster, 1989.

Merriam, Eve. *Halloween ABC*. Illustrated by Lane Smith. Macmillan, 1987. Ages 6–10.

Munari, Bruno. *Bruno Munari's ABC*. World Publishing, 1960.

Neumeier, Marty, and Byron Glaser. *Action Alphabet*. Greenwillow, 1985.

Piatti, Celestino. *Celestino Piatti's Animal ABC*. Translated by Jon Reid. Atheneum, 1966.

Piers, Helen. *Puppy's ABC*. Oxford, 1987.

Provensen, Alice, and Martin Provensen. *A Peaceable Kingdom: The Shaker ABCEDARIUS*. Viking, 1978. Ages 6–8.

Sendak, Maurice. "The Nutshell Library." *Alligators All Around*. Harper, 1962.

Tudor, Tasha. *A Is for Annabelle*. Walck, 1954.

Van Allsburg, Chris. *The Z Was Zapped*. Houghton Mifflin, 1987. Ages 6–10.

Watson, Clyde. *Applebet*. Illustrated by Wendy Watson. Farrar, 1982.

Wildsmith, Brian. *Brian Wildsmith's ABC*. Watts, 1962. Ages 6–10.

Wilner, Isabel. *B Is for Bethlehem: A Christmas Alphabet*. Illustrated by Elisa Kleven. Dutton, 1990.

Yolen, Jane. *All in the Woodland Early: An ABC Book*. Illustrated by Jane Breskin Zalben. Collins, 1979.

Counting Books

These books are generally suitable for ages 4 to 7. Ages will be provided only for those books intended for an older audience.

Aker, Susan. *What Comes in 2's, 3's & 4's?* Illustrated by Bernie Karlin. Simon & Schuster, 1990.

Anno, Mitsumasa. *Anno's Counting Book*. Crowell, 1977. Ages 7–9.

Aylesworth, Jim. *One Crow: A Counting Rhyme*. Illustrated by Ruth Young. Lippincott, 1988. Ages 5–7.

Bang, Molly. *Ten, Nine, Eight*. Greenwillow, 1983.

Carle, Eric. *My Very First Book of Numbers*. Crowell, 1974.

———. *1,2,3 to the Zoo*. Philomel, 1968.

Dunrea, Olivier. *Deep Down Underground*. Macmillan, 1989.

Ehlert, Lois. *Fish Eyes: A Book You Can Count On*. Harcourt, 1990.

Ernst, Lisa Campbell. *Up to Ten and Down Again*. Lothrop, 1986.

Feelings, Muriel. *Moja Means One: Swahili Counting Book*. Illustrated by Tom Feelings. Dial, 1971.

Hoban, Tana. *1, 2, 3*. Greenwillow, 1985.

———. *26 Letters and 99 Cents*. Greenwillow, 1987.

Hutchins, Pat. *1 Hunter*. Greenwillow, 1982.

Kitchen, Bert. *Animal Numbers*. Dial, 1987.

Langstaff, John. *Over in the Meadow*. Illustrated by Feodor Rojankovsky. Harcourt, 1957.

Lindbergh, Reeve. *Midnight Farm*. Illustrated by Susan Jeffers. Dial, 1987.

Lynn, Sara. *123*. Little, Brown, 1986.

McMillan, Bruce. *Counting Wildflowers*. Lothrop, 1986.

Oxenbury, Helen. *Numbers of Things*. Watts, 1968.

Peek, Merle. *The Balancing Act: A Counting Book*. Clarion, 1987.

Reiss, John. *Numbers*. Bradbury, 1971.

Rowan, Dick. *Everybody In! A Counting Book*. Bradbury, 1968.

Sendak, Maurice. "The Nutshell Library." *One Was Johnny*. Harper, 1962.

Sis, Peter. *Waving: A Counting Book*. Greenwillow, 1988.

Tafuri, Nancy. *Who's Counting?* Greenwillow, 1986.

Testa, Fulvio. *If You Take a Pencil*. Dial, 1982.

Wildsmith, Brian. *Brian Wildsmith's 1, 2, 3's*. Watts, 1965.

Concept Books

These books are generally suitable for ages 3 to 5.

Baer, Gene. *Thump, Thump, Rat-a-Tat-Tat*. Illustrated by Lois Ehlert. Harper, 1989.

Barton, Byron. *Building a House*. Greenwillow, 1981.

———. *Dinosaurs, Dinosaurs*. Crowell, 1989.

———. *Machines at Work*. Crowell, 1987.

Carle, Eric. *My Very First Book of Shapes*. Crowell, 1974.

———. *My Very First Book of Colors*. Crowell, 1974.

Crews, Donald. *Flying*. Greenwillow, 1986.

———. *Freight Train*. Greenwillow, 1978.

———. *Truck*. Greenwillow, 1980.

Ehlert, Lois. *Growing Vegetable Soup*. Harcourt, 1987.

Emberley, Rebecca. *Jungle Sounds*. Little, Brown, 1989.

Florian, Douglas. *A Summer Day*. Greenwillow, 1988.

———. *A Winter Day*. Greenwillow, 1987.

Fowler, Susi Gregg. *When Summer Ends*. Illustrated by Marisabina Russo. Greenwillow, 1989.

Gerstein, Mordicai. *The Sun's Day*. Harper, 1989.

Hoban, Tana. *Is It Red? Is It Yellow? Is It Blue?* Greenwillow, 1978.

———. *Look Again!* Macmillan, 1971.

———. *Over, Under, and Through and Other Spatial Concepts*. Macmillan, 1973.

———. *Push Pull, Empty Full: A Book of Opposites*. Macmillan, 1972.

Hughes, Shirley. *Alfie Gets in First*. Lothrop, 1982.

———. *Alfie Gives a Hand*. Lothrop, 1984.

———. *Angel Mae*. Lothrop, 1989.

———. *The Big Concrete Lorry*. Lothrop, 1990.

———. *Out and About*. Lothrop, 1988.

———. "Nursery Collection." *Bathwater's Hot*. Lothrop, 1985. (Others in the series: *Noisy; When We Went to the Park*.)

Isadora, Rachel. *I Hear*. Greenwillow, 1985. (Also in the series: *I Touch,* 1985; *I See,* 1985.)

Kalan, Robert. *Blue Sea*. Illustrated by Donald Crews. Greenwillow, 1979.

Kightley, Rosalinda. *Opposites*. Little, Brown, 1986.

———. *Shapes*. Little, Brown, 1986.

Krauss, Ruth. *A Hole Is to Dig*. Illustrated by Maurice Sendak. Harper, 1952.

Levey, Judith S., editor. *Macmillan Picture Wordbook*. Macmillan, 1990.

Lipkind, William. *Finders Keepers*. Illustrated by Nicolas Mordvinoff. Harcourt, 1951.

Lynn, Sara. *Colors*. Little, Brown, 1986.

Martin, Bill, Jr., and John Archambault. *Listen to the Rain*. Illustrated by James Endicott. Holt, 1988.

McCloskey, Robert. *Time of Wonder*. Viking 1957.

McDonald, Golden. pseud. (Margaret Wise Brown). *The Little Island*. Illustrated by Leonard Weisgard. Doubleday, 1946.

McMillan, Bruce. *Becca Backward, Becca Frontward: A Book of Concept Pairs*. Lothrop, 1986.

———. *Dry or Wet?* Lothrop, 1988.

———. *Super Super Superwords*. Lothrop, 1989.

———. *Time To . . . .* Lothrop, 1989.

Narahashi, Keiko. *I Have a Friend*. Macmillan, 1987.

Parnall, Peter. *Winter Barn*. Macmillan, 1986.

Pearson, Susan. *My Favorite Time of the Year*. Illustrated by John Wallner. Harper, 1988.

Reiss, John. *Colors*. Bradbury, 1969.

———. *Shapes*. Bradbury, 1974.

Rice, Eve. *Oh, Lewis!* Macmillan, 1974.

Rockwell, Anne, and Harlow Rockwell. *The Toolbox*. Macmillan, 1971.

Rogers, Fred. *Making Friends*. Photographs by Jim Judkis. Putnam, 1987.

———. *Moving*. Photographs by Jim Judkis. Putnam, 1987.

Scarry, Richard. *My First Word Book*. Random House, 1986.

———. *Richard Scarry's Biggest Word Book Ever!* Random House, 1985.

Schwartz, David M. *If You Made a Million*. Illustrated by Steven Kellogg. Photographs by George Ancona. Lothrop, 1989.

Serfozo, Mary. *Who Said Red?* Illustrated by Keiko Narahashi. Macmillan, 1988.

Shulevitz, Uri. *Rain Rain Rivers*. Scribner's, 1967.

Spier, Peter. *Fast-Slow High-Low*. Doubleday, 1972.

Tafuri, Nancy. *In a Red House*. Greenwillow, 1987.

Testa, Fulvio. *If You Look Around You*. Dutton, 1983.

verDorn, Bethea. *Moon Glows*. Illustrated by Thomas Graham. Arcade, 1990.

Voake, Charlotte. *Mrs. Goose's Baby*. Little, Brown, 1989.

Walsh, Ellen Stoll. *Mouse Paint*. Harcourt, 1989.

Winthrop, Elizabeth. *Shoes*. Illustrated by William Joyce. Harper, 1986.

Wolde, Gunilla. "Betsy Books." *This Is Betsy*. Random, 1975. (Also in series: *Betsy's Baby Brother,* 1975; *Betsy's First Day at Nursery School,* 1976; and *Betsy and the Doctor,* 1978.)

Wolff, Ashley. *A Year of Beasts*. Dutton, 1986.

———. *A Year of Birds*. Dodd, Mead, 1984.

Wordless Books

These books are generally suitable for ages 3 to 6. Ages will be provided only for those books intended for an older audience.

Alexander, Martha. *Bobo's Dream*. Dial, 1970.

Anno, Mitsumasa. *Anno's Journey*. Collins, 1978. Ages 8–10.

———. *Topsy-Turvies—Pictures to Stretch the Imagination*. Walker/Weatherhill, 1970.

Briggs, Raymond. *The Snowman*. Random, 1978.

Carle, Eric. *Do You Want to Be My Friend?* Harper, 1971.

Collington, Peter. *The Angel and the Soldier Boy*. Knopf, 1987.

———. *On Christmas Eve*. Knopf, 1990.

Day, Alexandra. *Carl Goes Shopping*. Farrar, 1989.

Demarest, Chris L. *Orville's Odyssey*. Prentice–Hall, 1986.

Dupasquier, Philippe. *The Great Escape*. Houghton, 1988.

Hutchins, Pat. *Changes, Changes*. Macmillan, 1971.

Krahn, Fernando. *Who's Seen the Scissors?* Dutton, 1975.

Martin, Rafe. *Will's Mammoth*. Illustrated by Stephen Gammell. Putnam, 1989.

Mayer, Mercer. *A Boy, a Dog, and a Frog*. Dial, 1967. (Others in the series: *Frog, Where Are You?,*

1969; *A Boy, a Dog, and a Friend,* 1971; *Frog on His Own,* 1973; *Frog Goes to Dinner,* 1974; *One Frog Too Many,* with Marianna Mayer, 1975.)

———. *The Great Cat Chase.* Four Winds, 1974.

McCully, Emily Arnold. *The Christmas Gift.* Harper, 1988.

———. *New Baby.* Harper, 1988.

———. *School.* Harper, 1987.

Ormerod, Jan. *Moonlight.* Lothrop, 1982.

———. *Sunshine.* Lothrop, 1981.

Prater, John. *The Gift.* Viking, 1986. Ages 6–8.

Spier, Peter. *Noah's Ark.* Doubleday, 1977. Ages 6–8.

———. *Oh, Were They Ever Happy!* Doubleday, 1978. Ages 6–8.

———. *Peter Spier's Rain.* Doubleday, 1982.

Tafuri, Nancy. *Early Morning in the Barn.* Greenwillow, 1983.

———. *Follow Me!* Greenwillow, 1990.

Wiesner, David. *Free Fall.* Lothrop, 1988. Ages 6–10.

———. *Tuesday.* Clarion, 1991. Ages 6–10.

Winter, Paula. *Sir Andrew.* Crown, 1980.

Picture Storybooks

Ackerman, Karen. *Song and Dance Man.* Illustrated by Stephen Gammell. Knopf, 1988. Ages 6–8.

Agee, Jon. *The Incredible Painting of Felix Clousseau.* Farrar, 1988. Ages 7–9.

Aiken, Joan. The Moon's Revenge. Illustrated by Alan Lee. Knopf, 1987. Ages 5–7.

Alexander, Martha. *Nobody Asked Me If I Wanted a Baby Sister.* Dial, 1971. Ages 5–7.

Allard, Harry. *Miss Nelson Is Missing.* Illustrated by James Marshall, Houghton, 1977. Ages 6–8.

———. *The Stupids Have a Ball.* Illustrated by James Marshall. Houghton, 1977. Ages 6–8.

Allard, Harry, and James Marshall. *Miss Nelson Has a Field Day.* Illustrated by James Marshall. Houghton, 1985. Ages 6–8.

Anholt, Catherine. *Truffles in Trouble.* Little, Brown, 1987. Ages 6–8.

———. *Truffles Is Sick.* Little, Brown, 1987. Ages 6–8.

Aragon, Jane Chelsea. *Winter Harvest.* Illustrated by Leslie Baker. Little, Brown, 1989. Ages 6–8.

Ardizzone, Edward. *Little Tim and the Brave Sea Captain.* Walck, 1955. Ages 6–8.

Arnold, Ted. *No Jumping on the Bed!* Dial, 1987. Ages 5–7.

Aruego, Jose. *Look What I Can Do.* Scribner's, 1971. Ages 5–7.

Babbitt, Natalie. *The Devil's Other Storybook.* Farrar, 1987. Ages 6–8.

———. *Nellie: A Cat on Her Own.* Farrar, 1989. Ages 6–8.

Baker, Jeannie. *Where the Forest Meets the Sea.* Greenwillow, 1988. Ages 8–10.

Baker, Olaf. *Where the Buffaloes Begin.* Illustrated by Stephen Gammell. Warne, 1981. Ages 8–10.

Bang, Molly. *The Paper Crane.* Greenwillow, 1985. Ages 8–10.

Barber, Antonia. T*he Mousehole Cat.* Illustrated by Nicola Bayley. Macmillan, 1990. Ages 6–8.

Barracca, Debra, and Sal Barracca. *The Adventures of Taxi Dog.* Illustrated by Mark Buehner. Dial, 1990. Ages 6–8.

Baylor, Byrd. *The Best Town in the World.* Illustrated by Ronald Himler. Scribner's, 1983. Ages 7–9.

———. *Hawk, I'm Your Brother.* Illustrated by Peter Parnall. Scribner's, 1976. Ages 7–9.

———. *The Other Way to Listen.* Illustrated by Peter Parnall. Scribner's, 1978. Ages 7–9.

Bemelmans, Ludwig. *Madeline.* Viking, 1939. Ages 5–7.

———. *Madeline's Rescue.* Viking, 1953. Ages 5–7.

Birdseye, Tom. *Air Mail to the Moon.* Illustrated by Stephen Gammell. Holiday, 1988. Ages 6–8.

Blos, Joan W. *Old Henry.* Illustrated by Stephen Gammell. Morrow, 1987. Ages 7–9.

Brett, Jan. T*he Wild Christmas Reindeer.* Putnam, 1990. Ages 6–8.

Broger, Achim. *The Santa Clauses.* Illustrated by Ute Krause. Dial, 1986. Ages 6–8.

Brooks, Ron. *Timothy and Gramps.* Bradbury, 1978. Ages 6–8.

Brown, Marc. *Arthur's Baby.* Little, Brown, 1987. Ages 5–7.

———. *D. W. All Wet.* Little, Brown, 1988. Ages 5–7.

Brown, Margaret Wise. *Goodnight Moon.* Illustrated by Clement Hurd. Harper, 1947. Ages 4–6.

———. *The Runaway Bunny.* Illustrated by Clement Hurd. Harper, 1942. Ages 4–6.

Brown, Ruth. *Our Puppy's Vacation*. Dutton, 1987. Ages 5–7.

Browne, Anthony. *Gorilla*. Knopf, 1985. Ages 7–9.

———. *Piggybook*. Knopf, 1986. Ages 8–10.

Bunting, Eve. *Ghost's Hour, Spook's Hour*. Illustrated by Donald Carrick. Clarion, 1987. Ages 7–9.

———. *The Wall*. Illustrated by Ronald Himler. Clarion, 1990. Ages 7–9.

———. *The Wednesday Surprise*. Illustrated by Donald Carrick. Clarion, 1989. Ages 6–10.

Burningham, John. *Grandpa*. Crown, 1985. Ages 5–7.

———. *Mr. Gumpy's Motor Car*. Harper, 1976.

Burton, Virginia Lee. *The Little House*. Houghton, 1942. Ages 5–7.

———. *Mike Mulligan and His Steam Shovel*. Houghton, 1939. Ages 5–7.

Butler, Dorothy. *My Brown Bear Barney*. Illustrated by Elizabeth Fuller. Greenwillow, 1989. Ages 5–7.

Carle, Eric. *The Grouchy Ladybug*. Crowell, 1971. Ages 5–7.

———. *The Mixed-Up Chameleon*. Crowell, 1975. Ages 6–8.

———. *The Very Busy Spider*. Philomel, 1984. Ages 5–7.

Carlstrom, Nancy White. *Blow Me a Kiss, Miss Lilly*. Illustrated by Amy Schwartz. Harper, 1990. Ages 5–7.

Carrick, Carol. *Ben and the Porcupine*. Illustrated by Donald Carrick. Clarion, 1981. Ages 6–8.

———. *What Happened to Patrick's Dinosaurs?* Illustrated by Donald Carrick. Clarion, 1986. Ages 6–8.

Carrick, Donald. *Harald and the Great Stag*. Clarion, 1988. Ages 6–8.

Caudill, Rebecca. *A Pocketful of Cricket*. Illustrated by Evaline Ness. Holt, 1964. Ages 6–8.

Cazet, Denys. *Never Spit on Your Shoes*. Orchard, 1990. Ages 6–10.

Cecil, Laura, editor. *Listen to This*. Illustrated by Emma Chishester Clark. Greenwillow, 1988. Ages 6–8.

Cherry, Lynne. *The Great Kapok Tree: A Tale of the Amazon Rainforest*. Harcourt, 1990. Ages 6–10.

Chetwin, Grace. *Box and Cox*. Illustrated by David Small. Bradbury, 1990. Ages 7–9.

Clifton, Lucille. *Amifika*. Illustrated by Thomas Di-Grazia. Dutton, 1977. Ages 6–8.

———. *My Friend Jacob*. Illustrated by Thomas Di-Grazia. Dutton, 1980. Ages 6–8.

Cohen, Caron Lee. *Whiffle Squeek*. Illustrated by Ted Rand. Dodd, 1987. Ages 6–8.

Cole, Brock. *The Giant's Toe*. Farrar, 1986. Ages 6–8.

———. *The Winter Wren*. Farrar, 1984. Ages 6–8.

Coltman, Paul. *Tog the Ribber; or Granny's Tale*. Illustrated by Gillian McClure. Farrar, 1985. Ages 6–8.

Cooney, Barbara. *Hattie and the Wild Waves: A Story from Brooklyn*. Viking, 1990. Ages 6–8.

———. *Island Boy*. Viking, 1988. Ages 6–10.

———. *Miss Rumphius*. Viking, 1982. Ages 6–10.

Cooney, Nancy Evans. *The Umbrella Day*. Illustrated by Melissa Bay Mathis. Putnam, 1989. Ages 5–7.

Craft, Ruth. *The Winter Bear*. Illustrated by Erik Blegvad. Atheneum, 1975. Ages 6–8.

Craven, Carolyn. *What the Mailman Brought*. Illustrated by Tomie dePaola. Putnam, 1987. Ages 5–7.

Crowe, Robert. *Clyde Monster*. Illustrated by Kay Chorao. Dutton, 1976. Ages 5–7.

Daly, Niki. *Not So Fast Songololo*. Atheneum, 1986. Ages 6–8.

Day, Alexandra. *Frank and Ernest*. Scholastic, 1988. Ages 6–10.

———. *Frank and Ernest Play Ball*. Scholastic, 1990. Ages 6–10.

de Brunhoff, Jean. *The Story of Babar*. Random House, 1933. Ages 6–8.

de Brunhoff, Jean, and Laurent de Brunhoff. *Babar's Anniversary Album: 6 Favorite Stories*. Random House, 1981. Ages 6–8.

Denslow, Sharon Phillips. *Night Owls*. Illustrated by Jill Kastner. Bradbury, 1990. Ages 5–7.

Denton, Terry. *Felix and Alexander*. Houghton, 1988. Ages 5–7.

dePaola, Tomie. *The Art Lesson*. Putnam, 1989. Ages 6–8.

———. *Nana Upstairs, Nana Downstairs*. Putnam, 1973. Ages 6–8.

———. *Strega Nona*. Prentice–Hall, 1975. Ages 5–7.

Drescher, Henrik. *Simon's Book,* Lothrop, 1983. Ages 7–9.

Dubanevich, Arlene. *Pigs at Christmas*. Bradbury, 1986. Ages 6–8.

Duncan, Lois. *Songs from Dreamland.* Illustrated by Kay Chorao. Knopf, 1989. Ages 6–8.

Duvoisin, Roger. *Petunia.* Knopf, 1950. Ages 6–8.

Engel, Diana. *Josephina Hates Her Name.* Morrow, 1989. Ages 5–7.

Ernst, Lisa Campbell. *Ginger Jumps.* Bradbury, 1990. Ages 4–6.

Ets, Marie Hall. *Gilberto and the Wind.* Viking, 1963. Ages 6–8.

Ets, Marie Hall, and Aurora Labastida. *Nine Days to Christmas.* Illustrated by Marie Hall Ets. Viking, 1959. Ages 7–9.

Euvremer, Teryl. *The Thieves of Peck's Pocket.* Crown, 1990. Ages 6–8.

Everitt, Betsy. *Frida the Wondercat.* Harcourt, 1990. Ages 6–8.

Faulkner, Matt. *The Amazing Voyage of Jackie Grace.* Scholastic, 1987. Ages 6–8.

Flack, Marjorie. *The Story About Ping.* Illustrated by Kurt Wiese. Viking, 1933. Ages 7–9.

Fleischman, Sid. *The Scarebird.* Illustrated by Peter Sis. Greenwillow, 1988. Ages 7–9.

Forrester, Victoria. *Poor Gabriella: A Christmas Story.* Illustrated by Susan Seddon. Calligraphy by John Prestianni. Atheneum, 1986. Ages 7–9.

Fox, Mem. *Hattie and the Fox.* Illustrated by Patricia Mullins. Bradbury, 1987. Ages 6–8.

———. *Night Noises.* Illustrated by Terry Denton. Gulliver, 1989. Ages 6–8.

———. *Shoes from Grandpa.* Illustrated by Patricia Mullins. Orchard, 1990. Ages 6–8.

———. *Wilfred Gordon McDonald Partridge.* Illustrated by Julie Vivas. Kane/Miller, 1985. Ages 6–8.

Freeman, Don. *Corduroy.* Viking, 1968. Ages 3–5.

———. *A Pocket for Corduroy.* Viking, 1978. Ages 3–5.

Friedman, Ina. *How My Parents Learned to Eat.* Illustrated by Allen Say. Houghton, 1984. Ages 7–9.

Gág, Wanda. *Millions of Cats.* Coward–McCann, 1928. Ages 4–6.

Galbraith, Kathryn. *Laura Charlotte.* Illustrated by Floyd Cooper. Philomel, 1990. Ages 6–8.

Garland, Michael. *My Cousin Katie.* Crowell, 1989. Ages 6–8.

Gerstein, Mordicai. *The Mountains of Tibet.* Harper, 1987. Ages 7–9.

Goode, Diane. *I Hear a Noise.* Dutton, 1988. Ages 5–7.

Gould, Deborah. *Grandpa's Slide Show Harness.* Lothrop, 1987. Ages 6–8.

Gray, Nigel. *A Country Far Away.* Illustrated by Philippe Dupasquier. Orchard, 1989. Ages 7–9.

Greenfield, Eloise. *Nathaniel Talking.* Illustrated by Jan Spivey Gilchrist. Writers and Readers, 1989. Ages 6–8.

———. *She Come Bringing Me That Little Baby Girl.* Illustrated by John Steptoe. Lippincott, 1974. Ages 6–8.

Grifalconi, Ann. *The Village of Round and Square Houses.* Little, Brown, 1986. Ages 6–8.

Griffith, Helen V. *Grandaddy's Place.* Illustrated by James Stevenson. Greenwillow, 1987. Ages 7–9.

Gross, Theodore. *Faro, Everyone Asked about You.* Illustrated by Sheila White Samton. Philomel, 1990. Ages 6–8.

Grossman, Bill. *Tommy at the Grocery Store.* Illustrated by Victoria Chess. Harper, 1989. Ages 6–10.

Hader, Berta, and Elmer Hader. *The Big Snow.* Macmillan, 1948. Ages 6–8.

Hall, Donald. *Ox–Cart Man.* Illustrated by Barbara Cooney. Viking, 1979. Ages 7–9.

Heide, Florence Parry, and Judith Heide Gilliland. *The Day of Ahmed's Secret.* Illustrated by Ted Lewin. Lothrop, 1990. Ages 6–10.

Hendershot, Judith. *In Coal Country.* Illustrated by Thomas B. Allen. Knopf, 1987. Ages 7–9.

Henkes, Kevin. *Julius, the Baby of the World.* Greenwillow, 1990. Ages 5–7.

———. *Shiela Rae the Brave.* Greenwillow, 1987. Ages 5–7.

Hest, Amy. *The Midnight Eaters.* Illustrated by Karen Gundersheimer. Four Winds, 1989. Ages 6–8.

Hilton, Nette. *Dirty Dave.* Illustrated by Roland Harvey. Orchard, 1990. Ages 6–8.

Hissey, Jane. *Little Bear's Trousers.* Putnam, 1987. Ages 4–6.

———. *Old Bear.* Putnam, 1986. Ages 4–6.

Hoban, Russell. *A Baby Sister for Frances.* Illustrated by Lillian Hoban. Harper, 1964. (Others in the series: *Bedtime for Frances,* illustrated by Garth Williams, 1969; *Best Friends for Frances.* Illustrated by Lillian Hoban, 1969; *A Bargain for Frances,* illustrated by Lillian Hoban. Harper, 1970.) Ages 4–6.

Hoberman, Mary Ann. *Mr. and Mrs. Muddle.* Illustrated by Catharine O'Neill. Little, Brown, 1988. Ages 4–6.

Hodges, Margaret. *The Wave.* Illustrated by Blair Lent. Houghton, 1957. Ages 7–9.

Hood, Thomas. *Before I Go to Sleep.* Illustrated by Maryjane Begin-Callanan. Putnam, 1990. Ages 5–7.

Houselander, Caryll. *Petook: An Easter Story.* Illustrated by Tomie dePaola. Holiday, 1988. Ages 7–9.

Houston, Gloria. *The Year of the Perfect Christmas Tree: An Appalachian Story.* Illustrated by Barbara Cooney. Dial, 1988. Ages 7–9.

Howard, Elizabeth Fitzgerald. *Chita's Christmas Tree.* Illustrated by Floyd Cooper. Bradbury, 1989. Ages 6–8.

Howe, James. *Pinky and Rex Get Married.* Illustrated by Melissa Sweet. Atheneum, 1990. Ages 5–7.

———. *There's a Monster Under My Bed.* Illustrated by David Rose. Atheneum, 1986. Ages 5–7.

Hughes, Shirley. *An Evening at Alfie's.* Lothrop, 1985. Ages 5–7.

Hurd, Edith Thacher. *I Dance in My Red Pajamas.* Illustrated by Emily Arnold McCully. Harper, 1982. Ages 6–8.

———. *The Pea Patch Jig.* Crown, 1986. Ages 6–8.

Ichikawa, Satomi. *Nora's Castle.* Putnam, 1986. Ages 5–7.

Isadora, Rachel. *Ben's Trumpet.* Greenwillow, 1979. Ages 6–10.

———. *The Pirates of Bedford Street.* Greenwillow, 1988. Ages 6–10.

Johnson, Angela. *Tell Me a Story, Mama.* Illustrated by David Soman. Orchard, 1989. Ages 6–8.

———. *When I Am Old with You.* Illustrated by David Soman. Orchard, 1990. Ages 7–9.

Johnson, Crockett. *Harold and the Purple Crayon.* Harper, 1955. Ages 5–7.

Johnson, Tony. *The Quilt Story.* Illustrated by Tomie dePaola. Putnam, 1985. Ages 6–8.

———. *Yonder.* Illustrated by Lloyd Bloom. Dial, 1988. Ages 6–8.

Jonas, Ann. *The Quilt.* Greenwillow, 1984. Ages 7–9.

———. *When You Were A Baby.* Greenwillow, 1982. Ages 6–8.

Joyce, William. *A Day with Wilbur Robinson.* Harper, 1990. Ages 6–8.

Jukes, Mavis. *Like Jake and Me.* Illustrated by Lloyd Bloom. Knopf, 1984. Ages 6–8.

Kahl, Virginia. *The Duchess Bakes a Cake.* Scribner's, 1955. Ages 6–8.

Kalman, Maira. *Max Makes a Million.* Viking, 1990. Ages 7–9.

Kasza, Keiko. *The Pigs' Picnic.* Putnam, 1988. Ages 6–8.

Keats, Ezra Jack. *Goggles.* Macmillan, 1969. Ages 5–7.

———. *Peter's Chair.* Harper, 1967. Ages 4–6.

———. *The Snowy Day.* Viking, 1962. Ages 4–6.

———. *Whistle for Willie.* Viking, 1964. Ages 5–7.

Keller, Holly. *Geraldine's Big Snow.* Greenwillow, 1988. Ages 6–8.

Kellogg, Steven. *Pinkerton, Behave!* Dial, 1979. Ages 6–8.

———. *Prehistoric Pinkerton.* Dial, 1987. Ages 6–8.

———. *The Mysterious Tadpole.* Dial, 1977. Ages 6–8.

Kennaway, Mwalimu and Adrienne. *Awful Aardvark.* Little, Brown, 1989. Ages 6–8.

Kesey, Ken. *Little Tricker the Squirrel Meets Big Double the Bear.* Illustrated by Barry Moser. Viking, 1990.

Khalsa, Dayal Kaur. *Cowboy Dreams.* Clarkson N. Potter, 1990. Ages 7–9.

———. *My Family Vacation.* Clarkson N. Potter, 1988. Ages 7–9.

Kimmel, Eric A. *The Chanukkah Guest.* Illustrated by Giora Carmi. Holiday, 1990. Ages 7–9.

Kinsey-Warnock, Natalie. *The Wild Horses of Sweetbriar.* Illustrated by Ted Rand. Dutton, 1990. Ages 7–9.

Kitamura, Satoshi. *UFO Diary.* Farrar, 1989. Ages 7–9.

Komaiko, Leah. *Annie Bananie.* Illustrated by Laura Cornell. Harper, 1987. Ages 6–8.

Kraus, Robert. *Leo the Late Bloomer.* Illustrated by José Aruego. Crowell, 1971. Ages 7–9.

———. *Owliver.* Illustrated by José Aruego and Ariane Dewey. Windmill, 1974. Ages 6–8.

Krause, Ute. *Pig Surprise.* Dial, 1989. Ages 6–8.

Kuskin, Karla. *The Philharmonic Gets Dressed.* Illustrated by Marc Simont. Harper, 1982. Ages 6–10.

Lasker, Joe. *A Tournament of Knights.* Crowell, 1986. Ages 8–10.

Lasky, Kathryn. *Sea Swan.* Illustrated by Catherine Stock. Macmillan, 1988. Ages 7–9.

Latimer, Jim. *Going the Moose Way Home.* Illustrated by Donald Carrick. Scribner's, 1988. Ages 6–8.

Lattimore, Deborah Nourse. *The Lady With the Ship on Her Head.* Harcourt, 1990. Ages 8–10.

Leaf, Margaret. *Eyes of the Dragon.* Illustrated by Ed Young. Lothrop, 1987. Ages 7–9.

Leaf, Munro. *The Story of Ferdinand.* Illustrated by Robert Lawson. Viking, 1936. Ages 7–9.

LeGuin, Ursula K. *Catwings Return.* Illustrated by S. D. Schindler. Orchard, 1989. Ages 6–8.

Lent, Blair. *Bayberry Bluff.* Houghton, 1987. Ages 7–9.

———. *John Tabor's Ride.* Little, Brown, 1966. Ages 7–9.

Levine, Abby. *What Did Mommy Do Before You?* Illustrated by DyAnne DiSalvo-Ryan. Whitman, 1988. Ages 5–7.

Levinson, Riki. *Watch the Stars Come Out.* Illustrated by Diane Goode. Dutton, 1985. Ages 7–9.

Lexau, Joan. *Benjie on His Own.* Illustrated by Don Bolognese. Dial, 1970. Ages 6–8.

Lindbergh, Reeve. *The Day the Goose Got Loose.* Illustrated by Steven Kellogg. Dial, 1990. Ages 5–7.

Lionni, Leo. *Alexander and the Wind-up Mouse.* Pantheon 1967. Ages 6–8.

———. *The Biggest House in the World.* Pantheon, 1968. Ages 5–7.

———. *Inch by Inch.* Astor–Honor, 1960. Ages 5–7.

———. *Swimmy.* Pantheon, 1963. Ages 6–8.

Locker, Thomas. *Sailing with the Wind.* Dial, 1986. Ages 6–8.

———. *Where the River Begins.* Dial, 1984. Ages 6–8.

Loriot, reteller. *Peter and the Wolf.* Illustrated by Jörg Müller. (Original story by Sergei Prokofiev.) Knopf, 1986. Ages 6–10.

Luenn, Nancy. *Nessa's Fish.* Illustrated by Neil Waldman. Atheneum, 1990. Ages 7–9.

Lyon, George Ella. *Come a Tide.* Illustrated by Stephen Gammell. Orchard, 1990. Ages 6–8.

———. *A Regular Rolling Noah.* Illustrated by Stephen Gammell. Bradbury, 1986. Ages 6–8.

Macaulay, David. *Why the Chicken Crossed the Road.* Houghton, 1987. Ages 8–10.

MacLachlan, Patricia. *Mama One, Mama Two.* Illustrated by Ruth Lercher Bornstein. Harper, 1982. Ages 8–10.

———. *Through Grandpa's Eyes.* Illustrated by Deborah Ray. Harper, 1979. Ages 7–9.

Mahy, Margaret. *The Great White Man-Eating Shark: A Cautionary Tale.* Illustrated by Jonathan Allen. Dial, 1990. Ages 8–10.

———. *17 Kings and 42 Elephants.* Illustrated by Patricia McCarthy. Dial, 1987. Ages 6–10.

Manson, Christopher. *Two Travellers.* Holt, 1990. Ages 6–8.

Marshall, James. *George and Martha.* Houghton, 1972. Ages 6–8.

———. *George and Martha Round and Round.* Houghton, 1988. Ages 6–8.

Martin, Bill, Jr., and John Archambault. *Knots on a Counting Rope.* Illustrated by Ted Rand. Holt, 1987. Ages 6–8.

———. *White Dynamite and Curly Kid.* Illustrated by Ted Rand. Holt, 1986. Ages 6–8.

Martin, Jacqueline Briggs. *Bizzy Bones and the Lost Quilt.* Illustrated by Stella Ormai. Lothrop, 1988. Ages 6–8.

Mayer, Mercer. *There's a Nightmare in My Closet.* Dial, 1968. Ages 5–7.

McAfee, Annalena. *Kirsty Knows Best.* Illustrated by Anthony Browne. Knopf, 1988. Ages 5–7.

McCloskey, Robert. *Blueberries for Sal.* Viking, 1948. Ages 5–7.

———. *Make Way for Ducklings.* Viking, 1941. Ages 5–7.

———. *One Morning in Maine.* Viking, 1952. Ages 7–9.

McCully, Emily Arnold. *The Evil Spell.* Harper, 1990. Ages 6–8.

McKissack, Patricia C. *Flossie and the Fox.* Illustrated by Rachel Isadora. Dial, 1986. Ages 7–9.

———. *Nettie Jo's Friends.* Illustrated by Scott Cook. Knopf, 1989. Ages 7–9.

Mosel, Arlene, adapter. *The Funny Little Woman.* Illustrated by Blair Lent. Dutton, 1972. Ages 6–8.

Naylor, Phyllis Reynolds. *Keeping a Christmas Secret.* Illustrated by Lena Shiffman. Atheneum, 1989. Ages 6–8.

Ness, Evaline. *Sam, Bangs and Moonshine*. Holt, 1966. Ages 6–8.

Nixon, Joan Lowery. *Beats Me, Claude*. Illustrated by Tracey Campbell Pearson. Viking, 1986. Ages 6–8.

Noble, Trinka H. *Jimmy's Boa and the Big Splash Birthday Bash*. Illustrated by Steven Kellogg. Dial, 1989. Ages 6–8.

Nolan, Dennis. *Dinosaur Dream*. Macmillan, 1990. Ages 6–8.

Oakley, Graham. *The Church Mice Adrift*. Atheneum, 1977. Ages 6–8.

———. *The Church Mouse*. Atheneum, 1972. Ages 6–8.

Paxton, Tom. *Englebert the Elephant*. Illustrated by Steven Kellogg. Morrow, 1990. Ages 6–8.

Pearson, Susan. *Izzie*. Illustrated by Robert Andrew Parker. Dial, 1975. Ages 6–8.

Peet, Bill. *Cyrus the Unsinkable Sea Serpent*. Houghton, 1975. Ages 5–7.

———. *Merle the High Flying Squirrel*. Houghton, 1974. Ages 5–7.

Peters, Lisa Westberg. *Good Morning River!* Illustrated by Deborah Kogan Ray. Arcade, 1990. Ages 6–8.

Pittman, Helena Clare. *Once When I Was Scared*. Illustrated by Ted Rand. Dutton, 1988. Ages 5–7.

Polacco, Patricia. *Babushka's Doll*. Simon and Schuster, 1990. Ages 6–8.

———. *The Keeping Quilt*. Simon and Schuster, 1988. Ages 6–8.

———. *Thunder Cake*. Putnam, 1990. Ages 6–8.

Politi, Leo. *Song of the Swallows*. Scribner's, 1949. Ages 6–8.

Pomerantz, Charlotte. *The Chalk Doll*. Illustrated by Frane Lessac. Harper, 1989. Ages 7–9.

Potter, Beatrix. *The Tale of Peter Rabbit*. Warne, 1902. (See 20 other titles in the series.) Ages 5–7.

Provensen, Alice, and Martin Provensen. *The Glorious Flight Across the Channel with Louis Blériot*. Viking, 1983. Ages 8–10.

———. *Shaker Lane*. Viking, 1987. Ages 7–9.

Pryor, Bonnie. *The Porcupine Mouse*. Illustrated by Maryjane Begin. Morrow, 1988. Ages 5–7.

Purdy, Carol. *Least of All*. Illustrated by Tim Arnold. Macmillan, 1987. Ages 6–8.

Radin, Ruth Yaffe. *A Winter Place*. Illustrated by Mattie Lou O'Kelley. Little, Brown, 1982. Ages 6–8.

Rand, Gloria. *Salty Sails North*. Illustrated by Ted Rand. Holt, 1990. Ages 6–8.

Ransome, Arthur. *The Fool of the World and the Flying Ship*. Illustrated by Uri Shulevitz. Farrar, 1968. Ages 6–8.

———. *My Dog, Trip*. Holiday, 1987. Ages 6–8.

Ray, Deborah Kogan. *Mr. and Mrs. Pig's Evening Out*. Atheneum, 1976. Ages 6–8.

Rayner, Mary. *Mrs. Pig Gets Cross: And Other Stories*. Dutton, 1987. Ages 6–8.

Rey, Hans A. *Curious George*. Houghton, 1941. (See others in the Curious George series.) Ages 5–7.

Rice, Eve. *Peter's Pockets*. Illustrated by Nancy Winslow Parker. Greenwillow, 1989. Ages 6–8.

Ringgold, Faith. *Tar Beach*. Crown, 1991. Ages 8–10.

Rogers, Jacqueline. *The Christmas Pageant*. Grosset, 1989. Ages 6–8.

Rogers, Jean. *Runaway Mittens*. Illustrated by Rie Muñoz. Greenwillow, 1988. Ages 5–7.

Rubel, Nicole. *It Came from the Swamp*. Dial, 1988. Ages 6–8.

Russo, Marisabina. *Waiting for Hannah*. Greenwillow, 1989. Ages 6–8.

Ryan, Cheli Duran. *Hildilid's Night*. Illustrated by Arnold Lobel. Macmillan, 1971. Ages 6–8.

Rylant, Cynthia. *Mr. Grigg's Work*. Illustrated by Julie Downing. Orchard, 1989. Ages 7–9.

———. *The Relatives Came*. Illustrated by Stephen Gammell. Bradbury, 1985. Ages 6–10.

———. *When I Was Young in the Mountains*. Illustrated by Diane Goode. Dutton, 1982. Ages 7–9.

Sanders, Scott Russell. *Aurora Means Dawn*. Illustrated by Jill Kastner. Bradbury, 1989. Ages 7–9.

Schertle, Alice. *William and Grandpa*. Illustrated by Lydia Dabcovich. Lothrop, 1989. Ages 6–8.

Schotter, Roni. *Captain Snap and the Children of Vinegar Lane*. Illustrated by Marcia Sewall. Watts, 1989. Ages 6–8.

Schroeder, Alan. *Ragtime Tumpie*. Illustrated by Bernie Fuchs. Little, Brown, 1989. Ages 6–8.

Schwartz, Amy. *Anabelle Swift, Kindergartner*. Orchard, 1988. Ages 5–7.

————. *Oma and Bobo.* Bradbury, 1987. Ages 5–7.

Schwartz, Henry. *How I Captured a Dinosaur.* Illustrated by Amy Schwartz. Orchard, 1989. Ages 6–8.

Scott, Ann Herbert. *Sam.* Illustrated by Symeon Shimin. McGraw-Hill, 1967. Ages 7–9.

Seligson, Susan. *The Amazing Amos and the Greatest Couch on Earth.* Illustrated by Howie Schneider. Little, Brown, 1989. Ages 6–8.

Sendak, Maurice. *In the Night Kitchen.* Harper, 1970. Ages 7–9.

————. *Where the Wild Things Are.* Harper, 1963. Ages 5–7.

Seuss, Dr. pseud. (Theodor S. Geisel). *And To Think That I Saw It On Mulberry Street.* Vanguard, 1937. Ages 5–7.

————. *The 500 Hats of Bartholomew Cubbins.* Vanguard, 1938. Ages 5–7.

————. *Horton Hatches the Egg.* Random, 1940. Ages 6–8.

————. *Oh, the Places You'll Go!* Random, 1990. Ages 6–8.

————. *Thidwick the Big-hearted Moose.* Random, 1948. Ages 6–8.

Sharmat, Marjorie Weinman. *I'm Not Oscar's Friend Anymore.* Illustrated by Tony DeLuna. Dutton, 1975. Ages 6–8.

Shulevitz, Uri. *Dawn.* Farrar, 1974. Ages 6–8.

————. *One Monday Morning.* Scribner's, 1967. Ages 6–8.

Siebert, Diane. *Heartland.* Illustrated by Wendell Minor. Harper, 1989. Ages 8–10.

————. *Sierra.* Illustrated by Wendell Minor. Harper, 1991. Ages 8–10.

Slobodkina, Esphyr, *Caps for Sale.* Addison-Wesley, 1947. Ages 4–6.

Small, David. *Imogene's Antlers.* Crown, 1985. Ages 6–8.

Spier, Peter. *Bored—Nothing To Do!* Doubleday, 1978. Ages 7–9.

Steig, William. *The Amazing Bone.* Farrar, 1976. Ages 7–9.

————. *Caleb and Kate.* Farrar, 1977. Ages 7–9.

————. *Doctor DeSoto.* Farrar, 1982. Ages 7–9.

————. *Sylvester and the Magic Pebble.* Simon and Schuster, 1969. Ages 7–9.

Steptoe, John. *Baby Says.* Lothrop, 1988. Ages 5–7.

————. *Stevie.* Harper, 1969. Ages 5–7.

Stevenson, James. *July.* Greenwillow, 1990. Ages 6–8.

————. *That Dreadful Day.* Greenwillow, 1985. Ages 6–8.

————. *What's Under My Bed?* Greenwillow, 1983. Ages 5–7.

————. *Will You Please Feed Our Cat?* Greenwillow, 1987. Ages 6–8.

Stevenson, Robert Louis. *Block City.* Illustrated by Ashley Wolff. Dutton, 1988. Ages 6–8.

Stock, Catherine. *Armien's Fishing Trip.* Morrow, 1990. Ages 6–8.

Stolz, Mary. *Storm in the Night.* Illustrated by Pat Cummings. Harper, 1988. Ages 6–8.

Swope, Sam. *The Araboolies of Liberty Street.* Illustrated by Barry Root. Clarkson N. Potter, 1989. Ages 6–8.

Tejima. *Fox's Dream.* Translated from Japanese by Susan Matsui. Philomel, 1987. Ages 6–8.

Tennyson, Noel. *The Lady's Chair and the Ottoman.* Lothrop, 1987. Ages 6–8.

Testa, Fulvio. *Wolf's Favor.* Dial, 1986. Ages 6–8.

Thomas, Jane Resh. *Saying Goodbye to Grandma.* Illustrated by Marcia Sewall. Clarion, 1988. Ages 7–9.

Tompert, Ann. *Grandfather Tang's Story.* Illustrated by Robert Andrew Parker. Crown, 1990. Ages 7–9.

Tresselt, Alvin. *White Snow, Bright Snow.* Illustrated by Roger Duvoisin. Lothrop, 1947. Ages 4–6.

Trivas, Irene. *Emma's Christmas.* Orchard, 1988. Ages 5–7.

Turkle, Brinton. *Do Not Open.* Dutton, 1981. Ages 5–7.

Turner, Ann. *Heron Street.* Illustrated by Lisa Desimini. Harper, 1989. Ages 6–8.

Udry, Janice May. *The Moon Jumpers.* Illustrated by Maurice Sendak. Harper, 1959. Ages 5–7.

Ungerer, Tomi. *The Beast of Monsieur Racine.* Farrar, 1971. Ages 6–8.

Updike, David. *An Autumn Tale.* Illustrated by Robert Andrew Parker. Pippin Press, 1988. Ages 6–8.

Van Allsburg, Chris. *Jumanji.* Houghton, 1981. Ages 6–10.

Van Laan, Nancy. *Possum Come a–Knockin'.* Illustrated by George Booth. Knopf, 1990. Ages 7–9.

Vincent, Gabrielle. *Where Are You, Ernest and Celestine?* Greenwillow, 1986. Ages 6–8.

Viorst, Judith. *Alexander and the Terrible, Horrible, No Good, Very Bad Day.* Illustrated by Ray Cruz. Atheneum, 1972. Ages 5–7.

————. *Alexander Who Used to Be Rich Last Sunday.* Illustrated by Ray Cruz. Atheneum, 1978. Ages 6–8.

————. *I'll Fix Anthony.* Illustrated by Arnold Lobel. Harper, 1969. Ages 4–6.

Waber, Bernard. *Ira Says Goodbye.* Houghton, 1988. Ages 6–8.

————. *Ira Sleeps Over.* Houghton, 1972. Ages 6–8.

Wahl, Jan. *Humphrey's Bear.* Illustrated by William Joyce. Holt, 1987. Ages 5–7.

Wallace, Barbara Brooks. *Argyle.* Illustrated by John Sandford. Abingdon, 1987. Ages 5–7.

Walter, Mildred Pitts. *My Mama Needs Me.* Illustrated by Pat Cummings. Lothrop, 1983. Ages 5–7.

Watson, Wendy. *Tales for a Winter's Eve.* Farrar, 1988. Ages 6–8.

Wayland, April Halprin. *To Rabbittown.* Illustrated by Robin Spowart. Scholastic, 1989. Ages 6–8.

Weller, Frances Ward. *Riptide.* Illustrated by Robert J. Blake. Philomel, 1990. Ages 6–8.

Wells, Rosemary. *Shy Charles.* Dial, 1988. Ages 4–6.

————. *Timothy Goes to School.* Dial, 1981. Ages 5–7.

Wiesner, David. *Hurricane.* Clarion, 1990. Ages 7–9.

Wild, Margaret. *Mr. Nick's Knitting.* Illustrated by Dee Huxley. Harcourt, 1989. Ages 6–8.

————. *The Very Best of Friends.* Illustrated by Julie Vivas. Harcourt, 1990. Ages 6–8.

Wildsmith, Brian. *Daisy.* Pantheon, 1984. Ages 6–8.

Wilhelm, Hans. *I'll Always Love You.* Crown, 1985. Ages 6–8.

Willard, Nancy. *The Mountains of Quilt.* Illustrated by Tomie dePaola. Harcourt, 1987. Ages 7–9.

————. *Night Story.* Illustrated by Ilse Plume. Harcourt, 1986. Ages 7–9.

Williams, Margery. *The Velveteen Rabbit.* Illustrated by William Nicholson. Doubleday, 1922. Ages 6–8.

Williams, Vera B.. *A Chair for My Mother.* Greenwillow, 1982. Ages 6–8.

————. *Something Special for Me.* Greenwillow, 1983. Ages 6–8.

————. *Stringbean's Trip to the Shining Sea.* Illustrated by author and Jennifer Williams. Greenwillow, 1988. Ages 7–9.

Willis, Val. *The Secret in the Matchbox.* Illustrated by John Shelley. Farrar, 1988. Ages 6–8.

Winter, Jeanette. *Come Out to Play.* Knopf, 1986. Ages 5–7.

Winthrop, Elizabeth. *Bear and Mrs. Duck.* Illustrated by Patience Brewster. Holiday, 1988. Ages 5–7.

Wood, Audrey. *Heckedy Peg.* Illustrated by Don Wood. Harcourt, 1987. Ages 6–8.

Xiong, Blia, reteller. *Nine-in-One Grr! Grr!,* adapted by Cathy Spagnoli. Illustrated by Nancy Hom. Children's Book Press, 1990. Ages 6–8.

Yashima, Taro. pseud. (Jun Iwamatsu). *Crow Boy.* Viking, 1955. Ages 7–9.

Yolen, Jane. *Owl Moon.* Illustrated by John Schoenherr. Putnam, 1987. Ages 6–8.

————. *Piggins.* Illustrated by Jane Dyer. Harcourt, 1987. Ages 6–8.

Yorinks, Arthur. *Company's Coming.* Illustrated by David Small. Crown, 1988. Ages 7–9.

————. *Hey, Al.* Illustrated by Richard Egielski. Farrar, 1986. Ages 7–9.

Ziefert, Harriet. *A New Coat for Anna.* Illustrated by Anita Lobel. Knopf, 1986. Ages 6–8.

Zimelman, Nathan. *Treed by a Pride of Irate Lions.* Illustrated by Toni Goffe. Little, Brown, 1990. Ages 6–8.

Zolotow, Charlotte. *If It Weren't for You.* Illustrated by Ben Shecter. Harper, 1966. Ages 6–8.

————. *Mr. Rabbit and the Lovely Present.* Illustrated by Maurice Sendak. Harper, 1962. Ages 5–7.

————. *Say It!* Illustrated by James Stevenson. Greenwillow, 1980. Ages 6–8.

————. *Something Is Going to Happen.* Illustrated by Catherine Stock. Harper, 1988. Ages 6–8.

————. *William's Doll.* Illustrated by William Pène du Bois. Harper, 1972. Ages 6–8.

Easy-to-Read and Pattern Books

These books are generally suitable for ages 4 to 8.

Bonsall, Crosby. *The Case of the Cat's Meow.* Harper, 1965.

————. *The Case of the Scaredy Cats.* Harper, 1971.

Bulla, Clyde Robert. *The Chalk Box Kid.* Illustrated by Thomas B. Allen. Random, 1987.

————. *The Christmas Coat*. Illustrated by Sylvie Wickstrom. Knopf, 1990.

Byars, Betsy. *Hooray for the Golly Sisters!* Illustrated by Sue Truesdell. Harper, 1990.

Cherry, Lynne. *Who's Sick Today?* Dutton, 1988.

Coerr, Eleanor. *Chang's Paper Pony*. Illustrated by Deborah Kogan Ray. Harper, 1988.

————. *The Josefina Story Quilt*. Illustrated by Bruce Degen. Harper, 1986.

Cohen, Caron Lee. *Three Yellow Dogs*. Illustrated by Peter Sis. Greenwillow, 1986.

Cohen, Miriam. *First Grade Takes a Test*. Illustrated by Lillian Hoban. Greenwillow, 1980.

————. *It's George!* Illustrated by Lillian Hoban. Greenwillow, 1988.

————. *When Will I Read?* Illustrated by Lillian Hoban. Greenwillow, 1977.

Cole, Joanna, and Stephanie Calmenson, compilers. *Ready . . . Set . . . Read!: The Beginning Reader's Treasury*. Illustrated by Anne Burgess and Chris Demarest. Doubleday, 1990.

de Regniers, Beatrice Schenk. *May I Bring a Friend?* Illustrated by Beni Montresor. Atheneum, 1964.

Ehrlich, Amy. *Leo, Zack, and Emmie*. Illustrated by Steven Kellogg. Dial, 1981.

Emberley, Barbara. *Drummer Hoff*. Illustrated by Ed Emberley. Prentice-Hall, 1967.

Gage, Wilson. *Squash Pie*. Illustrated by Glen Rounds. Greenwillow, 1976.

Griffith, Helen V. *Alex and the Cat*. Illustrated by Joseph Low. Greenwillow, 1982.

Hellen, Nancy. *The Bus Stop*. Orchard, 1988.

Hoban, Lillian. *Arthur's Prize Reader*. Harper, 1978.

————. *Arthur's Great Big Valentine*. Harper, 1989.

Hopkins, Lee Bennett, selector. *Good Books, Good Times*. Illustrated by Harvey Stevenson. Harper, 1990.

Hutchins, Pat. *The Doorbell Rang*. Greenwillow, 1986.

————. *Rosie's Walk*. Macmillan, 1968.

————. *Tidy Titch*. Greenwillow, 1991.

————. *What Game Shall We Play?* Greenwillow, 1990.

————. *The Wind Blew*. Macmillan, 1974.

————. *Titch*. Macmillan, 1971.

Johnson, Crockett. *A Picture for Harold's Room*. Harper, 1960.

Kessler, Leonard. *Kick, Pass, and Run*. Harper, 1966.

Kraus, Robert. *Where Are You Going, Little Mouse?* Illustrated by José Aruego and Ariane Dewey. Greenwillow, 1986.

Lobel, Arnold. *Mouse Soup*. Harper, 1977.

————. "Frog and Toad Series." *Frog and Toad Are Friends*. Harper, 1970. (Others in the series: *Frog and Toad Together*, 1972; *Frog and Toad All Year*, 1976; *Days with Frog and Toad*, 1979.)

Martin, Bill, Jr. *Brown Bear, Brown Bear, What Do You See?* Illustrated by Eric Carle. Holt, 1983.

McDonald, Megan. *Is This a House for Hermit Crab?* Illustrated by S. D. Schindler. Orchard, 1990.

Minarik, Else Holmelund. *Little Bear*. Illustrated by Maurice Sendak. Harper, 1957. (Others in the *Little Bear* series: *Father Bear Comes Home*, 1959; *Little Bear's Friend*, 1960; *Little Bear's Visit*, 1961; *A Kiss for Little Bear*, 1968.)

Moore, Lilian. *I'll Meet You at the Cucumbers*. Illustrated by Sharon Wooding. Atheneum, 1988.

Porte, Barbara Ann. *Harry in Trouble*. Illustrated by Yossi Abolafia. Greenwillow, 1989.

Rosen, Michael, reteller. *We're Going on a Bear Hunt*. Illustrated by Helen Oxenbury. Macmillan, 1989.

Rylant, Cynthia. *Henry and Mudge and the Happy Cat*. Illustrated by Sucie Stevenson. Bradbury, 1990.

Seuss, Dr. pseud. (Theodor S. Geisel). *The Cat in the Hat*. Random, 1957.

————. *The Cat in the Hat Comes Back*. Random, 1958.

————. *Fox in Sox*. Random, 1965.

Shaw, Nancy. *Sheep in a Jeep*. Illustrated by Margot Apple. Houghton, 1986.

————. *Sheep on a Ship*. Illustrated by Margot Apple. Houghton, 1989.

Titherington, Jeanne. *A Child's Prayer*. Greenwillow, 1989.

————. *Pumpkin Pumpkin*. Greenwillow, 1986.

Van Leeuwen, Jean. *Oliver and Amanda's Christmas*. Illustrated by Ann Schweninger. Dial, 1989.

Weiss, Nicki. *Where Does the Brown Bear Go?* Greenwillow, 1989.

Wellington, Monica. *All My Little Ducklings*. Dutton, 1989. Wells, Rosemary. *Noisy Nora*. Dial, 1973.

Williams, Sue. *I Went Walking*. Illustrated by Julie Vivas. Harcourt, 1990.

Winter, Jeanette. *Follow the Drinking Gourd*. Knopf, 1988.

Wood, Audrey. *The Napping House*. Illustrated by Don Wood. Harcourt, 1984.

Zolotow, Charlotte. *Do You Know What I'll Do?* Illustrated by Garth Williams. Harper, 1958.

Picture Books for Older Readers

Anno, Mitsumasa. *Anno's Britain*. Philomel, 1982. Ages 9–YA.

———. *Anno's Magical ABC: An Anamorphic Alphabet*. Illustrated by Masaichiro Anno. Philomel, 1981. Ages 9–YA.

———. *Anno's U.S.A*. Philomel, 1983. Ages 8–10.

Browne, Anthony. *The Tunnel*. Knopf, 1990. Ages 8–10.

Burkert, Nancy Ekholm. *Valentine and Orson*. Farrar, 1989. Ages 9–YA.

Capote, Truman. *A Christmas Memory*. Illustrated by Beth Peck. Knopf, 1989. Ages 8–10.

Cendrars, Blaise. *Shadow*. Illustrated by Marcia Brown. Scribner's, 1982. Ages 8–10.

Durell, Ann, and Marilyn Sachs, editors. *The Big Book for Peace*. Dutton, 1990. Ages 8–10.

Fields, Julia. *The Green Lion of Zion Street*. Illustrated by Jerry Pinkney. Macmillan, 1988. Ages 8–10.

Gallaz, Christophe, and Roberto Innocenti. *Rose Blanche*. Illustrated by Roberto Innocenti. Creative Education, 1985. Ages 9–YA.

Hodges, Margaret. *Saint George and the Dragon*. Illustrated by Trina Schart Hyman. Little, Brown, 1984. Ages 8–10.

Lattimore, Deborah Nourse. *The Flame of Peace: A Tale of the Aztecs*. Harper, 1987. Ages 8–10.

———. *The Sailor Who Captured the Sea: A Story of the Book of Kells*. Harper, 1991. Ages 9–YA.

Macaulay, David. *Black and White*. Houghton, 1990. Ages 8–10.

McDermott, Gerald. *Arrow to the Sun: A Pueblo Indian Tale*. Viking, 1974. Ages 8–10.

Müller, Jörg. *The Changing City*. Atheneum, 1977. Ages 9–YA.

Musgrove, Margaret. *Ashanti to Zulu*. Illustrated by Leo and Diane Dillon. Dial, 1976. Ages 8–10.

Price, Leontyne. *Aïda*. Illustrated by Leo and Diane Dillon. Harcourt, 1990. Ages 8–10.

Say, Allen. *El Chino*. Houghton, 1990. Ages 8–10.

———. *The Lost Lake*. Houghton, 1989. Ages 8–10.

Sendak, Maurice. *Outside Over There*. Harper, 1981. Ages 9–YA.

Steiner, Jörg. *The Bear Who Wanted to Be a Bear*. Illustrated by Jörg Müller. Atheneum, 1977. Ages 8–10.

———. *Rabbit Island*. Illustrated by Jörg Müller. Harcourt, 1978. Ages 8–10.

Van Allsburg, Chris. *The Mysteries of Harris Burdick*. Houghton, 1984. Ages 8–10.

———. *The Wreck of the Zephyr*. Houghton, 1983. Ages 8–10.

Ward, Lynd. *The Biggest Bear*. Houghton, 1952. Ages 7–9.

Willard, Nancy. *Pish, Posh, said Hieronymous Bosh*. Illustrated by Leo and Diane and Lee Dillon. Harcourt, 1991. Ages 9–YA.

Wisniewski, David. *Elfwyn's Saga*. Lothrop, 1990. Ages 8–10.

———. *Rain Player*. Houghton, 1991. Ages 8–10.

Illustrated Traditional and Modern Folktales

Aardema, Verna. *Rabbit Makes a Monkey of Lion: A Swahili Tale*. Illustrated by Jerry Pinkney. Dial, 1989. Ages 5–7.

———. *Why Mosquitoes Buzz in People's Ears*. Illustrated by Leo and Diane Dillon. Dial, 1975. Ages 5–7.

Andersen, Hans Christian. *The Little Match Girl*. Illustrated by Rachel Isadora. Putnam, 1987. Ages 7–9.

———. *The Tinderbox*. Illustrated by Barry Moser. Little, Brown, 1990. Ages 6–8.

Anno, Mitsumasa, reteller. *Anno's Aesop: A Book of Fables by Aesop and Mr. Fox*. Orchard, 1989. Ages 7–9.

Bach, Alice, and J. Cheryl Exum. *Moses' Ark: Stories from the Bible*. Illustrated by Leo and Diane Dillon. Delacorte, 1989. Ages 6–8.

Baker, Keith. *The Magic Fan*. Harcourt, 1989. Ages 7–9.

Berenzy, Alix. *A Frog Prince*. Holt, 1989. Ages 5–7.

Brett, Jan. *Beauty and the Beast*. Clarion, 1989. Ages 6–8.

———. *The Mitten*. Putnam, 1989. Ages 5–7.

Briggs, Raymond. *Jim and the Beanstalk*. Coward–McCann, 1970. Ages 5–7.

Brown Marcia. *Dick Whittington and His Cat*. Scribner's, 1950. Ages 6–8.

———. *Once a Mouse*. Scribner's, 1961. Ages 7–9.

Chaikin, Miriam, adaptor. *Exodus*. Illustrated by Charles Mikolaycak. Holiday, 1987. Ages 6–8.

Clark, Margaret, reteller. *The Best of Aesop's Fables.* Illustrated by Charlotte Voake. Little, Brown, 1990. Ages 7–9.

Climo, Shirley. *The Eygptian Cinderella.* Illustrated by Ruth Heller. Crowell, 1989. Ages 7–9.

Conover, Chris, reteller. *Mother Goose and the Sly Fox.* Farrar, 1989. Ages 6–8.

Cook, Scott, illustrator. *The Gingerbread Boy.* Knopf, 1987. Ages 5–7.

Cooney, Barbara. *Chanticleer and the Fox.* Crowell, 1958. Ages 6–8.

Cooper, Susan, reteller. *The Selkie Girl.* Illustrated by Warwick Hutton. McElderry, 1986. Ages 7–9.

Day, Edward C. *John Tabor's Ride.* Illustrated by Dirk Zimmer. Knopf, 1989. Ages 6–8.

DeFelice, Cynthia C. *The Dancing Skeleton.* Illustrated by Robert Andrew Parker. Macmillan, 1989. Ages 6–8.

dePaola, Tomie, reteller. *The Legend of the Indian Paintbrush.* Putnam, 1988. Ages 6–8.

———. *Tomie dePaola's Favorite Nursery Tales.* Putnam, 1986. Ages 4–6.

Eisen, Armand, reteller. *Goldilocks and the Three Bears.* Illustrated by Lynn Bywaters Ferris. Knopf, 1987. Ages 5–7.

Esbensen, Barbara Juster, reteller. *The Star Maiden: An Ojibway Tale.* Illustrated by Helen K. Davie. Little, Brown, 1988. Ages 7–9.

Field, Eugene. *Wynken, Blynken and Nod.* Illustrated by Susan Jeffers. Dutton, 1982. Ages 4–6.

Fonteyn, Margot. *Swan Lake.* Illustrated by Trina Schart Hyman. Harcourt, 1989. Ages 8–10.

Frasconi, Antonio. *The House That Jack Built.* Harcourt, 1958. Ages 6–8.

Galdone, Paul. *The Gingerbread Boy.* Clarion, 1975. Ages 4–6.

———. *The House That Jack Built.* McGraw-Hill, 1961. Ages 6–8.

———. *Old Mother Hubbard and Her Dog.* McGraw-Hill, 1960. Ages 5–7.

———, reteller. *Three Little Kittens.* Clarion, 1986. Ages 5–7.

Geisert, Arthur. *The Ark.* Houghton, 1988. Ages 6–8.

Geras, Adèle. *My Grandmother's Stories: A Collection of Jewish Folk Tales.* Illustrated by Jael Jordan. Knopf, 1990. Ages 8–10.

Gerstein, Mordicai, reteller. *The Seal Mother.* Dial, 1986. Ages 7–9.

———. *Tales of Pan.* Harper, 1986. Ages 7–9.

Goble, Paul. *Beyond the Ridge.* Bradbury, 1989. Ages 8–10.

———. *The Girl Who Loved Wild Horses.* Bradbury, 1978. Ages 7–9.

———, reteller. *Iktomi and the Berries: A Plains Indian Story.* Orchard, 1989. Ages 7–9.

———, reteller. *Iktomi and the Boulder: A Plains Indian Story.* Orchard, 1988. Ages 7–9.

Greene, Ellin. *The Legend of the Christmas Rose.* Illustrated by Charles Mikolaycak. Holiday, 1990. Ages 6–8.

Grimm, Jacob and Wilhelm. *The Bremen Town Musicians.* Illustrated by Joseph Palecek. Translated by Anthea Bell. Picture Book Studio, 1988. Ages 6–8.

Hadithi, Mwenye. *Crafty Chameleon.* Illustrated by Adrienne Kennaway. Little, Brown, 1987. Ages 6–8.

———. *Hot Hippo.* Illustrated by Adrienne Kennaway. Little, Brown, 1986. Ages 6–8.

———. *Lazy Lion.* Illustrated by Adrienne Kennaway. Little, Brown, 1990. Ages 6–8.

Hale, Lucretia. *The Lady Who Put Salt in Her Coffee.* Adapted and illustrated by Amy Schwartz. Harcourt, 1989. Ages 7–9.

Haley, Gail E. *Jack and the Fire Dragon.* Crown, 1988. Ages 6–8.

———. *A Story, A Story: An African Tale.* Atheneum, 1970. Ages 6–8.

Hamilton, Virginia, reteller. *The People Could Fly: American Black Folktales.* Illustrated by Leo and Diane Dillon. Knopf, 1985. Ages 6–10.

Haugaard, Eric Christian. *Prince Boghole.* Illustrated by Julie Downing. Macmillan, 1987. Ages 6–8.

———. *Princess Horrid.* Illustrated by Diane Dawson Hearn. Macmillan, 1990. Ages 6–8.

Heyer, Marilee, reteller. *The Weaving of a Dream: A Chinese Folktale.* Viking, 1986. Ages 7–9.

Hodges, Margaret. *The Arrow and the Lamp.* Illustrated by Donna Diamond. Little, Brown, 1989. Ages 7–9.

Hogrogian, Nonny. *The Cat Who Loved to Sing.* Knopf, 1988. Ages 5–7.

———. *One Fine Day.* Macmillan, 1971. Ages 5–7.

Hooks, William H. *The Ballad of Belle Dorcas*. Illustrated by Brian Pinkney. Knopf, 1990. Ages 7–9.

———, reteller. *Moss Gown*. Illustrated by Donald Carrick. Clarion, 1987. Ages 7–9.

Huck, Charlotte. *Princess Furball*. Illustrated by Anita Lobel. Greenwillow, 1989. Ages 6–8.

Hutton, Warwick, adaptor. *Adam and Eve: The Bible Story*. Macmillan, 1987. Ages 6–8.

———, reteller. *Moses in the Bulrushes*. Atheneum, 1986. Ages 6–8.

———, reteller. *Theseus and the Minotaur*. Macmillan, 1989. Ages 8–10.

Ishii, Momoko, reteller. *The Tongue–Cut Sparrow*. Translated from Japanese by Katherine Paterson. Illustrated by Suekichi Akaba. Lodestar, 1987. Ages 7–9.

Ivimey, John W. *The Complete Story of the Three Blind Mice*. Illustrated by Paul Galdone. Clarion, 1987. Ages 6–8.

Jarrell, Randall, translator. *Snow-White and the Seven Dwarfs*. Illustrated by Nancy Ekholm Burkert. Farrar, 1972. Ages 7–9.

Johnston, Tony. *The Badger and the Magic Fan: A Japanese Folktale*. Illustrated by Tomie dePaola. Putnam, 1990. Ages 6–8.

Karlin, Barbara, reteller. *Cinderella*. Illustrated by James Marshall. Little, Brown, 1989. Ages 6–8.

Kellogg, Steven, reteller. *Johnny Appleseed*. Morrow, 1988. Ages 6–8.

———. *Pecos Bill*. Morrow, 1986. Ages 6–8.

Kent, Jack. *The Fat Cat: A Danish Folktale*. Parents', 1971. Ages 6–8.

Kismaric, Carole. *The Rumor of Pavel and Paali: A Ukrainian Folktale*. Illustrated by Charles Mikolaycak. Harper, 1988. Ages 7–9.

Langstaff, John, and Feodor Rojankovsky. *Frog Went A- Courtin'*. Illustrated by Feodor Rojankovsky. Harcourt, 1955. Ages 6–8.

Le Tord, Bijou. *The Deep Blue Sea*. Orchard, 1990. Ages 6–8.

Lester, Julius, reteller. (Original tale by Joel Chandler Harris.) *The Tales of Uncle Remus: The Adventures of Brer Rabbit*. Illustrated by Jerry Pinkney. Dial, 1987. (See also: *More Tales of Uncle Remus: Further Adventures of Brer Rabbit, His Friends, Enemies, and Others, 1988; Further Tales of Uncle Remus, 1990*.) Ages 7–9.

———. *How Many Spots Does a Leopard Have?: And Other Tales*. Illustrated by David Shannon. Scholastic, 1989. Ages 7–9.

Lindbergh, Reeve. *Johnny Appleseed*. Illustrated by Kathy Jakobsen. Little, Brown, 1990. Ages 6–8.

Lobel, Arnold. *Fables*. Harper, 1980. Ages 6–8.

Lottridge, Celia Barker. *The Name of the Tree: A Bantu Folktale*. Illustrated by Ian Wallace. Macmillan, 1990. Ages 6–8.

Mahy, Margaret, reteller. *The Seven Chinese Brothers*. Illustrated by Jean and Mou–sien Tseng. Scholastic, 1990. Ages 6–8.

Marshall, James, reteller. *Goldilocks and the Three Bears*. Dial, 1988. Ages 5–7.

———. *Fox Be Nimble*. Dial, 1990. Ages 5–7.

———. *The Three Little Pigs*. Dial, 1989. Ages 5–7.

Martin, Rafe, reteller. *Foolish Rabbit's Big Mistake*. Illustrated by Ed Young. Putnam, 1985. Ages 6–8.

Mayer, Marianna. *The Twelve Dancing Princesses*. Illustrated by K. Y. Craft. Morrow, 1989. Ages 6–8.

McCurdy, Michael. *The Devils Who Learned to Be Good*. Little, Brown, 1987. Ages 6–8.

McDermott, Gerald. *Tim O'Toole and the Wee Folk*. Viking, 1990. Ages 6–8.

McVitty, Walter, reteller. *Ali Baba and the Forty Thieves*. Illustrated by Margaret Early. Abrams, 1989. Ages 6–8.

Menotti, Gian Carlo. *Amahl and the Night Visitors*. Illustrated by Michele Lemieux. Morrow, 1986. Ages 8–10.

Mollel, Tololwa M. *The Orphan Boy*. Illustrated by Paul Morin. Clarion, 1990. Ages 7–9.

Nesbit, E. *Melisande*. Illustrated by P. J. Lynch. Harcourt, 1989. Ages 8–10.

Ness, Evaline. *Old Mother Hubbard and Her Dog*. Holt, 1972. Ages 5–7.

Newton, Pam. *The Stonecutter: An Indian Folktale*. Putnam, 1990. Ages 7–9.

O'Shea, Pat, reteller. *Finn Mac Cool and the Small Men of Deeds*. Illustrated by Steven Lavis. Holiday, 1987. Ages 7–9.

Parks, Van Dyke, and Malcolm Jones, adaptors and retellers. (Original story by Joel Chandler Harris.) *Jump!: The Adventures of Brer Rabbit*. Illustrated by Barry Moser. Harcourt, 1986. (See also: *Jump Again!: More Adventures of Brer Rabbit, 1987; Jump on Over!: The Adventures of Brer Rabbit and His Family, 1989*.) Ages 7–9.

Paterson, Katherine. *The Tale of the Mandarin Ducks*. Illustrated by Leo and Diane Dillon. Lodestar, 1990. Ages 7–9.

Paxton, Tom, reteller. *Belling the Cat: And Other Aesop's Fables*. Illustrated by Robert Rayevsky. Morrow, 1990. Ages 8–10.

Perrault, Charles. *Cinderella*. Illustrated by Marcia Brown. Scribner's, 1954. Ages 5–7.

Pieńkowski, Jan, illustrator. *Easter: the King James Version*. Knopf, 1989. Ages 6–8.

Quayle, Eric, reteller. *The Shining Princess: and Other Japanese Legends*. Illustrated by Michael Foreman. Arcade, 1989. Ages 7–9.

Rogasky, Barbara, reteller. *The Water of Life*. Illustrated by Trina Schart Hyman. Holiday, 1986. Ages 7–9.

Rounds, Glen, reteller. *Old MacDonald Had A Farm*. Holiday, 1989. Ages 4–6.

San Souci, Robert D. *The Talking Eggs: A Folktale from the American South*. Illustrated by Jerry Pinkney. Dial, 1989. Ages 7–9.

Snyder, Dianne. *The Boy of the Three-Year Nap*. Illustrated by Allen Say. Houghton, 1988. Ages 7–9.

Stamm, Claus. *Three Strong Women: A Tall Tale from Japan*. Illustrated by Jean and Mou-sien Tseng. Viking, 1990. Ages 6–8.

Stanley, Diane. *Fortune*. Morrow, 1990. Ages 6–8.

Steptoe, John, reteller. *Mufaro's Beautiful Daughters: An African Tale*. (From G. M. Theal's Kaffir Folktales.) Lothrop, 1987. Ages 6–8.

———. *The Story of Jumping Mouse*. Lothrop, 1984. Ages 7–9.

Stevens, Janet, adaptor. *How the Manx Cat Lost Its Tail*. Harcourt, 1990. Ages 6–8.

———. *The Town Mouse and the Country Mouse: An Aesop Fable*. Holiday, 1987. Ages 6–8.

Stolz, Mary. *Zekmet, the Stone Carver: A Tale of Ancient Eygpt*. Illustrated by Deborah Nourse Lattimore. Harcourt, 1988. Ages 8–10.

Testa, Fulvio, illustrator. *Aesop's Fables*. Barron, 1989. Ages 8–10.

Turkle, Brinton. *Deep in the Forest*. Dutton, 1976. Ages 6–8.

Vernon, Adele. *The Riddle*. Illustrated by Robert Rayevsky and Vladimir Radunsky. Dodd, 1987. Ages 6–8.

Wallner, John, reteller. *Good King Wenceslas*. Putnam, 1990. Ages 6–8.

Watson, Richard Jesse, reteller. *Tom Thumb*. Harcourt, 1989. Ages 6–8.

Wilde, Oscar. *The Happy Prince*. Illustrated by Ed Young. Simon and Schuster, 1989. Ages 7–9.

Williams, Linda. *The Little Old Lady Who Was Not Afraid of Anything*. Illustrated by Megan Lloyd. Crowell, 1986. Ages 6–8.

Williams-Ellis, Amabel, selector. *Tales from the Enchanted World*. Illustrated by Moira Kemp. Little, Brown, 1988. Ages 7–9.

Wisniewski, David. *Elfwyn's Saga*. Lothrop, 1990. Ages 8–10.

———. *The Warrior and the Wise Man*. Lothrop, 1989. Ages 7–9.

Yolen, Jane. *Tam Lin*. Illustrated by Charles Mikolaycak. Harcourt, 1990. Ages 7–9.

Young, Ed. *Lon Po Po: A Red–Riding Hood Story from China*. Philomel, 1989. Ages 6–8.

Zelinsky, Paul O., reteller. *Rumpelstiltskin*. (From the German of the Brothers Grimm.) Dutton, 1986. Ages 6–8.

Zemach, Margot. *It Could Always Be Worse: A Yiddish Folk Tale*. Farrar, 1976. Ages 6–8.

———. *The Three Little Pigs: An Old Story*. Farrar, 1988. Ages 6–8.

Zimmermann, H. Werner. *Henny Penny*. Scholastic, 1989. Ages 5–7.

Illustrated Books of Poetry

Note the distinction between *poems* and *stories told in verse*. Heavily illustrated poems are listed here. Illustrated stories told in verse are included under the heading of Picture Storybooks.

Adoff, Arnold. *Flamboyan*. Illustrated by Karen Barbour. Harcourt, 1988. Ages 8–10.

Blegvad, Lenore. *This Little Pig-a-Wig and Other Rhymes about Pigs*. Illustrated by Erik Blegvad. Atheneum, 1978. Ages 5–7.

Bryan, Ashley. *Turtle Knows Your Name*. Atheneum, 1989. Ages 7–9.

Cassedy, Sylvia. *Roomrimes: Poems*. Illustrated by Michele Chessare. Crowell, 1987. Ages 6–8.

Chorao, Kay. *The Baby's Good Morning Book*. Dutton, 1986. Ages 3–5.

cummings, e.e. *hist whist*. Illustrated by Deborah Kogan Ray. Crown, 1989. Ages 8–10.

———. *Little Tree*. Illustrated by Deborah Kogan Ray. Crown, 1987. Ages 7–9.

dePaola, Tomie. *Tomie dePaola's Book of Poems*. Putnam, 1988. Ages 6–10.

Fisher, Aileen. *Listen Rabbit*. Illustrated by Symeon Shimin. Crowell, 1964. Ages 7–9.

Frank, Josette, selector. *Snow Toward Evening: A Year in a River Valley/Nature Poems*. Illustrated by Thomas Locker. Dial, 1990. Ages 8–10.

Gackenbach, Dick, adaptor. *Timid Timothy's Tongue Twisters*. Holiday, 1986. Ages 6–10.

Hoberman, Mary Ann. *Fathers, Mothers, Sisters, Brothers: A Collection of Family Poems*. Illustrated by Marylin Hafner. Little, 1991. Ages 6–10.

Hopkins, Lee Bennett, editor. *Dinosaurs*. Illustrated by Murray Tinkelman. Harcourt, 1987. Ages 6–8.

Kennedy, X. J. *Fresh Brats*. Illustrated by James Watts. Macmillan, 1990. Ages 6–10.

Larrick, Nancy, compiler. *Cats Are Cats*. Illustrated by Ed Young. Philomel, 1988. Ages 6–10.

————, editor. *Mice Are Nice*. Illustrated by Ed Young. Putnam, 1990. Ages 6–10.

Lenski, Lois. *Sing a Song of People*. Illustrated by Giles Laroche. Little, Brown, 1987. Ages 6–10.

Lewis, J. Patrick. *A Hippopotamusn't and Other Animal Verses*. Illustrated by Victoria Chess. Dial, 1990. Ages 6–8.

Lewis, Richard. *In the Night, Still Dark*. Illustrated by Ed Young. Atheneum, 1988. Ages 7–9.

Little, Lessie Jones. *Children of Long Ago*. Illustrated by Jan Spivey Gilchrist. Putnam, 1988. Ages 6–10.

Longfellow, Henry Wadsworth. *Paul Revere's Ride*. Illustrated by Ted Rand. Dutton, 1990. Ages 8–10.

Merriam, Eve. *Halloween ABC*. Illustrated by Lane Smith. Macmillan, 1987. Ages 8–10.

————. *You Be Good & I'll Be Night: Jump-On-the-Bed Poems*. Illustrated by Karen Lee Schmidt. Morrow, 1988. Ages 6–8.

Petersham, Maud, and Miska Petersham. *The Rooster Crows: A Book of American Rhymes and Jingles*. Macmillan, 1945. Ages 6–10.

Pooley, Sarah, selector. *A Day of Rhymes*. Knopf, 1988. Ages 6–10.

Prelutsky, Jack, selector. *Poems of A. Nonny Mouse*. Illustrated by Henrik Drescher. Knopf, 1989. Ages 6- 10.

————. *Tyrannosaurus Was a Beast: Dinosaur Poems*. Illustrated by Arnold Lobel. Greenwillow, 1988. Ages 6–8.

Singer, Marilyn. *Turtle in July*. Illustrated by Jerry Pinkney. Macmillan, 1989. Ages 8–10.

Sneve, Virginia Driving Hawk, selector. *Dancing Teepees: Poems of American Indian Youth*. Illustrated by Stephen Gammell. Holiday, 1989. Ages 9–YA.

Steig, Jeanne. *Consider the Lemming*. Illustrated by William Steig. Farrar, 1988. Ages 7–9.

Stevenson, Robert Louis. *A Child's Garden of Verses*. Chronicle, 1989. Ages 6–10.

Swann, Brian. *A Basket Full of White Eggs: Riddle Poems*. Illustrated by Ponder Goembel. Orchard, 1988. Ages 6–10.

Thayer, Ernest Lawrence. *Casey at the Bat*. Illustrated by Barry Moser. Godine, 1988. Ages 8–10.

Whipple, Laura, compiler. *Eric Carle's Animals Animals*. Illustrated by Eric Carle. Philomel, 1989. Ages 6–10.

C h a p t e r **5**

Traditional Literature

Listen!

Quiet your faces; be crossed every thumb;
  Fix on me deep your eyes . . .
And out of my mind a story shall come—
  Old, and lovely, and wise.
                    —Walter de la Mare

Visual narratives told by ancient cave paintings in Europe, Asia, and Australia tell us that prehistoric humans had stories to tell long before they had a written language. For thousands of years before writing was discovered, the best of these stories were preserved through the art of storytelling, from one generation to the next. Surely these stories survived because people enjoyed hearing them. Even today, their entertainment value cannot be denied. But particularly for the early humans, these stories served a more serious purpose in addressing the fundamental questions: Who are we? Where did we come from? and Why do people and nature behave as they do? In folk literature we have our most ancient stories and a priceless literary heritage that links us to our beginnings as thinking beings.

Definition and Description

Traditional literature is that body of ancient stories and poems that grew out of the human quest to understand the natural and spiritual worlds and that was preserved through time by the oral tradition of storytelling and was eventually written down. Having no known or identifiable authors, these stories and poems are attributed to entire groups of people or cultures. Although in ancient times some traditional stories may have been told as truth or may have been thought to contain elements of truth, today we consider them to be mostly or wholly fantasy.

Traditional literature includes several different types of stories, but because they were all shared orally for so long, they have many features in common. For example, plots are generally shorter than in other genres of literature because all but the essential details were omitted during countless retellings. Action, in turn, is concentrated, which kept audiences alert and interested. Characters in traditional literature tend to have only one outstanding quality, which made them easy to identify. In these stories there is no doubt about who is good and who is bad. Settings are unimportant and are described and referred to in the vaguest of terms, such as "In the beginning . . ." or "Long ago in a land far away . . . ." The language is full of rhythm and melody and yet sparse, since lengthy explanations and descriptions were also pared down or eliminated by countless retellings. Style is characterized by stock beginnings and endings ("Once upon a time" and "they lived happily ever after"), motifs or recognizable patterns (use of the number 3, as in 3 sisters, 3 wishes), and repetition of refrains or chants ("Mirror, mirror, on the wall . . . "). Themes most common in these stories are good versus evil, the power of perseverance, and explanations for the ways of the world. One feature that makes these stories particular favorites of young children is that they almost always have a happy ending.

Folklore is still being created, particularly in some of the developing countries where the oral tradition is still the chief means of communication. In our country, urban legends, jokes, and jump-rope rhymes are all part of the constantly evolving body of folklore. These stories and rhymes are of unknown origin, but because they are certainly not ancient, they will not be treated in this chapter. We must also note those stories written in the style of folk stories but by known authors. Because this body of modern, or literary, folktales has known authors and is not of ancient origin, it will be discussed in Chapter 6, Modern Fantasy.

Values of Traditional Literature for Children

Traditional literature has survived for several thousand years because it is highly entertaining. This is its greatest value for children of today.

- Traditional stories are highly entertaining to young children and make an excellent and welcomed next step into literature after nursery rhymes. Children, especially those between the ages of 3 and 8, derive great pleasure from hearing traditional stories again and again for reasons that are easily understandable. The action is immediate and exciting and the characters are easy to love or hate. Moreover, the underdog or smallest character is usually the winner. Additional reasons include short, rhyming chants that can be spoken with the storyteller; magic spells that make the impossible happen; and wrong-doing that is punished with satisfying swiftness and certainty.
- Traditional literature is an excellent source of stories for storytelling.

- Hearing traditional stories helps children to develop a strong sense of story, which in turn provides them with a good foundation for understanding other literary genres. The stock phrases, repetition, and uncomplicated characters typical of traditional tales help children without much story experience to make sense of, remember, and keep up with the action and characters in these stories.

- Knowing the characters and situations of traditional literature is part of being culturally literate. Children who grow up unfamiliar with this body of literature will be at a disadvantage when allusions to traditional literature are made in conversations and in print.

- Traditional literature provides an interesting way for children to be introduced to the diverse cultural groups of their country and other countries. Every cultural group has its body of folklore that, to some extent, reveals the characteristics and values of the people or gives insights into what makes the culture unique. Today, much of this folklore has been collected, translated, published, and made available to children. By introducing children to folklore from many lands and by comparing variants of the same story from different cultures, teachers and librarians are building a solid foundation for multicultural and international understanding.

- Because characters in traditional stories are easily identifiable as good or bad and because evil in these stories is punished with clear-cut finality, many people believe that hearing traditional literature helps children to sort out good and evil in the world and to identify with the good.

Others raise concerns that the gruesome violence sometimes found in traditional stories harms or traumatizes children. In recent times, many traditional stories have been rewritten to omit the violence, as in the Disney versions of folktales. In a "softened" version of "Snow White," the evil stepmother is either forgiven by the heroine or banished from the kingdom. More authentic versions of the tale end like this:

> *Then she [the stepmother] railed and cursed, and was beside herself with disappointment and anger. First she thought she would not go to the wedding; but then she felt she should have no peace until she went and saw the bride. And when she saw her she knew her for Snow-white, and could not stir from the place for anger and terror. For they had ready red-hot iron shoes, in which she had to dance until she fell down dead. (From Jakob Grimm and Wilhelm Grimm,* Household Stories, *translated by Lucy Crane [Macmillan, 1886].)*

Critics of the softened versions of traditional tales claim that altering the stories robs them of their power, their appeal, and their psychological benefit to children who, in the original versions, are reassured that the evil stepmother (or big bad wolf, or wicked ogre, etc.) is gone forever and cannot come back to hurt them. As parents, teachers, and librarians, you will be in a position to choose which versions of traditional literature to share. We believe that the unaltered versions, shared within the security of the family or classroom, have the greater benefit to children.

Evaluation and Selection of Traditional Literature

For thousands of years, people of all ages were the intended audience for traditional stories. In fact, this is still true in the few preliterate societies existing today. In our scientifically enlightened times, these stories have come to be seen as childlike in their use of the supernatural and magic. As a result, today's main audience for these stories is children between the ages of 3 and 8. The following list of evaluation criteria was developed with this audience in mind.

- A traditional tale, even though written down, should preserve the narrative, or storytelling, style and should sound as though it is being told.
- A traditional tale should preserve the flavor of the culture or country of its origin through the use of colloquialisms, unusual speech patterns, a few easily understood foreign terms, or proper names common to the culture.
- Since many versions and many retellings of traditional tales are currently available, those chosen should be neither too complicated nor too simplified to appeal to the audience.
- Retold versions of traditional tales must preserve the essential content that made the stories vital to people for thousands of years and that makes them relevant to children of today.
- In illustrated versions of traditional literature, text and illustrations must be of high quality, and illustrations must match the tone of the text and help to capture the essence of the culture of origin.
- In evaluating collections of traditional literature, it is important to consider all of the criteria listed above, as well as the number and variety of tales in the collection and the quality of reference aids, such as table of contents and indexes.

Because traditional stories have, by definition, simple plots and characterizations, some adults may think that the language in these stories should also be very simple. However, having simple plots and characterization does not preclude traditional tales from having a rich literary style. Even very young children are fascinated by the chants, stylistic flourishes, and colorful vocabulary that are characteristic of masterful storytelling.

With the current trend toward gorgeously and generously illustrated versions of traditional literature, there are instances when it would be tempting to base one's evaluation and selection mainly on illustrations. Not all illustrators are equally skillful as writers and artists, however. Furthermore, important aspects of traditional tales can be left out in retellings. For example, the well-known folktale, "Little Red Riding Hood" was used for centuries to warn children of the dangers that exist in the world and the sad results of careless behavior. If this tale is softened to the extent that no one is harmed and no one is punished, it loses its real meaning for children of today. Careful attention to quality and content of writing in traditional stories must always be a part of evaluation.

Historical Overview of Traditional Literature

Perhaps the world's first stories grew out of the dreams, wishes, ritual chants, or re-tellings of the notable exploits of our primitive ancestors. No one knows. Little can be said about the early history of this genre except that these stories existed only in oral form for thousands of years.

The first known English publication of any traditional literature was that of *Aesop's Fables* in 1484 by William Caxton, the printer. Although this work was instantly popular, further collections of traditional stories in print were slow to come, due mainly to the Puritans, who disapproved of any and all popular literature. During the Puritan Movement, which lasted roughly from 1500 to 1700, traditional literature retained its popularity with the common people through the *chapbook,* named after the chap-men, or peddlers, who sold them. These inexpensive paper books of between 32 and 64 pages contained stories of adventure and humor that were loosely based on the epics, legends, and folk heroes of traditional literature.

As the Romantic Movement gradually replaced the Puritan Movement in Europe in the eighteenth century, traditional literature was accepted by all levels of society once more. The first evidence of this change in attitude was the publication by Charles Perrault in 1697 in France of eight "courtly" tales under the title *Tales of Mother Goose.* Included in this collection were "Cinderella," "The Sleeping Beauty," "Little Red Riding Hood," and "Puss in Boots." The popularity of this publication is evidenced by its many editions in both France and England, but it was another 100 years before the next collection of traditional literature appeared.

The publication in 1812 of Jakob and Wilhelm Grimm's *Nursery and Household Tales,* which included such tales as "Rumpelstilskin," "Snow White and the Seven Dwarfs," and "Hansel and Gretel," gave the world some of its best-loved stories. As the nineteenth century progressed, other important collections of traditional literature appeared in Europe and England for the first time. In Norway, Peter Christian Asbjörnsen and Jörgen Moe collected such folktales as "The Three Billy Goats Gruff," "East o' the Sun and West o' the Moon," "Henny Penny," and "Pancake," and published them in 1851 in book form under the title *The Norwegian Folktales.* In England, Joseph Jacobs compiled from already printed sources his *English Fairy Tales* (1894), which included "The Three Bears," "The Three Little Pigs," and "The Little Red Hen." Jacobs's adaptations of many tales for a child audience is an important part of his contribution. By the time the Scot, Andrew Lang, published his valuable four-volume collection of folktales from around the world (*The Blue, Red, Green,* and *Yellow Fairy Books,* 1889–1894), the value and importance of traditional literature had been generally accepted. Milestones in the development of traditional literature are highlighted in Table 5–1.

The popularity of traditional literature with children has continued to grow in the twentieth century due, in part, to a renewed interest in storytelling. Other trends contributing to the popularity of this genre are the publication of illustrated retellings of single works of traditional literature, publication of cultural variants of traditional tales from around the world, and publication of newly discovered ethnic folk literature of

Table 5–1   Milestones in the Development of Traditional Literature

Date	Event	Significance
Prehistory–1500s	Oral storytelling.	Oral tradition kept ancient stories alive and provided literature to common people.
1484	*Aesop's Fables* published by William Caxton in England.	First known publication of traditional literature.
1500–1700	Puritan Movement.	Prevented the publication of traditional literature by the legitimate press.
	Chapbooks emerge.	Helped keep interest in traditional heroes alive during Puritan Movement.
1697	*Tales of Mother Goose* published by Charles Perrault in France.	First written version of folktales.
1700s	Romantic Movement.	Traditional fantasy promoted and embraced in Europe.
1812	Wilhelm & Jakob Grimm published *Nursery and Household Tales* in Germany.	Contributed to a sense of national identity in Germany. Helped to popularize folk literature worldwide.
1851	Asbjörnsen and Moe published *The Norwegian Folktales* in Norway.	Contributed to a sense of national identity in Norway. Helped to popularize folk literature worldwide.
1894	Joseph Jacobs published *English Fairy Tales* in England.	Adapted many tales for a child audience.
1889–94	Andrew Lang published 4 volumes of folktales from around the world.	Growing popularity and knowledge of folktales worldwide.

many Canadian and U.S. minorities in collections and single, illustrated works. Surely these trends indicate a healthy respect for the importance of our folk literary heritage, as well as general recognition of the worth of all traditional literature.

Types of Traditional Literature

For the beginning student of traditional literature, classification of stories can be confusing. For one thing, not everyone uses the same terms when referring to certain types of traditional stories. For another, we have a large body of modern stories written by known authors in the style of the traditional ones but that are not of ancient and unknown origin and, therefore, not "traditional" in the strict sense.

We have chosen the term *traditional literature* to refer to the entire body of stories passed down from ancient times by the oral tradition. The term *folktale* is sometimes used in the same way. The term *retold tale* refers to a version of a tale that is obviously based on an earlier, well-known tale but in which the language and bits of the plot have been altered to modernize or further dramatize the story. Nowadays, retold tales are often accompanied by completely new and original illustrations that sometimes give remarkable insights into the deeper meaning or relevancy of these tales. *Variant,* a term often used in reference to folktales, refers to a story that shares fundamental elements of plot or character with an archetypal story type, and therefore is said to be in the same story family. There are hundreds of variants of "Cinderella," for example, from all over the world. All of the following types of traditional literature occur in variant and retold tale versions.

Myths

Myths are those stories that recount and explain the origins of the world and the phenomena of nature. They are sometimes referred to as *creation stories.* Myths may have originated in ancient religious rituals. The characters in these stories are mainly gods and goddesses, with occasional mention of humans, and the setting is high above earth in the home of the gods. Though often violent, myths nonetheless mirror human nature and the essence of our sometimes primitive emotions, instincts, and desires. Some folklorists believe that myths are the foundation of all other ancient stories. The best-known mythologies are of Greek, Roman, and Norse origin.

Many excellent collections of myths are currently available for children. (See the list at the end of this chapter.) In addition, single myths are often published in picture book format. (See the list at the end of Chapter 4.) The complexity and symbolism often found in myths make them appropriate for an older audience (9 years and up) than is usual with traditional literature. Some myths have been simplified for a younger audience, but oversimplification robs these stories of their power and appeal.

Epics and Ballads

Epics are long stories of human adventure and heroism recounted in many episodes. Some epics are told in verse. Epics are grounded in mythology, and their characters can be both human and divine. However, the hero is always human, or, in some cases, superhuman, as was Ulysses in the *Odyssey,* Beowulf in the epic of that name, and Roland in *The Song of Roland.* The setting is earthly but not always realistic.

The ballad shares most of the characteristics of the epic, except that it is meant to be sung and for this reason was written in poetic verse. Though now found only in prose accounts, the character of Robin Hood first appeared in *The Ballad of Robin Hood.*

Legends and Tall Tales

Legends are stories based on either real or supposedly real individuals and their marvelous deeds. Legendary characters such as King Arthur, Lancelot, and Merlin, and legendary settings such as Camelot are a tantalizing mix of realism and fantasy. Although the feats of the heroes of legend defy belief today, in ancient times these stories were considered factual.

Tall tales are also highly exaggerated accounts of the exploits of persons, both real and imagined, so they may be considered a subcategory of legends, albeit of much more recent origin. In the evolution of the tall tale, however, as each teller embroidered upon the hero's abilities or deeds, the tales became outlandishly exaggerated and were valued more for their humor and braggadocio than for their factual content. Legends, in contrast, are more austere in tone. Well-known North American tall-tale heroes are Pecos Bill, Paul Bunyan, John Henry, and Johnny Appleseed.

Folktales

Folktales are those stories that grew out of the lives and imaginations of the people, or folk. Folktales have always been children's favorite type of traditional literature. One of the most interesting and important characteristics of these tales is their universality. No theories adequately explain this phenomenon, but the folktales of all cultures, regardless of geography or other surface cultural differences, are remarkably similar.

Folktales vary in content as to their original intended audiences. Long ago, the nobility and their courtiers heard stories of the heroism, valor, and benevolence of people like themselves—the ruling classes. In contrast, the stories heard by the common people portrayed the ruling classes as unjust or hard taskmasters whose riches were fair game for those common folk who were quick witted or strong enough to acquire them.

Some people use the terms *folktale* and *fairy tale* interchangeably. In fact, the majority of these stories have no fairies or magic characters in them, so to use one term in place of the other can be confusing and erroneous. We categorize fairy tales under *magic tales,* a kind of folktale having magic characters such as fairies.

The following is a list of the most prevalent kinds of folktales. Note that some folktales have characteristics of two or more folktale categories.

Cumulative   The cumulative tale uses repetition, accumulation, and rhythm to make an entertaining story out of the barest of plots. Because of its simplicity, rhythm, and humor, the cumulative tale has special appeal to the 3- to 5-year-olds. "The Gingerbread Boy," with its run-away cookie and his growing host of pursuers, is a good example of this kind of tale.

Humorous   The humorous tale is one that revolves around a character's incredibly stupid and funny mistakes. These tales are also known as *noodleheads, sillies, drolls,* and *numbskulls.* They have endured, no doubt, for their comic appeal and the guaranteed laughter they evoke. Some famous noodleheads are the Norwegian husband who kept house (and nearly demolished it) and Clever Elsie, who was so addlebrained that she got herself confused with someone else and was never heard from again.

Beast Beast tales feature talking animals and exaggerated action. Usually the characters are animals, but they can include humans. Young children accept and enjoy these talking animals, and older children can appreciate the fact that the animals symbolize humans. "The Three Bears," perhaps the best-loved folktale of all, is a good example of a beast tale.

Magic Magic tales, also known as *wonder tales* or *fairy tales,* contain elements of magic or enchantment in characters, plots, or settings. Fairies, elves, pixies, brownies, witches, magicians, genies, and fairy godparents are pivotal characters in these stories, and they use magic objects or words to weave their enchantments. Talking mirrors, 100-year naps, glass palaces, enchanted forests, thumb-sized heroines, and magic kisses are the stuff of magic tales.

Pourquoi Pourquoi tales explain phenomena of nature. The word *pourquoi* is French for *why,* and these tales can be understood as primitive explanations for the many "why" questions early humans asked. The strong connection between these tales and myths is obvious, which is why some folklorists identify pourquoi tales as the simplest myths. An example of a pourquoi tale is "Why the Sun and the Moon Live in the Sky."

Realistic Realistic tales are those whose characters, plot, and setting could conceivably have occurred. There is no magic in these tales, and any exaggeration is limited to the possible. Only a few realistic tales exist. Among them, "Dick Whittington and His Cat," which is based on an actual character, is perhaps the best known.

Fables

The fable is a simple story that incorporates characters, typically animals, whose actions teach a moralistic lesson or universal truth. Often, the moral is stated at the end of the story. Throughout history, fables have appealed to adults as well as to children, for the best of these stories are both simple and wise. Moreover, their use of animals as symbols for human behavior have made them safe, yet effective, political tools. Perhaps because of their adult appeal, fables were put into print far earlier than other forms of traditional literature.

Aesop's fables are the best-known collection of fables in the Western world, but other collections deserve our notice. From Persia, there are the *Panchatantra Tales;* from India, the *Jataka Tales;* and from France, the collected fables of Jean de La Fontaine.

Religious Stories

Stories based on religious writings or taken intact from religious manuscripts are considered to be religious stories. These stories may recount milestones in the development of a religion and its leadership, or they may present a piece of religious doctrine in narrative form. Stories of the latter sort are usually called *parables*.

Scholars of religion, language, and mythology have found a definite thread of continuity from myth and folk narrative to early religious thinking and writing. Many of the stories, figures, and rituals described in the sacred scriptures of Christianity, Hinduism, and Buddhism, among other religions, have their roots in ancient mythology.

Regardless of whether one considers the religious stories to be fact or fiction, the important point is that these wonderful stories should be shared with children. Because religion in the classroom is potentially controversial, however, many teachers and librarians do not feel comfortable sharing stories with any religious connection. This is unfortunate, since many wonderful stories and some superlative literature, as well as characters, sayings, and situations essential to the culturally literate person, are therefore missed.

Modern Folktales

The main difference between this literature and traditional literature is that it is a creation of the recent past or of the present and is written by known authors. For this reason, modern folktales will be discussed in the following chapter.

Traditional literature, that wealth of ancient stories accumulated over the course of human existence, is one of the treasures of our species. We listen to these endlessly fascinating stories, we reflect on them, and they help to tell us who we are. Good companions of our childhood, they easily become part of us and stay with us throughout our lives. Every child deserves access to this wonderful literary heritage.

Notable Retellers, Collectors, and Illustrators of Traditional Literature

Aesop, supposed Greek slave of the sixth century B.C. and author of a collection of classic fables.

Peter Christian Asbjørnsen, nineteenth-century Norwegian collector of folktales.

Marcia Brown, seven of her nine Caldecott Awards or Honor Book Awards are for illustrating folktales. *Cinderella; Once a Mouse.*

Nancy Ekholm Burkert, author and illustator whose meticulously detailed, authentic illustrations bring depth to folktales. *Snow White and the Seven Dwarfs* (translated by Randall Jarrell).

Walt Disney, animated film producer whose greatly sentimentalized versions of folktales popularized the genre. "Snow White and the Seven Dwarfs."

Leonard Everett Fisher, author and illustrator of Greek and Mexican mythology. *Theseus and the Minotaur.*

Paul Galdone, illustrator of numerous classic folktales. *The Gingerbread Boy; Androcles and the Lion.*

Jakob and Wilhelm Grimm, nineteenth-century German folktale collectors.

Margaret Hodges, reteller of traditional stories. *Saint George and the Dragon.*

Warwick Hutton, reteller and illustrator of Bible stories. *Adam and Eve: The Bible Story; Jonah and the Great Fish.*

Trina Schart Hyman, reteller and illustrator of classic folktales. *Little Red Riding Hood; The Sleeping Beauty.*

Joseph Jacobs, nineteenth-century English compiler and adaptor of folktales for children.

Jean de La Fontaine, seventeenth-century French author of fables.

Andrew Lang, nineteenth-century Scottish collector of folktales from around the world.

James Marshall, reteller and illustrator of humorously irreverent versions of classic folktales. *Goldilocks and the Three Bears.*

Jörgen Moe, nineteenth-century Norwegian collector of folktales.

Patricia Polacco, author and illustrator of Russian folk stories. *Thundercake.*

Ed Young, Chinese-American illustrator of Chinese folktale variants. *Lon Po-Po: A Red Riding Hood Story from China.*

Paul O. Zelinsky, illustrator whose realistic oil paintings provide insights into the meaning of folktales. *Hansel and Gretel; Rumpelstilskin.*

Margot Zemach, author and illustrator of humorous folktales from many countries. *It Could Always Be Worse: A Yiddish Folk Tale.*

Lisbeth Zwerger, Austrian who won the 1990 Hans Christian Andersen Award for her watercolor illustrations of folktales. *Little Red Cap.*

Recommended Traditional Literature

Ages refer to approximate interest levels. YA = young adult.

Myths and Epics

Asimov, Isaac. *Words from the Myths.* Illustrated by William Barss. Houghton, 1961. Ages 9–YA.

Baker, Betty. *At the Center of the World.* Illustrated by Murray Tinkelman. Macmillan, 1973. Ages 8–10.

Barth, Edna. *Cupid and Psyche.* Illustrated by Ati Forberg. Seabury, 1976. Ages 9–12.

Colum, Padraic. *The Children of Odin.* Illustrated by Willy Pogany. Macmillan, 1920. Ages 9–12.

Coolidge, Olivia. *Greek Myths.* Illustrated by Edouard Sandoz. Houghton, 1949. Ages 9–12.

———. *Legends of the North.* Illustrated by Edouard Sandoz. Houghton, 1951. Ages 9–12.

Crossley-Holland, Kevin, editor. *The Faber Book of Northern Legends.* Illustrated by Alan Howard. Faber, 1983. Ages 9–12.

d'Aulaire, Ingri, and Edgar Parin d'Aulaire. *Book of Greek Myths.* Doubleday, 1962. Ages 8–10.

———. *Norse Gods and Giants.* Doubleday, 1967. Ages 8- 10.

Evslin, Bernard. *Hercules.* Illustrated by Joseph A. Smith. Morrow, 1984. Ages 9–12.

Evslin, Bernard, Dorothy Evslin, and Ned Hoopes. *Heroes and Monsters of Greek Myth.* Illustrated by William Hunter. Scholastic, 1970. Ages 9–12.

Farmer, Penelope. *Beginnings: Creation Myths of the World.* Illustrated by Antonio Frasconi. Atheneum, 1979. Ages 9–12.

———. *Daedalus and Icarus.* Illustrated by Chris Connor. Harcourt, 1971. Ages 9–12.

Fisher, Leonard Everett. *The Olympians: Great Gods and Goddesses of Ancient Greece.* Holiday, 1984. Ages 9- 12.

Gates, Doris. *The Golden God: Apollo.* Illustrated by Constantinos CoConis. Viking, 1973. Ages 9–12.

———. *Lord of the Sky: Zeus.* Illustrated by Robert Handeville. Viking, 1972. Ages 9–12.

———. *Two Queens of Heaven, The Story of Demeter and Aphrodite.* Illustrated by Trina Schart Hyman. Viking, 1973. Ages 9-12.

———. *The Warrior Goddess: Athena.* Illustrated by Don Bolognese. Viking, 1972. Ages 9–12.

Green, Roger Lancelyn. *Tales of the Greek Heroes.* Penguin Books, 1958. Ages 9–12.

Hamilton, Virginia, reteller. *In the Beginning: Creation Stories from Around the World.* Illustrated by Barry Moser. Harcourt, 1988. Ages 9–12.

Hodges, Margaret. *The Gorgon's Head.* Illustrated by Charles Mikolaycak. Little, Brown, 1972. Ages 8–10.

———. *Persephone and the Springtime, A Greek Myth.* Illustrated by Arvis Stewart. Little, Brown, 1973. Ages 9–12.

Leach, Maria. *How the People Sang the Mountains Up: How and Why Stories.* Illustrated by Glen Rounds. Viking, 1967. Ages 8–10.

Low, Alice. *The Macmillan Book of Greek Gods and Heroes.* Illustrated by Arvis Stewart. Macmillan, 1985. Ages 9–12.

McDermott, Gerald. *Daughter of Earth: A Roman Myth.* Delacorte, 1984. Ages 9–12.

Proddow, Penelope, translator. *Demeter and Persephone.* Illustrated by Barbara Cooney. Doubleday, 1972. Ages 9–12.

Serraillier, Ian. *The Clashing Rocks: The Story of Jason.* Illustrated by William Stobbs. Walck, 1964. Ages 9–12.

———. *A Fall from the Sky: The Story of Daedalus.* Illustrated by William Stobbs. Walck, 1966. Ages 9–12.

———. *The Gorgon's Head: The Story of Perseus.* Illustrated by William Stobbs. Walck, 1962. Ages 9–12.

———. *Heracles the Strong.* Illustrated by Rocco Negri. Walck, 1970. Ages 9–12.

———. *The Way of Danger: The Story of Theseus.* Illustrated by William Stobbs. Walck, 1963. Ages 9–12.

Legends and Tall Tales

Bird, E. J. *Ten Tall Tales.* Carolrhoda, 1984. Ages 8–10.

Blair, Walter. *Tall Tale America: A Legendary History of Our Humorous Heroes.* Illustrated by Glen Rounds. Coward-McCann, 1944. Ages 7–9.

Day, Edward C. *John Tabor's Ride.* Illustrated by Dirk Zimmer. Knopf, 1989. Ages 8–10.

Dewey, Ariane. *The Narrow Escapes of Davy Crockett.* Greenwillow, 1990. Ages 8–10.

———. *Pecos Bill.* Greenwillow, 1983. Ages 7–9.

Fisher, Leonard Everett. *Jason and the Golden Fleece.* Holiday, 1990. Ages 9–12.

Fleischman, Sid. *McBroom and the Beanstalk.* Illustrated by Walter Lorraine. Little, Brown, 1978. (Others in the *McBroom* series: *McBroom Tells a Lie; McBroom and the Great Race; McBroom's Ghost; McBroom's Zoo; McBroom's Ear; McBroom and the Big Wind; McBroom's Almanac* .) Ages 6–8.

Gleiter, Jan, and Kathleen Thompson. *Paul Bunyan and Babe the Blue Ox.* Illustrated by Yoshi Miyake. Raintree, 1985. Ages 7–9.

Hastings, Selina. *Sir Gawain and the Green Knight.* Illustrated by Juan Wijngaard. Lothrop, 1981. Ages 9–12.

———. *Sir Gawain and the Loathly Lady.* Illustrated by Juan Wijngaard. Lothrop, 1985. Ages 9–12.

Hodges, Margaret. *Saint George and the Dragon.* Illustrated by Trina Schart Hyman. Little, Brown, 1984. Ages 8–10.

Keats, Ezra Jack. *John Henry, An American Legend.* Pantheon, 1965. Ages 8–10.

Kellogg, Steven, reteller. *Paul Bunyan.* Morrow, 1984. Ages 6–8.

———. reteller. *Pecos Bill.* Morrow, 1986. Ages 6–8.

Pyle, Howard. *The Merry Adventures of Robin Hood.* Scribner's, 1946/1883. Ages 9–12.

———. *Some Merry Adventures of Robin Hood.* Scribner's, 1954. Ages 9-12.

———. *The Story of King Arthur and His Knights.* Scribner's, 1984/1883. Ages 9-12.

Rounds, Glen. *Washday on Noah's Ark: A Story of Noah's Ark According to Glen Rounds.* Holiday, 1985. Ages 6–8.

Sutcliff, Rosemary. *The Light Beyond the Forest: The Quest for the Holy Grail.* Dutton, 1980. Ages 9–12.

———. *The Road to Camlann.* Dutton, 1982. Ages 9–12.

———. *The Sword and the Circle.* Dutton, 1981. Ages 9–12.

Folktales

Aardema, Verna. *The Riddle of the Drum.* Illustrated by Tony Chen. Four Winds, 1979. Ages 6–8.

———, reteller. *Traveling to Tondo: A Tale of the Nkundo of Zaire.* Illustrated by Will Hillenbrand. Knopf, 1990. Ages 7–9.

———. *Who's in Rabbit's House?* Illustrated by Leo and Diane Dillon. Dial, 1977. Ages 5-7.

———. *Why Mosquitoes Buzz in People's Ears.* Illustrated by Leo and Diane Dillon. Dial, 1975. Ages 5–7.

Arkhurst, Joyce Cooper. *The Adventures of Spider: West African Folk Tales*. Illustrated by Jerry Pinkney. Little, Brown, 1964. Ages 6–8.

Asbjörnsen, Peter Christian, and Jörgen E. Moe. *The Three Billy Goats Gruff*. Illustrated by Marcia Brown. Harcourt, 1957. Ages 6–8.

Bang, Molly. *Dawn*. Morrow, 1983. Ages 6–8.

Barth, Edna. *Cupid and Psyche: A Love Story*. Illustrated by Ati Forberg. Houghton Mifflin, 1976. Ages 7–9.

Bishop, Gavin. *Chicken Licken*. Oxford, 1984. Ages 6–8.

Briggs, Raymond. *Jim and the Beanstalk*. Coward, 1970. Ages 5–7.

Brown, Marcia. *The Bun: A Tale from Russia*. Harcourt, 1972. Ages 6–8.

———. *Stone Soup*. Scribner's, 1947. Ages 6–8.

Bryan, Ashley. *Beat the Story-Drum, Pum-Pum*. Atheneum, 1980. Ages 6–8.

———. *The Dancing Granny*. Atheneum, 1977. Ages 6-8.

Carew, Jan. *The Third Gift*. Illustrated by Leo and Diane Dillon. Little, Brown, 1974. Ages 7–9.

Cauley, Lorinda Bryan. *Goldilocks and the Three Bears*. Putnam, 1982. Ages 4–6.

Chase, Richard. *The Jack Tales*. Illustrated by Berkeley Williams, Jr. Houghton Mifflin, 1943. Ages 6–8.

Chaucer, Geoffrey. *Canterbury Tales*. Adapted by Barbara Cohen. Illustrated by Trina Schart Hyman. Lothrop, 1988. Ages 8–10.

Cole, Joanna. *Bony-Legs*. Illustrated by Dirk Zimmer. Four Winds, 1983. Ages 4–6.

Cooper, Susan, reteller. *The Silver Cow*. Illustrated by Warwick Hutton. Atheneum, 1983. Ages 8–10.

———. *Tam Lin*. Illustrated by Warwick Hutton. McElderry, 1991. Ages 8–10.

Corrin, Sara and Stephen, retellers. *The Pied Piper of Hamelin*. Illustrated by Errol Le Cain. Harcourt, 1989. Ages 7–9.

d'Aulaire, Ingri, and Edgar Parin d'Aulaire, editors and illustrators. *East of the Sun and West of the Moon*. Viking, 1969/1938. Ages 7–9.

De Beaumont, Madame. *Beauty and the Beast*. Translated and illustrated by Diane Goode. Bradbury, 1978. Ages 7–9.

de la Mare, Walter. *Molly Whuppie*. Illustrated by Errol Le Cain. Farrar, 1983. Ages 6–8.

dePaola, Tomie. *Strega Nona*. Prentice-Hall, 1975. Ages 6–8.

De Roin, Nancy. *Jataka Tales: Fables from the Buddha*. Illustrated by Ellen Lanyon. Houghton, 1975. Ages 7–9.

Dewey, Ariane. *Febold Feboldson*. Greenwillow, 1984. Ages 6–8.

French, Fiona. *Snow White in New York*. Oxford, 1986. Ages 7–10.

Galdone, Paul. *Cinderella*. McGraw-Hill, 1978. Ages 5–7.

———. *Henny Penny*. Seabury, 1968. Ages 5–7.

———. *The Little Red Hen*. Seabury, 1973. Ages 5–7.

———. *The Three Billy Goats Gruff*. Seabury, 1973. Ages 5–7.

———. *What's in Fox's Sac? An Old English Tale*. Clarion, 1982. Ages 6–8.

Garner, Alan. *Alan Garner's Book of British Fairy Tales*. Illustrated by Derek Collard. Delacorte, 1985. Ages 6–8.

Goble, Paul. *Buffalo Woman*. Bradbury, 1984. Ages 7–9.

———. *The Girl Who Loved Wild Horses*. Bradbury, 1978. Ages 7–9.

Grimm, Jakob, and Wilhelm Grimm. *The Bremen-Town Musicians*. Retold and illustrated by Ilse Plume. Doubleday, 1980. Ages 6–8.

———. *The Bremen Town Musicians*. Translated by Elizabeth Shub. Illustrated by Janina Domanska. Greenwillow, 1980. Ages 6–8.

———. *Favorite Tales from Grimm*. Retold by Nancy Garden. Illustrated by Mercer Mayer. Four Winds, 1982. Ages 6–8.

———. *Hans in Luck*. Illustrated by Felix Hoffman. Atheneum, 1975. Ages 6-8.

———. *Hansel and Gretel*. Illustrated by Anthony Browne. Watts, 1981. Ages 6-8.

———. *Hansel and Gretel*. Translated by Elizabeth D. Crawford. Illustrated by Lisbeth Zwerger. Morrow, 1979. Ages 6–8.

———. *Hansel and Gretel*. Illustrated by Paul Galdone. McGraw-Hill, 1982. Ages 6–8.

———. *Hansel and Gretel*. Retold by Rika Lesser. Illustrated by Paul O. Zelinsky. Dodd Mead, 1984. Ages 7–9.

———. *The Juniper Tree and Other Tales from Grimm*. Edited by Lore Segal and Maurice

Sendak. Translated by Randall Jarrell. Illustrated by Maurice Sendak. Farrar, 1976. Ages 6–8.

———. *Little Red Cap.* Translated by Elizabeth D. Crawford. Illustrated by Lisbeth Zwerger. Morrow, 1983. Ages 6-8.

———. *Little Red Riding Hood.* Illustrated by Trina Schart Hyman. Holiday, 1982. Ages 6-8.

———. *Rumpelstiltskin.* Retold and illustrated by Paul O. Zelinsky. Dutton, 1986. Ages 7–9.

———. *The Seven Ravens.* Translated by Elizabeth D. Crawford. Illustrated by Lisbeth Zwerger. Morrow, 1981. Ages 7–9.

———. *The Seven Ravens.* Illustrated by Felix Hoffman. Harcourt, 1963. Ages 7–9.

———. *The Sleeping Beauty.* Retold and illustrated by Warwick Hutton. Atheneum, 1979. Ages 7–9.

———. *The Sleeping Beauty.* Retold and illustrated by Trina Schart Hyman. Little, Brown, 1974. Ages 7–9.

———. *Snow-White and the Seven Dwarfs.* Translated by Randall Jarrell. Illustrated by Nancy Ekholm Burkert. Farrar, 1972. Ages 8-10.

———. *Tales from Grimm.* Translated and illustrated by Wanda Gág. Coward-McCann, 1936. Ages 7–9.

———. *Thorn Rose or The Sleeping Beauty.* Illustrated by Errol Le Cain. Bradbury, 1975. Ages 6–8.

———. *Tom Thumb.* Illustrated by Felix Hoffman. Atheneum, 1973. Ages 6–8.

———. *The Twelve Dancing Princesses.* Illustrated by Errol Le Cain. Viking, 1978. Ages 7–9.

Hague, Kathleen, and Michael Hague. *East of the Sun and West of the Moon.* Illustrated by Michael Hague. Harcourt, 1980. Ages 7–9.

Haley, Gail E. *A Story, A Story.* Atheneum, 1970. Ages 6–8.

———. *Jack and the Bean Tree.* Crown, 1986. Ages 6–8.

Hamilton, Virginia. *The Magical Adventures of Pretty Pearl.* Harper, 1983. Ages 7–9.

———. *The People Could Fly.* Illustrated by Leo and Diane Dillon. Knopf, 1985. Ages 8–10.

Harris, Joel Chandler. *Jump! The Adventures of Brer Rabbit.* Adapted by Van Dyke Parks. Illustrated by Barry Moser. Harcourt, 1986. (See also: *Jump Again!: More Adventures of Brer Rabbit,*

Harcourt, 1987; *Jump on Over! The Adventures of Brer Rabbit and His Family,* Harcourt, 1990.) Ages 6–8.

Haviland, Virginia. *Favorite Fairy Tales Told in India.* Illustrated by Blair Lent. Little, Brown, 1973. Ages 7–9.

———. *Favorite Fairy Tales Told in Italy.* Illustrated by Evaline Ness. Little, Brown, 1965. Ages 7–9.

———. *Favorite Fairy Tales Told in Norway.* Illustrated by Leonard Weisgard. Little, Brown, 1961. Ages 7–9.

———, editor. *North American Legends.* Illustrated by Ann Strugnell. Collins, 1979. Ages 7–9.

Highwater, Jamake. *Anpao: An American Indian Odyssey.* Illustrated by Fritz Scholder. Lippincott, 1977. Ages 9–12.

Hodges, Margaret. *The Fire Bringer: A Paiute Indian Legend.* Illustrated by Peter Parnall. Little, Brown, 1972. Ages 8–10.

Hogrogian, Nonny. *One Fine Day.* Macmillan, 1971. Ages 4–6.

Hooks, William H. *The Ballad of Belle Dorcas.* Illustrated by Brian Pinkney. Knopf, 1990. Ages 8–10.

———, reteller. *Moss Gown.* Illustrated by Donald Carrick. Clarion, 1987. Ages 7-9.

Huck, Charlotte. *Princess Furball.* Illustrated by Anita Lobel. Greenwillow, 1989. Ages 6-8.

Hutton, Warwick. *Beauty and the Beast.* Atheneum, 1975. Ages 7–9.

Ivimey, John W. *Three Blind Mice.* Illustrated by Victoria Chess. Little, Brown, 1990. Ages 7–9.

Jagendorf, Moritz A. *Noodlehead Stories from Around the World.* Illustrated by Shane Miller. Vanguard, 1957. Ages 6–8.

Jaquith, Priscilla. *Bo Rabbit Smart for True: Folktales from the Gullah.* Illustrated by Ed Young. Philomel, 1981. Ages 8–10.

Kellogg, Stephen. *Chicken Little.* Morrow, 1985. Ages 4–6.

———. *Paul Bunyan.* Morrow, 1984. Ages 6–8.

Kimmel, Eric. *Baba Yaga: A Russian Folktale.* Illustrated by Megan Lloyd. Holiday, 1991. Ages 7–9.

Lang, Andrew, reteller. *Aladdin.* Illustrated by Errol Le Cain. Viking, 1981. Ages 6–8.

Lester, Julius. *The Knee-high Man and Other Tales.* Illustrated by Ralph Pinto. Dial, 1972. Ages 7–9.

————, reteller. *The Tales of Uncle Remus: The Adventures of Brer Rabbit.* Dial, 1987. (See also: *More Tales of Uncle Remus: Further Adventures of Brer Rabbit, His Friends, Enemies, and Others.* Dial, 1988.) Ages 7–9.

Lindbergh, Reeve. *Johnny Appleseed.* Illustrated by Kathy Jakobsen. Little, Brown, 1990. Ages 6–8.

Louie, Ai-Ling. *Yeh-Shen: A Cinderella Story from China.* Illustrated by Ed Young. Philomel, 1982. Ages 7–9.

Mahy, Margaret. *The Seven Chinese Brothers.* Illustrated by Jean and Mon-sien Tseng. Scholastic, 1990. Ages 6–8.

Marshak, Samuel. *The Month-Brothers: A Slavic Tale.* Translated by Thomas P. Whitney. Illustrated by Diane Stanley. Morrow, 1983. Ages 6–8.

Marshall, James, reteller. *Goldilocks and the Three Bears.* Dial, 1988. Ages 6-8.

————. *Red Riding Hood.* Dial, 1987. Ages 6–8.

Martin, Eva, reteller. *Canadian Fairy Tales.* Illustrated by László Gál. Little, Brown, 1984. Ages 7–9.

Mayer, Mercer. *East of the Sun and West of the Moon.* Four Winds, 1980. Ages 7–9.

McDermott, Gerald. *Anansi the Spider.* Holt, 1972. Ages 6–8.

Mosel, Arlene. *The Funny Little Woman.* Illustrated by Blair Lent. Dutton, 1972. Ages 6–8.

————. *Tikki Tikki Tembo.* Illustrated by Blair Lent. Holt, 1968. Ages 6–8.

Ness, Evaline. *Tom Tit Tot.* Scribner's, 1965. Ages 4–6.

Paterson, Katherine. *The Tale of the Mandarin Ducks.* Illustrated by Leo and Diane Dillon. Lodestar, 1990. Ages 7–9.

Perrault, Charles. *Cinderella.* Illustrated by Marcia Brown. Scribner's, 1954. Ages 6–8.

————. *Cinderella, or The Little Glass Slipper.* Illustrated by Errol Le Cain. Bradbury, 1973. Ages 6–8.

————. *The Glass Slipper: Charles Perrault's Tales of Times Past.* Translated by John Bierhorst. Illustrated by Mitchell Miller. Four Winds, 1981. Ages 6–8.

————. *Little Red Riding Hood.* Illustrated by Beni Montresor. Doubleday, 1991. Ages 8–10.

————. *Puss in Boots.* Illustrated by Fred Marcellino. Farrar, 1990. Ages 6–8.

————. *Puss in Boots.* Illustrated by Marcia Brown. Scribner's, 1952. Ages 6–8.

————. *The Sleeping Beauty.* Translated and illustrated by David Walker. Crowell, 1976. Ages 6–8.

Ransome, Arthur. *The Fool of the World and the Flying Ship.* Illustrated by Uri Schulevitz. Farrar, 1968. Ages 6–8.

Robinson, Gail. *Raven the Trickster.* Illustrated by Joanna Troughton. Atheneum, 1982. Ages 6–8.

Sawyer, Ruth. *Journey Cake, Ho!* Illustrated by Robert McCloskey. Viking, 1953. Ages 4–6

Schwartz, Alvin. *Flapdoodle: Pure Nonsense from American Folklore.* Illustrated by John O'Brien. Lippincott, 1980. Ages 6–12.

————. *Witcracks: Jokes and Jests from American Folklore.* Illustrated by Glen Rounds. Lippincott, 1973. Ages 6–12.

Silverman, Maida. *Anna and the Seven Swans.* Illustrated by David Small. Morrow, 1984. Ages 7–9.

Singer, Isaac Bashevis. *The Golem.* Illustrated by Uri Shulevitz. Farrar, 1982. Ages 8–10.

————. *Mazel and the Shlimazel, or the Milk of the Lioness.* Illustrated by Margot Zemach. Farrar, 1967. Ages 8–10.

————. *When Shlemiel Went to Warsaw and Other Stories.* Translated by the author and Elizabeth Shub. Illustrated by Margot Zemach. Farrar, 1968. Ages 8–10.

Sleator, William. *The Angry Moon.* Illustrated by Blair Lent. Little, Brown, 1970. Ages 7–9.

Stamm, Claus. *Three Strong Women: A Tale from Japan.* Illustrated by Jean and Mon-sien Tseng. Viking, 1990. Ages 6–8.

Steel, Flora Annie. *Tattercoats.* Illustrated by Diane Goode. Bradbury, 1976. Ages 6–8.

Steptoe, John, reteller. *Mufaro's Beautiful Daughters: An African Tale.* Lothrop, 1987. Ages 6–8.

Tashjian, Virginia. *Once There Was and Was Not, Armenian Tales Retold.* Illustrated by Nonny Hogrogian. Little, Brown, 1966. Ages 7-9.

Tejima. *Ho-Limlim: A Rabbit Tale from Japan.* Philomel, 1990. Ages 6–8.

Toye, William. *The Loon's Necklace.* Illustrated by Elizabeth Cleaver. Oxford, 1977. Ages 7–9.

Whitney, Thomas P. *Vasilisa the Beautiful.* Illustrated by Nonny Hogrogian. Macmillan, 1970. Ages 6–8.

Yagawa, Sumiko. *The Crane Wife.* Translated by Katherine Paterson. Illustrated by Suekichi Akaba. Morrow, 1981. Ages 6–8.

Young, Ed. *Lon Po Po: A Red Riding-Hood Story from China.* Philomel, 1989. Ages 7–9.

Zemach, Harve. *Duffy and the Devil.* Illustrated by Margot Zemach, Farrar, 1973. Ages 6–8.

———. *It Could Always Be Worse.* Farrar, 1977. Ages 6–8.

Fables

Aesop. *Aesop's Fables.* Selected and illustrated by Michael Hague. Holt, 1985. Ages 7–9.

———. *Aesop's Fables.* Illustrated by Heidi Holder. Viking, 1981. Ages 7–9.

———. *The Lion and the Mouse.* Illustrated by Ed Young. Doubleday, 1980. Ages 6–8.

Anno, Mitsumasa, reteller. *Anno's Aesop: A Book of Fables by Aesop and Mr. Fox.* Orchard, 1989. Ages 7–9.

Brown, Marcia. *Once a Mouse.* Scribner's, 1961. Ages 6–8.

Cauley, Lorinda Bryan, reteller. *The Town Mouse and the Country Mouse.* Putnam, 1984. Ages 6–8.

Galdone, Paul. *Three Aesop Fox Fables.* Seabury, 1971. Ages 6–8.

Lobel, Arnold. *Fables.* Harper, 1980. Ages 6–8.

Paxton, Tom, reteller. *Belling the Cat and Other Aesop's Fables.* Illustrated by Robert Rayevsky. Morrow, 1990. Ages 7–9.

Religious Stories

Bible, New Testament. *Christmas: The King James Version.* Illustrated by Jan Pieńkowski. Knopf, 1984. Ages 6–10.

Bierhorst, John, translator. *Spirit Child: A Story of the Nativity.* Illustrated by Barbara Cooney. Morrow, 1984. Ages 7–9.

Bolliger, Max, reteller. *Noah and the Rainbow.* Translated by Clyde Robert Bulla. Illustrated by Helga Aichinger. Crowell, 1972. Ages 6–8.

Chaikin, Miriam. *Joshua in the Promised Land.* Illustrated by David Frampton. Clarion, 1982. Ages 7–9.

Cohen, Barbara. *I Am Joseph.* Illustrated by Charles Mikolaycak. Lothrop, 1980. Ages 7–9.

dePaola, Tomie. *The Legend of Old Befana.* Harcourt, 1980. Ages 6–8.

———. *The Story of Three Wise Kings.* Putnam, 1983. Ages 6–8.

———. *Tomie dePaola's Book of Bible Stories.* Putnam, 1990. Ages 6–10.

Evslin, Bernard. *Signs and Wonders: Tales from the Old Testament.* Illustrated by Charles Mikolaycak. Four Winds, 1981. Ages 6–10.

Fisher, Leonard Everett. *The Seven Days of Creation.* Holiday, 1981. Ages 7–9.

Graham, Lorenz. *David He No Fear.* Illustrated by Ann Grifalconi. Crowell, 1971. Ages 7–9.

———. *Every Man Heart Lay Down.* Illustrated by Colleen Browning. Crowell, 1970. Ages 7–9.

———. *Hongry Catch Foolish Boy.* Illustrated by James Brown, Jr. Crowell, 1973. Ages 7–9.

———. *A Road Down in the Sea.* Illustrated by Gregorio Prestopino. Crowell, 1970. Ages 7–9.

Hutton, Warwick. *Jonah and the Great Fish.* Atheneum, 1983. Ages 6–8.

Mikolaycak, Charles. *Babushka: An Old Russian Folktale.* Holiday, 1984. Ages 6–8.

Robbins, Ruth. *Baboushka and Three Kings.* Illustrated by Nicolas Sidjakov. Parnassus, 1960. Ages 6–8.

Spier, Peter. *The Book of Jonah.* Doubleday, 1985. Ages 6–8.

———. *Noah's Ark.* Doubleday, 1977. Ages 6–8.

Turner, Philip. *Brian Wildsmith's Illustrated Bible Stories.* Illustrated by Brian Wildsmith. Watts, 1969. Ages 6–10.

Vivas, Julie. *The Nativity.* Harcourt, 1988. Ages 6–10.

Weil, Lisl. *Esther.* Atheneum, 1980. Ages 7–9.

Winthrop, Elizabeth. *A Child Is Born.* Illustrated by Charles Mikolaycak. Holiday, 1983. Ages 6–8.

———. *He Is Risen.* Illustrated by Charles Mikolaycak. Holiday, 1985. Ages 6–8.

Chapter 6

Modern Fantasy

The Question

*People always say to me
"What do you think you'd like to be
When you grow up?"
And I say "Why,
I think I'd like to be the sky
Or be a plane or train or mouse
Or maybe be a haunted house
Or something furry, rough and wild . . .
Or maybe I will stay a child."*

—Karla Kuskin

Modern fantasy has its roots in traditional fantasy from which motifs, characters, stylistic elements, and, at times, themes have been drawn. Many of the most revered works of children's literature fall under the genre of modern fantasy. *The Adventures of Pinocchio, Alice's Adventures in Wonderland, The Wizard of Oz, The Wind in the Willows, Winnie-the-Pooh, Pippi Longstocking,* and *Charlotte's Web* immediately come to mind. The creation of stories that are highly imaginative—yet believable—is the hallmark of this genre.

Definition and Description

Modern fantasy refers to the body of literature in which the events, the settings, or the characters are outside the realm of possibility. A fantasy is a story that cannot happen in the real world, and for this reason it has been called the literature of the fanciful impossible. In these stories, animals talk, inanimate objects come to life, people are giants or thumb-sized, imaginary worlds are inhabited, and future worlds are explored, just to name a few of the possibilities. Modern fantasies are written by known authors, and this distinguishes the genre from traditional literature in which the tales are handed down through the oral tradition and have no known author. Although the events could not happen in real life, modern fantasies often contain truths that help the reader to understand today's world.

The *cycle format* in which one book is linked to another through characters, settings, or both is especially prevalent in modern fantasy. Elleman (1987) states, "Events in [fantasy] cycle books are often strung out over three or four volumes. Authors attempt to make each novel self-contained with varying degrees of success, but usually readers need the entire series for full impact" (p. 418). The cycle format appeals to readers who become attached to certain characters and then delight in reading the next book.

Values of Modern Fantasy for Children

When reading a work of fantasy, children can delight in imagining other worlds and the limitless possibilities this opens up in the human mind. Fantasy enables the reader to see the realities that extend beyond the normal range of human vision.

• Children can develop their imaginations through the vicarious experience of entering a different world from the present one. Trying to imagine something that does not exist in reality and putting shape, color, form, and sound to it can be challenging as well as enjoyable. For many readers of fantasy, television may seem boring because the images and sounds are provided, leaving little to the imagination.

• Children can increase their ability to think divergently through modern fantasy. In fantasies, the normal "rules" of the physical world are suspended, permitting the reader to gain a new perspective on the world of reality. Children can consider other ways of living, other ways the world might have been, or perhaps other ways the world might become. In addition, the ordinary becomes more thought provoking when compared to the extraordinary.

• Modern fantasy provides a temporary escape from reality. Everyone enjoys an occasional vacation from daily life. In addition, not all children's lives are easy and lighthearted. Children whose grim experiences make realistic stories seem artificial may relish the opportunity to visit the world of fantasy where good overcomes evil and justice prevails. Getting lost in a story, leaving behind the everyday world and its baggage of reality lets the young reader, temporarily at least, become thin, graceful, athletic, loved, curly haired or straight haired, and, of course, a little older—a whole new person, a participant in another world.

• Modern fantasy can entertain through its humor. The suspension of reality, a trait of fantasy, gives authors the leeway to produce humorous situations. Two universal sources of humor are exaggeration and the ridiculous or far-fetched; both of these characteristics are often found in modern fantasies. In Carlo Collodi's *The Adventures of Pinocchio,* the reader is delighted by the ever-longer nose as Pinocchio tells more lies, and in E. B. White's *Charlotte's Web,* the reader is amused and touched by the phrase *SOME PIG* found in Charlotte's spider web to describe Wilbur.

• Children can be inspired by an author's treatment of serious themes in modern fantasies. Within the context of fantastic situations or characters, strong messages in modern fantasy seem less somber or didactic than if presented within the framework of serious realistic fiction. The theme of love conquers evil can sometimes be accepted more readily in a fantasy than in realistic fiction, where such a message can appear overly sentimental or preachy.

Evaluation and Selection of Modern Fantasy

The usual standards for fine fiction must also be met by authors of modern fantasy. Believable and well-rounded characters who develop and change, well-constructed plots, well-described settings with internal consistency, a style appropriate to the story, and worthy themes are elements to be expected in all fiction. In addition, the following criteria apply specifically to modern fantasy.

• Authors of modern fantasy have the challenge of persuading readers to open themselves up to believing that which is contrary to reality, strange, whimsical, or magical, yet has an internal logic and consistency. Sometimes authors will accomplish this through beginning the story in a familiar and ordinary setting with typical, contemporary, human beings as characters. A transition is then made from this realistic world to the fantasy world. An example of this literary device is found in C. S. Lewis's *The Lion, the Witch, and the Wardrobe* in which the children in the story enter a wardrobe in an old house only to discover that the back of the wardrobe leads into the land of Narnia, a fantasy world with unusual characters. Other fantasies begin in the imagined world, but manage, through well-described settings and consistent well-rounded characters, to make this new reality believable. Either way, the plot, characters, and setting must be so well developed that the child reader is able to suspend disbelief and to accept the impossible as real.

• For a modern fantasy to be truly imaginative, the author must provide a unique setting. In some stories, the setting may move beyond the realistic in both time (moving to the past, future, or holding time still) and place (imagined worlds), whereas in others only one of these elements (place or time) will go beyond reality. Moreover, a modern fantasy author's creation must be original, a fresh vision from a mind with special insight.

Historical Overview of Modern Fantasy

Imaginative literature did not appear until the eighteenth century. These stories were not intended primarily for children but were political satires that came to be enjoyed by children as well as adults. *Gulliver's Travels* (1726) by the Irish clergyman, Jonathan Swift, is the most noteworthy of such books. In this adult satire ridiculing the antics of the English court and its politics, the hero Gulliver travels to strange, imaginary places, one inhabited by 6-inch Lilliputians, another inhabited by giants. These imaginary worlds were described in fascinating detail and with sufficient humor to appeal to a child audience.

Charles Kingsley's *The Water Babies* (1863) took a contemporary child and set him in another world. Kingsley's unique tale was marred by heavy didactic passages; however, it paved the way for the classic masterpiece of fantasy. In England in 1865, Charles Lutwidge Dodgson, an Oxford don who used the pen name Lewis Carroll, wrote *Alice's Adventures in Wonderland* that tells of a fantastic journey Alice takes to an imaginary world. The total absence of didacticism replaced by humor and fantasy resulted in the book's lasting appeal and world fame. Other fantasies that originated in England shortly after the appearance of *Alice* include *The Light Princess* (1867) and *At the Back of the North Wind* (1871) by George MacDonald, *The Magic Fishbone* (1868) by Charles Dickens, and *Just-So Stories* (1902) by Rudyard Kipling. This early development of modern fantasy for children in England was unrivaled by any other country and established the standard for the genre worldwide.

Modern fantasy has continued to thrive in England during the twentieth century. Noteworthy contributions from England include Beatrix Potter's *The Tale of Peter Rabbit* (1902), *The Wind in the Willows* (1908) by Kenneth Grahame, *The Velveteen Rabbit* (1922) by Margery Bianco, *Winnie-the-Pooh* (1926) by A. A. Milne, *Mary Poppins* (1934) by Pamela Travers, *The Hobbit* (1937) by J. R. R. Tolkien, *The Lion, the Witch, and the Wardrobe* (1950) by C. S. Lewis, *The Borrowers* (1953) by Mary Norton, and *The Children of Green Knowe* (1955) by Lucy M. Boston.

Early books of modern fantasy from other countries include *The Adventures of Pinocchio* (1881) by Carlo Collodi (Carlo Lorenzini) from Italy and *Journey to the Center of the Earth* (1864), *Twenty Thousand Leagues Under the Sea* (1869), and *Around the World in Eighty Days* (1872) by the Frenchman, Jules Verne. Verne's works are considered the first science fiction novels and remain popular today with adults and children. Later in France, Jean de Brunhoff wrote an internationally popular series of animal fantasies about a family of elephants. The first of these was *The Story of Babar* (1937).

Some works of fantasy from Scandinavia also deserve recognition. Hans Christian Andersen, a Dane, published many modern folktales, stories very similar in literary elements to the traditional tales. However, Hans Christian Andersen was the originator of most of his tales, for which his own life experiences were the inspiration. "The Ugly Duckling," "The Emperor's New Clothes," and "Thumbelina" are three of the most loved of Andersen's stories. His tales were published in 1835 and are considered the first modern fairy tales. In 1907, Selma Lagerlöf produced *The Wonderful Adventures of Nils,* a geographic sortie around Sweden by a small boy-turned-elf who flies on the back of a goose. Almost half a century later, another Swedish author, Astrid Lindgren, produced *Pippi Longstocking* (1945). Pippi, a lively, rambunctious, and very strong heroine who throws caution to the wind, lives an independent life of escapades envied by children the world over. From Finland in 1964 came the *The Tales of*

Moominvalley by Tove Jansson, the first of a series of books focusing on small imaginary creatures called Moomins, who hibernate in the winter and frolic and adventure in the summer.

The United States also produced some outstanding early modern fantasies, beginning with *The Wonderful Wizard of Oz* (1900) by L. Frank Baum, which is considered the first classic U.S. modern fantasy for children. Other landmark U.S. works of modern fantasy are the memorable animal fantasy *Rabbit Hill* (1944) by Robert Lawson; *Charlotte's Web* (1952) by E. B. White, the best-known and best-loved U.S. work of fantasy; *The Book of Three* (1964), the first of the Prydain Chronicles by Lloyd Alexander; and *A Wrinkle in Time* (1962) by Madeleine L'Engle, considered a modern classic in science fiction for children.

Science fiction, the most recent development in modern fantasy, is said to owe its birth to the nineteenth-century novels of Jules Verne (*Journey to the Center of the Earth,* 1864 and *20,000 Leagues Under the Sea,* 1869) and H. G. Wells (*Time Machine,* 1895). Adults, not children, were the primary audience for these novels, however. It was not until the twentieth century that science fiction began to be aimed specifically at children. The *Tom Swift* series by Victor Appleton (collective pseudonym for the Stratemeyer Syndicate), although stilted in style and devoid of female characters, can be considered the first science fiction for children, appearing in 1910 (*Tom Swift and His Airship*) with additional titles appearing in rapid succession.

The founding in 1926 of *Amazing Stories,* a magazine devoted solely to works of science fiction, was instrumental in launching science fiction as a legitimate literary form. Robert Heinlein, a recognized writer of science fiction for adults, published *Rocket Ship Galileo* in 1947, a tale of three teenagers' journey to the moon on an atomic-powered rocket ship. The great success of this children's book was a milestone for children's science fiction. Then, in 1962, Madeleine L'Engle's novel, *A Wrinkle in Time,* was published. From this point forward, many science fiction novels for children began to appear. In the late 1960s and 1970s, the theme of mind control was popular. John Christopher's Tripods trilogy and William Sleator's *House of Stairs* are good examples. Space travel and future worlds were frequent science fiction topics in the 1980s. Examples are H. M. Hoover's *The Shepherd Moon* (1984) and Pamela Sargent's *Earthseed* (1987). Milestones in the development of modern fantasy are highlighted in Table 6–1.

Modern fantasy is a genre for children that remains strong, especially in Great Britain and other English-speaking countries. Although personified toys and animals remain popular and prevalent in children's books, growth in this genre appears to be in stories in which fantasy is interwoven into other genres—science fiction, science fantasy, and historical fantasy. This blurring of traditional genres can also be seen in the interesting mixture of the logic of realistic mystery stories with supernatural elements, as in the popular mysteries of John Bellairs and Mary Downing Hahn. Modern fantasy is likely to continue to be a popular genre with children and authors, both in the more traditional modes as well as in the current direction of hybrid stories. The rich literary works of modern fantasy will continue to challenge children's imaginations and enhance their lives.

Table 6–1   Milestones in the Development of Modern Fantasy

Date	Event	Significance
1726	*Gulliver's Travels* by Jonathan Swift (England)	An adult novel prototype for children's fantasy adventures
1835	*Fairy Tales* by Hans Christian Andersen (Denmark)	First modern folktales
1864	*Journey to the Center of the Earth* by Jules Verne (France)	First science fiction novel (for adults)
1865	*Alices' Adventures in Wonderland* by Lewis Carroll (England)	First children's masterpiece of modern fantasy
1881	*The Adventures of Pinocchio* by Carlo Collodi (Italy)	Early classic personified toy story
1900	*The Wonderful Wizard of Oz* by L. Frank Baum (U.S.A)	First classic U.S. modern fantasy for children
1908	*Wind in the Willows* by Kenneth Grahame (England)	Early classic animal fantasy
1910	*Tom Swift and His Airship* by Victor Appleton (U.S.A.)	First science fiction novel for children
1926	*Winnie-the-Pooh* by A. A. Milne (England)	Early classic personified toy story
1926	*Amazing Stories,* science fiction magazine begun	Formal recognition of science fiction as a literary genre
1937	*The Hobbit* by J. R. R. Tolkien (England)	Early quest adventure with a cult following
1945	*Pippi Longstocking* by Astrid Lindgren (Sweden)	Classic unusual-character fantasy
1947	*Rocket Ship Galileo* by Robert Heinlein (U.S.A.)	Science fiction novel for children about a journey to the moon
1950	*The Lion, the Witch, and the Wardrobe* by C. S. Lewis (England)	Early classic quest adventure for children, first of the Narnia series
1952	*Charlotte's Web* by E. B. White (U.S.A.)	Classic U.S. animal fantasy
1953	*The Borrowers* by Mary Norton (England)	Classic little people fantasy
1962	*A Wrinkle in Time* by Madeline L'Engle (U.S.A.)	Classic U.S. science fiction novel for children
1964	*The Book of Three* by Lloyd Alexander (U.S.A.)	First book in classic quest series, the Prydain Chronicles

Types of Modern Fantasy

In modern fantasy, as in other genres, the distinctions between types are not totally discrete. The types of modern fantasy listed below are a starting point for thinking about the variety of fantastic stories, motifs, themes, and characters that gifted authors have created. Additional categories could be listed, and you will find that some stories may fit appropriately in more than one category. For example, *The Root Cellar* by Janet Lunn has been discussed as an historical fantasy due to its authentic historical setting, but inclusion of spirits from the past also make this story a candidate for the label of Supernatural Events and Mystery Fantasy.

Modern Folktales

Modern folktales, or *literary folktales* as they are also called, are tales told in a form similar to that of a traditional tale with the accompanying typical elements: little character description, strong conflict, fast-moving plot with a sudden resolution, vague setting, and, in some cases, magical elements. But these modern tales have a known, identifiable author who has written the tale in this form. In other words, the tales do not spring from the cultural heritage of a group of people through the oral tradition but rather from the mind of one creator. However, this distinction does not matter at all to children, and they delight in these tales as much as they do in the old folktales.

The tales of Hans Christian Andersen are the earliest and best known of these modern tales. More recently, others, including Jane Yolen (*The Girl Who Loved the Wind* and *The Emperor and the Kite*) and Robin McKinley (*Beauty*) have become known for their modern folktales.

Modern folktales are an important counterbalance to traditional tales. As was noted in Chapter 5, many of the traditional tales present an old-fashioned, stereotypic view of women and girls. Many of the modern tales present more assertive female characters who are clearly in charge of their own destinies. Examples include *The Practical Princess* and *Petronella* by Jay Williams.

Animal Fantasy

Animal fantasies are stories in which animals behave as human beings in that they experience emotions, talk, and have the ability to reason. Usually the animals in fantasies will (and should) retain many of their animal characteristics. In the best of these animal fantasies, the author will interpret the animal for the reader in human terms without destroying the animal's integrity or removing it from membership in the animal world. For example, a rabbit character in an animal fantasy will retain her natural abilities of speed and camouflage to outsmart her adversaries. At the same time, however, the author will permit the reader to see human qualities such as caring and love by having the rabbit carry on conversations with family members.

Animal fantasies can be read to very young children who enjoy the exciting but reassuring adventures in books. Examples are *The Tale of Peter Rabbit* by Beatrix Potter and *Runaway Bunny* by Margaret Wise Brown. Books for children in primary grades include somewhat longer stories, often in a humorous vein, such as Beverly Cleary's mouse stories, *Runaway Ralph* and *The Mouse and the Motorcycle;* Deborah and James Howe's humor-filled books, *Bunnicula,* and *Howliday Inn;* and Michael Bond's *Paddington Bear.* Enjoyable animal fantasies for the young reader often have easy-to-follow, episodic plots.

Fully developed novels of modern fantasy with subtle and complex characterizations and a progressive plot are especially suitable for reading aloud to children in their elementary school years. *Charlotte's Web* by E. B. White remains a favorite read-aloud book; *The Cricket in Times Square* by George Selden is also popular. A beautifully written book with richly drawn characterizations is *Wind in the Willows* by Kenneth Grahame, who describes in artistic detail the life of animal friends along a riverbank. This book features an episodic plot structure but has a challenging style appropriate to intermediate-grade students. *The Lemming Condition* by Alan Arkin, a short novel with a progressive plot, is also appreciated by intermediate-grade students who enjoy discussing the risks of being a follower. Although the interest in animal fantasy peaks at age 8 or 9, many children and adults continue to enjoy well-written animal fantasies. In animal fantasies for older readers, an entire animal world is usually created with all of the relationships among its members that might be found in a novel portraying human behavior. *Mrs. Frisby and the Rats of NIMH* by Robert C. O'Brien, *Watership Down* by Richard Adams, and *Redwall* by Brian Jacques are examples of complex, fully developed animal fantasy novels for readers in fifth grade up to adult.

Personified Toys and Objects

Stories in which admired objects or beloved toys are brought to life and believed in by a child or adult character in the story are the focus of this type of fantasy. An early classic example of these stories is *The Adventures of Pinocchio* by Carlo Collodi (Carlo Lorenzini), in which a mischievous puppet comes to life, runs away from his master, and has many exciting and dangerous escapades. In these stories, the object, toy, or doll becomes real to the human protagonist and, in turn, becomes real to the child reader (who has perhaps also imagined a toy coming to life). An example of a personified machine story can be found in Virginia Lee Burton's *Mike Mulligan and His Steam Shovel,* in which a close relationship exists between a steam shovel and his human operator. The responsibilities of parenthood are often assumed by the child protagonist who must nourish, protect, assist, and extricate the toy-come-to-life from various predicaments. This motif of responsibility is found in the recent story, *The Castle in the Attic,* by Elizabeth Winthrop. Personified toy and object stories appeal to children from preschool through upper-elementary grades.

Unusual Characters and Strange Situations

Some authors approach fantasy through reality, but take it beyond reality to the ridiculous or exaggerated. Generally those stories can be best described as having unusual characters or strange situations. Without doubt, *Alice's Adventures in Wonderland* by Lewis Carroll is the best known of this type of modern fantasy. More recent writers of modern fantasy have had such strange situations as a boy sailing across the Atlantic Ocean in a giant peach (*James and the Giant Peach* by Roald Dahl) and such unusual characters as a perfect, factory-made boy (*Konrad* by Christine Nöstlinger).

Modern fantasy appeals to readers of all ages. Florence Parry Heide's *The Shrinking of Treehorn* portrays a young boy who, one day, starts to shrink, but no one notices. The story is fascinating for middle-school students. Jean Merrill's *The Pushcart War* also is enjoyed by somewhat older students. This preposterous and amusing satire tells of a struggle between pushcart peddlers and truck drivers in New York City. In *Tuck Everlasting,* Natalie Babbitt explores the theme of immortality and its consequences, a provocative theme for children and adults.

Worlds of Little People

Some authors have written about worlds inhabited by miniature people who have developed a culture of their own in this world or who live in another world. In Mary Norton's *The Borrowers,* small people live in our world but take our leavings to create their own world. It is, of course, eventually human beings who threaten their existence and cause them to seek safety elsewhere. Carol Kendall has described the Land Between the Mountains where the Minnipins live in *The Gammage Cup,* a story about little people struggling against the pressure to conform. Stories of little people delight children because they can identify with the indignities foisted upon little and powerless people and because the "big people" in these stories are invariably outdone by the more ingenious little people.

Supernatural Events and Mystery Fantasy

Many recent fantasies evoke the supernatural. One common form of supernatural literature found in children's books is the ghost story. Some ghost stories intrigue younger children, especially when the topic is treated humorously and reassuringly, as in *The Ghosts of Hungryhouse Lane* by Sam McBratney, in which children find out about three ghosts in their new home but unearth ways to satisfy the needs of the ghosts.

Ghosts in children's books can be fearful threats or helpful protectors. The ghost of the priest in John Bellairs's *The Curse of the Blue Figurine* is the very soul of evil, whereas *Whispers from the Dead* by Joan Lowery Nixon features a ghost who prevents a murder.

Many authors write mysteries for children in which the solution is partially supernatural or arrived at with supernatural assistance. An author who is well known for many such fantasy mysteries is John Bellairs.

Historical Fantasy

Historical fantasy, sometimes called *time-warp fantasy,* is a story in which a present-day protagonist goes back in time to a different era. A contrast between the two time periods is shown to readers through the modern-day protagonist's discoveries of and astonishment with earlier customs. Historical fantasies must fully and authentically develop the historical setting, both time and place, just as in a book of historical fiction. Canadian Janet Lunn in *The Root Cellar* succeeds in producing this type of mixed-genre story. Kevin Major's *Blood Red Ochre,* an historical fantasy, alternates chapters between the present and past time. Belinda Hurmence in *A Girl Called Boy* and David Wiseman in *Jeremy Visick* also present interesting historical fantasies that will appeal to intermediate-grade students and older.

Quest Stories

Quest stories are adventure stories with a search motif. The quest may be pursuit for a lofty purpose, such as justice or love, or for a rich reward, such as a magical power or a hidden treasure. Quest stories that are serious in tone are sometimes called *high fantasy.* Many of these novels are set in medieval times and are reminiscent of the search for the holy grail. In these high fantasies, an imaginary other world fully portrays the society, its history, family tree, geographic location, population, religion, customs, and traditions. The conflict in these tales usually centers on the struggle between good and evil. Often, characters are drawn from myth and legend. The protagonist is engaged in a struggle against external forces of evil and internal temptations of weakness. Thus, the quest usually represents a journey of self-discovery and personal growth for the protagonist, in addition to the search for the reward. *The Hobbit,* written by J. R. R. Tolkien in 1937, is one of the first of these high fantasies and retains a cult of followers even today. Because of the greater complexity of these novels, their allure is for children in fifth grade and higher, including adults, of course. Good examples are C. S. Lewis's series starting with *The Lion, the Witch, and the Wardrobe,* Lloyd Alexander's series starting with *The Book of Three,* and Susan Cooper's series starting with *Over Sea, Under Stone.*

Science Fiction and Science Fantasy

Science fiction is a form of imaginative literature that provides a picture of something that could happen based on real scientific facts and principles. Therefore, story elements in science fiction must have the appearance of scientific plausibility or technical possibility. Hypotheses about the future of humankind and the universe presented in science fiction appear plausible and possible to the reader because settings and events are built on extensions of known technologies and scientific concepts.

In novels of science fiction such topics as mind control, genetic engineering, space technologies and travel, visitors from outer space, and future political and social systems all seem possible to the readers. These novels especially fascinate many young people because they feature characters who must learn to adjust to change and to become new persons, two aspects of living that adolescents also experience. In addition, science fiction stories may portray the world, or one very much like it, that young people will one day inhabit; for this reason, science fiction has sometimes been called *prophetic fiction.*

Science fiction is a type of fiction that you will want to know about because of its growing popularity among children and adolescents. If you are reluctant to read science fiction, or have never read it, you may want to start with some books by William

Sleator (*Interstellar Pig; The Duplicate*), H. M. Hoover (*Children of Morrow; This Time of Darkness*), or John Christopher (*The White Mountains*).

The distinction between science fiction and science fantasy is not clearly defined or universally accepted. *Science fantasy* is a popularized type of science fiction in which a scientific explanation, though not necessarily plausible, is offered for imaginative leaps into the unknown. Science fantasy presents a world that often mixes elements of mythology and traditional fantasy with scientific or technological concepts, resulting in a setting that has some scientific basis but never has or never could exist. A worthy example is *Collidescope* by Grace Chetwin. These novels, which usually appear in series, appeal to adolescents and young adults and, like many series, are sometimes formulaic and of mixed quality.

The *science fantasy gamebook* is a recent trend in science fantasy that appeals to a wide age range of young people, particularly boys, from age 8 to upper teen years. Gamebooks involve fantasies developed in numbered segments so that the reader may choose from alternatives in determining the story outcome. These science fantasies, book adaptations of the computer games programmed for participation and decision making, usually contain violent scenes and characters. Marshall (1988) points out that because of the violent nature of these gamebooks some adults tend to be concerned, whereas others "see the popularity of the books as a change from the well-documented findings that interest in reading declines fast, in teenage boys" (p. 44). For example, see *Talisman of Death* by Steve Jackson and Ian Livingstone.

Modern fantasy has appeal for persons with nonliteral minds, for people who go beyond the letter of a story to its spirit. Children, with their lively imaginations, are especially open to reading fantasies. The many types and topics within this genre—animal fantasies, little people stories, tales of personified toys, mystery fantasies, stories of unusual people and situations, quest tales, science fiction, and so on—offer children a breadth of inspiring and delightful entertainment. Since the level of conceptual difficulty varies considerably in this genre, modern fantasy offers many excellent stories for children from youngest to oldest.

References

Elleman, B. (1987). Current trends in literature for children. *Library Trends, 35* (3): 413–426.

Marshall, M. R. (1988). *An introduction to the world of children's books* (2nd ed.). Brookfield, VT: Gower.

Notable Authors of Modern Fantasy

Lloyd Alexander, author of high fantasy based on Welsh mythology, noted for the Prydain series with *The Book of Three* and four other titles.

Natalie Babbitt, author of *Tuck Everlasting,* a book about immortality.

John Bellairs, author of mysteries containing supernatural elements. The *House with a Clock in Its Walls* is the first book of a trilogy.

Lucy M. Boston, author of English historical fantasies set in a mysterious old house. *The Chil-*

dren from Green Knowe; A Stranger at Green Knowe.

John Christopher, British science fiction author who created the Tripods trilogy set in the twenty-first century. *The White Mountains; When the Tripods Came .*

Carlo Collodi, (pseud. for Carlo Lorenzini), Italian author who created the classic puppet tale, *Pinocchio,* in 1880.

Susan Cooper, author of high fantasies based on Arthurian legends. *Over Sea, Under Stone* is the first in a five-book series.

Roald Dahl, British author of many popular fantasies known for humor and exaggerated characters. *James and the Giant Peach; Charlie and the Chocolate Factory.*

Sylvia Engdahl, science fiction author who created a future society in *Enchantress from the Stars.*

Kenneth Grahame, author of *The Wind in The Willows,* the British classic about animal life on a riverbank.

Virginia Hamilton, African-American author of stories with supernatural elements. *Sweet Whispers, Brother Rush; Justice and Her Brothers.*

H. M. Hoover, young adult science fiction writer who presents future worlds. *Children of Morrow.*

Monica Hughes, science fiction author whose themes often center on the role of free will. *The Keeper of the Isis Light.*

Dick King-Smith, British author of animal fantasies. *Pigs Might Fly; Babe: The Gallant Pig.*

Robert Lawson, author of animal fantasies and fictionalized biographies. *Rabbit Hill; Ben and Me.*

Ursula Le Guin, creator of the Earthsea trilogy, a quest adventure series set in a world of magic. *The Wizard of Earthsea; The Tombs of Atuan.*

Madeleine L'Engle, noted for a popular science fiction milestone book, *A Wrinkle in Time,* and its sequels.

C. S. Lewis, British creator of the Chronicles of Narnia, a series of adventure quest stories. *The Lion, the Witch, and the Wardrobe.*

Astrid Lindgren, Swedish creator of the irrepressible Pippi of *Pippi Longstocking.*

Margaret Mahy, New Zealand author of fantasies with supernatural elements. *The Visitors; The Changeover.*

Anne McCaffrey, science fiction author who writes of Menolly, a young woman with special musical talents in *Dragonsong.*

Robin McKinley, author of quest tales with a female protagonist and a mythical setting. *The Blue Sword; The Hero and the Crown.*

A. A. Milne, British author of the whimsical classic, *Winnie-the-Pooh.*

Mary Norton, British author of *The Borrowers,* a series of little people stories.

George Selden, author of humorous animal fantasies. *The Cricket in Times Square; The Genie of Sutton Place.*

William Sleator, author of science fiction novels. *Interstellar Pig; The Duplicate.*

J. R. R. Tolkien, British author of *The Hobbit,* well-known fantasy set in Middle-earth, an imaginary world.

E. B. White, author of the classic animal fantasy, *Charlotte's Web.*

Patricia Wrightson, Australian author of modern fantasies drawing on Aboriginal myths. *The Nargun and the Stars.*

Recommended Modern Fantasy Books

Ages refer to approximate interest levels. YA = young adult readers

Adams, Richard. *Watership Down.* Macmillan, 1974. Ages 12–YA.

Aiken, Joan. *The Wolves of Willoughby Chase.* Illustrated by Pat Marriott. Doubleday, 1963. Ages 10–13.

Alcock, Vivien. *The Stonewalkers.* Delacorte, 1983. Ages 10–13.

Alexander, Lloyd. *The Beggar Queen.* Dutton, 1984. Ages 10–13.

―――. *The Book of Three.* Holt, 1964. Ages 10–YA. The first of the Prydain Chronicles, a series of five quest fantasies, including *The Black Cauldron, The Castle of Llyr, The High King, and Taran Wanderer.*

———. *The Cat Who Wished to Be a Man.* Dutton, 1978. Ages 9–12.

———. *The First Two Lives of Lukas-Kasha.* Dutton, 1978. Ages 9–12.

———. *The Kestrel.* Dutton, 1982. Ages 10–YA.

———. *The Marvelous Misadventures of Sebastian.* Dutton, 1970. Ages 9–12.

———. *The Remarkable Journey of Prince Jen.* Dutton, 1991. Ages 10–YA.

———. *Westmark.* Dutton, 1981. Ages 10-YA.

———. *The Wizard in the Tree.* Illustrated by Laszlo Kubinyi. Dutton, 1975. Ages 10–YA.

Andersen, Hans Christian. *The Fir Tree.* Illustrated by Nancy Burkert. Harper, 1970. Ages 8-11. (Andersen's *Fairy Tales* were first published in 1835.)

———. *The Nightingale.* Illustrated by Nancy Burkert. Translated by Eva Le Gallienne. Harper, 1965. Ages 7–10.

———. *The Snow Queen.* Illustrated by Susan Jeffers. Dial, 1982. Ages 8–10.

———. *The Steadfast Tin Soldier.* Illustrated by Marcia Brown. Translated by M. R. James. Scribner's, 1953. Ages 7–10.

———. *Thumbelina.* Illustrated by Lisbeth Zwerger. Translated by Anthea Bell. Picture Book Studio, 1985. Ages 6-9.

———. *The Ugly Duckling.* Illustrated by Alan Marks. Translated by Anthea Bell. Picture Book Studio, 1989. Ages 6–9.

Arkin, Alan. *The Lemming Condition.* Illustrated by Joan Sandin. Harper, 1976. Ages 10–YA.

Atwater, Richard and Florence. *Mr. Popper's Penguins.* Illustrated by Robert Lawson. Little, 1938. Ages 8–11.

Babbitt, Natalie. *The Devil's Other Storybook.* Farrar, 1987. Ages 8-11.

———. *Knee-Knock Rise.* Farrar, 1970. Ages 9–12.

———. *The Search for Delicious.* Farrar, 1969. Ages 9–12.

———. *Tuck Everlasting.* Farrar, 1975. Ages 10–YA.

Bailey, Carolyn. *Miss Hickory.* Illustrated by Ruth Gannett. Viking, 1968. Ages 8–11.

Barrie, Sir James. *Peter Pan.* Illustrated by Nora Unwin. Scribner's, 1911. Ages 8–11.

Baum, L. Frank. *The Wonderful Wizard of Oz.* Illustrated by W. W. Denslow. Morrow, 1900. Ages 8–11.

Bellairs, John. *The Curse of the Blue Figurine.* Dial, 1983. Ages 10-YA.

———. *A Figure in the Shadows.* Illustrated by Mercer Mayer. Dial, 1975. Ages 10–13.

Bond, Michael. *A Bear Called Paddington.* Illustrated by Peggy Fortnum. Houghton, 1960. Ages 7–10.

Bond, Nancy. *Another Shore.* McElderry, 1988. Ages 11–YA.

———. *A String in the Harp.* Atheneum, 1976. Ages 11–14.

Boston, Lucy M. *The Children of Green Knowe.* Illustrated by Peter Boston. Harcourt, 1955. Ages 8-11. The first of a series of fantasies set in an English mansion. Others include *An Enemy at Green Knowe, The River at Green Knowe, and Treasure of Green Knowe.*

Brittain, Bill. *Dr. Dredd's Wagon of Wonders.* Illustrated by Andrew Glass. Harper, 1987. Ages 8–12.

———. *The Wish Giver.* Illustrated by Andrew Glass. Harper, 1983. Ages 9–12.

Butterworth, Oliver. *The Enormous Egg.* Illustrated by Louis Darling. Little, Brown, 1956. Ages 8–11.

Carroll, Lewis. pseud. (Charles Lutwidge Dodgson). *Alice's Adventures in Wonderland* and *Through the Looking Glass.* First published in 1865. A recent edition is illustrated by Anthony Browne. Knopf, 1988. Ages 9–13.

Cassedy, Sylvia. *Behind the Attic Wall.* Crowell, 1983. Ages 10-13.

———. *Lucie Babbidge's House.* Crowell, 1989. Ages 9–12.

Charbonneau, Eileen. *The Ghosts of Stony Clove.* Orchard, 1988. Ages 10–YA.

Cleary, Beverly. *The Mouse and the Motorcycle.* Illustrated by Louis Darling. Morrow, 1965. Ages 7-11.

———. *Ralph S. Mouse.* Illustrated by Paul O. Zelinsky. Morrow, 1982. Ages 7–11.

———. *Runaway Ralph.* Illustrated by Louis Darling. Morrow, 1970. Ages 7-11.

Collodi, Carlo. pseud. (Carlo Lorenzini). *The Adventures of Pinocchio.* Illustrated by Attilio Mussino. Translated by Carol Della Chiesa. Macmillan, 1881.

Conrad, Pam. *Stonewords: A Ghost Story.* Harper, 1990. Ages 8-12.

Cooper, Susan. *Over Sea, Under Stone.* Illustrated by Margery Gill. Harcourt, 1965. Ages 10-YA. This is the first of a five-book Arthurian quest series, including *The Dark Is Rising, Greenwitch, The Grey King,* and *Silver on the Tree.*

Cresswell, Helen. *Moondial.* Macmillan, 1987. Ages 10-YA.

Dahl, Roald. *Charlie and the Chocolate Factory.* Illustrated by Joseph Schindelman. Knopf, 1964. Ages 8–11.

———. *James and the Giant Peach.* Illustrated by Nancy E. Burkert. Knopf, 1961. Ages 8–11.

———. *Matilda.* Illustrated by Quentin Blake. Viking, 1988. Ages 8–11.

Dickinson, Peter. *Heartsease.* Little, 1969. Ages 10–YA.

———. *Merlin Dreams.* Illustrated by Alan Lee. Delacorte, 1988. Ages 10–YA.

———. *The Weathermonger.* Little, 1969. Ages 10-YA.

Fleischman, Sid. *The Midnight Horse.* Illustrated by Peter Sis. Greenwillow, 1990.

Fleming, Ian. *Chitty-Chitty-Bang-Bang: The Magical Car.* Illustrated by John Burningham. Random, 1964. Ages 8–11.

Garfield, Leon. *The Empty Sleeve.* Delacorte, 1988. Ages 10–YA.

Garner, Alan. *Elidor.* Walck, 1967. Ages 9–12.

———. *The Owl Service.* Walck, 1968. Ages 9–12.

Godden, Rumer. *The Dolls' House.* Illustrated by Tasha Tudor. Viking, 1960. Ages 7-10.

———. *Impunity Jane.* Illustrated by Adrienne Adams. Viking, 1954. Ages 7–10.

Grahame, Kenneth. *The Wind in the Willows.* Illustrated by E. H. Shepard. Scribner's, 1908. Ages 9–12.

Hahn, Mary Downing. *The Doll in the Garden; A Ghost Story.* Clarion, 1989. Ages 9–12.

———. *Wait Till Helen Comes: A Ghost Story.* Clarion, 1986. Ages 9–13.

Hamilton, Virginia. *Justice and Her Brothers.* Greenwillow, 1978. Ages 12–YA.

———. *The Magical Adventures of Pretty Pearl.* Harper, 1983. Ages 11–YA.

———. *Sweet Whispers, Brother Rush.* Philomel, 1982. Ages 11–YA.

Heide, Florence Parry. *The Shrinking of Treehorn.* Illustrated by Edward Gorey. Holiday, 1971. Ages 7–10.

Hilgartner, Beth. *The Feast of the Trickster.* Houghton, 1991. Ages 12–YA.

Howe, Deborah, and James Howe. *Bunnicula; A Rabbit-Tale of Mystery.* Illustrated by Alan Daniel. Atheneum, 1979. Ages 8–11.

Howe, James. *Howliday Inn.* Atheneum, 1982. Ages 8–11.

Hunter, Mollie. *The Kelpie's Pearls.* Illustrated by Joseph Cellini. Funk & Wagnalls, 1966. Ages 9–12.

———. *The Mermaid Summer.* Harper, 1988. Ages 9–YA.

———. *A Stranger Came Ashore.* Harper, 1975. Ages 11–YA.

Hurmence, Belinda. *A Girl Called Boy.* Clarion, 1982. Ages 10–13.

Jacques, Brian. *Mariel of Redwall.* Illustrated by Gary Chalk. Philomel, 1992. Ages 11–YA.

———. *Mattimeo.* Illustrated by Gary Chalk. Philomel, 1990. Ages 11–YA.

———. *Mossflower.* Philomel, 1988. Ages 11–YA.

———. *Redwall.* Illustrated by Gary Chalk. Philomel, 1987 Ages 11–YA.

Jansson, Tove. *Finn Family Moomintroll.* Walck, 1965. Ages 7–10.

Jarrell, Randall. *The Bat-Poet.* Illustrated by Maurice Sendak. Macmillan, 1967. Ages 8–12.

Jones, Diana Wynne. *Castle in the Air.* Greenwillow, 1991. Ages 11–YA.

———. *Howl's Moving Castle.* Greenwillow, 1986. Ages 11–YA.

———. *The Lives of Christopher Chant.* Greenwillow, 1988. Ages 10–13.

Juster, Norton. *The Phantom Tollbooth.* Illustrated by Jules Feiffer. Random, 1961. Ages 10–13.

Kelleher, Victor. *The Red King.* Dial, 1990. Ages 12–YA.

Kendall, Carol. *The Gammage Cup.* Illustrated by Erik Blegvad. Harcourt, 1959. Ages 9–13.

Kesey, Ken. *Little Tricker the Squirrel Meets Big Double the Bear.* Illustrated by Barry Moser. Viking, 1990. Ages 8–11.

Key, Alexander. *Escape to Witch Mountain.* Illustrated by Leon B. Wisdom, Jr. Westminster, 1968. Ages 10–12.

———. *The Forgotten Door.* Westminster, 1965. Ages 10–12.

King-Smith, Dick. *Ace: The Very Important Pig.* Illustrated by Lynette Hemmant. Crown, 1990. Ages 7–11.

———. *Babe: The Gallant Pig.* Illustrated by Mary Rayner. Crown, 1985. Ages 7–11.

———. *Harry's Mad.* Illustrated by Jill Bennett. Crown, 1987. Ages 7–9.

———. *Pigs Might Fly.* Illustrated by Mary Rayner. Viking, 1982. Ages 8–11.

Kipling, Rudyard. *Just So Stories.* Doubleday, 1902. Ages 6–10.

Klause, Annette Curtis. *The Silver Kiss.* Delacorte, 1990. Ages 12–YA.

Langton, Jane. *The Astonishing Stereoscope.* Illustrated by Erik Blegvad. Harper, 1971. Ages 9–12.

———. *The Fledging.* Harper, 1980. Ages 10–YA.

Lawson, Robert. *Ben and Me.* Little, 1939. Ages 9–12.

———. *Rabbit Hill.* Viking, 1944. Ages 8–11.

Le Guin, Ursula K. *Catwings.* Illustrated by S. D. Schindler. Orchard, 1988. Ages 7–10.

———. *Catwings Return.* Illustrated by S. D. Schindler. Orchard, 1989. Ages 7–10.

———. *The Farthest Shore.* Atheneum, 1972. Ages 11–YA.

———. *Tehanu: The Last Book of Earthsea.* Atheneum, 1990. Ages 12–YA.

———. *The Tombs of Atuan.* Atheneum, 1971. Ages 11–YA.

———. *A Wizard of Earthsea.* Parnassus, 1968. Ages 11–YA.

Lewis, Clive Staples. *The Lion, the Witch, and the Wardrobe.* Illustrated by Pauline Baynes. Macmillan, 1950. Ages 9–12. The first in a series of quest fantasies, including *The Horse and His Boy, The Last Battle, The Magician's Nephew, Prince Caspian, The Silver Chair,* and *The Voyage of the Dawn Treader.*

Lindgren, Astrid. *Pippi Longstocking.* Translated by Florence Lamborn. Viking, 1950. Ages 8–11.

Lisle, Janet Taylor. *The Lampfish of Twill.* Illustrated by Wendy Anderson Halperin. Orchard, 1991. Ages 9–13.

Lively, Penelope. *The Ghost of Thomas Kempe.* Illustrated by Antony Maitland. Dutton, 1973. Ages 9–12.

Lunn, Janet. *The Root Cellar.* Scribner's, 1983. Ages 10-13.

Mahy, Margaret. *Dangerous Spaces.* Viking, 1991. Ages 8–12.

———. *The Haunting.* Atheneum, 1983. Ages 10–YA.

———. *Memory.* McElderry, 1988. Ages 11–YA.

———. *The Tricksters.* McElderry, 1987. Ages 11–YA.

Major, Kevin. *Blood Red Ochre.* Doubleday, 1989. Ages 12–YA.

Marshall, James. *Rats on the Roof: And Other Stories.* Dial, 1991. Ages 6–9.

Mayne, William. *Earthfasts.* Dutton, 1967. Ages 12–YA.

McBratney, Sam. *The Ghosts of Hungryhouse Lane.* Holt, 1989. Ages 7-10.

McGowen, Tom. *The Magician's Apprentice.* Dutton, 1987. Ages 10-13.

McDonald, George. *At the Back of the North Wind.* Illustrated by George and Doris Hauman. Macmillan, 1871.

McKillip, Patricia A. *The Riddle-Master of Hed.* Atheneum, 1976. Ages 10–13.

McKinley, Robin. *Beauty: A Retelling of the Beauty and the Beast.* Harper, 1978. Ages–YA.

———. *The Blue Sword.* Greenwillow, 1982. Ages 11–YA.

———. *The Hero and the Crown.* Greenwillow, 1984. Ages 11–YA.

Merrill, Jean. *The Pushcart War.* Illustrated by Ronni Solbert. Harper, 1964. Ages 10–YA.

Michels, Tilde. *Rabbit Spring.* Harcourt, 1988. Ages 7–10.

Milne, A. A. *The House at Pooh Corner.* Illustrated by Ernest Shepard. Dutton, 1928. Ages 6–9.

———. *Winnie-the-Pooh.* Illustrated by Ernest Shepard. Dutton, 1926. Ages 6–9.

Nixon, Joan Lowery. *Whispers from the Dead.* Delacorte, 1989. Ages 10–YA.

Norton, Andre. *Lavender-green Magic.* Illustrated by Judith Gwyn Brown. Crowell, 1974. Ages 11–YA.

Norton, Mary. *The Borrowers*. Illustrated by Beth and Joe Krush. Harcourt, 1953. Ages 8–11. This is the first of a series of little people fantasies, including *The Borrowers Afield, The Borrowers Afloat, The Borrowers Aloft,* and *The Borrowers Avenged*.

Nöstlinger, Christine. *Konrad*. Watts, 1977. Ages 8–11.

Park, Ruth. *Playing Beatie Bow*. Atheneum, 1982. Ages 10–YA.

Pearce, Philippa. *Tom's Midnight Garden*. Lippincott, 1959. Ages 9–12.

Pierce, Meredith Ann. *The Darkangel*. Little, Brown, 1982. Ages 12–YA.

Price, Susan. *The Ghost Drum: A Cat's Tale*. Farrar, 1987. Ages 8–12.

Rodowsky, Colby. *The Gathering Room*. Farrar, 1981. Ages 10–YA.

Sandburg, Carl. *Rootabaga Stories*. Illustrated by Maud and Miska Petersham. Harcourt, 1922. Ages 8–12.

Selden, George. *Chester Cricket's New House*. Illustrated by Garth Williams. Farrar, 1960. Ages 8–11.

———. *The Cricket in Times Square*. Illustrated by Garth Williams. Farrar, 1960. Ages 8–11.

———. *Harry Cat's Pet Puppy*. Illustrated by Garth Williams. Farrar, 1974. Ages 8–11.

———. *Tucker's Countryside*. Illustrated by Garth Williams. Farrar, 1969. Ages 8–11.

Sharp, Margery. *The Rescuers*. Illustrated by Garth Williams. Little, Brown, 1959. Ages 7–10.

Sherman, Josepha. *Child of Faerie, Child of Earth*. Walker, 1992. Ages 11–YA.

Snyder, Zilpha Keatley. *Below the Root*. Illustrated by Alton Raible. Atheneum, 1975. Ages 10–YA.

Steig, William. *Abel's Island*. Farrar, 1976. Ages 8–11.

———. *Dominic*. Farrar, 1972. Ages 8–11.

Sutcliff, Rosemary. *The Light Beyond the Forest*. Dutton, 1980. Ages 12–YA.

———. *The Road to Camlaan: The Death of King Arthur*. Dutton, 1982. Ages 12–YA.

Tolkien, J. R. R. *The Hobbit*. Houghton, 1938. Ages 10–YA.

Travers, P. L. *Mary Poppins*. Illustrated by Mary Shepard. Harcourt, 1934. Ages 9–12.

Voigt, Cynthia. *Building Blocks*. Atheneum, 1984. Ages 9–11.

Westall, Robert. *Ghost Abbey*. Scholastic, 1989. Ages 10–YA.

White, E. B. *Charlotte's Web*. Illustrated by Garth Williams. Harper, 1952. Ages 8–11.

———. *Stuart Little*. Illustrated by Garth Williams. Harper, 1945. Ages 8–11.

Williams, Jay. *Petronella*. Parents' Magazine, 1973. Ages 6–9.

———. *The Practical Princess and Other Liberating Fairy Tales*. Parents' Magazine, 1978. Ages 6–9.

Winthrop, Elizabeth. *The Castle in the Attic*. Holiday, 1985. Ages 8–12.

Wiseman, David. *Jeremy Visick*. Houghton, 1981. Ages 10–13.

Wrede, Patricia C. *Dealing with Dragons*. Harcourt, 1990. Ages 9–12.

Wrightson, Patricia. *Balyet*. McElderry, 1989. Ages 10–13.

———. *A Little Fear*. Atheneum, 1983. Ages 10–13.

———. *The Nargun and the Stars*. Atheneum, 1974. Ages 10–13.

Yolen, Jane. *Dragon's Blood*. Delacorte, 1982. Ages 10–13.

———. *The Emperor and the Kite*. Illustrated by Ed Young. World, 1967. Ages 7–10.

———. *The Girl Who Loved the Wind*. Illustrated by Ed Young. Crowell, 1972. Ages 7–10.

Science Fiction and Science Fantasy

Alcock, Vivien. *The Monster Garden*. Delacorte, 1988. Ages 10–14.

Cameron, Eleanor. *The Wonderful Flight to the Mushroom Planet*. Illustrated by Robert Henneberger. Little, 1954.

Chetwin, Grace. *Collidescope*. Bradbury, 1990. Ages 11–YA.

Christopher, John. *Beyond the Burning Lands*. Macmillan, 1971. Ages 11–YA.

———. *The City of Gold and Lead*. Macmillan, 1967. Ages 11–YA.

———. *The Guardians*. Macmillan, 1970. Ages 11–YA.

———. *The Pool of Fire*. Macmillan, 1968. Ages 11–YA.

———. *The White Mountains*. Macmillan, 1967. Ages 11–YA.

Conly, Jane Leslie. *Racso and Rats of NIMH*. Illustrated by Leonard Lubin. Harper, 1986. Ages 9–12.

Dickinson, Peter. *Eva*. Delacorte, 1989. Ages 12–YA.

Engdahl, Sylvia. *Enchantress from the Stars*. Atheneum, 1970. Ages 11–YA.

———. *The Far Side of Evil*. Atheneum, 1971. Ages 11–YA.

———. *This Star Shall Abide*. Atheneum, 1972. Ages 11–YA.

Hoover, H. M. *Away Is a Strange Place to Be*. Dutton, 1989. Ages 9–12.

———. *Children of Morrow*. Four Winds, 1973. Ages 11–YA.

———. *Orvis*. Viking, 1987. Ages 10–YA.

———. *The Shepherd Moon*. Viking, 1984. Ages 11–YA.

———. *This Time of Darkness*. Viking, 1980. Ages 11–YA.

Hughes, Monica. *Devil on My Back*. Atheneum, 1985. Ages 9–YA.

———. *The Dream Catcher*. Atheneum, 1987. Ages 9–YA.

———. *The Keeper of the Isis Light*. Atheneum, 1984. Ages 9–YA.

L'Engle, Madeleine. *A Swiftly Tilting Planet*. Farrar, 1978.

———. *A Wind in the Door*. Farrar, 1973.

———. *A Wrinkle in Time*. Farrar, 1962.

McCaffrey, Anne. *Dragonsinger*. Atheneum, 1977. Ages 11–YA.

———. *Dragonsong*. Atheneum, 1976. Ages 11–YA.

O'Brien, Robert C. *Mrs. Frisby and the Rats of NIMH*. Illustrated by Zena Bernstein. Atheneum, 1971. Ages 9–12.

Paton Walsh, Jill. *The Green Book*. Illustrated by Lloyd Bloom. Farrar, 1982. Ages 8–11.

Pinkwater, Daniel Manus. *Alan Mendelson, the Boy from Mars*. Dutton, 1979. Ages 10–YA.

———. *Fat Men from Space*. Dodd, 1977. Ages 8–11.

Rubinstein, Gillian. *Beyond the Labyrinth*. Watts, 1990. Ages 12–YA.

Sargent, Pamela. *Earthseed*. Harper, 1983. Ages 12–YA.

Service, Pamela F. *Stinker from Space*. Scribner's, 1988. Ages 9–12.

Sleator, William. *The Boy Who Reversed Himself*. Dutton, 1986. Ages 10–YA.

———. *The Duplicate*. Dutton, 1988. Ages 11–YA.

———. *House of Stairs*. Dutton, 1974. Ages 11–YA.

———. *Interstellar Pig*. Dutton, 1984. Ages 11–YA.

Chapter 7

Realistic Fiction

Listening to grownups quarreling,

standing in the hall against the
wall with my little brother, blown
like leaves against the wall by their
voices, my head like a pingpong ball
between the paddles of their anger:
I knew what it meant
to tremble like a leaf.

Cold with their wrath, I heard
the claws of the rain
pounce. Floods
poured through the city,
skies clapped over me,
and I was shaken, shaken
like a mouse
between their jaws.

—Ruth Whitman

Children's lives are sometimes sad and harsh. Realistic stories of today openly address these situations as well as the happy and humorous situations of life. Children of all ages appreciate stories about people who seem like themselves or who are involved in familiar activities. These realistic fiction stories have appealed to children for many years and continue to do so today.

Definition and Description

Realism in literature is a complex, multifaceted concept. Marshall (1988) considers various components of realism in literature, including factual, situational, emotional, and social. *Factual realism* is provided by the description of actual persons, places, and events in a book. When this occurs, the facts need to be accurately recorded. For example, usually in historical fiction and occasionally in realistic fiction, the names and locations of actual places are included in the story, with accurate and complete descriptions. *Situational realism* is provided by a situation that is not only possible but quite likely, often in an identifiable location with characters of an identifiable age and social class, making the whole treatment believable. The survival story, which often hinges on a life-threatening situation, is an example of a story built on situational realism. *Emotional realism* is provided by the appearance of believable feelings and relationships among characters. Rite-of-passage or growing-up stories often employ emotional realism. *Social realism* is provided by an honest portrayal of society and its conditions of the moment, including both healthy and adverse conditions. In almost all good realistic stories several of these components of realism occur, with varying degrees of emphasis.

Realistic fiction refers to stories that could really happen to people and animals; that is, it is within the realm of possibility that such events could occur or could have occurred. The protagonists of these stories are fictitious characters created by the author, but their actions and reactions are quite like those of real people or real animals. Sometimes events in these stories are exaggerated or outlandish—hardly probable but definitely possible. These stories, too, fit under the definition of realistic fiction.

Contemporary realism is a term used to describe stories that take place in the present time and portray attitudes and mores of the present culture. Unlike realistic books of several decades ago that depicted only happy families and were never controversial, today's contemporary realism often focuses on current societal issues, such as alcoholism, racism, poverty, and homelessness. These contemporary books still tell of the happy, funny times in children's lives, but they also include the harsh, unpleasant times that are, sadly, also a part of many children's lives. Child abuse and neglect, peer problems, the effects of divorce on children, drug abuse, physical and mental disabilities, disillusionment, and alienation from the mainstream of society are all topics included in the contemporary realistic novel.

Authors of contemporary realistic fiction set their stories in the present or recent past. But, in time, features of these stories, such as dialogue and allusions to popular culture, customs, and dress become dated and the stories are therefore no longer contemporary, though still realistic. Older stories that obviously no longer describe today's world, though they may have once been contemporary realistic fiction, are now simply realistic fiction.

The *problem novel* is a contemporary realistic story in which the conflict overwhelms the plot and characterization. For instance, a problem novel might have the protagonist suffering from child abuse and therefore contemplating suicide, only to find that her best friend is a drug addict and that her banker father has bilked thousands of pensioners out of their retirement funds! The problem novel is written to provide the author with a soapbox from which to lecture or a vehicle for capitalizing on whichever societal problem is currently at the forefront. Generally, these stories lack depth, have weak character development and consist of little, if any, plot. Problem novels remind us that it is always necessary to read literature carefully in order to find books worthy of children's attention.

Topics for realistic fiction are drawn from all aspects of life. Stories of humorous, everyday escapades of well-adjusted children in happy families are a popular form of realistic fiction. Beverly Cleary's stories of Ramona Quimby and her family immediately come to mind. Stories about animals portrayed realistically also are included in this genre. Usually in these stories an animal is featured along with a human being as story protagonists. The close relationship that evolves between the human being and the animal becomes the focus of the story. And, of course, the animal is not personified, but retains normal animal characteristics. Marguerite Henry's horse stories (*Misty of Chincoteague, Brighty of the Grand Canyon*) and Wilson Rawls's dog story (*Where the Red Fern Grows*) are examples of realistic animal stories that have been enjoyed by children for years. Other topics common to realistic fiction are mysteries, adventures, romances, sports stories, and children from other countries.

Values of Realistic Fiction for Children

Although a work of realistic fiction may be several times older than the child who reads it, it can still have great value for the child. Some books never lose their appeal and their ability to speak to the reader. The following values can be found in both older and contemporary realistic fiction.

- Realistic fiction stories are easy for children to relate to and enjoy. Children can often see their own lives, or lives much like their own, in these stories. Intermediate-grade children report on reading interest surveys that realistic fiction is their favorite genre. Of course, some children may prefer other categories, but realistic fiction does hold high appeal for many children at all grade levels.
- Realistic fiction permits children to see how other people live their lives and solve their problems. By understanding human relationships through stories, children can come to a better understanding of themselves and their own relationships with others.
- Some works of realistic fiction depict the lives of children from other cultures. In reading these stories, children can discover different ways people live their daily lives as well as explore the many commonalities in basic human values across cultures.

- Children can become aware that not all children's lives are as warm and secure as theirs may be and, as a result, they may become more sensitive to problems being experienced by other children.
- *Bibliotherapy,* using selected books to help children deal with their social and emotional problems, often draws books from this genre. Realistic fiction can help children realize that everyone faces problems in life—neighborhood bullies, siblings, social rejections—and, by reading of the problems others face, children can be better prepared to confront the challenges of their own lives.

Evaluation and Selection of Realistic Fiction

The criteria for evaluating realistic fiction are the same as for any work of fiction. Well-developed characters who manifest change as a result of significant life events, a well-structured plot with sufficient conflict and suspense to hold the reader's interest, a time and place suitable to the storyline, and a worthy theme are basic literary elements expected of any work of fiction, including works of realistic fiction.

- Some realistic novels portray adverse and discouraging social situations, such as homelessness and poverty; yet it remains important that the stories permit some cause for optimism. Children need to believe that they have some control over their lives. Furthermore, children need to trust that this world can be a good place in which to live and that it can be made a better place through the efforts of individuals. Finally, children need to understand that problems can be overcome or ameliorated.
- Themes in realistic stories often convey moral values, such as the rewards of kindness and generosity to others. However, these moral values must spring naturally from the story, as a byproduct of the story itself, not as the main reason for the story. At times, adults write books for children with the sole intent of teaching or preaching, and the story itself is nothing more than a thin disguise for a heavy-handed moral lesson. This may have been acceptable in the past, but today a good story must be the *raison d' être* of a children's book. The moral must not overwhelm the story, but may be its logical outcome.
- A novel of realistic fiction must be believable, even though all aspects may not be probable. Some adults and children have a tendency to criticize a story when the events are not probable. An example is *Homecoming* by Cynthia Voigt in which four children manage to travel hundreds of miles alone with almost no money to reach their grandmother's house. Admittedly this storyline may be improbable, yet it is certainly possible. Other aspects of *Homecoming* are more ordinarily realistic; for example, the characters are well developed and the relationships among the characters seem quite ordinary. Sometimes an author goes closer to the edge of the believable range in order to produce a more exciting, suspense-filled story. Reading the humdrum activities of daily life without embellishment, even though real, would certainly bore readers. In fiction, the story is of paramount importance and the sac-

rifice of some probability for a good story does not usually interfere with the pleasure children gain from a book. It may instead help to create interest in the story.

Selection of realistic fiction for classroom and library collections and for read-alouds should be balanced among the different types of realistic stories. A steady diet of humorous read-alouds does not offer the richness of experience to children that they deserve, nor does it provide for the varied reading interests of a group of children. It is extremely important to read aloud some books with females as main characters, and some with males as main characters, and some with minorities as main characters. The Edgar Allan Poe Award for Juvenile Mystery Novels can be helpful to you in selecting good mysteries—the most popular story type of all for intermediate-grade students. This award was established in 1961 by the Mystery Writers of America and is awarded annually in order to honor U.S. authors of mysteries for children. The list of winners is included in Appendix A.

Historical Overview of Realistic Fiction

The earliest realistic stories were didactic ones intending to teach morality and manners to young readers. The characters of the children's stories of the 1700s were usually wooden, lifeless boys and girls whose lives were spent in good works; however, in England during this period two significant events affecting the future of children's literature occurred. *Robinson Crusoe* by Daniel Defoe was published in 1719 for adults, but became a popular book among children. This forerunner of the adventure-survival story for children recounts the tale of a shipwrecked sailor who struggles against the forces of nature for survival on an island. Then in 1744, John Newbery began to publish, expressly for a child audience, books of realistic fiction intended to entertain as well as to educate. These two events laid the groundwork for establishing children's literature as a separate branch of literature.

The first type of realistic fiction for children that avoided the heavy didactic persuasion was the adventure story. Imitators of *Robinson Crusoe* were many, including the very popular *Swiss Family Robinson* by Johann Wyss of Switzerland in 1812. Later adventure stories of renown from England were *Treasure Island* (1883) and *Kidnapped* (1886) by Robert Louis Stevenson and from the United States, *The Adventures of Tom Sawyer* (1876) and *The Adventures of Huckleberry Finn* (1884) by Samuel Clemens (pseud. Mark Twain). Clemens, through the addition of sharp humor and characters who were in many ways less than admirable but nonetheless appealing, took an important step toward increased realism in stories.

Realistic family stories also came on the scene during the 1800s with *Little Women* (1868) by Louisa May Alcott and *Five Little Peppers and How They Grew* (1880), the first of a series of family stories by Harriet M. Lothrop (pseud. Margaret Sydney). The family story remains a favorite in the twentieth century, with early memorable books such as *Rebecca of Sunnybrook Farm* (1903) by Kate Douglas Wiggins, the series *Anne of Green Gables* (1908) by Canadian Lucy Maud Montgomery, and *The*

Secret Garden (1909) by Frances Hodgson Burnett of England. Since Anne of *Anne of Green Gables* and Mary of *The Secret Garden* were orphans, the books by Burnett and Montgomery can be considered precursors of adjustment stories that addressed the special needs of children with problems. Stories of happy and often large families continued to thrive and peaked in the 1940s and 1950s in family story series about the Moffat family by Eleanor Estes and about the Melendy family by Elizabeth Enright. Beverly Cleary's *Henry Huggins* stories and Sydney Taylor's *All-of-a-Kind Family* series continued this tradition into the 1950s and 1960s. These stories are often referred to as the *happy family* stories, and, compared with much of today's contemporary realism for children, these stories do seem almost lighthearted.

Children from other lands is another theme that can be found in many realistic stories for children. *Hans Brinker, or The Silver Skates* (1865) by Mary Mapes Dodge and *Heidi* (1880) by Johanna Spyri of Switzerland are set in Holland and Switzerland respectively and were two of the earliest *other lands* books. In the United States, Kate Seredy was awarded a Newbery Medal for *The Good Master* (1934), which was set in Hungary. One of the purposes of these early stories appeared to be an understanding and appreciation of foreign cultures. This theme continues to be seen in recent books published both by U.S. authors and by authors from other countries whose works are later published in the United States.

Realistic animal stories for children began to appear in the latter half of the nineteenth century. *Black Beauty* (1877) by Anna Sewell was a plea for humane treatment of animals and, though quite sentimental in places and completely personified, is still appreciated by some readers. *Beautiful Joe* (1894) by Margaret Marshall Saunders of Canada was a sentimental but well-loved dog story from this era. In 1894, Rudyard Kipling's *The Jungle Books,* exciting animal stories set in India, appeared, and these stories continue to hold the attention of readers today. Animal stories showing the maturing of the young human protagonist who assists the animal in the story have remained popular throughout the twentieth century. Canadian authors, such as Sheila Burnford, have been especially recognized for their contributions to this type of story.

Regional stories and stories about children of minority groups began to appear with more frequency in the 1940s. *Strawberry Girl* (1945) by Lois Lenski featured rural Florida, and was one of the first regional stories. *In My Mother's House* (1941) by Ann Nolan Clark featured Pueblo Indians and *Bright April* (1946) by Marguerite De Angeli discussed prejudice toward African Americans; however, it was only in the 1960s and 1970s that books written by minorities began to achieve national recognition. *Zeely* (1967) by Virginia Hamilton and *Stevie* (1969) by John Steptoe portray African-American childhood experiences and are two of the earliest and most noteworthy books representing this trend toward increased minority authorship—a trend that remains popular today.

A new era in realistic fiction for children was ushered in with the publication of *Harriet the Spy* by Louise Fitzhugh in 1964. This story of an unhappy and, at times, unpleasant girl depicted Harriet, her parents, and her classmates as anything but ideal or sympathetic human beings. This trend toward a more graphic and explicitly truthful

Table 7–1   Milestones in the Development of Realistic Fiction

Date	Event	Significance
1719	*Robinson Crusoe* by Daniel Defoe (England)	Early survival/adventure on a desert island; many imitators
1812	*Swiss Family Robinson* by Johann Wyss (Switzerland)	Most successful imitation of *Robinson Crusoe*
1865	*Hans Brinker, or The Silver Skates* by Mary Mapes Dodge (U.S.A.)	An early story set in another land (Holland)
1867	*Little Women* by Louisa May Alcott (U.S.A.)	An early family story of great popularity
1876	*The Adventures of Tom Sawyer* by Mark Twain (U.S.A.)	Classic adventure story set along the Mississippi
1877	*Black Beauty* by Anna Sewell (England)	Early horse story deploring inhumane treatment of animals
1880	*Heidi* by Joanna Spyri (Switzerland)	An early international story popular in the United States
1883	*Treasure Island* by Robert Louis Stevenson (England)	Classic adventure story with pirates
1894	*Beautiful Joe* by Margaret M. Saunders (Canada)	Early dog story, popular and sentimental
1908	*Anne of Green Gables* by L. M. Montgomery (Canada)	Early family story about an orphan and her new family
1911	*The Secret Garden* by Frances Hodgson Burnett (U.S.A.)	A classic sentimental novel of two children adjusting to life
1934	*The Good Master* by Kate Seredy (U.S.A.)	Newbery winner set in Hungary
1938	*The Yearling* by Marjorie Kinnan Rawlings (U.S.A.)	Classic animal story and coming-of-age story
1941	*In My Mother's House* by Ann Nolan Clark (U.S.A.)	Early story featuring Native Americans
1945	*Strawberry Girl* by Lois Lenski (U.S.A.)	Regional story set in Florida
1960	*The Incredible Journey* by Sheila Burnford (Canada)	Classic animal survival story with two dogs and a cat
1964	*Harriet the Spy* by Louise Fitzhugh (U.S.A.)	The beginning of the new realism movement
1970	*Are You There, God? It's Me, Margaret* by Judy Blume (U.S.A.)	Early book with frank treatment of sex
1972	*The Planet of Junior Brown* by Virginia Hamilton (U.S.A.)	Realistic novel featuring minority main characters by an African-American author

portrayal of life and the inclusion of many topics previously considered taboo continued to grow in children's books in the 1970s and 1980s and still prevails today. For example, Judy Blume's books are especially frank about sexual development and the emotional reactions to that development. Other controversial topics such as death, divorce, drugs, pacifism, alcoholism, and handicaps, which have always been a part of childhood, became permissible topics in children's books. Parents and other adults began to be shown, at times, as less than perfect, and families began to be portrayed as they truly are, not as one might believe they should be. This newer, franker brand of realism, sometimes referred to as the *new realism,* changed the world of children's books. The rosy cheer and avoidance of unpleasantness of earlier times were replaced by head-on discussion of all topics reflective of contemporary experience. The new realism books may be less lighthearted than their predecessors, but they are also more truthful and more real. Milestones in the development of realistic fiction are highlighted in Table 7–1.

Types of Realistic Fiction

The subject matter of realistic fiction includes the child's whole world of relationships with self and others: the joys, sorrows, challenges, adjustments, anxieties, and satisfactions of human life. A single realistic book will often treat more than one aspect of human life within its pages; however, each book emphasizes one or the other of these aspects by which it is defined.

Family Situations

Stories about the *nuclear family*, children and their relationships with parents and siblings, are a natural subject of books for children. Childhood for most children is spent in close contact with family members. Family stories for younger children often portray a happy child with loving parents. In these stories the everyday activities are shown—from brushing teeth to cooking dinner. Easy chapter books appealing to newly independent readers can be found within this type. These stories often show the child at play and sometimes explore sibling relationships as well. *Anastasia Krupnik* by Lois Lowry and *Ramona Quimby, Age 8* by Beverly Cleary are good examples of this type of book.

Extended families can also be found in children's books. Aunts, uncles, grandparents, and cousins are important in the real lives of many children and may also be enjoyed in stories written for children. Sometimes a book will tell of a child being raised by a member of the extended family; other times a relative is portrayed as a supportive family member. See *Arthur for the Very First Time* by Patricia MacLachlan and *The Unmaking of Rabbit* by Constance C. Greene.

The *alternative family* of today's world is also depicted in family stories. Not all family stories present the safe and secure world of healthy, intact families. Separation, divorce, single-parent families, and reconstructed families of stepparents and stepchildren are often the backdrop of stories today. For example, see *The Night Daddy* by Maria Gripe, *Mom, the Wolfman and Me* by Norma Klein, and *Something to Count On* by Emily Moore. The difficulty children and adults encounter in adjusting to these new family situations becomes the primary conflict in some stories. Temporary family situations, such as foster care for children, are also described in books about family life. It is important for children to see families other than the typical mother, father, and two children portrayed positively in books.

Peer Relationships

In addition to adapting to one's family situation, children must also learn to cope with their peers. Many realistic stories show children struggling for *acceptance by peers* in a group situation. School settings are common in these stories. Examples include *Blubber* by Judy Blume and *Skinnybones* by Barbara Park. Neighborhoods, clubhouses, and summer camps are other common settings. For instance, see *The Goats* by Brock Cole and *Hecate, William McKinley, MacBeth, and Me, Elizabeth* by E. L. Konigsburg.

Developing *close friendships* is another focus of stories about peer relationships. These friends may be the same sex or the opposite sex, the same age or very different age, or the same culture or different culture. A concern for friendship and how to be a good friend to someone are shared traits of these stories. *Bridge to Terabithia* by Katherine Paterson and *Onion John* by Joseph Krumgold are good examples of this type of book.

Growth and Maturity

From birth to age 10, most children's lives revolve around family, friends, and classmates, but during the preteen and teen years a shift toward *self-discovery and independence* occurs. During these years, rapid growth and change are seen in the physical, emotional, moral, and intellectual domains of life. These changes are reflected in books for adolescent children aged 10 and older. Sometimes books that deal with the trials and tribulations encountered during growth from childhood to adulthood are called *rite-of-passage* books, such as *A Fine White Dust* by Cynthia Rylant and *The 18th Emergency* by Betsy Byars.

Children become aware of their *growing sexuality* during preteen and teen years as they begin to mature. Some stories for older teens show attraction between members of the opposite sex as well as members of the same sex, with the beginning of sexual activity sometimes shown in relationships. See *I'll Get There, It Better Be Worth the Trip* by John Donovan and *Then Again, Maybe I Won't* by Judy Blume.

Maturity is achieved through *facing and overcoming fears*. These fears may be of internal forces as well as external dangers. Stories of dealing with fears of emotional and psychological dangers feature protagonists who fear being different, making commitments, being rejected, and sometimes are excessively fearful of life itself. For example, see *Different Dragons* by Jean Little.

Facing physical danger, an external force, also contributes to the maturing process. Stories of *survival and adventure* are ones in which the young protagonist must rely on will and ingenuity to survive a life-threatening situation. Although most survival stories are set in isolated places, a growing number are being set in cities where gangs, drug wars, and abandonment are indeed life threatening. Adventure stories may be set in any environment where the protagonist has freedom of action. *Hatchet* by Gary Paulsen and *Scorpions* by Walter Dean Myers are examples of this type of book.

Acceptance of Cultural Differences

Part of growing up is the discovery that not all people are the same; part of becoming a healthy and humane adult is accepting the differences in oneself and in others. Today's children are growing up in a multicultural society in which an understanding and appreciation of cultural and linguistic differences among peoples are essential for societal harmony and cooperation. *Multicultural books* are those in which the main characters are from a racial, language, religious, or ethnic minority such as African Americans, Asian Americans, Hispanic Americans, Jewish Americans, or Native Americans. These books can be instrumental in developing in all children new understanding and appreciation for others as well as providing characters with whom minority children themselves may more readily identify. *Yellow Bird and Me* by Joyce Hansen is a good example. Each year more authors and illustrators from minority groups are becoming recognized for their contributions to children's literature.

As our earth hastens toward becoming an international community, children will be members of an international community. Books set in *foreign countries* may be written by U.S. authors about life in another culture or by a foreign author about her own country. These books can help children develop an awareness of people from other countries and an appreciation for children whose lives differ from their own. Examples include *Buster's World* by Bjarne Reuter and *Wolf* by Gillian Cross. For further discussion of multicultural and international children's literature of a variety of genres, refer to Chapter 10.

Popular Topics in Realistic Fiction

Certain types of realistic fiction are consistently sought out by children for their independent reading. Although the quality of some of these books may be mediocre, others are well written and deserve children's attention. What these books provide is relatively appealing and easy-to-read stories for the developing reader. By reading many of these stories, children improve their vocabularies, comprehension, and fluency at this stage of their reading development. You can help students by making them aware of the best books available in these categories.

Sports stories often present a story in which a child protagonist struggles to become accepted as a member of a team and does eventually succeed through determination and hard work. *Wild Pitch* by Matt Christopher is a good example of a sports story. Although traditionally written with boys as the main characters, some sports stories are now available that feature girls as protagonists.

Mysteries, popular with boys and girls, range from simple "whodunits" to complex character stories. The element of suspense is a strong part of the appeal of these stories. Mysteries have won more state children's choice awards than any other type of story, which suggests that mysteries are truly favorites of children. See *Encyclopedia Brown* by Donald J. Sobol and *The Dollhouse Murders* by Betty Ren Wright.

Humorous stories are ones featuring characters caught up in silly situations or involved in funny escapades. Children often are amused by the incongruities presented in these predicament stories. Other humorous stories draw on word play for their humor. *Bagthorpes Unlimited* by Helen Cresswell is a good example of a humorous story.

Animal stories remain an ever-popular genre with children, with dog and horse stories being the most popular of these. In realistic animal stories, the animal protagonist behaves like an animal and is not personified. Usually a child is also a protagonist in these stories. Examples are *The Black Stallion* by Walter Farley and *The Incredible Journey* by Sheila Burnford.

Series stories have appealed to children for generations. The Nancy Drew series and Hardy Boys series, with their quick-moving, linear plots, ordinary vocabulary, and easy syntax, offer children the satisfaction of reading a chapter book on their own. The young reader knows that this series book, once completed, can be quickly followed by another similar book from the same shelf. The ease of reading and the ease of availability make the series books popular with the newly independent reader. These series books are called *formula fiction* and appear as mysteries, fantasy and science fantasy adventures, and romances. The authors who are hired by a syndicate follow a set structure in developing each book. Three or four plots and a set number of characters are established and implemented in the writing of each book of the series.

Many recent series released in quantity are *romances,* such as *Babysitters Club, Sweet Valley Twins, Wild Fire,* and *Sweet Dreams.* Although no one claims that they are literature, their success in the market cannot be ignored. Elleman (1987) points out that an especially unfortunate aspect of these series romances is their dependence on stereotyped characters and reflection of white, middle-class, suburban life. The stereotyping of girls in traditional roles in which success is too often defined in terms of popularity among boys is a debilitating message to convey to today's girls.

Stories in the realistic fiction genre present familiar situations with which children can readily identify, often reflect contemporary life, and portray settings not much different from the homes, schools, towns, and cities known to today's children. The protagonists of these stories are frequently testing themselves as they grow toward adulthood; young readers of these stories can therefore empathize and gain insight into their own life predicaments. Your challenge will be to stay abreast of good realistic stories in order to provide a wide range of books that will both entertain, encourage, and inspire your students.

References

Elleman, B. (1987). Current trends in literature for children. *Library Trends, 35* (3), 413–426.

Marshall, M. R. (1988). *An introduction to the world of children's books* (2nd ed.) Brookfield, VT: Gower.

Notable Authors of Realistic Fiction

Judy Blume, writer of popular, sometimes controversial, novels focusing on problems of preteens and teens. *Are You There God? It's Me, Margaret; Tales of a Fourth Grade Nothing.*

Sue Ellen Bridgers, author of adolescent novels on family relationships. *All Together Now.*

Sheila Burnford, Canadian author of a popular animal survival story, *The Incredible Journey.*

Betsy Byars, author of stories about children who face and overcome family and personal problems. *The Pinballs; Summer of the Swans.*

Matt Christopher, author of many sports stories. *Dirt Bike Racer.*

Beverly Cleary, writer of humorous family stories about everyday happenings. *Ramona Quimby, Age 8; Dear Mr. Henshaw.*

Vera and Bill Cleaver, authors of Appalachian-based realistic fiction. *Where the Lilies Bloom.*

Louise Fitzhugh, author of *Harriet the Spy* that ushered in the new realism movement.

Paula Fox, recipient of Hans Christian Andersen Medal who writes stories about family relationships. *Blowfish Live in the Sea; One–Eyed Cat.*

Jean Craighead George, author of ecological fiction and survival in nature stories. *Julie of the Wolves; My Side of the Mountain.*

Bette Greene, author of stories about friendships among African-American adolescents. *Philip Hall Likes Me, I Reckon Maybe.*

Maria Gripe, Swedish author of contemporary realistic novels featuring alternative family types. *The Night Daddy.*

Virginia Hamilton, author of stories about the African-American experience. *Zeely; The Planet of Junior Brown.*

Tormod Haugen, 1990 Hans Christian Andersen medalist, Norwegian author of sensitive stories about troubled adolescents. *Zeppelin; The Night Birds.*

Marguerite Henry, author of many horse stories. *King of the Wind; Misty of Chincoteague.*

James Houston, Canadian author of survival stories. *Frozen Fire; White Fang.*

Elaine L. Konigsburg, writer of sensitive and humorous stories of preteens and teens. *From the Mixed-Up Files of Mrs. Basil E. Frankweiler; (George).*

Jean Little, Canadian author who writes family-adjustment stories. *Mine for Keeps; Mama's Going to Buy You a Mockingbird.*

Sharon Bell Mathis, author of African-American family experiences. *The Hundred Penny Box.*

Nicholasa Mohr, author of adolescent novels set in Puerto Rican neighborhoods of New York City. *Nilda.*

Farley Mowat, author of popular animal stories set in Canada. *Owls in the Family.*

Walter Dean Myers, author of novels about African-American adolescents in city settings. *Scorpions; Fast Sam, Cool Clyde, and Stuff.*

Peggy Parish, author of *Amelia Bedelia* series of humorous books on literalmindedness.

Katherine Paterson, author of stories featuring relationships with peers and family. *The Great Gilly Hopkins; Bridge to Terabithia.*

Gary Paulsen, author of nature survival adventures often set in northern United States or Canada. *Hatchet; Dogsong.*

Ellen Raskin, writer of intriguing, complex mysteries. *The Westing Game; Figgs & Phantoms.*

Wilson Rawls, author of poignant animal stories set in the Ozarks. *Where the Red Fern Grows; Summer of the Monkeys.*

Jan Slepian, books on overcoming handicaps and adjusting to change. *The Broccoli Tapes; The Alfred Summer.*

Alfred Slote, author of sports stories. *The Trading Game; Hang Tough, Paul Mather.*

Zilpha Keatley Snyder, author of mystery stories. *The Famous Stanley Kidnapping Case; The Egypt Game.*

Donald Sobol, author of mystery series for transitional readers. *Encyclopedia Brown* series.

Ivan Southall, Australian author of high-risk adventure stories. *Ash Road; To the Wild Sky.*

Colin Thiele, Australian author of adventure stories who often includes Aboriginal characters. *Fire in the Stone; Storm Boy.*

Cynthia Voigt, author of stories about the Tillerman family of four children and their friends. *Dicey's Song; A Solitary Blue.*

Laurence Yep, author of novels about the Asian-American experience. *Child of the Owl; Dragonwings.*

Recommended Realistic Fiction Books

Ages refer to approximate interest levels. YA= young adult readers.

Avi. *Nothing But the Truth*. Orchard, 1991. Ages 12–YA.

Bauer, Marion Dane. *On My Honor*. Clarion, 1986. Ages 8–12.

Bawden, Nina. *Kept in the Dark*. Lothrop, 1982. Ages 10–YA.

——. *The Outside Child*. Lothrop, 1989. Ages 10–YA.

Block, Francesca Lia. *Witch Baby*. Harper Collins, 1991. Ages 14–YA.

Blume, Judy. *Are You There God? It's Me, Margaret*. Bradbury, 1970. Ages 10–YA.

——. *Blubber*. Bradbury, 1974. Ages 9–12.

——. *It's Not the End of the World*. Bradbury, 1972. Ages 12–YA.

——. *Tales of a Fourth Grade Nothing*. Illustrated by Roy Doty. Dutton, 1972. Ages 8–12.

Bonham, Frank. *Durango Street*. Dutton, 1965. Ages 12–YA.

Bridgers, Sue Ellen. *All Together Now*. Knopf, 1979. Ages 11–YA.

Brooks, Bruce. *Everywhere*. HarperCollins, 1990. Ages 11–YA.

——. *The Moves Make the Man*. Harper, 1984. Ages 11–YA.

Brooks, Martha. *Two Moons in August*. Little, Brown, 1992 Ages 12–YA.

Burch, Robert. *Queenie Peavy*. Illustrated by Jerry Lazare. Viking, 1966. Ages 10–YA.

Burnford, Sheila. *The Incredible Journey*. Illustrated by Carl Burger. Little, 1961. Ages 8–11.

Buss, Fran Leeper, and Daisy Cubias. *Journey of the Sparrows*. Dutton, 1991. Ages 12–YA.

Byars, Betsy C. *After the Goat Man*. Illustrated by Ronald Himler. Viking, 1974. Ages 9–12.

——. *Bingo Brown, Gypsy Lover*. Viking, 1990. Ages 11–YA.

——. *The Burning Questions of Bingo Brown*. Viking, 1988. Ages 9–12.

——. *Cracker Jackson*. Viking, 1985. Ages 10–14.

——. *The House of Wings*. Illustrated by Daniel Schwartz. Viking, 1972. Ages 8–12.

——. *The Night Swimmers*. Illustrated by Troy Howell. Delacorte, 1980. Ages 8–11.

——. *The Summer of the Swans*. Illustrated by Ted CoConis. Viking, 1970. Ages 9–12.

Cameron, Ann. *More Stories Julian Tells*. Illustrated by Ann Strugnell. Knopf, 1986. Ages 7–11.

Cameron, Eleanor. *Julia's Magic*. Illustrated by Gail Owens. Dutton, 1984. Ages 9–12.

——. *That Julia Redfern*. Dutton, 1982. Ages 9–12.

Carter, Alden R. *Up Country*. Putnam, 1989. Ages 12–YA.

Cassedy, Sylvia. *M. E. and Morton*. Crowell, 1987. Ages 11–YA.

Christopher, Matt. *Tackle Without a Team*. Illustrated by Margaret Sanfilippo. Little, Brown, 1989. Ages 10–14.

Cleary, Beverly. *Dear Mr. Henshaw*. Illustrated by Paul Zelinsky. Morrow, 1983. Ages 9–12.

——. *Ramona and Her Father*. Illustrated by Alan Tiegreen. Morrow, 1977. Ages 7–10.

——. *Ramona and Her Mother*. Illustrated by Alan Tiegreen. Morrow, 1977. Ages 7–10.

——. *Ramona Quimby, Age 8*. Illustrated by Alan Tiegreen. Morrow, 1981. Ages 7–10.

——. *Ramona the Brave*. Illustrated Alan Tiegreen. Morrow, 1975. Ages 5–8.

——. *Ramona the Pest*. Illustrated by Louis Darling. Morrow, 1968. Ages 5–8.

——. *Strider*. Illustrated by Paul O. Zelinsky. Morrow, 1991. Ages 9–13.

Cleaver, Vera and Bill. *I Would Rather Be a Turnip*. Lippincott, 1971. Ages 11–13.

——. *Lady Ellen Grae*. Illustrated by Ellen Raskin. Lippincott, 1968. Ages 9–12.

——. *Trial Valley*. Lippincott, 1977. Ages 11–YA.

——. *Where the Lillies Bloom*. Illustrated by Jim Spanfeller. Lippincott, 1969. Ages 11–YA.

Clements, Bruce. *Tom Loves Anna Loves Tom*. Farrar, 1990. Ages 12–YA.

Cohen, Barbara. *Thank You, Jackie Robinson*. Illustrated by Richard Cuffari. Lothrop, 1974. Ages 8–11.

Cole, Brock. *Celine*. Farrar, 1989. Ages 12–YA.

——. *The Goats*. Farrar, 1987. Ages 11–YA.

Corbett, Scott. *Grave Doubts.* Little, Brown, 1982. Ages 9–12.

Corcoran, Barbara. *Annie's Monster.* Atheneum, 1990. Ages 10–YA.

Cormier, Robert. *The Chocolate War.* Pantheon, 1974. Ages 12–YA.

———. *The Bumblebee Flies Anyway.* Pantheon, 1983. Ages 13–YA.

———. *We All Fall Down.* Delacorte, 1991. Ages 13–YA.

Cresswell, Helen. *Bagthorpes Liberated: Being the Seventh Part of the Bagthorpe Saga.* Macmillan, 1989. Ages 8–12.

———. *Ordinary Jack.* Macmillan, 1977. Ages 8–12.

Cross, Gillian. A *Map to Nowhere.* Holiday, 1989. Ages 10–13.

———. *On the Edge.* Holiday, 1985. Ages 10–13.

———. *Roscoe's Leap.* Holiday, 1987. Ages 10–13.

———. *Wolf.* Holiday, 1991. Ages 10–13.

Crutcher, Chris. *Athletic Shorts: Six Short Stories.* Greenwillow, 1991. Ages 13–YA.

Davis, Jenny. *Goodbye and Keep Cold.* Watts, 1987. Ages 13–YA.

Doherty, Berlie. *Granny Was a Buffer Girl.* Watts, 1988. Ages 13–YA.

———. *White Peak Farm.* Watts, 1990. Ages 11–YA.

Eckert, Allan W. *Incident at Hawk's Hill.* Illustrated by John Schoenherr. Little, Brown, 1971. Ages 10–YA.

Ehrlich, Amy. *Where It Stops, Nobody Knows.* Dial, 1988. Ages 12–YA.

Ellis, Sarah. *A Family Project.* Macmillan, 1988. Ages 10–14.

———. *Next-Door Neighbors.* Macmillan, 1990. Ages 9–13.

Estes, Eleanor. *The Moffats.* Illustrated by Louis Slobodkin. Harcourt, 1941. Ages 7–10.

———. *The Hundred Dresses.* Illustrated by Louis Slobodkin. Harcourt, 1944. Ages 8–11.

Fine, Anne. *Alias Madame Doubtfire.* Little, Brown, 1988. Ages 9–12.

———. *The Book of the Banshees.* Little, Brown, 1992. Ages 11–YA.

———. *My War with Goggle-Eyes.* Little, Brown, 1989. Ages 11–14.

Fitzhugh, Louise. *Harriet the Spy.* Harper, 1964. Ages 9–12.

———. *The Long Secret.* Harper, 1965. Ages 9–12.

Fox, Paula. *Blowfish Live in the Sea.* Bradbury, 1970. Ages 12–YA.

———. *How Many Miles to Babylon?* Illustrated by Paul Giovanipoulos. White, 1967. Ages 11–YA.

———. *Monkey Island.* Watts, 1991. Ages 9–12.

———. *The Moonlight Man.* Bradbury, 1986. Ages 11–YA.

———. *One-Eyed Cat.* Bradbury, 1984. Ages 9–12.

———. *The Village by the Sea.* Watts, 1988. Ages 10–13.

Gardiner, John Reynolds. *Stone Fox.* Illustrated by Marcia Sewall. Crowell, 1980. Ages 7–11.

Garfield, Leon. *The December Rose.* Viking, 1987. Ages 10–YA.

Geller, Mark. *What I Heard.* Harper, 1987. Ages 10–13.

George, Jean Craighead. *The Cry of the Crow.* Harper, 1980. Ages 10–13.

———. *Julie of the Wolves.* Illustrated by John Schoenherr. Harper, 1972. Ages 11–YA.

Gilson, Jamie. *Sticks and Stones and Skeleton Bones.* Illustrated by Dee deRosa. Lothrop, 1991. Ages 8–11.

Gipson, Fred. *Old Yeller.* Illustrated by Carl Burger. Harper, 1956. Ages 10–YA.

Gordon, Sheila. *Waiting for the Rain: A Novel of South Africa.* Watts, 1987. Ages 11–YA.

Grant, Cynthia D. *Keep Laughing.* Atheneum, 1991. Ages 12–YA.

Greene, Bette. *Phillip Hall Likes Me, I Reckon Maybe.* Illustrated by Charles Lilly. Dial, 1974. Ages 9–12.

Greene, Constance C. *Al(exandra) the Great.* Viking, 1982. Ages 8–12.

———. *Beat the Turtle Drum.* Illustrated by Donna Diamond. Viking, 1976. Ages 10–YA.

———. *A Girl Called Al.* Illustrated by Byron Barton. Viking, 1969. Ages 8–12.

Haas, Jessie. *Keeping Barney.* Greenwillow, 1982. Ages 9–12.

———. *The Sixth Sense: And Other Stories.* Greenwillow, Ages 11–YA.

Hall, Barbara. *Dixie Storms.* Harcourt, 1990. Ages 12–YA.

Hamilton, Virginia. *Cousins*. Putnam, 1990. Ages 9–13.

———. *The Planet of Junior Brown*. MacMillan, 1971. Ages 12–YA.

Hansen, Joyce. *The Gift-Giver*. Clarion, 1980. Ages 9–12.

———. *Yellow Bird and Me*. Clarion, 1986. Ages 9–12.

Harris, Rosemary. *Zed*. Farber, 1982. Ages 11–YA.

Haugen, Tormod. *The Night Birds*. Translated from the Norwegian by Sheila LaFarge. Delacorte, 1982. Ages 10–14.

Henry, Marguerite. *King of the Wind*. Illustrated by Wesley Dennis. Rand, 1948. Ages 7–11.

———. *Misty of Chincoteague*. Illustrated by Wesley Dennis. Rand, 1947. Ages 7–11.

Hermes, Patricia. *Mama, Let's Dance*. Little, 1991. Ages 10–YA

Holman, Felice. *Slake's Limbo*. Scribner's, 1974. Ages 10–13.

Houston, James A. *Frozen Fire*. Atheneum, 1977. Ages 11–YA.

Hughes, Dean. *Family Pose*. Atheneum, 1989. Ages 10–13.

Hunt, Irene. *Up a Road Slowly*. Follett, 1966. Ages 11–YA.

Hurwitz, Johanna. *Class Clown*. Illustrated by Sheila Hamanaka. Morrow, 1987. Ages 6–9.

———. *Russell and Elisa*. Morrow, 1989. Ages 6–9.

Keller, Beverly. *No Beasts! No Children!* Lothrop, 1983. Ages 8–12.

Kerr, M. E. *Fell*. Harper, 1987. Ages 13–YA.

———. *Fell Down*. HarperCollins, 1991. Ages 12–YA.

Kinsey–Warnock, Natalie. *The Canada Geese Quilt*. Illustrated by Leslie W. Bowman. Dutton, 1989. Ages 8–12.

Kjelgaard, Jim. *Big Red*. Illustrated by Bob Kuhn. Holiday, 1945. Ages 9–12.

Klein, Norma. *Mom, the Wolf Man, and Me*. Pantheon, 1972. Ages 11–YA.

Klein, Robin. *Enemies*. Illustrated by Noela Young. Dutton, 1989. Ages 9–12.

Kline, Suzy. *Herbie Jones and the Class Gift*. Illustrated Richard Williams. Putnam, 1987. Ages 8–11.

———. *What's the Matter with Herbie Jones?* Illustrated by Richard Williams. Putnam, 1986. Ages 8–11.

Konigsburg, E. L. *From the Mixed-Up Files of Mrs. Basil E. Frankweiler*. Atheneum, 1967. Ages 9–12.

———. *(George)*. Atheneum, 1970. Ages 11–YA.

———. *Journey to an 800 Number*. Atheneum, 1982. Ages 10–13.

L'Engle, Madeleine. *Meet the Austins*. Vanguard, 1960. Ages 9–12.

Levin, Betty. *The Trouble with Gramary*. Greenwillow, 1988. Ages 10–13.

Lisle, Janet Taylor. *Afternoon of the Elves*. Watts, 1989. Ages 9–12.

Little, Jean. *Mama's Going to Buy You a Mockingbird*. Viking, 1985. Ages 10–13.

———. *Mine for Keeps*. Illustrated by Lewis Parker. Little, 1962. Ages 9–12.

———. *Take Wing*. Little, Brown, 1968. Ages 9–12.

Lord, Bette Bao. *In the Year of the Boar and Jackie Robinson*. Illustrated by Marc Simont. Harper, 1984. Ages 8–11.

Lowry, Lois. *All About Sam*. Illustrated by Diane de Groat. Houghton, 1988. Ages 8–12.

———. *Anastasia at Your Service*. Illustrated by Diane de Groat. Houghton, 1982. Ages 8–12.

———. *Anastasia Krupnik*. Houghton, 1985. Ages 8–12.

———. *Attaboy, Sam!* Illustrated by Diane de Groat. Houghton, 1992. Ages 7–11.

———. *The One Hundredth Thing About Caroline*. Houghton, 1983. Ages 8–12.

———. *Rabble Starkey*. Houghton, 1987. Ages 10–13.

———. *A Summer to Die*. Houghton, 1977. Ages 10–13.

Maartens, Maretha. *Paper Bird: A Novel of South Africa*. Translated by Madeleine van Biljon. Clarion, 1991. Ages 10–YA.

MacLachlan, Patricia. *The Facts and Fictions of Minna Pratt*. Harper, 1988. Ages 7–11.

———. *Journey*. Illustrated by Barry Moser. Delacorte, 1991. Ages 10–14.

Mahy, Margaret. *The Catalogue of the Universe*. McElderry, 1986. Ages 14–YA.

———. *Underrunners*. Viking, 1992. Ages 12–YA.

Major, Kevin. *Hold Fast.* Delacorte, 1980. Ages 13–YA.

Marino, Jan. *The Day That Elvis Came to Town.* Little, Brown, 1991. Ages 12–YA.

Mark, Jan. *Handles.* Atheneum, 1985. Ages 11–YA.

———. *Thunder and Lightnings.* Crowell, 1979. Ages 11–YA.

Marsden, John. *So Much to Tell You.* Joy Street, 1989. Ages 12–YA.

Mathis, Sharon Bell. *The Hundred Penny Box.* Illustrated by Leo and Diane Dillon. Viking, 1975. Ages 7–10.

Merrill, Jean. *The Pushcart War.* Illustrated by Ronni Solbert. Harper, 1964. Ages 11–YA.

Mohr, Nicholasa. *Felita.* Illustrated by Ray Cruz. Dial, 1979. Ages 8–11.

Myers, Walter Dean. *The Mouse Rap.* Harper, 1990. Ages 11–YA.

———. *Scorpions.* Harper, 1988. Ages 10–YA.

———. *Somewhere in the Darkness.* Scholastic, 1992. Ages 12–YA.

Naidoo, Beverley. *Chain of Fire.* Illustrated by Eric Velasquez. Lippincott, 1990. Ages 11–YA.

———. *Journey to Jo'burg: A South African Story.* Illustrated by Eric Velasquez. Lippincott, 1986. Ages 8–12.

Naylor, Phyllis Reynolds. *Reluctantly Alice.* Atheneum, 1991. Ages 8–11.

———. *Shiloh.* Atheneum, 1991. Ages 8–11.

Newman, Robert. *The Case of the Frightened Friend.* Atheneum, Ages 10–13.

———. *The Case of the Murdered Players.* Atheneum, 1985. Ages 10–13.

———. *The Case of the Vanishing Corpse.* Atheneum, 1980. Ages 10–13.

Park, Barbara. *Almost Starring Skinnybones.* Knopf, 1988. Ages 9–12.

———. *Skinnybones.* Knopf, 1982. Ages 9–12.

Paterson, Katherine. *Bridge to Terabithia.* Illustrated by Donna Diamond. Crowell, 1977. Ages 9–13.

———. *The Great Gilly Hopkins.* Crowell, 1978. Ages 9–12.

———. *Jacob Have I Loved.* Crowell, 1980. Ages 12–YA.

Paulsen, Gary. *Hatchet.* Bradbury, 1987. Ages 9–12.

———. *The Monument.* Delacorte, 1991. Ages 11–YA.

———. *Woodsong.* Bradbury, 1990. Ages 11–YA.

Pearce, Philippa. *The Way to Sattin Shore.* Illustrated by Charlotte Voake. Greenwillow, 1984. Ages 10–13.

Peck, Richard. *Remembering the Good Times.* Delacorte, 1985. Ages 11–YA.

Pfeffer, Susan Beth. *The Year Without Michael.* Bantam, 1987. Ages 12–YA.

Phipson, Joan. *Hit and Run.* Atheneum, 1985. Ages 10–YA.

Plummer, Louise. *My Name Is Sus5an Smith. The 5 Is Silent.* Delacorte, 1991. Ages 13–YA.

Porte, Barbara Ann. *I Only Made Up the Roses.* Greenwillow, 1987. Ages 12–YA.

Procházková, Iva. *The Season of Secret Wishes.* Translated by Elizabeth D. Crawford. Lothrop, 1989. Ages 9–12.

Reuter, Bjarne. *Buster's World.* Translated from the Danish by Anthea Bell. Dutton, 1989. Ages 9–12.

———. *The Sheik of Hope Street.* Dutton, 1991. Ages 9–12.

Rodowsky, Colby. *H, My Name Is Henley.* Farrar, 1982. Ages 10–13.

———. *Sydney. Herself.* Farrar, 1989. Ages 11–YA.

Rylant, Cynthia. *A Blue-Eyed Daisy.* Bradbury, 1985. Ages 9–12.

———. *A Fine White Dust.* Bradbury, 1986. Ages 9–12.

———. *Every Living Thing.* Illustrated by S. D. Schindler. Bradbury, 1985. Ages 11–YA.

Sachs, Marilyn. *The Bears' House.* Illustrated by Louis Glanzman. Doubleday, 1971. Ages 9–12.

Shreve, Susan. *The Gift of the Girl Who Couldn't Hear.* Morrow, 1991. Ages 10–13.

Slepian, Jan. *The Alfred Summer.* Macmillan, 1980. Ages 10–12.

———. *The Broccoli Tapes.* Philomel, 1989. Ages 10–13.

———. *Lester's Turn.* Macmillan, 1981. Ages 10–13.

Slote, Alfred. *Hang Tough, Paul Mather.* Lippincott, 1973. Ages 9–12.

———. *The Trading Game.* Lippincott, 1990. Ages 9–12.

Smith, Doris Buchanan. *The Pennywhistle Tree.* Putnam, 1991. Ages 9–12.

———. *Return to Bitter Creek.* Viking, 1986. Ages 10–13.

———. *A Taste of Blackberries.* Illustrated by Charles Robinson. Crowell, 1973. Ages 9–12.

Smith, Robert Kimmel. *Bobby Baseball.* Illustrated by Alan Tiegreen. Delacorte, 1989. Ages 8–11.

Snyder, Zilpha Keatley. *The Changeling.* Atheneum, 1970. Ages 9–12.

———. The *Egypt Game.* Illustrated by Alton Raible. Atheneum, 1967. Ages 10–13.

Southall, Ivan. *Let the Balloon Go.* Bradbury, 1968. Ages 9–12.

Spence, Eleanor. *The Devil Hole.* Lothrop, 1977. Illustrated by Malcolm Green. Ages 10–13.

Sperry, Armstrong. *Call It Courage.* Macmillan, 1940. Ages 8–12.

Spinelli, Jerry. *Maniac Magee.* Little, Brown, 1990. Ages 9–12.

Staples, Suzanne Fisher. *Shabanu: Daughter of the Wind.* Knopf, 1989. Ages 12–YA.

Stolz, Mary. *The Bully of Barkham Street.* Illustrated by Leonard Shortall. Harper, 1963.

———. *A Dog on Barkham Street.* Harper, 1960. Ages 8–11.

Talbert, Marc. *Pillow of Clouds.* Dial, 1991. Ages 11–YA.

Taylor, Sydney. *All-of-a-Kind Family* Illustrated by Helen John. Follett, 1951. Ages 7–10.

Taylor, Theodore. *The Cay.* Doubleday, 1969. Ages 9–12.

———. *The Trouble with Tuck.* Doubleday, 1981. Ages 7–10.

Thesman, Jean. *The Rain Catchers.* Houghton, 1991. Ages 12–YA.

Thiele, Colin. *Shadow Shark.* Harper, 1988. Ages 10–13.

Ure, Jean. *Plaque.* Harcourt, 1991. Ages 12–YA.

Voigt, Cynthia. *Dicey's Song.* Atheneum, 1982. Ages 9–12.

———. *A Solitary Blue.* Atheneum, 1983. Ages 10–YA.

———. *Sons from Afar.* Atheneum, 1987. Ages 10–YA.

Walter, Mildred Pitts. *Have a Happy* ———. Illustrated by Carole Byard. Lothrop, 1989. Ages 9–12.

———. *Justin and the Best Biscuits in the World.* Illustrated by Catherine Stock. Lothrop, 1986. Ages 8–11.

Weller, Frances Ward. *Boat Song.* Macmillan, 1987. Ages 9–12.

Wojciechowska, Maia. *Shadow of a Bull.* Illustrated by Alvin Smith. Atheneum, 1964. Ages 9–12.

Wolff, Virginia Euwer. *Probably Still Nick Swansen.* Holt, 1988. Ages 11–YA.

Yarbrough, Camille. *The Shimmershine Queens.* Putnam, 1988. Ages 9–12.

Chapter **8**

Historical Fiction

Buffalo Dusk

The buffaloes are gone.
And those who saw the buffaloes are gone.
Those who saw the buffaloes by thousands and how they
*   pawed the prairie sod into dust with their hoofs,*
*   their great heads down pawing on in a great pageant*
*   of dusk,*
Those who saw the buffaloes are gone.
And the buffaloes are gone.

—Carl Sandburg

Historical fiction brings history to life by placing appealing child characters in accurately described historical settings. By telling the stories of these characters' everyday lives as well as presenting their triumphs and failures, authors of historical fiction provide young readers with the human side of history, making it more real and more memorable.

Definition and Description

Historical fiction is realistic fiction set in a time remote enough from the present to be considered history. That is, although the story is imaginary, it is within the realm of possibility that such events could have occurred at that time in history. In these stories historical facts blend with imaginary characters and plot. The facts are actual historical events, authentic period settings, and real historical figures. An imaginary story is constructed around these facts. In the *Reference Guide to Historical Fiction for Children and Young Adults,* Adamson (1987) states:

Historical fiction recreates a particular historical period with or without histori-
cal figures as incidental characters. It is generally written about a time period in
which the author has not lived or no more recently than one generation before its
composition. For example, fiction written in 1987 must be set, at the latest, in 1967,
to be considered historical. Fiction written in 1930 but set in 1925 does not fulfill
this criterion for legitimate historical fiction. (p. ix)

In the most common form of historical fiction, the main characters of the story are imaginary, but some secondary characters may be actual historical figures. An example of this type of historical fiction is the 1944 Newbery Award winner, *Johnny Tremain* by Esther Forbes. Set in the U.S. Revolutionary War period, this story tells of Johnny, a fictitious character, who is apprenticed to a silversmith. In the course of the story, Samuel Adams, John Hancock, and Paul Revere are introduced as minor characters.

In another form of historical fiction, the past is described complete with the social traditions, customs, morals, and values of the period but with no mention of an actual historical event nor actual historical figures as characters. The physical location is also accurately reconstructed for the readers. An example of this story type is *The Witch of Blackbird Pond* by Elizabeth George Speare. The Puritan way of life in Connecticut in the 1600s is depicted in this story about young Kit from Barbados who becomes involved in a witchcraft trial. The locales and traditions are accurate reconstructions of Puritan life of that era, whereas the characters, dialogue, day-to-day events, and details are fictitious. Both these forms of historical stories qualify as historical fiction under the definition of this genre.

A third type of historical story is one in which elements of fantasy are found, and therefore is not within the realm of possibility. For example, time warps and other supernatural features may be found in Canadian Janet Lunn's *The Root Cellar* and in Belinda Hurmence's *A Girl Called Boy*. These stories are *historical fantasy* and are included in Chapter 6, Modern Fantasy. Picture books in the historical fiction genre are discussed in Chapter 4, Picture Books.

Values of Historical Fiction for Children

Historical fiction can enliven the dry facts of history by presenting those facts through the everyday lives of children living long ago. Reading about and recognizing the feelings and thoughts a child of that era might experience enable young readers of today to relate on a more personal level with the events and people of history. Of course, with historical fiction—as with any form of good literature—the primary value is enjoyment and reading pleasure. Other values of historical fiction include the following:

- Readers see that their lives have been affected by those who lived before them. They also realize that their lives will affect the lives of those who will come after them.

- The human, everyday side of history is seen. Children understand that history was made by people like themselves.
- Children understand how people lived and enjoyed their lives in different historical times.
- An appreciation of the universality of human needs across history is developed.
- Children learn about their own ethnic or national heritage.
- Readers acquire a sense of time and, gradually, a sense that history is stories of what happened in the past.
- Readers develop greater interest in the study of social studies—history, geography, and anthropology.

Evaluation and Selection of Historical Fiction

Historical fiction must first be evaluated for its story strength. It must tell an engaging story. The author must develop rounded, complex characters with whom children can identify. The author should also develop a universal theme that is worthy and thought provoking, without becoming didactic. In addition, the author of historical fiction must present historical facts with as much accuracy and objectivity as books of history. This means that a setting must be described in sufficient detail as to provide an authentic sense of that time and that place without overwhelming the story. Details such as hair and clothing styles, home architecture and furnishings, foods and food preparation, and modes of transportation must be subtly woven into the story to provide a convincing, authentic period setting. The characters must act within the traditions and norms of their times.

Expressing the language or dialect of the period presents a particular challenge to the author of historical stories. Dialogue that occurs within the text often becomes problematic for the writer. If the speech of the period is greatly different from today, then the author faces a decision: remain true to the language of the time but cause readers difficulties in comprehending, or present the language in today's dialect but lose the flavor and authenticity of the language of the period. In any case, it seems important that the language not jar the reader by its obvious inappropriateness, nor lose the reader by its extreme difficulty. Most children's authors strive to attain the middle ground—some flavor of a language difference but modified in order to be understandable to the child reader. Young listeners adapt easily to dialects when they are modeled well by their teachers, and may even find occasion to use the dialect to lend flavor to their subsequent writing.

In summary, the criteria for evaluating historical fiction are

- An engrossing story with well-developed characters
- An interesting plot
- Worthy but subtle themes
- An authentic, well-described setting that informs the reader but does not overwhelm the story

- Historical accuracy in describing places, events and facts, morals, manners, customs, and behaviors of the people

The Scott O'Dell Award, an award established in 1981 by the author Scott O'Dell and administered by the *Bulletin of the Center for Children's Books,* honors what is judged to be the most outstanding work of children's historical fiction published in the previous year. The work must be written by a U.S. citizen and be set in the New World. The list of the Scott O'Dell Award winners found in Appendix A can be a source for selecting outstanding historical fiction for use with students. The National Council of Social Studies publishes a list of the most notable trade books in the field of social studies from the preceding year in a fall issue of its journal, *Social Education.* This list includes many works of historical fiction, as well as nonfiction works, and is a useful source to locate recent books of this genre.

Early Books and Trends in Historical Fiction

Although historical stories were written for children as early as the 1800s, few titles remain of interest from those early years. The early books placed an emphasis on exciting events and idealized real-life characters—much in the style of heroic legends. Howard Pyle's works were an exception to this pattern. Two of his historical novels, *Otto of the Silver Hand* (1888) and *Men of Iron* (1891), set in the Middle Ages, approach in quality many of the more recent works. However, few other stories written prior to World War I had memorable characters presented as well-rounded, complex individuals. Most of these stories seem unconvincing today.

Between World War I and World War II, historical stories appeared in which well-developed characters involved in realistic events were portrayed in authentic period settings. In 1928, Eric Kelly won the Newbery Medal for the *The Trumpeter of Krakow,* set in Poland in the Middle Ages. This exciting adventure features two children who outwit the Tartars who have captured one of their fathers. From the 1930s, a few truly remarkable books remain popular with children today. *Calico Bush* (1931) by Rachel Field tells the story of Marguerite Ledoux, a French servant girl who settles in Maine in 1743. Between 1932 and 1943, the first eight books of the *Little House* series by Laura Ingalls Wilder were published. These stories have continued to grow in popularity, partially as a result of the long-lasting television series based on the books. *Caddie Woodlawn* by Carol Ryrie Brink tells the story of Caddie, a tomboy growing up in Wisconsin during the 1860s; this story was first published in 1936 and is still read with enjoyment by children today. *Johnny Tremain* by Esther Forbes was awarded the Newbery Award in 1944. This Revolutionary era novel is considered a children's classic.

After World War II, we saw a flowering of historical fiction for children in both English and American literature. Many outstanding books were published in the 15 years following World War II. Examples are *The Door in the Wall* by Marguerite deAngeli, published in 1949; *The Buffalo Knife* by William O. Steele, published in 1952; *The Courage of Sarah Noble* by Alice Dalgliesh, published in 1954; *The Sword in the Tree* by Clyde Robert Bulla, published in 1956; *Calico Captive,* published in 1957, and *The Witch of Blackbird Pond,* published in 1958, by Elizabeth George Speare; *The Cabin Faced West* by Jean Fritz, published in 1958; and *The Lantern Bearers* by Rosemary Sutcliff, published in 1959. In 1954, the Laura Ingalls Wilder Award was awarded to (and named for) Laura Ingalls Wilder, an author of historical fiction. This award, the "Hall of Fame" of children's authors and illustrators, honors an author or illustrator whose books, published in the United States, have made a substantial and lasting contribution to children's literature. By 1960, the genre of historical fiction was well established as a fine resource for children's enjoyment and enrichment. Milestones in the development of historical fiction are highlighted in Table 8–1.

Historical fiction continues to flourish today. Minority authors have written a number of excellent works based on the early experiences of their cultural groups in North America; for example, see *Song of the Trees* and its sequels by Mildred Taylor and *Journey to Topaz* and its sequel by Yoshiko Uchida. Of special note are also many outstanding, recently published books set during the years leading up to and including World War II. The establishment in 1981 of the Scott O'Dell Award for Historical Fiction has begun to offer additional recognition for authors of this genre. In 1989, Elizabeth George Speare was selected to receive the Laura Ingalls Wilder Award for the entire body of her work, which comprises four outstanding works of historical fiction for children.

Topics in Historical Fiction

Two ways of considering the topics treated in historical fiction novels are by the universal themes presented in the books and by the historical periods in which the books are set. First, some *common themes* that can be found within historical fiction novels for children are suggested with titles of books in which the theme is developed. Next, six *historical periods* in which historical fiction novels can be found are reviewed in capsule form.

Themes in Historical Fiction

Common themes that extend across time and place in historical stories can be an approach for presenting historical fiction to children. For example, a theme, such as seeking new frontiers, is explored through a small group of books set in different times and places. Some possible themes for development in this manner are listed below with suggestions of books that might be selected for the study of the theme. Other themes may be discovered when you read historical fiction novels and consider the commonalities to be found among them.

TABLE 8–1   Milestones in the Development of Historical Fiction

Date	Event	Significance
1888	*Otto of the Silver Hand* by Howard Pyle	Early recognized work of historical fiction
1928	The Newbery Award given to *The Trumpeter of Krakow* by Eric Kelly	National recognition for an early work of historical fiction
1932–1943	Publication of the first eight books of the *Little House* series by Laura Ingalls Wilder	Classic historical fiction
1944	*Johnny Tremain* by Esther Forbes given the Newbery Award	Classic historic adventure set during the American Revolution era
1949–1960	Many historical novels published, including *The Door in the Wall,* by Marguerite de Angeli, *Witch of Blackbird Pond* by Elizabeth George Speare, *The Lantern Bearers* by Rosemary Sutcliff	Dramatic increase in the quality and quantity of historical novels for children
1954	Establishment of the Laura Ingalls Wilder Award, first awarded to Wilder	Recognition of an historical fiction author for the entire body of her historical fiction work
1961	Scott O'Dell's *Island of the Blue Dolphins* awarded the Newbery Medal	Landmark book of historical fiction with a strong female protagonist from a minority culture
1962	Scott O'Dell awarded the Hans Christian Andersen Prize	International recognition of a U.S. author of historical novels
1971	*Journey to Topaz* by Yoshiko Uchida	Early historical work about and by a minority—Japanese American
1975	*The Song of the Trees* by Mildred Taylor	First in a series of story books about an African-American family's struggle starting in the Depression era
1981	Establishment of the Scott O'Dell Award	Award given for an outstanding historical novel set in North America brings recognition to the genre
1989	Elizabeth George Speare awarded the Laura Ingalls Wilder Award	Recognition of an author of historical fiction for her substantial contribution to children's literature

Seeking New Frontiers

The Cabin Faced West by Jean Fritz.
Little House in the Big Woods by Laura Ingalls Wilder.
Wagon Wheels by Barbara Brenner.
Beyond the Divide by Kathryn Lasky.
The Far-off Land by Rebecca Caudill.
On to Oregon by Honoré Morrow.

Search for Freedom from Persecution

Jump Ship to Freedom by James Lincoln Collier and Christopher Collier.
The Island on Bird Street by Uri Orlev.
The Upstairs Room by Johanna Reiss.
The Wild Children by Felice Holman.
Sing Down the Moon by Scott O'Dell.
The Endless Steppe by Esther Hautzig.
The Witch of Blackbird Pond by Elizabeth George Speare.

Effects of War

My Brother Sam Is Dead by James Lincoln Collier and Christopher Collier.
Zoar Blue by Janet Hickman.
Across Five Aprils by Irene Hunt.
Summer of My German Soldier by Bette Greene.
Shades of Gray by Carolyn Reeder.

Family Closeness in Times of Adversity

Journey Home by Yoshiko Uchida.
Journey to America by Sonia Levitin.
Roll of Thunder, Hear My Cry by Mildred Taylor.
Upon the Head of the Goat by Aranka Siegal.
Sounder by William H. Armstrong.

Periods of History in Fiction

The natural relationship of historical fiction stories to the study of history and geography suggests building whole units of study around periods of both world and U.S. history in which good stories for children are set. The following capsule statements on six historical periods will give you an idea of how this might be organized. At the end of the chapter (under Recommended Books), you will find works of historical fiction organized by these six historical periods.

Beginnings of Civilization up to 3,000 B.C.

This period represents prehistoric cultures and civilizations. Early peoples (Java, Neanderthals, Cro-Magnons) and early civilizations in the Middle East and Asia are included. Egyptians, Syrians, and Phoenicians developed civilizations, and Hebrews produced a religious faith, Judaism, that resulted in the Old Testament. The subcontinent of India was the site of Aryan civilizations. Chinese dynasties were responsible for excellent works of art and agricultural systems of irrigation.

Civilizations of the Ancient World, 3,000 B.C. to A.D. 600

The Greek city-states are followed by a period of Roman rule in western Europe. Christianity was founded in Jerusalem and spread throughtout Europe. Ancient Asia was the site of enduring civilizations that bred two remarkable men born about A.D. 560: the Indian religious leader, Buddha, and the Chinese philosopher, Confucius. Both had a lasting influence on their civilizations.

Civilizations of the Medieval World, 600 to 1500

The eastern part of the Roman Empire maintained its stability and preserved the civilization from the capital of Constantinople. This civilization, the Byzantine Empire, created a distinct culture and branch of the Christian Church—the Orthodox Church—which influenced Russia to adopt both the religion and the culture. Following the fall of the Roman Empire, western Europe dissolved into isolated separate regions without strong governments. Many of the responsibilities of government were carried out by the Christian Church. The Church dominated the economic, political, cultural, and educational life of the Middle Ages in western Europe. These feudal societies eventually gave rise to the separate nations of modern Europe. During this era, early African and American civilizations arose independently. The great civilizations of China and Japan continued to flourish throughout these centuries.

Emergence of Modern Nations, 1500 to 1800

The Renaissance, a literary and artistic movement, swept western Europe. Many important developments of this period included the invention of the printing press, a new emphasis on reason, a reformation of the Christian Church, and advances in science. During this same period, central governments throughout Europe increased their power. Spain, then France, dominated Europe in the 1500s and 1600s. In the 1700s, Russia, Austria, and Prussia rose to power. This was also a time when Europeans explored and settled in Africa, India, and the Americas. The Portuguese and Spanish took the lead in explorations and acquired many foreign colonies. England, the Netherlands, France, and Russia also colonized and influenced East Asia, India, Africa, and the Americas.

Revolutions created new governments and new nations. The American Revolution (1776–1781) created a new nation; the French Revolution in 1789 affected the direction of governments toward democracy in all of Europe. Napoleon built an empire across Europe, resulting in the uniting of European nations to defeat Napoleon. The nations of Latin America also began to gain their independence. China expanded gradually under the Ming and Ch'ing dynasties. Japan prospered under the Tokugawa shogunate. The United States and Canada were the sites of rapid population increases due to immigration; the settlements in North America were predominantly along the eastern coasts. Some westward expansion was beginning in the United States and Canada.

Development of Industrial Society, 1800 to 1914

The 1800s were marked by a rapid shift from agricultural societies to industrial societies. Great Britain was an early site for this change. The factory system developed and prospered, while working and living conditions deteriorated for the worker. New technology—railroad trains, steamboats, the telegraph and telephone—affected transportation and communications. Advances in science and medicine helped explain the nature of life and improved the quality of life. Education developed into an important institution in western Europe and North America. Europe underwent revolutions that readjusted boundaries and eventually led to the unification of new nations.

The westward movement was fully realized as pioneers settled across the United States and Canada. The building of railroads hastened the establishment of new settlements. Native Americans struggled for survival in the face of these massive population shifts. Black slavery had existed in the American colonies from earliest days, but in the 1800s, slavery became a social and economic issue resulting in the Civil War (1861–1865). Slavery was abolished and the Union was preserved at the cost of 600,000 lives and a major rift between the North and the South.

The United States grew in economic and political strength. An age of imperialism resulted in firm control of large areas of the world by other world powers such as England, France, and Belgium. Great Britain dominated India, parts of Africa, and continued its influence over Canada, Australia, and New Zealand, while Japan became a powerful force in east Asia.

World Wars in the Twentieth Century, 1914 to 1945

This era includes World War I (1914–1918) in Europe, in which the United States and Canada joined and fought with the Allies (Great Britain, France, Russia, Greece, and Rumania); the between-wars period that included the Great Depression; Hitler's rise to power in 1933; and World War II (1939–1945) in Europe and Asia, in which Canada and the United States joined forces with England, France, and Russia to battle Germany, Italy, and Japan. In 1917, the Bolshevik Revolution established a communist government in Russia. In 1931, Great Britain recognized Canada, Australia, New Zealand, and South Africa as completely independent. However, each nation declared its loyalty to the British monarch and continued its cultural ties with Great Britain. The Holocaust during World War II—the persecution and killing of Jewish and other people by the Nazi regime—stands out as one of the most atrocious periods in modern history.

Many fine works of historical fiction for children can now be found. Children have an opportunity to live vicariously the lives of people from long ago—people from different cultures and from different parts of the world.

Reference

Adamson, L. G. (1987). *A reference guide to historical fiction for children and young adults*. Westport, CT: Greenwood Press.

Notable Authors of Historical Fiction

Patricia Beatty, author of U.S. and British historical novels. *Hail Columbia; Turn Homeward, Hannalee.*

Patricia Clapp, author of novels set in U.S. colonial and Revolutionary War eras. *I'm Deborah Sampson: A Soldier in the War of the Revolution.*

James Lincoln Collier and Christopher Collier, authors of novels set in U.S. Revolutionary War era. *My Brother Sam Is Dead.*

Esther Forbes, author of 1944 Newbery Award winner, *Johnny Tremain,* set in U.S. Revolutionary War period.

Erik Christian Haugaard, author of historical novels set in many different eras, including the Viking explorations and England in the Middle Ages. *Messenger for Parliament.*

Mollie Hunter, Scottish writer whose novels are set in early Scotland. *The Stronghold.*

Scott O'Dell, author of many stories based on Native-American and Mexican-American cultures. *Island of the Blue Dolphins.*

Hans Peter Richter, author of holocaust novels set in Germany during World War II. *Friedrich.*

Elizabeth George Speare, winner of Scott O'Dell, Newbery, and Laura Ingalls Wilder Awards for her works of historical fiction. *The Sign of the Beaver.*

Rosemary Sutcliff, English author of many memorable books recreating the early history of England. *Song for a Dark Queen.*

Mildred Taylor, author of seven stories of an African-American land-owning family, beginning in the 1930s and set in rural Mississippi. *Roll of Thunder, Hear My Cry.*

Yoshiko Uchida, author of historical novels about the life of Japanese Americans during the Depression and during and immediately following World War II. *Journey to Topaz.*

Laura Ingalls Wilder, author of *Little House* series based on the Ingalls family experiences as pioneers in the Midwest.

Laurence Yep, author of historical fiction about Chinese Americans and their adjustments to life in the United States. *Dragonwings.*

Alki Zei, author of international historical novels set in Greece, three books of which have won the Batchelder Award. *The Sound of Dragon's Feet.*

Recommended Historical Fiction Books

Ages refer to approximate interest levels. YA = young adult readers. Locales and dates of settings are noted.

Beginnings of Civilization up to 3000 B.C.

Behn, Harry. *The Faraway Lurs.* World, 1963. Ages 12–15. Northern Europe, 3500 B.C.

Linevski, A. *An Old Tale Carved Out of Stone.* Translated by Maria Polushkin. Crown, 1973. Ages 10–14. Early Siberia.

Osborne, Chester. *The Memory String.* Atheneum, 1984. Ages 8–12. Siberian Peninsula, 25,000 B.C.

Steele, William O. *The Magic Amulet.* Harcourt, 1979. Ages 10–14. North America, 10,000 B.C.

Treece, Henry. *The Dream-Time.* Meredith, 1968. Ages 11–14. British Isles, 11,000 B.C..

Wibberley, Leonard. *Attar of the Ice Valley.* Farrar, 1968. Ages 11–YA. Europe, 50,000 B.C.

Civilizations of the Ancient World, 3000 B.C. to A.D. 600

Hunter, Mollie. *The Stronghold.* Harper, 1974. Ages 9–12. British Isles, 100 B.C.

McGraw, Eloise Jarvis. *Mara, Daughter of the Nile.* Penguin, 1953. Ages 11–YA. Ancient Egypt, 1550 B.C.

Paton Walsh, Jill. *Children of the Fox.* Farrar, 1978. Ages 10–14. Ancient Persia, 400 B.C.

Speare, Elizabeth George. *The Bronze Bow*. Houghton, 1961. Ages 10–14. Jerusalem, A.D. 30.

Sutcliff, Rosemary. *Song for a Dark Queen*. Crowell, 1978. Ages 10–14. British Isles, A.D. 50.

———. *Sun Horse, Moon Horse*. Dutton, 1978. Ages 10–14. British Isles, 100 B.C.

Civilizations of the Medieval World, 600 to 1500

Bulla, Clyde Robert. *Viking Adventure*. Crowell, 1963. Ages 7–10. Norway, 900s.

De Angeli, Marguerite. *The Door in the Wall*. Doubleday, 1949. Ages 9–12. England, 1300s.

Haugaard, Erik Christian. *Hakon of Rogen's Saga*. Houghton, 1963. Ages 9–12. Vikings, 900s.

Kelly, Eric. *The Trumpeter of Krakow*. Macmillan, 1928. Ages 11–14. Poland, 1400s.

Skurzynski, Gloria. *Manwolf*. Houghton, 1981. Ages 10–14. Poland, 1380s.

———. *What Happened in Hamelin*. Four Winds, 1979. Ages 10–14. Germany, 1200s.

Stolz, Mary. *Pangur Ban*. Harper, 1988. Ages 11–14. Ireland, 800s, 1100s.

The Emergence of Modern Nations, 1500 to 1800

Avi. *The Fighting Ground*. Lippincott, 1984. Ages 10–14. U.S. Revolutionary War era, 1770s.

———. *Night Journeys*. Pantheon, 1979. Ages 8–11. U.S. colonial era, 1770s.

Caudill, Rebecca. *The Far-off Land*. Viking, 1964. Ages 11–14. U.S. frontier, 1780s.

Clapp, Patricia. *Constance: A Story of Early Plymouth*. Lothrop, 1968. Ages 10–14. U.S. colonial era, 1620s.

———. *I'm Deborah Sampson: A Soldier in the War of the Revolution*. Lothrop, 1977. Ages 9–12. U.S., 1770s.

———. *Witches' Children: A Story of Salem*. Lothrop, 1982. Ages 10–YA. U.S. colonial era, 1690s.

Collier, James Lincoln, and Christopher Collier. *Jump Ship to Freedom*. Delacorte, 1981. Ages 9–12. U.S. slavery, 1780s.

———. *My Brother Sam Is Dead*. Four Winds, 1974. Ages 10–14. U.S. Revolutionary War era, 1770s.

———. *War Comes to Willy Freeman*. Delacorte, 1983. Ages 9–12. U.S., African Americans, 1780s.

Colver, Anne. *Bread-and-Butter Journey*. Holt, 1970. Ages 7–10. U.S. pioneers, 1780s.

Dalgliesh, Alice. *The Courage of Sarah Noble*. Scribner's, 1954. Ages 7–9. U.S. pioneers, early 1700s.

Fleischman, Paul. *Saturnalia*. Harper, 1990. Ages 12–YA. Boston, Narraganset Indians, 1680s.

Forbes, Esther. *Johnny Tremain*. Houghton, 1943. Ages 10–13. U.S. Revolutionary War era, 1770s.

Fritz, Jean. *The Cabin Faced West*. Coward, 1958. Ages 7–10. U.S. pioneers, 1700s.

Gauch, Patricia. *This Time, Tempe Wick?* Coward, 1974. Ages 7–10. U.S. Revolutionary War era, 1780s.

Haugaard, Erik Christian. *A Messenger for Parliament*. Houghton, 1976. Ages 10–14. England, 1640s.

Hunter, Mollie. *The 13th Member*. Harper, 1971. Ages 12–YA. Scotland, 1500s.

O'Dell, Scott. *The Captive*. Houghton, 1979. Ages 10–14. Mexico, 1500s.

———. *Sarah Bishop*. Houghton, 1980. Ages 10–14. U.S. Revolutionary War era, 1770s.

Petry, Ann. *Tituba of Salem Village*. Crowell, 1964. Ages 10–14. U.S. colonial era, 1690s.

Speare, Elizabeth George. *The Sign of the Beaver*. Houghton, 1983. Ages 8–12. Maine frontier, 1700s.

———. *The Witch of Blackbird Pond*. Houghton, 1958. Ages 10–14. U.S. colonial era, 1680s.

Sutcliff, Rosemary. *Bonnie Dundee*. Dutton, 1984. Ages 10–14. Scotland, 1600s.

The Development of Industrial Society, 1800 to 1914

Aiken, Joan. *The Teeth of the Gale*. Harper, 1988. Ages 9–YA. Spain, 1820s.

Angell, Judie. *One-Way to Ansonia*. Bradbury, 1985. Ages 10–YA. U.S. immigrants, 1890s.

Armstrong, William H. *Sounder*. Harper, 1969. Ages 9–12. U.S. South, African Americans, early 1900s.

Avi. *The True Confessions of Charlotte Doyle*. Orchard, 1990. Ages 8–12. England, United States, 1830s.

Beatty, Patricia. *Charley Skedaddle*. Morrow, 1987. Ages 11–14. U.S. Civil War, 1860s.

————. *Jayhawker.* Morrow, 1991. Ages 10–14. Kansas, slavery, underground railroad, 1800s.

————. *Turn Homeward, Hannalee.* Morrow, 1984. Ages 10–14. U.S. Civil War, 1860s.

Bilson, Geoffrey. *Death over Montreal.* Kids Can Press, 1982. Ages 8–11. Scotland, Canada, 1830s.

Blos, Joan. *A Gathering of Days: A New England Girl's Journal,* 1830–32. Scribner's, 1979. Ages 7–11. U.S. frontier, 1830s.

Brandis, Marianne. *The Tinderbox.* Porcupine's Quill, 1982. Ages 11–14. Canada, 1830s.

Brenner, Barbara. *Wagon Wheels.* Harper, 1978. Ages 7–9. U.S. pioneers, African Americans, 1870s.

Brink, Carol Ryrie. *Caddie Woodlawn.* Macmillan, 1935. Ages 8–11. Wisconsin frontier, 1860s.

Conrad, Pam. *Prairie Songs.* Harper, 1985. Ages 10–14. Nebraska, late 1800s.

De Felice, Cynthia. *Weasel.* Macmillan, 1990. Ages 9–12. Ohio frontier, 1830s.

Fleischman, Paul. *The Borning Room.* Harper, 1991. Ages 11–YA. Ohio farm life, 1800s.

————. *Coming-and-Going Men: Four Tales.* Illustrated by Randy Gaul. Harper, 1985. Ages 11–YA. Vermont, 1800.

Fox, Paula. *The Slave Dancer.* Bradbury, 1973. Ages 11–YA. U.S. slave trade, 1840s.

Fritz, Jean. *Brady.* Coward, 1960. Ages 9–12. Pennysylvania, slavery, 1830s.

German, Tony. *A Breed Apart.* McClelland and Stewart, 1985. Ages 11–YA. Canadian Northwest, early 1800s.

Hamilton, Virginia. *The Bells of Christmas.* Illustrated by Lambert Davis. Harcourt, 1989. Ages 8–11. Ohio, African Americans, 1890s.

Hansen, Joyce. *Which Way Freedom?* Walker, 1986. Ages 11–YA. U.S., slavery, Civil War era.

Harris, Christie. *Cariboo Trail.* Longman, 1957. Ages 12–14. U.S., Minnesota, western Canada, 1860s.

Harvey, Brett. *Cassie's Journey: Going West in the 1860's.* Illustrated by Deborah Kogan Ray. Holiday, 1988. Ages 7–9. U.S. frontier, 1860s.

Hickman, Janet. *Zoar Blue.* Macmillan, 1978. Ages 9–12. U.S. Civil War era, 1860s.

Highwater, Jamake. *Legend Days.* Harper, 1984. Ages 10–YA. U.S., Northern Plains Indians, 1800s.

Holman, Felice. *The Wild Children.* Scribner's, 1983. Ages 9–12. Russia, early 1900s.

Hudson, Jan. *Sweetgrass.* Tree Frog Press, 1984; Philomel, 1989. Ages 11–YA. Canada, Dakota Indians, 1830s.

Hunt, Irene. *Across Five Aprils.* Follett, 1964. Ages 10–YA. U.S. Civil War era, 1860s.

Lasky, Kathryn. *Beyond the Divide.* Macmillan, 1983. Ages 12–YA. U.S. frontier, mid-1800s.

————. *The Night Journey.* Warne, 1981. Ages 10–14. Russia, United States, early 1900s.

Lunn, Janet. *Shadow in Hawthorn Bay.* Scribner's, 1986/Dennys, 1986. Ages 12–YA. Canada frontier, early 1800s.

MacLachlan, Patricia. *Sarah, Plain and Tall.* Harper, 1985. Ages 7–10. U.S. frontier, 1850s.

Moeri, Louise. *Save Queen of Sheba.* Dutton, 1981. Ages 9–12. U.S. frontier, 1800s.

Monjo, F. N. *The Drinking Gourd.* Harper, 1970. Ages 6–9. New England, underground railroad, 1850s.

Morrow, Honoré. *On to Oregon!* Morrow, 1954. Ages 9–12. U.S. frontier, 1840s.

O'Dell, Scott. *Island of the Blue Dolphins.* Houghton, 1960. Ages 10–14. Pacific island, Native Americans, mid-1800s.

————. *Sing Down the Moon.* Houghton, 1970. U. S., Navajo Indians, 1860s.

Paterson, Katherine. *Lyddie.* Dutton, 1991. Ages 12–YA. Massachusetts, mill life, mid-1800s.

Pullman, Philip. *The Ruby in the Smoke.* Knopf, 1987. Ages 14–YA. London, 1800s.

Reeder, Carolyn. *Shades of Gray.* Macmillan, 1989. Ages 9–12. U.S. Civil War era, 1860s.

Smucker, Barbara. *Underground to Canada.* Clarke Irwin, 1977. Ages 12–YA. Canada, Ontario, 1800s.

Turner, Ann. *Grasshopper Summer.* Macmillan, 1989. Ages 9–12. U.S., Kentucky to Dakota Territory, 1870s.

Wilder, Laura Ingalls. *Little House in the Big Woods.* Harper, 1932. Ages 7–10. Wisconsin frontier, 1800s.

Yep, Laurence. *Dragonwings.* Harper, 1979. Ages 9–12. California, early 1900s.

————. *The Serpent's Children.* Harper, 1984. Ages 9–12. China, 1830s.

Zei, Alki. *The Sound of Dragon's Feet.* Dutton, 1979. Ages 10–14. Russia, late 1800s.

World Wars in the Twentieth Century, 1914 to 1945

Bawden, Nina. *Henry*. Illustrated by Joyce Powzyk. Lothrop, 1988. Ages 9–12. England, World War II era.

Chang, Margaret, and Raymond Chang. *In the Eye of the War*. Macmillan, 1990. Ages 10–12. China, World War II.

DeJong, Meindert. *House of Sixty Fathers*. Harper, 1956. Ages 8–12. China, World War II.

Frank, Rudolf. *No Hero for the Kaiser*. Translated by Patricia Crampton. Illustrated by Klaus Steffens. Lothrop, 1986 (originally published in 1931). Ages 10–YA. Poland, World War I.

Garrigue, Sheila. *The Eternal Spring of Mr. Ito*. Bradbury, 1985. Ages 8–11. Canada, Japanese-Canadian internment, World War II.

Greene, Bette. *Summer of My German Soldier*. Dial, 1973. U.S., World War II.

Hahn, Mary Downing. *Stepping on the Cracks*. Clarion, 1991. Ages 10–13. U.S., Maryland, World War II.

Hautzig, Esther. *The Endless Steppe*. Harper, 1968. Ages 10–14. Russia, Jews, World War II.

Heuck, Sigrid. *The Hideout*. Translated from the German by Rika Lesser. Dutton, 1988. Ages 9–12. Germany, Jews, World War II.

Hooks, William H. *Circle of Fire*. Atheneum, 1982. Ages 9–12. Rural North Carolina, Ku Klux Klan, 1930s.

Hughes, Monica. *Blaine's Way*. Irwin, 1986. Ages 12–YA. Canada, World War II.

Hunter, Bernice Thurman. *That Scatterbrain Booky*. Scholastic–TAB, 1981. Ages 12–YA. Canada, Depression, 1930s.

Kogawa, Joy. *Naomi's Road*. Oxford, 1986. Ages 9–12. Canada, British Columbia, Japanese Canadian internment, World War II.

Levitin, Sonia. *Journey to America*. Atheneum, 1970. Ages 10–14. Germany, Jews, World War II era.

Little, Jean. *From Anna*. Harper, 1972. Ages 9–12. Canada, 1930s. Germany, Canada, 1930s.

Lowry, Lois. *Number the Stars*. Houghton, 1989. Ages 8–12. Denmark, World War II.

Lyon, George Ella. *Borrowed Children*. Watts, 1988. Ages 10–14. Kentucky, Depression era, 1930s.

Magorian, Michelle. *Good Night, Mr. Tom*. Harper, 1982. Ages 11–14. England, World War II.

Matas, Carol. *Lisa's War*. Scribner's, 1989. Ages 10–13. Denmark, Jews, World War II.

Morpurgo, Michael. *Waiting for Anya*. Viking, 1991. Ages 10–14. Southern France, Jews, World War II.

Orlev, Uri. *The Island on Bird Street*. Translated from the Hebrew by Hillel Halkin. Houghton, 1983. Ages 9–13. Poland, Jews, World War II.

———. *The Man from the Other Side*. Translated from the Hebrew by Hillel Halkin. Houghton, 1991. Ages 12–YA. Poland, Jews, World War II.

Paulsen, Gary. *The Cookcamp*. Orchard, 1991. Ages 10–13. U.S., road crew, World War II.

Pelgrom, Els. *The Winter When Time Was Frozen*. Translated from the Dutch by Maryka and Rafael Rudnik. Morrow, 1980. Ages 9–12. Holland, World War II.

Reiss, Johanna. *The Upstairs Room*. Crowell, 1972. Ages 10–14. Holland, Jews, World War II.

Richter, Hans Peter. *Friedrich*. Translated from the German by Edite Kroll. Holt, 1970. Ages 10–14. Germany, Jews, World War II.

Siegal, Aranka. *Upon the Head of the Goat: A Childhood in Hungary 1939–44*. Farrar, 1981. Ages 12–YA. Hungary, World War II.

Taylor, Mildred. *Road to Memphis*. Dial, 1990. Ages 12–YA. U.S. South, African Americans, 1941.

———. *Roll of Thunder, Hear My Cry*. Dial, 1976. Ages 10–14. U.S. South, African Americans, 1930s.

———. *Let the Circle Be Unbroken*. Dial, 1981. Ages 10–14. U.S. South, African Americans, 1930s.

Taylor, Theodore. *The Cay*. Doubleday, 1969. Ages 8–12. Caribbean, World War II era.

Uchida, Yoshiko. *Journey to Topaz*. Illustrated by Donald Carrick. Scribner's, 1971. Ages 10–14. U.S., internment of Japanese Americans, World War II.

Vos, Ida. *Hide and Seek*. Translated from the Dutch by Terese Edelstein and Inez Smidt. Houghton, 1991. Ages 9–13. Jews, World War II.

Westall, Robert. *The Kingdom by the Sea*. Farrar, 1991. Ages 10–13. England, World War II.

Zei, Alki. *Petros' War*. Translated from the Greek by Edward Fenton. Dutton, 1972. Ages 12–YA. Greece, World War II.

————. *Wildcat Under Glass.* Translated from the Greek by Edward Fenton. Holt, 1968. Ages 11–YA. Greece, 1930s.

Post-World War II Era, 1946 to 1960s

Bauer, Marion Dane. *Rain of Fire.* Clarion, 1983. Ages 10–13. U.S., post–World War II era.

de Jenkins, Lyll Becerra. *The Honorable Prison.* Lodestar, 1988. Ages 12–YA. South America, 1950s.

Doyle, Brian. *Angel Square.* Groundwood Books, 1984. Ages 9–12. Canada, Ottawa, post-World War II.

Härtling, Peter. *Crutches.* Translated from the German by Elizabeth D. Crawford. Lothrop, 1988. Ages 9–14. Austria, post-World War II.

Hewitt, Marsha, and Claire MacKay. *One Proud Summer.* Women's Press, 1981. Ages 10–YA. Canada, Quebec, 1946.

Sacks, Margaret. *Beyond Safe Boundaries.* Lodestar, 1989. Ages 12–YA. South Africa, Jews. 1960s.

Slepian, Jan. *Risk n' Roses.* Putnam, 1990. Ages 11–14. Bronx, New York, 1948.

Talbert, Marc. *The Purple Heart.* HarperCollins, 1992. Ages 10–13. U.S., Vietnam War era.

Uchida, Yoshiko. *Journey Home.* Illustrated by Charles Robinson. Atheneum, 1978. Ages 10–13. U.S., Japanese Americans, post-World War II.

Chapter 9

Nonfiction

Questions at Night

Why
Is the sky?

What starts the thunder overhead?
Who makes the crashing noise?
Are the angels falling out of bed?
Are they breaking all their toys?

Why does the sun go down so soon?
Why do the night-clouds crawl
Hungrily up to the new-laid moon
And swallow it, shell and all?

If there's a bear among the stars,
As all the people say,
Won't he jump over those pasture-bars
And drink up the Milky Way?

Does every star that happens to fall
Turn into a firefly?
Can't it ever get back to Heaven at all?
And why
Is the sky?

—Louis Untermeyer

Children are naturally curious. Their interest in the world around them is boundless. Teachers, librarians, and parents want to nourish that curiosity with lively, intelligent answers and provocative questions. But as modern science continues to open up the world to investigation and to provide massive amounts of new information almost daily, those who guide children's learning quickly find that they need help in answering children's many questions. Nonfiction books are an excellent source of information for children and the adults who guide their learning.

Definition and Description

By now it should be understood that in children's literature there are no absolute genre definitions. For example, nonfiction for children is not limited to works containing only facts. Instead, this genre can best be defined in terms of emphasis. The content emphasis of children's nonfiction is documented fact; its primary purpose is to inform. In contrast, the content of fictional literature is largely, if not wholly, a product of the imagination, and the purpose is to entertain. Because of the emphasis of its purpose, nonfiction is often called *informational literature*.

Some countries now recognize a third type of literature that has elements of both fiction and nonfiction and call it *faction*. Mogens Jansen, president of the Danish National Association of Reading Teachers, describes *faction* as "'nonfiction' the presentation of which is mainly sustained by 'fiction elements': the well-told nonfiction which has fictional overtones, but *is* nonfictional—and absolutely correct" (Jansen, 1987, p. 16).

Although North America has not designated faction as an independent genre, but considers it a part of nonfiction, adults who deal with books and children are well aware of this type of literature and its appeal to 8- to 12-year-old boys, in particular. Today a great number of books present factual information on a ribbon of narrative. Examples are *Cathedral* by David Macaulay and *My Place in Space* by Robin and Sally Hirst, illustrated by Roland Harvey with Joe Levine.

Nonfiction can be written on any aspect of the physical, biological, and social world, including what is known of outer space. Thus, it should come as no surprise that in most children's collections in school and public libraries well over half of the titles are nonfiction, with some estimates as high as 70 percent. In school libraries, at least, more nonfiction circulates than fiction, and informed sources say that more than half of children's books being published currently are nonfiction. Although fictional literature is better known to the general public (due to book awards and a tendency for adults to equate children's literature with stories), nonfiction is enormously popular with children as recreational reading material.

Some comment on the formats of nonfiction books is in order. Book format has to do with how information is presented on the book page, rather than with the information itself. Any topic could conceivably be presented in a number of different ways. The most common distinct formats in which informational books for children are currently being produced are as follows:

- *Nonfiction chapter book.* This format, widely used in nonfiction, features a large amount of text that is organized into chapters. Graphics and illustrations are common in the more recent nonfiction chapter books but are still less important than the text. Almost all biographies, with the exception of picture book biographies, appear in this format. Examples include *Rescue: The Story of How Gentiles Saved Jews in the Holocaust* by Milton Meltzer and *Amos Fortune, Free Man* by Elizabeth Yates.

- *Informational picture book.* This format features large, uncomplicated illustrations and brief text in large typeface on oversized pages. The illustrations help to convey the information. The main types of informational picture books are concept books, including ABC and counting books (discussed in Chapter 5), and picture book biographies. Examples include *A Picture Book of Eleanor Roosevelt* by David A. Adler, illustrated by Robert Casilla, and *The King's Day* by Aliki.

- *Science and social science concept picture book.* Originally conceived for 4- to 8-year-olds, this book presents one or two scientific or social concepts via brief, uncomplicated text accompanied by numerous, large illustrations. It also encourages participation by including an experiment or hands-on activity. These books are now available for older children as well. *Evolution* by Joanna Cole, illustrated by Aliki, is a good example of this type of book.

- *Photo essay.* Presentation of information in the photo essay is equally balanced between text and illustration. Excellent, information-bearing photographs, and crisp, condensed writing style are hallmarks of this nonfictional format. Photo essays are generally written for children in the intermediate grades and up. Examples include *Lincoln: A Photobiography* by Russell Freedman and *The American Family Farm* by George Ancona, text by Joan Anderson.

- *Fact books.* Presentation of information in these books is mainly through lists, charts, and tables. Examples include almanacs, books of world records, and sports trivia and statistics books. For example, see *The Guinness Book of World Records* published annually by Sterling Publishing Company.

Values of Nonfiction for Children

When the best nonfictional literature is shared regularly with children, the ultimate benefit to them is that they acquire a love of learning. In addition, the following important values of children's nonfiction are worth considering.

- High-quality nonfiction provides accurate information in understandable and interesting language and illustrations, proving to children that learning can be enjoyable.
- Nonfiction provides children with a ready source of factual information about their personal questions, interests, hobbies, and problems.
- Nonfiction can be an excellent resource for content area classes, providing varied sources of information about topics and different points of view about issues.

- The best nonfiction offers students excellent models of the scientific method of observation, hypothesis formulation, data gathering, experimentation, and evaluation.
- Well-written biographies can inspire children to overcome obstacles and formulate goals and can help them to understand and accept themselves and others.

Teachers stand to benefit from good nonfiction as much as children, if they use it as a resource for their content area teaching. It stands to reason that the examples, anecdotes, and interesting facts chosen by world-class researchers and writers might add considerably to most teachers' presentations. Besides, good teaching demands that classroom resources not be confined to the single point of view and selective coverage offered by the average school textbook. It is much more interesting and instructive for children to be presented with a variety of resources to be read, heard, or seen, and then discussed and compared.

Evaluation and Selection of Nonfiction

Criteria for evaluating children's nonfiction bear some similarity to those for evaluating fiction, since authors of both kinds of literature have stories to tell. In nonfiction, however, the story must be true; for this reason, evaluation and selection of nonfiction present challenges not met when evaluating other genres of children's literature.

The criteria listed below will help you to distinguish the worthier books of nonfiction from the not so worthy. However, it is important to remember that every work of nonfiction need not meet every criterion to be worthy and that no one book can cover a topic completely. By offering children a variety of satisfactory books to be read and compared, you more than compensate for the shortcomings of a good-but-not-great book.

- Children's nonfiction must be written in a clear, direct, easily understandable style. Good writing is the backbone of good informational literature. Over the years, a tight, compressed writing style has come to be favored in nonfictional text. Successful authors of nonfiction stimulate their readers' interest and involvement by using such stylistic devices as questions and the second-person pronoun *you*, as in "Have you ever wondered how chameleons change colors?" Their tone is conversational, enthusiastic, and engaging without losing sight of the fact that the pursuit of knowledge is serious. A lighter tone and humor can make learning fun, as proven by Jean Fritz in her books about U.S. Revolutionary era leaders.

Style of writing in nonfiction extends to the writing of captions for illustrations and other reference aids. Though brief, these pieces of text serve the vital function of explaining the significance of illustrations or of drawing the reader's attention to important or interesting details pictured.

- Facts must be accurate. Authors of adult nonfiction prove the accuracy of their facts through documentation by way of footnotes, reference citations, and end-of-chapter reference notes. But these devices complicate text and are decidedly unpopular with young readers. The problem for children's nonfiction book editors then becomes whether to have a readable, uncluttered text or a well-documented but less readable text. Most editors today opt for the readable text. An author's credentials have no direct relationship to his or her ability to write competently about a topic and are no guarantee that a book of nonfiction is accurate or well written. Therefore, evaluators must be careful to check the resources or resource persons used by the author as listed in the introduction, reference lists, or appendix as indicators of the book's accuracy.

Accuracy also means currency of information. A book's publication date is one indication of its currency. A more reliable check is to compare the information with that found in other recently published sources on the topic.

To be accurate, a work of nonfiction must also distinguish between fact, theory, and opinion. When not clearly stated as such, theories or opinions are flagged in good nonfiction by carefully placed phrases such as "may be," "is believed to be," or "perhaps."

From their earliest years, children enjoy stories about animals and objects that behave just as humans do. As you learned in Chapter 3, attributing human qualities to animals, material objects, or forces is called *personification* and is part of the charm of works of traditional and modern fantasy. In nonfiction, however, this same device is to be avoided, because the implication is factually inaccurate. Saying in a work of nonfiction that a horse "feels proud to carry his master" is an example of this device.

Another rhetorical device to be avoided in nonfiction is *teleology,* or giving humanlike purpose to natural phenomena. You will often hear people give Mother Nature credit for the weather or for the beauty of a landscape, and this is perfectly acceptable in our daily conversation. But to explain the forces of nature in such human terms in a work of nonfiction is unscientific.

- The book must be attractive to the child. It must look interesting and inviting enough for a child to want to find out what it has to offer. Factors contributing to the attractiveness of a work of nonfiction are the cover, quality of illustrations, balance of text and illustrations, amount and use of space on the page, and size of type. Dense text that fills up each page and dull, infrequent illustrations can make a book unattractive to young readers.

- Design and organization of the book must aid conceptual understanding and encourage analytical thinking. Judicious use of subheadings can make text much easier to read and comprehend. Reference aids such as tables of contents, indexes, pronunciation guides, glossaries, maps, charts, and tables also serve to make information in books easier to find and retrieve, more comprehensible, and more complete. In evaluating a work of nonfiction, you should ask yourself if subheadings and reference aids are needed and then whether the provided aids adequately serve their purposes and are logically placed.

Presentation of information should be from known to unknown, general to specific, or simple to more complex. Information presented in these ways is not only easier to understand but it also provides models for students' own expository writing.

• Stereotyping must be avoided both by fair and proper representation of races, religions, ethnic groups, age groups, and sexes in text and illustrations and by avoidance of sexist or racist language. Consider the following excerpt from a nonfiction trade book about the country of Italy:

> *Italian people are very varied, but there are certain marks which many of them have in common: a dark skin, lively movements and quick speech. Those who live in the north are tough, and make good businessmen. Those of the south are easygoing and less efficient. (Martin, 1966, unpaginated)*

As this passage shows, stereotyping can be committed through overgeneralization and can convey gross inaccuracies. The best nonfiction goes beyond mere avoidance of sexist or racist language and stereotyped images in text and illustrations. It also shows positive images of cultural diversity.

• Format and artistic medium should be appropriate for the content. The exactness, clarity, and precision of photography, for example, make this medium useful to authors whose purpose is to present the world as it is. Sometimes, however, a drawing is preferable to a photograph when an illustrator wishes to highlight a specific feature by omitting irrelevant details. Engineered paper or pop-up illustrations are appropriate when three dimensions are required to give an accurate sense of placement of the parts of a whole, as in human anatomy.

• Depth and complexity of subject treatment must be appropriate for the intended audience. One of your first concerns when evaluating a work of nonfiction for depth and complexity is whether the topic is covered adequately for the intended audience. All vital steps in a process should be included and various viewpoints on controversial issues should be considered. Skillful authors of nonfiction for young children are able to explain concepts in simple and understandable language. Oversimplification, however, can easily misinform. If an explanation must be simplified to the extent that facts must be altered before a child can begin to understand, perhaps the concept or topic should be taken up when the child is older.

Selecting the best of nonfiction for children can be a challenge. With an annual North American production of over 2,000 new nonfiction titles on such divergent and complicated topics as black holes and the internal combustion engine, few individuals have time to read more than a fraction of the new titles, let alone know enough about the topics to be able to judge the technical accuracy of these books. Many teachers and librarians find the following professional review sources helpful in identifying the outstanding informational books on topics of interest to them and their students.

Eyeopeners by Beverly Kobrin: A good, general introduction to children's nonfiction and an annotated list of 500 recommended informational books

The Kobrin Letter: A monthly newsletter that reviews informational books, both new and old, on selected topics

Appraisal: Children's Science Books: A quarterly periodical featuring reviews by content specialists of books with more advanced scientific content

"Outstanding Science Trade Books for Children": An annual, annotated list of notable books in the field of science

"Notable Children's Trade Books in the Field of Social Studies": An annual, annotated list of notable books in the field of social studies

For further information on these sources, see the Reference List in Appendix G.

In addition to these review sources, the Orbis Pictus Award for Outstanding Nonfiction for Children offers you yet another source of good nonfiction titles. The National Council of Teachers of English (NCTE) announces at its November convention the award winner, up to five Honor Books, and other outstanding nonfiction choices published during the previous year. For a complete listing of the Orbis Pictus award winners and honor books, see Appendix A.

Historical Overview of Nonfiction

The history of children's nonfiction begins in 1657 with the publication of John Amos Comenius's *Orbis Pictus, The World in Pictures*. Not only was this the first children's picture book but it was also a work of nonfiction. This auspicious beginning for nonfiction was cut short, however, by the Puritan Movement. For nearly 200 years the vast majority of books published for and read by children were intended more for moralistic instruction than for information.

Although books of nonfiction continued to be written in the eighteenth and nineteenth centuries, much of the growth and development of this genre occurred in the twentieth century. Writing in 1953 about history and biography for children, Elizabeth Nesbitt commented, "In comparison with the present, the early 1900's seem poverty-striken in these two fields, in regard to both number of books and to significance of presentation" (Meigs, Eaton, Nesbitt, & Viguers, 1953, p. 392). The growth of public school and library systems in the United States and Canada called for more nonfiction trade books to meet the curricular demands of schools. With few exceptions, however, much of the children's nonfiction written during the first half of the twentieth century was decidedly unremarkable in quality.

Then, in 1957, the former Soviet Union launched *Sputnik*, the first artificial space satellite, and the United States was galvanized into action in an effort to catch up and win the race for space and technology. The National Defense Education Act funneled federal money into science education, and children's book publishers responded with a wave of improved science trade books on every conceivable topic. The gush of federal funding and the emphasis on science in schools lasted through most of the 1960s, during which time nonfiction continued a gradual evolution in style and format and a growing trend toward publication in series. Generous use of illustrations in nonfiction, introduced in the "picture histories" and "picture geographies" of the 1940s and 1950s, was taken to a new level in the science concept picture book, which appeared in the early 1960s (Giblin, 1988). These books, exemplified by the *Let's Read and Find Out* series (Crowell), successfully delivered science concepts to preschool and primary-grade audiences for the first time by using numerous, large, high-quality illustrations. Popular with children accustomed to watching television, this trend toward more illustrations and less text in nonfiction has continued to the present time and has resulted in the adoption (from *Life* magazine), development, and refinement of yet another format for children's nonfiction—the photo essay.

As the stature of nonfiction rose and more top-flight authors and illustrators were engaged in its production, the quality of research, writing, and art in these books improved. The inaccuracies of fictionalizing, the dullness of lengthy and stiff or overly sentimental prose, and the incidental nature of infrequent and colorless illustrations common in nonfiction through the 1950s were no longer tolerated. A lighter, yet factual, tone balanced with high-quality, informative illustrations and graphics emerged as the preferred nonfiction style of the 1980s (Elleman, 1987).

Meanwhile, children's biographies were greatly affected by the more liberal attitudes and relaxed topic restrictions that revolutionized children's fiction in the 1960s. Prior to this time, certain subjects (ethnic minorities, women, infamous people) and topics (the subjects' personal weaknesses, mistakes, and tragedies) were not often found in children's biographies. It was thought that subjects worthy of being commemorated should be placed on a pedestal. By the mid-1960s, this had changed, as Russell Freedman (1988) pointed out in his Newbery Award acceptance speech. "The hero worship of the past has given way to a more realistic approach, which recognizes the warts and weaknesses that humanize the great" (p. 447).

Long in the literary shadow of fiction (less than 10 percent of the Newbery winners were nonfiction as of 1980), nonfiction finally achieved equal stature in the 1980s. Nancy Willard won a Newbery Award for her biographical poem, *A Visit to William Blake's Inn: Poems for Innocent and Experienced Travelers* (Harcourt Brace Jovanovich, 1981), and Russell Freedman won a Newbery Award for his photo essay, *Lincoln: A Photobiography* (Holiday House, 1987) in 1988. Moreover, six works of nonfiction were among the Newbery Honor Books between 1980 and 1990.

As the decade of the nineties began, it was widely recognized in the children's book industry that nonfiction was *the* hot topic in book selection for the young. But this surge of interest in nonfiction was not the result of massive government funding, as in the 1950s and 1960s. Rather, it was the result of parents and librarians who were willing to supply their children with the best learning materials possible.

The trend toward respect and recognition of children's nonfiction culminated in 1990 with the establishment of the Orbis Pictus Award for Outstanding Nonfiction for Children. This award program, sponsored by the National Council of Teachers of English, is for the purpose of promoting and recognizing excellence in the writing of nonfiction for children. The award itself is made annually to the author of what has been judged to be the most outstanding work of nonfiction (excluding textbooks, historical fiction, folklore, and poetry) published during the previous year. Named in

TABLE 9–1 Milestones in the Development of Nonfiction for Children

Date	Event	Significance
1657	*Orbis Pictus* by John Amos Comenius	First known work of nonfiction for children
1671	*A Token for Children, Being an Exact Account of the Conversions, Holy and Exemplary Lives and Joyful Deaths of Several Young Children* by James Janeway	A didactic biography believed to be the most widely read children's book in the Puritan era
1683	*New England Primer*	First concept book for American children; reflected didacticism of the Puritan era
1921	*The Story of Mankind* by Hendrik Van Loon	Won the first Newbery award; greatly influenced children's books with its lively style and creative approach
1939	*Abraham Lincoln* by Ingri and Edgar Parin d'Aulaire	One of the first picture book biographies for younger children
1940	*Daniel Boone* by James H. Daugherty	First biography to win the Newbery Award
1948	*The Story of the Negro* by Arne Bontemps	The first important history of the Negro
1952	*Diary of a Young Girl* by Anne Frank	Classic autobiography; helped many to understand the tragedy of the Jewish holocaust
1960	*Let's-Read-and-Find-Out* series by Branley and Roma	Introduced the science concept picture book for young children
1969	*To Be a Slave* by Julius Lester	African-American biography chosen as Newbery Honor Book
1987	*Lincoln: A Photobiography* by Russell Freedman	First nonfictional photo essay to win a Newbery Award
1990	First Orbis Pictus Award for Nonfiction (*The Great Little Madison* by Jean Fritz)	Nonfiction as a genre is recognized

honor of Comenius's book written some 300 years earlier, this award calls to mind how far children's nonfiction has come. Milestones in the development of nonfiction for children are highlighted in Table 9–1.

Topics of Nonfiction

Although nonfiction is confined to one chapter in this book, it is by far the largest single genre in children's literature in that everything known to humankind is a conceivable topic. Organization of such an enormous variety of topics could, of course, be done in a variety of satisfactory ways, one of which is the scientific approach used here. First, the world of information is divided into the biological, the physical, the social, and the applied sciences, and then the humanities and biography are dealt with separately.

The Biological Sciences

The biological sciences deal with living organisms and the laws and phenomena that relate to any organism or group of organisms. A topic particularly interesting to children within this field is the human body—its anatomy, senses, nutrition, reproduction, health, handicaps, and heredity. Equally interesting to children are information books about pets and their care, breeding, and training, as well as the habits, habitats, life cycles, and migrations of wild animals. Ecology and the environment will be of interest and concern to more and more children who recognize the fragility of our global ecology and their responsibility to help protect it from destruction. Informational books can help children to understand what harms our ecology and to learn how they can participate in its protection and healing. Examples include *Going Green: A Kid's Handbook to Saving the Planet* by John Elkington, Julia Hailes, Douglas Hill, and Joel Makower, illustrated by Tony Ross, and *The Human Body* by Jonathan Miller, designed by David Pelham.

The Physical Sciences

The physical sciences, sometimes referred to as the natural sciences, deal primarily with nonliving materials. Rocks, land forms, oceans, the stars, and the atmosphere and its weather and seasons are all likely topics that children could learn about within the fields of geology, geography, oceanography, astronomy, and meteorology that comprise the physical sciences. Not only will children be able to satisfy their curiosity about such topics in this category as volcanoes and earthquakes but teachers will find the many books about the planets and our solar system helpful in presenting these topics in class. Examples include *Weather Words and What They Mean* by Gail Gibbons and *Volcano: The Eruption and Healing of Mount St. Helens* by Patricia Lauber.

The Social Sciences

The social sciences deal with the institutions and functioning of human society and the interpersonal relationships of individuals as members of society. Through books in this field children can learn about various forms of government, religions, different countries and their cultures, money, and transportation. Most children have a natural interest in books about careers, family relationships, and leisure activities and will appreciate finding answers to their questions without always having to ask an adult. An example is *A Family in Thailand* by Ruth and Neil Thomson.

The Applied Sciences

The applied sciences deal with the practical applications of pure science that people have devised. All machines, for example, from simple levers to super computers, from bicycles to space rockets, are part of this field, and many children are naturally interested in finding out how they work. Interest in the applied sciences can be developed in children by pointing out how their lives are affected by these applications.

For example, children get sick and medicine helps to cure them. How? Children get hungry and food appears. What are the processes by which the food is produced, prepared, packaged, and marketed? Children like toys and buy them in stores. Who designs the toys and how are they manufactured? The answers to questions like these can be found in today's nonfictional literature. For example, see *The Way Things Work* by David Macaulay and *Milk* by Donald Carrick.

A specific type of book within the applied sciences—the experiment or how-to book—capitalizes on children's natural curiosity and fondness for hands-on activities. Its contents range from directions for conducting various scientific experiments to cookbooks, guides to hobbies, and directions for small construction projects, like clubhouses. For example, see *How to Make a Chemical Volcano and Other Mysterious Experiments* by Alan Kramer.

The Humanities

The humanities deal with those branches of learning that primarily have a cultural or artistic character. Of greatest interest to children and their teachers are books about the fine arts of drawing, painting, and sculpture; the performing arts of singing, dancing, making instrumental music, and acting; and handicrafts of all sorts. Since many children are artistically creative and often study dance, music, and drawing, they can be led to read about the arts and artists to learn new techniques or to draw inspiration from others' experiences. Others might read these books to decide whether they are interested in trying to develop their artistic talent. Some books make the arts more accessible or real to children by explaining what to look for in paintings or an opera, for example, or by revealing the hard work required of an artist to achieve a spectacular performance or an intriguing work of art. Examples include *A Very Young Musician* by Jill Krementz and *Great Painters* by Piero Ventura.

Biography

A biography deals with the life of an actual person of the past or present with the intent of commemorating the subject and inspiring the reader by example. Biographers report the experiences, influences, accomplishments, and legacies of their subjects. An *autobiography* is about the author's own life. *Self Portrait: Trina Schart Hyman* by Trina Schart Hyman is an example of an autobiography.

In adult nonfiction, biographies must be completely documented to be acceptable. In biographies for children, more latitude is allowed, and biographers use varying degrees of invention. This invention ranges from choosing what aspect of the subject the biographer wants to emphasize as the theme of the book (e.g., great energy or love of freedom) to actually inventing fictional characters and conversation.

Biographies, then, can be classified by degree of documentation, as follows:

• *Authentic biographies.* In this type of biography, all factual information is documented through eyewitness accounts, written documents, letters, diaries, and, more recently, audio and videotape recordings. Details in the lives of people who lived long ago, such as conversations, are often difficult to document, however. So, for the sake of art, biographers must use such devices as interior monologue (telling what someone probably thought or said to himself or herself based on known actions), indirect discourse (reporting the gist of what someone said without using quotation marks), attribution (interpretation of known actions to determine probable motives), and inference to make their stories lively and appealing and worth children's time to read. Skillful biographers such as Jean Fritz are able to employ these devices without altering the truth or fictionalizing. Still, it is advisable to read and compare several biographies of a subject, if possible, in order to counteract any bias an author might have. *The Great Little Madison* by Jean Fritz is an example of an authentic biography.

• *Fictionalized biography.*   This type of biography is also based on careful research, but the author creates dramatic episodes from known facts by using imagined conversation. The conversation is, of course, carefully structured around what pertinent facts are known, but the actual words are invented by the author. An example of this type of biography is *Carry On, Mr. Bowditch* by Jean Lee Latham.

• *Biographical fiction.*   This type of biography allows much artistic license, including invented dialogue, fictional secondary characters, and some reconstructed action. The known achievements of the biographical subjects are reported accurately, but in other respects these works are as much fiction as fact. Examples include *Anthony Burns: The Defeat and Triumph of a Fugitive Slave* by Virginia Hamilton and *Johnny Appleseed* by Steven Kellogg.

Biographies can also be classified by coverage of the subject's life. Quality in biography for young readers, as determined by accuracy of information, coverage, and writing style, will vary. In evaluating the following types of biographies, you will want to look for a balance between the need for adequate coverage and the tolerance that the target child audience has for detail.

• The *complete biography* covers the entire life of the subject from birth to death. An example is *Columbus and the World Around Him* by Milton Meltzer.

• The *partial biography* covers only part of the life of the subject. Biographies for very young children will often be of this type, as will, of course, the biographies of living persons. An example is *Teammates* by Peter Golenbock, illustrated by Paul Bacon.

• The *collected biography* includes the life stories of several people in one book, organized into chapters. An example is *Indian Chiefs* by Russell Freedman.

• The *biography series* is a multivolume set of books with each book containing one separate biography. Most series of this type feature subjects with some common attribute, accomplishment, or skill, such as leadership or legendary sports ability. For example, the *Women of Our Time* series, published by Viking, includes biographies on such subjects as Grandma Moses, Babe Didrikson, Diana Ross, and Margaret Thatcher; and the *First Biographies* series by David

A. Adler, published by Holiday House, written for beginning independent readers in grades 2 through 4, includes biographies on such subjects as Thomas Jefferson, Martin Luther King, and Jackie Robinson.

As never before, today's nonfictional literature for children is able to meet the needs and interests of young readers in quality, variety, and reader appeal. With these books, children's appetites for learning can be fed while their curiosity for more information is piqued.

References

Elleman, Barbara. (1987). Current trends in literature for children. *Library Trends, 35*(3), 413–426.

Freedman, Russell. (1988). Newbery medal acceptance. *The Horn Book, 64*(4), 444–451.

Giblin, James Cross. (1988). The rise and fall and rise of juvenile nonfiction, 1961–1988. *School Library Journal, 35*(2), 27–31.

Jansen, Mogens. (1987). *A little about language, words, and concepts—or what may happen when children learn to read.* Translated by Lotte Rosbak Juhl. Dragör, Denmark: Landsforeningen af Læsepædagoger.

Martin, Rupert. (1966). *Looking at Italy.* New York: Lippincott.

Meigs, C., Eaton, A. T., Nesbitt, E., & Viguers, R. H. (1953). *A critical history of children's literature.* New York: Macmillan.

Untermeyer, Louis. (1969). "Questions at Night," in *The Golden Treasury of Poetry.* London: Collins.

Notable Authors of Nonfiction

Aliki, author/illustrator of informational picture books for older readers. *The King's Day; A Medieval Feast.*

Rhoda Blumberg, author of accounts of important explorations in U.S. history. *The Incredible Journey of Lewis and Clark; Commodore Perry in the Land of the Shogun.*

Clyde Robert Bulla, author of biographies for beginning independent readers. *Squanto, Friend of the White Man.*

Joanna Cole, author of a variety of informational books for beginning independent readers. *Magic School Bus* series.

Ingri and Edgar Parin d'Aulaire, authors/illustrators of several oversized picture book biographies for 5- to 7-year-olds. *Christopher Columbus; Abraham Lincoln.*

Russell Freedman, author of biographies of famous Americans and of informational books about U.S. history. *Lincoln: A Photobiography; Children of the Wild West.*

Jean Fritz, biographer of political leaders during the U.S. Revolutionary War era. *Can't You Make Them Behave, King George?; And Then What Happened, Paul Revere?*

Gail Gibbons, author/illustrator of numerous informational books for the 5- to 7-year-old that explains how everyday things work or get done. *The Post Office Book; Check It Out! The Book About Libraries.*

Virginia Hamilton, biographer of several important African Americans. *Anthony Burns: The Escape and Trial of a Fugitive Slave; W.E.B. DuBois.*

Jill Krementz, author of nonfiction series on children's hobbies and coping with difficult situations. *How It Feels to be Adopted.*

Kathryn Lasky, author of well-regarded works of photojournalism and works concerning archaeology. *Sugaring Time; Dinosaur Dig.*

Patricia Lauber, author of definitive nonfiction on popular topics such as volcanoes, mummies, and dinosaurs. *Volcano: The Eruption and Healing of Mt. St. Helens; Tales Mummies Tell.*

David Macaulay, author/illustrator of several books of faction about construction of monumental buildings and informational picture books for older readers. *Cathedral; The Way Things Work.*

Milton Meltzer, author who presents the minority perspective in historical informational books. *The Black Americans: A History in Their Own Words.*

Dorothy Hinshaw Patent, zoologist who writes informational books about animals. *Farm Animals; Whales: Giants of the Deep.*

Laurence Pringle, author of many informational books that express concern for the environment. *Nuclear Energy: Troubled Past, Uncertain Future.*

Anne Rockwell, creator of concept books for preschoolers. *Willy Can Count.*

Jack Denton Scott, author of photo essays about well-known American birds and animals. *Alligator; Little Dogs of the Prairie.*

Millicent E. Selsam, author of informational books about plants and "A First Look" nonfiction series for primary-grade children. *The Amazing Dandelion; A First Look at Animals That Eat Other Animals.*

Seymour Simon, author of over 100 science-related books that often contain practical activities. *The Planets* series; *Icebergs and Glaciers.*

Diane Stanley, author of picture book biographies for older readers. *Good Queen Bess; The Story of Elizabeth I of England; Shaka, King of the Zulus.*

Yoshiko Uchida, author of an autobiographical account of the internment of Japanese-Americans during World War II. *Journey to Topaz; Journey Home.*

Recommended Nonfiction Books

Ages refer to approximate reading levels. YA = young adult readers.

Biography

Adler, David A. *A Picture Book of Eleanor Roosevelt.* Holiday, 1991. (See others in the *First Biographies series.*) Ages 6–8.

Adoff, Arnold. *Malcolm X.* Crowell, 1970. Ages 8–10.

Blair, Gwenda. *Laura Ingalls Wilder.* Illustrated by Thomas B. Allen. Putnam, 1981. Ages 8–10.

Blumberg, Rhoda. *Commodore Perry in the Land of the Shogun.* Lothrop, 1985. Ages 9–12.

———. *The Incredible Journey of Lewis and Clark.* Lothrop, 1987. Ages 9–12.

Bulla, Clyde Robert. *Squanto, Friend of the White Man.* Illustrated by Peter Burchard. Crowell, 1954. Ages 7–9.

Cleary, Beverly. *A Girl from Yamhill: A Memoir.* Morrow, 1988. Ages 8–10.

d'Aulaire, Ingri, and Edgar Parin. *Abraham Lincoln.* Doubleday, 1939, 1957. Ages 7–9.

———. *Columbus.* Doubleday, 1955. Ages 7–9.

Freedman, Russell. *Franklin Delano Roosevelt.* Clarion, 1990. Ages 9–12.

———. *Indian Chiefs.* Holiday, 1987. Ages 9–12.

———. *Lincoln: A Photobiography.* Clarion, 1987. Ages 9–12.

———. *The Wright Brothers: How They Invented the Airplane.* Holiday, 1991. Ages 9–12.

Fritz, Jean. *And Then What Happened, Paul Revere?* Illustrated by Tomie dePaola. Coward/McCann, 1973. Ages 8–10.

———. *Bully for You, Teddy Roosevelt!* Putnam, 1991. Ages 8–10.

———. *Can't You Make Them Behave, King George?* Illustrated by Tomie dePaola. Coward/McCann, 1976. Ages 8–10.

———. *China Homecoming.* Putnam, 1985. Ages 8–10.

———. *The Double Life of Pocahontas.* Illustrated by Ed Young. Putnam, 1983. Ages 8–10.

———. *The Great Little Madison*. Putnam, 1989. Ages 9–12.

———. *Homesick: My Own Story*. Illustrated by Margot Tomes. Putnam, 1982. Ages 8–10.

———. *Make Way for Sam Houston*. Illustrated by Elsie Primavera. Putnam, 1986. Ages 8–10.

———. *Stonewall*. Illustrated by Stephen Gammell. Putnam, 1979. Ages 8–10.

———. *Traitor: The Case of Benedict Arnold*. Putnam, 1981. Ages 9–12.

———. *What's the Big Idea, Ben Franklin?* Illustrated by Margot Tomes. Coward/McCann,1978. Ages 8–10.

———. *Where Do You Think You're Going, Christopher Columbus?* Illustrated by Margot Tomes. Putnam, 1980. Ages 8–10.

———. *Where Was Patrick Henry on the 29th of May?* Illustrated by Margot Tomes. Coward/McCann, 1975. Ages 8–10.

———. *Why Don't You Get a Horse, Sam Adams?* Illustrated by Trina Schart Hyman. Coward/McCann, 1974. Ages 8–10.

———. *Will You Sign Here, John Hancock?* Illustrated by Trina Schart Hyman. Coward/McCann, 1976. Ages 8–10.

Gerrard, Roy. *Sir Francis Drake: His Daring Deeds*. Farrar, 1988. Ages 9–12.

Golenbock, Peter. *Teammates*. Illustrated by Paul Bacon. Harcourt, 1990. Ages 7–9.

Hamilton, Virginia. *Anthony Burns: The Defeat and Triumph of a Fugitive Slave*. Knopf, 1988. Ages 11 and up.

Hyman, Trina Schart. *Self-Portrait: Trina Schart Hyman*. Addison-Wesley, 1981. Ages 7–9.

Kellogg, Steven. *Johnny Appleseed*. Morrow, 1988. Ages 6–8.

Lasker, Joe. *The Great Alexander the Great*. Viking, 1983. Ages 7–9.

Latham, Jean Lee. *Carry On, Mr. Bowditch*. Houghton, 1955. Ages 10–12.

Lindberg, Reeve. *Johnny Appleseed*. Illustrated by Kathy Jacobsen. Little, Brown, 1990. Ages 6–8.

Lyons, Mary E. *Sorrow's Kitchen: The Life and Folklore of Zora Neale Hurston*. Scribners, 1990. Ages 12–YA.

Meltzer, Milton. *Columbus and the World Around Him*. Watts. 1990. Ages 12–YA.

———. *Dorothea Lange, Life Through the Camera*.

Illustrated by Donna Diamond. Viking, 1985. Ages 9–12.

———. *George Washington and the Birth of Our Nation*. Watts, 1986. Ages 12–YA.

———. *Starting from Home: A Writer's Beginnings*. Viking, 1988. Ages 9–12.

Peet, Bill. *Bill Peet: An Autobiography*. Houghton, 1989. Ages 8–10.

Sandburg, Carl. *Abe Lincoln Grows Up,* reprinted from *Abraham Lincoln: The Prairie Years*. Illustrated by James Daugherty. Harcourt, 1928. Ages 9–12.

Say, Allen. *El Chino*. Houghton, 1990. Ages 8–10.

Stanley, Diane, and Peter Vennema. *Good Queen Bess: The Story of Elizabeth I of England*. Four Winds, 1990. Ages 8–10.

———. *The Last Princess: The Story of Princess Ka'iulani of Hawaii*. Four Winds, 1991. Ages 8–10.

———. *Shaka: King of the Zulus*. Illustrated by Diane Stanley. Morrow, 1988. Ages 7–9.

Uchida, Yoshiko. *Journey to Topaz*. Scribner's, 1971. (Sequel: *Journey Home,* Atheneum, 1978.) Ages 9–12.

Willard, Nancy. *A Visit to William Blake's Inn: Poems for Innocent and Experienced Travelers*. Illustrated by Alice and Martin Provensen. Harcourt, 1981. Ages 8–10.

Women of Our Time Series. Viking. Ages 9–12.

Yates, Elizabeth. *Amos Fortune, Free Man*. Illustrated by Nora S. Unwin. Dutton, 1950. Ages 8–12.

Zemach, Margot. *Self–Portrait, Margot Zemach*. Addison-Wesley, 1978. Ages 8–10.

Informational Books

Abells, Chana Byers. *The Children We Remember*. Photographs from the Archives of Yad Vashem, the Holocaust Martyrs' and Heroes' Remembrance Authority, Jerusalem, Israel. Greenwillow, 1986. Ages 12–YA.

Alexander, Sally Hobart. *Mom Can't See Me*. Photographs by George Ancona. Macmillan, 1990. Ages 4–6.

Aliki (Brandenburg). *How a Book Is Made*. Crowell, 1986. Ages 6–8.

————. *The King's Day: Louis XIV of France.* Crowell, 1989. Ages 7–9.

————. *A Medieval Feast.* Crowell, 1983. Ages 8–10.

Ancona, George. *The American Family Farm.* Text by Joan Anderson. Harcourt, 1989. Ages 8–10.

Ancona, George and Mary Beth. *Handtalk Zoo.* Photographs by George Ancona. Four Winds, 1989. Ages 6–8.

Anderson, Joan. *Born to the Land: An American Portrait.* Photographs by George Ancona. Harcourt, 1989. Ages 7–9.

————. *The First Thanksgiving Feast.* Photographs by George Ancona. Clarion, 1984. Ages 7–9.

Anno, Mitsumasa. *Anno's Math Games I.* Philomel, 1987. (*Math Games II,* 1989; *Math Games III,* 1991). Ages 6–10.

Arnold, Caroline. *Dinosaurs Down Under: And Other Fossils from Australia.* Photographs by Richard Hewett. Clarion, 1990. Ages 8–10.

————. *Saving the Peregrine Falcon.* Photographs by Richard R. Hewett. Carolrhoda, 1985. Ages 8–10.

Arnosky, Jim. *Deer at the Brook.* Lothrop, 1986. Ages 6–8.

————. *Raccoons and Ripe Corn.* Lothrop, 1987. Ages 6–8.

Aruego, Jose, and Ariane Dewey. *We Hide, You Seek.* Greenwillow, 1979. Ages 4–6.

Baer, Edith. *This Is the Way We Go to School: A Book About Children Around the World.* Illustrated by Steve Bjorkman. Scholastic, 1990. Ages 6–10.

Ballard, Robert D. *Exploring the Titanic.* Illustrated by Ken Marschall. Scholastic, 1988. Ages 7–9.

Banish, Roslyn. *Let Me Tell You About My Baby.* Harper, 1988. Ages 7–9.

Barton, Byron. *I Want to Be an Astronaut.* Crowell, 1988. Ages 7–9.

Bash, Barbara. *Tree of Life: The World of the African Baobab.* Little, Brown, 1989. Ages 7–9.

Blumberg, Rhoda. *Commodore Perry in the Land of the Shogun.* Lothrop, 1985. Ages 9–12.

————. *The Great American Gold Rush.* Bradbury, 1989. Ages 9–12.

————. *The Incredible Journey of Lewis and Clark.* Lothrop, 1987. Ages 9–12.

Branley, Franklyn M. *The Christmas Sky,* revised edition. Illustrated by Stephen Fieser. Crowell, 1990. Ages 6–8.

————. *Eclipse: Darkness in Daytime,* revised edition. Illustrated by Donald Crews. Crowell, 1988. Ages 6–8.

————. *Uranus: The Seventh Planet.* Illustrated by Yvonne Buchanan. Crowell, 1989. Ages 6–8.

Brinkloe, Julie. *Fireflies!* Macmillan, 1985. Ages 6–8.

Brown, Laurene Krasny, and Marc Brown. *Dinosaurs Alive and Well!: A Guide to Good Health.* Little, Brown, 1990. Ages 6–8.

————. *Dinosaurs' Divorce: A Guide for Changing Families,* Atlantic Monthly Press, 1986. Ages 6–8.

Brown, Marc. *Your First Garden Book.* Atlantic-Little, 1981. Ages 4–6.

Bunting, Eve. *The Wall.* Illustrated by Ronald Himler. Clarion, 1990. Ages 6–8.

Cajacob, Thomas, and Teresa Burton. *Close to the Wild: Siberian Tigers in a Zoo.* Photographs by Thomas Cajacob. Carolrhoda, 1986. Ages 7–9.

Carrick, Donald. *Milk.* Greenwillow, 1985. Ages 5–7.

Ceserani, Gian Paolo. *Grand Constructions.* Illustrated by Piero Ventura. Putnam, 1983. Ages 9–YA.

Charlip, Remy and Mary Beth. *Handtalk Birthday: A Number and Story Book in Sign Language.* Photographs by George Ancona. Four Winds, 1987. Ages 7–9.

Cohn, Janice. *I Had a Friend Named Peter: Talking to Children About the Death of a Friend.* Illustrated by Gail Owens. Morrow, 1987. Ages 6–10.

Cole, Joanna. *Evolution.* Illustrated by Aliki. Crowell, 1990. Ages 6–8.

————. *A Gift from Saint Francis: The First Creche.* Illustrated by Michelle Lemieux. Morrow, 1989. Ages 7–9.

————. *A Horse's Body.* Photographs by Jerome Wexler. Morrow, 1981. (Others in the series: *A Snake's Body,* 1981; *A Cat's Body,* 1982; *A Big Bird's Body,* 1983.) Ages 6–8.

————. *The Human Body: How We Evolved.* Illustrated by Walter Gaffney-Kessel and Juan Carlos Barberis. Morrow, 1987. Ages 6–8.

————. *Large As Life: Nighttime Animals Life Size.* Illustrated by Kenneth Lilly. Knopf, 1985. Ages 6–8.

————. *The Magic Schoolbus: At the Waterworks.* Illustrated by Bruce Degen. Scholastic, 1986. Ages 7–9.

————. *The Magic Schoolbus: Inside the Earth.* Illustrated by Bruce Degen. Scholastic, 1987. Ages 7–9.

————. *The Magic Schoolbus: Inside the Human Body.* Illustrated by Bruce Degen. Scholastic, 1989. Ages 7–9.

————. *The Magic Schoolbus: Lost in the Solar System.* Illustrated by Bruce Degen. Scholastic, 1990. Ages 7–9.

————. *My Puppy Is Born.* Photographs by Jerome Wexler. Morrow, 1973 (revised and expanded, 1991). Ages 6–8.

Day, Alexandra. *Frank and Ernest.* Scholastic, 1988. Ages 7–9.

————. *Frank and Ernest Play Ball.* Scholastic, 1990. Ages 7–9.

dePaola, Tomie. *Charlie Needs a Cloak.* Prentice-Hall, 1973. Ages 6–8.

————. *My First Chanukah.* Putnam, 1987. Ages 6–8.

DeSantis, Kenny. *A Dentist's Tools.* Photographs by Patricia A. Agre. Dodd, 1988. Ages 6–8.

————. *A Doctor's Tools.* Photographs by Patricia A. Agre. Dodd, 1985. Ages 6–8.

Dunrea, Oliver. *Deep Down Underground.* Macmillan, 1989. Ages 7–9.

Ehlert, Lois. *Eating the Alphabet: Fruits and Vegetables from A–Z.* Harcourt, 1989. Ages 4–6.

————. *Growing Vegetable Soup.* Harcourt, 1987. Ages 4–6.

Ehrlich, Amy. *The Story of Hanukkah.* Illustrated by Ori Sherman. Dial, 1989. Ages 7–9.

Elkington, John, Julia Hailes, Douglas Hill, and Joel Makower. *Going Green: A Kid's Handbook to Saving the Planet.* Illustrated by Tony Ross. Puffin, 1990. Ages 8–12.

Ellis, Veronica Freeman. *Afro-Bets First Book About Africa.* Illustrated by George Ford. Just Us Books, 1990. Ages 4–6.

Esbensen, Barbara Juster. *Great Northern Diver: The Loon.* Illustrated by Mary Barrett Brown. Little, Brown, 1990. Ages 8–10.

Fisher, Leonard Everett. *The Great Wall of China.* Macmillan, 1986. Ages 9–12.

————. *The Wailing Wall.* Macmillan, 1989. Ages 9–12.

Flacklam, Margery. *Do Not Disturb: The Mysteries of Animal Hibernation and Sleep.* Illustrated by Pamela Johnson. Little, Brown, 1989. Ages 8–12.

————. *And Then There Was One: The Mysteries of Extinction.* Illustrated by Pamela Johnson. Little, Brown, 1990. Ages 8–12.

Freedman, Russell. *Dinosaurs and Their Young.* Illustrated by Leslie Morrill. Holiday, 1983. Ages 8–10.

————. *Sharks.* Holiday, 1985. Ages 8–10.

Fritz, Jean. *Shh! We're Writing the Constitution.* Illustrated by Tomie dePaola. Putnam, 1987. Ages 8–10.

Gelfand, Marilyn. *My Great-Grandpa Joe.* Photographs by Rosmarie Hausherr. Four Winds, 1986. Ages 7–9.

George, Jean C. *One Day in the Woods.* Illustrated by Gary Allen. Crowell, 1988. (See also: *One Day in the Tropical Rain Forest,* 1990.) Ages 7–9.

George, William T. *Box Turtle at Long Pond.* Illustrated by Lindsay Barrett George. Greenwillow, 1989. Ages 6–8.

Gibbons, Gail. *Trains.* Holiday, 1987. Ages 5–7.

————. *Up Goes the Skyscraper!* Four Winds, 1986. Ages 5–7.

————. *Weather Words and What They Mean.* Holiday, 1990. Ages 6–8.

Giblin, James Cross. *From Hand to Mouth: Or, How We Invented Knives, Forks and Spoons and the Tablemanners To Go With Them.* Harper, 1987. Ages 6–10.

Girard, Linda Walvoord. *Adoption Is for Always.* Illustrated by Judith Friedman. Albert Whitman, 1986. Ages 8–10.

Goodall, Jane. *The Chimpanzee Family Book.* Photographs by Michael Neugebauer. Picture Book Studio, 1989. Ages 8–10.

Goodall, John. *The Story of an English Village.* Atheneum, 1979. Ages 7–9.

Goor, Ron and Nancy. *Insect Metamorphosis: From Egg to Adult.* Photographs by Ron Goor. Atheneum, 1990. Ages 7–9.

Hausherr, Rosemarie. *Children and the AIDS Virus: A Book for Children, Parents, and Teachers.* Clarion, 1989. Ages 8–12.

——. *My First Kitten.* Four Winds, 1985. Ages 6–8.

Hirschi, Ron. *Who Lives in . . . the Mountains?* Photographs by Galen Burrell. Putnam, 1989. Ages 6–8.

——. *Who Lives in . . . the Prairies?* Photographs by Galen Burrell. Putnam, 1989. Ages 6–8.

Hirst, Robin, and Sally Hirst. *My Place in Space.* Illustrated by Roland Harvey with Joe Levine. Orchard, 1988. Ages 12–YA.

Hoyt–Goldsmith, Diane. *Totem Pole.* Photographs by Lawrence Migdale. Holiday, 1990. Ages 7–9.

Isaacson, Philip M. *Round Buildings, Square Buildings, and Buildings that Wiggle Like a Fish.* Knopf, 1988. Ages 8–10.

Janeczko, Paul B. *The Place My Words Are Looking For: What Poets Say About and Through Their Work.* Bradbury, 1990. Ages 9–12.

Jasperson, William. *Cranberries.* Houghton, 1991. Ages 8–10.

——. *Ice Cream.* Macmillan, 1988. Ages 8–10.

Jenness, Aylette. *Families: A Celebration of Diversity, Commitment, and Love.* Houghton, 1990. Ages 8–10.

Johnston, Ginny, and Judy Cutchins. *Scaly Babies: Reptiles Growing Up.* Morrow, 1988. Ages 7–9.

Kitzinger, Sheila. *Being Born.* Photographs by Lennart Nilsson. Grosset, 1986. Ages 6–YA.

Kohl, MaryAnn F. *Mudworks.* Bright Ring Publishing, 1989. Ages 5–7.

Koralek, Jenny. *Hanukkah: The Festival of Lights.* Illustrated by Juan Wijngaard. Lothrop, 1990. Ages 7–9.

Kramer, Alan. *How to Make a Chemical Volcano and Other Mysterious Experiments.* Franklin Watts, 1989. Ages 8–10.

Krementz, Jill. *A Very Young Musician.* Simon & Schuster, 1991. (See others in *A Very Young . . .* series) Ages 8–10.

Kuklin, Susan. *Thinking Big: The Story of a Young Dwarf.* Lothrop, 1986. Ages 7–9.

Kuskin, Karla. *Jerusalem, Shining Still.* Illustrated by David Frampton. Harper, 1987. Ages 8–10.

Lasker, Joe. *Merry Ever After: The Story of Two Medieval Weddings.* Viking, 1976. Ages 8–10.

Lasky, Kathryn. *Dinosaur Dig.* Illustrated by Christopher Knight. Morrow, 1990. Ages 8–10.

——. *Sugaring Time.* Photographs by Christopher Knight. Macmillan, 1983. Ages 8–10.

——. *Traces of Life: The Origins of Humankind.* Illustrated by Whitney Powell. Morrow, 1990. Ages 9–12.

Lauber, Patricia. *Dinosaurs Walked Here and Other Stories Fossils Tell.* Bradbury, 1987. Ages 8–12.

——. *Journey to the Planets.* Crown, 1982. Ages 8–12.

——. *The News about Dinosaurs.* Bradbury, 1989. Ages 8–12.

——. *Seeds Pop! Stick! Glide!* Photographs by Jerome Wexler. Crown, 1981. Ages 8–12.

——. *Volcano: The Eruption and Healing of Mount St. Helens.* Bradbury, 1986. Ages 9–12.

Lavies, Bianca. *Backyard Hunter: The Praying Mantis.* Dutton, 1990. Ages 7–9.

——. *Lily Pad Pond.* Dutton, 1989. Ages 7–9.

——. *Tree Trunk Traffic.* Dutton, 1989. Ages 7–9.

Leedy, Loreen. *Messages in the Mailbox: How to Write a Letter.* Holiday, 1991. Ages 7–9.

Lester, Julius. *To Be a Slave.* Dial, 1968. Ages 12–YA.

Lewis, Naomi. *Swan.* Illustrated by Deborah King. Lothrop, May 1986. Ages 7–9.

Mabey, Richard. *Oak and Company.* Illustrated by Clare Roberts. Greenwillow, 1983. Ages 6–8.

Macaulay, David. *Castle.* Houghton, 1977. Ages 10–YA.

——. *Cathedral: The Story of its Own Construction.* Houghton, 1973. Ages 10–YA.

——. *The Way Things Work.* Houghton, 1988. Ages 10–YA.

Machotka, Hana. *What Do You Do at a Petting Zoo?* Morrow, 1990. Ages 6–8.

Maestro, Betsy. *The Story of the Statue of Liberty.* Illustrated by Giulio Maestro. Lothrop, 1986. Ages 9–12.

Matthews, Downs. *Polar Bear Cubs.* Photographs by Dan Guravich. Simon and Schuster, 1989. Ages 6–8.

McClung, Robert M. *America's Endangered Birds: Programs & People Working to Save Them.* Illustrated by George Founds. Morrow, 1979. Ages 9–12.

McFarlan, Donald, ed. *The Guinness Book of World Records*. Sterling Publishing Company. Published annually. Ages 7–13.

McKissack, Patricia, and Frederick McKissack. *The Civil Rights Movement in America from 1865 to the Present*. Childrens Press, 1987. Ages 9–YA.

McLaughlin, Molly. *Earth Worms, Dirt, and Rotten Leaves: An Exploration in Ecology*. Macmillan, 1988. Ages 9–12.

McNulty, Faith. *Peeping in the Shell: A Whooping Crane is Hatched*. Illustrated by Irene Brady. Harper, 1986. Ages 8–10.

Meltzer, Milton. *The American Revolutionaries: A History in Their Own Words 1750–1800*. Crowell, 1988. Ages 12–YA.

———. *Rescue: The Story of How Gentiles Saved Jews in the Holocaust*. Harper, 1988. Ages 12–YA.

———. *Voices from the Civil War: A Documentary History of the Great American Conflict*. Crowell, 1989. Ages 12–YA.

Miller, Jonathan. *The Human Body*. Designed by David Pelham. Viking, 1983. Ages 9–12.

Morris, Ann. *Bread, Bread, Bread*. Photographs by Ken Heyman. Lothrop, 1989. Ages 8–10.

Müller, Jörg. *The Changing City*. Atheneum, 1977. Ages 8–12.

———. *The Changing Countryside*. Atheneum, 1977. Ages 8–12.

Munro, Roxie. *Christmastime in New York City*. Dodd, 1987. Ages 6–8.

———. *The Inside-Outside Book of Washington, D.C.* Ages 6–8. Dutton, 1987.

Murphy, Jim. *The Boy's War: Confederate and Union Soldiers Talk About the Civil War*. Clarion, 1990. Ages 12–YA.

Newlands, Anne. *Meet Edgar Degas*. Lippincott, 1989. Ages 7–9.

Norsgaard, E. Jaediker. *How to Raise Butterflies*. Photographs by Campbell Norsgaard. Putnam, 1988. Ages 7–9.

O'Dell, Scott. *Sing Down the Moon*. Houghton, 1970. (Also listed under historical fiction.) Ages 9–12.

Parker, Nancy Winslow, and Joan Richards Wright. *Bugs*. Illustrated by Nancy Winslow Parker. Greenwillow, 1987. Ages 7–9.

Patent, Dorothy Hinshaw. *Farm Animals*. Photographs by William Muñoz. Holiday, 1984. Ages 6–8.

———. *A Picture Book of Cows*. Photographs by William Muñoz. Holiday, 1982. Ages 6–8.

———. *Where the Bald Eagles Gather*. Photographs by William Muñoz. Clarion, 1984. Ages 6–8.

Patterson, Dr. Francine. *Koko's Kitten*. Photographs by Ronald H. Cohn. Scholastic, 1985. Ages 6–10.

———. *Koko's Story*. Photographs by Ronald H. Cohn. Scholastic, 1988. Ages 6–10.

Perle, Lila. *The Great Ancestor Hunt: The Fun of Finding Out Who You Are*. Clarion, 1989. Ages 8–10.

Peters, Lisa Westberg. *The Sun, the Wind, and the Rain*. Illustrated by Ted Rand. Holt, 1988. Ages 7–9.

Peterson, Jeanne Whitehouse. *I Have a Sister, My Sister Is Deaf*. Illustrated by Deborah Ray. Harper, 1977. Ages 7–9.

Polacco, Patricia. *Meteor!* Dodd, 1987. Ages 7–9.

Pope, Joyce. *Kenneth Lilly's Animals: A Portfolio of Paintings*. Illustrated by Kenneth Lilly. Lothrop, 1988. Ages 8–10.

Pringle, Laurence. *Death Is Natural*. Four Winds, 1977. Ages 7–9.

———. *Dinosaurs and People: Fossils, Facts, and Fantasies*. Harcourt, 1978. Ages 7–9.

———. *Dinosaurs and Their World*. Harcourt, 1968. Ages 7–9.

———. *Global Warming: Assessing the Greenhouse Threat*. Arcade, 1990. Ages 7–9.

———. *Throwing Things Away: From Middens to Resource Recovery*. Crowell, 1988. Ages 8–10.

Ride, Sally, and Susan Okie. *To Space and Back*. Lothrop, 1986. Ages 9–12.

Robbins, Ken. *Tools*. Four Winds, 1983. Ages 6–8.

Rockwell, Ann. *Things That Go*. Dutton, 1986. Ages 4–6.

Rockwell, Anne, and Harlow Rockwell. *The Supermarket*. Macmillan, 1979. Ages 4–6.

Rockwell, Harlow. *My Dentist*. Greenwillow, 1975. Ages 3–5.

———. *My Doctor*. Macmillan, 1973. Ages 3–5.

———. *My Nursery School*. Greenwillow, 1976. Ages 3–5.

Rogasky, Barbara. *Smoke and Ashes: The Story of the Holocaust*. Holiday, 1988. Ages 12–YA.

Rogers, Fred. *Making Friends*. Photographs by Jim Judkis. Putnam, 1988. Ages 4–6.

————. *Moving*. Photographs by Jim Judkis. Putnam, 1988. Ages 4–6.

Rosenberg, Maxine B. *Brothers and Sisters*. Photographs by George Ancona. Clarion, 1991. Ages 6–8.

Ryder, Joanne. *Where Butterflies Grow*. Illustrated by Lynne Cherry. Lodestar, 1989. Ages 7–9.

————. *White Bear, Ice Bear*. Illustrated by Michael Rothman. Morrow, 1989. Ages 7–9.

Sancha, Sheila. *The Luttrell Village: Country Life in the Middle Ages*. Crowell, 1982. Ages 9–12.

Sattler, Helen Roney. *Dinosaurs of North America*. Illustrated by Anthony Rao. Lothrop, 1981. Ages 6–8.

————. *The Illustrated Dinosaur Dictionary*. Illustrated by Pamela Carroll, Anthony Rao, and Christopher Santuro. Lothrop, 1983. Ages 6–10.

Schmitt, Lois. *Smart Spending: A Young Consumer's Guide*. Scribner's, 1989. Ages 7–9.

Schwartz, Lynne Sharon. *The Four Questions*. Illustrated by Ori Sherman. Dial, 1989. Ages 8–10.

Scott, Jack Denton. *Alligator*. Photographs by Ozzie Sweet. Putnam, 1984. Ages 7–9.

————. *Swans*. Photographs by Ozzie Sweet. Putnam, 1988. Ages 7–9.

Selsam, Millicent E. *Cotton*. Photographs by Jerome Wexler. Morrow, 1982. Ages 7–9.

————. *How to Be a Nature Detective*. Illustrated by Ezra Jack Keats. Harper, 1963. Ages 7–9.

Selsam, Millicent, and Joyce Hunt. *Keep Looking!*. Illustrated by Normand Chartier. Macmillan, 1989. Ages 7–9.

Sewall, Marcia. *The Pilgrims of Plimoth*. Atheneum, 1986. Ages 8–10.

Simon, Seymour. *Jupiter*. Morrow, 1985. (Others in The Planets series: *Mars,* 1987; *Saturn,* 1985; *Uranus,* 1987.) Ages 8–10.

————. *The Long Journey from Space*. Crown, 1982.

Ages 8–10.

————. *The Long View Into Space*. Crown, 1979. Ages 8–10.

————. *The Paper Airplane Book*. Illustrated by Byron Barton. Viking, 1971. Ages 8–10.

————. *The Smallest Dinosaur*. Illustrated by Anthony Rao. Crown, 1982. Ages 7–9.

————. *Soap Bubble Magic*. Illustrated by Stella Ormai. Lothrop, 1985. Ages 7–9.

————. *Storms*. Morrow, 1989. Ages 8–10.

————. *The Stars*. Morrow, 1986. Ages 8–10.

————. *The Sun*. Morrow, 1986. Ages 8–10.

————. *Volcanoes*. Morrow, 1988. Ages 8–10.

Spier, Peter. *We the People: The Constitution of the United States of America*. Doubleday, 1987. Ages 8–10.

Thomson, Ruth, and Neil Thomson. *A Family in Thailand*. Lerner Publications, 1988. (See others in *A Family in . . .* series.) Ages 7–9.

Turner, Glennette Tilly. *Take a Walk In Their Shoes*. Illustrated by Ellen C. Fox. Dutton/Cobblehill, 1989. Ages 8–10.

Udry, Janice May. *A Tree Is Nice*. Illustrated by Marc Simont. Harper, 1956. Ages 5–7.

Van Loon, Hendrik Willem. *The Story of Mankind*. Liveright, 1921, 1984. Ages 9–12.

Ventura, Piero. *Great Painters*. Translated by Geoffrey Culverwell. Putnam, 1984. Ages 9–YA.

Wexler, Jerome. *Flowers, Nuts, Seeds*. Prentice–Hall, 1988. Ages 7–9.

Wilcox, Charlotte. *Trash*. Photographs by Jerry Bushey. Carolrhoda, 1988. Ages 8–10.

Wilkes, Angela. *My First Nature Book*. Knopf, 1990. Ages 6–8.

Yoshida, Toshi. *Elephant Crossing*. Putnam, 1989. Ages 7–9.

————. *Young Lions*. Putnam, 1989. Ages 7–9.

Chapter 10

Multicultural and International Literature

All the Colors of the Race

All the colors of the race
are
> *in my face, and just behind my face:*
>> *behind my eyes:*
> *inside my head.*

And inside my head, I give my self a place
> *at the end of a long*
>> *line   forming*
>>> *it self into a*
>>>> *circle.*
And I am holding out my hands.
> —Arnold Adoff

If people were not concerned about the differences between them, there would be no reason for this chapter. But difference—whether racial, cultural, religious, or physical—has always concerned humans, eliciting pride, curiosity, or fear, depending on the point of view. Over 200 years ago our nation was founded on the principle that all people are created equal; and yet, even today, we are far from achieving tolerance and appreciation of those different from ourselves.

This chapter is presented in two parts. The first part focuses on literature written about the major racial, religious, and language minorities in the United States. The second part focuses on literature written originally for children living in other lands but also read and enjoyed by children in the United States.

SECTION ONE: MULTICULTURAL LITERATURE

Definition and Description

Multicultural literature refers to those trade books, regardless of genre, having as the main character a person who is a member of a racial, religious, or language minority. This section of the chapter will focus on the five most populous minority groups in the United States, each of which has an established and growing body of children's literature that describes that experience. These groups are African American; Asian American (including people of Chinese, Japanese, Korean, and Vietnamese descent); Hispanic American (including Cuban Americans, Mexican Americans, Puerto Ricans, and others of Spanish descent); Jewish American; and Native American (a general term referring to the many tribes of American Indians.)

Reference to a minority implies the existence of a larger, different group—a majority. In this case, the majority is the white, Anglo-Saxon population and the literature that describes it. Until recently, this was the only group well represented in U.S. children's books.

Values of Multicultural Literature for Children

Multicultural literature has value for both minority and majority children. As a multicultural society, the United States benefits from cooperation and friendship among all people living within its borders. The violence and destruction that often result from racial and religious prejudice hurt everyone. From a minority perspective, one step toward effective, confident citizenship in a multicultural society is an understanding of one's particular social and cultural heritage. From a majority perspective, the first thing that people must do in order to accept those different from themselves is to learn about them, and reading is one of the best ways to do this. Knowledge gained through reading then makes understanding possible, and understanding often leads to appreciation.

Multicultural literature, then, is valuable for the following reasons:

- Minority children who see people like themselves positively represented in high-quality multicultural literature derive self-esteem and pride in their own heritage. Every child has a right to self-respect.
- Reading multicultural literature is a way for majority children (and their parents, teachers, and librarians) to learn about or to become aware of minority peoples and their cultures. Majority children who find only people like themselves represented in literature could easily get the impression that they are somehow better or more worthy as a group than others. Multicultural literature shows majority children that other groups are not only worthy but have something to teach the majority. Also, school-based studies have shown that emotional involvement and vicarious experience with minority characters through

works of multicultural literature reduce students' prejudices toward the minority. (For a summary of these studies, see *Social Education,* April/May, 1988.)

• Multicultural literature often addresses issues and problems peculiar to minority children from the perspective of a minority character in the story. Reading about such problems as racial or religious prejudice and how book characters deal with these problems may help some minority children to cope with the same problems themselves.

Evaluation and Selection of Multicultural Literature

With respect to multicultural literature, your first concern as a teacher, librarian, or parent should be that well-written books of this kind are available to the children under your care. This task is often not as simple as it may at first seem. Some cultural groups in the United States are not yet well represented in children's books. Also, a wide variety of the most current and best multicultural books are not readily available everywhere. Someone, perhaps you, has to take the time and the effort to learn about, read, evaluate, and then introduce the best of this literature into a school or community. The following criteria should be considered when evaluating multicultural books:

• Some evaluation criteria remain constant regardless of the type of literature. Multicultural literature should exhibit high literary and artistic quality, worthy themes, and appropriate reading levels for the intended audience.

• Racial and cultural stereotyping should be avoided; instead, multifaceted, well-rounded minority characters should be found in these stories. The nature of stereotyping is that it unfairly assigns a fixed image or fixed characteristics to everyone within a group, thereby denying everyone within the group the right to any individuality or choice. No one likes to be the victim of stereotyping.

Traditional racial, religious, and language minority stereotypes that have developed over the years in the United States make clear the damage and unwarranted denigration that can result from the practice. In evaluating children's books, you will want to be alert to any portrayal of African Americans as coarse-featured, musical, and poor; of Asian Americans as sly, overly diligent, and obsequious; of Hispanic Americans as lazy, holiday-minded, and impoverished; of Jewish Americans as greedy, aggressive, and penurious; and of Native Americans as savage, primitive, and warlike. Books perpetuating such stereotypes have no place in the classroom.

• Positive images of minority characters should be evident. Good multicultural books go beyond avoidance of stereotypes to provide characters and situations that project positive, believable images of minorities in family, school, work, and play.

• Cultural details must be accurate. Much of what distinguishes the literature of a particular minority group from that of other groups is found in the details, such as idioms and dialect used in dialogue, descriptions of clothing, hairstyles, and food, architecture of homes, and customs. Just as important, these details must be accurate when describing subgroups *within* a minority group. For example, customs of Native

Americans vary greatly from tribe to tribe. Gross overgeneralization is not only inaccurate but is a form of stereotyping.

• In selecting multicultural books for a young readership, variety is a key concern. Not only should there be books about the minorities represented in a classroom but there should be books about the many other minorities living in this country. Likewise, there should be multicultural books of varying genres and multicultural characters in these books from a variety of backgrounds.

Variety also extends to authorship. Multicultural books written by both minority authors and majority authors should be readily available to children. In her landmark book, *Shadow and Substance,* Rudine Sims (1982) established a classification system for books about African Americans that can be applied to any minority literature and can be helpful in evaluation and selection of these books. Adapting her labels and definitions to include all multicultural literature, there are:

> *Social conscience books.*   These books about minorities are written to help both majority and minority readers know the condition of their fellow humans. Examples are *The Slave Dancer* by Paula Fox and *Iggie's House* by Judy Blume.

> *Melting pot books.*   These books are written for both minority and majority readers on the assumption that both need to be informed that nonwhite children are exactly like other American children, except for the color of their skins or their religious preference. Examples include *A Snowy Day* by Ezra Jack Keats and *Jennifer, Hecate, Macbeth, William McKinley, & Me, Elizabeth* by E. L. Konigsburg.

> *Culturally conscious books.*   These books are written primarily (though not exclusively) by minority authors for a specific minority group of readers in which an attempt is made to reveal the true, unique character of that minority culture. Examples are *Stevie* by John Steptoe and *Roll of Thunder, Hear My Cry* by Mildred Taylor.

Having examples of all three types of multicultural books in your classroom will assure that your students will be able to read from the perspective of both the minority author and the white author. Minority students in particular should have the experience of reading stories written about children like themselves from the perspective of someone within their minority group.

Several book selection aids focus on multicultural books. *Multicultural Children's and Young Adult Literature: A Selected Listing of Books 1980–90 by and about People of Color* is a carefully selected, regularly updated, annotated listing of multicultural books of all genres produced by the University of Wisconsin, Madison's Cooperative Children's Book Center. *The Black Experience in Children's Literature,* an annotated book list published about every five years by the New York Public Library, offers a comprehensive collection of African-American books in print at the time of publication. The nearly 500 entries in the latest edition (1989) are organized by United States, South and Central American, and Caribbean, African, and British titles. *Literature for*

Children about Asians and Asian Americans: Analysis and Annotated Bibliography, with Additional Reading for Adults (Jenkins & Austin, 1987) is arranged by nation and subdivided into genres. *Literature by and about the American Indian* (Stensland, 1979) is an annotated, retrospective bibliography of nearly 800 children's and young adult titles of all genres having to do with North American Indians. A more recent resource on books about Native Americans, *Books without Bias: Through Indian Eyes, Vol. 2* (Slapin & Seale, 1988), also contains articles, essays, and poems written by Native Americans. *Resource Reading List 1990: Annotated Bibliography of Resources by and about Native People* (Verrall & McDowell, 1990) focuses on Native Canadians. *Books in Spanish for Children and Young Adults* (Schon, 1989), a guide for choosing Spanish language books for Hispanic children, is organized by country of origin, including a large section on the United States. These books are of all genres, and some are bilingual. (For further information on these resources, see Appendix G.)

The professional review sources are valuable guides to selecting the most recent multicultural books. *Booklist, School Library Journal, The Bulletin of the Center for Children's Books* and *Horn Book Magazine* all regularly call attention to multicultural books, and sometimes gather helpful lists of these books by minority group, book genre, or intended audience. (For further information on Book Selection Aids, see Appendix G.)

Book awards for special content also can guide teachers and librarians toward high-quality multicultural books. The best known of these is the Coretta Scott King Award, founded in 1969 and, since 1979, sponsored by the American Library Association. This annual award is given to the African-American author and (since 1974) illustrator whose books published in the preceding year are judged to be the most outstanding inspirational and educational literature for children. (For a complete list of award winners, see Appendix A.)

In recent years small presses have given teachers and librarians yet another source of multicultural books. Several of these publishers have focused on multicultural literature, and so their catalogues seem a treasure trove for those looking for minority literature. Children's Press, Children's Book Press, and Carolrhoda Books deserve special notice for their multicultural publications.

Evaluating, selecting, and then bringing multicultural literature to your classroom, though essential, is not enough to assure that your students will actually read the books. Since children, without adult guidance, tend to choose books about children like themselves (Rudman, 1984), you must also purposefully expose majority children to multicultural books through reading aloud, booktalking, and selecting particular titles for small group reading.

Historical Overview of Multicultural Literature

Minority groups living in the United States were long ignored as subjects for children's books. On the few occasions that minorities did appear in children's books, they did so as crudely stereotyped characters, objects of ridicule, or shadowy secondary characters. Helen Bannerman's *The Story of Little Black Sambo* (1900), Claire Bishop's *The Five Chinese Brothers* (1938), Sara Cone Bryant's *Epaminondas and His Auntie* (1907), and Hugh Lofting's *The Voyages of Dr. Dolittle* (1922) come under this category. Today, books such as these have either been rewritten to eliminate the racism or have disappeared from children's library shelves.

Although many of the Newbery Award winners and honor books of the 1920s and 1930s were set in foreign countries, almost none had to do with U.S. minorities. Laura Adams Armer's novel about Native Americans, *Waterless Mountain,* the Newbery winner in 1932, was the only exception.

The 1940s offered little improvement. Although Florence Crannell Means wrote sympathetic and informative novels such as *The Moved-Outers* (1945) about American ethnic minorities during the 1930s and 1940s, negative stereotypes, such as those of Native Americans as savages projected in Newbery winners *Daniel Boone* by James Daugherty (1939) and *The Matchlock Gun* by Walter D. Edmonds (1941) were more prevalent by far.

The first harbinger of change came in 1949 when an African-American author, Arne Bontemps, won a Newbery Honor Award for his *Story of the Negro* and became the first member of a minority to receive this honor. A more sympathetic attitude toward American minorities, at least in literature, emerged in the 1950s, as evidenced by the positive treatment of minority characters in such Newbery winners as *Amos Fortune, Free Man* by Elizabeth Yates (1950) and *. . . And Now Miguel* by Joseph Krumgold (1953).

The Civil Rights movement of the 1960s focused attention on the social inequities and racial injustices that prevailed in the United States. The spirit of the times resulted in two landmark publications. The first of these was *The Snowy Day* by Ezra Jack Keats (1962), the first Caldecott Award-winning book to have an African American as the protagonist. The great popularity of this book no doubt encouraged other authors, both minority and majority, to produce books with minority protagonists. The second publication was a powerful article by Nancy Larrick entitled "The All-White World of Children's Books." In this article, which appeared in the September 11, 1965, issue of *Saturday Review,* Larrick reported that in nearly all U.S. children's books the African American was either omitted entirely or scarcely mentioned (p. 63). American trade book publishers, the education system, and the public library system were called upon to fill this void.

For a time, the spirit of social consciousness born in the 1960s had good results. In 1966, the Council on Interracial Books for Children was founded and helped to promote young, African-American authors. In 1969, the Coretta Scott King Award was established to recognize distinguished writing in children's books by African-American authors. Also, a number of books with minority protagonists or minority themes were chosen as Newbery winners in the early seventies: *Sounder* by William H. Armstrong won in 1970; *Julie of the Wolves* by Jean Craighead George won in 1973; and *The Slave Dancer* by Paula Fox won in 1974. Judging from this record, the establishment had accepted minorities as protagonists in award-winning books; but it was not until 1975 that a minority author, Virginia Hamilton, author of *M. C. Higgins, the Great,* won a Newbery Award.

In quick succession, other minority authors were recognized for their outstanding literary and artistic efforts. In 1976, Leo Dillon (in collaboration with his wife, Diane Dillon) won a Caldecott Award for *Why Mosquitoes Buzz in People's Ears* (Aardema, 1975) and Sharon Bell Mathis and Laurence Yep received Newbery Honor Awards for *The Hundred Penny Box* and *Dragonwings,* respectively. The following year, 1977, Mildred D. Taylor, author of *Roll of Thunder, Hear My Cry,* became the second African American to win the Newbery Award. After 1975, the prevailing opinion among U.S. children's book publishers and professional reviewers seemed to be that members of a minority group were the ones most able to write authoritatively about the minority experience. White authors were no longer as likely to win major awards for writing about minorities as they were in the early 1970s.

The politically conservative 1980s were not conducive to a continued flowering of multicultural literature in the United States. Fewer books with minority characters or themes were published and fewer minority authors won awards than in the 1970s. Toward the end of the decade, however, the climate improved. Several small presses devoted exclusively to multicultural literature were founded. Currently there is a renewed interest in multicultural literature, and an increasing number of minority authors and illustrators is entering the field.

TABLE 10–1   Milestones in the Development of Multicultural Literature

Date	Event	Significance
1932	*Waterless Mountain* by Armer wins Newbery Medal	One of the few children's books about minorities in the first half of the twentieth century
1945	*The Moved-Outers* by Means wins Newbery Honor	A move away from stereotyped depiction of minorities begins
1949	*Story of the Negro* by Bontemps wins Newbery Honor	First minority author to win a Newbery Honor
1950	*Song of the Swallows* by Politi wins Caldecott Award	First picture book with an Hispanic-American protagonist to win the Caldecott Award
1962	*The Snowy Day* by Keats wins Caldecott Award	First picture book with an African-American protagonist to win the Caldecott Award
1965	"The All–White World of Children's Books" by Larrick published in *Saturday Review*	Called the nation's attention to the lack of multicultural literature
1969	Coretta Scott King Award founded	African-American literature and authors begin to be promoted and supported
1975	*M. C. Higgins, the Great* by Hamilton wins Newbery Award	First book by a minority author to win the Newbery Award
1976	*Why Mosquitoes Buzz In People's Ears* illustrated by Leo and Diane Dillon wins Caldecott Award	First picture book illustrated by an African American to win the Caldecott Award
1990	*Lon Po Po: A Red-Riding Hood Story from China* translated and illustrated by Ed Young wins Caldecott Award	First picture book illustrated by an Asian American to win the Caldecott Award

As minority groups intermingle with each other and with the white population, children of mixed heritage will be born. Already this group is growing fast. Perhaps the experience of growing up with a mixed heritage will be a topic featured in the multicultural literature of the future. Milestones in the development of multicultural literature are highlighted in Table 10–1.

Types of Multicultural Literature

Although the last several decades have seen positive changes in the status of multi-cultural literature in the United States, there is still a marked shortage of books of this kind. Minority authors and illustrators of children's books are also in short supply.

A newfound public interest in family heritage that began in the 1980s in the United States began to be reflected in minority literature by the end of the decade. Interest in books about ethnic heritage has helped minority authors and illustrators to regain some of the publishing momentum of the 1970s. Awakening to the meaning and importance of one's heritage is a theme that weaves across all genres of literature in all minority groups.

African-American Literature

Of all minority groups living in the United States, African Americans have produced the largest and most rapidly growing body of children's literature. Every genre is well represented in African-American literature, but none better than poetry. Because it is so personal, poetry portrays a culture well, as is evident in the sensitive yet powerful work of poets Arnold Adoff, Gwendolyn Brooks, Nikki Giovanni, Eloise Greenfield, and Langston Hughes. For example, see *Honey, I Love and Other Love Poems* by Eloise Greenfield.

Tapping into their rich oral tradition, African Americans have contributed Anansi the Spider, Brer Rabbit, High John the Conqueror, and John Henry the Steel Drivin' Man to the list of favorite U.S. folklore characters. Even today, authors are bringing folktales to the United States from Africa. Examples include *Why Mosquitoes Buzz in Peoples' Ears* by Verna Aardema and *The Village of Round and Square Houses* by Ann Grifalconi.

In some cases, African Americans have reclaimed their tales by retelling (without racist elements) stories first written down in this country by white authors, as Julius Lester has done in his retelling of Joel Chandler Harris's *The Tales of Uncle Remus: The Adventures of Brer Rabbit*. More recent memories and family stories have begun to be written by African-American authors as modern folktales. For example, see *Mirandy and Brother Wind* by Patricia McKissack.

African Americans have told the stories of their lives in the United States through both historical fiction and realistic fiction. The stories for older readers often include harsh but painfully accurate accounts of racial oppression, as in Mildred Taylor's historical fiction saga of the close-knit Logan family (*The Song of the Trees; Roll of Thunder, Hear My Cry; Let the Circle Be Unbroken;* and *The Road to Memphis*) and in Virginia Hamilton's contemporary realistic novel, *The Planet of Junior Brown* or Walter Dean Myers's *The Scorpions*. The characters, settings, and incidents created by these authors will be recognized by many African Americans who have lived through similar experiences; others will appreciate these stories as windows on understanding today's racial situation. Teachers can see to it that such stories are balanced, however, with more positive, encouraging contemporary stories.

Recently, African-American faces have begun to appear more frequently in picture books. While these books tend to address universal topics rather than those dealing specifically with race, they can still be culturally conscious. The work of illustrators Donald Crews, Leo Dillon, Muriel and Tom Feelings, Jerry Pinkney, and John Steptoe deserves special notice. Examples include the *Everett Anderson* series by Lucille Clifton and *Aïda* retold by Leontyne Price and illustrated by Leo and Diane Dillon.

African-American nonfiction is mainly biography. In the 1960s and 70s, a large percentage of these biographical subjects were sports heroes, but more recent subjects have come from a broader spectrum of achievement. For example, see *Anthony Burns: The Defeat and Triumph of a Fugitive Slave* by Virginia Hamilton.

Asian-American Literature

Asian-American children's literature is mainly represented in the United States by stories about Chinese Americans and Japanese Americans, possibly because these groups have lived as minorities in this country longer than others such as Vietnamese Americans. A major theme in much of the fiction and nonfiction for older readers is the oppression that drove the people out of their homelands and the prejudice that they faced as minorities in this country. A more positive theme is that of learning to appreciate one's cultural heritage while adjusting to life in the United States. Examples include *Dragonwings* and *Child of the Owl* by Laurence Yep and *In the Year of the Boar and Jackie Robinson* by Bette Bao Lord.

Traditional stories from Asia retold in English have contributed many interesting folktales and folktale variants to American children's libraries. Characters generally thought of as European, such as Little Red Riding Hood and Cinderella, have their Asian counterparts. Examples are *Lon Po Po: A Red-Riding Hood Story from China* translated by Ed Young and *Yeh Shen: A Cinderella Story from China* by Ai-Lang Louie, illustrated by Ed Young.

Asian-American artists have brought the sophisticated style and technical artistry of the Orient to U.S. children's book illustration. Ed Young's use of screenlike panels, Allen Say's precision, and Yoshi's unusual fabric paintings are especially noteworthy. Examples are *The Boy of the Three-Year Nap* by Diane Snyder, illustrated by Allen Say, and *Who's Hiding Here?* by Yoshi.

The body of Asian-American children's literature is small. Nonfiction, poetry, and fantasy are almost unrepresented, with the notable exception of Rhoda Blumberg's

1986 Newbery Honor book, a work of nonfiction, *Commodore Perry in the Land of the Shogun*. There is no special U.S. award for Asian-American literature.

Hispanic-American Literature

Of the five major U.S. minority groups, Hispanic Americans currently have the smallest body of children's literature and an insufficient amount of high-quality literature. This is especially regrettable since Hispanic Americans are the fastest growing of the large minority groups in the United States. Those books available are mainly about Puerto Ricans and Mexican Americans, with the works of Nicholasa Mohr being outstanding examples. Leo Politi's books about Mexican Americans have been popular for many years, but do not describe the current minority experience. An example is *Felita* by Nicholasa Mohr.

Some developments hold promise for improvement in the status of Hispanic-American literature. The rise of small press publishers, such as Children's Book Press, which focus on Hispanic-American literature, has already resulted in more literature being written for and about this group. The trend toward marketing more Spanish-English bilingual texts in the United States also will improve the availability of Hispanic-American books, particularly to younger children who are learning to read. For example, see *Uncle Nacho's Hat/El Sombrero del Tío Nacho* adapted by Harriet Rohmer, Spanish version by Rosalina Zubizarreta.

Jewish-American Literature

Without doubt the terrible experience of the Jewish holocaust in Europe during the 1930s and 1940s has had a tremendous influence on Jewish-American children's literature. The prejudice and cruelty that led to the holocaust and the nightmare of the death camps themselves are recurring themes in both fiction and nonfiction for older readers. Since many Jewish people immigrated to the United States as the Nazi threat grew in Europe, much holocaust literature has been written by eyewitnesses or by those whose relatives were victims. Examples are *The Upstairs Room* by Johanna Reiss, *Upon the Head of the Goat* by Aranka Siegal, and *Smoke and Ashes: The Story of the Holocaust* by Barbara Rogasky.

Jewish emigration from Europe during the war years brought to the United States many outstanding artists whose work has greatly influenced children's book illustration. Two subjects often presented in Jewish-American picture books are Jewish holidays and folktales. Illustrated Jewish folktale collections, particularly those by Isaac Bashevis Singer, offer excellent, witty stories and high literary quality. Examples include *Hershel and the Hanukkah Goblins* by Eric Kimmel, illustrated by Trina Schart Hyman; *Zlateh the Goat and Other Stories* by Isaac Bashevis Singer, illustrated by Maurice Sendak; and *It Could Always Be Worse* by Margot Zemach.

The Jewish-American community has produced numerous excellent authors and illustrators of children's books. Literary creativity is promoted through two book award programs: the National Jewish Book Awards and the Association of Jewish Libraries Awards.

Native-American Literature

Almost from the moment that white explorers landed on this continent some 500 years ago, Native Americans have suffered at the hands of what soon became the white majority. Consequently, in books written from the Native-American perspective, oppression by the white population is a pervasive theme. Appreciation, celebration, and protection of nature, central tenets of Native-American cultures, are other recurrent themes in this body of literature. Examples are *Sing Down the Moon* by Scott O'Dell and *Legend Days* by Jamake Highwater.

Although much has been written *about* Native Americans, relatively little has been written *by* members of this minority group. Native Americans who are known for their children's books include Virginia Drivinghawk Sneve for her novels and poetry and Shonto Begay for his illustrations. Examples are *When Thunders Spoke* by Virginia Driving Hawk Sneve and *The Mud Pony* by Caron Lee Cohen, illustrated by Shonto Begay.

Numerous other writers and illustrators have told and retold the folktales and history of Native Americans in picture books, historical fiction, and informational books. Paul Goble is particularly well known for his impressively illustrated retellings of the legends of the Plains Indians, as are Scott O'Dell for his award-winning works of historical fiction featuring young Native-American women, and Canadian James Houston for his Inuit Indian survival stories. The body of nonfictional works about Native Americans is particularly rich, with the works of Ann Nolan Clark, Russell Freedman, Milton Meltzer, and Alex Bealer being outstanding. Examples include *The Girl Who Loved Wild Horses* by Paul Goble, *Island of the Blue Dolphins* by Scott O'Dell, and *Only the Names Remain: The Cherokees and the Trail of Tears* by Alex Bealer.

SECTION TWO: INTERNATIONAL LITERATURE

Definition and Description

International literature in the United States is defined as literary selections originally published for the children in a country other than the United States in a language of that country and later published in the United States. The key elements of this definition are the book's country of origin and the determination of the primary audience for the book. If a book was written and published in France for French children, then translated and published for U.S. children, it is considered an international book in the United States. Books classified as international literature by this definition include:

1. English language books, written and published originally in English in another country, such as Canada or Australia, then published or distributed in the United States.
2. Translated books, written and published in a foreign language and then translated into English and published in the United States.

3. Foreign language books, written and published in a foreign language in another country for children of that country and later published or distributed in the United States in the foreign language.

If a book is written and published in the United States about Australian life, then the primary audience is U.S. children and the book is not considered international. Such books written and published in the United States about other countries are included in the lists of recommended books in the genre chapters.

Sometimes it is difficult to ascertain a book's country of origin. The publishing history page is the most reliable source of this information. (Note that in some foreign books this publishing history is placed at the end of the book.) In any case, a careful reading will inform you of the book's original date and place of publication.

Values of International Literature for Children

The value of international children's literature in developing an understanding and appreciation for other cultures is undeniable.

- Through this literature, the history, traditions, and people of other countries are brought to life.
- By interpreting events in the everyday lives of their characters and by depicting long-term changes in the characters' lives, authors present a truer and more understandable picture of life in other countries than does the crisis-prone, single-event coverage of television and newspapers.
- Compelling stories build students' interest in the people and places they are reading about and pave the way to a deeper understanding and appreciation of the geography and history content encountered in textbooks.
- Literature written by natives of the country or region under study gives authenticity and an international perspective to classroom materials.
- Through international literature, children are given an opportunity to enjoy the best-loved stories of their peers around the world. This, in turn, can help students develop a bond of shared experience with children of other nations and acquire cultural literacy with a global perspective.

Evaluation and Selection of International Literature

International books, both chapter books and picture books, should first be judged by the standards for all good literature. Particular attention must be given to translated works. These works should exhibit a good, fluent writing style that is not stilted or awkward. Some flavor of the country of origin should remain. For example, place and character names should usually remain true to the original text in order to foster in children a tolerance and an appreciation of other languages and customs. Some translated books include a glossary of foreign words, meanings, and pronunciations. This permits readers to risk new and different words and sounds with no loss of confidence. Although too many words left untranslated can be annoying to the reader, a few can be enjoyable and provoke an interest in foreign languages. The translation should not violate the tone of the book by being so idiomatic as to jar the reader. For example, a book from Czechoslovakia rings untrue if the translation of the young people's language sounds like hip American slang or street talk.

Teachers and librarians may note in some international books differences in writing and illustrating styles. International chapter books for intermediate and upper-grade readers lean toward introspection by the main character. Examples are 1990 Hans Christian Andersen Medalist Tormod Haugen's *Night Birds* and *Zeppelin*. Students could be alerted to the differences and asked to reflect on why the author may have chosen that manner of telling the story. In some cases, illustrations in international books are more abstract than is usual for U.S. picture books. Aspects of plot and theme in these books are heavily embedded in the pictorial details. For example, many layers of meaning can be unraveled with repeated readings of the story personifying the months of the year in *December's Travels,* illustrated by Dušan Kállay, 1988 Hans Christian Andersen Medalist.

With the increase of internationalism in all domains of our social and cultural life, more international children's books are becoming available in the United States. To locate international children's book titles, a number of selection sources will prove helpful. *Bookbird,* the International Board on Books for Young People (IBBY) journal, announces recent international award-winning books and national award winners from many nations and is, therefore, an important source for current information on international books. It also features articles on international children's literature. The *USBBY Newsletter* from the United States section of IBBY, and the international page of *Reading Today,* the bulletin of the International Reading Association, highlight events of interest in the United States and other countries related to this field.

The lists of past winners of the Hans Christian Andersen Award, the Mildred L. Batchelder Award, and the British, Australian, New Zealand, and Canadian awards for children's books are excellent sources of international titles and authors. (See Appendix A.) The major children's book review sources include reviews of notable international books in their monthly review columns. (See Appendix G for lists of these journals.) *Booklist,* a review journal published by the American Library Association, has occasional summary booklists on translated books and on foreign language books.

The newsletters, *The Bulletin* and *The Dragon Lode,* of the children's literature special interest groups of the National Council of Teachers of English (NCTE) and the International Reading Association (IRA) have columns devoted to international book reviews. The parent organizations may be contacted for membership information on special interest groups.

Marianne Carus, who grew up in Nazi Germany, made a commitment when founding the children's magazine, *Cricket,* to include "translated stories from as many countries as possible and about as many cultures as possible" because of her belief that "the earlier in life we lay the foundation for international understanding and tolerance, the sounder will be the bridges built later and the more ready for peaceful traffic and exchange back and forth" (Carus, 1980, pp. 174–175). This outstanding magazine, a good source for short read-alouds, features U.S. and international short stories of high quality for children from ages 6 to 12. Although international children's books are published each year by many of the largest U.S. publishers, their numbers are relatively small. Many small press publishers have taken the lead in this field and in publishing multicultural books. A publication that lists small, alternative publishers of children's books with a description of their emphases is *Alternative Press Publishers of Children's Books: A Directory* (4th edition) by Kathleen T. Horning. (For further information see Appendix G.)

A few publishers have specialized in international children's books and deserve special mention here.

African Imprints Library Services, 410 West Falmouth Highway, Box 350, West Falmouth, MA 02574. This catalogue includes recent children's books available from 20 African nations.

Atheneum/Margaret K. McElderry Books, Macmillan Publishing Company, 866 Third Avenue, New York, NY 10022. This company publishes picture books and chapter books from other English-speaking countries and translated children's chapter books. Margaret K. McElderry, a children's book editor, is recognized for her leadership in bringing more translated children's books to the United States.

Farrar, Straus, and Giroux, 19 Union Square West, New York, NY 10003. As a result of a translation and distribution agreement with the largest Swedish publisher of children's books, Rabén and Sjögren, this company publishes a number of translated Swedish books every year.

Kane/Miller Book Publishers, P.O. Box 529, Brooklyn, NY 11231-0005. This small press specializes in translated foreign children's picture books from around the world under the "Cranky Nell" imprint.

Lerner Publications Company/Carolrhoda Books, Inc., 241 First Avenue North, Minneapolis, MN 55401. This company publishes many multicultural and international nonfiction and fiction children's books.

Picture Book Studio, P.O. Box 9139, 10 Central Street, Saxonville, MA 01701. This company publishes many international picture books, some being collaborative works between Europeans and Americans.

Tundra Books of Northern New York, Box 1030, Plattsburgh, NY 12901. This company specializes in Canadian and French/English bilingual books for children.

Turton and Chambers Ltd., Station Road, Woodchester Stroud, Glos GL5 5EQ, England. This firm specializes in translating into English and publishing foreign children's books for distribution in England and Australia. Books can be ordered by catalog from England.

Wellington Publishing Company, P.O. Box 14877, Chicago, IL 60614. This small press specializes in translated children's books.

Historical Overview of International Literature

Much of the children's literature available in the United States during the seventeenth, eighteenth, nineteenth, and early twentieth centuries came from Europe. These early children's books are an important part of our cultural heritage, but we seldom think of the fact that they were originally published in other countries and many in other

TABLE 10–2 Early Milestones in International Children's Literature

Date	Event	Significance
1648	*Orbis Pictus* by John Amos Comenius	Earliest nonfiction picture book
1697	*Tales of Mother Goose* by Charles Perrault	Early folktales from France
1719	*Robinson Crusoe* by Daniel Defoe	Two early adult adventure books from England, adopted by children
1726	*Gulliver's Travels* by Jonathan Swift	
1812	*Nursery and Household Tales* by Jakob and Wilhelm Grimm	Traditional folktales from Germany
1833	*Fairy Tales* by Hans Christian Andersen	Early modern folktales from Denmark
1846	*Book of Nonsense* by Edward Lear	Early humorous poetry from England
1865	*Alice's Adventures in Wonderland* by Lewis Carroll	Classic English modern fantasy
1880	*Heidi* by Johanna Spyri	Early realistic story from Switzerland
1881	*The Adventures of Pinocchio* by Carlo Collodi	Modern fantasy from Italy
1883	*Treasure Island* by Robert Louis Stevenson	Adventure tale from England by a Scottish author
1885	*A Child's Garden of Verses* by Robert Louis Stevenson	Classic collection of Golden Age poems from England
1894	*The Jungle Book* by Rudyard Kipling	Animal stories set in India by an English author
1901	*The Tale of Peter Rabbit* by Beatrix Potter	Classic English picture book
1906	*The Wonderful Adventures of Nils* by Selma Lagerlöf	A fantasy trip around Sweden
1908	*Wind in the Willows* by Kenneth Grahame	Animal fantasy from England
1908	*Anne of Green Gables* by Lucy M. Montgomery	Realistic family story from Canada
1926	*Winnie-the-Pooh* by A. A. Milne	Personified toy story from England
1928	*Bambi* by Felix Salten	Personified deer story from Germany
1931	*The Story of Babar* by Jean de Brunhoff	Personified elephant fantasy from France
1945	*Pippi Longstocking* by Astrid Lindgren	Classic fantasy from Sweden
1949	*Finn Family Moomintroll* by Tove Jansson	Fantasy about small creatures in Finland

languages. They are so familiar to us in United States that we consider them our children's classics, and indeed they have become so. Table 10–2 lists a sampling of international children's classics published from the end of the seventeenth century up to World War II.

With the rapid growth in the U.S. children's book field in the twentieth century, the flow of books from other countries became overshadowed by large numbers of U.S. publications. In addition, during World War II, little cultural exchange occurred across international borders. The end of World War II saw a change in the international mood, and two developments occurred that had far-reaching effects on the children's book field: (1) children's books in translation began to be published in unprecedented numbers (Carus, 1980) and (2) the international children's book field was established and fostered by an international organization, awards, and publishers' bookfairs of children's books.

The first development—a wider exchange of international children's books—brought many memorable books to the United States from other countries. As was true prior to World War II, most of the international children's literature available in the United States was from European countries. This trend continues today, with one exception—Japan. Many Japanese picture books have been translated and published in the United States and have received considerable recognition. The best known of the Japanese artists in the United States is Mitsumasa Anno. Although more international books are now being published, books from other countries have stiff competition from U.S. books and have not always been commercial successes—making this field risky for publishers. The contributions of publishers who publish international titles need to be recognized, and a concerted effort among all book professionals is needed to make these books available to children in their libraries and schools.

The second development—the establishment of an international children's book field—was advanced by Jella Lepman, who described these early developments in *A Bridge of Children's Books* (1969). Lepman, a German-born Jew who left Germany during World War II for England, returned to Germany after the war to work in the field of children's books as a way to promote international understanding and world peace. Lepman began a traveling exhibit of children's books for German children, which in 1949 was established as the International Youth Library (IYL) in Munich. The IYL is the largest collection of children's books from around the world and currently holds well over 400,000 books. In reflecting on these accomplishments, Lepman concludes in her book that "in many parts of the world children were holding books in their hands and meeting over a bridge of children's books" (p. 154).

Lepman also worked with others from many countries in establishing the International Board on Books for Young People (IBBY) in 1953. IBBY is organized by sections from member countries. The members of national sections are children's book editors, agents, librarians, publishers, educators, translators, authors, illustrators—anyone who works in the children's book field. In 1956, IBBY founded the Hans Christian Andersen Medal, an international award program that honors outstanding authors of children's literature. The first recipient of this medal was Eleanor Farjeon of Great Britain. The medal is given every two years, and in 1966 an award to outstanding illustrators was added. Alois Carigiet of Switzerland was the 1966 Medal winner for illustrations. (See Appendix A for other Hans Christian Andersen Award winners.) In 1963, IBBY founded *Bookbird,* an international quarterly periodical on literature for children and young people. IBBY holds a biennial world congress in September; the first congress held in North America was in Williamsburg, Virginia, in 1990.

In 1967, the Biennale of Illustrations Bratislava (BIB), an international exposition of children's book illustrations, was established and takes place every other year in Bratislava, Czechoslovakia. An international jury selects prize-winning children's book illustrations for a Grand Prix, the highest award, and recognizes honor books.

In 1968, the first Mildred L. Batchelder Award was announced by the American Library Association in honor of a U.S. publisher of the most distinguished translated children's book published in the preceding year. This award is given annually to encourage the translation and publication of international books in the United States. (See Appendix A for the award list.)

An international children's bookfair is convened in Bologna, Italy, every April for children's book publishers. This forum has proved to be an important one for the international exchange of children's books—a time when publishers display their best in the interests of attracting publishers from other nations to publish the new books in their own countries. Three prizes are awarded at this fair, one selected by a jury of children from ages 6 to 9.

TABLE 10–3   Milestones in the Develpment of an International Children's Book Field

Date	Event	Significance
1949	Founding of the International Youth Library in Munich, Germany	A center for the collection and study of world children's literature
1953	Establishment of the International Board on Books for Young People (IBBY)	An organization for exchange among professionals working in the international children's book field
1956	IBBY awards the Hans Christian Andersen Medal to Eleanor Farjeon, England	The first international award for authors of children's books
1966	IBBY awards the Hans Christian Andersen Medal to Alois Carigiet, France	The first international award for illustrators of children's books
1966	Children's book fair begun in Bologna, Italy	An international exchange for publishers of children's books; award given for the best books
1966	*Bookbird,* quarterly journal from IBBY begun	A journal for international exchange on children's literature
1967	Establishment of the Biennale of Illustrations Bratislava	An international exposition of children's book illustrations
1968	The Mildred L. Batchelder Award given to Knopf for Erich Kästner's *The Little Man*	An award established by the American Library Association to recognize U.S. publishers of translated children's books
1990	IBBY held its biennial congress in Williamsburg, Virginia	First IBBY Congress held in North America

The future of international children's literature depends upon our success in several arenas. First, we must encourage the development of stronger national literatures from developing nations where most literature remains at the stage of the oral tradition. We must also promote more literary exchange with nations whose literature is now growing rapidly in order to bring more of the world's best literature to our children's attention. Finally, we must support those organizations that can assist in these endeavors. Milestones in the development of an international children's book field are highlighted in Table 10–3.

International Books by World Regions

Quite logically, the international books most often available in the United States have been and continue to be books from other English-speaking countries. These *English language* books originate in many different countries, but the largest numbers of them come from Great Britain, Australia, Canada, and New Zealand. Although the books do not require translation, they are often published in the United Sates with other changes: spelling, characters' names, place names, and, sometimes titles and cover illustrations. These changes are made ostensibly in order to increase the marketability of the books in this country, and may indeed accomplish that end in some cases. Due to the shared primary language and some cultural commonalities among these nations, the literary exchange has been relatively easy. Teachers are often surprised to discover that one of their favorite authors is British, Canadian, or Australian. An example is *The Jolly Postman* by Janet and Allan Ahlberg. However, many English language books do feature cultural attitudes and customs not typically found in the United States that warrant comparison and discussion by students. The major awards and award winners from English-speaking countries are listed in Appendix A.

Translated books come to the United States from around the world, but the largest numbers come from Europe. Today, many books come from Sweden, Norway, Denmark, from Switzerland, the Netherlands, Germany, France, and Belgium, and in considerably smaller numbers from eastern European countries, especially Czechoslovakia and the former Soviet Union. A few books come from Italy and Spain. An example from Norway is *Two Short and One Long* by Nina Aamundsen.

Translated children's literature from Asia originates mostly in Japan, but books from Korea, China and Thailand can occasionally be found. Japan has an extremely sophisticated field of book illustrating, and many beautifully illustrated picture books are now making their way into the U.S. market. An example from Sri Lanka is *The Umbrella Thief* by Sybil Wettasinghe.

African nations have produced little children's literature that has been exported to the United States. The reasons for this are many, but probably the most influential one is that of economics. Publishing books is expensive, especially in full color, thus the publishing industry is not firmly established in developing countries. An example from Ghana is *Cat in Search of a Friend* by Meshack Asare. Central and South American countries suffer from similar economic problems and the field of children's literature is less advanced. However, books from Costa Rica, Colombia, and Venezuela are arriving recently in more substantial numbers. An example from Venezuela is *The Night of the Stars* by Douglas Gutiérrez and María Fernandez Oliver.

The difficulties of locating and translating good books from non-English-speaking countries contribute to the dearth of available titles. Certain publishing companies have been attempting to overcome this dearth of foreign literature in our country by focusing solely on foreign children's literature, whereas other publishers have made a concerted effort to increase the percentage of foreign books among their titles. These efforts are encouraging. As more librarians, teachers, and parents become interested in purchasing this body of literature, more publishers will become willing to meet the market need.

There is reason to hope that the current unrest between cultures will not always be the case. Ethnic prejudice and bias are not natural behaviors; they are learned. One of the most intriguing challenges to those who work with children is to combat the ignorance that is at the root of racial, cultural, and religious prejudice and intolerance. Children's literature, particularly the rich multicultural and international selections currently available, is a powerful tool in this effort, for it shows that the similarities between all people are much more fundamental than the differences.

References

Carus, M. (1980). Translation and internationalism in children's literature. *Children's Literature in Education, 11*(4), 171–179.

Damjan, M. (1986). *December's travels*. Illustrated by Dušan Kállay. Translated by Anthea Bell. New York: Dial.

Haugen, T. (1982). *Night birds*. Translated by Sheila LaFarge. New York: Delacorte.

Haugen, T. (1991). *Zeppelin*. Translated by David Jacobs. Stroud, England: Turton & Chambers Ltd.

Larrick, N. (1965). The all-white world of children's books. *Saturday Review* (September 11), 63–65, 84–85.

Lepman, J. (1969). *A bridge of children's books*. Chicago: American Library Association.

Rudman, M. (1984). *Children's literature: An issues approach* (2nd ed.). New York: Longman.

Sims, R. (1982). *Shadow and substance: Afro-American experience in contemporary children's fiction*. Urbana, IL: NCTE.

Notable Authors and Illustrators of Multicultural Literature

African American

Verna Aardema, reteller of African folktales. *Bringing the Rain to Kapiti Plain; Why Mosquitoes Buzz in People's Ears.*

Arnold Adoff, author of several books of poetry about the African-American experience. *Black Is Brown Is Tan*

Ashley Bryan, collector, teller, and illustrator of African songs and folktales. *I'm Going to Sing: Black American Spirituals.*

Lucille Clifton, author of the *Everett Anderson* series of picture story books. *Everett Anderson's Good-bye.*

Leo and Diane Dillon, illustrators of two Caldecott Award-winning books. Leo Dillon is the first African American to win a Caldecott Award. *Why Mosquitoes Buzz in People's Ears; Ashanti to Zulu.*

Virginia Hamilton, award-winning author whose books about African Americans include realistic fiction, mystery, fantasy, myth, and biography. *M. C. Higgins, the Great; Zeely.*

Langston Hughes, leading African-American poet of the twentieth century; not primarily a children's poet. *The Dream Keeper.*

Ezra Jack Keats, author/illustrator whose picture book character, Peter, was the first African-American protagonist in a Caldecott Award-winning book. *The Snowy Day; Peter's Chair.*

Julius Lester, author of nonfiction and collector and reteller of African-American folktales. *To Be a Slave.*

Patricia McKissack, author of modern African-American folktales and informational books. *Mirandy and Brother Wind.*

Walter Dean Myers, author of sometimes gritty contemporary realistic fiction about African Americans growing up. *The Scorpions; Fallen Angels.*

Jerry Pinkney, illustrator whose light-filled watercolors capture the beauty of African Americans. *The Talking Eggs.*

John Steptoe, first African-American author/illustrator to gain fame in the United States. *Stevie; Mufaro's Beautiful Daughters.*

Mildred Taylor, author whose award-winning books of historical fiction chronicle the experience of growing up Black in southern United States in the 1940s and 50s. *Roll of Thunder, Hear My Cry; The Friendship.*

Asian American

Yoshiko Uchida, author of autobiographical accounts of U.S. imprisonment of Japanese-American citizens during World War II. *Journey to Topaz; Journey Home.*

Taro Yashima, author/illustrator of some of the first picture books with Asian protagonists. *Crow Boy; Umbrella.*

Paul Yee, author who writes about the Chinese Canadian experience. *Tales from Gold Mountain: Stories of the Chinese in the New World.*

Laurence Yep, author of historical and contemporary realistic fiction about growing up as an Asian American. *Dragonwings; Child of the Owl.*

Ed Young, first Asian-American illustrator to win the Caldecott Award. *Lon Po Po: A Red-Riding Hood Story from China.*

Hispanic American

Leo Politi, author/illustrator of several award-winning picture books having Hispanic-American characters. *Pedro, the Angel of Olvera Street; Juanita.*

Nicholasa Mohr, author of several novels about Puerto Rican life in New York City. *Felita; Going Home.*

Jewish American

Milton Meltzer, author of important nonfictional works about several U.S. minorities. *Remember the Days: A Short History of the Jewish American.*

Isaac Bashevis Singer, Nobel prize-winning author of several collections of tales that tell much about Jewish traditions and customs. *When Shlemiel Went to Warsaw and Other Stories.*

Native American

John Bierhorst, collector of traditional literature of Native Americans and South American and Mexican Indians. *The Fire Plume: Legends of the American Indians.*

Ann Nolan Clark, author of many works of nonfiction for and about Native Americans. *Secret of the Andes.*

Paul Goble, reteller and illustrator of the folktales and legends of the Native Americans of the Great Plains. *The Girl Who Loved Wild Horses.*

Jamake Highwater, author of the Ghost Horse Cycle in which many aspects of the Native American heritage are examined. *Legend Days.*

Scott O'Dell, author of several works of award-winning historical fiction featuring strong female Native-American heroines. *Island of the Blue Dolphins.*

Virginia Driving Hawk Sneve, author of contemporary realistic novels about life on Native-American reservations. *When Thunders Spoke.*

Notable Authors, Illustrators, and Translators of International Literature

Lena Anderson, Swedish illustrator of the *Linnea* books by Christina Björk, and her own *Baby Bunny* series.

Mitsumasa Anno, Japanese author/illustrator of sophisticated wordless picture books and concept books; 1984 recipient of the Hans Christian Andersen Award. *Topsy Turvies: Pictures to Stretch the Imagination* and *Anno's Journey.*

Jeannie Baker, Australian artist who uses relief collages in her illustrations. *Where the Forest Meets the Sea* and *Home in the Sky.*

Graeme Base, Australian illustrator of large, elaborate format picture books. *Animalia* and *The Eleventh Hour.*

Anthea Bell, British award-winning translator from German, Dutch, and Danish languages. Translated *Buster's World* by Bjarne Reuter and *Konrad* by Christine Nöstlinger.

Quentin Blake, British illustrator popular for his irreverently humorous style. *Quentin Blake's ABC* and *Nonstop Nonsense* by Margaret Mahy.

Cecil Bödker, Danish author of stories set in Africa; recipient of 1976 Hans Christian Andersen Award. *The Leopard.*

Anthony Browne, British author/illustrator whose stark realism reveals modern social ills. *Wally the Wimp* and *Gorilla.*

Patricia Crampton, British translator from German, Dutch, and Scandinavian languages into English. Winner of the 1984 Astrid Lindgren Translation Prize. Translated *No Hero for the Kaiser* by Rudolf Frank.

Elizabeth D. Crawford, U.S. translator from German, French, and Dutch; translated *Crutches* and *Old John* by Peter Härtling, and *Hansel and Gretel* illustrated by Lisbeth Zwerger.

Roald Dahl, British author of extremely popular and wildly humorous modern fantasies. *James and the Giant Peach* and *Charlie and the Chocolate Factory.*

Peter Dickinson, British author of science fiction. *Heartsease* and *Tulku.*

Mem Fox, Australian author of picture storybooks often employing Australian animals. *Possum Magic* and *Koala Lou.*

Maria Gripe, Swedish author of contemporary realistic fiction novels; recipient of the 1974 Hans Christian Andersen Medal. *The Night Daddy* and *Hugo and Josephine.*

Ted Harrison, Canadian illustrator particularly noted for his interpretations of the frozen north. *A Northern Alphabet* and *The Cremation of Sam McGee* by Robert Service.

Peter Härtling, German author of World War II historical fiction novels. *Crutches* and *Old John.*

Erik Christian Haugaard, British author noted for historical fiction novels. *Hakon of Rogen's Saga* and *Cromwell's Boy.*

Tormod Haugen, Norwegian author of introspective novels for adolescents; recipient of 1990 Hans Christian Andersen Award. *Night Birds* and *Zeppelin.*

James Houston, Canadian author of survival stories and tales of Inuit Indians. *The Falcon Bow* and *The White Archer.*

Monica Hughes, Canadian author of contemporary fiction and science fiction. *The Keeper of the Isis Light* and *The Dream Catcher.*

Tove Jansson, Finnish creator of the *Moomin* fantasy stories; recipient of the 1966 Hans Christian Andersen Award. *Finn Family Moomintroll.*

Dušan Kállay, Czechoslovakian illustrator and winner of the Bratislava Grand Prix and the 1988 Hans Christian Andersen Award. Illustrated *December's Travels* by Mischa Damjan.

Dennis Lee, Canadian poet known for humorous poetry. *Alligator Pie* and *Garbage Delight.*

Astrid Lindgren, Swedish author of classic fantasy, *Pippi Longstocking,* and realistic novels; second recipient of the Hans Christian Andersen Medal. *The Brothers Lionheart.*

Jean Little, Canadian author of realistic chapter books featuring children with emotional and physical disabilities. *Mine for Keeps* and *Mama's Going to Buy You a Mockingbird.*

Janet Lunn, Canadian author of historical time fantasy novels. *The Root Cellar* and *Shadow in Hawthorn Bay.*

Margaret Mahy, New Zealand author of modern fantasies with supernatural elements. *The Haunting* and *The Changeover.*

Kevin Major, Canadian award-winning author of popular adolescent novels. *Hold Fast* and *Blood Red Ochre.*

Lucy M. Montgomery, Canadian author of *Anne of Green Gables* stories.

Farley Mowat, Canadian author of animal stories. *Owls in the Family* and *Never Cry Wolf.*

Mary Norton, British author of *The Borrowers* series about personified little people.

Christine Nöstlinger, Austrian author of humorous fantasy; 1984 recipient of the Hans Christian Andersen Award. *Konrad.*

Lygia Bojunga Nunes, Brazilian author who received the 1982 Hans Christian Andersen Award for her personified animal stories. *The Companions.*

A. Philippa Pearce, British author of modern fantasies and contemporary mysteries. *Tom's Midnight Garden* and *The Way to Sattin Shore.*

Stéphane Poulin, Canadian artist known for the *Josephine* cat stories and a bilingual ABC. *Ah! belle cité / A Beautiful City ABC.*

Bohumil Říha, Czechoslovakian author; recipient of the 1980 Hans Christian Andersen Award. *New Gulliver.*

Ivan Southall, Australian author of realistic adventure stories. *Josh; Ash Road;* and *Let the Balloon Go.*

Rosemary Sutcliff, British author of historical fiction novels. *The Lantern Bearers* and *Bonnie Dundee.*

Colin Thiele, Australian author of realistic novels whose isolated settings reveal the enormity of the country. *Fire in the Stone* and *Storm Boy.*

Julie Vivas, Australian illustrator of picture books. *Possum Magic* and *Wilfred Gordon McDonald Partridge.*

Brian Wildsmith, British illustrator noted for his innovative and modernistic designs. *Brian Wildsmith's ABC* and *Brian Wildsmith's Mother Goose.*

Patricia Wrightson, Australian author of contemporary novels with Aboriginal folk spirits; received the Hans Christian Andersen Award in 1988. *The Nargun and the Stars* and *A Little Fear.*

Alki Zei, Greek author of historical fiction novels; three-time recipient of the Mildred L. Batchelder Award. *Wildcat Under Glass* and *The Sound of Dragon's Feet.*

Lisbeth Zwerger, Austrian illustrator and recipient of the 1990 Hans Christian Andersen Award; particularly noted for her illustrations of traditional folktales, including tales of the Brothers Grimm. *Hansel and Gretel* and *Little Red Cap.*

Recommended Multicultural Books

Ages refer to approximate interest levels. YA = young adult readers.

African American

Aardema, Verna. *Bringing the Rain to Kapiti Plain: A Nandi Tale.* Illustrated by Beatriz Vidal. Dial, 1981. Ages 7–9.

———. *Why Mosquitoes Buzz in People's Ears.* Illustrated by Leo and Diane Dillon. Dial, 1975. Ages 5–7.

Adoff, Arnold. *Black Is Brown Is Tan.* Harper, 1973. Ages 8–10.

———. *Malcolm X.* Crowell, 1970. Ages 8–10.

Armstrong, William H. *Sounder.* Harper, 1969. Ages 9–12.

Bontemps, Arne. *The Story of the Negro.* Knopf, 1948. Ages 9–12.

Bryan, Ashley. *Turtle Knows Your Name.* Atheneum, 1989. Ages 6–8.

Burgess, Barbara Hood. *Oren Bell.* Delacorte, 1991. Ages 8–10.

Carew, Jan. *Children of the Sun.* Illustrated by Leo and Diane Dillon. Little, Brown, 1980. Ages 6–8.

Clifton, Lucille. *Everett Anderson's Good-bye.* Illustrated by Ann Grifalconi. Holt, 1988. Ages 5–7.

Collier, James, and Christopher Collier. *Jump Ship to Freedom.* Delacorte, 1981. (Others in the

Arabus Family Saga: *War Comes to Willy Freeman*, 1983; *Who Is Carrie?*, 1984.) Ages 9–12.

Courlander, Harold. *The Crest and the Hide: And Other African Stories of Heroes, Chiefs, Bards, Hunters, Sorcerers, and Common People.* Illustrated by Monica Vachula. Coward-McCann, 1982. Ages 8–10.

Davis, Ossie. *Langston: A Play.* Delacorte, 1982. Ages 8–10.

De Treviño, Elizabeth Borton. *I, Juan de Pareja.* Farrar, 1965. Ages 9–12.

Ellis, Veronica Freeman. *Afro-Bets First Book About Africa.* Just Us Books, 1990. Ages 4–6.

Feelings, Muriel. *Jambo Means Hello: Swahili Alphabet Book.* Dial, 1974. Ages 6–8.

———. *Moja Means One: Swahili Counting Book.* Illustrated by Tom Feelings. Dial, 1971. Ages 6–8.

Flournoy, Valerie. *The Patchwork Quilt.* Illustrated by Jerry Pinkney. Dial, 1985. Ages 5–7.

Fox, Paula. *The Slave Dancer.* Bradbury, 1973. Ages 9–12.

Greene, Bette. *Philip Hall Likes Me. I Reckon Maybe.* Illustrated by Charles Lilly. Dial, 1974. Ages 8–10.

Greenfield, Eloise. *Honey, I Love and Other Love Poems.* Viking, 1978. Ages 6–10.

———. *Nathaniel Talking.* Illustrated by Jan Spivey Gilchrist. Black Butterfly, 1989. Ages 6–10.

———. *Under the Sunday Tree.* Illustrated by Amos Ferguson. Harper, 1988. Ages 6–10.

Grifalconi, Ann. *The Village of Round and Square Houses.* Little, Brown, 1986. Ages 7–9.

Haley, Gail. *A Story, a Story.* Atheneum, 1970. Ages 7–9.

Hamilton, Virginia. *The All Jahdu Storybook.* Illustrated by Barry Moser. Harcourt, 1991. Ages 7–9.

———. *Cousins.* Philomel, 1990. Ages 9–12.

———. *The House of Dies Drear.* Illustrated by Eros Keith. Macmillan, 1968. (See sequel: *The Mystery of Drear House,* Greenwillow, 1987.) Ages 9–12.

———. *M. C. Higgins, the Great.* Macmillan, 1974. Ages 9–12.

———. *The Magical Adventures of Pretty Pearl.* Harper, 1983. Ages 7–9.

———. *The Planet of Junior Brown.* Macmillan, 1971. Ages 12–YA.

———. *The People Could Fly: American Black Folktales.* Illustrated by Leo and Diane Dillon. Knopf, 1985. Ages 7–9.

———. *Zeely.* Illustrated by Symeon Shimin. Macmillan, 1967. Ages 7–9.

Harris, Joel Chandler. *Jump! the Adventures of Brer Rabbit.* Adapted by Van Dyke Parks. Illustrated by Barry Moser. Harcourt, 1986. (See also: *Jump Again! More Adventures of Brer Rabbit,* 1987.) Ages 7–9.

Haskins, Francine. *I Remember "121."* Children's Book Press, 1991. Ages 6–8.

Hoffman, Mary. *Amazing Grace.* Illustrated by Caroline Binch. Dial, 1991. Ages 6–8.

Howard, Elizabeth Fitzgerald. *Aunt Flossie's Hats (and Crab Cakes Later).* Illustrated by James Ransome. Clarion, 1991. Ages 6–8.

Hurmence, Belinda. *A Girl Called Boy.* Clarion, 1982. Ages 9–12.

Joseph, Lynn. *A Wave in Her Pocket: Stories from Trinidad.* Illustrated by Brian Pinkney. Clarion, 1991. Ages 7–9.

Lester, Julius. *How Many Spots Does a Leopard Have?* Illustrated by David Shannon. Scholastic, 1989. Ages 7–9.

———, reteller. *The Tales of Uncle Remus: The Adventures of Brer Rabbit.* Illustrated by Jerry Pinkney. Dial, 1987. (See also: *More Tales of Uncle Remus: Further Adventures of Brer Rabbit, His Friends, Enemies, and Others,* 1988.) Ages 7–9.

———. *To Be a Slave.* Dial, 1968. Ages 9–12.

Lewin, Hugh. *Jafta.* Illustrated by Lisa Kopper. Carolrhoda, 1983. (See others in the *Jafta* series.) Ages 7–9.

Lyons, Mary E. *Sorrow's Kitchen: The Life of Zora Neale Hurston.* Scribner's, 1990. Ages 12–YA.

Mathis, Sharon Bell. *The Hundred Penny Box.* Illustrated by Leo and Diane Dillon. Viking, 1975. Ages 7–9.

McDermott, Gerald. *Anansi the Spider: A Tale from the Ashanti.* Holt, 1972. Ages 7–9.

McKissack, Patricia. *Mirandy and Brother Wind.* Illustrated by Jerry Pinkney. Knopf, 1988. Ages 7–9.

McKissack, Patricia, and Frederick McKissack. *A Long Hard Journey: The Story of the Pullman Porter.* Walker, 1989. Ages 8–10.

Meltzer, Milton. *The Black Americans: A History in Their Own Words, 1619–1983.* Crowell, 1984. Ages 12–YA.

Monjo, F. N. *The Drinking Gourd.* Illustrated by Fred Brenner. Harper, 1970. Ages 6–8.

Musgrove, Margaret. *Ashanti to Zulu: African Traditions.* Illustrated by Leo and Diane Dillon. Dial, 1976. Ages 8–10.

Myers, Walter Dean. *Now Is Your Time: The African-American Struggle for Freedom.* Harper, 1991. Ages 9–12.

———. *Scorpions.* Harper, 1988. Ages 9–12.

Price, Leontyne. *Aida.* Illustrated by Leo and Diane Dillon. Harcourt, 1990. Ages 8–10.

Ringgold, Faith. *Tar Beach.* Crown, 1991. Ages 6–8.

Sanfield, Steve. *The Adventures of High John the Conqueror.* Illustrated by John Ward. Watts, 1989. Ages 9–12.

Steptoe, John. *Mufaro's Beautiful Daughters.* Lothrop, 1987. Ages 7–9.

Taylor, Mildred. *Roll of Thunder, Hear My Cry.* Dial, 1976. (See others in the Logan family saga: *The Song of the Trees,* 1975; *Let the Circle Be Unbroken,* 1981; *Road to Memphis,* 1990.) Ages 9–12.

Turner, Glennette Tilley. *Take a Walk in Their Shoes.* Cobblehill, 1989. Ages 9–12.

Walter, Mildred Pitts. *Brother to the Wind.* Illustrated by Leo and Diane Dillon. Lothrop, 1985. Ages 6–8.

———. *Justin and the Best Biscuits in the World.* Illustrated by Catherine Stock. Lothrop, 1986. Ages 6–8.

Weik, Mary Hays. *The Jazz Man.* Illustrated by Ann Grifalconi. Atheneum, 1966. Ages 6–8.

Yarbrough, Camille. *Cornrows.* Illustrated by Carole Byard. Coward-McCann, 1979. Ages 6–8.

Yates, Elizabeth. *Amos Fortune, Free Man.* Illustrated by Nora S. Unwin. Dutton, 1950. Ages 8–10.

Asian American

Blumberg, Rhoda. *Commodore Perry in the Land of the Shogun.* Lothrop, 1985. Ages 9–12.

Brown, Tricia. *Lee Ann: The Story of a Vietnamese-American Girl.* Photographs by Ted Thai. Putnam, 1991. Ages 6–8.

Choi, Sook Nyul. *Year of Impossible Goodbyes.* Houghton, 1991. Ages 9–12.

Clark, Ann Nolan. *To Stand Against the Wind.* Viking, 1978. Ages 9–12.

Dooley, Norah. *Everybody Cooks Rice.* Illustrated by Peter J. Thornton. Carolrhoda, 1991. Ages 6–8.

Friedman, Ina R. *How My Parents Learned to Eat.* Illustrated by Allen Say. Houghton, 1984. Ages 7–9.

Ishii, Momoko. *The Tongue-Cut Sparrow.* Illustrated by Suekichi Akaba. Translated by Katherine Paterson. Dutton, 1987. Ages 7–9.

Levin, Ellen. *I Hate English!* Illustrated by Steve Bjorkman. Scholastic, 1989. Ages 7–9.

Lord, Bette Bao. *In the Year of the Boar and Jackie Robinson.* Illustrated by Marc Simont. Harper, 1984. Ages 7–9.

Morimoto, Junko. *My Hiroshima.* Viking, 1990. Ages 8–10.

Nelson, Theresa. *And One for All.* Orchard, 1989. Ages 12–YA.

Nhuong, Huynh Quang. *The Land I Lost: Adventures of a Boy in Vietnam.* Illustrated by Vo-Dinh Mai. Harper, 1982. Ages 9–12.

Pelligrini, Nina. *Families Are Different.* Holiday, 1991. Ages 6–8.

Snyder, Dianne. *The Boy of the Three-Year Nap.* Illustrated by Allen Say. Houghton, 1988. Ages 7–9.

Tompert, Ann. *Grandfather Tang's Story: A Tale With Tangrams.* Illustrated by Robert Andrew Parker. Crown, 1990. Ages 7–9.

Uchida, Yoshiko. *Journey to Topaz.* Scribner's, 1971. (See sequel: *Journey Home,* Atheneum, 1978.) Ages 9–12.

Wallace, Ian. *Chin Chiang and the Dragon's Dance.* Atheneum, 1984. Ages 7–9.

Xiong, Blia. *Nine-in-One, Grr! Grr!* Adapted by Cathy Spagnoli. Illustrated by Nancy Hom. Children's Book Press, 1989. Ages 6–8.

Yee, Paul. *Tales from Gold Mountain: Stories of the Chinese in the New World.* Macmillan, 1990. Ages 8–10.

Yep, Laurence. *Child of the Owl.* Harper, 1977. Ages 12–YA.

————. *Dragonwings*. Harper, 1975. Ages 9–12.

————. *The Rainbow People*. Harper, 1989. Ages 9–12.

————. *The Star Fisher*. Morrow, 1991. Ages 12–YA.

————. *Tongues of Jade*. Illustrated by David Wiesner. HarperCollins, 1991. Ages 8–12.

Yoshi. *Who's Hiding Here?* Picture Book Studio, 1987. Ages 3–5.

Hispanic American

Aardema, Verna. *Borreguita and the Coyote*. Illustrated by Petra Mathers. Knopf, 1991. Ages 6–8.

————. *The Riddle of the Drum: A Tale from Tizapan, Mexico*. Illustrated by Tony Chen. Four Winds, 1979. Ages 7–9.

Belpré, Pura. *Once in Puerto Rico*. Illustrated by Christine Price. Warne, 1973. Ages 8–10.

Buss, Fran Leeper, with assistance of Daisy Cubias. *Journey of the Sparrows*. Lodestar, 1991. Ages 9–12.

Carlson, Lori M., and Cynthia L. Ventura, eds. *Where Angels Glide at Dawn: New Stories from Latin America*. Illustrated by José Ortega. Lippincott, 1990. Ages 12–YA.

Castañeda, Omar S. *Among the Volcanoes*. Lodestar, 1991. Ages 12–YA.

Clark, Ann Nolan. *Secret of the Andes*. Illustrated by Jean Charlot. Viking, 1952. Ages 9–12.

————. *Year Walk*. Viking, 1975. Ages 9–12.

Delacre, Lulu. *Arroz con Leche: Popular Songs and Rhymes from Latin America*. Scholastic, 1989. Ages 6–10.

DeMessieres, Nicole. *Reina the Galgo*. Dutton, 1981. Ages 8–10.

De Treviño, Elizabeth Borton. *El Güero: A True Adventure Story*. Illustrated by Leslie W. Bowman. Farrar, 1989. Ages 8–10.

Durros, Arthur. *Abuela*. Dutton, 1991. Ages 6–8.

Ets, Marie Hall, and Aurora Labastida. *Nine Days to Christmas: A Story of Mexico*. Illustrated by Marie Hall Ets. Viking, 1959. Ages 6–8.

Griego y Maestas, José, and Rudolfo A. Anaya. *Cuentos: Tales from the Hispanic Southwest*. Illustrated by Jaime Valdez. Museum of New Mexico, 1980. Ages 7–9.

Hall, Lynn. *Danza!* Scribner's, 1981. Ages 7–9.

Haseley, Dennis. *Ghost Catcher*. Illustrated by Lloyd Bloom. Harper, 1991. Ages 6–8.

Hinojosa, Francisco, adaptor. *The Old Lady Who Ate People*. Illustrated by Leonel Maciel. Little, Brown, 1984. Ages 6–8.

Holman, Felice. *Secret City, U.S.A.* Scribner's, 1990. Ages 8–10.

Jagendorf, M. A., and R. S. Boggs. *The King of the Mountains: A Treasury of Latin American Folk Stories*. Vanguard, 1960. Ages 7–9.

Krumgold, Joseph. *. . . And Now Miguel*. Illustrated by Jean Charlot. Crowell, 1953. Ages 8–10.

Kurtycz, Marcos, and Ana Garcia Kobeh. *Tigers and Opossums: Animal Legends*. Little, Brown, 1984. Ages 7–9.

Mangurian, David. *Children of the Incas*. Macmillan, 1979. Ages 8–10.

Meyer, Carolyn, and Charles Gallenkamp. *The Mystery of the Ancient Maya*. Atheneum, 1985. Ages 8–10.

Millard, Anne. *The Incas*. Illustrated by Richard Hook. Warwick, 1980. Ages 7–9.

Mohr, Nicholasa. *Felita*. Illustrated by Ray Cruz. Dial, 1979. Ages 8–10.

O'Dell, Scott. *Carlota*. Houghton, 1981. Ages 9–12.

Politi, Leo. *Song of the Swallows*. Scribner's, 1949. Ages 6–8.

Rohmer, Harriet, adapter. *Uncle Nacho's Hat*. Illustrated by Veg Reisberg. Children's Book Press, 1989 (Bilingual, English-Spanish). Ages 6–8.

Soto, Gary. *Baseball in April and Other Stories*. Harcourt, 1990. Ages 9–12.

Winter, Jonah. *Diego*. Illustrated by Jeanette Winter. Knopf, 1991 (Bilingual, English-Spanish). Ages 7–9.

Zubizarreta, Rosalma, Harriet Rohmer, & David Schecter. From a poem by Alejandro Cruz Martinez. *The Woman Who Outshone the Sun*. Illustrated by Fernando Olivera. Children's Book Press, 1991 (Bilingual, English-Spanish). Ages 6–8.

Jewish American

Adler, David A. *A Picture Book of Hanukkah*. Illustrated by Linda Heller. Holiday, 1982. Ages 6–8.

————. *A Picture Book of Jewish Holidays.* Illustrated by Linda Heller. Holiday, 1981. Ages 6–8.

Barrie, Barbara. *Lone Star.* Delacorte, 1990. Ages 9–12.

Ehrlich, Amy. *The Story of Hanukkah.* Illustrated by Ori Sherman. Dial, 1989. Ages 6–8.

Geras, Adèle. *My Grandmother's Stories: A Collection of Jewish Folk Tales.* Illustrated by Jael Jordan. Knopf, 1990. Ages 8–10.

Goldin, Barbara Diamond. *Cakes and Miracles: A Purim Tale.* Illustrated by Erika Weihs. Viking, 1991. Ages 7–9.

Hutton, Warwick. *Moses in the Bulrushes.* Atheneum, 1986. Ages 6–8.

Hautzig, Esther. *The Endless Steppe: A Girl in Exile.* Crowell, 1968. Ages 9–12.

Kimmel, Eric, adapter. *Days of Awe: Stories for Rosh Hashanah and Yom Kippur.* Illustrated by Erika Weihs. Viking, 1991. Ages 8–10.

————. *Hershel and the Hanukkah Goblins.* Illustrated by Trina Schart Hyman. Holiday, 1989. Ages 7–9.

Lasky, Kathryn. *The Night Journey.* Warne, 1981. Ages 9–12.

Levitin, Sonja. *Journey to America.* Atheneum, 1970. (See sequel: *Silver Days,* 1989.) Ages 12–YA.

Livingston, Myra Cohn. *Poems for Jewish Holidays.* Illustrated by Lloyd Bloom. Holiday, 1986. Ages 6–10.

Lowry, Lois. *Number the Stars.* Houghton, 1989. Ages 7–9.

Meltzer, Milton. *Never to Forget: The Jews of the Holocaust.* Harper, 1976. Ages 12–YA.

————. *Remember the Days: A Short History of the Jewish American.* Illustrated by Harvey Dinnerstein. Doubleday, 1974. Ages 12–YA.

————. *Rescue: The Story of How Gentiles Saved Jews in the Holocaust.* Harper, 1988. Ages 9–12.

Orlev, Uri. *The Island on Bird Street.* Translated by Hillel Halkin. Houghton, 1984. Ages 9–12.

————. *The Man from the Other Side.* Translated by Hillel Halkin. Houghton, 1991. Ages 9–12.

Reiss, Johanna. *The Upstairs Room.* Crowell, 1972. Ages 9–12.

Richter, Hans Peter. *Friedrich.* Translated by Edite Kroll. Holt, 1970. (See sequel: *I Was There,* 1972.) Ages 9–12.

Rogasky, Barbara. *Smoke and Ashes: The Story of the Holocaust.* Holiday, 1988. Ages 12–YA.

Schwartz, Amy. *Mrs. Moskowitz and the Sabbath Candlesticks.* Jewish Publication Society, 1985. Ages 7–9.

Siegal, Aranka. *Upon the Head of the Goat: A Childhood in Hungary 1939–1944.* Farrar, 1981. (See sequel: *Grace in the Wilderness: After the Liberation, 1945–1948,* 1985.) Ages 9–12.

Singer, Isaac Bashevis. *The Golem.* Illustrated by Uri Shulevitz. Farrar, 1982. Ages 8–10.

————. *When Shlemiel Went to Warsaw & Other Stories.* Illustrated by Margot Zemach. Farrar, 1968. Ages 8–10.

Singer, Isaac Bashevis, and Elizabeth Schub, translator. *Zlateh, the Goat, and Other Stories.* Illustrated by Maurice Sendak. Harper, 1966. Ages 7–9.

Slepian, Jan. *Risk n' Roses.* Putnam, 1990. Ages 8–10.

Zemach, Margot. *It Could Always Be Worse.* Farrar, 1977. Ages 6–8.

Native American

Aliki. *Corn Is Maize: The Gift of the Indians.* Crowell, 1976. Ages 6–8.

Andrews, Jan. *Very Last First Time.* Illustrated by Ian Wallace. McElderry, 1986. Ages 6–8.

Armer, Laura Adams. *Waterless Mountain.* Longmans, 1931. Ages 9–12.

Ashabranner, Brent. *Morning Star, Black Sun: The Northern Cheyenne Indians and America's Energy Crisis.* Photographs by Paul Conklin. Dodd, 1982. Ages 9–12.

————. *To Live in Two Worlds: American Indian Youth Today.* Photographs by Paul Conklin. Dodd, 1984. Ages 9–12.

Ata, Te. *Baby Rattlesnake.* Adapted by Lynn Moroney. Illustrated by Veg Reisberg. Children's Book Press, 1989. Ages 4–6.

Baker, Betty. *Rat Is Dead and Ant Is Sad.* Illustrated by Mamoru Funai. Harper, 1981. Ages 6–8.

Baker, Olaf. *Where the Buffaloes Begin.* Illustrated by Stephen Gammell. Warne, 1981. Ages 7–9.

Baylor, Byrd. *The Desert Is Theirs.* Illustrated by Peter Parnall. Scribner's, 1975. Ages 7–9.

————. *A God on Every Mountain Top: Stories of Southwest Indian Mountains.* Illustrated by Carol Brown. Scribner's, 1981. Ages 8–10.

————. *Hawk, I'm Your Brother.* Illustrated by Peter Parnall. Scribner's, 1976. Ages 8–10.

————. *Moonsong.* Illustrated by Ronald Himler. Scribner's, 1982. Ages 8–10.

Bealer, Alex. *Only the Names Remain: The Cherokees and the Trail of Tears.* Little, Brown, 1972. Ages 9–12.

Benchley, Nathaniel. *Only Earth and Sky Last Forever.* Harper, 1972. Ages 11–YA.

Bierhorst John, editor. *Black Rainbow: Legends of the Incas and Myths of Ancient Peru.* Farrar, 1976. Ages 9–12.

————. *Doctor Coyote: A Native American Aesop's Fables.* Illustrated by Wendy Watson. Macmillan, 1987. Ages 7–9.

————, editor. *The Hungry Woman: Myths and Legends of the Aztecs.* Morrow, 1984. Ages 8–10.

————, editor. *The Monkey's Haircut and Other Stories Told by the Maya.* Illustrated by Robert Andrew Parker. Morrow, 1986. Ages 8–10.

————, translator. *Spirit Child: A Story of the Nativity.* Illustrated by Barbara Cooney. Morrow, 1984. Ages 6–8.

————, editor. *The Whistling Skeleton: American Indian Tales of the Supernatural.* Illustrated by Robert Andrew Parker. Four Winds, 1982. Ages 7–9.

Bulla, Clyde Robert, and Michael Syson. *Conquista!* Illustrated by Ronald Himler. Crowell, 1978. Ages 7–9.

Coatsworth, Emerson, and David Coatsworth, editors. *The Adventures of Nanabush: Ojibway Indian Stories.* Illustrated by Francis Kagige. Atheneum, 1980. Ages 8–10.

Cohen, Caron Lee. *The Mud Pony.* Illustrated by Shonto Begay. Scholastic, 1988. Ages 6–8.

DeArmond, Dale, reteller. *The Boy Who Found the Light.* Little, Brown, 1990. Ages 8–10.

dePaola, Tomie. *The Legend of the Bluebonnet.* Putnam, 1983. Ages 6–8.

Ekoomiak, Normie. *Arctic Memories.* Holt, 1990 (Bilingual, English-Inuktitut). Ages 9–12.

Fleischman, Paul. *Saturnalia.* Harper, 1990. Ages 12–YA.

Freedman, Russell. *Buffalo Hunt.* Holiday, 1988. Ages 9–12.

————. *Indian Chiefs.* Holiday, 1987. Ages 9–12.

George, Jean Craighead. *Julie of the Wolves.* Harper, 1972. Ages 9–12.

————. *The Talking Earth.* Harper, 1983. Ages 9–12.

Goble, Paul. *Beyond the Ridge.* Bradbury, 1989. Ages 8–10.

————. *The Gift of the Sacred Dog.* Bradbury, 1980. Ages 8–10.

————. *The Girl Who Loved Wild Horses.* Bradbury, 1978. Ages 6–8.

————. *Iktomi and the Buffalo Skull.* Orchard, 1991. (See other *Iktomi* trickster tales.) Ages 7–9.

Haseley, Dennis. *The Scared One.* Illustrated by Deborah Howland. Warne, 1983. Ages 7–9.

Highwater, Jamake. *Anpao: An American Indian Odyssey.* Illustrated by Fritz Scholder. Lippincott, 1977. Ages 9–12.

————. *The Ceremony of Innocence.* Harper, 1985. Ages 9–12.

————. *I Wear the Morning Star.* Harper, 1986. Ages 9–12.

————. *Legend Days.* Harper, 1984. Ages 9–12.

Hobbs, Will. *Bearstone.* Atheneum, 1989. Ages 9–12.

Hoyt-Goldsmith, Diane. *Totem Pole.* Photographs by Lawrence Migdale. Holiday, 1990. Ages 6–8.

Hudson, Jan. *Sweetgrass.* Philomel, 1989. Ages 12–YA.

Keegan, Marcia. *Pueblo Boy: Growing Up in Two Worlds.* Cobblehill, 1991. Ages 7–9.

Kesey, Ken. *The Sea Lion.* Illustrated by Neil Waldman. Viking, 1991. Ages 8–10.

Luenn, Nancy. *Nessa's Fish.* Atheneum, 1990. Ages 7–9.

Marrin, Albert. *War Clouds in the West: Indians and Cavalrymen 1860–1890.* Atheneum, 1984. Ages 9–12.

Martin, Bill, and John Archambault. *Knots on a Counting Rope.* Holt, 1987. Ages 6–8.

Miles, Miska. *Annie and the Old One.* Illustrated by Peter Parnall. Little, Brown, 1971. Ages 7–9.

Mowat, Farley. *Lost in the Barrens.* Illustrated by Charles Geer. McClelland and Stewart, 1984. Ages 9–12.

O'Dell, Scott. *Black Star, Bright Dawn*. Houghton, 1988. Ages 9–12.

———. *Island of the Blue Dolphins*. Houghton, 1960. Ages 9–12.

———. *Sing Down the Moon*. Houghton, 1970. Ages 12–YA.

Paulsen, Gary. *Dogsong*. Bradbury, 1988. Ages 12–YA.

Robinson, Gail. *Raven the Trickster: Legends of the North American Indians*. Illustrated by Joanna Troughton. Atheneum, 1982. Ages 8–10.

Seattle, Chief. *Brother Eagle, Sister Sky*. Illustrated by Susan Jeffers. Dial, 1991. Ages 6–10.

Sneve, Virginia Driving Hawk, selector. *Dancing Teepees: Poems of American Indian Youth*. Illustrated by Stephen Gammell. Holiday, 1989. Ages 9–12.

———. *High Elk's Treasure*. Illustrated by Oren Lyons. Holiday, 1972. Ages 9–12.

———. *Jimmy Yellow Hawk*. Illustrated by Oren Lyons. Holiday, 1972. Ages 9–12.

———. *When Thunder Spoke*. Illustrated by Oren Lyons. Holiday, 1974. Ages 9–12.

Speare, Elizabeth George. *The Sign of the Beaver*. Houghton, 1983. Ages 8–10.

Steptoe, John. *The Story of Jumping Mouse*. Lothrop, 1984. Ages 7–9.

Toye, William. *The Loon's Necklace*. Illustrated by Elizabeth Cleaver. Oxford, 1977. Ages 7–9.

Recommended International Books

Ages refer to approximate interest levels. YA = young adult readers. Country of original publication is noted.

English Language Books

Ahlberg, Janet, and Allan Ahlberg. *Each Peach Pear Plum*. Viking, 1979. Ages 3–6. U.K.

Aiken, Joan. *Bridle the Wind*. Delacorte, 1983. Ages 11–YA. U.K.

———. *The Wolves of Willoughby Chase*. Doubleday, 1962. Ages 11–YA. U.K.

Alcock, Vivien. *The Cuckoo Sister*. Delacorte, 1986. Ages 12–YA. U.K.

Allen, Pamela. *Who Sank the Boat?* Putnam, 1982. Ages 4–7. Australia.

Andrews, Jan. *Very Last First Time*. Illustrated by Ian Wallace. Macmillan, 1986. Canadian.

Argent, Kerry, and Rod Trinca. *One Woolly Wombat*. Kane/Miller, 1985. Ages 3–6. Australia.

Asare, Meshack. *Cat in Search of a Friend*. Kane/Miller, 1986. Ages 4–10. Ghana.

Baker, Jeannie. *Where the Forest Meets the Sea*. Greenwillow, 1987. Ages 7–12. Australia.

Base, Graeme. *Animalia*. Viking, 1986. Ages 6–YA. Australia.

Bell, William. *Forbidden City*. Doubleday, 1990. Ages 12–YA. Canada.

Blades, Ann. *Mary of Mile 18*. Tundra, 1971. Ages 7–10. Canada.

Brooks, Martha. *Paradise Café and Other Stories*. Little, Brown, 1988. Ages 12–YA. Canada.

Brott, Ardyth. *Jeremy's Decision*. Illustrated by Michael Martchenko. Kane/Miller, 1990. Ages 4–7. Canada.

Browne, Anthony. *Gorilla*. Knopf, 1985. Ages 5–8. U.K.

———. *Willy the Champ*. Knopf, 1986. Ages 4–8. U.K.

Burnford, Sheila. *The Incredible Journey*. Little, Brown, 1961. Ages 8–12. Canada.

Burningham, John. *Mr. Gumpy's Motor Car*. Crowell, 1976. Ages 4–8. U.K.

Bush, John. *The Fish Who Could Wish*. Illustrated by Korky Paul. Kane/Miller, 1991. Ages 4–8. U.K.

Catterwell, Thelma. *Sebastian Lives in a Hat*. Illustrated by Kerry Argent. Kane/Miller, 1990. Ages 2–5. Australia.

Christopher, John. *Fireball*. Dutton, 1981. Ages 10–YA. U.K.

———. *The White Mountains*. Macmillan, 1967. Ages 10–YA. U.K.

Clark, Mavis Thorpe. *If the Earth Falls In.* Houghton, 1975. Ages 9–12. Australia.

Cresswell, Helen. *The Secret World of Polly Flint.* Macmillan, 1984. Ages 9–12. U.K.

Dahl, Roald. *Matilda.* Illustrated by Quentin Blake. Viking, 1988. Ages 9–12. U.K.

Dickinson, Peter. *Merlin Dreams.* Delacorte, 1988. Ages 10–13. U.K.

Ellis, Sarah. *Next-Door Neighbors.* Macmillan, 1989. Ages 10–12. Canada.

Fox, Mem. *Possum Magic.* Illustrated by Julie Vivas. Abingdon, 1987. Ages 4–7. Australia.

———. *Wilfrid Gordon McDonald Partridge.* Illustrated by Julie Vivas. Kane/Miller, 1985. Ages 5–10. Australia.

Freeman, Bill. *Danger on the Tracks.* Lorimer, 1987. Ages 11–YA. Canada.

Garfield, Leon. *The December Rose.* Viking, 1987. Ages 10–YA. U.K.

Gay, Marie-Louise. *Moonbeam on a Cat's Ear.* Stoddart, 1986. Ages 5–8. Canada.

Gordimer, Nadine, and David Goldblatt. *Lifetimes Under Apartheid.* Knopf, 1986. Ages 11–YA. South Africa.

Gordon, Sheila. *Waiting for the Rain: A Novel of South Africa.* Watts, 1987. Ages 11–YA. South Africa.

Graham, Bob. *Crusher Is Coming!* Viking, 1987. Ages 7–10. Australia.

———. *Greetings from Sandy Beach.* Kane/Miller, 1992. Ages 4–8. Australia.

Hathorn, Elizabeth. *The Tram to Bondi Beach.* Illustrated by Julie Vivas. Kane/Miller, 1989. Ages 4–8. Australia.

Haugaard, Erik C. *Leif the Unlucky.* Houghton, 1982. Ages 11–YA. U.K.

Houston, James. *The Falcon Bow.* Macmillan, 1986. Ages 10–13. Canada.

———. *The White Archer: An Eskimo Legend.* Harcourt, 1990. Ages 9–13. Canada.

Hughes, Monica. *Blaine's Way.* Irwin, 1986. Ages 12–YA. Canada.

———. *The Dream Catcher.* Atheneum, 1987. Ages 10–YA. Canada.

———. *Hunter in the Dark.* Atheneum, 1983. Ages 11–YA. Canada.

———. *Keeper of the Isis Light.* Nelson, 1980. Ages 11–YA. Canada.

Ingpen, Robert, adapter and illustrator. *Click Go the Shears.* Collins, 1984. Ages 6–10. Australia.

Jam, Teddy. *Night Cars.* Illustrated by Eric Beddows. Watts, 1988. Ages 5–8. Canada.

Kelleher, Victor. *Master of the Grove.* Penguin, 1982. Ages 11–YA. Australia.

———. *Taronga.* Viking, 1986. Ages 11–YA. Australia.

Khalsa, Dayal Kaur. *Tales of a Gambling Grandma.* Tundra, 1986. Ages 6–9. Canada.

Klein, Robin. *Hating Alison Ashley.* Viking, 1987. Ages 9–12. Australia.

Kogawa, Joy. *Naomi's Road.* Illustrated by Matt Gould. Oxford, 1986. Ages 9–12. Canada.

Lee, Dennis. *Alligator Pie.* Macmillan, 1974. Ages 5–10. Canada.

———. *Jelly Belly.* Macmillan, 1983. Ages 5–10. Canada.

Lewis, C. S. *The Lion, the Witch, and the Wardrobe.* Macmillan, 1950. Ages 10–YA. U.K.

Little, Jean. *Different Dragons.* Illustrated by Laura Fernandez. Viking, 1986. Canada.

———. *Mama's Going to Buy You a Mockingbird.* Viking, 1985. Ages 10–YA. Canada.

Lunn, Janet. *Amos' Sweater.* Illustrated by Kim LaFave. Groundwood, 1988. Ages 5–9. Canada.

———. *The Root Cellar.* Scribner's, 1983. Ages 11–YA. Canada.

———. *Shadow in Hawthorn Bay.* Scribner's, 1987. Ages 11–YA. Canada.

Mahy, Margaret. *The Blood-and-Thunder Adventure on Hurricane Peak.* McElderry, 1989. Ages 9–12. New Zealand.

———. *The Haunting.* Atheneum, 1983. Ages 10–YA. New Zealand.

Major, Kevin. *Blood Red Ochre.* Delacorte, 1989. Ages 13–YA. Canada.

———. *Hold Fast.* Delacorte, 1980. Ages 13–YA. Canada.

Mark, Jan. *Thunder and Lightnings.* Crowell, 1979. Ages 10–YA. U.K.

Matas, Carol. *Lisa's War.* Scribner's, 1989. Ages 10–YA. Canada.

McKee, David. *Tusk Tusk.* Kane/Miller, 1990. Ages 5–9. U.K.

Melling, O. R. *The Singing Stone.* Viking, 1986. Ages 11–YA. Canada.

Mollel, Tololwa M. *The Orphan Boy*. Illustrated by Paul Morin. Clarion, 1991. Ages 5–8. Canada.

Montgomery, Lucy M. *Anne of Green Gables*. Bantam, 1908. Ages 9–13. Canada.

Moore, Inga. *The Truffle Hunter*. Kane/Miller, 1987. Ages 4–9. U.K.

Mowat, Farley. *Owls in the Family*. Little, Brown, 1962. Ages 8–11. Canada.

Muller, Robin. *The Magic Paintbrush*. Doubleday, 1989. Ages 5–9. Canada.

Munsch, Robert. *Pigs*. Illustrated by Michael Martchenko. Annick, 1989. Ages 5–8. Canada.

Naidoo, Beverley. *Chain of Fire*. Lippincott, 1990. Ages 11–YA. South Africa.

———. *Journey to Jo'burg*. Lippincott, 1986. Ages 10–YA. South Africa.

Norton, Mary. *The Borrowers*. Harcourt, 1953. Ages 8–12. U.K.

Ottley, Reginald. *No More Tomorrow*. Harcourt, 1971. Ages 9–YA. Australia.

Park, Ruth. *Playing Beatie Bow*. Macmillan, 1980. Ages 10–YA. Australia.

Paterson, A. B. *Waltzing Matilda*. Illustrated by Desmond Digby. HarperCollins, 1991. Ages 4–10. Australia.

Pearce, Philippa. *Tom's Midnight Garden*. Lippincott, 1959. Ages 9–12. U.K.

Phipson, Joan. *Hit and Run*. Macmillan, 1986. Ages 11–YA. Australia.

———. *Six and Silver*. Illustrated by Margaret Horder. Harcourt, 1971. Ages 10–YA. Australia.

Poulin, Stéphane. *Benjamin and the Pillow Saga*. Annick, 1990. Ages 5–9. Canada.

———. *Have You Seen Josephine?* Tundra, 1988. Ages 5–8. Canada.

Richler, Mordecai. *Jacob Two-Two Meets the Hooded Fang*. Bantam, 1987. Ages 5–8. Canada.

Rodda, Emily. *Pigs Might Fly*. Illustrated by Noela Young. Greenwillow, 1986. Ages 8–11. Australia.

Rousseau, May. *Everyone Is Dressing Up*. Kane/Miller, 1991. Ages 2–5. Canada.

Rubinstein, Gillian. *Space Demons*. Dial, 1986. Ages 10–14. Australia.

Service, Robert. *The Cremation of Sam McGee*. Illustrated by Ted Harrison. Greenwillow, 1986. Ages 10–YA. Canada.

Smucker, Barbara. *Incredible Jumbo*. Viking, 1990. Ages 10–YA. Canada.

———. *Jacob's Little Giant*. Illustrated by Laura Fernandez. Penguin, 1987. Ages 8–11. Canada.

———. *Underground to Canada*. Puffin, 1978. Ages 11–YA. Canada.

Southall, Ivan. *Ash Road*. Greenwillow, 1978. Ages 10–YA. Australia.

———. *Josh*. Macmillan, 1988. Ages 12–YA. Australia.

———. *Rachel*. Farrar, 1986. Ages 11–YA. Australia.

Speare, Jean. *A Candle for Christmas*. Illustrated by Ann Blades. Macmillan, 1986. Ages 7–10. Canada.

Spence, Eleanor. *The Devil Hole*. Illustrated by Malcolm Green. Lothrop, 1977. Ages 10–13. Australia.

Stone, Ted. *The Ghost of Peppermint Flats and Other Stories*. Western Producer Prairie, 1989. Ages 9–12. Canada.

Sutcliff, Rosemary. *Flame-colored Taffeta*. Farrar, 1986. Ages 10–YA. U.K.

Thiele, Colin. *Fire in the Stone*. Harper, 1974. Ages 10–YA. Australia.

Thomas, Valerie. *Winnie the Witch*. Illustrated by Korky Paul. Kane/Miller, 1987. Ages 4–8. U.K.

Trezise, Percy. *Turramulli the Giant Quinkin*. Illustrated by Dick Roughsey. Gareth Stevens, 1988. Ages 5–9. Australia.

Trinka, Rod, and Kerry Argent. *One Woolly Wombat*. Illustrated by Kerry Argent. Kane/Miller, 1982. Ages 5–7. Australia.

Vaughn, Marcia K. *Wombat Stew*. Illustrated by Pamela Lofts. Silver Burdett, 1986. Ages 4–7. Australia.

Wagner, Jenny. *The Bunyip of Berkeley's Creek*. Illustrated by Ron Brooks. Bradbury, 1973. Ages 6–9. Australia.

———. *John Brown, Rose and the Midnight Cat*. Illustrated by Ron Brooks. Bradbury, 1977. Australia.

Wallace, Ian. *Ching Chiang & the Dragon's Dance*. Macmillan, 1984. Ages 4–8. Canada.

———. *Morgan the Magnificient*. Macmillan, 1988. Ages 5–9. Canada.

Westall, Robert. *Ghost Abbey*. Scholastic, 1989. Ages 11–YA. U.K.

————. *The Promise.* Scholastic, 1990. Ages 12–YA. U.K.

Wildsmith, Brian. *Fishes.* Oxford, 1985. Ages 4–8. U.K.

Wrightson, Patricia. *The Nargun and the Stars.* Macmillan, 1986. Ages 9–13. Australia.

Yee, Paul. *The Curses of Third Uncle.* Illustrated by Don Besco. Lorimer, 1986. Ages 10–YA. Canada.

————. *Tales from Gold Mountain: Stories of the Chinese in the New World.* Macmillan, 1990. Ages 7–12. Canada.

Translated Books

Aamundsen, Nina R. *Two Short and One Long.* Houghton, 1990. Ages 9–13. Norway.

Aleichem, Sholom. *Holiday Tales of Sholom Aleichem.* Translated from the Yiddish by Aliza Shevrin. Macmillan, 1985. Israel.

Anno, Mitsumasa and Others. *All in a Day.* Translated from the Japanese. Putnam, 1987. Ages 3–11. Japan.

Barbot, Daniel. *A Bicycle for Rosaura.* Illustrated by Morella Fuenmayor. Kane/Miller, 1991. Ages 4–8. Venezuela.

Beck, Martine. *The Wedding of Brown Bear and White Bear.* Illustrated by Marie H. Henry. Translated by Aliyah Morgenstern. Little, Brown, 1990. Ages 4–8. France.

Beckman, Gunnel. *Mia Alone.* Translated from the Swedish by Joan Tate. Dell, 1978. Ages 12–YA. Sweden.

Bergman, Tamar. *Along the Track.* Translated from the Hebrew by Michael Swirsky. Houghton, 1991. Ages 10–YA. Israel.

————. *The Boy from Over There.* Translated from the Hebrew by Hillel Halkin. Houghton, 1988. Ages 12–YA. Israel.

Björk, Christina. *Linnea in Monet's Garden.* Illustrated by Lena Anderson. Translated by Joan Sandin. Farrar (R & S), 1987. Ages 7–11. Sweden.

————. *Linnea's Windowsill Garden.* Illustrated by Lena Anderson. Translated from the Swedish by Joan Sandin. Farrar (R & S), 1988. Ages 7–11. Sweden.

Bödker, Cecil. *The Leopard.* Translated from the Danish by Gunnar Poulsen. Atheneum, 1975. Ages 10–14. Denmark.

Bohdal, Susi. *The Magic Honey Jar.* Translated from the German by Anthea Bell. North-South (Holt), 1987. Ages 4–8. Austria.

Bojunga-Nunes, Lygia. *The Companions.* Illustrated by Larry Wilkes. Translated by Ellen Watson. Farrar (R & S), 1989. Ages 7–10. Brazil.

Bos, Burny. *Prince Valentino.* Illustrated by Hans de Beer. North-South, 1990. Ages 5–8. Netherlands.

Bour, Daniéle. *The House from Morning to Night.* Kane/Miller, 1985. Ages 3–8. France.

Bröger, Achim. *The Day Chubby Became Charles.* Illustrated by Emily Arnold McCully. Translated from the German by Renée Vera Cafiero. Lippincott, 1990. Ages 8–11. Germany.

Brunhoff, Jean de. *The Story of Babar.* Translated from the French by Merle Haas. Random, 1933. France.

Calders, Pere. *Brush.* Illustrated by Carme Solé Vendrell. Translated by Marguerite Feitlowitz. Kane/Miller, 1986. Ages 3–7. Spain.

Carrier, Roch. *The Hockey Sweater.* Translated from the French by Sheila Fischman. Tundra, 1984. Canada.

Clément, Claude. *The Painter and the Wild Swans.* Illustrated by Frédéric Clément. Translated from the French by Robert Levine. Dial, 1986. Ages 7–11. Canada.

————. *The Voice of the Wood.* Illustrated by Frédéric Clément. Translated by Lenny Hort. Dial, 1989. Ages 7–11. France.

Cohen, Peter. *Olson's Meat Pies.* Illustrated by Olaf Landström. Translated by Richard E. Fisher. Farrar (R & S), 1989. Ages 5–9. Sweden.

Collodi, Carlo. *The Adventures of Pinocchio.* Translated from the Italian by Marianna Mayer. Macmillan, 1981. Ages 6–9. Italy.

Damjan, Mischa. *December's Travels.* Illustrated by Dusan Kállay. Translated from the German by Anthea Bell. Dial, 1986. Ages 5–9. Germany.

Dekkers, Midas. *Arctic Adventures.* Translated from the Dutch. Watts, 1987. Ages 10–14. Netherlands.

Donnelly, Elfie. *So Long, Grandpa*. Translated from the German by Anthea Bell. Crown, 1981. Ages 8–11. Germany.

Duran, Cheli, editor. *The Yellow Canary Whose Eye Is So Black: Poems from Spanish-speaking Latin America*. Translated by Cheli Duran. Macmillan, 1977. Ages 12–YA.

Eriksson, Eva. *The Tooth Trip*. Translated from the Swedish. Carolrhoda, 1985. Ages 4–7. Sweden.

Escudié, René. *Paul and Sebastian*. Illustrated by Ulises Wensell. Translated by Roderick Townley. Kane/Miller, 1988. Ages 4–8. France.

Fährmann, Willi. *The Long Journey of Lukas B*. Translated from the German by Anthea Bell. Bradbury, 1985. Ages 11–YA. Germany.

Frank, Anne. *Anne Frank: The Diary of a Young Girl*. Translated from the Dutch by B. M. Mooyaart. Doubleday, 1967. Netherlands.

Frank, Rudolph. *No Hero for the Kaiser*. Translated from the German by Patricia Crampton. Lothrop, 1986. Ages 12–YA. Germany.

Friis-Baastad, Babbis. *Don't Take Teddy*. Translated from the Norwegian by Lise Sömme McKinnon. Scribner's, 1967. Ages 9–12. Norway.

Fukami, Haruo. *An Orange for a Bellybutton*. Translated by Cathy Hirano. Carolrhoda, 1990. Ages 5–8. Japan.

Gallaz, Christopher, and Roberto Innocenti. *Rose Blanche*. Translated from the French by Martha Coventry and Richard Graglia. Creative Education, 1985. Ages 9–YA. France.

Gehrts, Barbara. *Don't Say a Word*. Translated from the German by Elizabeth D. Crawford. Macmillan, 1986. Ages 11–YA. Germany.

Grimm Brothers. *Hansel and Gretel*. Illustrated by Lisbeth Zwerger. Translated by Elizabeth D. Crawford. Picture Book Studio, 1988. Ages 5–8. Germany.

Gripe, Maria. *Agnes Cecilia*. Translated from the Swedish by Rika Lesser. Harper, 1990. Ages 12–YA. Sweden.

———. *Elvis and His Secret*. Translated from the Swedish by Sheila LaFarge. Dell, 1979. Ages 8–11. Sweden.

———. *The Night Daddy*. Translated from the Swedish by Gerry Bothmer. Delacorte, 1971. Ages 9–12. Sweden.

Härtling, Peter. *Crutches*. Translated from the German by Elizabeth D. Crawford. Lothrop, 1988. Ages 11–YA. Germany.

———. *Old John*. Translated from the German by Elizabeth D.Crawford. Lothrop, 1990. Ages 10–12. Germany.

Haugen, Tormod. *Night Birds*. Translated from the Norwegian by Sheila LaFarge. Delacorte, 1982. Norway.

Heine, Helme. *Prince Bear*. McElderry, 1989. Ages 6–9. Germany.

Hertz, Ole. *Tobias Has a Birthday*. Translated from the Danish by Tobi Tobias. Carolrhoda, 1983. Ages 4–9. Denmark.

Heuck, Sigrid. *The Hideout*. Translated from the German by Rika Lesser. Dutton, 1988. Ages 10–13. Germany.

Hidaka, Masako. *Girl from the Snow Country*. Translated from the Japanese by Amanda Mayer Stinchecum. Kane/Miller, 1986. Ages 4–8. Japan.

Holm, Anne. *North to Freedom*. Translated from the Danish by L. W. Kingsland. Harcourt, 1984. Ages 10–13. Denmark.

Isami, Iksuyo. *The Fox's Egg*. Translated by Cathy Hirano. Carolrhoda, 1989. Ages 4–8. Japan.

Jansson, Tove. *Finn Family Moomintroll*. Translated by Elizabeth Portch. Farrar, 1989. Ages 6–9. Finland.

Johansen, H. *7 × 7 Tales of a Sevensleeper*. Illustrated by Käthi Bhend. Translated by Christopher Franschelli. Dutton, 1989. Ages 6–8. Switzerland.

Kaldhol, Marit. *Goodbye Rune*. Illustrated by Wenche Öyen. Translated from the Norwegian. Kane/Miller, 1987. Ages 5–10. Norway.

Kästner, Erich. *The Little Man*. Translated from the German by James Kirkup. Knopf, 1966. Ages 8–12. Germany.

Korschunow, Irina. *The Foundling Fox*. Illustrated by Reinhard Michl. Translated from the German by James Skofield. Harper, 1985. Ages 4–8. Switzerland.

———. *Small Fur Is Getting Bigger*. Illustrated by Reinhard Michl. Translated by James Skofield. Harper, 1990. Ages 6–9. Switzerland.

Krause, Ute. *Pig Surprise*. Dial, 1989. Ages 5–8. Germany.

Kullman, Harry. *The Battle Horse.* Translated from the Swedish by George Blecher and Lone Thygesen-Blecher. Bradbury, 1981. Ages 12–YA. Sweden.

Lagercrantz, Rose, and Samuel Lagercrantz. *Is It Magic?* Illustrated by Eva Erikkson. Translated by Paul Norlen. Farrar (R & S), 1990. Ages 4–7.

Likhanov, Albert. *Shadows Across the Sun.* Translated from the Russian by Richard Lourie. Harper, 1983. Ages 10–YA. Russia.

Lindgren, Astrid. *Lotta's Bike.* Illustrated by Ilon Wiklund. Farrar (R & S), 1989. Ages 3–6. Sweden.

———. *Pippi Longstocking.* Illustrated by Louis S. Glanzman. Translated by Florence Lamborn. Viking, 1950. Ages 8–11. Sweden.

———. *Rasmus and the Vagabond.* Translated from the Swedish by Gerry Bothmer. Puffin, 1960. Ages 9–12. Sweden.

———. *Ronia, the Robber's Daughter.* Translated from the Swedish by Patricia Crampton. Viking, 1983. Ages 10–YA. Sweden.

Lindström, Eva. *The Cat Hat.* Translated by Stephen Croall. Kane/Miller, 1989. Ages 7–9. Sweden.

Maartens, Maretha. *Paper Bird.* Translated from the Afrikaans by Madeleine van Biljon. Clarion, 1991. Ages 9–12. South Africa.

Mandelbaum, Pili. *You Be Me, I'll Be You.* Kane/Miller, 1990. Ages 5–8. Belgium.

Marshak, Samuel. *The Month Brothers; A Slavic Tale.* Translated from the Russian by Thomas Whitney. Morrow, 1983. Ages 5–9. Russia.

———. *The Pup Grew Up.* Illustrated by Vladimir Radunsky. Translated by Richard Pevear. Holt, 1989. Ages 7–10. Russia.

Maruki, Toshi. *Hiroshima No Pika.* Translated from the Japanese. Lothrop, 1982. Ages 9–YA. Japan.

Mebs, Gudrun. *Sunday's Child.* Translated from the German by Sarah Gibson. Dial, 1986. Ages 8–11. Switzerland.

Michels, Tilde. *Rabbit Spring.* Illustrated by Käthi Bhend. Translated by Alison James. Harcourt, 1988. Ages 6–9. Switzerland.

Morgenstern, Susie Hoch. *It's Not Fair!* Illustrated by Kathie Abrams. Translated from the French. Farrar, 1983. Ages 9–12. France.

Nilsson, Ulf. *If You Didn't Have Me.* Illustrated by Eva Eriksson. Translated from the Swedish by George Blecher and Lone Thygesen-Blecher. McElderry, 1987. Ages 7–10. Sweden.

Nomura, Takaaki. *Grandpa's Town.* Translated by Amanda Mayer Stinchecum. Kane/Miller, 1991. Ages 4–8. Japan.

Nöstlinger, Christine. *The Cucumber King.* Translated from the German by Anthea Bell. Bergh, 1984. Ages 6–9. Austria.

———. *Konrad.* Translated from the German by Anthea Bell. Watts, 1977. Ages 9–12. Austria.

Orlev, Uri. *The Island on Bird Street.* Translated from the Hebrew by Hillel Halkin. Houghton, 1984. Ages 9–12. Israel.

———. *The Man from the Other Side.* Houghton, 1991. Ages 10–13. Israel.

Pelgrom, Els. *The Winter When Time Was Frozen.* Translated from the Dutch by Maryka and Raphael Rudnik. Morrow, 1980. Ages 11–14. Netherlands.

Preussler, Otfried. *The Tale of the Unicorn.* Illustrated by Gennady Spirin. Translated by Lenny Hort. Dial, 1989. Ages 5–8. Germany.

Rettich, Margret. *Suleiman the Elephant.* Translated from the German by Elizabeth D. Crawford. Lothrop, 1986. Ages 6–9. Germany.

Reuter, Bjarne. *Buster's World.* Translated from the Danish by Anthea Bell. Dutton, 1989. Ages 9–12. Denmark.

Richter, Hans Peter. *Friedrich.* Translated from the German by Edite Kroll. Holt, 1970. Ages 11–YA. Germany.

Sales, Francesc. *Ibrahim.* Illustrated by Eulàlia Sariola. Translated by Marc Simont. Lippincott, 1989. Ages 8–12. Spain.

Sato, Satoru. *I Wish I Had a Big, Big Tree.* Illustrated by Tsutomu Murakami. Translated by Hitomi Jitodai and Carol Eisman. Lothrop, 1989. Ages 5–8. Japan.

Schami, Rafik. *A Hand Full of Stars.* Translated from the German by Rika Lesser. Dutton, 1990. Ages 10–YA. Germany.

Schmidt, Annie M. G. *Pink Lemonade.* Illustrated by Linda Cares. Translated by Henrietta ten Harmsel. Eerdmans, 1981. Ages 6–10. Netherlands.

Schubert, Ingrid, and Dieter Schubert. *The Magic Bubble Trip.* Kane/Miller, 1985. Ages 3–8. Netherlands.

Siekkinen, Raija. *The Curious Faun.* Illustrated by Hannu Taina. Translated by Tim Steffa. Carolrhoda, 1990. Ages 6–9. Finland.

———. *Mister King.* Illustrated by Hannu Taina. Translated by Tim Steffa. Carolrhoda, 1987. Ages 6–9. Finland.

Singer, Isaac. *When Schlemiel Went to Warsaw & Other Stories.* Translated from the Yiddish by Elizabeth Shub. Farrar, 1968. Ages 7–10. Israel.

———. *Zlateh the Goat & Other Stories.* Translated from the Yiddish by Elizabeth Shub. Harper, 1984. Ages 7–10. Israel.

Solotareff, Grégoire. *Don't Call Me Little Bunny.* Farrar, 1988. Ages 4–8. France.

———. *The Ogre and the Frog King.* Translated from the French. Greenwillow, 1988. Ages 4–8. France.

Spyri, Johanna. *Heidi.* Crown, 1880. Ages 9–12. Switzerland.

Steiner, Jörg. *Rabbit Island.* Translated from the German by Ann Conrad Lammers. Harcourt, 1978. Ages 8–12.

Sundvall, Viveca. *Mimi and the Biscuit Factory.* Illustrated by Eva Erikkson. Translated by Eric Bibb. Farrar (R & S), 1989. Ages 4–7. Sweden.

Svedberg, Ulf. *Nicky the Nature Detective.* Illustrated by Lena Anderson. Farrar (R & S), 1988. Ages 7–11.

Takeshita, Fumiko. *The Park Bench.* Illustrated by Mamoru Suzuki. Translated by Ruth A. Kanagy. Kane/Miller, 1988. Ages 3–8. Japan.

Tejima, Keizaburo. *Owl Lake.* Translated from the Japanese. Putnam, 1987. Ages 4–9. Japan.

Tolstoy, Leo. *The Lion and the Puppy and Other Stories for Children.* Illustrated by Claus Sievert. Translated from the Russian by James Riordan. Holt, 1988. Ages 9–YA. Russia.

Van Iterson, S. R. *Pulga.* Translated from the Dutch by Alexander and Alison Gode. Morrow, 1972. Ages 10–14. Netherlands.

Vincent, Gabrielle. *Ernest and Celestine.* Greenwillow, 1982. Ages 3–7. France.

Wettasinghe, Sybil. *The Umbrella Thief.* Kane/Miller, 1987. Ages 4–8. Sri Lanka.

Zei, Alki. *Petros' War.* Translated from the Greek by Edward Fenton. Dutton, 1972. Ages 10–14. Greece.

———. *The Sound of Dragon's Feet.* Translated from the Greek by Edward Fenton. Dutton, 1979. Ages 9–12. Greece.

———. *Wildcat Under Glass.* Translated from the Greek by Edward Fenton. Holt, 1968. Ages 10–YA. Greece.

Chapter **11**

Planning the Literature Curriculum

Sixty seconds make a minute—
How much good can I do in it?
Sixty minutes make an hour—
All the good that's in my power.
                    —Traditional

Successful teaching rarely happens by accident; usually it is the result of careful planning. Good teachers employ both long-range and short-range planning to organize the presentation of content, to assure students' mastery of certain processes, and to encourage students to develop their own value systems and attitudes. Only through careful planning can all three of these important aspects of teaching be included in a school day.

This chapter deals with long-range planning for literature instruction (short-range planning is dealt with in Chapter 12). It begins with a discussion of different ways that literature is integrated into the elementary school curriculum. The latter part of the chapter introduces some practical guidelines for long-term planning for literature.

Curriculum Models in Literacy

A critical goal of teachers in grades K through 8 is to help students become literate—that is, able to read and write. Inservice and preservice teachers of the 1990s will encounter two different approaches to literacy subscribed to in U.S. schools and teacher training institutions: the basal reader approach and the whole language approach. Underlying the differences in these two approaches are the different learning theories upon which each is based. Your approach to literacy development will depend on your own philosophy of teaching and learning—the ideas you believe in strongly enough to act on.

The philosophy you accept will affect every aspect of your teaching: the materials you choose and how you present them to your students, how you arrange your classroom furniture, the activities you engage your students in, how you behave in class, and how you encourage your students to behave. In the following discussion it is important to note the theoretical differences underlying each curriculum model in literature and to begin to form your own philosophy of learning and literacy development.

Literature-Based Reading

Literature-based reading is an approach to teaching reading through the exclusive use of trade books. Literature-based reading fits within a larger philosophy of teaching and learning called the *whole language approach to literacy.* The learning theory on which whole language teaching and literature-based reading are based is that children learn by searching for meaning in the world around them, constantly forming hypotheses, testing them to see if they work, and subsequently accepting or rejecting them. For young children, language has meaning only when it is used in *wholes* (stories, conversations, messages, etc.) and when they have sufficient prior knowledge to support the acquisition of new knowledge. Consequently, from the very beginning of literature-based reading instruction, children are presented with whole (not fragmented) language, mostly in the form of excellent stories. As they hear and see these stories, they naturally begin to form hypotheses about sound-symbol relationships, accepting those that seem to work and rejecting those that do not.

The best example of whole language learning is *spoken language,* which nearly every child acquires effortlessly and with great success by age 5 or 6. Children learn to speak by being immersed in oral language from the time they are born. They listen to people talk and attend to the contexts of this speech. They are urged to talk, and their efforts, however approximate or bumbling, are applauded and supported so long as their meaning comes through. They constantly practice using oral language in natural, interest-driven ways until their attempts at speaking get them what they want.

Teachers using the literature-based approach to reading adopt the key features of oral language learning by structuring a classroom environment in which children are immersed in good literature. In these classrooms, children hear literature read aloud several times a day, they see good readers reading voluntarily, they discover that good books can entertain them and tell them things they want to know, and they constantly practice reading books that they themselves have chosen because they are interested in the topics.

Key elements of the literature-based reading classroom include:

- Daily reading aloud of good literature by the teacher
- Quantities of good trade books in the classroom (five or more books per child) selected to match specific interests and approximate reading abilities of the students in the class

- Reading experiences that stand on the merits of the literature alone (i.e., stories are not inevitably followed by exercises)
- Daily silent reading by students of books that they choose
- Daily opportunities for students to share their reactions to books orally
- Daily opportunities for students to respond to literature in a variety of ways, including writing, drama, and art
- Reading skills taught when needed, and then within meaningful contexts and never in isolation
- Frequent individual student-teacher reading conferences

Decisions about what to teach, when to teach it, and what materials to use are made by the teacher in the whole language classroom. These decisions and the responsibility for materials selection and acquisition may make literature-based reading more demanding of teachers' professional judgment than other reading instruction methods; however, when it is managed well, this approach has proven to be very effective, not only in teaching students to read but also in creating a positive attitude toward reading. The stimulus of new and exciting materials and students' unique personal responses to them can make teaching less rote and more exciting.

The absence of a prescribed, lockstep program is one of the greatest strengths of literature-based reading, but it also makes this approach vulnerable to many abuses. Using quantities of mediocre literature to teach children to read is one example of this kind of abuse. Another is failing to select a wide variety of literature that includes multicultural and international titles, poetry, and a balance of genres and character types. Yet another is the practice of regularly using class sets of single trade books with a predetermined reading schedule and fill-in-the-blank worksheets—a practice that has more in common with procedures followed in the traditional basal reading approach than in a literature-based approach.

There is no one right way to teach literature-based reading. The method cannot be packaged. Your best protection against bogus claims, materials, and practices is to have a complete understanding of the theory behind whole language. *Transitions* by Regie Routman (1988), *Literature-Based Reading Programs at Work* (1987), edited by Hancock and Hill, and *Whole Language: Theory in Use* (1985) edited by Judith Newman are a few of the excellent, practical resources available to provide this information. (For further information on these resources, see Appendix G.)

Basal Reading Program Supplemented by Children's Literature

Just as children bring a variety of learning styles and needs to the task of learning, so do teachers bring a variety of teaching styles and needs to teaching. A single approach to teaching reading cannot suit all teachers or all students. The most common approach to the teaching of reading is the *basal reading approach supplemented by children's literature.*

The basal reading program has been the traditional approach to teaching reading in U.S. elementary schools for decades. According to Durkin (1987), it "is composed of a series of readers said to be written at successively more difficult levels" (p. 417).

The core materials include a student reader, a teacher's manual, student workbooks, ditto masters, and tests. The strength of the basal program is that it provides teachers with an organized instructional framework upon which to build (Lapp, Flood, & Farnan, 1992). In other words, the teacher using this approach does not have to develop his entire reading program by selecting all materials and planning all related activities. Basal reading programs offer teachers considerable guidance and help with the decisions and challenges involved in teaching children to read.

The learning theory upon which basal reading materials have been based for most of this century is that learning complex skills begins with mastering the simplest components of that skill before attempting the next larger components, and so on until the whole skill is learned. In terms of learning to read, this means that the letters of the alphabet are learned first, followed by letter-sound patterns, words, then sentences. Finally, when the components of reading are learned, whole works of literature, such as stories, plays, and poems, are read. As late as the beginning of the 1980s, the embodiment of this philosophy was the basal reader—with its emphasis on progressive skill and subskill mastery and its use of short and simple sentences and a controlled vocabulary. The concern with basals of the 1950s, 60s, and 70s was with the limitations of the story selections—specifically, the controlled vocabulary, the uninteresting plots, and the poor writing style. Fortunately, this is no longer the case.

In the 1980s, U.S. publishers of basal readers made some changes in their products. These changes were made in response to two indicators: (1) criticism by teachers and teacher educators about the low literary quality and the lockstep system in basals and (2) the convincing literacy statistics from New Zealand (100 percent literacy), where a national literature-based reading program was begun nearly 30 years ago. The quality of stories written specifically for the basals was improved. Multicultural characters began to appear in basal stories with more frequency than in the past. Most importantly, excerpts from high-quality trade books and some whole, albeit brief, literary works were integrated into basal readers. These changes were incorporated while retaining the skill-based instruction (particularly phonics instruction for beginning readers) regarded by researchers as important to well-rounded reading programs (Anderson, Hiebert, Scott, & Wilkinson, 1985).

Even with these changes, basals are not designed to be a complete substitute for trade books. Even though some basal stories are good literature, not excerpted or adapted, the brevity of these selections is a problem for intermediate grades. Most students in these grades are capable of reading novel-length chapter books and should be doing so on a regular basis in their school reading program. Students in classes where anthologies and basal readers are used exclusively are denied the all-important self-selection of reading material from a wide variety of books.

Perhaps basal readers are most effective when used in concert with a wide variety of trade books that reflect students' interests and reading abilities. In this arrangement, the basal provides guidance and structure to both teaching and learning, while the trade books provide the variety, opportunity for self-selection, and interest that motivates children to want to read.

Ideally, each teacher should be allowed to choose the approach to teaching reading that best suits his philosophy of learning and teaching style. In many school districts across the United States, however, the use of a basal approach to teaching reading is mandated. Even so, many teachers in this situation have begun to move away from a slavish, "read-every-page-or-bust" attitude toward these programs. They have found ways to improve their teaching of reading by using their basal programs in innovative ways that eliminate some of the skills exercises of this approach and allow time for literature as well. Some guidelines drawn from the example of these teachers are:

- Use only the best literary selections the basal offers. Substitute good trade literature for the rest.
- Let students read some of the better written basal selections simply for enjoyment. It is the joy and wonder of reading marvelous tales or interesting information that motivates children to learn to read, not the tests on their comprehension of these stories. Use the time saved from skill, drill, and comprehension questions for silent reading.
- Eliminate the stigma of ability grouping by forming heterogeneous reading groups. Use the time saved from conducting 3 or 4 different reading lessons to hold individual reading conferences.
- Use basal readers' phonics lessons and drills only when, in the teacher's opinion, an individual student or group of students will benefit from them. (This need is exhibited by students in their individual reading conferences and in their writing.) Children do not learn according to an imposed schedule, but only when they are ready to learn. Use the time saved from ineffective exercises to read aloud from good books or for silent reading from self-choice books.
- Avoid comprehension questions at the end of basal reading lessons that trivialize the stories or demean the students. Use the time saved to allow children to share their personal reactions to the story, to offer literary criticisms of the selection, or to respond to the story in writing, drama, or art.
- Make phonics instruction a regular but brief (10–15 minutes) part of primary-grade reading instruction. Avoid letting phonics instruction become the main attraction of reading. That role should be reserved for good stories.

Integrated Day and Thematic Learning

Based on the British Primary School model of instruction, the integrated day and thematic learning curriculum models in literacy are grounded in whole language theory and a literature-based approach to reading. The central tenet of the integrated day model is that all aspects of the curriculum—reading, language arts, social studies, health, math, science, and physical education—are organized around or focused on a theme or topic. For example, if the chosen topic is mammals, the students would:

- Practice their reading by listening to and reading story books about mammals
- Write extensively (fiction and nonfiction) about mammals
- Learn to identify characteristics of mammals from informational trade books and science textbooks

- Investigate through observation, interviews, and research how certain nonhuman mammals affect humans' lives
- Monitor over several months the health, feeding habits, weight, and growth of a mammalian class pet
- Use this knowledge to create bulletin boards, artwork, dramas, and books of all sorts

With this approach to teaching, children investigate content more deeply than in nonintegrated approaches and begin to see that their learning to read and write has practical, worthwhile uses.

Another central feature of the integrated day model is the use of literature across the curriculum. This means using works of literature as teaching materials in the content areas. The logic for this practice is sound. Many trade books contain information relevant to the topics studied in school. Moreover, this information is presented through captivating and sometimes beautifully illustrated narratives. Thus, the information is interesting to students and therefore more comprehensible and memorable. When using literature across the curriculum, teachers and students are not confined to the textbook as the sole resource. With a librarian's assistance, you can find several resources on most topics. Using several sources of information has always been considered prudent, both in and out of school, since doing so usually provides fuller factual coverage of topics and leads to wiser, more informed decisions on issues.

Thematic learning is similar to the integrated day approach in that there is a focus on a theme or topic, but this model usually involves a specific portion of the curriculum only—language arts and reading, or science, for example.

For obvious reasons both the integrated day and the thematic learning models will work best in self-contained classrooms. But even in situations where classes are departmentalized, teachers can team up through joint planning to deliver thematic units of instruction across the curriculum. For example, seventh-grade history and language arts teachers could coordinate the study of the American Civil War with classroom reading and discussion of such books as *Across Five Aprils* (Hunt, 1964), *Rifles for Watie* (Keith, 1957), *Shades of Gray* (Reeder, 1989), *The Boys' War: Confederate and Union Soldiers Talk about the Civil War* (Murphy, 1990), *The Perilous Road* (Steele, 1958), and *Turn Homeward, Hannalee* (Beatty, 1984).

Themes and topics used in the integrated day and thematic learning approaches are chosen by the teacher on the basis of current students' needs and interests, current events, and prior successes with previously developed thematic units. The length of time spent on any one theme or topic can vary from a year to a day, but several weeks' duration is the norm.

Two pitfalls of integrated day and thematic learning curriculum models must be avoided. The first is choosing a unit theme or topic solely on the basis of having at hand a number of related books and without regard for its interest to students or its suitability to curricular goals. Remember: The unit theme or topic drives literature selection, not vice versa. The second pitfall is choosing literature just because it relates to the theme or topic but with no regard to its quality or appropriateness for the students. Boring books make boring thematic instructional units.

Organization of Curriculum

Literature is more than a collection of well-written stories and poems. Literature also has its own body of knowledge, which some school systems and teachers believe should be a part of the K–8 curriculum. A term sometimes used to label this treatment of literature is *discipline-based literature instruction*. The object of such a course of study is to teach children the mechanics of literature: the terms used to define it, its components or elements, its genres, and the craft of creating it. Some teachers plan for a year-long strand of literature instruction organized variously by topic or theme, by author or illustrator, by genre, or by literary element. In each case, there should be goals for the course of study, a specific set of children's trade books to be read or heard by each child during the course of study, guidelines for selection of materials, a schedule, and criteria for evaluating the course of study.

Theme or Topic

Teachers who choose to organize a study of literature by theme or topic want their students generally to become aware of the power of literature to explain the human condition. Themes and topics will vary according to ages and circumstances of students. For example, primary-grade children will be interested in themes and topics having to do with school and family life. Those in the middle grades, on the other hand, will be more intrigued by themes and topics dealing with the discovery and use of inner resources to become more independent or even to survive.

Possible themes that a seventh- or eighth-grade class might explore through a year include:

> Surviving in the Modern World
> Alienation
> Coping with Parents and Younger Siblings
> Teen-Agers Through History: The Same Old Problems?
> Dependence and Independence
> The Future World
> Beneath the Skin: What Is the True Nature of Difference?

Possible themes and topics for a younger group might include:

> Families Come in All Shapes and Sizes
> School Now and in the Past
> Use Your Wits
> The Importance of Having Good Friends
> Stories from Other Countries
> Old Ones and Young Ones Together
> Famous People Were Children Too

Using this approach, each child reads or listens to the book or books chosen by the teacher to accompany each theme. Following the reading, students explore the theme through discussion, writing, drama, art, and further reading on the theme or topic.

Author or Illustrator

The goal of a curriculum in literature organized by author or illustrator is to make students more familiar with the works and styles of selected children's book authors and illustrators. An additional goal may be knowledge of the authors' or illustrators' lives insofar as these life experiences influenced the subjects' works. The choice of authors and illustrators will naturally be guided both by students' reading interests and the teacher's desire to introduce students to important authors, illustrators, and their works. The number of works chosen to represent an author or illustrator will vary, but even when an author's books are lengthy, more than one work is recommended.

As a class experiences a sampling of the chosen author's or illustrator's work, attention will be focused on trademark stylistic elements such as unusual use of words or color or media, as well as themes, characters, character types, or settings common to these works. Later, information about the person's life can be introduced through reports, audio- and videotaped interviews, and even guest appearances by the author or illustrator. Many resources, including biographies and biographical reference volumes, such as *Something about the Author* (Olendorf), provide information about children's book authors and illustrators. (For more information about this resource, see Appendix G.)

Success of author and illustrator studies is not necessarily defined by wholesale student approval of the featured artists. Students must be allowed to decide whether they like a person's work or not and should be encouraged to discover why. Wholesale *disapproval* by students of the works of a featured author or illustrator, however, is an important form of *teacher* evaluation that should not be ignored. In such a case, the teacher's choice of author or books to be studied was not appropriate for this purpose and should be reconsidered. Students are evaluated informally through observation of their recognition of featured authors' or illustrators' works and their ability to compare literary and artistic styles of various authors and illustrators.

Genre

By organizing a literature curriculum around literary genres, teachers provide a context for students to learn about the various types of literature and the characteristics of each. In the beginning, the teacher will have to direct students' attention to similarities in books of like genre—for example, that works of historical fiction are always set in the past or that characters in folktales are two-dimensional. Soon, however, students will begin to read with more genre awareness and will enjoy finding common elements within genres and differences between genres.

One advantage of this plan is that students over the school year can be exposed to a wide variety of literature. Knowledge of different genres gives students useful schemata—frameworks for understanding borne of prior experience—for story types.

A genre approach can work in all grade levels, given thoughtful selection of titles and delivery of literary concepts. Planning involves choosing the genres to be studied, selecting the representative children's books for each, and determining the order in which the genres will be studied. One of the few recent, year-long, planned literature programs available, *Celebrate Literature* (Fox & Sauer, 1989), uses a genre approach for grades K–6.

Literary Element

When teachers say that their teaching of literature is organized by literary element, they are usually referring to the elements of fiction (as presented in Chapter 3): plot, character, setting, theme, and style. Other elements, such as artistic styles, media, and book format, could be addressed as well.

The goal of a literature curriculum organized by literary element is to give students a better understanding of the craft of writing so that they can read more perceptively and appreciatively and possibly apply this knowledge to their own writing. Since this approach is analytical and somewhat abstract, it is more appropriate for students in fourth grade or above.

Careful selection of children's books to accompany the investigation of each literary element is crucial to the success of this approach. The featured element must be prominent and must have been used by the author with extraordinary skill. In addition, the story itself must captivate young readers. Note that in this approach, books of various genres can be grouped to demonstrate the same literary element.

Students' acquaintance with the literary elements can go far beyond mere definition. Close reading of key passages reveals the author's craft at developing character, establishing mood, and authenticating setting. Re-creation of these elements through art, drama, and writing then gives students a personal and more complete understanding of these elements.

When planning for a curriculum in literature, a teacher has the option of remaining with one of the approaches for the entire year or of using a variety of approaches.

Developing the Literature Curriculum

Gaining a solid understanding of the theory behind the curriculum models and approaches outlined in the previous two sections is a necessary first step in planning successfully for a literature curriculum. Once a teacher chooses an approach to teaching literacy, the theory upon which the approach is based serves as a guide in the remaining practical considerations in the overall task of planning.

Designing a Classroom Reading Environment

Much can be learned about a teacher's philosophy of learning and teaching simply by taking a look around the classroom. The two classrooms depicted in Figures 11–1 and 11–2 were purposely designed to emphasize the differences possible in classroom

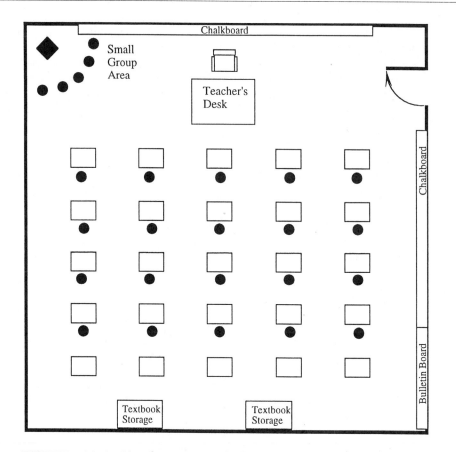

FIGURE   11–1   Teacher-Centered Classroom

arrangement. What sorts of interactions seem to be encouraged in these classrooms as indicated by the arrangement of desks?

The teacher-centered classroom arrangement (Figure 11–1) implies a teacher-centered environment: The teacher is the center of attention and the main source of information. The preponderant type of discourse in this classroom is most likely whole-class lecture, and its direction is from teacher to student. The interactive classroom arrangement (Figure 11–2) implies a more student-centered environment. Various types of discourse seem to be encouraged here: student-to-student discussions, small group activities, and teacher-student conferences. The direction of this discourse is as much from student to student and student to teacher as it is teacher to student.

In addition to room arrangement, other aspects of a classroom reveal the nature of what goes on from day to day. What materials and resources are most apparent? What is the nature of displays and bulletin boards? What level of thinking and inquiry is indicated by the student work on display? Teachers who recognize the importance

FIGURE 11–2 Interactive Classroom

of good literature to the teaching of reading will design an attractive and comfortable classroom reading environment.

Many teachers promote reading and reading-related activities by designating a specific area of the classroom as the *reading center.* The reading center is made conducive to reading by being located as far as possible from noisy activities and by being outfitted with comfortable seating (carpeting, pillows, soft chairs) and lots of conveniently placed and easy-to-find books, as in the interactive classroom in Figure 11–2. The reading center houses the classroom library and can be the setting for independent silent reading, paired and small group reading, and whole-class read-aloud sessions during the day. Low shelving can serve many purposes: boundaries for the center; sound buffers; and storage for books, book circulation records, book club order forms, and audio- and videotapes relating to books.

The reading center is a logical place to display students' book-related writing and artwork, such as student-produced books, students' book reviews, charts showing the class's favorite books and authors, and letters to and from authors and illustrators. Walls and bulletin boards in this way become an integral part of the reading center.

Teachers with self-contained classrooms might have several centers each devoted to a specific curricular subject such as science or health, math, and writing. By outfitting each center with appropriate books and displaying student writing and art related to their work in these areas, teachers naturally integrate the subject areas and show students the relationships between them. The interactive classroom shown in Figure 11–2 shows how this might be arranged. Another noticeable feature of the interactive classroom is the proximity and availability of books. Providing students with a rich supply of trade literature is also the result of planning.

Building a Classroom Library Collection

Most, if not all, the responsibility for acquiring a sufficiently large and varied collection of books in your classroom will be yours. With perseverance, it can be done. Most classroom libraries have a permanent collection as well as a collection that comes from the school or public library and changes regularly. Beginning teachers who are willing to plan ahead with their school and public librarians can borrow enough books for adequate temporary classroom libraries while they build their own collections. Even after a large permanent collection is established, a rotating selection from the school and public library can be coordinated with specific units of study, providing depth and breadth to the unit content and to the students' learning experience.

Careful selection of titles for the classroom library makes the most of limited resources. Children's librarians can provide invaluable advice in selecting titles for a classroom library and should be consulted. If this is not an option, browsing in a well-stocked children's bookstore and consulting publishers' catalogues are alternative ways of finding out what is available. Publishers of children's books issue one or two catalogues annually in which they describe their new publications and list their previous publications that are currently available (the backlist). If your school or public librarian does not have these catalogues, publishers will supply them on request. Some teachers use catalogues to get an overview of what is available before going to a bookstore.

Your own permanent trade book collection can be built inexpensively by using several proven approaches. These include:

- Requesting an allocation from your principal or PTO for purchase of books
- Writing a small grant proposal ($250–$1000) to your school district or professional organization for purchase of trade books
- Taking advantage of bonus books offered by student paperback book clubs
- Informing students' parents that you are building a collection and would like to have first refusal of any children's books that they plan to discard

- Establishing a "give a book to the classroom" policy for parents who want to celebrate their child's birthday or a holiday at school in some way
- Frequenting garage sales and library book sales, where good books can often be purchased for pennies

Most bookstores offer a 20 percent discount to teachers who use their own money to buy books to add to their classroom collections. An alternative to the bookstore is the book "jobber," or wholesale dealer for many publishers. Jobbers offer even greater discounts to teachers, sometimes up to 40 percent, but it is important to remember that most jobbers do not carry small press publications. Your school librarian probably uses a jobber and can assist you in setting up a staff account with the same firm. Some of the larger firms include Baker & Taylor, Brodart, and Ingram Book Company.

With these methods and sources, classroom collections grow quickly. From the beginning, you will need to devise a coding system for your permanent collection to streamline shelving and record keeping. Many teachers find that color coding their books by genre with colored tape on the spines works well. If at all possible, students should be trained and given the responsibility for color coding, checking in and out, repairing, and reshelving books.

Remember that the whole point of building a classroom library is to promote reading, not to provide a handsome display. Inevitably, if children use their classroom library, books will be lost and damaged. Severe reprimands for losing or damaging a book may work against your ultimate goal.

Outlining a Year-Long Curriculum

Planning for the school year permits the teacher to have resources available when they are needed. In outlining for a year-long literature curriculum, several steps must be taken.

Determining the Approach   A teacher must first determine which literature curriculum he will teach: topic/theme, author/illustrator, genre, or literary element. Another alternative is to create a hybrid literature curriculum by including aspects of several of these approaches in the plan.

Establishing Goals   *Goals* in a literature curriculum are those aims one expects to accomplish by the end of the course of study. The term *objectives* refers to short-range aims to be accomplished day by day or week by week. Central to this part of the planning process is deciding on the literary concepts to be taught. Since goals largely determine the parameters of the course of study, they must be established early in the planning process.

Goals for a literature curriculum are established by individual teachers and sometimes by schools or school districts. Likely goals for a fifth-grade teacher, let us call him Mr. Ortiz, who has determined to use a mixed genre/author approach to teaching literature would be:

- Students will enjoy reading a variety of genres of literature.
- Students will be familiar with the characteristics of traditional literature, modern fantasy, historical fiction, contemporary realistic fiction, mystery, and science fiction, and will be able to classify a book as belonging to one of the featured genres when reading it.
- Students will become familiar with several leading authors of each of the above genres and will be able to identify characteristics of the writing of each author.

Determining Units of Study   After goals have been identified and set, the next step in outlining a literature curriculum is to determine the units of study through which the literature content will be delivered. In this way, a tentative schedule can be set in order to foresee needs in terms of time and materials.

Selecting Focus Books   Each unit will require certain trade books for reading aloud or for class study. Early selection of these titles is important for several reasons. Balance in the overall book selection, for instance, is achieved much more easily in the planning stages. *Balance in book selection* means that the set of books presents a diversity of characters (type, sex, age, ethnicity, place of origin), settings (urban, rural, familiar, foreign), and themes. Early selection of focus books also gives a teacher or librarian time to procure multiple copies. A third advantage of early selection is being able to estimate the time necessary for each unit. Some units will take longer than others, depending on such variables as the extent of content to be covered, the length and difficulty of books to be read, and the type and complexity of planned book extension activities. A likely list of units, books, and featured authors for Mr. Ortiz would be:

Unit 1: Traditional Literature

Mythology

The Macmillan Book of Greek Gods and Heroes by Alice Low. Illustrated by Arvis Stewart.
Theseus and the Minotaur adapted by Leonard Everett Fisher.

Legends

The Legend of King Arthur retold by Robin Lister. Illustrated by Alan Baker.
Sir Gawain and the Loathly Lady by Selina Hastings. Illustrated by Juan Wijngaard.
Dragon Slayer: The Story of Beowulf by Rosemary Sutcliff.

Folktales

Snow White and the Seven Dwarfs translated by Randall Jarrell. Illustrated by Nancy Eckholm Burkert.
Snow White in New York by Fiona French.

Read-Aloud

Sir Gawain and the Green Knight by Selina Hastings. Illustrated by Juan Wijngaard.

Unit 2: Modern Fantasy

Tuck Everlasting by Natalie Babbitt.
A Stranger Came Ashore by Mollie Hunter.
Konrad by Kristine Nostlinger.

Read-Aloud

The Lion, the Witch, and the Wardrobe by C. S. Lewis.

Featured Author: C. S. Lewis

Unit 3: Historical Fiction (the U.S. westward expansion)

Save Queen of Sheba by Louise Moeri.
On to Oregon by Honoré Morrow.
I Am Regina by Sally Keehn.
Caddie Woodlawn by Carol Ryrie Brink.

Read-Aloud

Wait for Me, Watch for Me, Eula Bee by Patricia Beatty.

Featured Author: Patricia Beatty

Unit 4: Contemporary Realistic Fiction

Bridge to Terabithia by Katherine Paterson.
Child of the Owl by Laurence Yep.
Secret City, U.S.A. by Felice Holman.
Two Short and One Long by Nina Ring Aamundsen.

Read-Aloud

Zeely by Virginia Hamilton.

Featured Author: Virginia Hamilton

Unit 5: Mystery

Peppermints in the Parlor by Barbara Brooks Wallace.
The Mystery of Dies Drear by Virginia Hamilton.
The Egypt Game by Zilpha Keatley Snyder.
The Dollhouse Murders by Betty Ren Wright.

Read-Aloud

The Westing Game by Ellen Raskin.

Featured Author: Ellen Raskin

Unit 6: Science Fiction

The Green Book by Jill Paton Walsh.
The White Mountains by John Christopher.
Collidescope by Grace Chetwin.
The Duplicate by William Sleator.

Read-Aloud

A Wrinkle in Time by Madeleine L'Engle.

Featured Author: Madeleine L'Engle

An issue often discussed in children's literature circles is the efficacy of a *literary canon* of children's literature, an official list of children's books judged by experts to be worthy of inclusion in a literature curriculum. Elementary teachers and librarians have largely rejected the idea of a literary canon mainly because its sole criterion for selection is literary excellence, with no consideration for a book's appeal or relevance to children. Moreover, teachers know that they are in the best position to select books that match their students' interests and their own planned curricula. A literary canon is rarely revised and quickly becomes dated. Being so rigid and select, it cannot reflect the varied and changing interests of a particular group of children. Although the term *literary canon* most often refers to a nationally recognized booklist, teachers should be aware that when they stick rigidly to the same set of books year after year, they are, in effect, proclaiming that their own personal literary canon of children's literature is more important than the needs and interests of the children they teach.

Scheduling   With an overview of the plan established, the teacher can begin to set dates and time allotments for each unit and for activities within units. With each year of experience, the teacher's time estimates become more accurate. At this point, it is still easy to adjust the year-long plan if it becomes obvious that too much or too little has been planned.

Planning makes it possible to integrate the literature curriculum with other areas of study. For example, Mr. Ortiz can schedule his literature unit on historical fiction to coincide with his U.S. history unit on the westward expansion.

Fleshing Out the Units of Study

Thinking through, organizing, and writing down the details of daily lessons and activities is the final step in planning for a literature curriculum. Two methods of organizing the details of units of study are webs and literature units.

Webs   Webbing is a way of creating a visual overview of a unit of study complete with its focus, related book titles, and activities. Ideas for a web are generated through brainstorming. The main advantage of webbing is that the process clarifies and even suggests ties or associations between concepts, books, and activities. Webs can be organized around a theme or topic, a single book, a book genre, an author or illustrator, or a literary concept. Activities can be drawn from all skill areas—writing, reading, listening, thinking, speaking, art, crafts, drama, and music. The web in Figure 11–3 is the likely result of Mr. Ortiz's webbing organized around the genre of historical fiction with attention to a featured author.

Information about and examples of webs are available in several resources. *The WEB* (Wonderfully Exciting Books), a quarterly book review journal produced by the Reading Center at The Ohio State University, includes a literature web in every issue. *Webbing with Literature: Creating Story Maps with Children's Books* by Karen D'Angelo Bromley (1991) explores webbing as a way for children to respond to literature. Teachers who use webbing as a way to plan literature units will appreciate the many topics, themes, and resources suggested in *Book Links,* a journal published by the American Library Association. (For further information on these resources, see Appendix G.)

A disadvantage of webbing is that there is no indication of the chronology of events or time allotments. Eventually the web must be transferred to a more linear format, which is similar to the literature unit.

Literature Units The literature unit resembles an outline organized by day or by week. Specificity will vary according to the needs and experience of the teacher, but each day's plan usually includes the following components:

- *Objectives.* These are short-term aims that can conceivably be met by the end of the day or week. For example, Mr. Ortiz may state as an objective for the second week of his historical fiction unit that he will read aloud Chapters 6–10 of Patricia Beatty's *Wait for Me, Watch for Me, Eula Bee.* During that same week, a likely objective for his students would be that they note and share descriptions of pioneers' dress, modes of transportation, food, and travel routes in the various books of historical fiction that they are reading independently or in small groups, and that they begin to notice the attention to accuracy of details in works of historical fiction.
- *Procedures and methods.* This part of the unit tells what the teacher does, in what order, and with what materials. Mr. Ortiz's procedures may call for him to let his students choose a way to "put themselves in the shoes" of either the Native Americans or the pioneers and to exhibit some of the injustices or hardships suffered by either group during the white settling of the west. He suggests some of the ways this might be done (dramatize a book episode, assume the persona of a book character and write a letter to the class from the pioneer trail, draw a scene as suggested in a book) and asks students to suggest other ways. Likewise, he projects what materials are likely to be needed for these activities so that he might have them on hand.
- *Evaluation.* Teachers must consider how they intend to evaluate each day's activities both in terms of how well they worked (a form of self-evaluation) and how well the students met the objectives.

Because units of study are several weeks long, they usually include a culminating activity that gives students an opportunity to reflect on what they have learned, review major points, and sometimes celebrate the focus of the unit in some way. Mr.

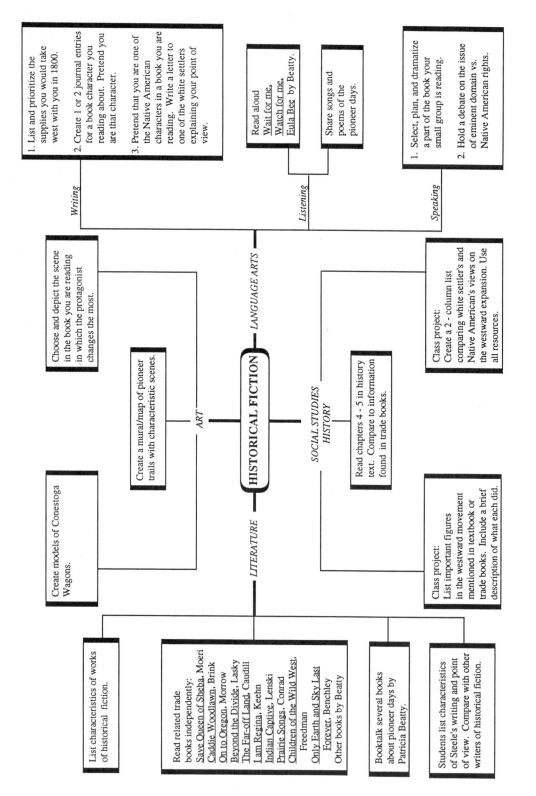

Writing

1. List and prioritize the supplies you would take west with you in 1800.
2. Create 1 or 2 journal entries for a book character you are reading about. Pretend you are that character.
3. Pretend that you are one of the Native American characters in a book you are reading. Write a letter to one of the white settlers explaining your point of view.

Listening

Read aloud Wait for me, Watch for me, Eula Bee by Beatty.

Share songs and poems of the pioneer days.

Speaking

1. Select, plan, and dramatize a part of the book your small group is reading.
2. Hold a debate on the issue of eminent domain vs. Native American rights.

Choose and depict the scene in the book you are reading in which the protagonist changes the most.

Create a mural/map of pioneer trails with characteristic scenes.

Create models of Conestoga Wagons.

ART

LANGUAGE ARTS

HISTORICAL FICTION

SOCIAL STUDIES
HISTORY

Read chapters 4 - 5 in history text. Compare to information found in trade books.

Class project:
Create a 2 - column list comparing white settler's and Native American's views on the westward expansion. Use all resources.

Class project:
List important figures in the westward movement mentioned in textbook or trade books. Include a brief description of what each did.

LITERATURE

List characteristics of works of historical fiction.

Read related trade books independently:
Save Queen of Sheba, Moeri
Caddie Woodlawn, Brink
On to Oregon, Morrow
Beyond the Divide, Lasky
The Far-off Land, Caudill
I am Regina, Keehn
Indian Captive, Lenski
Prairie Songs, Conrad
Children of the Wild West,
Freedman
Only Earth and Sky Last
Forever, Benchley
Other books by Beatty

Booktalk several books about pioneer days by Patricia Beatty.

Students list characteristics of Steele's writing and point of view. Compare with other writers of historical fiction.

FIGURE 11–3 Literature Web

Ortiz's students might conclude their historical fiction/westward movement unit with a wagon train evening of songs, stories, and food described in the books and other resources they have read.

An overall unit evaluation is valuable to a teacher, particularly if he intends to use the unit with another group of students. Revisions can make the unit even more successful in succeeding years. The unit plan should indicate how the unit will be evaluated.

Professionally developed literature units occur in such resource books as *Focus Units in Literature: A Handbook for Elementary School Teachers* by Joy Moss (1984). Beginning teachers may find good ideas in such resources but should avoid considering these units as complete or unalterable. Rather, these prepared units should be tailored by you to reflect your students' prior experiences, interests, and abilities, and your goals and objectives.

Implementing a Schoolwide Curriculum in Literature

Having a schoolwide curriculum in literature has many benefits for teachers and students and is worth pursuing. The main benefit to students is that their teachers' efforts will be coordinated from year to year. Repetition of content and titles will be avoided and continuity will be improved. The main benefits to teachers are that ideas, expertise, and materials will be shared and planning will be facilitated by knowing what experiences with literature incoming students have had or should have.

The impetus for planning a schoolwide curriculum in literature often comes from one person or a small group of people committed to the idea. In your school, that person could be you. The task of developing a schoolwide literature curriculum, however, should be shared by a committee that has a representative from each grade level and the library media specialist. Having someone on the committee who is knowledgeable about children's books is essential.

A literature curriculum committee's function is to determine what literature content will be presented at each grade level. A set of trade books appropriate for delivering the literature curriculum at each grade level can also be suggested by the committee, although the ultimate choice of books to be used in a classroom will be the individual teacher's decision. Literature curriculum committees often select and update their schoolwide read-aloud list. Such a list helps to prevent duplication of teachers' read-aloud choices at different grade levels and to assure that students hear a well-balanced selection of books over the years. Having such a list may also convince some teachers to begin a read-aloud program.

Censorship   Another task of the literature curriculum committee is to establish guidelines for school personnel to use in selecting books and for dealing with would-be censors of curriculum or library materials. Being able to prove that any book found in a school or classroom library has met stated selection criteria protects teachers against claims that the material has been negligently or capriciously allowed into a school library. The following criteria are often included in school selection policies:

- The book must be favorably reviewed in national professional review journals.
- The book must be included on one or more national recommended lists. (Lists such as the ALA's annual Notable Books list should be stated.)

It makes sense for a school to have and use written criteria for evaluating and selecting books that students are going to be asked or invited to read. You would be wise to find out if your school has a book selection policy and, if not, help develop one.

In dealing with censorship attempts, teachers should let their actions be guided by two precepts: (1) a parent has the right to object to his or her child's reading or listening to a specific book, and that right should be respected; and (2) a parent does not have the right to deny everyone else the right to read or hear a book. Teachers often find that censorship problems can be solved by being flexible. For example, if a parent objects to a book that is being read aloud to his or her child, the teacher can allow that child to visit another classroom or the media center when the book is being read.

Teachers and library media specialists also have found that a written procedure is helpful in bringing order and reason into discussions with parents who want to censor school materials. Most procedures call for teachers to give would-be censors a complaint form and ask them to specify their concerns in writing. There are advantages to such a system: Both teachers and parents are given time to reflect on the issue and to control their emotions; and the would-be censor is given time to read the book in its entirety, if he or she has not done so already. Developing a written procedure and a complaint form for dealing with a would-be censor are important tasks for the literature curriculum committee.

The American Library Association's Office for Intellectual Freedom has several publications about censorship such as *Censorship and Selection: Issues and Answers for Schools* (copublished by the American Association of School Administrators, 1988) that provide important and helpful information to schools on this topic. (For a catalog of all ALA publications, write to ALA Publishing, 50 East Huron Street, Chicago, IL 60611.)

One form of school censorship is so subtle that most teachers, librarians, and students are unaware that it is happening, which makes it almost more harmful than publicized cases. This form of censorship occurs when teachers or librarians, for whatever reason, select such a narrow assortment of books for classroom use as to omit perfectly acceptable genres, topics, character types, and authors. Your best defense against this kind of censorship is an awareness of the harm that it can do.

The Library Media Center   The well-stocked, efficiently run library media center is the heart of a school, and the knowledgeable media center director has his finger on the pulse of each classroom. Gone are the days when the library was synonymous with dry speeches about the Dewey Decimal System and the proper way to do research reports. Lately, as literature-based reading and literature across the curriculum have gained acceptance, library media specialists and teachers have been moving toward a shared responsibility for teaching. They work as a team to provide students with the richest educational experience that their combined resources can provide. Teachers tell librarians their resource needs, and librarians help teachers by identifying and locating appropriate resources, keeping teachers updated with the newest literature and suggesting ways to present books to students. For these reasons, the librarian should be encouraged to play a key role in planning and developing a school-wide curriculum in literature.

Bookfairs and School Bookstores   Bookfairs and school bookstores are two ways that schools can bring literature to children and their parents. Both entities are important in the overall development of a schoolwide literature curriculum. A bookfair is a book sale that is organized by a book vendor, such as a bookstore owner, and held in the school building for one or more days. Books are attractively displayed so that children and their parents can browse and select items for purchase. Bookfairs always call attention to literature and reading and can even be considered a reading motivator. They are especially appropriate in areas where there are no children's bookstores or well-stocked libraries.

Bookfairs send strong messages to children and their parents about a school's stance on reading and about what sorts of reading materials teachers and librarians in the school endorse. Children and parents who attend bookfairs in which joke collections, scented stickers, stamps, commercialized series books, coloring books, and posters are prominent will assume that this is what reading means to the teachers in these schools. Bookfairs in which a wide variety of good literature is prominent send an entirely different (and more defensible) message about reading to parents and children. Excellent bookfairs are the result of careful planning and active involvement in selection of books by teachers and school librarians. Book selection should not be left solely to the book vendor.

The school bookstore is a permanent part of the school. It is often a Parent-Teacher Organization project and is run by parent volunteers, but students and teachers are often enlisted or volunteer to help run the store. Most books are sold at cost, but arrangements are sometimes made for any profits to support a giveaway program in which students exchange credits for good performance in class for books.

Book selection is just as important to the school bookstore as to the school bookfair and for the same reasons. Teachers and librarians should be actively involved in selecting their bookstore stock and in advising parents on selections. Teachers who are involved in book selection can arrange for titles related to their unit themes and topics to be available in the bookstore.

Parent Involvement   In most communities parents and other adult members of students' families want to be involved in some way in their children's learning. In some instances parents are willing to help in classrooms on a regular basis. These people and their efforts must be integrated into the teacher's plans. In a school with an established curriculum in literature, teachers can develop a list of suggestions for using parent volunteers in the literature program. Such a list would be especially useful for new teachers. Some of the ways that parents can help teachers include the following:

- Listen to children read orally
- Read aloud to small groups or individual students
- Take children to the school library
- Type, assemble, and bind the storybooks that children write
- Read stories on audiotapes for listening
- Help maintain the classroom library (code, repair, shelve, check out books)
- Fill out book club orders
- Make book bags for carrying books back and forth from home
- Type lists of good read-aloud books for children to take home and share with parents

Parental involvement in literature also means getting support for the school reading program at home. Parents are almost always willing to promote their children's academic efforts at home if they are told how to do it. Many teachers give parents lists of activities that support reading, including brief, carefully worded explanations where necessary. Some typical suggestions include:

- Read to your child at night. (Lists of good read-alouds can be sent home regularly.)
- Listen to your child read aloud.
- Participate in shared reading with your child. (Shared reading techniques for beginning readers are explained in Chapter 12.)
- Take your child to the library to select books.
- Give books to your child as gifts. (Lists of good gift book suggestions can be sent home prior to birthdays and holidays.)

Guest Authors and Illustrators   Professional children's authors and illustrators often visit schools to speak to children about their careers and their books. Teachers are usually instrumental in selecting, inviting, and organizing these visits. Guest authors and illustrators may be chosen on the basis of availability, but more often they are chosen because of the students' interest in their books or the relevancy of their work to a topic that students are studying.

The standard procedure is to contact the marketing director or editor of the author's or artist's publishing house to determine availability and terms. Since most established children's authors and illustrators charge an honorarium and travel expenses, schools within a system often share the author and the costs.

Careful selection, pre-visit promotion and preparation, and scheduling can result in author or illustrator visits that are inspiring to all concerned. At the very least, planners will want to assure that many copies of the guest's books are bought, distributed, and widely read by students for weeks before the guest arrives. As the day of the visit approaches, children can be led to think about and respond to the guest's books in many ways, to develop thought-provoking and worthwhile questions to ask the guest speaker, and to find out as much as possible about the individual. A visit from an author or illustrator can be the culminating event in an instructional unit or of an entire year-long literature curriculum. It deserves careful planning.

Many state reading associations have developed lists of children's authors and illustrators who live in state. These lists can usually be found in public libraries.

Evaluating the Literature Program

Ongoing evaluation is part of responsible teaching, since it reveals strengths and weaknesses in instruction and indicates where revision is suggested. In today's schools, reading and math skills are given the lion's share of attention in standardized evaluation programs, and all too often no attention is paid to children's growth in literary understanding. But many teachers believe that student growth in literary understanding and appreciation is important and should be assessed. The question, then, is How?

Observation and Assessment of Student Learning Evaluation of students in relation to a literature curriculum will focus mainly on the curriculum's effect on student behaviors rather than on the students' grasp of concepts. Consequently, the evaluation will be accomplished primarily by observing students rather than by testing them. An important principle to remember when planning for evaluation of teaching and learning is that evaluation must parallel the goals and objectives of the instructional plan. To look for conceptual understandings or behaviors in students when those concepts or behaviors have not been taught or encouraged is to invite failure and disappointment.

Experienced teachers often develop checklists to use in observation and assessment of various aspects of their literature programs. Also, generic checklists can be developed by teams of teachers and librarians at each grade level in a school and then tailored by individual teachers to fit their own specific plans.

Checklist for Student Involvement with Books Some of the behaviors that teachers look for in their students' interaction with literature will vary by grade level and the students' development. Other behaviors will show up on checklists for all grade levels. For example, preschool or first-grade teachers would be likely to look for evidence that their students know the terms *author* and *illustrator,* use the terms correctly in their discussions of books, and recognize the work of specific authors and illustrators. Middle-grade teachers, on the other hand, would be more likely to look for evidence that students are choosing and reading novel-length stories independently. Teachers at all grade levels will be looking for evidence that their students are enjoying reading and voluntarily choosing to read. The following generic checklist gives an idea of what such an evaluation instrument might look like.

Checklist for Student Involvement with Literature

Behavior	Yes	No	Comment
Reading			
Student reads voluntarily and willingly	___	___	_____
Student enjoys reading	___	___	_____
Student reads during silent reading time	___	___	_____
Student reads for entertainment	___	___	_____
Student reads for information	___	___	_____
Student reads a variety of books	___	___	_____
Response to Literature			
Student talks intelligently about books read or heard	___	___	_____
Student shares responses to books with peers	___	___	_____
Student attends during read-aloud sessions	___	___	_____
Student is able to discuss a book in terms of character	___	___	_____
plot	___	___	_____
setting	___	___	_____
theme	___	___	_____
style	___	___	_____
Student is able to accept that different people may have different responses to the same story	___	___	_____
Student is able to relate stories to personal experience, where applicable	___	___	_____
Selection of Literature			
Student knows how to select appropriate books for independent reading	___	___	_____
Student is developing a personal preference in literature	___	___	_____
Student tries new book genres	___	___	_____

Checklist for Classroom Environment The environment of a classroom is determined mainly by what the resident teacher values in learning and teaching. These values, in turn, determine how the classroom is arranged, which materials are available, and what sorts of events and activities are regularly scheduled. The following checklist incorporates all of these features.

Checklist for Promoting Literature through Classroom Environment

Feature	Yes	No	Comment
Physical Plant			
Desks are arranged to promote student-to-student discussion	___	___	_____
Room arrangement provides quiet areas for reading and thinking	___	___	_____
Reading area is well lighted	___	___	_____
Reading area has comfortable seating	___	___	_____
Reading area has adequate and convenient shelving for books	___	___	_____
Reading area is well organized and orderly	___	___	_____
Student response projects are displayed	___	___	_____
Materials			
Classroom has a trade book library	___	___	_____
Classroom library is adequate in			
scope (variety of genres)	___	___	_____
depth (variety of books within a genre)	___	___	_____
providing for varying reading abilities	___	___	_____
recent books	___	___	_____
multicultural and international books	___	___	_____
Classroom has a temporary collection	___	___	_____
Temporary collection			
addresses gaps in permanent collection	___	___	_____
is exchanged regularly	___	___	_____
provides for varying student interests	___	___	_____
is coordinated with topics of study	___	___	_____
Classroom library materials are			
easy for students to reach and reshelve	___	___	_____
coded and organized logically	___	___	_____

Scheduling

Time is provided for self-choice reading every day	—	—	_____
Time is provided for browsing and selection of books regularly	—	—	_____
Time is provided for response to literature	—	—	_____

Checklist for Teaching Activities   Success in making children lovers of books and reading certainly does not depend upon generous supplies of equipment or a certain physical layout, although these can facilitate the job. In the end, it is what the teacher does with literature that makes the biggest impression on children. Activities that make the learning experience positive and nonthreatening are generally the most successful with children. This point of view is evident in the following checklist of teaching activities.

Checklist for Promoting Literature through Teaching Activities

Teaching Activity	Yes	No	Comment
Making Literature Enjoyable			
Read aloud daily	—	—	_____
Select books for read-aloud that			
reflect students' interests	—	—	_____
represent a wide variety of genres	—	—	_____
Share poetry orally on a regular basis	—	—	_____
Share stories through storytelling	—	—	_____
Motivating Students to Read			
Introduce books regularly through booktalks	—	—	_____
Encourage student response to literature			
by asking open-ended or divergent questions	—	—	_____
by encouraging varied responses			
oral response	—	—	_____
written response	—	—	_____
graphic response	—	—	_____
Allow students to choose books for independent reading	—	—	_____

Modeling Reading Behaviors

Read during silent reading time ___ ___ _____

Talk enthusiastically about books read ___ ___ _____

Show students how to select books ___ ___ _____

Showing the Relevance of Literature

Integrate literature across the curriculum ___ ___ _____
   health/science ___ ___ _____
   social studies/history ___ ___ _____
   language arts ___ ___ _____
   reading ___ ___ _____
   math ___ ___ _____

Encouraging Literature Appreciation

Present a year-long literature curriculum ___ ___ _____

Reaching Beyond the Classroom

Send read-aloud suggestions to parents ___ ___ _____

Encourage parents to visit library with
their children ___ ___ _____

Invite parents and community leaders to
be guest readers for read-aloud ___ ___ _____

Evaluation

Record student growth
   in understanding of literary concepts ___ ___ _____
   in choices of books to read ___ ___ _____
   in attitude toward reading ___ ___ _____

References

Anderson, R. C., Hiebert, E. H., Scott, J. A., & Wilkinson, I. A. (1985). *Becoming a nation of readers: The report of the commission on reading.* Champaign, IL: Center for the Study of Reading.

Beatty, P. (1978). *Wait for me, watch for me, Eula Bee.* New York: Morrow.

Bromley, K. D. (1991). *Webbing with literature: Creating story maps with children's books.* Boston: Allyn and Bacon.

Durkin, D. (1987). *Teaching young children to read* (4th ed.). Boston: Allyn and Bacon.

Fox, C., & Sauer, M. (1989). *Celebrate literature: A comprehensive curriculum for children in grades K–6.* Logan, IA: Perfection Form, Inc.

Lapp, D., Flood, J., & Farnan, N. (1992). Basal readers and literature: A tight fit or a mismatch? In K. D. Wood & A. Moss (Eds.), *Exploring literature in the classroom: Content and methods* (pp. 33–57). Norwood, MA: Christopher-Gordon.

Moss, J. F. (1984). *Focus units in literature: A handbook for elementary school teachers.* Urbana, IL: National Council of Teachers of English.

Riechman, H. F. (1988). *Censorship and selection: Issues and answers for schools.* Chicago: American Library Association and American Association of School Administrators.

Chapter 12

Developing Teaching Strategies

Reading

> . . . We get no good
> By being ungenerous even to a book,
>   And calculating profits . . . so much help
> By so much reading. It is rather when
> We gloriously forget ourselves and plunge
> Soul-forward, headlong, into a book's profound,
> Impassioned for its beauty and salt of truth—
> 'Tis then we get the right good from a book.
>   —Elizabeth Browning

The teacher is the key to a well-planned, effective literature program. In the previous chapter, long-term aspects of planning and preparing for the literature program were addressed. This chapter will focus on the strategies teachers need to carry out such a program. Having students experience and respond to literature are two major responsibilities that a teacher must assume in order to ensure a good literature program.

Experiencing Literature

Many teaching strategies can be used to provide students with opportunities to experience enjoyable, exciting, and thought-provoking literature. Students experience prose, poetry, fiction, and nonfiction (1) by having it read aloud to them by a skillful oral reader; (2) by reading it silently to themselves; (3) through shared reading activities with a parent, librarian, teacher, or peer; (4) through stories told to them; (5) through choral poetry; and (6) through other media such as audio- and videotapes.

Reading Aloud by Teachers

Reading aloud to students is a powerful way to provide them with literary experiences; it is the centerpiece of a curriculum in literature. Beginning in their infancy and throughout their elementary school years and beyond, children should hear books read aloud. Although some teachers at the intermediate-grade level do not read aloud, this teaching strategy is just as important in the development of readers at this stage as it is in kindergarten.

Some of the more important reasons that teachers read aloud are:

1. To provide students with exciting and stimulating experiences in reading matter that may be too difficult for them to read to themselves but not beyond their ability to enjoy and appreciate
2. To build background and interest in subject matter that will soon be taught in an upcoming content area unit of instruction
3. To introduce new genres of literature or new literary concepts, such as a particular element of fiction or poetry
4. To contribute to students' knowledge of their literary heritage by reading aloud the works of notable authors and illustrators, as well as the masterpieces of traditional literature
5. To assist students in developing their meaning vocabularies, their ability to comprehend connected discourse, and their ability to think critically
6. To make students aware of the delight to be found in books and poems—a delight that they can later provide to themselves through reading good books
7. To have the opportunity to share emotional, funny, exciting, and stimulating moments with students

Three distinct aspects of the read-aloud experience need to be examined in order to make it as effective a teaching strategy as possible. Those aspects are (1) selecting the literature to read, (2) preparing the students for read-aloud time, and (3) reading the book aloud. Each of these aspects needs to be taken into consideration for a successful read-aloud experience.

Book Selection   Regardless of the book you choose to read aloud, it is essential that you read the book to yourself before reading it to a class. When you preread a book, you can determine whether you find the story enjoyable and worthy of children's time and whether you believe it is of an appropriate level of difficulty for your students. You also can begin to note ways in which the story lends itself to student response.

Over the course of a school year you will want to read aloud a variety of literature: poems, picture books, and chapter books of different genres and types. You will also want to ensure a balance of males and females as main characters in the books, and main characters from different backgrounds and settings, including multicultural and international ones.

The most recognized works in children's literature, though sometimes complex, deserve to be shared with students over the course of their elementary school years.

When a book or poem is challenging for students, you need to be prepared to guide their understanding. Without this help, many children would never experience and enjoy some of the more difficult, but worthy, pieces of literature. Conversely, you will want to avoid choosing books for reading aloud that students can and will consume eagerly on their own, reserving those books for students' independent reading.

When first reading aloud to a new class, however, you will want to start with shorter and easier works, known to be popular with students, and gradually build up to longer and more challenging works as you become better acquainted with your students, their interests, and their abilities. Likewise, in selecting poems to read to your class, you should begin with selections with proven appeal. Narrative poems, for example, are enjoyed by elementary-grade students, especially ones that rhyme and have a distinct rhythm. Subjects of poems popular with students include humor, well-liked familiar experiences, and animals. For more discussion of students' preferences in literature, refer to Chapters 1 and 3.

Preparation   Once a selection is made, the next step is to prepare the class for read-aloud time. For students to profit from read-aloud experiences, they need to be attentive. You can prepare students for reading aloud by having them remove distractions, such as pencils and other objects, from their immediate vicinity; by having them sit quietly in the designated place for read-aloud time; and by asking them to be ready to listen. If the book has concepts that you believe will baffle your students, you may want to clarify those before beginning to read.

Introduce the book by stating the title, author, and illustrator of the book, even with the smallest children. This will teach children that books are written by real people called authors, and that the illustrations are made by people called illustrators. Sometimes you may want to ask the students to predict what they believe the story will be about from looking at the cover and the title; other times you may want to explain briefly why you chose this book to read to them. For example, you may say that you are going to read this book because "it's another story by one of our favorite authors, William Steig" or "the book will tell us more about what it was like to live on the prairie in the nineteenth century." Introductions should be kept short. They serve the purpose of preparing students to be attentive to and interested in the story.

In preparing for reading aloud, some teachers set up a tape recorder so they can record the read-aloud sessions. The tapes may be used by students who were absent and by other students who enjoy hearing repetitions of the story while following along in the book. Next, strategies for reading aloud picture books, chapter books, and poems need to be considered.

Reading Aloud Picture Books Effectively   Consider the following steps:

• Position yourself close to the class so that all students can see the pictures. Many teachers choose to have students gather on the floor (if it is carpeted) in a semi-circle around the teacher who sits in a low chair just above the students. In this way the students can approach more closely than they can on chairs or at desks.

● Show the pictures as you read the book. Most teachers accomplish this by holding the book out to the side where both students and teacher can see it at the same time. If you find this unmanageable, you can turn the book back and forth for you, and then for the students, to see each page. Some primary-grade teachers become expert at upside-down reading and can hold the book in front of them while reading it. Whatever system you use will be fine so long as students see the pictures as you read the book. Remember that in a good picture book the text and pictures are carefully integrated to convey the story as a whole. Hearing and seeing picture books should be simultaneous.

● After the introduction, begin reading the book aloud, placing emphasis on the meaning of the story. Think of reading aloud as a type of mini-dramatic performance. Read enthusiastically and provide drama through taking on different voices for different characters, pausing for effect at exciting moments, and varying your voice in pitch (low to high), in volume (soft to loud), and in pace (slow to fast). Good oral readers often start the reading with a soft voice, of medium pace and pitch, so that as the story builds they can alter pitch, volume, and pace for special effects.

● Your body movements and facial expressions can also be used to enhance the drama of the read-aloud experience. Leaning forward during a scary, suspenseful part of a story and smiling or chuckling during a funny part can convey to the students your involvement in the story.

● Maintain eye contact with your students. Be sure you are aware of their nonverbal responses to this reading experience. Good eye contact with the students helps you to maintain class control and permits you to observe when a word of explanation may be needed.

● Read the book from beginning to end without interruptions except on an as-needed basis. Constant interruptions of the story by too many explanations or side comments interfere with the students' enjoyment of the story. On the other hand, if an illustration has a key element that needs to be observed to understand the story, then pointing it out when on that page may be worthwhile. If a child makes a spontaneous comment, then recognize the response quickly and go on. Interruptions by the teacher should be made only to prevent confusion, misunderstanding, or longer interruptions by students.

● Some books, such as concept books and interactive books, do call for interruptions in the read-aloud process. This is particularly true for informational books.

Reading Aloud Chapter Books Effectively Many of the same considerations discussed in reading aloud picture books also hold true with chapter book read-alouds. Of course, chapter books have few if any illustrations, so holding the book for students to see the pictures is not necessary. In addition, chapter books are usually read aloud over a relatively long period of time from a few days to many weeks. In a qualitative study conducted by Lynch-Brown and Tomlinson (1988) on reading aloud in grades 4 to 6, it was found that experienced teachers reading aloud novel-length chapter books include four identifiable phases in the process:

1. *Orientation.* This brief, pre-book phase of the read-aloud experience includes an introduction of the author and title of the book, predictions about the story based on the title, statements by the teacher on the story setting, location of the story setting on a map, and elicitation of student knowledge of the time and place of the setting. This orientation phase is completed during the the first session of the read-aloud experience and then the teacher begins reading aloud.

2. *Exposition.* This phase typically lasts from four to seven days. It is a period of protracted reading aloud, involving few planned extension activities. It is as though the teacher allows the book to get its grip on the students' imaginations and does not want to break the spell of the book with any diversions. Teachers note students' non-verbal responses, such as facial expressions or restlessness, which might indicate confusion or lack of understanding, and quickly supply any clarification or information needed. In this phase, students are given the opportunity to share their responses to the book, as they are throughout the read-aloud experience.

The teachers view this phase as a difficult but important period for bringing the students into the story. Some teachers help their students through this period by summarizing the story events at the end of each day's reading during the first several days. Some teachers report negative student reactions to the stories during this phase until the establishment of characters, setting, and problem is supplanted by the rising action of the plot with the conflict and suspense reaching full play.

3. *Extension.* It is during this phase that the teacher generally reads the middle and end of the story. Students are thoroughly engrossed with the story at this point and want the teacher to read on as quickly as possible. A characteristic of this phase is that enrichment activities are interspersed with the oral reading by the teacher. In contrast to the activities seen in the exposition phase, these activities tend to carry the students beyond the book.

4. *Completion.* Like the orientation phase, this phase is quite brief, generally confined to one session beginning after the oral reading is finished. During this phase the teacher encourages students to discuss their affective responses to the completed book in order to interpret it and savor it. In this phase the teacher conducts brief activities sufficient to bring closure to the read-aloud experience without giving the flavor of a rehash.

Listed below are some practices that teachers have used successfully during the exposition and extension phases of chapter book read-alouds to help "hook" the students on the book and to keep them tuned in and involved.

- Keep a chart of the characters—their names, relationships, and roles in the story— as the characters appear. This strategy is especially helpful if the story has a large number of characters. For example, in *The Westing Game* (1978) by Ellen Raskin, the many characters of this mystery must be remembered for the plot to make sense.
- Design and display a map of the story setting in order to track the events of the story in sequence. In most quest fantasies this visual aid can assist students in following the characters' journey for the quest.

- Develop a time line, somewhat like a horizontal mural, on which the dates are set at intervals above the line and the story events placed below the line at the appropriate date. For historical fiction and biographies a time line can serve as a mnemonic device for the storyline as well as for the historic events of the era. For this purpose the dates and historic events would be noted on a third tier of the time line.

Although each teacher may handle the chapter book read-aloud situation differently, all teachers in the 1988 study took their cues from the students and from the book, letting students' verbal and nonverbal responses and the plot and setting of the book guide them in their choice of strategies.

Reading Aloud Poetry Effectively   Poetry should be read aloud to students on a regular basis, daily if possible. Brief, positive encounters with one or two poems at a time are best. Too many poems in one sitting may overwhelm students or become tedious. In addition, the following points will help you to read poetry well:

- The most important rule to keep in mind is that poetry should be read for its meaning. Stress the meaning elements of the poem just as you do when reading prose. Often, the words in poetry are phrased such that you must continue past the end of the line to the next line before pausing. In other words, the breaks must be determined by the meaning units of the poem, not by the lines.
- A corollary of the first rule is that a reader should not overemphasize the beat of the poem. Doing so results in an annoying singsong effect. The natural rhythm of the poem will be felt in a more interesting way if you avoid an unnatural, meaningless reading and let the poetic language provide the rhythm.
- Poetry should be enunciated clearly. Each sound and each syllable of a poem are important and must be heard to be appreciated. This often means that you will need to slow down your normal reading pace in order to give full value to each sound.
- Poetry needs to be performed and dramatized. Take some chances and try out different effects (using different voices, elongating words, singing, shouting, pausing dramatically, etc.) as you read poems aloud.
- Poems may need to be read aloud a number of times because the many meanings of a poem may be perceived only after its literal sense is known. Also, favorite poems can be enjoyed again and again, as teachers and students savor one more reading.

Some teachers report that they do not share poetry with their students because of their uncertainty of how to read it aloud. By practicing the poems ahead of time and by reading poetry frequently, a teacher can overcome this reluctance. The rewards to both students and teachers are worth the effort.

Silent Reading by Students

Another way for students to experience good literature is to read it to themselves. Indeed, the ultimate goal of a literature program is to turn students into readers who, of their own free will, read self-selected, good literature with enjoyment, understanding, and appreciation. To assist students in becoming independent, lifelong readers, teachers in grades K–8 need to set aside time each day for students to read silently in these formative years of reading development. The amount of time for silent reading must be tailored to the reading attention spans of students. Kindergarten and first-grade students may spend only 5 to 10 minutes reading independently, but fourth- and fifth-grade students will often read silently up to an hour.

Many schools have instituted sustained silent reading (SSR) programs on a school-wide basis in order to promote the reading habit in students. In these SSR programs a certain time each day is set aside for all students, teachers, librarians, coaches, principals, custodians, and office and kitchen staff to take a "reading break." The philosophy behind SSR programs is that students need to see adults who read and who place a high priority on reading. In SSR programs, students read materials of their own choosing and are not required to write book reports or give oral reports on these materials.

Whether or not you are in a school with an SSR program, you will want to provide your students with silent reading time each day. Teachers often indicate that their students have time to read because they can read as soon as their other work is finished. This practice is not adequate in that generally the same students never finish their work and, of course, never have time to read; and these are sometimes the very students who most need encouragement to become avid readers.

Here are some tips for having successful silent reading periods.

- Have a well-stocked classroom collection of books. See Chapter 11 for more information on this.
- Conduct booktalks regularly so students become aware of books they may wish to read. These booktalks can be given by teachers and librarians. Many librarians keep a file of booktalks they have given and will gladly serve as resource persons for teachers in preparing booktalks.
- Utilize other techniques to introduce books to students. For example, displaying new books attractively in the classroom and showing videos of notable authors talking about their books and craft are effective in "selling" books to children.
- Schedule the same time each day for silent reading and adhere to it. Permit no activities other than silent reading during this time. Allow enough time for students to get well into their books and to achieve some level of satisfaction from the reading.
- Insist on attentiveness to books during this time. With primary-grade students quiet talking in pairs about books or individual lipreading aloud may be on-task behavior, but children in intermediate grades can probably read silently and should be expected to do so.

- Spend the silent reading period engrossed in books, setting yourself as an example of a reader. Be knowledgeable of and interested in the books the students are reading.
- Provide students with an opportunity to talk *voluntarily* with you or one another about their books after the silent reading period is over.

Booktalks

A booktalk is an oral presentation by a teacher, a librarian, or a student who tells about a book in order to stimulate the students' interest in the book and motivate them to read it. Booktalks are not book reports, analyses of the author's style, or the old-fashioned book report with characters, setting, theme, and plot (Bodart, 1980). Booktalks have been used effectively for years by librarians who have developed this strategy into an art for the purpose of encouraging students to check out books from the library. Teachers can give booktalks on 5 to 10 books each week from their classroom and school library collections and in this way entice students to read and experience good literature.

Booktalks can be given on any book, but they are especially needed to inspire students to read chapter books. Because chapter books take longer to read and have few illustrations, students truly appreciate booktalks on the books' content to assist them in making wise reading choices. Booktalks can be judged a success when students read the books following the booktalks.

Some teachers who give frequent booktalks also advocate having students give booktalks in order to induce other students to read the suggested books. A regular feature of "Reading Rainbow," the public television program about children's books, is children giving booktalks. One teacher taped two or three of these "Reading Rainbow" booktalks and showed them in class in order to help her students learn how to give good booktalks. The following are recommendations for giving a good booktalk.

- Be sure you have read the book before trying to do a booktalk on it.
- Booktalk books that you have liked, wholly or in part, or that you think your students will enjoy. Sincere enthusiasm for a book is stimulating and infectious.
- Have the book available to show to the students as you give the booktalk. Format aspects—such as cover illustrations, length, size, and shape of the books—which also influence book choices, can be weighed by students only if they can see the book.
- Keep the booktalk brief, no more than two minutes. Don't tell too much about the book or the students will see no reason to read it. For most books, four to six sentences will suffice. At first you will want to write out your booktalks until you have a sure feel for how to give them.
- Tell the topic and something about the action in the story, but *do not tell the plot*. Feature a scene or character the story revolves around, but do not discuss the scene that gives away the ending.

- Some booktalks may feature a short excerpt from the book. This excerpt will be an interesting beginning of the book or a suspenseful event—but the outcome is, of course, not told.
- You may want to compare the book with other books known to the students, suggesting that if they liked a certain book they may enjoy this one. Other times you may wish to point out that the book is by a favorite author and recall for the students the other titles by the author.
- A booktalk can be about a group of books that share the same theme; in this case you will want to talk briefly about each book and how it fits with the others.

The following is an example of a short booktalk:

The Slave Dancer *(1974) by Paula Fox. Back in the 1800s, Jessie Bollier played his fife on the docks of New Orleans for spare change from passersby. But one day he was thrown into a canvas bag and taken aboard a slave ship destined for Africa. The ship's captain wanted a fife player on board so that the black slaves who are going to be transported back from Africa will exercise and remain healthy on the return trip. Thus, Jessie, a white boy, finds himself to be the first slave on board. The story of Jessie's journey and the people he met—some of them cruel and some kind—are told in this book,* The Slave Dancer, *which is based on an incident that really happened.*

After you have given the booktalk, place the book back on the reading table for students to peruse and to consider for reading. Over time, you should give booktalks on a variety of books at different levels of reading difficulty, on different topics, and with male and female protagonists from both majority and minority groups, in order to appeal to the wide range of interests and abilities that exist among students in a classroom.

Shared Reading

Shared reading is a term being used here to describe a number of teaching strategies that attempt to draw on the natural literacy learning that has long occurred in book-loving homes around the world. These various strategies provide children with opportunities to experience good literature as they are learning to read. The strategies have in common a semi-structured modification of the parent-child interaction with repeated readings of favorite books as the child gradually acquires an understanding of print and its relationship to our sound system or to the words we speak. A list of predictable books suitable for use in shared reading activities can be found in Appendix C.

Shared-Book Experience   Don Holdaway is well known for proposing an adaptation of the home-learning experience. He proposed the shared-book experience and developed Big Books, enlarged-text books of approximately 24" × 30", in order to replicate the home-learning strategy with groups of beginning readers in school settings. A typical classroom teaching-learning sequence of shared-book experience as proposed by Holdaway (1982) can be summarized in five steps:

- *Opening activity.* Favorite poems and songs are repeated by the students and teacher while the teacher points to the text of a Big Book. Then a new poem or song is taught.
- *Review of a familiar story.* The teacher and students review a favorite story in an enlarged format. This story is used to teach skills in context. Students participate by saying the story in unison. Sometimes the story is then informally dramatized.
- *Language play.* The teacher involves the students in alphabet games, rhymes, and songs that use letter names. The purpose is to have fun with words and sounds and to avoid isolated phonic drills.
- *Presentation of a new story.* The teacher and students read aloud a new story from a Big Book. The teacher encourages students to use word-solving strategies by observing context and by predicting to confirm new vocabulary words.
- *Output activities.* Students read independently from a wide selection of favorites, participate in art activities stemming from the new story, and compose original stories often using structures from the new story. Sometimes several children enjoy playing school—one acting as teacher—while they read a favorite story together. (p. 299)

This sequence encapsulates the strategy developed by Holdaway and his colleagues in New Zealand to use children's books in classrooms in a manner similar to the one used by many parents whose preschoolers readily and naturally learned to read.

Assisted Reading   The natural reading approach has been adapted for various situations. For example, Hoskisson, Sherman, and Smith (1974) proposed assisted reading as a strategy to use with impaired readers. In assisted reading, the learner and the adult sit side by side with a book. The learner reads aloud until she has difficulty, at which point the adult supplies the word.

Paired Reading   Paired reading is guided practice with a lead reader who reads in a soft voice and invites the child to fill in words when a pause occurs and the child knows the word. A good resource for the classroom is John Ciardi's *You Read to Me, I'll Read to You* (1962), a book of poems designed for paired reading. Paired reading can also be enjoyed by two children of compatible personalities who read back and forth to one another.

In all of these strategies, well-chosen literature is important; the nature of the experience is companionable, not authoritative; and the child reader must see the text and hear the words simultaneously. Sometimes the adult places a finger under each word as it is being read in order to draw the child's attention to the print. Selecting favorite, loved stories is essential because the success of these strategies is contingent on frequent rereadings of the same book. Although the primary purpose of these strategies is to provide a favorable situation in which children can acquire literacy, the effect of the strategies can be the promotion of a love of literature.

Storytelling

Storytelling is the oldest medium for sharing literature. Oral literature flourished for thousands of years before writing was invented and books became commonly available. When a teacher tells stories, another delightful means for children to experience literature becomes available to her class. By bringing stories to life through personal expression and interpretation, a storyteller establishes a close communication with her audience. A storyteller begins by selecting a good story. Next, she practices it until she is able to tell it with ease, and then she tells it to different audiences again and again.

Selection of a Story   Good stories take time to find. First, you must genuinely like the story. To find possible stories for telling, begin with collections of folktales and short stories. Read some of these until you find a few you especially like. Then consider these two points:

- The first stories you tell should take no longer than 10 minutes. As you develop your gifts of storytelling, you may want to tell longer stories.
- Good stories for telling usually have few characters (from two to five), high conflict, action that builds to a climax, and a quick conclusion that ties together all the threads of the story. Humorous elements are also worth seeking.

Preparation for Telling   Once you have selected a story to tell, outline the story content in terms of the plot. Many storytellers note on 3" × 5" cards the title and source of the tale, the characters' names and story events, and any other information that may be helpful. These cards can then be consulted quickly just before telling a story. A story file can be a nice resource to keep as more stories are prepared for telling. Carol Fox, a storyteller from Illinois, reports that she tapes her stories and then uses them to refresh her memory for later retellings.

Practice   Tell the story aloud to yourself again and again. Do not memorize the story, but keep in mind the characters and sequence of main story events. Each time you tell the story, it will change a bit, becoming more and more your own story as you include personal touches.

The children's imaginations and your voice and facial expressions are the foundations for good storytelling experiences. Some storytellers find props useful, whereas others believe props diminish the closeness between audience and storyteller. If used, props should enhance the story, not overpower or distract from it. Experiment with props to find out what works best for you. They can be simple—such as a hat, a stick-on mustache, or a stuffed toy—or more elaborate—such as a mask, a puppet, or a costume.

When puppets are used, a separate puppet is made for each character and is held by the storyteller while the character is speaking. Puppets can be purchased or made by the storyteller. Another more elaborate use of props is the feltboard story—a storytelling aid some teachers especially enjoy. Pictures or objects are attached to a feltboard or display board and are moved around during the story. Cumulative stories especially lend themselves to feltboard presentations.

The art of storytelling can be developed with practice. Teachers who tell stories in their classrooms report that their students are appreciative listeners and soon begin telling stories themselves.

Choral Poetry

Choral poetry is interpreting and saying a poem together as a group activity. These poems may either be practiced and recited aloud or rehearsed and read aloud. Students enjoy this way of experiencing poetry because they have a participatory role in the activity. Most poetry, intended to be listened to, is suitable for choral presentation.

Selection At first, select a short poem from one to four stanzas until your students develop some skill in memorizing and performing poems. Humorous narrative poems are good first choices.

Memorization For most choral presentations the first step is for the teacher to select and read aloud a poem that is well liked by the students. Then each line or pair of lines is said by the teacher and repeated by the students until they know them. It is preferable for the students to repeat the lines *after* the teacher and for the teacher to avoid reciting with the class, so that the students will commit the poem to memory instead of waiting for the teacher's voice. Once the entire poem is learned in this way, then variations can be added for performing the poem.

Although students need to rehearse a poem in order to intone it similarly, some longer poems with older students who read well will not be memorized but practiced and read together as a group.

Arrangements Options for reading a poem chorally include unison, two- or three-part, solo voices, cumulative buildup, and simultaneous voices, as explained below.

- In unison choral speaking, the students learn the poem and recite it together as a group. Two-part or three-part choral poetry is usually based on arranging students into voice types (for example, high, medium, and low) to achieve different effects and selecting lines of the poem for each group to recite or read.
- Solo voices can be added to either of these presentations and are sometimes used for asking a question or making an exclamation.
- Some poems lend themselves to cumulative buildup presentations. A cumulative buildup is effected by having, for example, only two voices say the first line, then two more join in on the second line, and then two more, gradually building to a crescendo until the entire class says the last line or stanza.

- Poems can be presented by simultaneous recitation, a presentation similar to a musical round. In this case, group one begins the poem and recites it all the way through. When group one begins the third line, for example, then group two starts the first line and the two groups recite simultaneously until the end. Other groups can, of course, be added.

Many other variations can be developed for use in choral presentations. Let imagination be your guide. Words and lines can be spun into ghostly moans, or barked, or sung, or repeated. Choreography adds visual impact, as do simple props. As soon as children learn that poems do not have to be read sedately through exactly as written, they will begin to find excitement and deeper meaning in poetry.

Performance   Incorporating action, gestures, body movements, and finger plays can produce more interesting and enjoyable presentations. Occasionally performing a well-honed choral poem for an audience can bring pride to young performers. Remember, the best audiences are close by—the class next door, the principal, the librarian, the custodian, or a visiting parent. Students truly enjoy this nonthreatening way of sharing poetry. Stimulate creativity by reading different poems and allowing various interpretations to reveal the imagination and insight of your students.

Audiotapes and Videotapes

Many tapes are available today to bring literature to students. Recently some well-known actors have made excellent audio recordings of some favorite children's stories. Animated and iconographic videos are also readily available. *Animated videos* are cartoons or images that move; *iconographic videos* are films in which the camera moves over static illustrations. A few videos are movies based on children's books and performed by actors. Predictably, these vary widely in quality.

Some audiovisual media re-creations are artistically well done and deserve to be considered as another means for students to experience literature. Generally it is preferable to have students read the book first and form their own images of the story. Then, after viewing the tape, students can make comparisons between the book and the tape.

Audio- and videotapes are usually available in school libraries, through school districts' media repositories, or from nearby public libraries. Book clubs sometimes offer audiotapes to teachers with the purchase of a certain number of books by the class.

Responding to Literature

When students experience a story by listening to it, or by reading it, or by viewing it, they may naturally wish to respond or express their reactions to the experience in some way. In sharing their responses with others, students profit by recapturing the experience through translating it to a new form or medium; they develop a better understanding of what they experienced by organizing and deepening their feelings and thoughts on the experience; they discover that others' experiences with the same book may not have been the same as theirs; and they bring closure to the experience.

Although it is important to give students opportunities to respond to books, not every book needs or merits a lengthy response. The peals of laughter and the moans of sorrow during the actual reading of the story are sometimes response enough. But with other books, students need opportunities to explore further their thoughts and feelings. Teachers can elicit student responses to literature through oral expression, written expression, and the graphic arts.

Oral Response

Students love to talk, and what better to talk about than a sincerely felt shared book experience? Rosenblatt (1978) reminds us that no two people have the same prior experiences and that it is the transaction that occurs between the text, the reader, and the present context that provokes a particular response. Teachers may generate opportunities for students to share their individual insights to literary experiences in many different ways.

Discussions   Perhaps the most often used means of eliciting students' responses is through discussions. *Whole-class discussion* usually accompanies the reading aloud of a book to the class. In these discussions comprehension is assumed and the discussion centers on the different ways students feel and think about the book, its characters, its events, and its outcome. Thus, to stimulate a good class discussion, a teacher will encourage students to share their individual responses to open-ended questions, not seek supposedly right answers in order to check comprehension or recall. In a class discussion, the teacher has the pivotal role as discussion leader. The discussion tends to be a teacher-to-students, students-to-teacher format. And with a large class, only some of the students will have an opportunity to express their viewpoints.

Another format for students to discuss their responses to literature is the *literature response group*. In literature response groups, students share their responses with peers about a book they have read as a group or a book read aloud by the teacher to the whole class. One of the goals of literature response groups is to have all children learn to work with one another and to value the opinions and views of others.

Groups can be established by the desire to read the same book, by friendship, by heterogeneous assignment by the teacher, or by random assignment. Small groups are usually set up with two to six students for optimal functioning. Students who have less skill working in groups often function better in dyads or triads. The small group discussion is a student-to-student form of communication and permits students more control over the discussion and more roles to perform as group members. For example, students may assume the role of leader, recorder, arbiter, listener, or devil's advocate. The advantages of small group discussions are that students are in control, have more opportunities to express their opinions, and can become more actively involved. Unless students have been taught to work together, however, groups do not function well. Small group model discussions with the teacher as a participating member and joint planning by teacher and class before groups begin working can set rules, goals, and timelines.

Individual conferences between a teacher and a student are another means of discovering students' responses to literature. Although a teacher may choose to set up conferences daily, occasional conferences in which the student comes prepared to talk about a book she has recently finished can be instructive for the teacher and motivating for the student. The conference is focused on what the student thought and felt about the book. Some teachers ask the student to read aloud a favorite part of the story and tell why it was selected. Individual conferences are from 5 to 10 minutes long, and usually end with considering the next book the student will read or the response activity the student has planned.

Eliciting a good discussion with substantial student participation is not an easy art. First of all, it is essential to remember that comprehension of the story is assumed and that the teacher's (or group leader's) purpose is not to test the students on the meaning of the story. Beyond this, certain strategies for promoting discussions need to be considered for use in leading class discussions, in guiding literature response groups, and in interacting with students in individual conferences. Whether you, as the teacher, will be leading the discussion or guiding your students in the art of discussion leader, the questions to be posed are very important.

Questioning   Common sense tells us that a question that can be answered by yes, no, or a single word or phrase will not lead to an interactive discussion. The question, "Did you like the story?" may result in a simple "yes." "Which part of the story did you like best and what did you like about it?" is likely to elicit a more detailed response.

Divergent questions have no one right answer but a number of possible answers. They naturally provoke more discussion than convergent questions for which only one answer is correct. Examples of each of these question types follow. They are tailored to the book, *Sylvester and the Magic Pebble* (1969) by William Steig.

- "Was Sylvester turned into a rock or a lion?" ("A rock.") This question is convergent; it can be answered by a single word.
- "What did you think would happen to Sylvester after he became a rock?" ("I thought he would get rolled down the hill and the pebble would tumble on top of him and he would turn back into a donkey." "I thought he would have to be a rock forever." "I thought his dad would find the magic pebble and turn him back into a donkey.") This question is divergent; it stimulates many different answers, each of which is possible or correct. The response to this question results in more than a single word or phrase.
- "Who is the main character of the story?" ("Sylvester.") This convergent question tests the students' literal comprehension of the story and can be answered by only one word. Such a question does not provoke discussion.

- "Do you like Sylvester?" This question, though divergent, can be answered in a word. A better way to phrase this question is "Why do you like or dislike Sylvester?" or "How do you feel about Sylvester?" The question remains divergent but now may also result in discussion.

The best ideas for questions to stimulate book discussions flow directly from your response to the particular book and why you want the students to experience the book. Usually you will have students read works of fiction for the aesthetic experience they will have with it—enjoyment, appreciation, emotional involvement, deeper understanding of life, and so on. In this case, your questions need to permit students to talk about their experiences. Divergent questions are best suited to this goal. Your questions will tell your students what you believe is important in reading. If your questions are convergent ones about the plot, characters, and setting, then you are telling your students that reading fiction is a type of egg hunt for the particular eggs laid by this author and previously located by you. On the other hand, if you ask divergent questions that permit them to explore their individual experiences with a work of fiction, students will soon discover that you really want to understand their feelings and thoughts about books.

The purpose of reading informational books, though perhaps partially aesthetic, is usually efferent; that is, the reader's attention is centered on what should be retained as a residue after the actual reading event. Locating specific pieces of information to support an argument, or comparing information from two or more sources are examples of reasons for efferent reading of literature. Convergent questions in this case would reflect that purpose and be acceptable. Questions that stimulate more than a single-word answer are still, of course, preferable. Certainly, nonfiction may be read for more than information acquisition, just as fiction may be read for more than aesthetic purposes. For example, historical fiction novels may be read aloud by teachers with a dual goal: involvement in a powerful vicarious experience and acquisition of some understandings about life during a particular era. But keeping in mind the purposes for reading will guide you in formulating good questions.

Taking notes on the interesting, provocative, funny, heart-wrenching, and problematic characters and scenes of a book is a good starting point for question development. Such questions will be specific to a book and are preferable, but formula questions can be adapted to different books and may help you in designing good questions based on specific books. Some formula questions are listed here.

- What important ideas did you find conveyed in this story?
- What made certain parts of this book so funny? Sad? Exciting? Tell which part you are thinking of and why you think it is funny (sad, exciting).
- How do you think the story should have ended and why do you think that?
- How would you have acted if you had been (book character)?
- What do you think the author's main message (theme) was in this story? Explain why you agree or disagree with the message.
- Which part of the story did you like best or least and why?

- Which character did you like best or least and why?
- How is this story similar to other ones we have read?
- How is this story similar to (a specific story)? Compare the stories and tell which you liked better and why.
- Which character do you identify with? Tell why and how you identify with him or her.
- What has happened in your life that you are reminded of by this story (character, situation)?
- What would you have done in (character)'s predicament?
- What do you think about (character)?
- What would (character) have done if . . . .

Following Up   Another facet of leading a discussion is the followup question. Once a student has given an answer, take that answer and build on it with a question that asks the student to expand or carry the answer to another realm. For example, after the student has said that she expected Sylvester to remain a rock forever, you might ask her to explore how Sylvester would adjust to being a rock and whether and how his parents would adjust. In turn, asking other students to tell how and why they believe otherwise about a part of the story is a way to help students discover that each person's experience with the book may be different.

Waiting   What happens if no one answers the question you asked? This is not likely to happen, because students like to talk; but a good discussion leader knows the value of *waiting*. Wait long enough and someone will finally respond. Too often discussion leaders jump in and answer their own questions before students have had a chance to think of what their thoughts are on the point being raised. Some teachers find that asking students to jot notes about the book experience during and after reading gives them time to reflect on their experiences with the book and helps them to formulate their thoughts and feelings for later expression during the discussion.

Creative Drama   Creative drama is informal drama that lends itself readily to the reenactment of story experiences. In discussing the features of creative drama, McCaslin (1990) urges teachers and librarians to keep the following in mind.

- The drama is based on a piece of literature.
- Dialogue is created by the actors: lines are not written or memorized.
- Improvisation is an essential element.
- Movement on "stage" by actors is an integral part of creative drama.
- Scenery and costumes are not used, although an occasional prop may assist the children's imaginations.
- Drama, a process rather than a product, means that it is not performed for an audience. The performances are for the benefit of the participants. Several different dramas or different dramatic interpretations of the same piece of literature can occur simultaneously in the classroom.

Creative drama is an enjoyable and rewarding oral language activity that can be used with students at all grade levels from kindergarten to high school. A single scene from a chapter book may be enacted, or a picture book or short story may be dramatized in its entirety. The most suitable stories to start with are relatively simple ones, having from two to six characters and high action. Many folktales fit this description and lend themselves to being enacted.

The steps to follow in guiding creative drama in the classroom are:

- Once a story is selected, the students listen to it being read to them or they read it independently.
- Next, they decide if they like the story enough to want to act it out. If so, they then listen to it again or read it, paying particular attention to the characters and the story scenes in sequence.
- The students then list the characters and the scenes on the chalkboard or on chart paper.
- They cast the play by assigning parts to actors. If enough students are interested in dramatizing the same story, you may want to assign two or more casts of actors immediately. In this way each cast of characters can observe the performances of the others and learn from them.
- Next, each cast uses the list of scenes to review the plot, ensuring that all actors recall the events. Discuss the characters at this time, too, having students describe the actions, talk, and appearance for each.
- Give the cast of characters a few minutes to decide how to handle the performance and then run through it. The first attempt may be a bit bumpy, but by the second time through it usually goes quite smoothly.
- After completing the drama, the class or the group of students then evaluates its success. McCaslin (1990) suggests these questions:
    1. Did they tell the story?
    2. What did you like about the opening scene?
    3. Did the characters show that they were excited? (angry, unhappy, etc.)
    4. When we play it again, can you think of anything that would improve it?
    5. Was anything important left out? (p. 174)

Due to its improvisational nature and absence of costumes and scenery, creative drama appropriately places importance on the learning and experiencing process, not on performance, and it permits drama to become a frequent means of responding to literature in the classroom.

Readers' Theatre   Readers' theatre is the oral presentation of literature by two or more actors, and usually a narrator, reading from a script. Children's literary response is made evident through expressive oral reading and their group interpretation. This form of response is especially enjoyable for children who are able to read aloud with some fluency. Features typically associated with readers' theatre are:

- The readers and narrator typically remain on the "stage" throughout the production.

- Readers use little movement, suggesting action with simple gestures and facial expressions.
- Chairs or stools are used for readers and narrator to sit on, and performers usually remain seated throughout the performance. Sometimes certain readers sit with their backs to the audience to suggest that they are not in that scene.
- No costumes or stage settings are necessary, and at most should be suggestive, rather than complete or literal, so as to permit the imaginations of the audience to have full rein. The use of sound effects may enhance the performance and give the impression of a radio play.

Scripts can be developed for readers' theatre by the teacher or by older students adapting a work of literature enjoyed by the class. Picture books readily lend themselves to adaptation, as do short stories. Some teachers have successfully adapted well-selected scenes from a favorite chapter book. The qualities to seek in a promising story are lots of natural-sounding dialogue, strong characterization, drama or humor, and a satisfactory ending. If the original work has extensive dialogue, the script writing is very easy. The script begins with a list of characters and an opening statement by the narrator. Following the introduction, the dialogue is written into script form, with the narrator scripted for the remaining nondialogue, narrative parts.

Scripts can also be purchased, but finding scripts that are both well written and adapted from the literature you wish to use in your classroom may prove difficult. Using any play script you can find defeats the purpose of providing students with an alternate form of response to their literary experiences. Remember: As with most things, developing the first script is the most difficult. Once you have done it, you will find out how easy it is. Intermediate-grade students take readily to script development once they have a model to imitate. Readers' theatre can become a frequently selected response option of literature response groups.

Choice of literature to use can include virtually any literary genre—biographies, letters, diaries, and journals. Poetry selected and arranged for readers' theatre on a particular theme infuses an interesting variation into this form of drama. Paul Fleischman's *Joyful Noise: Poems for Two Voices* (1988) and *I Am Phoenix: Poems for Two Voices* (1985) are collections of poetry for older children written in a manner already suitable for a readers' theatre presentation. Variations on readers' theatre can be accomplished through the addition of background music, choral poems, and brief scenes from different stories tied together by a common theme, among other options to enliven this dramatic enactment of literature.

Preparation for a readers' theatre presentation is a good opportunity for students to strengthen their oral reading abilities and to try out their expressive skills. The group typically reads through the script once or twice, and then works on refining the interpretive aspects of each performer. Decisions need to be made on the arrangement of chairs and speakers for greatest visual effect. Following each presentation, an evaluation is made by the group with the goal of improving future performances.

McCaslin (1990) states that "the simplicity of production and effectiveness of result make it [readers' theatre] singularly desirable in schools with inadequate stage facilities and where rehearsal time is at a premium" (p. 263). For these same reasons, readers' theatre is extremely well-suited to classroom reenactments of literary experiences. In readers' theatre, the students have the opportunty to translate their experiences with a literary work to a new medium—the medium of drama—with considerable ease and pleasure.

Story Tellings and Retellings   Children who hear good stories read aloud by teachers, librarians, and parents often recapture those happy experiences by making the stories their own through story retellings. In addition, in their natural play activities during preschool years, children enjoy roleplaying and making up their own stories to tell to a playmate, real or imagined. The foundation for children's storytelling comes from the children's language environment—the talk they have heard and the stories that have been read to them. As young students learn to tell and retell stories, they reinforce their concept of story and are provided with opportunities for oral language development and expansion. Children who can tell a story with a beginning, middle, and an end have the groundwork laid for later writing activities. You will note that story tellings and retellings by children are different in purpose than storytelling by teachers, as discussed in an earlier section of this chapter. Teachers tell stories as one of many ways of sharing literature with their students.

Teachers can foster the telling and retelling of stories by structuring a classroom environment that is conducive to this activity. Setting off an area of the classroom where children can gather for quiet talk and equipping it with some props such as story puppets, feltboards with cut-out story figures, toy story characters (stuffed animals, dolls, plastic and metal figures), wordless books, and children's favorite storybooks can entice children into telling and retelling their favorite stories. Some children take the book shared by the teacher during storytime and page through it, retelling the story from the pictures; others take story puppets and re-create the story or make up an entirely new adventure with the same characters.

Tape recorders also inspire younger students to record and listen to their favorite stories, while older students find a tape recorder an incentive for developing radio shows based on favorite books. Their favorite choral poetry and readers' theatre performances are both well suited to radio show productions.

Written Response

Written language activities are an important means for students to respond to their experiences with literature.

Expression of Ideas and Feelings   The simplest and most direct way for teachers to elicit written responses to stories is to ask students to write their ideas and feelings about a book or poem listened to or read. Questions to stimulate written response may be formulated according to the same guidelines suggested for designing discussion questions earlier in this chapter. Divergent, open-ended questions, rather than convergent questions, will elicit students' feelings and ideas about a scene, a character, or the story as a whole, and will help students explore their personal involvement with the story.

Each student's writing ability must be considered in selecting an appropriate writing activity. Emergent writers may find it possible to write the name of their favorite character and draw a picture of that character; more able writers may be able to write a detailed character description.

Literature Journals and Records   Some teachers have found a literature journal—in which students make frequent written responses to books read—a motivating tool for students. Teachers read and comment on the entries periodically and students gain a sense of pride in their reading accomplishments.

In some cases, reactions to books by one student can be enjoyed by the rest of the class. One teacher clipped blank response sheets with columns for responses (Author, Title, Reaction) inside the front cover of books in the classroom collection. After reading the book, a student enters her name and her views on the book. Other students enjoy reading the book to see if their reaction will be the same. Some teachers have had students write 4" × 6" notecards about each book as it is read. These cards are kept on file in the library corner so that each new reader can add her impressions to the card.

Models for Stories and Poems   When children read and listen to stories, they accumulate vocabulary, sentence structures, stylistic devices, and story ideas and structures. Well-written stories and poems serve as models for children in their own writing. When an 8-year-old boy who wrote extremely well-developed, interesting stories was asked how he learned to make up such good stories, he replied, "It's really a secret, but I'll tell you if you won't tell my teacher. I don't really make up the stories. When I was little, my mother read lots of books to me, then in school my teachers read a lot more. So what I do is take a beginning from one of the stories, a middle from another, and the end from another. And then I make up a title." Children who have a rich literary background have a well-stocked storehouse of beginnings, middles, and endings to put to use in their speaking and writing.

Modeling after different literary forms can be used to extend book and poem experiences. Writing a story modeled after another story can be an enjoyable re-creation of the experience. In modeling, the student adapts a story form or idea into a new creation. Examples are:

- Students create another episode using the same characters.
- Students write a different ending to the story read.
- Students take the perspective of another character in the story and recast the story with a shift in point of view. Two examples of a change in point of view can be found in Jon Scieszka's *The True Story of the 3 Little Pigs by A. Wolf* (1989), which gives the Big Bad Wolf's version, and Scieszka's *The Frog Prince Continued* (1991), which tells the shocking truth about "happily ever after."
- Students develop readers' theatre scripts, writing a story in a new form.
- Students write a prequel to a story.

- Students take a story set in the past and rewrite it with a modern-day setting. Alternatively, a character from the historical narrative can become a visitor to modern times.

Poems can also be modeled. A favorite writing activity is to read many poems of one poetic form, then analyze the form to reveal the characteristics of its structure. Quatrains, cinquains, haiku, and limericks can all be used as models with students once they have an appreciation for poetry and the specific poetic form. Some poets have suggested other models and patterns for students to follow in writing poetry. Kenneth Koch's *Rose, Where Did You Get That Red?* (1973) and *Wishes, Lies, And Dreams* (1970), Barbara Juster Esbensen's *A Celebration of Bees: Helping Children Write Poetry* (1975), Lee Bennett Hopkins's *Pass the Poetry, Please!* (1987), and David McCord's *One at a Time* (1977) are useful resources for teachers who want to encourage students to compose poems. (See Appendix G for further information and annotations of these books.)

Traditional Book Reports   Requiring students to list author, title, date, genre, setting, main characters, and a summary of the plot seldom causes students to delve more deeply into their experiences with literature. Traditional book reports are usually viewed by students as tedious busywork. Although book reports are assigned by teachers in order to cause students to read, students often report that they never read the books they report on, but rather read the bookflap, a page or two at the beginning and end, and write the report. More promising ways to foster the reading habit are through a good read-aloud program, time set aside for silent reading, booktalks about lots of readily available literature, literature response groups in which students can show their excitement for stories, class discussions, and writing activities in which students' thoughts and feelings about books can be expressed.

Recently, some so-called literature response forms or worksheets have been published for use by teachers who are using literature-based reading approaches. Be cautious in your use of these worksheets. They need to be examined carefully because some of them are little more than disguised book report forms asking for plot, setting, characters, and theme. Such comprehension assessment may be justified occasionally in the reading class, but if your interest is to elicit students' responses to literature, stay away from worksheets.

Graphic Arts Response

Most students enjoy arts and crafts. Graphic design and display techniques can therefore be an enjoyable and effective way to communicate literary experiences with other students and to share book experiences with parents and visitors. *Graphic arts response* is the use of different art and graphic design and display techniques to organize, deepen, and bring closure to students' experiences with literature. These activities can be a way for students to recapture the literary experience while translating it to a new medium.

Pictures and Collages   Students can make pictures and collages to illustrate a favorite story or poem. Having a variety of materials available to choose from in designing their re-creations of literature increases students' enthusiasm and creativity. Paints, colored pencils, chalk, crayons, collage materials (cloth, yarn, lace, tissue paper), colored construction paper, and magazines with pictures and printed words for cutting up and shaping into pictures can be kept readily available for use in the classroom. Teachers foster good design by asking students to think about the purpose and desired effects and by pointing out interesting visual elements in other media, especially in picture books. For example, when students observe the different ways illustrators frame their pictures, outline figures, and use blank space and perspective for highlighting an object, they often can replicate and adapt these techniques for their own classroom design projects.

Teachers have often overused the activity of "draw a picture of the story" by assigning it too frequently, by not planning the activity adequately, and by permitting students little or no choice of media and project. An activity repeated to the point of monotony becomes little more than busywork to students. Remember that it may be unnecessary to have a response activity of any kind after reading a book or that a worthy response to a book would be finding another book by the same author and reading it next.

When more active response seems warranted, however, it is important to plan worthwhile ways for students to express those responses. Providing students with options on the form or shape the response will take and then planning collaboratively with the students on the execution of the project are the roles the teacher needs to assume. Your art specialists and school and public librarians can be of great assistance in helping you plan response activities.

Murals   Murals are made from a long roll of paper mounted horizontally on bulletin boards. The entire length of paper is usually divided into sections and often presents a chronology of the story events. Murals may feature a particular theme, such as animals from stories around the world, different kinds of homes the characters live in, personified dolls and toys from a unit on stories with personification, or various ways young story characters have overcome obstacles as they grow and mature. Groups of children decide on the theme or topic, design the segments, and allocate tasks to group members. Sometimes students work directly on the mounted mural, other times they cut it into sections and work at tables then tape it back together for mounting. This device is well suited for literature response groups whose members collaborate in selecting, planning, and implementing the mural. The product is often dramatic and showy, offering the group members a feeling of real accomplishment.

Roller Movies   This technique produces a simulated movie or filmstrip of a story. The pictures are designed, frame by frame, on a long roll of paper. Once completed, each end of the paper is taped to a dowel rod or broom handle, then the paper is rolled onto the feeder rod so that the beginning frame is viewed first when the paper is unrolled. The ends of each rod are inserted into holes on the sides of a cardboard box so the paper can be stretched from one roller to the other across the box opening and then rolled to the receiver rod to move the frames along. The box is turned on its side, TV style, to face the audience, and the story unfolds as the frames are rolled onto the receiver rod. A script is written by the group to go along with each frame. The need for group collaboration makes this an ideal project for literature response groups and the finished movie lends itself to story retellings.

Dioramas   A diorama is a three-dimensional display in which objects and figures are placed into a background or setting to create a scene. Dioramas are often made in classrooms by using shoeboxes set on the side, providing a framework on which to construct a setting, such as a floor, ceiling, and three walls of a room. Many materials may be used to make the figures, their background, furniture, and clothes, including modeling clay, collage materials, matchboxes, dried leaves, pine straw, and tiny dolls. Dioramas are especially well suited to individuals and pairs of students who may work alone or cooperatively in selecting and re-creating in miniature an important scene from a story.

Books and Big Books   Children can make their own stories and poems into books for a more finished presentation of their writing efforts. There are many different ways to make books in the classroom, ranging from the simple process of stapling together students' separate pictures on a topic with an illustrated cover to the more complex task of developing books with hard covers made of cardboard with pages covered in clear or patterned adhesive paper or fabric, and then sewn together and bound for a "real book" look.

Big Books are often modeled after a favorite picture book enjoyed by the class, with the pictures drawn by students and the text printed by the teacher on 24" × 30" heavy paper or poster board, which is then laminated, bound on metal rings, and hung on an easel. Many schools have laminators for use in these projects. Lamination is also done at many commercial copy and print shops at a moderate cost.

Making books is an activity most suited for individuals or pairs of students. However, a collaborative book organized around a theme or pattern can be made by a larger group in which each member contributes a story or poem. In this type of book, a table of contents with the names of each contributor offers recognition of all students while also calling students' attention to this useful part of a book. When students are first learning the steps of making books, considerable guidance from an adult is required. Parent volunteers and teacher aides can be shown how to provide this assistance. The step-by-step processes of making different types of books can be found in these sources:

- Aliki's *How a Book Is Made* (1984), a 32-page picture book for children, describes the stages of commercial book publishing, including the writing of the manuscript, the drawing of pictures, and the technical processes leading to printed and bound copies.
- Howard Greenfeld's *Books: From Writer to Reader* (1984), a 197-page book more for adult readers, also describes the stages of commercial publishing in a straightforward manner.

- Susan Purdy's *Books for You to Make* (1973), a 96-page book that will prove useful to children and adults, gives well-illustrated, detailed instructions on how to write, design, illustrate, and bind books. Many different bindings, from simple to complex, are described and illustrated.
- Harvey Weiss's *How to Make Your Own Books* (1974) is a fine source for different types of bindings and cover ideas. In addition, many types of books (flip books, scrolls, Japanese-style books, etc.) and how to make them by hand are described and illustrated in this 72-page book.

Completed books need to be displayed for admiration and made available for reading by others. A special place in the reading corner can be reserved to exhibit student-made books.

Newspapers and Newsletters   A collaborative endeavor in which students write about the books they have been reading and tell about their book-related projects can result in class newspapers and newsletters. Each issue of the paper can focus on a different topic, such as favorite authors, illustrators, story characters, and poetic forms. In some intermediate grade classrooms a different literature response group accepts editing responsibilities for the newsletter each month, selecting the focus, soliciting manuscripts, designing pages and making editorial decisions. The newsletters are sent home to parents with suggestions of good books to read and new authors to check out. Since computers are generally available in schools, individuals with word processing skills can usually be found, often among the students, to produce interesting newspapers and newsletters.

Time Lines, Maps, Diagrams, and Charts   A type of visual figure that details a period of time covered in a story is a *time line.* The figure is made by drawing a line on a long strip of mural paper, then placing the dates below the line at scaled intervals. The story events are logged in above the line. This graphic aid organizes the events of the story and can permit the students to compare events from a novel of historical fiction or from a biography with actual dates from history.

Time lines can be excellent visual aids when used in conjunction with reading aloud a progressive plot chapter book. The time line is set up with the dates, then the story events are recorded after each day's reading. The time line can also serve as a reminder of what has happened thus far as a review before beginning the next chapter.

Time lines can also be useful when students are reading a variety of material on a single period of history: biographies, historical fiction novels, and photoessays on World War II, for instance. Historical events from different sources can be compared for authenticity by using parallel time lines or by adding more tiers to the same time line. Individual students may develop time lines to follow the events of an entire series of books, such as science fiction novels and quest adventure stories.

Maps are especially suitable for charting the settings in chapter books of many genres. They can be designed by individuals or groups of students and make interesting and helpful visual aids for telling others about books. Some chapter books in which maps are included as part of the book can be used by students as models to imitate for drawing storymaps on other books. (For example, see the endpapers of *The Nargun and the Stars* [1974] by Patricia Wrightson, *The Book of Three* [1964] by Lloyd Alexander, and *Rabbit Hill* [1944] by Robert Lawson.) Maps are also suitable for laying out the events in picture books and books with a circular journey motif in which the protagonist leaves home, encounters adversity, overcomes it, and returns home.

A *diagram* presents textual material in visual form and can be used to illustrate arrangements and relations within a story. (For example, in *Linnea in Monet's Garden* [Björk, 1987] a family tree of Monet's family is displayed.) Many information books use diagrams, and students can develop ideas for presenting information through diagrams by perusing these books. Another Linnea story, *Linnea's Windowsill Garden*, has a diagram of plants and their seeds. Diagrams can also be developed to show relationships found in book series and long works, such as the Arthurian legends. Diagrams can be used by teachers and students to display the progression of a story, which is especially useful to help students understand unusual plot twists.

Charts give information in table form to show relationships, summarize information, and present facts in a capsule form. (For example, on page 8 of *Linnea's Almanac* [Björk, 1989] a chart showing species of birds and their feeding habits assists readers in the art of feeding winter birds.) When students use nonfiction books for studying content areas, they can be encouraged to consider visual means for presenting and summarizing the information gained.

Displays and Bulletin Boards   Displays are three-dimensional re-creations of a setting, a town, or a battle scene, for instance, placed on a large flat surface, such as a table or piece of plywood. The use of clay and cardboard for figures, papier mache for hills, colored construction paper for lakes and land surfaces, and so on permits students to design impressive displays from story settings. More artistically talented students can be given opportunities to excel in these design activities.

Designing and making bulletin boards provide groups of students with opportunities to demonstrate their book experiences in innovative ways. Planning bulletin boards and displays requires students to select an interesting and worthy focus or message in order to call attention to the display and to get the message across effectively by using only a few words.

Giving students choices of books to read and choices in the ways they respond to them is an essential component of a good curriculum in literature. This chapter presented a smorgasbord of ideas for having students experience literature and respond to those literary experiences.

References

Alexander, L. (1964). *The book of three*. New York: Holt.

Aliki (Brandenberg). (1986). *How a book is made*. New York: Harper & Row.

Björk, C. (1987). *Linnea in Monet's garden*. Illustrated by L. Anderson. Translated by J. Sandin. Stockholm: Rabén & Sjögren.

Björk, C. (1989). *Linnea's almanac.* Illustrated by L. Anderson. Translated by J. Sandin. Stockholm: Rabén & Sjögren.

Björk, C. (1988). *Linnea's windowsill garden.* Illustrated by L. Anderson. Translated by J. Sandin. Stockholm: Rabén & Sjögren.

Bodart, J. (1980). *Booktalk!* New York: H. W. Wilson.

Ciardi, J. (1962). *You read to me, I'll read to you.* New York: Lippincott.

Esbensen, B. J. (1975). *A celebration of bees: Helping children write poetry.* Minneapolis: Winston Press.

Fleischman, P. (1985). *I am phoenix: Poems for two voices.* New York: Harper & Row.

Fleischman, P. (1988). *Joyful noise: Poems for two voices.* New York: Harper & Row.

Fox, P. (1973). *The slave dancer.* New York: Bradbury.

Greenfeld, H. (1989). *Books: From writer to reader.* New York: Crown.

Holdaway, D. (1982). Shared book experience: Teaching reading using favorite books. *Theory into Practice, 21,* 293–300.

Hopkins, L. B. (1987). *Pass the poetry please!* New York: Harper & Row.

Hoskisson, K., Sherman, T. M., & Smith, L. L. (1974). Assisted reading and parent involvement. *The Reading Teacher, 27,* 710–714.

Koch, K. (1971). *Wishes, lies and dreams: Teaching children to write poetry.* New York: Random.

Koch, K. (1973). *Rose, where did you get that red?* New York: Random.

Lawson, R. (1944). *Rabbit hill.* New York: Viking.

Lynch-Brown, C., & Tomlinson, C. T. (1988). *Reading aloud novel-length chapter books: A qualitative study.* Paper presented at the International Reading Association Annual Conference, Toronto.

McCaslin, N. (1990). *Creative drama in the classroom* (5th ed.). New York: Longman.

McCord, D. (1977). *One at a time: Collected poems for the young.* Boston: Little, Brown.

Purdy, S. (1973). *Books for you to make.* Philadelphia: Lippincott.

Raskin, E. (1978). *The westing game.* New York: Dutton.

Rosenblatt, L. M. (1978). *The reader, the text, the poem: The transactional theory of the literary work.* Carbondale, IL: Southern Illinois University Press.

Scieszka, J. (1991). *The frog prince continued.* Illustrated by S. Johnson. New York: Viking.

Scieszka, J. (1989). *The true story of the three little pigs by A. Wolf.* Illustrated by L. Smith. New York: Viking.

Steig, W. (1969). *Sylvester and the magic pebble.* New York: Windmill.

Weiss, H. (1974). *How to make your own books.* New York: Crowell.

Wrightson, P. (1974). *The nargun and the stars.* New York: Atheneum.

Children's Book Awards

National, General Awards

The United States

The Caldecott Medal This award, sponsored by the Association of Library Service to Children Division of the American Library Association, is given to the illustrator of the most distinguished picture book for children published in the United States during the preceding year. Only U.S. residents or citizens are eligible for this award.

1938 *Animals of the Bible, A Picture Book.* Text selected from the King James Bible by Helen Dean Fish. Illustrated by Dorothy P. Lathrop. Lippincott (Bible, ages 3–8).

Honor Books:

Seven Simeons: A Russian Tale by Boris Artzybasheff. Viking (Traditional, ages 6–8).

Four and Twenty Blackbirds compiled by Helen Dean Fish. Illustrated by Robert Lawson. Stokes/ Lippincott (Traditional, ages 3–6).

1939 *Mei Li* by Thomas Handforth. Doubleday (Realism, ages 6–7).

Honor Books:

The Forest Pool by Laura Adams Armer. McKay/ Longmans (Realism, ages 6–7).

Wee Gillis by Munro Leaf. Illustrated by Robert Lawson. Viking (Realism, ages 5–7).

Snow White and the Seven Dwarfs. Translated and illustrated by Wanda Gág. Coward-McCann (Traditional, ages 3–6).

Barkis by Clare Turlay Newberry. Harper (Realism, ages 3–7).

Andy and the Lion by James Daugherty. Viking (Fantasy, ages 3–7).

1940 *Abraham Lincoln* by Ingri d'Aulaire and Edgar Parin d'Aulaire. Doubleday (Biography, ages 6–8).

Honor Books:

Cock-a-Doodle-Doo by Berta and Elmer Hader. Macmillan (Animal realism, ages 3–7).

Madeline by Ludwig Bemelmans. Viking (Realism, ages 5–7).

The Ageless Story by Lauren Ford. Dodd (Bible, ages 5–8).

1941 *They Were Strong and Good* by Robert Lawson. Viking (Biography, ages 6–7).

Honor Book:

April's Kittens by Clare Turlay Newberry. Harper (Realism, ages 3–6).

1942 *Make Way for Ducklings* by Robert McCloskey. Viking (Animal fantasy, ages 3–6).

Honor Books:

An American ABC by Maud and Miska Petersham. Macmillan (Alphabet, ages 3–6).

In My Mother's House by Ann Nolan Clark. Illustrated by Velino Herrera. Viking (Informational, ages 6–8).

Paddle-to-the-Sea by Holling Clancy Holling. Houghton (Informational, ages 6–8).

Nothing at All by Wanda Gág. Coward-McCann (Animal fantasy, ages 3–6).

1943   *The Little House* by Virginia Lee Burton. Houghton (Fantasy, ages 3–6).

Honor Books:

Dash and Dart by Mary and Conrad Buff. Viking (Realism, ages 3–6).

Marshmallow by Clare Turlay Newberry. Harper (Realism, ages 3–6).

1944   *Many Moons* by James Thurber. Illustrated by Louis Slobodkin. Harcourt (Modern folktale, ages 5–7).

Honor Books:

Small Rain: Verses From the Bible. Text arranged from the Bible by Jessie Orton Jones. Illustrated by Elizabeth Orton Jones. Viking (Bible, ages 3–7).

Pierre Pigeon by Lee Kingman. Illustrated by Arnold Edwin Bare. Houghton (Realism, ages 6–7).

The Mighty Hunter by Berta and Elmer Hader. Macmillan (Fantasy, ages 3–6).

A Child's Good Night Book by Margaret Wise Brown. Illustrated by Jean Charlot. Scott (Realism, ages 3–6).

Good Luck Horse by Chih-Yi Chan. Illustrated by Plato Chan. Whittlesey (Traditional, ages 6–7).

1945   *Prayer for a Child* by Rachel Field. Illustrated by Elizabeth Orton Jones. Macmillan (Realism, ages 3–6).

Honor Books:

Mother Goose: Seventy-Seven Verses with Pictures. Illustrated by Tasha Tudor. Walck (Traditional, ages 3–6).

In the Forest by Marie Hall Ets. Viking (Fantasy, ages 3–6).

Yonie Wondernose by Marguerite de Angeli. Doubleday (Realism, ages 6–7).

The Christmas Anna Angel by Ruth Sawyer. Illustrated by Kate Seredy. Viking (Modern folktale, ages 6–7).

1946   *The Rooster Crows* selected and illustrated by Maud and Miska Petersham. Macmillan (Mother Goose/Nursery rhymes, ages 3–6).

Honor Books:

Little Lost Lamb by Golden MacDonald. Illustrated by Leonard Weisgard. Doubleday (Realism, ages 3–6).

Sing Mother Goose by Opal Wheeler. Illustrated by Marjorie Torrey. Dutton (Nursery songs, ages 3–6).

My Mother Is the Most Beautiful Woman in the World retold by Becky Reyher. Illustrated by Ruth Gannett. Lothrop (Traditional, ages 5–7).

You Can Write Chinese by Kurt Wiese. Viking (Informational, ages 6–8).

1947   *The Little Island* by Golden MacDonald. Illustrated by Leonard Weisgard. Doubleday (Fantasy, ages 3–6).

Honor Books:

Rain Drop Splash by Alvin Tresselt. Illustrated by Leonard Weisgard. Lothrop (Informational, ages 5–7).

Boats on the River by Marjorie Flack. Illustrated by Jay Hyde Barnum. Viking (Informational, ages 6–7).

Timothy Turtle by Al Graham. Illustrated by Tony Palazzo. Viking (Animal fantasy, ages 3–6).

Pedro, the Angel of Olvera Street by Leo Politi. Scribner's (Realism, ages 3–6).

Sing in Praise: A Collection of the Best Loved Hymns by Opal Wheeler. Illustrated by Marjorie Torrey. Dutton (Informational, ages 3–8).

1948   *White Snow, Bright Snow* by Alvin Tresselt. Illustrated by Roger Duvoisin. Lothrop (Realism, ages 3–6).

Honor Books:

Stone Soup: An Old Tale by Marcia Brown. Scribner's (Traditional, ages 6–8).

McElligot's Pool by Dr. Seuss (pseud. for Theodor Geisel). Random (Fantasy, ages 3–6).

Bambino the Clown by George Schreiber. Viking (Realism, ages 5–7).

Roger and the Fox by Lavinia Davis. Illustrated by Hildegard Woodward. Doubleday (Realism, ages 5–7).

Song of Robin Hood edited by Anne Malcolmson. Illustrated by Virginia Lee Burton. Houghton (Traditional, ages 9 and up).

1949   *The Big Snow* by Berta and Elmer Hader. Macmillan (Animal realism, ages 3–6).

Honor Books:

Blueberries for Sal by Robert McCloskey. Viking (Realism, ages 3–6).

All Around Town by Phyllis McGinley. Illustrated by Helen Stone. Lippincott (Alphabet, ages 3–6).

Juanita by Leo Politi. Scribner's (Realism, ages 3–6).

Fish in the Air by Kurt Wiese. Viking (Fantasy, ages 5–7).

1950 ***Song of the Swallows*** by Leo Politi. Scribner's (Realism, ages 3–6).

Honor Books:

America's Ethan Allen by Stewart Holbrook. Illustrated by Lynd Ward. Houghton (Biography, ages 6–8).

The Wild Birthday Cake by Lavinia R. Davis. Illustrated by Hildegard Woodward. Doubleday (Realism, ages 5–6).

The Happy Day by Ruth Krauss. Illustrated by Marc Simont. Harper (Animal fantasy, ages 3–6).

Henry-Fisherman by Marcia Brown. Scribner's (Realism, ages 5–7).

Bartholomew and the Oobleck by Dr. Seuss (pseud. for Theodor Geisel). Random (Modern folktale, ages 5–7).

1951 ***The Egg Tree*** by Katherine Milhous. Scribner's (Realism, ages 3–6).

Honor Books:

Dick Whittington and His Cat. Translated and illustrated by Marcia Brown. Scribner's (Traditional, ages 6–8).

The Two Reds by Will (pseud. for William Lipkind). Illustrated by Nicolas (pseud. for Nicolas Mordvinoff). Harcourt (Fantasy, ages 3–6).

If I Ran the Zoo by Dr. Seuss (pseud. for Theodor Geisel). Random (Fantasy, ages 3–6).

T-Bone, the Baby-Sitter by Clare Turlay Newberry. Harper (Realism, ages 3–6).

The Most Wonderful Doll in the World by Phyllis McGinley. Illustrated by Helen Stone. Lippincott (Realism, ages 6–7).

1952 ***Finders Keepers*** by Will (pseud. for William Lipkind). Illustrated by Nicolas (pseud. for Nicolas Mordvinoff). Harcourt (Modern folktale, ages 3–6).

Honor Books:

Mr. T. W. Anthony Woo by Marie Hall Ets. Viking (Modern folktale, ages 3–6).

Skipper John's Cook by Marcia Brown. Scribner's (Realism, ages 5–7).

All Falling Down by Gene Zion. Illustrated by Margaret Bloy Graham. Harper (Informational, ages 3–6).

Bear Party by William Pène du Bois. Viking (Animal fantasy, ages 3–7).

Feather Mountain by Elizabeth Olds. Houghton (Modern folktale, ages 5–7).

1953 ***The Biggest Bear*** by Lynd Ward. Houghton (Realism, ages 3–7).

Honor Books:

Puss in Boots. Translated and illustrated by Marcia Brown. Scribner's (Traditional, ages 5–7).

One Morning in Maine by Robert McCloskey. Viking (Realism, ages 3–6).

Ape in a Cape: An Alphabet of Odd Animals by Fritz Eichenberg. Harcourt (Alphabet, ages 3–6).

The Storm Book by Charlotte Zolotow. Illustrated by Margaret Bloy Graham. Harper (Informational, ages 3–6).

Five Little Monkeys by Juliet Kepes. Houghton (Animal fantasy, ages 3–6).

1954 ***Madeline's Rescue*** by Ludwig Bemelmans. Viking (Realism, ages 3–6).

Honor Books:

Journey Cake, Ho! by Ruth Sawyer. Illustrated by Robert McCloskey. Viking (Traditional, ages 5–7).

When Will the World Be Mine? by Miriam Schlein. Illustrated by Jean Charlot. Scott (Animal fantasy, ages 3–6).

The Steadfast Tin Soldier by Hans Christian Andersen. Translated by M. R. James. illustrated by Marcia Brown. Scribner's (Modern folktale, ages 5–7).

A Very Special House by Ruth Krauss. Illustrated by Maurice Sendak. Harper (Fantasy, ages 3–6).

Green Eyes by Abe Birnbaum. Capitol (Animal fantasy, ages 3–6).

1955 ***Cinderella, or the Little Glass Slipper*** by Charles Perrault. Translated and illustrated by Marcia Brown. Scribner's (Traditional, ages 3–7).

Honor Books:

Book of Nursery and Mother Goose Rhymes compiled and illustrated by Marguerite de Angeli. Doubleday (Nursery rhymes, ages 3–6).

Wheel on the Chimney by Margaret Wise Brown. Illustrated by Tibor Gergely. Lippincott (Realism, ages 6–7).

The Thanksgiving Story by Alice Dalgliesh. Illustrated by Helen Sewell. Scribner's (Historical fiction [USA, 1700s], ages 5–7).

1956   *Frog Went A-Courtin'* retold by John Langstaff. Illustrated by Feodor Rojankovsky. Harcourt (Traditional, ages 3–7).

Honor Books:

Play With Me by Marie Hall Ets. Viking (Realism, ages 3–6).

Crow Boy by Taro Yashima. Viking (Realism, ages 5–7).

1957   *A Tree Is Nice* by Janice May Udry. Illustrated by Marc Simont. Harper (Informational, ages 3–7).

Honor Books:

Mr. Penny's Race Horse by Marie Hall Ets. Viking (Animal fantasy, ages 5–7).

1 Is One by Tasha Tudor. Walck. (Counting, ages 3–6).

Anatole by Eve Titus. Illustrated by Paul Galdone. McGraw (Animal fantasy, ages 5–7).

Gillespie and the Guards by Benjamin Elkin. Illustrated by James Daugherty. Viking (Realism, ages 6–7).

Lion by William Pène du Bois. Viking (Animal fantasy, ages 5–7).

1958   *Time of Wonder* by Robert McCloskey. Viking (Realism, ages 6–8).

Honor Books:

Fly High, Fly Low by Don Freeman. Viking (Animal fantasy, ages 3–6).

Anatole and the Cat by Eve Titus. Illustrated by Paul Galdone. McGraw (Animal fantasy, ages 3–6).

1959   *Chanticleer and the Fox* by Chaucer. Adapted and illustrated by Barbara Cooney. Crowell (Traditional, ages 5–7).

Honor Books:

The House That Jack Built ("La Maison Que Jacques a Bâtie"): A Picture Book in Two Languages by Antonio Frasconi. Harcourt (Informational, ages 5–8).

What Do You Say, Dear? A Book of Manners for All Occasions by Sesyle Joslin. Illustrated by Maurice Sendak. Scott (Fantasy, ages 3–6).

Umbrella by Taro Yashima. Viking (Realism, ages 3–6).

1960   *Nine Days to Christmas* by Marie Hall Ets and Aurora Labastida. Illustrated by Marie Hall Ets. Viking (Realism, ages 3–7).

Honor Books:

Houses from the Sea by Alice E. Goudey. Illustrated by Adrienne Adams. Scribner's (Informational, ages 5–7).

The Moon Jumpers by Janice May Udry. Illustrated by Maurice Sendak. Harper (Realism, ages 3–6).

1961   *Baboushka and the Three Kings* by Ruth Robbins. Illustrated by Nicolas Sidjakov. Parnassus (Traditional, ages 5–7).

Honor Book:

Inch by Inch by Leo Lionni. Obolensky (Animal fantasy, ages 3–6).

1962   *Once a Mouse* retold by Marcia Brown. Scribner's (Traditional, ages 5–7).

Honor Books:

The Fox Went Out on a Chilly Night: An Old Song by Peter Spier. Doubleday (Traditional, ages 3–6).

Little Bear's Visit by Else Minarik. Illustrated by Maurice Sendak. Harper (Animal fantasy, ages 3–7).

The Day We Saw the Sun Come Up by Alice Goudey. Illustrated by Adrienne Adams. Scribner's (Informational, ages 5–7).

1963   *The Snowy Day* by Ezra Jack Keats. Viking (Realism, ages 3–6).

Honor Books:

The Sun Is a Golden Earring by Natalia Belting. Illustrated by Bernarda Bryson. Holt (Modern folktale, ages 7–10).

Mr. Rabbit and the Lovely Present by Charlotte Zolotow. Illustrated by Maurice Sendak. Harper (Animal fantasy, ages 3–6).

1964   *Where the Wild Things Are* by Maurice Sendak. Harper (Fantasy, ages 3–7).

Honor Books:

Swimmy by Leo Lionni. Pantheon (Animal fantasy, ages 3–6).

All in the Morning Early by Sorche Nic Leodhas (pseud. for Leclaire Alger). Illustrated by Evaline Ness. Holt (Traditional, ages 3–6).

Mother Goose and Nursery Rhymes by Philip Reed. Atheneum (Traditional, ages 3–6).

1965   *May I Bring a Friend?* by Beatrice Schenk de Regniers. Illustrated by Beni Montresor. Atheneum (Fantasy, ages 5–7).

Honor Books:

Rain Makes Applesauce by Julian Scheer. Illustrated by Marvin Bileck. Holiday (Fantasy, ages 5–7).

The Wave by Margaret Hodges. Illustrated by Blair Lent. Houghton (Traditional, ages 6–9).

A Pocketful of Cricket by Rebecca Caudill. Illustrated by Evaline Ness. Holt (Realism, ages 5–7).

1966 *Always Room for One More* by Sorche Nic Leodhas (pseud. for Leclaire Alger). Illustrated by Nonny Hogrogian. Holt (Traditional, ages 3–6).

Honor Books:

Hide and Seek Fog by Alvin Tresselt. Illustrated by Roger Duvoisin. Lothrop (Realism, ages 5–7).

Just Me by Marie Hall Ets. Viking (Realism, ages 3–5).

Tom Tit Tot adapted by Joseph Jacobs. Illustrated by Evaline Ness. Scribner's (Traditional, ages 5–7).

1967 *Sam, Bangs and Moonshine* by Evaline Ness. Holt (Realism, ages 6–8).

Honor Book:

One Wide River to Cross adapted by Barbara Emberley. Illustrated by Ed Emberley. Prentice-Hall (Bible, ages 3–6).

1968 *Drummer Hoff* adapted by Barbara Emberley. Illustrated by Ed Emberley. Prentice-Hall (Traditional, ages 3–6).

Honor Books:

Frederick by Leo Lionni. Pantheon (Animal fantasy, ages 5–7).

Seashore Story by Taro Yashima. Viking (Realism, ages 6–8).

The Emperor and the Kite by Jane Yolen. Illustrated by Ed Young. World (Modern folktale, ages 5–7).

1969 *The Fool of the World and the Flying Ship: A Russian Tale* by Authur Ransome. Illustrated by Uri Shulevitz. Farrar (Traditional, ages 6–8).

Honor Book:

Why the Sun and the Moon Live in the Sky: An African Folktale by Elphinstone Dayrell. Illustrated by Blair Lent. Houghton (Traditional, ages 6–8).

1970 *Sylvester and the Magic Pebble* by William Steig. Windmill (Animal fantasy, ages 5–7).

Honor Books:

Goggles! by Ezra Jack Keats. Macmillan (Realism, ages 3–6).

Alexander and the Wind-Up Mouse by Leo Lionni. Pantheon (Animal fantasy, ages 3–6).

Pop Corn and Ma Goodness by Edna Mitchell Preston. Illustrated by Robert Andrew Parker. Viking (Modern folktale, ages 5–7).

Thy Friend, Obadiah by Brinton Turkle. Viking (Historical fiction [New England, 1700s], ages 3–7).

The Judge: An Untrue Tale by Harve Zemach. Illustrated by Margot Zemach. Farrar (Modern folktale, ages 5–7).

1971 *A Story, A Story: An African Tale* by Gail E. Haley. Atheneum (Traditional, ages 5–7).

Honor Books:

The Angry Moon retold by William Sleator. Illustrated by Blair Lent. Atlantic/Little, Brown (Traditional, ages 6–8).

Frog and Toad Are Friends by Arnold Lobel. Harper (Animal fantasy, ages 3–7).

In the Night Kitchen by Maurice Sendak. Harper (Fantasy, ages 5–7).

1972 *One Fine Day* by Nonny Hogrogian. Macmillan (Traditional, ages 5–7).

Honor Books:

If All the Seas Were One Sea by Janina Domanska. Macmillan (Traditional, ages 3–6).

Moja Means One: Swahili Counting Book by Muriel Feelings. Illustrated by Tom Feelings. Dial (Counting, ages 5–8).

Hildilid's Night by Cheli Duran Ryan. Illustrated by Arnold Lobel. Macmillan (Modern folktale, ages 3–6).

1973 *The Funny Little Woman* retold by Arlene Mosel. Illustrated by Blair Lent. Dutton (Traditional, ages 5–7).

Honor Books:

Hosie's Alphabet by Hosea Baskin, Tobias Baskin, and Lisa Baskin. Illustrated by Leonard Baskin. Viking (Alphabet, ages 6–9).

When Clay Sings by Byrd Baylor. Illustrated by Tom Bahti. Scribner's (Informational, ages 6–8).

Snow-White and the Seven Dwarfs by the Brothers Grimm. Translated by Randall Jarrell. Illustrated by Nancy Ekholm Burkert. Farrar (Traditional, ages 3–7).

Anansi the Spider: A Tale from the Ashanti adapted and illustrated by Gerald McDermott. Holt (Traditional, ages 6–8).

1974 *Duffy and the Devil* retold by Harve Zemach. Illustrated by Margot Zemach. Farrar (Traditional, ages 6–8).

Honor Books:

Three Jovial Huntsmen adapted and illustrated by Susan Jeffers. Bradbury (Traditional, ages 3–6).

Cathedral: The Story of Its Construction by David Macaulay. Houghton (Informational, ages 8 and up).

1975 ***Arrow to the Sun*** adapted and illustrated by Gerald McDermott. Viking (Traditional, ages 6–8).

Honor Book:

Jambo Means Hello: Swahili Alphabet Book by Muriel Feelings. Illustrated by Tom Feelings. Dial (Alphabet, ages 6–8).

1976 ***Why Mosquitoes Buzz in People's Ears*** retold by Verna Aardema. Illustrated by Leo and Diane Dillon. Dial (Traditional, ages 6–8).

Honor Books:

The Desert Is Theirs by Byrd Baylor. Illustrated by Peter Parnall. Scribner's (Informational, ages 6–8).

Strega Nona retold and illustrated by Tomie de Paola. Prentice-Hall (Traditional, ages 5–8).

1977 ***Ashanti to Zulu: African Traditions*** by Margaret Musgrove. Illustrated by Leo and Diane Dillon. Dial (Informational, ages 7–11).

Honor Books:

The Amazing Bone by William Steig. Farrar (Fantasy, ages 6–8).

The Contest by Nonny Hogrogian. Greenwillow (Traditional, ages 6–8).

Fish for Supper by M. B. Goffstein. Dial (Realism, ages 3–6).

The Golem: A Jewish Legend retold and illustrated by Beverly Brodsky McDermott. Lippincott (Traditional, ages 6–9).

Hawk, I'm Your Brother by Byrd Baylor. Illustrated by Peter Parnall. Scribner's (Realism, ages 7–9).

1978 ***Noah's Ark*** by Peter Spier. Doubleday (Bible/Wordless, ages 3–7).

Honor Books:

Castle by David Macaulay. Houghton (Informational, ages 8 and up).

It Could Always Be Worse retold by Margot Zemach. Farrar (Traditional, ages 5–7).

1979 ***The Girl Who Loved Wild Horses*** by Paul Goble. Bradbury (Fantasy, ages 6–8).

Honor Books:

Freight Train by Donald Crews. Greenwillow (Concept, ages 3–6).

The Way to Start a Day by Byrd Baylor. Illustrated by Peter Parnall. Scribner's (Informational, ages 6–9).

1980 ***Ox-Cart Man*** by Donald Hall. Illustrated by Barbara Cooney. Viking (Historical fiction [New England, 1800s], ages 5–8).

Honor Books:

Ben's Trumpet by Rachel Isadora. Greenwillow (Realism, ages 5–7).

The Treasure by Uri Shulevitz. Farrar (Traditional, ages 6–8).

The Garden of Abdul Gasazi by Chris Van Allsburg. Houghton (Fantasy, ages 6–8).

1981 ***Fables*** by Arnold Lobel. Harper (Animal fantasy, ages 3–6).

Honor Books:

The Bremen-Town Musicians retold and illustrated by Ilse Plume. Doubleday (Traditional, ages 5–7).

The Grey Lady and the Strawberry Snatcher by Molly Bang. Four Winds (Fantasy/wordless, ages 6–8).

Mice Twice by Joseph Low. Atheneum (Animal fantasy, ages 3–6).

Truck by Donald Crews. Greenwillow (Concept, ages 3–6).

1982 ***Jumanji*** by Chris Van Allsburg. Houghton (Fantasy, ages 6–8).

Honor Books:

A Visit to William Blake's Inn: Poems for Innocent and Experienced Travelers by Nancy Willard. Illustrated by Alice and Martin Provensen. Harcourt (Biography/Poetry, ages 7–10).

Where the Buffaloes Begin by Olaf Baker. Illustrated by Stephen Gammell. Warne (Traditional, ages 7–10).

On Market Street by Arnold Lobel. Illustrated by Anita Lobel. Greenwillow (Alphabet, ages 4–6).

Outside Over There by Maurice Sendak. Harper (Fantasy, ages 7–10).

1983 ***Shadow*** by Blaise Cendrars. Translated and illustrated by Marcia Brown. Scribner's (Traditional, ages 8–11).

Honor Books:

When I Was Young in the Mountains by Cynthia Rylant. Illustrated by Diane Goode. Dutton (Realism, ages 7–9).

A Chair for My Mother by Vera B. Williams. Greenwillow (Realism, ages 6–8).

1984 ***The Glorious Flight: Across the Channel with Louis Blériot*** by Alice and Martin Provensen. Viking (Historical fiction [France, 1909], ages 7–10).

Honor Books:

Ten, Nine, Eight by Molly Bang. Greenwillow (Counting, ages 3–6).

Little Red Riding Hood by the Brothers Grimm. Retold and illustrated by Trina Schart Hyman. Holiday (Traditional, ages 5–8).

1985 *Saint George and the Dragon* adapted by Margaret Hodges. Illustrated by Trina Schart Hyman. Little, Brown (Traditional, ages 9–12).

Honor Books:

Hansel and Gretel adapted by Rika Lesser. Illustrated by Paul O. Zelinksy. Dodd (Traditional, ages 6–8).

The Story of Jumping Mouse retold and illustrated by John Steptoe. Lothrop (Traditional, ages 7–10).

Have You Seen My Duckling? by Nancy Tafuri. Greenwillow (Animal fantasy, ages 4–6).

1986 *The Polar Express* by Chris Van Allsburg. Houghton (Fantasy, ages 5–9).

Honor Books:

The Relatives Came by Cynthia Rylant. Illustrated by Stephen Gammell. Bradbury (Realism, ages 6–9).

King Bidgood's in the Bathtub by Audrey Wood. Illustrated by Don Wood. Harcourt (Fantasy, ages 5–8).

1987 *Hey, Al* by Arthur Yorinks. Illustrated by Richard Egielski. Farrar (Fantasy, ages 7–10).

Honor Books:

The Village of Round and Square Houses by Ann Grifalconi. Little, Brown (Traditional, ages 7–9).

Alphabatics by Suse MacDonald. Bradbury (Alphabet, ages 4–6).

Rumpelstiltskin by the Brothers Grimm. Retold and illustrated by Paul O. Zelinsky. Dutton (Traditional, ages 6–9).

1988 *Owl Moon* by Jane Yolen. Illustrated by John Schoenherr. Philomel (Realism, ages 5–8).

Honor Book:

Mufaro's Beautiful Daughters retold by John Steptoe. Lothrop (Traditional, ages 6–9).

1989 *Song and Dance Man* by Karen Ackerman. Illustrated by Stephen Gammell. Knopf (Realism, ages 7–10).

Honor Books:

Free Fall by David Wiesner. Lothrop (Fantasy/Wordless, ages 7–10).

Goldilocks and the Three Bears retold and illustrated by James Marshall. Dial (Traditional, ages 5–8).

Mirandy and Brother Wind by Patricia McKissack. Illustrated by Jerry Pinkney. Knopf (Traditional, ages 7–9).

The Boy of the Three-Year Nap by Diane Snyder. Illustrated by Allen Say. Houghton (Traditional, ages 7–10).

1990 *Lon Po Po: A Red-Riding Hood Story from China* translated and illustrated by Ed Young. Philomel (Traditional, ages 5–8).

Honor Books:

Hershel and the Hanukkah Goblins by Eric Kimmel. Illustrated by Trina Schart Hyman. Holiday (Modern folktale, ages 7–10).

The Talking Eggs adapted by Robert D. San Souci. Illustrated by Jerry Pinkney. Dial (Traditional, ages 6–9).

Bill Peet: An Autobiography by Bill Peet. Houghton (Biography, ages 7–10).

Color Zoo by Lois Ehlert. Lippincott (Concept, ages 3–6).

1991 *Black and White* by David Macaulay. Houghton (Mystery, ages 8–12).

Honor Books:

Puss 'n Boots by Charles Perrault. Illustrated by Fred Marcellino. Farrar (Traditional, ages 5–7).

"More, More, More," Said the Baby: 3 Love Stories by Vera Williams. Greenwillow (Realism, ages 3–5).

1992 *Tuesday* by David Wiesner. Clarion (Fantasy/Wordless, ages 7–10).

Honor Book:

Tar Beach by Faith Ringgold. Crown (Realism/Multicultural [African-American], ages 6–9).

The Newbery Medal   This award, sponsored by the Association for Library Service to Children Division of the American Library Association, is given to the author of the most distinguished contribution to children's literature published during the preceding year. Only U.S. citizens or residents are eligible for this award.

1922 *The Story of Mankind* by Hendrik Willem Van Loon. Liveright (Informational, ages 12 and up).

Honor Books:

The Great Quest by Charles Boardman Hawes. Little, Brown (Historical fiction [New England, 1826], ages 11–YA).

Cedric the Forester by Bernard G. Marshall. Appleton (Historical fiction [England, 1200s], ages 11–YA).

The Old Tobacco Shop by William Bowen. Macmillan (Fantasy, ages 9–12).

The Golden Fleece and the Heroes Who Lived Before Achilles by Padraic Colum. Macmillan (Traditional fantasy, ages 9–13).

Windy Hill by Cornelia Meigs. Macmillan (Realism, ages 9–12).

1923 *The Voyages of Doctor Dolittle* by Hugh Lofting. Lippincott (Fantasy, ages 8–12).

(No record of the runners-up.)

1924 *The Dark Frigate* by Charles Boardman Hawes. Little, Brown (Historical fiction [England, 1600s], ages 10–YA).

(No record of the runners-up.)

1925 *Tales from Silver Lands* by Charles J. Finger. Illustrated by Paul Honoré. Doubleday (Traditional fantasy, ages 9–YA).

Honor Books:

Nicholas by Anne Carroll Moore. Putnam (Fantasy [Little people], ages 8–11).

Dream Coach by Anne and Dillwyn Parrish. Macmillan (Fantasy, ages 7–11).

1926 *Shen of the Sea* by Arthur Bowie Chrisman. Illustrated by Else Hasselriis. Dutton (Fantasy [Literary tales], ages 9–12).

Honor Book:

The Voyagers by Padraic Colum. Macmillan (Traditional fantasy/Informational, ages 10–12).

1927 *Smoky, the Cowhorse* by Will James. Scribner's (Animal realism, ages 9–12).

(No record of the runners-up.)

1928 *Gay-Neck, The Story of a Pigeon* by Dhan Gopal Mukerji. Illustrated by Boris Artzybasheff. Dutton (Animal realism, ages 9–YA).

Honor Books:

The Wonder Smith and His Son by Ella Young. McKay/Longmans (Traditional fantasy [Ireland], ages 10–YA).

Downright Dencey by Caroline Dale Snedeker. Doubleday (Historical fiction [New England, 1812], ages 9–13).

1929 *The Trumpeter of Krakow* by Eric P. Kelly. Illustrated by Angela Pruszynska. Macmillan (Historical Fiction [Poland, 1400s], ages 11–YA).

Honor Books:

The Pigtail of Ah Lee Ben Loo by John Bennett. McKay/Longmans (Fantasy/Poetry, ages 8–13).

Millions of Cats by Wanda Gág. Coward-McCann (Picture book; Fantasy, ages 5–7).

The Boy Who Was by Grace T. Hallock. Dutton (Historical fiction [Italy through 3000 years], ages 10–YA).

Clearing Weather by Cornelia Meigs. Little, Brown (Historical fiction [U.S. 1787], ages 11–YA).

The Runaway Papoose by Grace P. Moon. Doubleday (Realism/Multicultural, ages 8–11).

Tod of the Fens by Eleanor Whitney. Macmillan (Historical fiction [England 1400s], ages 11–YA).

1930 *Hitty: Her First Hundred Years* by Rachel Field. Illustrated by Dorothy P. Lathrop. Macmillan (Historical fantasy, ages 9–13).

Honor Books:

The Tangle-Coated Horse and Other Tales: Episodes from the Fionn Saga by Ella Young. Illustrated by Vera Brock. Longmans (Traditional, ages 10–13).

Vaino: A Boy of New Finland by Julia Davis Adams. Illustrated by Lempi Ostman. Dutton (Historical fiction [Finland, 1920s], ages 11–YA).

Pran of Albania by Elizabeth C. Miller. Doubleday (Realism, ages 11–YA).

The Jumping-Off Place by Marian Hurd McNeely. McKay/Longmans (Realism, ages 10–YA).

A Daughter of the Seine by Jeanette Eaton. Harper (Biography, ages 12–YA).

Little Blacknose by Hildegarde Hoyt Swift. Illustrated by Lynd Ward. Harcourt (Fantasy, ages 8–11).

1931 *The Cat Who Went to Heaven* by Elizabeth Coatsworth. Illustrated by Lynd Ward. Macmillan (Fantasy, ages 10–13).

Honor Books:

Floating Island by Anne Parrish. Harper (Fantasy, ages 8–11).

The Dark Star of Itza by Alida Malkus. Harcourt (Historical fiction [Mayan Empire], ages 11–YA).

Queer Person by Ralph Hubbard. Doubleday (Historical Fiction/Multicultural [Native American], ages 9–13).

Mountains Are Free by Julia Davis Adams. Dutton (Historical fiction [Switzerland], ages 11–YA).

Spice and the Devil's Cave by Agnes D. Hewes. Knopf (Historical fiction [Portugal, 1400s], ages 11–YA).

Meggy McIntosh by Elizabeth Janet Gray. Doubleday (Historical fiction [Scotland, USA, 1775], ages 10–YA).

Garram the Hunter: A Boy of the Hill Tribes by Herbert Best. Illustrated by Allena Best (Erick Berry). Doubleday (Realism [Africa], ages 9–13).

Ood-Le-Uk, the Wanderer by Alice Lide and Margaret Johansen. Illustrated by Raymond Lufkin. Little, Brown (Realism [Alaska], ages 11–14.

1932 ***Waterless Mountain*** by Laura Adams Armer. Illustrated by Sidney Armer and Laura Adams Armer. McKay/Longmans (Realism/ Multicultural [Native American], ages 9–13).

Honor Books:

The Fairy Circus by Dorothy Lathrop. Macmillan (Fantasy, ages 6–9).

Calico Bush by Rachel Field. Macmillan (Historical fiction, [USA, 1743], ages 9–13).

Boy of the South Seas by Eunice Tietjens. Coward-McCann (Realism, ages 9–12).

Out of the Flame by Eloise Lownsbery. McKay/ Longmans (Historical fiction [France, 1500s], ages 10–YA).

Jane's Island by Marjorie Hill Alee. Houghton (Realism, ages 9–13).

The Truce of the Wolf and Other Tales of Old Italy by Mary Gould Davis. Harcourt (Traditional fantasy, ages 8–13).

1933 ***Young Fu of the Upper Yangtze*** by Elizabeth Foreman Lewis. Illustrated by Kurt Wiese. Holt (Realism, ages 10–YA).

Honor Books:

Swift Rivers by Cornelia Meigs. Little, Brown (Historical fiction [USA, 1835], ages 10–13.

The Railroad to Freedom by Hildegarde Swift. Harcourt (Biography, ages 10–YA).

Children of the Soil by Nora Burglon. Doubleday (Realism, ages 9–12).

1934 ***Invincible Louisa: The Story of the Author of "Litte Women"*** by Cornelia Meigs. Little, Brown (Biography, ages 10–12).

Honor Books:

The Forgotten Daughter by Caroline Dale Snedeker. Doubleday (Historical fiction [Italy, 2nd century B.C.], ages 11–YA).

Swords of Steel by Elsie Singmaster. Houghton (Historical fiction [USA, 1859], ages 11–YA).

ABC Bunny by Wanda Gág. Coward-McCann (Picture book. Fantasy/Alphabet, ages 3–7).

Winged Girl of Knossos by Erik Berry. Appleton (Historical fiction [Ancient Greece], ages 10–YA).

New Land by Sarah L. Schmidt. McBride (Realism, ages 10–YA).

The Apprentice of Florence by Anne Kyle. Houghton (Historical fiction [Italy, 1400s], ages 11–YA).

The Big Tree of Bunlaby: Stories of My Own Countryside by Padraic Colum. Illustrated by Jack Yeats. Macmillan (Fantasy, ages 8–YA).

Glory of the Seas by Agnes D. Hewes. Illustrated by N. C. Wyeth. Knopf (Historical fiction [USA, 1850s], ages 11–YA).

1935 ***Dobry*** by Monica Shannon. Illustrated by Atanas Katchamakoff. Viking (Realism, ages 9–11).

Honor Books:

The Pageant of Chinese History by Elizabeth Seeger. McKay/Longmans (Informational, ages 11–YA).

Davy Crockett by Constance Rourke. Harcourt (Biography, ages 12–YA).

A Day on Skates: The Story of a Dutch Picnic by Hilda Van Stockum. Harper (Realism, ages 6–8).

1936 ***Caddie Woodlawn*** by Carol Ryrie Brink. Illustrated by Kate Seredy. Macmillan (Historical fiction [USA, 1860s], ages 9–12).

Honor Books:

Honk: The Moose by Phil Strong. Illustrated by Kurt Wiese. Dodd (Realism, ages 7–11).

The Good Master by Kate Seredy. Viking (Realism, ages 9–11).

Young Walter Scott by Elizabeth Janet Gray. Viking (Biography, ages 11–YA).

All Sail Set by Armstrong Sperry. Winston (Historical fiction [USA, 1851], ages 10–13).

1937 ***Roller Skates*** by Ruth Sawyer. Illustrated by Valenti Angelo. Viking (Realism, ages 8–10).

Honor Books:

Phoebe Fairchild: Her Book by Lois Lenski. Lippincott (Historical fiction [New England, 1830s], ages 9–12).

Whistler's Van by Idwal Jones. Viking (Realism, ages 9–13).

The Golden Basket by Ludwig Bemelmans. Viking (Realism, ages 6–9).

Winterbound by Margery Bianco. Viking (Realism, ages 11–YA).

Audubon by Constance Rourke. Harcourt (Biography, ages 11–YA).

The Codfish Musket by Agnes D. Hewes. Doubleday (Historical fiction [USA, 1780s], ages 11–YA).

1938 *The White Stag* by Kate Seredy. Viking (Traditional, ages 10–YA).

Honor Books:

Bright Island by Mabel L. Robinson. Random (Realism, ages 11–YA).

Pecos Bill by James Cloyd Bowman. Little, Brown (Traditional, ages 9–YA).

On the Banks of Plum Creek by Laura Ingalls Wilder. Harper (Historical fiction [USA, 1870s], ages 8–11.

1939 *Thimble Summer* by Elizabeth Enright. Holt (Realism, ages 8–11).

Honor Books:

Leader by Destiny: George Washington, Man and Patriot by Jeanette Eaton. Harcourt (Biography, ages 11–YA).

Penn by Elizabeth Janet Gray. Viking (Biography, ages 11 and up).

Nino by Valenti Angelo. Viking (Realism, ages 9–11).

"Hello, the Boat!" by Phyllis Crawford. Holt (Historica fiction [USA, 1817], ages 9–13).

Mr. Popper's Penguins by Richard and Florence Atwater. Little, Brown (Animal fantasy, ages 7–11).

1940 *Daniel Boone* by James H. Daugherty. Viking (Biography, ages 10–YA).

Honor Books:

The Singing Tree by Kate Seredy. Viking (Historical fiction [Eastern Europe, 1910s], ages 9–12).

Runner of the Mountain Tops by Mabel L. Robinson. Random (Biography, ages 11 and up).

By the Shores of Silver Lake by Laura Ingalls Wilder. Harper (Historical fiction [USA, 1880s], ages 8–10).

Boy with a Pack by Stephen W. Meader. Harcourt (Historical fiction [USA, 1837], ages 9–13).

1941 *Call it Courage* by Armstrong Sperry. Macmillan (Realism, ages 9–12).

Honor Books:

Blue Willow by Doris Gates. Viking (Historical fiction [USA, 1930s], ages 8–11).

Young Mac of Fort Vancouver by Mary Jane Carr. Crowell (Historical fiction [Canada, early 1800s], ages 10–YA).

The Long Winter by Laura Ingalls Wilder. Harper (Historical fiction [USA, 1880s], ages 9–13).

Nansen by Anna Gertrude Hall. Viking (Biography, ages 11 and up).

1942 *The Matchlock Gun* by Walter D. Edmonds.

Illustrated by Paul Lantz. Dodd (Historical fiction [Colonial America, 1757], ages 8–11).

Honor Books:

Little Town on the Prairie by Laura Ingalls Wilder. Harper (Historical fiction [USA, 1881], ages 8–10).

George Washington's World by Genevieve Foster. Scribner's (Informational/Biography, ages 10–YA).

Indian Captive: The Story of Mary Jemison by Lois Lenski. Lippincott (Historical fiction [USA, 1750s], ages 9–11).

Down Ryton Water by Eva Roe Gaggin. Illustrated by Elmer Hader. Viking (Historical fiction [England & Netherlands, 1600s], ages 12 and up).

1943 *Adam of the Road* by Elizabeth Janet Gray. Illustrated by Robert Lawson. Viking (Historical fiction [England, 1290s], ages 9–12).

Honor Books:

The Middle Moffat by Eleanor Estes. Harcourt (Realism, ages 8–10).

"Have You Seen Tom Thumb?" by Mabel Leigh Hunt. Lippincott (Biography, ages 10–YA).

1944 *Johnny Tremain* by Esther Forbes. Illustrated by Lynd Ward. Houghton (Historical fiction [Boston, 1770s], ages 12–YA).

Honor Books:

These Happy Golden Years by Laura Ingalls Wilder. Harper (Historical fiction [USA, 1880s], ages 8–10).

Fog Magic by Julia L. Sauer. Viking (Modern fantasy, ages 9–12).

Rufus M. by Eleanor Estes. Harcourt (Realism, ages 8–10).

Mountain Born by Elizabeth Yates. Coward-McCann (Animal realism, ages 9–11).

1945 *Rabbit Hill* by Robert Lawson. Viking (Animal fantasy, ages 7–9).

Honor Books:

The Hundred Dresses by Eleanor Estes. Harcourt (Realism, ages 7–9).

The Silver Pencil by Alice Dalgliesh. Scribner's (Realism, ages 10–YA).

Abraham Lincoln's World by Genevieve Foster. Scribner's (Informational/Biography, ages 10–YA).

Lone Journey: The Life of Roger Williams by Jeanette Eaton. Illustrated by Woodi Ishmael. Harcourt (Biography, ages 13–YA).

1946 *Strawberry Girl* by Lois Lenski. Lippincott (Historical fiction [Florida, early 1900s], ages 8–10).

Honor Books:

Justin Morgan Had a Horse by Marguerite Henry. Follett (Realism, ages 8–10).

The Moved-Outers by Florence Crannell Means. Houghton (Realism, ages 10–12).

Bhimsa, the Dancing Bear by Christine Weston. Scribner's (Realism, ages 8–10).

New Found World by Katherine B. Shippen. Viking (Informational, ages 10–YA).

1947 ***Miss Hickory*** by Carolyn Sherwin Bailey. Illustrated by Ruth Gannett. Viking (Fantasy/Toys and dolls, ages 7–9).

Honor Books:

The Wonderful Year by Nancy Barnes. Messner (Realism, ages 9–12).

The Big Tree by Mary and Conrad Buff. Viking (Informational, ages 9–13).

The Heavenly Tenants by William Maxwell. Harper (Fantasy, ages 10–YA).

The Avion My Uncle Flew by Cyrus Fisher. Appleton (Realism, ages 10–13).

The Hidden Treasure of Glaston by Eleanore M. Jewett. Viking (Historical fiction [England, 1172], ages 10–13).

1948 ***The Twenty-One Balloons*** by William Pène du Bois. Lothrop (Fantasy, ages 9–11).

Honor Books:

Pancakes-Paris by Claire Huchet Bishop. Viking (Realism, ages 8–11).

Li Lun, Lad of Courage by Carolyn Treffinger. Abingdon (Realism, ages 9–12).

The Quaint and Curious Quest of Johnny Longfoot, The Shoe-King's Son by Catherine Besterman. Bobbs-Merrill (Traditional, ages 8–10).

The Cow-Tail Switch, And Other West African Stories by Harold Courlander and George Herzog. Holt (Traditional, ages 8–13).

Misty of Chincoteague by Marguerite Henry. Illustrated by Wesley Dennis. Rand (Animal realism [horse], ages 9–12).

1949 ***King of the Wind*** by Marguerite Henry. Illustrated by Wesley Dennis. Rand (Historical fiction [Morocco, Europe, 1700s], ages 9–12).

Honor Books:

Seabird by Holling Clancy Holling. Houghton (Informational, ages 9–12).

Daughter of the Mountains by Louise Rankin. Viking (Realism, ages 9–11).

My Father's Dragon by Ruth S. Gannett. Random (Fantasy, ages 6–9).

Story of the Negro by Arna Bontemps. Knopf (Informational, ages 10 and up).

1950 ***The Door in the Wall*** by Marguerite de Angeli. Doubleday (Historical fiction [England, 1300s], ages 9–11).

Honor Books:

Tree of Freedom by Rebecca Caudill. Viking (Historical fiction [USA, 1780s], ages 10–12).

The Blue Cat of Castle Town by Catherine Coblentz. McKay/Longmans (Traditional, ages 9–YA).

Kildee House by Rutherford Montgomery. Doubleday (Realism, ages 8–12).

George Washington by Genevieve Foster. Scribner's (Biography, ages 8–11).

Song of the Pines by Walter and Marion Havighurst. Holt (Historical fiction [USA, 1850s], ages YA).

1951 ***Amos Fortune, Free Man*** by Elizabeth Yates. Illustrated by Nora Unwin. Dutton (Biography, ages 9–11).

Honor Books:

Better Known as Johnny Appleseed by Mabel Leigh Hunt. Lippincott (Biography, ages 11 and up).

Gandhi, Fighter Without a Sword by Jeanette Eaton. Morrow (Biography, ages 11–YA).

Abraham Lincoln, Friend of the People by Clara I. Judson. Follett (Biography, ages 9–13).

The Story of Appleby Capple by Anne Parrish. Harper (Fantasy, ages 6–8).

1952 ***Ginger Pye*** by Eleanor Estes. Harcourt (Realism, ages 8–10).

Honor Books:

Americans Before Columbus by Elizabeth Chesley Baity. Viking (Informational, ages 10 and up).

Minn of the Mississippi by Holling Clancy Holling. Houghton (Informational, ages 7–9).

The Defender by Nicholas Kalashnikoff. Scribner's (Realism, ages 9–13).

The Light at Tern Rock by Julia L. Sauer. Viking (Realism, ages 7–9).

The Apple and the Arrow by Mary and Conrad Buff. Houghton (Biography, ages 8–10).

1953 ***Secret of the Andes*** by Ann Nolan Clark. Illustrated by Jean Charlot. Viking (Realism/Multicultural [Native-American], ages 11–13).

Honor Books:

Charlotte's Web by E. B. White. Harper (Animal fantasy, ages 7–9).

Moccasin Trail by Eloise J. McGraw. Coward-McCann (Historical fiction [USA, 1830s], ages 11–YA).

Red Sails to Capri by Ann Weil. Viking (Historical fiction [Italy, 1826], ages 9–11).

The Bears on Hemlock Mountain by Alice Dalgliesh. Scribner's (Historical fiction [USA, 1800s], ages 6–9).

Birthdays of Freedom, Vol. 1 by Genevieve Foster. Scribner's (Informational/Biography, ages 10–13).

1954   *And Now Miguel* by Joseph Krumgold. Illustrated by Jean Charlot. Crowell (Historical fiction [New Mexico, 1940s], ages 9–12).

Honor Books:

All Alone by Claire Huchet Bishop. Viking (Realism, ages 8–11).

Shadrach by Meindert DeJong. Harper (Animal realism, ages 8–10).

Hurry Home, Candy by Meindert DeJong. Harper (Animal realism, ages 8–10).

Theodore Roosevelt, Fighting Patriot by Clara I. Judson. Follett (Biography, ages 9–11).

Magic Maize by Mary and Conrad Buff. Houghton (Realism, ages 8–11).

1955   *The Wheel on the School* by Meindert DeJong. Illustrated by Maurice Sendak. Harper (Realism, ages 8–11).

Honor Books:

The Courage of Sarah Noble by Alice Dalgliesh. Scribner's (Historical fiction [USA, 1707], ages 8–10).

Banner in the Sky by James Ramsey Ullman. Lippincott (Historical fiction [Europe, 1860s], ages 10–YA).

1956   *Carry On, Mr. Bowditch* by Jean Lee Latham. Houghton (Biography, ages 10–13).

Honor Books:

The Golden Name Day by Jennie D. Lindquist. Harper (Realism, ages 8–11).

The Secret River by Marjorie Kinnan Rawlings. Scribner's (Fantasy, ages 6–9).

Men, Microscopes and Living Things by Katherine B. Shippen. Viking (Informational, ages 10 and up).

1957   *Miracles on Maple Hill* by Virginia Sorensen. Illustrated by Beth and Joe Krush. Harcourt (Realism, ages 8–10).

Honor Books:

Old Yeller by Fred Gipson. Harper (Realism, ages 9–12).

The House of Sixty Fathers by Meindert DeJong. Harper (Historical fiction [China, 1940s], ages 9–13).

Mr. Justice Holmes by Clara I. Judson. Follett (Biography, ages 9–13).

The Corn Grows Ripe by Dorothy Rhoads. Viking (Realism, ages 9–11).

The Black Fox of Lorne by Marguerite de Angeli. Doubleday (Historical fiction [Scotland, tenth century], ages 9–12).

1958   *Rifles for Watie* by Harold Keith. Illustrated by Peter Burchard. Crowell (Historical fiction, [USA, 1860s], ages 10–YA).

Honor Books:

The Horsecatcher by Mari Sandoz. Westminster (Realism, ages 11–YA).

Gone-Away Lake by Elizabeth Enright. Harcourt (Realism, ages 8–11).

The Great Wheel by Robert Lawson. Viking (Historical fiction [U.S., 1890s], ages 9–12).

Tom Paine, Freedom's Apostle by Leo Gurko. Crowell (Biography, ages 11–YA).

1959   *The Witch of Blackbird Pond* by Elizabeth George Speare. Houghton (Historical fiction [USA, 1680s], ages 12–YA).

Honor Books:

The Family Under the Bridge by Natalie S. Carlson. Harper (Realism, 8–10).

Along Came a Dog by Meindert DeJong. Harper (Animal realism, ages 9–YA).

Chucaro: Wild Pony of the Pampa by Francis Kalnay. Harcourt (Animal realism, ages 9–13).

The Perilous Road by William O. Steele. Harcourt (Historical fiction [USA, 1860s], ages 9–13).

1960   *Onion John* by Joseph Krumgold. Illustrated by Symeon Shimin. Crowell (Realism, ages 9–12).

Honor Books:

My Side of the Mountain by Jean George. Dutton (Realism, ages 10–12).

America Is Born by Gerald Johnson. Morrow (Informational, ages 9–13).

The Gammage Cup by Carol Kendall. Harcourt (Fantasy [little people], ages 9–12).

1961   *Island of the Blue Dolphins* by Scott O'Dell. Houghton (Historical fiction [USA, 1800s]/Multicultural [Native American], ages 9–13).

Honor Books:

America Moves Forward by Gerald Johnson. Morrow (Informational, ages 9–13).

Old Ramon by Jack Schaefer. Houghton (Realism, ages 10–YA).

The Cricket in Times Square by George Selden. Farrar (Animal fantasy, ages 7–9).

1962 *The Bronze Bow* by Elizabeth George Speare. Houghton (Historical fiction [Jerusalem, first century A.D.], ages 12–YA).

Honor Books:

Frontier Living by Edwin Tunis. World (Informational, ages 10 and up).

The Golden Goblet by Eloise J. McGraw. Coward (Historical fiction [Ancient Egypt], ages 10–YA).

Belling the Tiger by Mary Stolz. Harper (Fantasy, ages 7–9).

1963 *A Wrinkle in Time* by Madeleine L'Engle. Farrar (Fantasy [science fiction], ages 9–12).

Honor Books:

Thistle and Thyme by Sorche Nic Leodhas (pseud. for Leclaire Alger). Holt (Traditional fantasy, ages 7–11).

Men of Athens by Olivia Coolidge. Houghton (Biography, ages 11–YA).

1964 *It's Like This, Cat* by Emily Cheney Neville. Harper (Realism, ages 10–YA).

Honor Books:

Rascal by Sterling North. Dutton (Animal realism, ages 9–11).

The Loner by Esther Wier. McKay/Longmans (Realism, ages 9–13).

1965 *Shadow of a Bull* by Maia Wojciechowska. Atheneum (Realism, ages 10–12).

Honor Book:

Across Five Aprils by Irene Hunt. Follett (Historical fiction [USA, 1860s], ages 10–13).

1966 *I, Juan de Pareja* by Elizabeth Borten de Treviño. Farrar (Biography, ages 10–12).

Honor Books:

The Black Cauldron by Lloyd Alexander. Holt (Fantasy, ages 10–12).

The Animal Family by Randall Jarrell. Pantheon (Fantasy, ages 10–13).

The Noonday Friends by Mary Stolz. Harper (Realism, ages 9–11).

1967 *Up a Road Slowly* by Irene Hunt. Follett (Realism, ages 10–YA).

Honor Books:

The King's Fifth by Scott O'Dell. Houghton (Historical fiction [Spain, 1500s], ages 10–12).

Zlateh the Goat and Other Stories by Isaac Bashevis Singer. Harper (Fantasy, ages 8–11).

The Jazz Man by Mary H. Weik. Atheneum (Realism, ages 9–12).

1968 *From the Mixed-Up Files of Mrs. Basil E. Frankweiler* by E. L. Konigsburg. Atheneum (Realism, ages 10–12).

Honor Books:

Jennifer, Hecate, Macbeth, William McKinley, and Me, Elizabeth by E. L. Konigsburg. Atheneum (Realism, ages 9–11).

The Black Pearl by Scott O'Dell. Houghton (Realism, ages 9–11).

The Fearsome Inn by Isaac Bashevis Singer. Scribner's (Fantasy, ages 10–YA).

The Egypt Game by Zilpha Keatley Snyder. Atheneum (Realism, ages 9–11).

1969 *The High King* by Lloyd Alexander. Holt (Fantasy [Quest], ages 10–12).

Honor Books:

To Be a Slave by Julius Lester. Dial (Informational, ages 11–YA).

When Shlemiel Went to Warsaw and Other Stories by Isaac Bashevis Singer. Farrar (Fantasy, ages 9 and up).

1970 *Sounder* by William H. Armstrong. Harper (Historical fiction [Southern U.S., early twentieth century], ages 10–13).

Honor Books:

Our Eddie by Sulamith Ish-Kishor. Pantheon (Realism, ages 11–YA).

The Many Ways of Seeing: An Introduction to the Pleasure of Art by Janet Gaylord Moore. World (Informational, ages 10 and up).

Journey Outside by Mary Q. Steele. Viking (Fantasy, ages 10–13).

1971 *Summer of the Swans* by Betsy Byars. Viking (Realism, ages 10–13).

Honor Books:

Kneeknock Rise by Natalie Babbitt. Farrar (Fantasy, ages 9–13).

Enchantress from the Stars by Sylvia Louise Engdahl. Atheneum (Fantasy [science fiction], ages 11–YA).

Sing Down the Moon by Scott O'Dell. Houghton (Historical fiction [USA, 1860s], ages 12–YA).

1972 *Mrs. Frisby and the Rats of NIMH* by Robert C. O'Brien. Atheneum (Animal fantasy, ages 10–12).

Honor Books:

Incident at Hawk's Hill by Allan W. Eckert. Little, Brown (Historical Fiction [Canada, 1870]/Animal realism, ages 10–12).

The Planet of Junior Brown by Virginia Hamilton. Macmillan (Realism, ages 11–YA).

The Tombs of Atuan by Ursula K. LeGuin. Atheneum (Fantasy [quest], ages 10 and up).

Annie and the Old One by Miska Miles. Little, Brown. (Picture book; Realism/Multicultural [Native-American], ages 8–10).

The Headless Cupid by Zilpha Keatley Snyder. Atheneum (Realism [mystery], ages 10–12).

1973 *Julie of the Wolves* by Jean Craighead George. Harper (Realism/Multicultural [Native-American], ages 10–13).

Honor Books:

Frog and Toad Together by Arnold Lobel. Harper (Picture book; Animal fantasy, ages 3–7).

The Upstairs Room by Johanna Reiss. Crowell (Historical fiction [Holland, 1940s], ages 9–13).

The Witches of Worm by Zilpha Keatley Snyder. Atheneum (Realism, ages 10–12).

1974 *The Slave Dancer* by Paula Fox. Bradbury (Historical fiction [U.S., Africa, 1840s], ages 10–13).

Honor Book:

The Dark Is Rising by Susan Cooper. Atheneum/McElderry (Fantasy [quest], ages 11–YA).

1975 *M. C. Higgins, the Great* by Virginia Hamilton. Macmillan (Realism/Multicultural [African-American], ages 10–13).

Honor Books:

Figgs & Phantoms by Ellen Raskin. Dutton (Realism, ages 10–13).

My Brother Sam Is Dead by James Lincoln Collier and Christopher Collier. Four Winds (Historical fiction [colonial America, 1700s], ages 10–YA).

The Perilous Gard by Elizabeth Marie Pope. Houghton (Historical fiction [England, 1558], ages 12–YA).

Philip Hall Likes Me. I Reckon Maybe by Bette Greene. Dial (Realism/Multicultural [African-American], ages 9–11).

1976 *The Grey King* by Susan Cooper. Atheneum/McElderry (Fantasy [quest], ages 11–YA).

Honor Books:

The Hundred Penny Box by Sharon Bell Mathis. Viking (Realism/Multicultural [African-American], ages 8–11).

Dragonwings by Lawrence Yep. Harper (Historical fiction [San Francisco, 1903–1909]/Multicultural [Chinese-American], ages 10–13).

1977 *Roll of Thunder, Hear My Cry* by Mildred D. Taylor. Dial (Historical fiction [Mississippi, 1934]/Multicultural [African-American], ages 9–13).

Honor Books:

Abel's Island by William Steig. Farrar (Animal fantasy, ages 8–10).

A String in the Harp by Nancy Bond. Atheneum/McElderry (Fantasy, ages 11–13).

1978 *The Bridge to Terabithia* by Katherine Paterson. Crowell (Realism, ages 9–11).

Honor Books:

Anpao: An American Indian Odyssey by Jamake Highwater. Lippincott (Traditional fantasy/Multicultural [Native-American], ages 10–12).

Ramona and Her Father by Beverly Cleary. Morrow (Realism, ages 7–9).

1979 *The Westing Game* by Ellen Raskin. Dutton (Realism [mystery], ages 10–12).

Honor Book:

The Great Gilly Hopkins by Katherine Paterson. Crowell (Realism, ages 9–12).

1980 *A Gathering of Days: A New England Girl's Journal, 1830–32* by Joan Blos. Scribner's (Historical fiction [New England, 1830s], ages 11–YA).

Honor Book:

The Road from Home: The Story of an Armenian Girl by David Kherdian. Greenwillow (Historical fiction [Turkey, Greece, 1907–1924], ages 11–YA).

1981 *Jacob Have I Loved* by Katherine Paterson. Crowell (Historical fiction [U.S., 1940s], ages 12–YA).

Honor Books:

The Fledgling by Jane Langton. Harper (Fantasy, ages 9–11).

A Ring of Endless Light by Madeleine L'Engle. Farrar (Fantasy [science fiction], ages 10–12).

1982 *A Visit to William Blake's Inn: Poems for Innocent and Experienced Travelers* by Nancy

Willard. Illustrated by Alice and Martin Provensen. Harcourt (Picture book; Poetry, ages 9–11).

Honor Books:

Ramona Quimby, Age 8 by Beverly Cleary. Morrow (Realism, ages 7–9).

Upon the Head of the Goat: A Childhood in Hungary, 1939–1944 by Aranka Siegal. Farrar (Historical fiction, ages 10–13).

1983 ***Dicey's Song*** by Cynthia Voigt. Atheneum (Realism, ages 9–12).

Honor Books:

The Blue Sword by Robin McKinley. Greenwillow (Fantasy [quest], ages 12–YA).

Dr. DeSoto by William Steig. Farrar (Picture book; Animal fantasy, ages 5–8).

Graven Images by Paul Fleischman. Harper (Fantasy, ages 10–12).

Homesick: My Own Story by Jean Fritz. Putman (Biography, ages 9–11).

Sweet Whispers, Brother Rush by Virginia Hamilton. Philomel (Fantasy/Multicultural [African American], ages 12–YA).

1984 ***Dear Mr. Henshaw*** by Beverly Cleary. Morrow (Realism, ages 8–10).

Honor Books:

The Sign of the Beaver by Elizabeth George Speare. Houghton (Historical fiction [colonial America], ages 9–11).

A Solitary Blue by Cynthia Voigt. Atheneum (Realism, ages 11–13).

Sugaring Time by Kathryn Lasky. Photographs by Christopher Knight. Macmillan (Informational, ages 9–13).

The Wish Giver by Bill Brittain. Harper (Fantasy, ages 9–12).

1985 ***The Hero and the Crown*** by Robin McKinley. Greenwillow (Fantasy [quest], ages 12–YA).

Honor Books:

Like Jake and Me by Mavis Jukes. Illustrated by Lloyd Bloom. Knopf (Picture book; Realism, ages 7–9).

The Moves Make the Man by Bruce Brooks. Harper (Realism/Multicultural [African-American], ages 11–YA).

One-Eyed Cat by Paula Fox. Bradbury (Realism, ages 9–12).

1986 ***Sarab, Plain and Tall*** by Patricia MacLachlan. Harper (Historical fiction [U.S. western frontier, 1800s], ages 8–10).

Honor Books:

Commodore Perry in the Land of the Shogun by Rhoda Blumberg. Lothrop (Informational, ages 9–13).

Dogsong by Gary Paulsen. Bradbury (Realism/Multicultural [Native American], ages 10–13).

1987 ***The Whipping Boy*** by Sid Fleischman. Greenwillow (Historical fiction [Medieval England], ages 9–11).

Honor Books:

On My Honor by Marion Dane Bauer. Clarion (Realism, ages 8–11).

Volcano: The Eruption and Healing of Mount St. Helens by Patricia Lauber. Bradbury (Informational, ages 8–13).

A Fine White Dust by Cynthia Rylant. Bradbury (Realism, ages 10–12).

1988 ***Lincoln: A Photobiography*** by Russell Freedman. Clarion/Houghton (Biography, ages 8–12).

Honor Books:

After the Rain by Norma Fox Mazer. Morrow (Realism, ages 12–YA).

Hatchet by Gary Paulsen. Bradbury (Realism, ages 9–13).

1989 ***Joyful Noise: Poems for Two Voices*** by Paul Fleischman. Harper (Poetry, ages 9–YA).

Honor Books:

In the Beginning: Creation Stories from Around the World by Virginia Hamilton. Harcourt (Traditional fantasy, ages 9–YA).

Scorpions by Walter Dean Myers. Harper (Realism/Multicultural [African-American, Hispanic-American], ages 10–13).

1990 ***Number the Stars*** by Lois Lowry. Houghton (Historical fiction [Denmark, 1940s], ages 8–10).

Honor Books:

Afternoon of the Elves by Janet Taylor Lisle. Orchard (Realism, ages 10–13).

Shabanu, Daughter of the Wind by Suzanne Fisher Staples. Knopf (Realism, ages 12–YA).

The Winter Room by Gary Paulsen. Orchard (Realism, ages 10–13).

1991 ***Maniac Magee*** by Jerry Spinelli. Little, Brown (Realism, ages 9–13).

Honor Book:

The True Confessions of Charlotte Doyle by Avi. Orchard (Historical fiction [England-U.S., 1830], ages 10–13).

1992 *Shiloh* by Phyllis Reynolds Naylor. Atheneum (Animal realism, ages 8–10).

Honor Books:

Nothing But the Truth by Avi. Orchard (Realism, ages 10–14).

The Wright Brothers: How They Invented the Airplane by Russell Freedman. Holiday (Informational/ Biography, ages 9–12).

Boston Globe—Horn Book Awards These awards, sponsored by *The Boston Globe* and *The Horn Book,* are given to an author for outstanding fiction or poetry for children, to an illustrator for outstanding illustration in a children's book, and, since 1976, to an author for outstanding nonfiction for children.

1967 Text: *The Little Fishes* by Erik Christian Haugaard. Houghton.

Illustration: *London Bridge Is Falling Down* by Peter Spier. Doubleday.

1968 Text: *The Spring Rider* by John Lawson. Crowell.

Illustration: *Tikki Tikki Tembo* by Arlene Mosel. Illustrated by Blair Lent. Holt.

1969 Text: *A Wizard of Earthsea* by Ursula K. Le Guin. Houghton.

Illustration: *The Adventures of Paddy Pork* by John S. Goodall. Harcourt.

1970 Text: *The Intruder* by John Rowe Townsend. Lippincott.

Illustration: *Hi, Cat!* by Ezra Jack Keats. Macmillan.

1971 Text: *A Room Made of Windows* by Eleanor Cameron. Atlantic/Little.

Illustration: *If I Built a Village* by Kazue Mizumura. Crowell.

1972 Text: *Tristan and Iseult* by Rosemary Sutcliff. Dutton.

Illustration: *Mr. Grumpy's Outing* by John Burningham. Holt.

1973 Text: *The Dark Is Rising* by Susan Cooper. Atheneum/McElderry.

Illustration: *King Stork* by Trina Schart Hyman. Little, Brown.

1974 Text: *M.C. Higgins, the Great* by Virginia Hamilton. Macmillan.

Illustration: *Jambo Means Hello* by Muriel Feelings. Illustrated by Tom Feelings. Dial.

1975 Text: *Transport 7–41–R* by T. Degens. Viking.

Illustration: *Anno's Alphabet* by Mitsumasa Anno. Crowell.

1976 Fiction: *Unleaving* by Jill Paton Walsh, Farrar.

Nonfiction: *Voyaging to Cathay: Americans in the China Trade* by Alfred Tamarin and Shirley Glubok. Viking.

Illustration: *Thirteen* by Remy Charlip and Jerry Joyner. Parents.

1977 Fiction: *Child of the Owl* by Laurence Yep. Harper.

Nonfiction: *Chance, Luck and Density* by Peter Dickinson. Atlantic/Little, Brown.

Illustration: *Granfa' Grig Had a Pig and Other Rhymes* by Wallace Tripp. Little, Brown.

1978 Fiction: *The Westing Game* by Ellen Raskin. Dutton.

Nonfiction: *Mischling, Second Degree: My Childhood in Nazi Germany* by Ilse Koehn. Greenwillow.

Illustration: *Anno's Journey* by Mitsumasa Anno. Philomel.

1979 Fiction: *Humbug Mountain* by Sid Fleischman. Atlantic/Little, Brown.

Nonfiction: *The Road from Home: The Story of an Armenian Girl* by David Kherdian. Greenwillow.

Illustration: *The Snowman* by Raymond Briggs. Random.

1980 Fiction: *Conrad's War* by Andrew Davies. Crown.

Nonfiction: *Building: The Fight Against Gravity* by Mario Salvadori. Atheneum/McElderry.

Illustration: *The Garden of Abdul Gasazi* by Chris Van Allsburg. Houghton.

1981 Fiction: *The Leaving* by Lynn Hall. Scribner's.

Nonfiction: *The Weaver's Gift* by Kathryn Lasky. Warne.

Illustration: *Outside Over There* by Maurice Sendak. Harper.

1982 Fiction: *Playing Beatie Bow* by Ruth Park. Atheneum.

Nonfiction: *Upon the Head of the Goat: A Childhood in Hungary, 1939–1944* by Aranka Siegal. Farrar.

Illustration: *A Visit to William Blake's Inn: Poems for Innocent and Experienced Travelers* by Nancy Willard. Illustrated by Alice and Martin Provensen. Harcourt.

1983 Fiction: *Sweet Whispers, Brother Rush* by Virginia Hamilton. Philomel.

Nonfiction: *Behind Barbed Wire: The Imprisonment of Japanese Americans During World War II.* by Daniel S. Davis. Dutton.

Illustration: *A Chair for My Mother* by Vera B. Williams. Greenwillow.

1984 Fiction: *A Little Fear* by Patricia Wrightson. McElderry/Atheneum.

Nonfiction: *The Double Life of Pocahontas* by Jean Fritz. Putnam.

Illustration: *Jonah and the Great Fish* retold and illustrated by Warwick Hutton. McElderry/Atheneum.

1985 Fiction: *The Moves Make the Man* by Bruce Brooks. Harper.

Nonfiction: *Commodore Perry in the Land of the Shogun* by Rhoda Blumberg. Lothrop.

Illustration: *Mama Don't Allow* by Thatcher Hurd. Harper.

1986 Fiction: *In Summer Light* by Zibby O'Neal. Viking Kestrel.

Nonfiction: *Auks, Rocks, and the Odd Dinosaur* by Peggy Thomson. Crowell.

Illustration: *The Paper Crane* by Molly Bang. Greenwillow.

1987 Fiction: *Rabble Starkey* by Lois Lowry. Houghton.

Nonfiction: *Pilgrims of Plimouth* by Marcia Sewall. Atheneum.

Illustration: *Mufaro's Beautiful Daughters* by John Steptoe. Lothrop.

1988 Fiction: *The Friendship* by Mildred Taylor. Dial.

Nonfiction: *Anthony Burns: The Defeat and Triumph of a Fugitive Slave* by Virginia Hamilton. Knopf.

Illustration: *The Boy of the Three-Year Nap* by Diane Snyder. Illustrated by Allen Say. Houghton.

1989 Fiction: *The Village by the Sea* by Paula Fox. Orchard.

Nonfiction: *The Way Things Work* by David Macaulay. Houghton.

Illustration: *Shy Charles* by Rosemary Wells. Dial.

1990 Fiction: *Maniac Magee* by Jerry Spinelli. Little, Brown.

Nonfiction: *The Great Little Madison* by Jean Fritz. Putnam.

Illustration: *Lon Po Po: A Red-Riding Hood Story from China* retold and illustrated by Ed Young. Philomel.

1991 Fiction: *The True Confessions of Charlotte Doyle* by Avi. Orchard.

Nonfiction: *Appalachia: The Voices of Sleeping Birds* by Cynthia Rylant. Illustrated by Barry Moser. Harcourt.

Illustration: *The Tale of the Mandarin Ducks* retold by Katherine Paterson. Illustrated by Leo and Diane Dillon. Lodestar.

Great Britain

Kate Greenaway Medal   This award, sponsored by the British Library Association, is given to the illustrator of the most distinguished work in illustration in a children's book first published in the United Kingdom during the preceding year.

1957   *Tim All Alone* by Edward Ardizzone. Oxford.

1958   *Mrs. Easter and the Storks* by V. H. Drummond. Faber.

1959   No award

1960   *Kashtanka and a Bundle of Ballads* by William Stobbs. Oxford.

1961   *Old Winkle and the Seagulls* by Elizabeth Rose. Illustrated by Gerald Rose. Faber.

1962   *Mrs. Cockle's Cat* by Philippa Pearce. Illustrated by Anthony Maitland. Kestrel.

1963   *Brian Wildsmith's ABC* by Brian Wildsmith. Oxford.

1964   *Borka* by John Burningham. Jonathan Cape.

1965   *Shakespeare's Theatre* by C. W. Hodges. Oxford.

1966   *Three Poor Tailors* by Victor Ambrus. Hamilton.

1967   *Mother Goose Treasury* by Raymond Briggs. Hamilton.

1968 *Charlie, Charlotte & the Golden Canary* by Charles Keeping. Oxford.
1969 *Dictionary of Chivalry* by Grant Uden. Illustrated by Pauline Baynes. Kestrel.
1970 *The Quangle-Wangle's Hat* by Edward Lear. Illustrated by Helen Oxenbury. Heinemann.
   Dragon of an Ordinary Family by Margaret Mahy. Illustrated by Helen Oxenbury. Heinemann.
1971 *Mr. Gumpy's Outing* by John Burningham. Jonathan Cape.
1972 *The Kingdom under the Sea* by Jan Piénkowski. Jonathan Cape.
1973 *The Woodcutter's Duck* by Krystyna Turska. Hamilton.
1974 *Father Christmas* by Raymond Briggs. Hamilton.
1975 *The Wind Blew* by Pat Hutchins. Bodley Head.
1976 *Horses in Battle* by Victor Ambrus. Oxford.
   Mishka by Victor Ambrus. Oxford.
1977 *The Post Office Cat* by Gail E. Haley. Bodley Head.
1978 *Dogger* by Shirley Hughes. Bodley Head.
1979 *Each Peach Pear Plum* by Janet and Allan Ahlberg. Kestrel.
1980 *The Haunted House* by Jan Piénkowski. Heinemann.
1981 *Mr. Magnolia* by Quentin Blake. Jonathan Cape.
1982 *The Highwayman* by Alfred Noyes. Illustrated by Charles Keeping. Oxford.
1983 *Long Neck and Thunder Foot*. Kestrel; and *Sleeping Beauty and Other Favorite Fairy Tales.* Gollancz. Both illustrated by Michael Foreman.
1984 *Gorilla* by Anthony Browne. Julia McRae Books.
1985 *Hiawatha's Childhood* by Errol LeCain. Faber.
1986 *Sir Gawain and the Loathly Lady* by Selina Hastings. Illustrated by Juan Wijngaard. Walker.
1987 *Snow White in New York* by Fiona French. Oxford.
1988 *Crafty Chameleon* by Mwenye Hadithi. Illustrated by Adrienne Kennaway. Hodder & Stoughton.
1989 *Can't You Sleep, Little Bear?* by Martin Waddell. Illustrated by Barbara Firth. Walker.

1990 *War Boy: A Country Childhood* by Michael Foreman. Arcade.
1991 *The Whale's Song* by Dyan Sheldon. Illustrated by Gary Blythe. Dial.

Carnegie Medal   This award, sponsored by the British Library Association, is given to the author of the most outstanding children's book first published in English in the United Kingdom during the preceding year.

1937 *Pigeon Post* by Arthur Ransome. Cape.
1938 *The Family from One End Street* by Eve Garnett. Muller.
1939 *The Circus Is Coming* by Noel Streatfield. Dent.
1940 *Radium Woman* by Eleanor Doorly. Heinemann.
1941 *Visitors from London* by Kitty Barne. Dent.
1942 *We Couldn't Leave Dinah* by Mary Treadgold. Penguin.
1943 *The Little Grey Men* by B. B. Eyre & Spottiswoode.
1944 No award
1945 *The Wind on the Moon* by Eric Linklater. Macmillan.
1946 No award
1947 *The Little White Horse* by Elizabeth Goudge. Brockhampton Press.
1948 *Collected Stories for Children* by Walter de la Mare. Faber.
1949 *Sea Change* by Richard Armstrong. Dent.
1950 *The Story of Your Home* by Agnes Allen. Transatlantic.
1951 *The Lark on the Wing* by Elfrida Vipont Foulds. Oxford.
1952 *The Wool-Pack* by Cynthia Harnett. Methuen.
1953 *The Borrowers* by Mary Norton. Dent.
1954 *A Valley Grows Up* by Edward Osmond. Oxford.
1955 *Knight Crusader* by Ronald Welch. Oxford.
1956 *The Little Bookroom* by Eleanor Farjeon. Oxford.
1957 *The Last Battle* by C. S. Lewis. Bodley Head.

1958 A Grass Rope by William Mayne. Oxford.
1959 *Tom's Midnight Garden* by Philippa Pearce. Oxford.
1960 *The Lantern Bearers* by Rosemary Sutcliff. Oxford.
1961 *The Making of Man* by I. W. Cornwall. Phoenix.
1962 *A Stranger at Green Knowe* by Lucy Boston. Faber.
1963 *The Twelve and the Genii* by Pauline Clarke. Faber.
1964 *Time of Trial* by Hester Burton. Oxford.
1965 *Nordy Banks* by Sheena Porter. Oxford.
1966 *The Grange at High Force* by Philip Turner. Oxford.
1967 No award
1968 *The Owl Service* by Alan Garner. Collins.
1969 *The Moon in the Cloud* by Rosemary Harris. Faber.
1970 *The Edge of the Cloud* by K. M. Peyton. Oxford.
1971 *The God Beneath the Sea* by Leon Garfield and Edward Blishen. Kestrel.
1972 *Josh* by Ivan Southall. Angus and Robertson.
1973 *Watership Down* by Richard Adams. Rex Collings.
1974 *The Ghost of Thomas Kempe* by Penelope Lively. Heinemann.
1975 *The Stronghold* by Mollie Hunter. Hamilton.
1976 *The Machine-Gunners* by Robert Westall. Macmillan.
1977 *Thunder and Lightnings* by Jan Mark. Kestrel.
1978 *The Turbulent Term of Tyke Tiler* by Gene Kemp. Faber.
1979 *The Exeter Blitz* by David Rees. Hamish Hamilton.
1980 *Tulku* by Peter Dickinson. Dutton.
1981 *City of Gold* by Peter Dickinson. Gollancz.
1982 *The Scarecrows* by Robert Westall. Chatto and Windus.
1983 *The Haunting* by Margaret Mahy. Dent.
1984 *Handles* by Jan Mark. Kestrel.
1985 *The Changeover* by Margaret Mahy. Dent.

1986 *Storm* by Kevin Crossley-Holland. Heinemann.
1987 *Granny was a Buffer Girl* by Berlie Doherty. Methuen.
1988 *The Ghost Drum* by Susan Price. Faber.
1989 *Pack of Lies* by Geraldine McCaughrean. Oxford.
1990 *My War with Goggle-Eyes* by Anne Fine. Joy Street.
1991 *Wolf* by Gillian Cross. Oxford.

Canada

Amelia Frances Howard-Gibbon Medal This award, sponsored by the Canadian Library Association, is given to an illustrator for the most distinguished illustrations in a children's book published in Canada during the preceding year. Only Canadian citizens are eligible for this award.

1971 *The Wind Has Wings* edited by Mary Alice Downie and Barbara Robertson. Illustrated by Elizabeth Cleaver. Oxford.
1972 *A Child in Prison Camp* by Shizuye Takashima. Tundra.
1973 *Au Dela Du Soleil/Beyond the Sun* by Jacques de Roussan. Tundra.
1974 *A Prairie Boy's Winter* by William Kurelek. Tundra.
1975 *The Sleighs of My Childhood/Les Traineaux de Mon Enfance* by Carlo Italiano. Tundra.
1976 *A Prairie Boy's Summer* by William Kurelek. Tundra.
1977 *Down by Jim Long's Stage: Rhymes for Children and Young Fish* by Al Pittman. Illustrated by Pam Hall. Breakwater.
1978 *The Loon's Necklace* by William Toye. Illustrated by Elizabeth Cleaver. Oxford.
1979 *A Salmon for Simon* by Betty Waterton. Illustrated by Ann Blades. Douglas & McIntyre.
1980 *The Twelve Dancing Princesses* retold by Janet Lunn. Illustrated by László Gál. Methuen.

1981 *The Trouble with Princesses* by Christie Harris. Illustrated by Douglas Tait. McClelland & Stewart.

1982 *Ytek and the Arctic Orchid : An Inuit Legend* by Garnet Hewitt. Illustrated by Heather Woodall. Douglas & McIntyre.

1983 *Chester's Barn* by Lindee Climo. Tundra.

1984 *Zoom at Sea* by Tim Wynne-Jones. Illustrated by Ken Nutt. Douglas & McIntyre.

1985 *Chin Chiang and the Dragon's Dance* by Ian Wallace. Groundwood.

1986 *Zoom Away* by Tim Wynne-Jones. Illustrated by Ken Nutt. Douglas & McIntyre.

1987 *Moonbeam on a Cat's Ear* by Marie-Louise Gay. Stoddard.

1988 *Rainy Day Magic* by Marie-Louise Gay. Hodder & Stoughton.

1989 *Amos's Sweater* by Janet Lunn. Illustrated by Kim LaFave. Douglas & McIntyre.

1990 *Til All the Stars Have Fallen: Canadian Poems for Children* selected by David Booth. Illustrated by Kady MacDonald Denton. Kids Can Press.

1991 *The Orphan Boy* by Tololwa M. Mollel. Illustrated by Paul Morin. Oxford.

Canadian Children's Book of the Year Award This award, sponsored by the Canadian Library Association, is given to the author of a children's book of outstanding literary merit. Since 1954, an equivalent award has been presented to the author of a children's book published in French. Only Canadian citizens are eligible for these awards.

1947 *Starbuck Valley Winter* by Roderick Haig-Brown. Collins.

1948 *Kristli's Trees* by Mabel Dunham. Hale.

1949 No award

1950 *Franklin of the Arctic* by Richard S. Lambert. McClelland & Stewart.

1951 No award

1952 *The Sun Horse* by Catherine Anthony Clark. Macmillan of Canada.

1953 No award

1954 No English award

Le Vénérable Francois de Montmorency-Laval by Émile S. J. Gervais. Comité des Fondateurs de l'Église Canadienne.

1955 No award

1956 *Train for Tiger Lily* by Louise Riley, Macmillan of Canada.

No French award

1957 *Glooskap's Country* by Cyrus Macmillan. Oxford.

No French award

1958 *Lost in the Barrens* by Farley Mowat. Little.

Le Chevalier du Roi by Beatrice Clément. Atelier.

1959 *The Dangerous Cove* by John F. Hayes. Copp Clark.

Un Drôle de Petit Cheval by Hélène Flamme. Leméac.

1960 *The Golden Phoenix* by Marius Barbeau and Michael Hornyansky. Walck/Oxford.

L' Été Enchanté by Paule Daveluy. Atelier.

1961 *The St. Lawrence* by William Toye. Oxford.

Plantes Vagabondes by Marcelle Gauvreau. Centre de Psychologie et de Pédagogie.

1962 No English award

Les Îles du Roi Maha Maha II by Claude Aubry. Pélican.

1963 *The Incredible Journey* by Sheila Burnford. Little, Brown.

Drôle D'Automne by Paul Daveluy. Pélican.

1964 *The Whale People* by Roderick Haig-Brown. Collins.

Férie by Cécile Chabot. Beauchemin.

1965 *Tales of Nanabozho* by Dorothy Reid. Oxford.

Le Loup de Nöel by Claude Aubry. Centre de Psychologie et de Pédagogie.

1966 *Tiktá Liktak* by James Houston. Kestrel/Longmans.

Le Chêne des Tempêtes by Andrée Mallet-Hobden. Fides.

The Double Knights by James McNeal. Walck.

Le Wapiti by Monique Corriveau. Jeunesse.

1967 *Raven's Cry* by Christie Harris. McClelland & Stewart.

No French award

1968 *The White Archer* by James Houston. Academic/Kestrel.

Légendes Indiennes du Canada by Claude Mélancon. Editions du Jour.

1969 *And Tomorrow the Stars* by Kay Hill. Dodd.

No French award

1970 *Sally Go Round the Sun* by Edith Fowke. McClelland & Stewart.

La Merveilleuse Histoire de la Naissance by Lionel Gendron. Les Editions de l'Homme.

1971 *Cartier Discovers the St. Lawrence* by William Toye. Oxford.

La Surprise de Dame Chenille by Henriette Major. Centre de Psychologie et de Pédagogie.

1972 *Mary of Mile 18* by Ann Blades. Tundra.
No French award

1973 *The Marrow of the World* by Ruth Nichols. Macmillan.

Le Petit Sapin Qui a Poussé sur Une Étoile by Simone Bussières. Laurentiennes.

1974 *The Miraculous Hind* by Elizabeth Cleaver. Holt.
No French award.

1975 *Alligator Pie* by Dennis Lee. Macmillan.
No French award

1976 *Jacob Two-Two Meets the Hooded Fang* by Mordecai Richler. McClelland & Stewart.
No French award

1977 *Mouse Woman and the Vanished Princesses* by Christie Harris. McClelland & Stewart.
No French award

1978 *Garbage Delight* by Dennis Lee. Macmillan.
No French award

1979 *Hold Fast* by Kevin Major. Clarke, Irwin.
No French award

1980 *River Runners: A Tale of Hardship and Bravery* by James Houston. McClelland & Stewart.
No French award

1981 *The Violin Maker's Gift* by Donn Kushner. Macmillan.
No French award

1982 *The Root Cellar* by Janet Lunn. Dennys.
No French award

1983 *Up to Low* by Brian Doyle. Douglas & McIntyre.
No French award

1984 *Sweetgrass* by Jan Hudson. Tree Frog Press.
No French award

1985 *Mama's Going to Buy You a Mockingbird* by Jean Little. Penguin.
No French award

1986 *Julie* by Cora Taylor. Western.
No French award

1987 *Shadow in Hawthorn Bay* by Janet Lunn. Dennys.
No French award

1988 *A Handful of Time* by Kit Pearson. Penguin.
No French award

1989 *Easy Avenue* by Brian Doyle. Groundwood.
No French award

1990 *The Sky Is Falling* by Kit Pearson. Penguin.
No French award

1991 *Redwork* by Michael Bedard. Dennys.
No French award

Australia

Australian Children's Books of the Year Awards   The Australian Children's Book Council sponsors three awards for excellence in children's books: The Picture Book of the Year Award; The Children's Book of the Year for Younger Readers (for books that bridge the gap between picture books and longer novels); and The Children's Book of the Year for Older Readers.

Australian Picture Book of the Year Award

1956 *Wish and the Magic Nut* by Peggy Barnard. Illustrated by Shelia Hawkins. Sands.

1957   No award

1958 *Piccaninny Walkabout* by Axel Poignant. Angus & Robertson.

1959–1964   No awards

1965 *Hugo's Zoo* by Elizabeth MacIntyre. Angus & Robertson.

1966–1968   No awards

1969 *Sly Old Wardrobe* by Ivan Southall. Illustrated by Ted Greenwood. Cheshire.

1970   No award

1971 *Waltzing Matilda* by A. B. Paterson. Illustrated by Desmond Digby.

1972–1973   No awards

1974 *The Bunyip of Berkeley's Creek* by Jenny Wagner. Illustrated by Ron Brooks. Kestrel.

1975 *The Man from Ironbark* by A. B. Paterson. Illustrated by Quentin Hole. Collins.

1976 *The Rainbow Serpent* by Dick Roughsey. Collins.

1977 *ABC of Monsters* by Deborah Niland. Hodder & Stoughton.

1978 *John Brown, Rose and the Midnight Cat* by Jenny Wagner. Illustrated by Ron Brooks. Kestrel.

1979 *The Quinkins* written and illustrated by Percy Trezise and Dick Roughsey. Collins.

1980 *One Dragon's Dream* by Peter Pavey. Nelson.

1981 No award

1982 *Sunshine* by Jan Ormerod. Kestrel.

1983 *Who Sank the Boat?* by Pamela Allen. Nelson.

1984 *Bertie and the Bear* by Pamela Allen, Nelson.

1985 No award
   Highly commended: *The Inch Boy* by Junko Morimoto. Collins.

1986 *Felix and Alexander* written and illustrated by Terry Denton. Oxford.

1987 *Kojuro and the Bears* adapted by Helen Smith. Illustrated by Junko Morimoto. Collins.

1988 *Crusher Is Coming!* by Bob Graham. Lothian.

1989 *Drac and the Gremlins* by Allan Baillie. Illustrated by Jane Tanner. Viking/Kestrel.

   The Eleventh Hour by Graeme Base. Viking/Kestrel.

1990 *The Very Best of Friends* by Margaret Wild. Illustrated by Julie Vivas. Margaret Hamilton.

1991 *Greetings from Sandy Beach* by Bob Graham. Lothian.

Australian Children's Book of the Year for Younger Readers Award

1982 *Rummage* by Cristobel Mattingley. Illustrated by Patricia Mullins. Angus & Robertson.

1983 *Thing* by Robin Klein. Illustrated by Allison Lester. Oxford.

1984 *Bernice Knows Best* by Max Dann. Illustrated by Ann James. Oxford.

1985 *Something Special* by Emily Rodda. Illustrated by Noela Young. Angus & Robertson.

1986 *Arkwright* by Mary Steele. Hyland House.

1987 *Pigs Might Fly* by Emily Rodda. Illustrated by Noela Young. Angus & Robertson.

1988 *My Place* by Nadia Wheatley and Donna Rawlins. Collins Dove.

1989 *The Best-Kept Secret* by Emily Rodda. Angus & Robertson.

1990 *Pigs and Honey* by Jeanie Adams. Omnibus.

1991 *Finders Keepers* by Emily Rodda. Omnibus.

Australian Children's Book of the Year for Older Readers Award

1946 *Karrawingi, the Emu* by Leslie Rees. Sands.

1947 No award

1948 *Shackleton's Argonauts* by Frank Hurley. Angus & Robertson.

1949 *Whalers of the Midnight Sun* by Alan Villiers. Angus & Robertson.

1950 No award

1951 *Verity of Sydney Town* by Ruth Williams. Angus & Robertson.

1952 *The Australia Book* by Eve Pownall. Sands.

1953 *Aircraft of Today and Tomorrow* by J. H. and W. D. Martin. Angus & Robertson.

   Good Luck to the Rider by Joan Phipson. Angus & Robertson.

1954 *Australian Legendary* by K. L. Parker. Angus & Robertson.

1955 *The First Walkabout* by H. A. Lindsay and N. B. Tindale. Kestrel.

1956 *The Crooked Snake* by Patricia Wrightson. Angus & Robertson.

1957 *The Boomerang Book of Legendary Tales* by Enid Moodie-Heddle. Kestrel.

1958 *Tiger in the Bush* by Nan Chauncy. Oxford.

1959 *Devil's Hill* by Nan Chauncy. Oxford.

   Sea Menace by John Gunn. Constable.

1960 *All the Proud Tribesmen* by Kylie Tennant. Macmillan.

1961 *Tangara* by Nan Chauncy. Oxford.

1962 *The Racketty Street Gang* by H. L. Evers. Hodder & Stoughton.

   Rafferty Rides a Winner by Joan Woodbery. Parrish.

1963 *The Family Conspiracy* by Joan Phipson. Angus & Robertson.
1964 *The Green Laurel* by Eleanor Spence. Oxford.
1965 *Pastures of the Blue Crane* by Hesba F. Brinsmead. Oxford.
1966 *Ash Road* by Ivan Southall. Angus & Robertson.
1967 *The Min Min* by Mavis Thorpe Clark. Lansdowne.
1968 *To the Wild Sky* by Ivan Southall. Angus & Robertson.
1969 *When Jays Fly to Barbmo* by Margaret Balderson. Oxford.
1970 *Uhu* by Annette Macarther-Onslow. Ure Smith.
1971 *Bread and Honey* by Ivan Southall. Angus & Robertson.
1972 *Longtime Passing* by Hesba F. Brinsmead. Angus & Robertson.
1973 *Family at the Lookout* by Noreen Shelly. Oxford.
1974 *The Nargun and the Stars* by Patricia Wrightson. Hutchinson.
1975 No award
1976 *Fly West* by Ivan Southall. Angus & Robertson.
1977 *The October Child* by Eleanor Spence. Oxford.
1978 *The Ice Is Coming* by Patricia Wrightson. Hutchinson.
1979 *The Plum-Rain Scroll* by Ruth Manley. Hodder & Stoughton.
1980 *Displaced Person* by Lee Harding. Hyland House.
1981 *Playing Beatie Bow* by Ruth Park. Nelson.
1982 *The Valley Between* by Colin Thiele. Rigby.
1983 *Master of the Grove* by Victor Kelleher. Penguin.
1984 *A Little Fear* by Patricia Wrightson. Hutchinson.
1985 *The True Story of Lilli Stubeck* by James Aldridge. Hyland House.
1986 *The Green Wind* by Thurley Fowler. Rigby.
1987 *All We Know* by Simon French. Angus & Robertson.
1988 *So Much to Tell You* by John Marsden. Walter McVitty Books.

1989 *Beyond the Labyrinth* by Gillian Rubinstein. Hyland House.
1990 *Came Back to Show You I Could Fly* by Robin Klein. Viking/Kestrel.
1991 *Strange Objects* by Gary Crew. Heinemann Australia.

New Zealand

Russell Clark Award for Illustrations This award is given to an illustrator for the most distinguished illustrations for a children's book published in New Zealand the previous year. Only citizens or residents of New Zealand are eligible for this award.

1978 *The House of the People* by Ron L. Bacon. Illustrated by Robert F. Jahnke. Collins.
1979 *Kim* by Bruce Treloar. Collins.
1980–1981 No awards
1982 *Mrs. McGinty and the Bizarre Plant* by Gavin Bishop. Oxford.
1983 No award
1984 *The Tree Witches* by Gwenda Turner. Penguin.
1985 *The Duck in the Gun* by Joy Cowley. Illustrated by Robyn Belton. Shortland.
1986 *A Lion in the Night* by Pamela Allen. Hamilton.
1987 *Taniwha* by Patricia Grace. Illustrated by Robyn Kahukiwa. Viking Kestrel.
1988 *The Magpies* by Denis Glover. Illustrated by Dick Frizzell.
1989 *Joseph's Boat* by Caroline Macdonald. Illustrated by Chris Gaskin. Hodder & Stoughton.
1990 *A Walk to the Beach* by Chris Gaskin.
1991 *Arthur and the Dragon* by David Elliot. Steck-Vaughn.
1992 *One Lonely Kakapo* by Sandra Morris. Hodder & Stoughton.

Esther Glen Award This award is given to an author for the most distinguished contribution to New Zealand children's literature during the previous year. Only New Zealand citizens or residents are eligible.

1945 *The Book of Wiremu* by Stella Morice. Angus & Robertson.
1946 No award
1947 *Myths and Legends of Maoriland* by A. W. Reed. Reed.
1948–1949 No awards
1950 *The Adventures of Nimble, Rumble and Tumble* by Joan Smith. Paul's Book Arcade.
1951–1958 No awards
1959 *Falter Tom and the Water Boy* by Maurice Duggan. Paul's Book Arcade.
1960–1963 No awards
1964 *The Story of a Little Boy* by Leslie C. Powell. Paul's Book Arcade.
1965–1969 No awards
1970 *A Lion in the Meadow* by Margaret Mahy. Dent.
1971–1972 No awards
1973 *The First Margaret Mahy Story Book* by Margaret Mahy. Dent.
1974 No award
1975 *My Cat Likes to Hide in Boxes* by Eve Sutton and Lynley Dodd. Hamish Hamilton.

1976–1977 No awards
1978 *The Lighthouse Keeper's Lunch* by Ronda Armitage. Deutsch.
1979 *Take the Long Path* by Joan de Hamel. Lutterworth.
1980 No award
1981 *The Year of the Yelvertons* by Katherine O'Brien. Oxford.
1982 *The Haunting* by Margaret Mahy. Dent.
1983 *Jacky Nobody* by Anne de Roo. Methuen.
1984 *Elephant Rock* by Caroline Macdonald. Hodder.
1985 *The Changeover* by Margaret Mahy. Dent.
1986 *Motherstone* by Maurice Gee. Oxford.
1987 No award
1988 *Alex* by Tessa Duder. Oxford.
1989 *The Mangrove Summer* by Jack Lazenby. Oxford.
1990 *Alex in Winter* by Tessa Duder. Oxford.
1991 *Agnes the Sheep* by William Taylor. Scholastic.
1992 *Alessandra: Alex in Rome* by Tessa Duder. Oxford.

Awards for a Body of Work

Hans Christian Andersen Award

This international award, sponsored by the International Board on Books for Young People, is given every two years to a living author and, since 1966, to a living illustrator whose complete works have made important international contributions to children's literature.

1956 Eleanor Farjeon (Great Britain)
1958 Astrid Lindgren (Sweden)
1960 Erich Kästner (Germany)
1962 Meindert DeJong (USA)
1964 René Guillot (France)
1966 Author: Tove Jansson (Finland)
    Illustrator: Alois Carigiet (Switzerland)
1968 Authors: James Krüss (Germany) and José Maria Sanchez-Silva (Spain)
    Illustrator: Jirí Trnka (Czechoslovakia)

1970 Author: Gianni Rodari (Italy)
    Illustrator: Maurice Sendak (USA)
1972 Author: Scott O'Dell (USA)
    Illustrator: Ib Spang Olsen (Denmark)
1974 Author: Maria Gripe (Sweden)
    Illustrator: Farshid Mesghali (Iran)
1976 Author: Cecil Bödker (Denmark)
    Illustrator: Tatjana Mawrina (USSR)
1978 Author: Paula Fox (USA)
    Illustrator: Otto S. Svend (Denmark)
1980 Author: Bohumil Riha (Czechoslovakia)
    Illustrator: Suekichi Akaba (Japan)
1982 Author: Lygia Bojunga Nunes (Brazil)
    Illustrator: Zbigniew Rychlicki (Poland)
1984 Author: Christine Nöstlinger (Austria)
    Illustrator: Mitsumasa Anno (Japan)
1986 Author: Patricia Wrightson (Australia)
    Illustrator: Robert Ingpen (Australia)

1988 Author: Annie M. G. Schmidt (Netherlands)
Illustrator: Dušan Kallay (Czechoslovakia)
1990 Author: Tormod Haugen (Norway)
Illustrator: Lisbeth Zwerger (Austria)
1992 Author: Virginia Hamilton (USA)
Illustrator: Kveta Pacovská (Czechoslovakia)

Laura Ingalls Wilder Award

This award, sponsored by the Association for Library Service to Children of the American Library Association, is given to a U.S. author or illustrator whose body of work has made a lasting contribution to children's literature. Awarded every five years until 1980, the award is now given every three years.

1954 Laura Ingalls Wilder
1960 Clara Ingram Judson
1965 Ruth Sawyer
1970 E. B. White
1975 Beverly Cleary
1980 Theodor S. Geisel (Dr. Seuss)
1983 Maurice Sendak

1986 Jean Fritz
1989 Elizabeth George Speare
1992 Marcia Brown

NCTE Excellence in Poetry for Children Award

This award, sponsored by the National Council of Teachers of English, is given to a living U.S. poet in recognition of his or her total body of poetry written for children ages 3 through 13. Awarded annually until 1982, the award is now given every three years.

1977 David McCord
1978 Aileen Fisher
1979 Karla Kuskin
1980 Myra Cohn Livingston
1981 Eve Merriam
1982 John Ciardi
1985 Lilian Moore
1988 Arnold Adoff
1991 Valerie Worth

Awards for Specific Genres or Groups

Mildred L. Batchelder Award

This award, sponsored by the ALA's Association for Library Service to Children, is given to the American publisher of a children's book considered to be the most outstanding of those books originally published in a country other than the United States in a language other than English, and subsequently translated and published in the United States during the previous year.

1968 *The Little Man* by Erich Kästner. Translated from German by James Kirkup. Illustrated by Rick Schreiter. Knopf.
1969 *Don't Take Teddy* by Babbis Friis-Baastad. Translated from Norwegian by Lise Sömme McKinnon. Scribner's.
1970 *Wildcat Under Glass* by Alki Zei. Translated from Greek by Edward Fenton. Holt.
1971 *In the Land of Ur: The Discovery of Ancient Mesopotamia* by Hans Baumann. Translat-

ed from German by Stella Humphries. Illustrated by Hans Peter Renner. Pantheon.
1972 *Friedrich* by Hans Peter Richter. Translated from German by Edite Kroll. Holt.
1973 *Pulga* by Siny Rose Van Iterson. Translated from Dutch by Alexander and Alison Gode. Morrow.
1974 *Petros' War* by Alki Zei. Translated from Greek by Edward Fenton, Dutton.
1975 *An Old Tale Carved Out of Stone* by Aleksandr M. Linevski. Translated from Russian by Maria Polushkin. Crown.
1976 *The Cat and Mouse Who Shared a House* written and illustrated by Ruth Hürlimann. Translated from German by Anthea Bell. Walck.
1977 *The Leopard* by Cecil Bödker. Translated from Danish by Gunnar Poulsen. Atheneum.
1978 No award
1979 *Konrad* by Christine Nöstlinger. Translated from German (Austrian) by Anthea Bell. Illustrated by Carol Nicklaus. Watts.

Rabbit Island by Jörg Steiner. Translated from German (Swiss) by Ann Conrad Lammers. Illustrated by Jörg Müller. Harcourt.

1980   *The Sound of Dragon's Feet* by Alki Zei. Translated from Greek by Edward Fenton. Dutton.

1981   *The Winter When Time Was Frozen* by Els Pelgrom. Translated from Dutch by Raphael and Maryka Rudnik. Morrow.

1982   *The Battle Horse* by Harry Kullman. Translated from Swedish by George Blecher and Lone Thygesen-Blecher. Bradbury.

1983   *Hiroshima No Pika* written and illustrated by Toshi Maruki. Translated from Japanese through Kurita-Bando Literary Agency. Lothrop.

1984   *Ronia, the Robber's Daughter* by Astrid Lindgren. Translated from Swedish by Patricia Crampton. Viking.

1985   *The Island on Bird Street* by Uri Orlev. Translated from Hebrew by Hillel Halkin. Houghton.

1986   *Rose Blanche* by Christophe Gallaz and Roberto Innocenti. Translated from French by Martha Coventry and Richard Graglia. Illustrated by Roberto Innocenti. Creative Education.

1987   *No Hero for the Kaiser* by Rudolf Frank. Translated from German by Patricia Crampton. Illustrated by Klaus Steffans. Lothrop.

1988   *If You Didn't Have Me* by Ulf Nilsson. Translated from Swedish by Lone Thygesen-Blecher and George Blecher. Illustrated by Eva Eriksson. McElderry.

1989   *Crutches* by Peter Härtling. Translated from German by Elizabeth D. Crawford. Lothrop.

1990   *Buster's World* by Bjarne Reuter. Translated from Danish by Anthea Bell. Dutton.

1991   *A Hand Full of Stars* by Rafik Schami. Translated from German by Rika Lesser. Dutton.

Honor Book:

Two Short and One Long by Nina Ring Aamundsen. Translated from Norwegian by the author. Houghton.

1992   *The Man from the Other Side* by Uri Orlev. Translated from Hebrew by Hillel Halkin. Houghton.

Coretta Scott King Awards

These awards, founded to commemorate Dr. Martin Luther King, Jr., and his wife, Coretta Scott King, for their work in promoting peace and world brotherhood, are given to an African-American author and, since 1974, an African-American illustrator whose children's books, published during the preceding year, made outstanding inspirational and educational contributions to literature for children and young people. The awards are sponsored by the Social Responsibilities Round Table of the American Library Association.

1970   *Martin Luther King, Jr.: Man of Peace* by Lillie Patterson. Garrard.

1971   *Black Troubador: Langston Hughes* by Charlemae Rollins. Rand.

1972   *17 Black Artists* by Elton C. Fax. Dodd.

1973   *I Never Had It Made* by Jackie Robinson as told to Alfred Duckett. Putnam.

1974   Author: *Ray Charles* by Sharon Bell Mathis. Crowell.

Illustrator: The same title, illustrated by George Ford.

1975   Author: *The Legend of Africana* by Dorothy Robinson. Johnson.

Illustrator: The same title, illustrated by Herbert Temple.

1976   Author: *Duey's Tale* by Pearl Bailey. Harcourt.

Illustrator: No award

1977   Author: *The Story of Stevie Wonder* by James Haskins. Lothrop.

Illustrator: No award

1978   Author: *Africa Dream* by Eloise Greenfield. Day/Crowell.

Illustrator: The same title, illustrated by Carole Bayard.

1979   Author: *Escape to Freedom* by Ossie Davis. Viking.

Illustrator: *Something on My Mind* by Nikki Grimes. Illustrated by Tom Feelings. Dial.

1980   Author: *The Young Landlords* by Walter Dean Myers. Viking.

Illustrator: *Cornrows* by Camille Yarbrough. Illustrated by Carole Bayard. Coward.

1981   Author: *This Life* by Sidney Poitier. Knopf.

Illustrator: *Beat the Story-Drum, Pum-Pum* by Ashley Bryan. Atheneum.

1982   Author: *Let the Circle Be Unbroken* by Mildred Taylor. Dial.

Illustrator: ***Mother Crocodile: An Uncle Amadou Tale from Senegal*** adapted by Rosa Guy. Illustrated by John Steptoe. Delacorte.

1983   Author: ***Sweet Whispers, Brother Rush*** by Virginia Hamilton. Philomel.

Illustrator: ***Black Child*** by Peter Mugabane. Knopf.

1984   Author: ***Everett Anderson's Good-Bye*** by Lucille Clifton. Holt.

Illustrator: ***My Mama Needs Me*** by Mildred Pitts Walter. Illustrated by Pat Cummings. Lothrop.

1985   Author: ***Motown and Didi*** by Walter Dean Myers. Viking.

Illustrator: No award

1986   Author: ***The People Could Fly: American Black Folktales*** by Virginia Hamilton. Knopf.

Illustrator: ***Patchwork Quilt*** by Valerie Flournoy. Illustrated by Jerry Pinkney.

1987   Author: ***Justin and the Best Biscuits in the World*** by Mildred Pitts Walter. Lothrop.

Illustrator: ***Half Moon and One Whole Star*** by Crescent Dragonwagon. Illustrated by Jerry Pinkney. Macmillan.

1988   Author: ***The Friendship*** by Mildred D. Taylor. Illustrated by Max Ginsburg. Dial.

Illustrator: ***Mufaro's Beautiful Daughters: An African Tale*** retold and illustrated by John Steptoe. Lothrop.

1989   Author: ***Fallen Angels*** by Walter Dean Myers. Scholastic.

Illustrator: ***Mirandy and Brother Wind*** by Patricia McKissack. Illustrated by Jerry Pinkney. Knopf.

1990   Author: ***A Long Hard Journey*** by Patricia and Frederick McKissack. Walker.

Illustrator: ***Nathaniel Talking*** by Eloise Greenfield. Illustrated by Jan Spivey Gilchrist. Black Butterfly Press.

1991   Author: ***Road to Memphis*** by Mildred D. Taylor. Dial.

Illustrator: ***Aida*** retold by Leontyne Price. Illustrated by Leo and Diane Dillon. Harcourt.

1992   Author: ***Now Is Your Time! The African-American Struggle for Freedom*** by Walter Dean Myers. HarperCollins.

Illustrator: ***Tar Beach*** by Faith Ringgold. Crown.

Edgar Allan Poe Award (Mystery)— Best Juvenile Novel Category

This award, sponsored by the Mystery Writers of America, is given to the author of the best mystery of the year written for young readers.

1961   ***The Mystery of the Haunted Pool*** by Phyllis A. Whitney. Westminster.

1962   ***The Phantom of Walkaway Hill*** by Edward Fenton. Doubleday.

1963   ***Cutlass Island*** by Scott Corbett. Atlantic/Little.

1964   ***The Mystery of the Hidden Hand*** by Phyllis A. Whitney. Westminster.

1965   ***The Mystery at Crane's Landing*** by Marcella Thum. Dodd.

1966   ***The Mystery of 22 East*** by Leon Ware. Westminster.

1967   ***Sinbad and Me*** by Kin Platt. Chilton.

1968   ***Signpost of Terror*** by Gretchen Sprague. Dodd.

1969   ***The House of Dies Drear*** by Virginia Hamilton. Macmillan.

1970   ***Danger at Black Dyke*** by Winifred Finlay. Phillips.

1971   ***The Intruder*** by John Rowe Townsend. Lippincott.

1972   ***Night Fall*** by Joan Aiken. Holt.

1973   ***Deathwatch*** by Robb White. Doubleday.

1974   ***The Long Black Coat*** by Jay Bennett. Delacorte.

1975   ***The Dangling Witness*** by Jay Bennett. Delacorte.

1976   ***Z for Zachariah*** by Robert C. O'Brien. Atheneum.

1977   ***Are You in the House Alone?*** by Richard Peck. Viking.

1978   ***A Really Weird Summer*** by Eloise Jarvis McGraw. Atheneum.

1979   ***Alone in Wolf Hollow*** by Dana Brookins. Clarion.

1980   ***The Kidnapping of Christina Lattimore*** by Joan Lowery Nixon. Harcourt.

1981   ***The Seance*** by Joan Lowery Nixon. Harcourt.

1982   ***Taking Terri Mueller*** by Norma Fox Mazer. Avon.

1983 *The Murder of Hound Dog Bates* by Robbie Branscum. Viking.

1984 *The Callender Papers* by Cynthia Voigt. Atheneum.

1985 *Night Cry* by Phyllis Reynolds Naylor. Atheneum.

1986 *The Sandman's Eyes* by Patricia Windsor. Delacorte.

1987 *Other Side of Dark* by Joan Lowery Nixon. Delacorte.

1988 *Lucy Forever and Miss Rosetree, Shrinks* by Susan Shreve. Holt.

1989 *Megan's Island* by Willo Davis Roberts. Atheneum.

1990 No award

1991 *Stonewords* by Pam Conrad. Harper.

Scott O'Dell Award for Historical Fiction

This award, donated by the author Scott O'Dell and administered by the Bulletin of the Center of Children's Books, is given to the author of a distinguished work of historical fiction for children or young adults set in the New World and published in English by a U.S. publisher.

1984 *The Sign of the Beaver* by Elizabeth George Speare. Houghton.

1985 *The Fighting Ground* by Avi (Wortis). Harper.

1986 *Sarah, Plain and Tall* by Patricia MacLachlan. Harper.

1987 *Streams to the River, River to the Sea: A Novel of Sacagawea* by Scott O'Dell. Houghton.

1988 *Charlie Skedaddle* by Patricia Beatty. Morrow.

1989 *The Honorable Prison* by Lyll Becerra de Jenkins. Lodestar.

1990 *Shades of Gray* by Carolyn Reeder. Macmillan.

1991 *A Time of Troubles* by Pieter van Raven. Scribner's.

1992 *Stepping on the Cracks* by Mary Downing Hahn. Clarion.

Orbis Pictus Award

This award, sponsored by NCTE's Committee on Using Nonfiction in the Elementary Language Arts Classroom, is given to an author in recognition of excellence in writing of nonfiction for children published in the United States in the preceding year.

1990 *The Great Little Madison* by Jean Fritz. Putnam.

Honor Books:

The Great American Gold Rush by Rhoda Blumberg. Bradbury.

The News About Dinosaurs by Patricia Lauber. Bradbury.

1991 *Franklin Delano Roosevelt* by Russell Freedman. Clarion.

Honor Books:

Arctic Memories by Normee Ekoomiak. Holt.

Seeing Earth from Space by Patricia Lauber. Orchard.

Phoenix Award

This award, sponsored by the Children's Literature Association, is given to the author of a book first published 20 years earlier. The book must have been originally published in English and cannot have been the recipient of a major children's book award.

1985 *Mark of the Horse Lord* by Rosemary Sutcliff. Walck.

1986 *Queenie Peavy* by Robert Burch. Viking.

1987 *Smith* by Leon Garfield. Constable.

1988 *The Rider and His Horse* by Eric Christian Haugaard. Houghton.

1989 *The Night Watchman* by Helen Cresswell. Macmillan.

1990 *Enchantress from the Stars* by Sylvia Louise Engdahl. Macmillan.

1991 *A Long Way from Verona* by Jane Gardam. Macmillan.

Other Notable Book Exhibitions and Awards

Biennale of Illustrations Bratislava

This biannual international exposition of books was begun in 1967 and is held in Bratislava, Czechoslovakia. A Grand Prix and five honor book awards are given to children's books for excellence in illustration.

American Institute of Graphic Arts Book Show

This annual book show features approximately 100 books, both children's and adult, selected for excellence in design and manufacture. Lists of books selected each year can be found in *AIGA Graphic Design USA* (Watson-Guptil).

New York Times Best Illustrated Children's Books of the Year

Sponsored by *The New York Times*, this list of 10 books appears annually in the *Times*. A three-member panel of experts chooses the books.

International Reading Association Children's Book Award

Sponsored by the Institute for Reading Research and administered by the International Reading Association, this international award is given annually to an author for a first or second book that shows unusual promise in the children's book field.

International Board on Books for Young People Honor List

Sponsored by the International Board on Books for Young People (IBBY), this biannual list is composed of three books (one for text, one for illustration, and one for translation) from each IBBY National Section to represent the best in children's literature published in that country in the past two years. The books selected are recommended as suitable for publication worldwide.

State Children's Choice Award Programs

ARIZONA: "Arizona Young Readers Award," founded 1977. (Grades K–4)

ARKANSAS: "Charlie May Simon Children's Book Award," founded 1970. (Grades 4–6)

CALIFORNIA: "California Young Reader Medals," founded 1975. (Four divisions: primary, intermediate, junior high, senior high)

COLORADO: "Colorado Children's Book Award," founded 1976. (Elementary grades); "Blue Spruce Award," founded 1985. (YA)

FLORIDA: "Florida Reading Association Children's Book Award," founded 1987. (Grades K–2); "Sunshine State Young Reader's Award," founded 1984. (Grades 3–8)

GEORGIA: "Georgia Children's Book Award," founded 1969. (Grades 4–8); "Georgia Children's Picture Storybook Award," founded 1976. (Grades K–3)

HAWAII: "Nene Award," founded 1964. (Grades 4–6)

ILLINOIS: "Rebecca Caudill Young Readers' Book Award," founded 1988. (Grades 4–8)

INDIANA: "Young Hoosier Award," founded 1975. (Two divisions: Grades 4–6, Grades 6–8)

IOWA: "Iowa Children's Choice Award" founded 1980. (Grades 3–6); "Iowa Teen Award," founded 1985. (Grades 6–9)

KANSAS: "William Allen White Children's Book Award," founded 1953. (Grades 4–8)

KENTUCKY: "Kentucky Bluegrass Award," founded 1983. (Division one, Grades K–3; Division two, Grades 4–8)

MARYLAND: "Maryland Children's Book Award," founded 1988. (Grades 3–6)

MASSACHUSETTS: "Massachusetts Children's Book Award," founded 1976. (Grades 4–6)

MICHIGAN: "Michigan Young Readers' Awards," founded 1980.

MINNESOTA: "Maud Hart Lovelace Book Award," founded 1979. (Grades 3–8)

MISSOURI: "Mark Twain Award," founded 1971. (Grades K–8)

NEBRASKA: "Golden Sower Award for Fiction," founded 1981. (Grades 4–6); "Golden Sower Award for Picture Book," founded 1983. (Grades K–3)

NEW HAMPSHIRE: "Great Stone Face Award," founded 1980. (Grades 4–6)

NEW JERSEY: "Garden State Children's Book Awards," founded 1977. (Three divisions: Easy to Read, Younger Fiction, Younger Nonfiction)

NEW MEXICO: "Land of Enchantment Book Award," founded 1981. (Grades 4–8)

NEVADA: "Nevada Young Readers' Award," founded 1988. (Three divisions: Grades K–3, 4–6, YA)

NORTH DAKOTA: "Flicker Tale Children's Book Award,"founded 1978. (Two categories: picture book and intermediate book)

OHIO: "Buckeye Children's Book Awards," founded 1982. (Three divisions: Grades K–2, 3–5, 6–8)

OKLAHOMA: "Sequoyah Children's Book Award," founded 1959. (Grades 3–6); "Sequoyah Young Adult Book Award," founded 1988. (Grades 7–9)

PACIFIC NORTHWEST: (Alaska; Alberta, Canada; British Columbia, Canada; Idaho; Montana; Oregon; Washington) "Pacific Northwest Young Reader's Choice Award," founded 1940. (Grades 4–8)

PENNSYLVANIA: "Keystone to Reading Book Award," founded 1984.

SOUTH CAROLINA: "South Carolina Children's Book Award," founded 1976. (Grades 4–8); "South Carolina Young Adult Book Award," founded 1980. (Grades 9–12)

SOUTH DOKOTA: "Prairie Pasque Children's Book Award," founded 1987. (Grades 4–6)

TENNESSEE: "Volunteer State Book Award," founded 1979. (Four divisions: Grades K–3, 4–6, 7–9, 10–12)

TEXAS: "The Texas Bluebonnet Award," founded 1979. (Grades 3–6)

UTAH: "Utah Children's Book Award," founded 1980. (Grades 3–6)

VERMONT: "Dorothy Canfield Fisher Children's Book Award," founded 1957. (Grades 4–8)

VIRGINIA: "Young Reader Award of the State of Virginia," founded 1981. (Four divisions: Grades Ps–3, 4–6, 7–9, 10–12)

WASHINGTON: "Washington Children's Choice Picture Book Award," founded 1982. (Grades K–3)

WEST VIRGINIA: "West Virginia Children's Book Award" founded 1984. (Grades 3–6)

WISCONSIN: "Golden Archer Award," founded 1974. (Grades 4–8); "Little Archer Award," founded 1976. (Grades K–3)

WYOMING: "Indian Paintbrush Book Award," founded 1986. (Grades 4–6); "Soaring Eagle Young Adult Book Award," founded 1988. (Two divisions: Grades 7–9, Grades 10–12)

Holiday Books

General

Alexander, Sue. *America's Own Holidays*. Illustrated by Leslie Morrill. Translated into Spanish by Sandra Martin Arnold. Watts, 1988.

Burnett, Bernice. *Holidays*. Watts, 1983.

Cazet, Denys. *December 24th*. Bradbury, 1986.

Devlin, Wende, and Harry Devlin. *Cranberry Birthday*. Four Winds, 1988. (Others in the *Cranberryport* series: *Cranberry Thanksgiving; Cranberry Halloween; Cranberry Valentine; Cranberry Christmas*.)

Dunkling, Leslie. *A Dictionary of Days*. Facts on File, 1988.

Gibbons, Gail. *Happy Birthday!* Holiday, 1986.

Gregory, Ruth W. *Anniversaries and Holidays* (4th ed.). American Library Association, 1983.

Grigoli, Valorie. *Patriotic Holidays and Celebrations*. Watts, 1985.

Hautzig, Esther. *Holiday Treats*. Illustrated by Yaro-slava. Macmillan, 1983.

Laird, Elizabeth. *Happy Birthday! A Book of Birthday Celebrations*. Illustrated by Satomi Ichikawa. Philomel, 1988.

Larrick, Nancy. *More Poetry for Holidays*. Illustrated by Harold Berson. Garrard, 1973.

Livingston, Myra Cohn, compiler. *Birthday Poems*. Illustrated by Margot Tomes. Holiday, 1989.

———. *Celebrations*. Illustrated by Leonard Everett Fisher. Holiday, 1985.

———. *Poems for Jewish Holidays*. Holiday, 1986.

Manning-Sanders, Ruth, compiler. *Festivals*. Illustrated by Raymond Briggs. Dutton, 1973.

Perl, Lila. *Piñatas and Paper Flowers; Holidays of the Americas in English and Spanish*. Illustrated by Victoria de Larrea. Clarion, 1983.

Van Straalen, Alice. *The Book of Holidays Around the World*. Dutton, 1986.

Fall Holidays

Adams, Adrienne. *A Halloween Happening*. Macmillan, 1981.

Alcott, Louisa May. *An Old-Fashioned Thanksgiving*. Illustrated by Michael McCurdy. Holiday, 1989.

Anderson, Joan. *First Thanksgiving Feast*. Photos by George Ancona. Clarion, 1984.

Baldwin, Margaret. *Thanksgiving*. Watts, 1983.

Barkin, Carol. *Scary Halloween Costume Book*. Lothrop, 1983.

Barkin, Carol, and Elizabeth James. *Happy Thanksgiving!* Illustrated by Giora Carmi. Lothrop, 1987.

Brown, Marc. *Arthur's Thanksgiving*. Little, Brown, 1984.

Bunting, Eve. *Scary, Scary Halloween*. Illustrated by Jan Brett. Ticknor & Fields, 1986.

Fritz, Jean. *Where Do You Think You Are Going, Christopher Columbus?* Putnam, 1980.

Gibbons, Gail. *Halloween*. Holiday, 1984.

————. *Thanksgiving Day*. Holiday, 1985.

Hoban, Lillian. *Arthur's Halloween Costume*. Harper, 1984.

Kroll, Steven. *Oh, What a Thanksgiving!* Illustrated by S. D. Schindler. Scholastic, 1988.

————. *One Tough Turkey*. Illustrated by John Wallner. Holiday, 1982.

Livingston, Myra Cohn, compiler. *Halloween Poems*. Illustrated by Stephen Gammell. Holiday, 1989.

————. *Thanksgiving Poems*. Illustrated by Stephen Gammell. Holiday, 1985.

Merriam, Eve. *Halloween ABC*. Illustrated by Lane Smith. Macmillan, 1987.

Penner, Lucille Recht. *The Thanksgiving Book*. Hastings, 1986.

Prelutsky, Jack. *It's Thanksgiving*. Illustrated by Marylin Hafner. Greenwillow, 1982.

Rose, David. *It Hardly Seems Like Halloween*. Lothrop, 1983.

Sandak, Cass R. *Columbus Day*. Crestwood, 1990.

Titherington, Jeanne. *Pumpkin Pumpkin*. Greenwillow, 1986.

Yolen, Jane. *Best Witches: Poems for Halloween*. Illustrated by Elise Primavera. Putnam, 1989.

Winter Holidays

Adams, Adrienne. *The Great Valentine's Day Balloon Race*. Macmillan, 1987.

Adler, David A. *Happy Hanukkah Rebus*. Illustrated by Jan Palmer. Viking, 1989.

————. *Martin Luther King, Jr.: Free at Last*. Illustrated by Robert Casilla. Holiday, 1986.

————. *A Picture Book of Hanukkah*. Holiday, 1985.

————. *A Picture Book of Martin Luther King, Jr.* Illustrated by Robert Casilla. Holiday, 1989.

Aliki. *Christmas Tree Memories*. HarperCollins, 1991.

Anderson, Joan. *Christmas on the Prairie*. Photos by George Ancona. Ticknor & Fields, 1985.

Barkin, Carol, and Elizabeth James. *Happy Valentine's Day!* Illustrated by Martha Weston. Lothrop, 1988.

Barth, Edna. *Shamrocks, Harps, and Shillelaghs: The Story of the Saint Patrick's Day Symbols*. Illustrated by Ursula Arndt. Clarion, 1977.

Bauer, Caroline Feller. *Halloween: Stories and Poems*. Illustrated by Peter Sis. Lippincott, 1989.

Bemelmans, Ludwig. *Madeline's Christmas*. Viking, 1985.

Brett, Jan. *Twelve Days of Christmas*. Dodd, 1986.

————. *The Wild Christmas Reindeer*. Putnam, 1990.

Bröger, Achim, adapter. *The Santa Clauses*. Illustrated by Ute Krause. Dial, 1986.

Brown, Tricia. *Chinese New Year*. Photos by Fran Ortiz. Holt, 1987.

Bulla, Clyde R. *The Christmas Coat*. Illustrated by Sylvie Wickstrom. Knopf, 1989.

Bunting, Eve. *St. Patrick's Day in the Morning*. Illustrated by Jan Brett. Clarion, 1980.

Capote, Truman. *A Christmas Memory*. Illustrated by Beth Peck. Knopf, 1989.

Carlson, Nancy. *Mysterious Valentine*. Carolrhoda, 1985.

Caudill, Rebecca. *A Certain Small Shepherd*. Holt, 1965.

Cazet, Denys. *Christmas Moon*. Bradbury, 1984.

Chaikim, Miriam. *Light the Candle: The Story and Meaning of Hanukkah*. Houghton, 1981.

Clifton, Lucille. *Everett Anderson's Christmas Coming*. Illustrated by Evaline Ness. Holt, 1971.

Collington, Peter. *On Christmas Eve*. Knopf, 1990.

Croll, Carolyn. *The Little Snowgirl*. Putnam, 1989.

Cummings, E. E. *Little Tree*. Illustrated by Deborah Kogan Ray. Crown, 1987.

Day, Alexandra. *Carl's Christmas*. Farrar, 1990.

Delacre, Lulu. *Las Navidades: Popular Christmas Songs from Latin America*. Scholastic, 1990.

dePaola, Tomie. *Family Christmas Tree Book*. Holiday, 1984.

————. *Merry Christmas, Strega Nona*. Harcourt, 1986.

————. *My First Chanukkah*. Putnam, 1989.

Donnelly, Liza. *Dinosaur's Christmas*. Scholastic, 1991.

Freedman, Russell. *Lincoln: A Photobiography*. Clarion, 1987.

Gibbons, Gail. *Christmas Time*. Holiday, 1985.

Giblin, James. *The Truth about Santa Claus*. Crowell, 1985.

Godden, Rumer. *The Story of Holly and Ivy*. Illustrated by Barbara Cooney. Viking, 1985.

Goldin, Barbara Diamond. *Just Enough Is Plenty: A Hanukkah Tale*. Viking, 1988.

————. *The World's Birthday: A Rosh Hashanah Story*. Harcourt, 1990.

Greene, Ellin. *The Legend of the Christmas Rose*. Illustrated by Charles Mikolaycak. Holiday, 1990.

Hamilton, Virginia. *The Bells of Christmas*. Illustrated by Lambert Davis. Harcourt, 1989.

Harrison, Michael, editor. *The Oxford Book of Christmas Poems*. Illustrated by Christopher Stuart-Clark. Oxford, 1984.

Hayes, Sarah. *Happy Christmas, Gemma*. Illustrated by Jan Ormerod. Lothrop, 1986.

Hirsh, Marilyn. *I Love Hanukkah*. Holiday, 1984.

Holabird, Katherine. *Angelina's Christmas*. Illustrated by Helen Craig. Crown, 1985.

Hopkins, Lee Bennett, editor. *Good Morning to You, Valentine*. Illustrated by Tomie dePaola. Harcourt, 1976.

Houston, Gloria. *The Year of the Perfect Christmas Tree: An Appalachian Story*. Illustrated by Barbara Cooney. Dial, 1988.

Hunt, Roderick. *The Oxford Christmas Book for Children*. Oxford, 1983.

Keats, Ezra Jack. *The Little Drummer Boy*. Words and music by Katherine Davis, Henry Onerati, and Harry Simeone. Macmillan, 1972.

Kimmel, Eric A. *The Chanukkah Guest*. Illustrated by Gloria Carmi. Holiday, 1990.

————. *Days of Awe: Stories for Rosh Hashanah and Yom Kippur*. Illustrated by Erika Weihs. Viking, 1991.

————. *Herschel and the Hanukkah Goblins*. Illustrated by Trina Schart Hyman. Holiday, 1989.

Kroll, Steven. *Santa's Crash-Bang Christmas*. Illustrated by Tomie dePaola. Holiday, 1977.

Lagerlöf, Selma. *The Legend of the Christmas Rose*. Retold by Ellin Greene. Illustrated by Charles Mikolaycak. Holiday, 1990.

Langstaff, John, editor. *What a Morning! The Christmas Story in Black Spirituals*. Illustrated by Ashley Bryan. McElderry, 1987.

Livingston, Myra Cohn, compiler. *Christmas Poems*. Illustrated by Trina Schart Hyman. Holiday, 1984.

————. *New Year's Poems*. Illustrated by Margot Tomes. Holiday, 1987.

————. *Valentine Poems*. Illustrated by Patience Brewster. Holiday, 1987.

Lubin, Leonard B. *Christmas Gift-Bringers*. Lothrop, 1989.

Manushkin, Fran. *Latkes and Applesauce: A Hanukkah Story*. Scholastic, 1990.

Merriam, Eve. *The Christmas Box*. Illustrated by David Small. Morrow, 1985.

Moeri, Louise. *Star Mother's Youngest Child*. Illustrated by Trina Schart Hyman. Houghton, 1975.

Moore, Clement Clarke. *The Night Before Christmas*. Illustrated by Wendy Watson. Clarion, 1990.

Munro, Roxie. *Christmastime in New York City*. Dodd, 1987.

Murphy, Shirley R. *The Song of the Christmas Mouse*. Illustrated by Donna Diamond. Harper, 1990.

Niland, Kilmeny. *A Bellbird in a Flame Tree*. Morrow/Tambourine, 1991.

Overton, Jenny. *The Thirteen Days of Christmas*. Illustrated by Joseph A. Smith. Greenwillow, 1987.

Parish, Peggy. *Merry Christmas, Amelia Bedelia*. Illustrated by Lynn Sweat. Greenwillow, 1986.

Pepper, Dennis, editor. *An Oxford Book of Christmas Stories*. Illustrated by Judy Brown and others. Oxford, 1987.

Polacco, Patricia. *Uncle Vova's Tree*. Philomel, 1989.

Prelutsky, Jack. *It's Valentine's Day*. Illustrated by Yossi Abolafia. Scholastic, 1983.

Robbins, Ruth. *Babouska and the Three Kings*. Illustrated by Nicolas Sidjakov. Parnassus, 1960.

Robinson, Barbara. *The Best Christmas Pageant Ever*. Illustrated by Judith G. Brown. Harper, 1972.

Rylant, Cynthia. *Children of Christmas: Stories for the Season.* Illustrated by S. D. Schindler. Orchard, 1987.

San Souci, Robert D. *The Christmas Ark.* Doubleday, 1991.

Sawyer, Ruth. *Joy to the World: Christmas Legends.* Illustrated by Trina Schart Hyman. Little, 1966.

Say, Allen. *Tree of Cranes.* Houghton, 1991.

Scheidl, Gerda Marie. *Four Candles for Simon.* Illustrated by Marcus Pfister. Translated from the German by Anthea Bell. North-South, 1987.

Seuss, Dr. *How the Grinch Stole Christmas.* Random, 1957.

Solotareff, Grégoire. *Noël's Christmas Secret.* Farrar, 1989.

Stevenson, James. *Night after Christmas.* Greenwillow, 1981.

Sussman, Susan. *Hanukkah: Eight Lights Around the World.* Illustrated by Judith Friedman. Whitman, 1988.

————. *There's No Such Thing as a Chanukkah Bush,* Sandy Goldstein. Whitman, 1983.

Trivas, Irene, reteller. *Emma's Christmas.* Orchard, 1988.

Van Allsburg, Chris. *Polar Express.* Houghton, 1985.

Vincent, Gabrielle. *Merry Christmas, Ernest and Celestine.* Greenwillow, 1984.

Walter, Mildred Pitts. *Have a Happy . . .* Illustrated by Carole Byard. Lothrop, 1989.

Waters, Kate, and Madeline Slovenz-Low. *Lion Dancer: Ernie Wan's Chinese New Year.* Photos by Martha Cooper. Scholastic, 1990.

Weil, Lisl. *Santa Claus Around the World.* Holiday, 1987.

Wells, Rosemary. *Max's Christmas.* Dial, 1986.

Wilson, Robina B. *Merry Christmas! Children at Christmastime Around the World.* Illustrated by Satomi Ichikawa. Putnam, 1983.

Spring Holidays

Adams, Adrienne. *The Easter Egg Artists.* Macmillan, 1981.

Berger, Gilda. *Easter and Other Spring Holidays.* Watts, 1983.

Gibbons, Gail. *Easter.* Holiday, 1989.

Greenfeld, Howard. *Passover.* Holt, 1978.

Houselander, Caryll. *Petook: An Easter Story.* Illustrated by Tomie dePaola. Holiday, 1988.

Livingston, Myra Cohn, compiler. *Poems for Mothers.* Holiday, 1988.

Milhous, Katherine. *The Egg Tree.* Macmillan, 1981.

Sharmat, Marjorie. *Hooray for Father's Day!* Holiday, 1987.

Summer Holidays

Day, Alexandra. *Frank and Ernest Play Ball.* Scholastic, 1990.

Giblin, James Cross. *Fireworks, Picnics, and Flags: The Story of the Fourth of July Symbols.* Clarion, 1983.

Joose, Barbara. *Fourth of July.* Knopf, 1985.

Keller, Holly. *Henry's Fourth of July.* Greenwillow, 1985.

Thayer, Ernest. *Casey at the Bat.* Illustrated by Wallace Tripp. Putnam, 1980.

Williams, Vera B. *Stringbean's Trip to the Shining Sea.* Illustrated by the author and Jennifer Williams. Greenwillow, 1988.

Predictable Books

Ahlberg, Janet and Allan. *Each Peach Pear Plum.* Scholastic, 1978.

Anholt, Catherine and Laurence. *What I Like.* Putnam, 1991.

Asch, Frank. *Monkey Face.* Parent's Magazine Press, 1977.

Baer, Gene. *Thump Thump Rat A Tat Tat.* Illustrated by Lois Ehlert. Harper, 1989.

Barrett, Judi. *Animals Should Definitely Not Act Like People.* Atheneum, 1980.

———. *Animals Should Definitely Not Wear Clothing.* Atheneum, 1977.

Brown, Margaret Wise. *Goodnight Moon.* Harper, 1947.

Brown, Ruth. *A Dark, Dark Tale.* Dial, 1981.

Burningham, John. *Mr. Gumpy's Outing.* Holt, 1970.

———. *Would You Rather . . .* Crowell, 1978.

Burton, Marilie. *Tail, Toes, Eyes, Ears, Nose.* Harper, 1988.

Butler, Dorothy. *My Brown Bear Barney.* Illustrated by Elizabeth Fuller. Greenwillow, 1988.

Carle, Eric. *The Grouchy Ladybug.* Crowell, 1977.

———. *The Very Busy Spider.* Philomel, 1985.

———. *The Very Hungry Caterpillar.* Collins, 1969.

Charlip, Remy. *Fortunately.* Parents' Magazine Press, 1964.

Cherry, Lynne. *Who's Sick Today.* Dutton, 1988.

Cole, Brock. *The King at the Door.* Doubleday, 1979.

Conover, Chris. *Six Little Ducks.* Crowell, 1976.

Cuyler, Margery. *That's Good, That's Bad.* Illustrated by David Catrow. Holt, 1991.

dePaola, Tomie. *The Comic Adventures of Old Mother Hubbard and Her Dog.* Harcourt, 1981.

de Regniers, Beatrice Schenk. *May I Bring a Friend?* Atheneum, 1972.

Demers, Jan. *What Do You Do with a . . . ?* Willowisp, 1985.

Deming, A.G. *Who Is Tapping at My Window?* Illustrated by Monica Wellington. Dutton, 1988.

Emberley, Barbara. *One Wide River to Cross.* Prentice-Hall, 1966.

Emberley, Barbara and Ed. *Drummer Hoff.* Prentice-Hall, 1967.

Evans, Katie. *Hunky Dory Ate It.* Illustrated by Janet Morgan Stoeke. Dutton, 1992.

Fox, Mem. *Shoes from Grandpa.* Orchard, 1990.

Gág Wanda. *Millions of Cats.* Coward-McCann, 1928.

Galdone, Paul. *The Gingerbread Boy.* Seabury, 1975.

———. *Henny Penny.* Scholastic, 1968.

———. *The Little Red Hen.* Scholastic, 1973.

———. *The Teeny, Tiny Woman.* Houghton, 1984.

Gerstein, Mordicai. *Roll Over!* Crown, 1984.

Goennel, Heidi. *My Day.* Little, Brown, 1988.

———. *My Dog.* Orchard, 1990.

Greely, Valerie. *White Is the Moon.* Macmillan, 1990.

Guarino, Deborah. *Is Your Mama a Llama?* Illustrated by Steven Kellogg. Scholastic, 1989.

Hayes, Sarah. *The Grumpalump.* Clarion, 1990.

Hellen, Nancy. *The Bus Stop.* Orchard, 1990.

———. *Old MacDonald Had a Farm.* Orchard, 1990.

Hennessy, B. G. *Jake Baked the Cake*. Illustrated by Mary Morgan. Viking, 1990.

Higgins, Don. *Papa's Going to Buy Me a Mockingbird*. Seabury, 1968.

Hill, Eric. *Where's Spot?* Putnam's, 1980.

Hoberman, Mary Ann. *A House Is a House for Me*. Viking, 1978.

Hogrogian, Nonny. *One Fine Day*. Macmillan, 1971.

Hutchins, Pat. *Rosie's Walk*. Macmillan, 1968.

———. *Titch*. Collier, 1971.

———. *What Shall We Play?* Greenwillow, 1990.

Joslin, Sesyle. *What Do You Say, Dear?* Addison-Wesley, 1958.

Kalan, Robert. *Jump, Frog, Jump*. Illustrated by Byron Barton. Mulberry, 1981.

Kochenmeister, Cherryl. *On Monday, When It Rained*. Photos by Tom Berthiaume. Houghton, 1989.

Kraus, Robert. *Leo the Late Bloomer*. Windmill, 1971.

Krauss, Ruth. *A Hole Is to Dig*. Harper, 1952.

Lobel, Arnold. *On Market Street*. Greenwillow, 1981.

Lyon, George Ella. *The Outside Inn*. Orchard, 1991.

McMillan, Bruce. *Play Day: A Book of Terse Verse*. Holiday, 1991.

Martin, Bill, Jr. *Brown Bear, Brown Bear*. Holt, 1970.

———. *Chicka Chicka Boom Boom*. Illustrated by Lois Ehlert. Simon & Schuster, 1989.

———. *Fire! Fire! Said Mrs. McGuire*. Holt, 1970.

———. *Polar Bear, Polar Bear, What Do You Hear?* Illustrated by Eric Carle. Holt, 1990.

Numeroff, Laura Joffe. *If You Give a Mouse a Cookie*. Harper, 1985.

Pizer, Abigail. *It's A Perfect Day*. Lippincott, 1990.

Polushkin, Maria. *Mother, Mother, I Want Another*. Crown, 1978.

Roe, Eileen. *All I Am*. Illustrated by Helen Cogancherry. Bradbury, 1990.

Rosen, Michael, reteller. *We're Going on a Bear Hunt*. Illustrated by Helen Oxenbury. McElderry, 1989.

Sawyer, Ruth. *Journey Cake, Ho!* Viking, 1953.

Seuss, Dr. *Green Eggs and Ham*. Random, 1960.

Shapiro, Arnold. *Who Says That?* Illustrated by Monica Wellington. Dutton, 1991.

Simon, Mina and Howard. *If You Were an Eel, How Would You Feel?* Follett, 1963.

Tafuri, Nancy. *Spots, Feathers, and Curly Tails*. Greenwillow, 1988.

Watanabe, Shigeo. *How Do I Put It On?* Collins, 1977.

Weiss, Nicki. *Where Does the Brown Bear Go?* Greenwillow, 1989.

Wells, Rosemary. *A Lion for Lewis*. Dial, 1982.

———. *Noisy Nora*. Dial, 1973.

Winter, Jeanette. *Hush Little Baby*. Pantheon, 1984.

Wood, Audrey. *The Napping House*. Harcourt, 1984.

Zemach, Harve. *The Judge*. Farrar, 1969.

Zemach, Margot. *Hush, Little Baby*. Dutton, 1976.

Zolotow, Charlotte. *If It Weren't for You*. Harper, 1966.

Transitional Books

Adler, David A. *Cam Jansen and the Mystery of the Stolen Diamonds*. Illustrated by Susanna Natti. Viking, 1980. (Others in the series: *Cam Jansen and the Mystery of the Dinosaur Bones*, 1983; *Cam Jansen and the Mystery of the Monster*, 1986.)

Aiken, Joan. *Arabel and Mortimer*. Illustrated by Quentin Blake. Doubleday, 1981.

———. *Mortimer Says Nothing*. Illustrated by Quentin Blake. Doubleday, 1981.

———. *Mortimer's Cross*. Illustrated by Quentin Blake. Harper, 1983.

Bang, Molly G. *Wiley and the Hairy Man*. Macmillan, 1976.

Baylor, Byrd. *I'm in Charge of Celebrations*. Illustrated by Peter Parnall. Charles Scribner, 1986.

Bennett, Lee. *I Loved Rose Ann*. Illustrated by Ingrid Fetz. Knopf, 1976.

Birdsong, Tom. *I'm Going to Be Famous*. Holiday House, 1986.

Bulla, Clyde Robert. *Shoeshine Girl*. Illustrated by Leigh Grant. Crowell, 1975.

Burningham, John. *Around the World in Eighty Days*. Merimac, 1979.

Byars, Betsy. *Beans on the Roof*. Illustrated by Melodye Rosales. Delacorte, 1988.

Cameron, Ann. *Stories Julian Tells*. Illustrated by Ann Strugnell. Knopf, 1984. (Others in the series: *More Stories Julian Tells*, 1986; *Julian's Glorious Summer*, 1987; *Julian, Dream Doctor*, 1990.)

Christian, Mary Blount. *The Phantom of the Operetta*. Illustrated by Kathleen Collins Howell. Dutton, 1986.

———. *Sebastian [Super Sleuth] and the Baffling Bigfoot*. Illustrated by Lisa McCue. Macmillan, 1990.

Clifford, Eth. *Harvey's Horrible Snake Disaster*. Houghton, 1986. (Others in the series: *Harvey's Marvelous Monkey Mystery*, 1987.)

Coerr, Eleanor. *The Josefina Story Quilt*. Illustrated by Bruce Degen. Harper, 1986.

Cohen, Barbara. *Gooseberries to Oranges*. Illustrated by Beverly Brodsky. Lothrop, 1982.

———. *Molly's Pilgrim*. Illustrated by Michael Deraney. Lothrop, 1983.

Conford, Ellen. *A Case for Jenny Archer*. Illustrated by Diane Palmisciano. Little, Brown, 1988. (Others in the series: *A Job for Jenny Archer*, 1988.)

Cunningham, Julia. *Oaf*. Illustrated by Peter Sis. Knopf, 1986.

Delton, Judy. *Grumpy Pumpkins*. Illustrated by Alan Tiegreen, 1988. (Others in the *Pee Wee Scouts* series: *Pee Wee Christmas*, 1988; *Cookies and Crutches; Camp Ghost-Away; Lucky Dog Days*.)

Duder, Tessa. *Jellybean*. Viking, 1986.

Edwards, Dorothy. *The Naughty Little Sister Storybook*. Illustrated by Shirley Hughes. Clarion, 1990.

Esbensen, Barbara Juster. *Words with Wrinkled Knees: Animal Poems*. Illustrated by John Stadler. Crowell, 1986.

Fleischman, Sid. *The Hey Hey Man*. Illustrated by Nadine Bernard Westcott. Little, Brown, 1979.

———. *McBroom and the Big Wind*. Illustrated by Walter Lorraine. Little, Brown, 1967. (Others in the series: *McBroom's Ear,* 1969; *McBroom's Zoo,* 1971.)

Foley, Patricia. *John and the Fiddler*. Illustrated by Marcia Sewall. Harper, 1990.

Galbraith, Kathryn O. *Roommates*. Illustrated by Mark Graham. Macmillan, 1990.

———. *Roommates and Rachel*. Illustrated by Mark Graham. Macmillan, 1991.

Gallaz, Christophe, and Roberto Innocenti. *Rose Blanche*. Translated by Martha Coventry and Richard Graglia. Illustrated by Roberto Innocenti. Creative Education, 1985.

Gardiner, John Reynolds. *General Butterfingers*. Illustrated by Cat Bowman Smith. Houghton, 1986.

Giff, Patricia Reilly. *Lazy Lions, Lucky Lambs*. Dell, 1985. (Others in the series: *The Candy Corn Contest,* Delacorte, 1986; *Mother Jackson Meets the Wall,* Doubleday, 1990.)

———. *The Winter Worm Business*. Dell, 1981. (See others in the Casey Valentine series.)

Greene, Carol. *Robin Hill*. Illustrated by Ellen Eagle. Harper, 1986.

Greenfield, Eloise. *Grandmama's Joy*. Illustrated by Carole Byard. Philomel, 1980.

Griffith, Helen V. *Caitlin's Holiday*. Illustrated by Susan Condie Lamb. Greenwillow, 1990.

Haugaard, Erik. *A Boy's Will*. Illustrated by Troy Howell. Houghton, 1983.

Henkes, Kevin. *Margaret & Taylor*. Greenwillow, 1984.

Herzig, Alison Cragin, and Jane Lawrence Mali. *Thaddeus*. Illustrated by Steven Gammell. Little, Brown, 1986.

Hiser, Constance. *Ghosts in Fourth Grade*. Illustrated by Cat Bowman Smith. Holiday, 1991.

Holland, Isabelle. *Henry and Grudge*. Illustrated by Liisa Chauncy Guida. Walker, 1986.

Horner, John R., and James Gorman. *Maia: A Dinosaur Grows Up*. Illustrated by Doug Henderson. Running Press, 1987.

Houston, James. *The Falcon Bow: An Arctic Legend*. Macmillan, 1986.

Hughes, Shirley. *The Big Alfie and Annie Rose Storybook*. Lothrop, 1989.

Hurwitz, Johanna. *Busybody Nora*. Illustrated by Susan Jeschke. Morrow, 1976.

———. *Russell and Elisa*. Illustrated by Lillian Hoban. Morrow, 1989.

Johansen, H. *7 × 7 Tales of a Sevensleeper*. Illustrated by Käthi Bhend. Translated by Christopher Franschelli. Dutton, 1989.

Jukes, Mavis. *Blackberries in the Dark*. Illustrated by Thomas B. Allen. Knopf, 1985.

Kamen, Gloria. *Kipling: Storyteller of East and West*. Atheneum, 1985.

King-Smith, Dick. *Sophie's Snail*. Illustrated by Claire Minter-Kemp. Delacorte, 1989.

Kinsey-Warnock, Natalie. *The Canada Geese Quilt*. Illustrated by Leslie W. Bowman. Dutton, 1989.

Kline, Susy. *Herbie Jones and the Monster Ball*. Illustrated by Richard Williams. Putnam, 1989.

———. *Horrible Harry's Secret*. Illustrated by Frank Remkiewicz. Viking, 1990.

Korschunow, Irina. *Adam Draws Himself a Dragon*. Translated from German by James Skofield. Illustrated by Mary Rahn. Harper, 1987.

———. *Small Fur*. Translated from German by James Skofield. Harper, 1988.

Kurelek, William, and Margaret S. Engelhart. *They Sought A New World: The Story of European Immigration to North America*. Tundra Books, 1985.

Lindgren, Astrid. *The Ghost of Skinny Jack*. Illustrated by Ilon Wikland. Viking, 1988.

Lydon, Kerry Raines. *A Birthday for Blue*. Illustrated by Michael Hays. Albert Whitman, 1989.

MacLachlan, Patricia. *Sarah, Plain and Tall*. Harper, 1985.

Maril, Nadja. *Me, Molly Midnight: The Artist's Cat*. Illustrated by Herman Maril. Stemmer House, 1977.

———. *Runaway Molly Midnight: The Artist's Cat*. Illustrated by Herman Maril. Stemmer House, 1980.

Marshall, James. *Rats on the Roof and Other Stories*. Dial, 1991.

Maruki, Toshi. *Hiroshima No Pika*. Lothrop, 1982.

Mathis, Sharon Bell. *The Hundred Penny Box.* Illustrated by Leo and Diane Dillon. Viking, 1975.

Matsuno, Masako. *A Pair of Red Clogs.* Illustrated by Kazue Mizumura. Collins, 1960.

Mattingly, Christobel. *Duck Boy.* Illustrated by Patricia Mullins. Atheneum, 1986.

———. *The Miracle Tree.* Illustrated by Marianne Yamaguchi. Harcourt, 1986.

McCutcheon, Elsie. *The Rat War.* Farrar, 1986.

Milne, A. A. *When We Were Very Young.* Illustrated by Ernest H. Shepard. Dutton, 1924.

Moskin, Marietta. *Day of the Blizzard.* Illustrated by Stephen Gammell. Coward, McCann, 1978.

Murphy, Shirley Rousseau. *The Song of the Christmas Mouse.* Illustrated by Donna Diamond. Harper, 1990.

Nabb, Magdalen. *Josie Smith.* Illustrated by Pirkko Vainio. McElderry Books, 1988.

O'Dell, Scott. *The Treasure of Topo-El-Bampo.* Illustrated by Lynd Ward. Houghton, 1972.

O'Neal, Zibby. *Grandma Moses: Painter of Rural America. (Women of Our Time series).* Illustrated by Donna Ruff. Paintings by Grandma Moses. Viking, 1986.

Parish, Peggy. *Amelia Bedelia Goes Camping.* Illustrated by Lynn Sweat. Greenwillow, 1985. (Others in the series: *Amelia Bedelia Helps Out; Amelia Bedelia.*)

Paton-Walsh, Jill. *Birdy and the Ghosties.* Illustrated by Alan Marks. Farrar, 1989.

Pearce, Philippa. *A Dog So Small.* Illustrated by Anthony Maitland. Viking, 1962.

Peck, Robert Newton. *Rabbits and Redcoats.* Illustrated by Laura Lydecker. Walker, 1976.

———. *Soup.* Knopf, 1974. (Others in the series: *Soup in the Saddle,* 1983; *Soup's Goat,* 1984; *Soup on Ice,* 1985.)

———. *Trig.* Illustrated by Pamela Johnson. Little, Brown, 1977.

Peretz, I. L. *The Seven Good Years and Other Stories.* Translated and adapted by Esther Hautzig. Illustrated by Deborah Kogan Ray. The Jewish Publication Society of America, 1984.

Pinkwater, Daniel M. *Jolly Roger: A Dog of Hoboken.* Lothrop, 1985.

Rabe, Berniece. *Margaret's Moves.* Illustrated by Julie Downing. Dutton, 1987.

Sharmat, Marjorie Weinman. *Chasing After Annie.* Illustrated by Marc Simont. Harper, 1981.

Shulevitz, Uri. *The Strange and Exciting Adventures of Jeremiah Hush.* Farrar, 1986.

Singer, Marilyn. *Where There's a Will, There's a Way.* Illustrated by Andrew Glass. Holt, 1986.

Smith, Janice Lee. *The Show-and-Tell War and Other Stories About Adam Joshua.* Illustrated by Dick Gackenbach. Harper, 1988. (Others in the series: *It's Not Easy Being George: Stories About Adam Joshua (And His Dog).* Harper, 1989.)

Sobol, Donald J. *Encyclopedia Brown Solves Them All.* Illustrated by Leonard Shortall, Scholastic, 1968. (Others in the series: *Encyclopedia Brown Tracks Them Down,* 1971; *Encyclopedia Brown's Book of Wacky Sports,* 1982; *Encyclopedia Brown Sets the Pace,* 1982.)

Steiner, Barbara. *Oliver Dibbs and The Dinosaur.* Illustrated by Eileen Christelow. Four Winds, 1986.

Sterman, Betsy and Samuel. *Too Much Magic.* Illustrated by Judy Glasser. Lippincott, 1987.

Stolz, Mary. *Belling the Tiger.* Illustrated by Beni Montressor. Harper, 1961.

———. *The Bully on Barkham Street.* Illustrated by Leonard Shortall. Harper, 1963.

———. *A Dog on Barkham Street.* Illustrated by Leonard Shortall. Harper, 1960.

———. *The Explorer on Barkham Street.* Illustrated by Emily A. McCully. Harper, 1985.

Taylor, Mildred D. *The Friendship.* Illustrated by Max Ginsburg. Dial, 1987.

Van De Wetering, Janwillem. *Hugh Pine and the Good Place.* Illustrated by Lynn Munsinger. Houghton, 1986.

Waddell, Martin. *Harriet and the Crocodiles.* Illustrated by Mark Burgess. Little, Brown, 1984.

Wallace-Brodeur, Ruth. *Stories from the Big Chair.* Illustrated by Diane de Groat. Macmillan, 1989.

Appendix E

Short Read-Alouds for Intermediate and Middle-Level Grades

Ages refer to approximate interest levels. YA = young adult readers.

Short Story Collections

Adams, Barbara Johnston. *Crime Mysteries*. Watts, 1988. Ages 11–YA.

Aiken, Joan. *Give Yourself a Fright: Thirteen Tales of the Supernatural*. Delacorte, 1989. Ages 11–YA.

———. *Past Eight O'Clock: Goodnight Stories*. Viking, 1987. Ages 8–11.

———. *Up the Chimney Down, and Other Stories*. Harper, 1985. Ages 10–14.

Alcock, Vivien. *Ghostly Companions: A Feast of Chilling Tales*. Delacorte, 1984. Ages 10–14.

Alexander, Lloyd. *The Town Cats, and Other Tales*. Dutton, 1977. Ages 8–11.

Babbitt, Natalie. *The Devil's Other Storybook*. Farrar, 1987. Ages 9–12.

———. *The Devil's Storybook*. Farrar, 1974. Ages 9–12.

Brooke, William J. *A Telling of the Tales: Five Stories*. Harper, 1990. Ages 9–12.

Brooks, Martha. *Paradise Café and Other Stories*. Little, Brown, 1990. Ages 12–YA.

Carlson, Lori M., and Cynthia Ventura, editors. *Where Angels Glide at Dawn: New Stories from Latin America*. Lippincott, 1990. Ages 10–14.

Carlson, Natalie Savage. *The Talking Cat, and Other Stories of French Canada*. Harper, 1952. Ages 8–11.

Carlstrom, Nancy White. *Light: Stories of a Small Kindness*. Illustrated by Desimini. Little, Brown, 1990. Ages 9–12.

Christian, Peggy. *The Old Coot*. Illustrated by Eileen Cristelow. Atheneum, 1991. Ages 8–11.

Conger, David, reteller. *Many Lands Many Stories: Asian Folktales.* Illustrated by Ruth Ra. Tuttle, 1987. Ages 9–14.

Coville, Bruce, editor. *Herds of Thunder, Manes of Gold: A Collection of Horse Stories and Poems.* Illustrated by Ted Lewin. Doubleday, 1990. Ages 9–YA.

Crutcher, Chris. *Athletic Shorts.* Greenwillow, 1991. Ages 12–YA.

d'Aulaire, Ingri, and Edgar Parin d'Aulaire. *Book of Greek Myths.* Doubleday, 1962. Ages 9–YA.

Drimmer, Frederick. *Born Different: The Amazing Stories of Some Very Special People.* Atheneum, 1988. Ages 11–14.

Durell, Ann, and Marilyn Sachs. *The Big Book for Peace.* Dutton, 1990. Ages 9–12.

Fleischman, Paul. *Coming-and-Going Men: Four Tales.* Harper, 1985. Ages 11–14.

———. *Graven Images: 3 Stories.* Harper, 1982. Ages 11-14.

Gallo, Donald R., editor. *Connections: Short Stories by Outstanding Writers for Young Adults.* Delacorte, 1989. Ages 12–YA.

Haas, Jessie. *The Sixth Sense and Other Stories.* Greenwillow, 1988. Ages 9–12.

Hamilton, Virginia. *In the Beginning: Creation Stories from Around the World.* Harcourt, 1988. Ages 9–13.

———. *The Dark Way: Stories from the Spirit World.* Harcourt, 1990. Ages 9–12.

———. *The People Could Fly: American Black Folktales.* Illustrated by Leo and Diane Dillon. Knopf, 1985. Ages 7–13.

Hughes, Ted. *Tales of the Early World.* Illustrated by Andrew Davidson. Farrar, 1991. Ages 10–14.

Jennings, Paul. *Unreal! Eight Surprising Stories.* Viking, 1991. Ages 9–12.

Joseph, Lynn. *A Wave in Her Pocket: Stories from Trinidad.* Illustrated by Brian Pinkney. Clarion, 1991. Ages 8–10.

Kennedy, Richard. *Collected Stories.* Harper, 1987. Ages 8–10.

Kipling, Rudyard. *The Jungle Books.* Penguin, 1964 (originally published in 1894). Ages 9–12.

———. *Just So Stories.* Illustrated by Safaya Salter. Holt, 1987 (originally published in 1902). Ages 8–11.

Konigsburg, E. L. *Altogether, One at a Time.* Atheneum, 1971. Ages 9–12.

———. *Throwing Shadows.* Atheneum, 1979. Ages 10–14.

L'Amour, Louis. *The Outlaws of Mesquite: Frontier Stories.* Bantam, 1990. Ages 12–YA.

Lester, Julius, reteller. *How Many Spots Does a Leopard Have? and Other Tales.* Illustrated by David Shannon. Scholastic, 1989. Ages 8–14. (See also: *More Tales of Uncle Remus, Further Adventures of Brer Rabbit, His Friends, Enemies, and Others; Further Tales of Uncle Remus; The Tales of Uncle Remus, the Adventures of Brer Rabbit.*)

Little, Jean. *Hey World, Here I Am!* Harper Collins, 1989. Ages 12–YA.

Lively, Penelope. *Uninvited Ghosts, and Other Stories.* Dutton, 1985. Ages 9–12.

Mahy, Margaret. *The Door in the Air and Other Stories.* Delacorte, 1991. Ages 9–12.

———. *Leaf Magic and Five Other Favorites.* Dent/Littlefield, 1985. Ages 8–11.

Martin, Eva. *Tales of the Far North.* Dial, 1987. Ages 9–12.

McManus, Patrick. *The Grasshopper Trap.* Holt, 1985. Ages 12–YA.

Morris, Johnny, editor. *The Faber Book of Animal Stories.* Faber, 1978. Ages 8–10.

Park, Ruth. *Things in Corners.* Viking, 1991. Ages 11–13.

Pearce, Philippa. *Who's Afraid? And Other Strange Stories.* Greenwillow, 1987. Ages 9–12.

Pettepiece, Thomas, and Anatoly Aleksin, editors. *Face to Face: A Collection of Stories by Celebrated Soviet and American Writers.* Philomel, 1990. Ages 10–14.

Quayle, Eric, reteller. *The Shining Princess and Other Japanese Legends.* Illustrated by Michael Foreman. Arcade, 1989. Ages 10–14.

Rapaport, Doreen. *Escape from Slavery: Five Journeys to Freedom.* Illustrated by Charles Lilly. Harper Collins, 1991. Ages 11–13.

Rochman, Hazel, editor. *Somehow Tenderness Survives: Stories of Southern Africa.* Harper Collins, 1988. Ages 12–YA.

Rounds, Glen. *Ol' Paul, the Mighty Logger.* Holiday, 1976. Ages 8–11.

Rylant, Cynthia. *A Couple of Kooks and Other Stories.* Watts, 1990. Ages 12–YA.

————. *Every Living Thing*. Bradbury, 1985. Ages 10–14.

San Souci, Robert D. *Short and Shivery: Thirty Chilling Tales*. Illustrated by Katherine Coville. Doubleday, 1987. Ages 9–12.

Schmid, Eleanore. *Cats' Tales: Feline Fairy Tales From Around the World*. Translated by Anthea Bell. North South, 1985. Ages 9–12.

Segel, Elizabeth, editor. *Short Takes: A Short Story Collection for Young Readers*. Lothrop, 1986. Ages 8–11.

Singer, Isaac Bashevis. *Naftali the Storyteller and His Horse, Sus, and Other Stories*. Farrar, 1976. Ages 9–12.

Soto, Gary. *Baseball in April, and Other Stories*. Harcourt, 1990. Ages 10–14.

Stoutenberg, Adrien. *American Tall Tales*. Illustrated by Richard M. Powers. Viking, 1966. Ages 8–11.

Thomas, Joyce Carol, editor. *A Gathering of Flowers: Stories About Being Young in America*. Harper, 1990. Ages 10–13.

Tolstoy, Leo. *The Lion and the Puppy, and Other Stories for Children*. Translated by James Riordan. Illustrated by Claus Sievert. Holt, 1988. Ages 9–12.

Walker, Barbara K., reteller. *A Treasury of Turkish Folktales for Children*. Shoe String Press, 1988.

White, Anne Terry. *The Golden Treasury of Myths and Legends*. Illustrated by Alice and Martin Provenson. Golden Press, 1959. Ages 8–YA.

Yee, Paul. *Tales from Gold Mountain: Stories of the Chinese in the New World*. Macmillan, 1989. Ages 9–12.

Yolen, Jane. *The Faery Flag: Stories and Poems of Fantasy and the Supernatural*. Orchard, 1989. Ages 10–14.

Yolen, Jane, and Martin H. Greenberg, editors. *Things that Go Bump in the Night: A Collection of Original Stories*. Harper, 1989. Ages 10–14.

Yolen, Jane, Martin H. Greenberg, and Charles G. Waugh, editors. *Dragons and Dreams: A Collection of New Fantasy and Science Fiction Stories*. Harper, 1986. Ages 9–12.

————, editors. *Spaceships & Spells: A Collection of New Fantasy and Science Fiction Stories*. Harper, 1987. Ages 10–13.

Zolotow, Charlotte, editor. *Early Sorrow: Ten Stories of Youth*. Harper, 1986. Ages 12–YA.

Picture Books

Note that additional picture books for older readers can be found in a list at the end of Chapter 4.

Bang, Molly. *The Paper Crane*. Greenwillow, 1985.

Briggs, Raymond. *When the Wind Blows*. Schocken, 1982.

Browne, Anthony. *Piggybook*. Knopf, 1986.

Carrick, Donald. *Morgan and the Artist*. Clarion, 1985.

Clément, Claude. *The Voice of the Wood*. Illustrated by Frédéric Clément. Dial, 1989.

Cooper, Susan. *The Silver Cow: A Welsh Tale*. Illustrated by Warwick Hutton. Atheneum, 1983.

Damjan, Mischa. *December's Travels*. Illustrated by Dusan Kállay. Dial, 1986.

Ekoomiak, Normee. *Arctic Memories*. Holt, 1990.

Freedman, Florence B. *Brothers: A Hebrew Legend*. Illustrated by Robert Andrew Parker. Harper, 1985.

Gallaz, Christophe and Roberto Innocenti. *Rose Blanche*. Illustrated by Roberto Innocenti. Translated from the French. Creative Education, 1985.

Gerrard, Roy. *Sir Cedric*. Farrar, 1984.

Goble, Paul. *Buffalo Woman*. Bradbury, 1984.

————. *Dream Wolf*. Bradbury, 1990.

Hamanaka, Sheila. *The Journey: Japanese Americans, Racism, and Renewal*. Orchard, 1990.

Hartford, John. *Steamboat in a Cornfield*. Crown, 1986.

Hastings, Selina. *Sir Gawain and the Loathly Lady*. Illustrated by Juan Wijngaard. Lothrop, 1985.

Hodges, Margaret. *Saint George and the Dragon*. Illustrated by Trina Schart Hyman. Little, Brown, 1984.

Hooks, William H. *The Ballad of Belle Dorcas*. Illustrated by Brian Pinkney. Knopf, 1990.

Keeping, Charles. *Sammy Streetsinger.* Oxford, 1984.

Maruki, Toshi. *Hiroshima No Pika.* Lothrop, 1980.

Oakley, Graham. *Henry's Quest.* Atheneum, 1986.

Paterson, Katherine. *The Tale of the Mandarin Duck.* Illustrated by Leo Dillon and Diane Dillon. Dutton, 1990.

Rylant, Cynthia. *Miss Maggie.* Illustrated by Thomas DiGrazia. Dutton, 1983.

Sales, Francesc. *Ibrahim.* Illustrated by Eulàlia Sariola. Translated by Marc Simont. Lippincott, 1989.

Say, Allen. *El Chino.* Houghton, 1990.

Scieszka, Jon. *The True Story of the Three Little Pigs! By A. Wolf.* Illustrated by Lane Smith. Viking, 1989.

Service, Robert William. *The Cremation of Sam McGee.* Illustrated by Ted Harrison. Greenwillow, 1986.

Siekkinen, Raija. *The Curious Faun.* Illustrated by Hannu Taina. Translated by Tim Steffa. Carolrhoda, 1990.

Stanley, Diane, and Peter Vennema. *Good Queen Bess: The Story of Elizabeth I of England.* Four Winds, 1990.

Turner, Ann. *Dakota Dugout.* Illustrated by Ronald Himler. Macmillan, 1985.

A p p e n d i x F

Children's Magazines

The following list includes some of the most popular children's magazines available to young people today. A more complete list of children's magazines may be found in Selma K. Richardson's *Magazines for Children* (American Library Association, 1990). The list below is organized by subject of primary emphasis.

Drama

Plays, the Drama Magazine for Young People. Scripts. Ages 6–17. 7 issues/year. Order from: Plays, 120 Boylston St., Boston, MA 02116.

Geography

World Newsmap of the Week/Headline Focus. News summaries, maps, teaching suggestions. Ages 10–17. Weekly. Order from: World Newsmap of the Week, Field Publications, 4343 Equity Dr., P.O. Box 16630, Columbus, OH 43216.

Health

Child Life. Articles, fiction, activities with an emphasis on nutrition and safety. Ages 9–11. 8 issues/year. Similar magazines for different age groups by the same publisher include *Humpty Dumpty's Magazine* (ages 4–6), *Children's Playmate Magazine* (ages 6–8), *Jack and Jill* (Ages 7–10), and *Children's Digest* (preteen). Order from: (Magazine title), P.O. Box 7133, Red Oak, IA 51591.

History

Calliope: World History for Young People. Articles, puzzles, plays. Themed issues. Ages 9–16. 5 issues/year.

Cobblestone: The History Magazine for Young People. Articles about U.S. history. Themed issues. Ages 9–15. 12 issues/year.

Order from: Cobblestone Publishing, Inc., 30 Grove St., Peterborough, NH 03458.

Language

Bonjour. Picture stories and features in French. Beginning French. 6 issues/year.

Das Rad. Picture stories and features in German. Beginning German. 6 issues/year.

¿Qué Tal? Picture stories and features in Spanish. Beginning Spanish. 6 issues/year.

Order from: (Magazine title), Scholastic, Inc., 2931 E. McCarty St., P.O. Box 3710, Jefferson City, MO 65102.

Language Arts

Scholastic Sprint. Plays, articles, stories, news for reading. Ages 9–11 (2nd-, 3rd-grade reading level). 14 issues/year.

Scholastic Action. Plays, articles, stories, news for reading. Ages 12–14 (2nd- through 4th-grade reading level). 14 issues/year.

Order from: (Magazine title), Scholastic, Inc., 2931 E. McCarty St., P.O. Box 3710, Jefferson City, MO 65102.

Writing! Articles, advice, and exercises for writing improvement. Ages 12–17. 9 issues/year. Order from: *Writing!,* Field Publications, 4343 Equity Dr., Columbus, OH 43228.

Literature

Cricket. Fiction, nonfiction, book reviews, activities. Ages 6–12. 12 issues/year. Order from: *Cricket,* P.O. Box 58342, Boulder, CO 80322.

Lady Bug. Fiction, poems, songs, and games. Ages 2–7. 12 issues/year. Order from: *Lady Bug,* P.O. Box 58342, Boulder, CO 80322.

Merlyn's Pen: The National Magazine of Student Writing. Fiction, poetry, and essays by students. Ages 12–16. 4 issues/year. Order from: *Merlyn's Pen,* P.O. Box 1058, East Greenwich, RI 02818.

Seedling Series: Short Story International. Stories from or set in countries other than the United States. Ages 9–12. 4 issues/year. Order from: *Seedling Series,* International Cultural Exchange, 6 Sheffield Rd., Great Neck, NY 11021.

Stone Soup: The Magazine by Children. Stories, poems, book reviews, and art by children through age 13. Ages 6–13. 5 issues/year. Order from: *Stone Soup,* Children's Art Foundation, P.O. Box 83, Santa Cruz, CA 95063.

Math

Scholastic Dynamath. Math puzzles, exercises, and activities. Ages 10–11. 9 issues/year.

Scholastic Math Magazine. Math problems, games, and activities. Ages 12–14. 14 issues/year.

Order from: Scholastic, Inc., 2931 E. McCarty St., P.O. Box 3710, Jefferson City, MO 65102.

Zillions. Articles about using money wisely. Ages 8–14. 6 issues/year. Order from: *Zillions,* P.O. Box 54861, Boulder, CO 80322.

Nature

Chickadee. Nonfiction, fiction, and puzzles about the environment and the sciences. Ages 6–9. 10 issues/year. Order from: *Chickadee,* P.O. Box 11314, Des Moines, IA 50340. In French: *Coulicou,* Les Éditions Héritage, Inc., 300 avenue Arran, Saint-Lambert, Quebec, J4K 1K5, Canada.

National Geographic World. Nonfiction articles and nature photography. Ages 8–13. 12 issues/year. Order from: *National Geographic World,* P.O. Box 2330, Washington, DC 20077.

OWL. Nonfiction articles about the environment, science, and technology; nature photography. Ages 9–12. 10 issues/year. Order from: *OWL,* P.O. Box 11314, Des Moines, IA 50340.

Ranger Rick. Nonfiction articles, nature project suggestions, and nature photography. Ages 6–12. 12 issues/year. Order from: *Ranger Rick,* National Wildlife Federation, 8925 Leesburg Pike, Vienna, VA 22184.

Your Big Backyard. Nature photography, puzzles, and games. Ages 3–5. 12 issues/year. Order from: *Your Big Backyard,* National Wildlife Federation, 8925 Leesburg Pike, Vienna, VA 22184.

Recreation

Boys' Life. Articles, fiction, projects, and features about outdoor life and sports. Ages 8–18. 12 issues/year. Order from: Boy Scouts of America, 1325 Walnut Hill Lane, P.O. Box 152079, Irving, TX 75015.

Hopscotch: The Magazine for Young Girls. Nonfiction articles and stories about activities and hobbies; poems and puzzles. 6 issues/year. Order from: *Hopscotch,* P.O. Box 1292, Saratoga Springs, NY 12866.

Science

Current Science. News in the earth, physical, and life sciences. Ages 11–15. 18 issues/year. Order from: *Current Science,* Field Publications, 4343 Equity Dr., Columbus, OH 43228.

Odyssey: Space Exploration and Astronomy for Young People. Articles and illustrations on astronomy, space exploration, and technology. Ages 8–14. 12 issues/year. Order from: *Odyssey,* Kalmbach Publishing Co., 21027 Crossroads Circle, P.O. Box 1612, Waukesha, WI 53187.

Science World. Articles, experiments, science news. Ages 12–16. 18 issues/year. Order from: *Science World,* Scholastic, Inc., 2931 E. McCarty St., P.O. Box 3710, Jefferson City, MO 65102.

Scienceland. Articles and illustrations about biology to promote scientific thinking; themed issues. Ages 5–8. 8 issues/year. Order from: *Scienceland,* 501 Fifth Ave., Suite 2108, New York, NY 10017.

SuperScience (Red Edition). Science lessons and activities to involve children in experimenting. Themed issues. Ages 6–8. 8 issues/year.

SuperScience (Blue Edition). Same general format as Red Edition. Ages 9–11. 8 issues/year. Order from: *SuperScience* (State "Red" or "Blue" Edition), Scholastic, Inc., 2931 E. McCarty St., Jefferson City, MO 65102.

3-2-1 Contact. Stories, puzzles, projects, experiments, questions and answers about science, nature, and technology. Ages 8–14. 10 issues/year. Order from: *3-2-1 Contact,* Children's Television Workshop, P.O. Box 53051, Boulder, CO 80322.

Social Studies

Faces: The Magazine About People. Articles and activities about anthropology and natural history. Ages 9–15. 10 issues/year. Order From: *Faces,* Cobblestone Publishing, Inc., 30 Grove St., Peterborough, NH 03458.

Junior Scholastic. Articles on U.S. history, current events, map skills and exercises. Ages 11–13. 18 issues/year. Order from: *Junior Scholastic,* Scholastic, Inc., 2931 E. McCarty St., P.O. Box 3710, Jefferson City, MO 65102.

Skipping Stones: A Multi-Ethnic Children's Forum. Articles for and by children about world cultures and cooperation. Ages 6–14. 4 issues/year. Order from: *Skipping Stones,* Aprovecho Institute, 80574 Hazelton Rd., Cottage Grove, OR 97424.

Appendix G

Professional Resources

Compiled and Annotated by Marie Louise Sorensen

Professional Readings

Books

Bader, B. (1976). *American picture books from No-ah's ark to the beast within.* New York: Macmillan.

This critical, comprehensive history of art in children's picture book publishing in the United States is particularly valuable because we often take for granted the seemingly unlimited capabilities of art reproduction available to us today. Bader describes the achievements of artists by putting them in the perspective of advances in reproduction techniques as they became available to the publishing industry.

Barton, B. (1986). *Tell me another: Storytelling and reading aloud at home, at school, and in the community.* Markham, Ontario: Pembroke Publishers. Distributed by Heinemann.

The author believes that reading aloud and storytelling are different versions of the same thing and that both can be used by teachers to create
memorable experiences for their students when incorporated into classroom activities.

Barton, B., & Booth, D. (1990). *Stories in the classroom: Storytelling, reading aloud, and roleplaying with children.* Portsmouth, NH: Heinemann.

The authors suggest a variety of followup activities to help teachers create and enrich their classrooms with what the authors refer to as the "storying" experience. Included are ideas for finding appropriate stories.

Bauer, C. F. (1977). *Handbook for storytellers.* Chicago: American Library Association.

Bauer uses storytelling to introduce her listeners to children's literature. She includes sections on getting started, sources for stories, multimedia approaches, and planning programs.

Bauer, C. F. (1983). *This way to books.* Drawings by Lynn Gates. New York: H. W. Wilson.

Bauer shares ideas to help librarians, teachers, and parents extend children's interest in read-

ing books. She includes information on storytelling, booktalks, presenting poetry, games, crafts, exhibits, and programs.

Bodart-Talbot, J. (1985–1988). *Booktalk!* (Vols. 2 and 3). *Booktalking for all ages and audiences.* New York: H. W. Wilson.

These resources explain the what, how, and why of booktalking, followed by prepared booktalks for all ages and audiences. The booktalks are categorized by age level and subject, and the last volume has a cumulative index.

Bromley, K. D. (1991). *Webbing with literature: Creating story maps with children's books.* Boston: Allyn and Bacon.

Bromley defines semantic webbing and explains the use of webs to enhance children's comprehension of literature in grades K–8. She includes chapters on the selection of quality literature and various ways of helping children respond to literature. The author also provides examples of webs for 50 award-winning books with additional brief annotations for another 145 books.

Burke, E. M. (1986). *Literature for the young child* (2nd ed.). Boston: Allyn and Bacon.

Burke correlates research about how children learn and make sense of their world with extensive information about young children's literature. Her practical ideas will be helpful to teachers wishing to incorporate literature into their programs for young children.

Butzow, C. M., and J. W. (1989). *Science through children's literature: An integrated approach.* Englewood, CO: Teachers Ideas Press/Libraries Unlimited.

This handbook provides a rationale for using children's literature as a springboard to science, with an emphasis on sharing ideas but encouraging teachers to plan such instruction on their own. The bibliographies include material on literature, whole language, and science activities. Some 33 science units for grades K–3 are presented, each revolving around a familiar children's book.

Carlsen, G. R., & Sherrill, A. (1988). *Voices of readers: How we come to love books.* Urbana, IL: National Council of Teachers of English.

The authors have excerpted from and categorized reading autobiographies written by Carlsen's students over a period of 30 years. The presentation and the analysis of these quotes in the readers' own words provides a compelling list of conditions that promote the making of readers.

Cullinan, B. E. (ed.). (1987). *Children's literature in the reading program.* Newark, DE: International Reading Association.

Advocating the incorporation of children's literature into the reading program on all grade levels, this book includes chapters by many well-known contributors who discuss a variety of aspects of literature-based reading, including implementation.

Cullinan, B. E. (1989). *Literature and the child* (2nd ed.). San Diego: Harcourt Brace Jovanovich.

Cullinan's textbook explains the function of literature in the life of a child, and then presents the various genre of children's literature. The last part of the book focuses on the literature of many cultures and the history of children's literature. Teaching ideas, profiles of authors, and information about landmarks in the field are interspersed throughout.

Esbensen, B. J. (1975). *A celebration of bees: Helping children write poetry.* Minneapolis: Winston Press.

Emphasizing that children's first experiences in writing poetry should be in group sessions, this teacher shares practical ideas that will help move children toward individual poetry writing.

Fox, C., & Sauer, M. (1989–1990). *Celebrate literature: A literature curriculum for grades K–6.* Logan, IA: Perfection Form.

These guides for each grade level provide specific ideas for integrating quality literature into the curriculum. The research-based suggestions include reading aloud, using libraries, and asking open-ended questions.

Glazer, J. I. (1991). *Literature for young children* (3rd ed.). New York: Merrill/Macmillan.

Well-written children's literature has much to offer children as they develop and grow. Those who work with preschool and primary-grade children will benefit from the research cited by Glazer and from her recommendations for integrating literature into programs for young children.

Hancock, J., & Hill, S. (eds.). (1987). *Literature-based reading programs at work.* Portsmouth, NH: Heinemann.

This book from Australia suggests solutions to the possible problems encountered when teachers implement a literature-based reading program. The authors also discuss how teachers' beliefs affect how they help children learn.

Hansen, J. (1987). *When writers read.* Portsmouth, NH: Heinemann.

Hansen describes the change—in both adults and children—that resulted when teachers and researchers working together in an elementary school discovered that the same principles used in the process approach to the teaching of writing could be applied to the teaching of reading. The author compares her current thinking with the way she used to do things as a classroom teacher in the late 1960s and 70s, emphasizing how children can be encouraged to develop strategies to help them learn to read.

Heard, G. (1989). *For the good of the earth and sun: Teaching poetry.* Portsmouth, NH: Heinemann.

Heard, a poet, describes her experiences with helping children and teachers learn about the process of writing poetry.

Hearne, B. (1990). *Choosing books for children: A commonsense guide* (revised, expanded, and updated). New York: Delacorte Press.

Hearne discusses her favorite children's books as a starting point for anyone interested in learning about children's literature and how to help children develop a love for literature.

Helbig, A. K., & Perkins, A. R. (1986). *Dictionary of American children's fiction, 1960–1984: Recent books of recognized merit.* New York: Greenwood Press.

This comprehensive reference includes works of fiction of at least 5000 words that were listed in

Children's Books: Awards & Prizes, *published by the Children's Book Council, as well as some additional titles of merit not recognized when they were published. Each commentary indicates other specific entries, including title, author, characters, and well-known places, where additional information on that book may be found. An earlier volume covers U. S. books published between 1859 and 1959. A two-volume reference work published in 1989 treats British children's literature of merit published from 1678 to 1985.*

Hickman, J., & Cullinan, B. E. (eds.). (1989). *Children's literature in the classroom: Weaving Charlotte's Web.* Needham Heights, MA: Christopher-Gordon Publishers.

This book is a tribute to Charlotte Huck written by her former students, with chapters on picture books, fantasy, historical fiction, and poetry, as well as sections on many aspects of implementing a literature-based reading program.

Hopkins, L. B. (1987). *Pass the poetry, please!* (revised, enlarged, and updated.). New York: Harper & Row.

Hopkins introduces his favorite works by 20 contemporary poets and enthusiastically makes suggestions for helping children appreciate poetry at home, in the classroom, and in the library. Bibliographies are included.

Huck, C. S., Hepler, S., & Hickman, J. (eds.). (1987). *Children's literature in the elementary school* (4th ed.). New York: Holt, Rinehart & Winston.

Designed to help teachers and other students become knowledgeable about all genres of children's literature, the authors of this textbook also offer ideas to help teachers plan and develop a literature program that will extend into all apsects of the elementary school curriculum. Many bibliographies are included.

Johnson, T. D., & Louis, D. R. (1987). *Literacy through literature.* Portsmouth, NH: Heinemann.

These Canadian-based authors share many ideas for introducing children to literature and then relate such activities to underlying assump-

tions and beliefs about how children learn to read.

Johnson, T. D., & Louis, D. R. (1990). *Bringing it all together: A program for literacy.* Portsmouth, NH: Heinemann.

In their second book of suggestions for those planning a literature program for the classroom, the authors discuss the theory behind their ideas, explaining that when readers begin to understand the philosophy on which literature programs are based, they will be able to develop and implement their own ideas.

Kimmel, M. M., & Segal, E. (1988). *For reading out loud! A guide to sharing books with children* (revised and expanded). New York: Delacorte.

Compiled by librarians who know and love books, this handbook includes comments on 125 books recommended for preschoolers and 175 for school-age listeners. The annotations, listed alphabetcially by title, include estimates on how much time to allow for reading selections aloud.

Koch, K. (1970). *Wishes, lies, and dreams: Teaching children to write poetry.* New York: Harper.

Koch describes how he worked with inner-city children who had never done much writing of any kind and encouraged them to express themselves by writing down their feelings.

Koch, K. (1973). *Rose, where did you get that red? Teaching great poetry to children.* New York: Random House.

Koch explains his approach to exposing children to adult poetry by providing samples of the lessons he used followed by examples of the poetry his students wrote in response. He includes an anthology of additional poetry.

Kulleseid, E. R. & Strickland, D. S. (1989). *Literature, literacy, and learning: Classroom teachers, library media specialists, and the literature-based curriculum.* Chicago: ALA.

After concisely explaining the theory and research behind literature-based reading programs, the authors describe the partnership of the school library media specialist and the classroom teacher. The Appendix includes a viewer's

guide to a video produced by Encyclopaedia Britannica Educational Corporation (1990, No. 4594) for use in conjunction with this booklet.

Lindgren, M. V. (ed.). (1991). *The multicolored mirror: Cultural substance in literature for children and young adults.* Madison, WI: Cooperative Children's Book Center.

This collection of thoughtful essays is based on presentations delivered at an April 1991 conference with the same title. The book has been expanded to include a list of resources offered as a starting point for those interested in increasing their awareness of available multicultural literature. Rudine Sims Bishop addresses the issue of evaluating books by and about African Americans. Kathleen T. Horning and Ginny Moore Kruse offer both an annotated bibliography of recommended books about people of color published in the early 1990s and an essay that briefly documents the changes that have resulted in the publication of more culturally sensitive books than were available a generation ago.

Lukens, R. (1990). *A critical handbook of children's literature* (4th ed.). Glenview, IL: Scott, Foresman/Little, Brown.

Lukens's explanation of the elements of literature and her descriptions of the various genre of children's literature have helped this book become a classic for learning the art of evaluation.

Martin, D. (1990). *The telling line: Essays on fifteen contemporary book illustrators.* New York: Delacorte.

Martin gets at the history of British children's picture book illustration by discussing publishing trends, printing techniques, and changing art styles in the field in the course of his interviews with 15 major graphic artists, including Raymond Briggs, Helen Oxenbury, and Brian Wildsmith.

McClure, A. A. (1990). *Sunrises and songs: Reading and writing poetry in an elementary classroom.* Portsmouth, NH: Heinemann.

This book describes how two teachers guided their fifth- and sixth-grade students into writing and reading poetry over a period of a year.

Lists of these teachers' favorite books of poetry are included.

McCord, D. (1977). *One at a time: His collected poems for the young.* Illustrated by Henry B. Kane. Boston: Little, Brown.

This compilation contains poems from five of David McCord's previous single volumes, with a subject index as well as a first line index.

Moss, J. F. (1984). *Focus units in literature: A handbook for elementary school teachers.* Urbana, IL: NCTE.

This handbook includes 13 units focusing on a wide variety of topics, with each including bibliographies, sample questions for class discussion, and other suggested activities. Also included are ideas for helping teachers create their own focus units.

Moss, J. F. (1990). *Focus on literature: A context for literacy learning.* Katonah, N.Y.: Richard C. Owen Publishers.

Moss offers an explanation of theoretical background, examples of literature units, bibliographies, and other practical suggestions for teachers who want to bring quality literature into their classrooms.

Neuman, J. (ed.). (1985). *Whole language: Theory in use.* Portsmouth, NH: Heinemann.

Includes essays on a variety of topics in which experienced teachers explain how their classroom practices have been affected by their understanding of whole language theory.

Norton, D. (1991). *Through the eyes of a child* (3rd ed.). New York: Merrill (an imprint of Macmillan).

Each chapter presents the characteristics, history, and representative titles of a particular genre, followed by suggestions for involving children in that type of literature. Educational research is frequently cited. The chapter on multicultural literature is followed by information on developing an appreciation for the minority cultures in our society. Extensive bibliographies are included throughout the book.

Pellowski, A. (1984). *The story vine: A source book of unusual and easy-to-tell stories from around*

the world. Illustrated by Lynn Sweat. New York: Macmillan.

Pellowski cites sources and uses drawings to illustrate how she tells some of her favorite stories with the aid of authentic props, such as string figures and pictures.

Pellowski, A. (1990). *The world of storytelling: A guide to the origins, development, and applications of storytelling* (revised and expanded). New York: H. W. Wilson.

Pellowski provides comprehensive information about the oral tradition and the history of storytelling. She stresses the responsibility of the storyteller to know and present background information about the various cultures from which stories are selected for telling. Bibliographies list books, articles, and manuals on storytelling, as well as a list of storytelling festivals held around the world.

Rhodes, L. K., & Dudley-Marling, C. (1988). *Readers and writers with a difference: A holistic approach to teaching learning disabled and remedial students.* Portsmouth, NH: Heinemann.

Rhodes and Dudley-Marling share strategies that have worked in their classrooms and offer recommendations for choosing reading materials. They explain how to use predictable books and they include an expanded bibliography of Rhodes's 1981 list of such books.

Routman, R. (1988). *Transitions: From literature to literacy.* Portsmouth, NH: Heinemann.

Explaining how she came to change the way she helps children learn to read, this author describes reading and writing as processes, and includes a section on evaluation. The last 100 pages are devoted to resources for the teacher, including an excellent bibliography of professional books and journal articles.

Routman, R. (1991). *Invitations: Changing as teachers and learners K–12.* Portsmouth, NH: Heinemann.

In her second book, Routman provides additional assistance to teachers committed to improving the way they teach. Having observed the teachers in her school district struggle with change, Routman believes that the issues all teachers confront are similar, regardless of what grade or age they teach. The comprehensive, annotated bibliography updates the resources in Routman's 1988 book.

Rudman, M. K. (1984). *Children's literature: An issues approach* (2nd ed.). New York: Longman.

Chapter 10 in this book describes an individualized reading program using children's literature. The rest of the book discusses criteria for evaluating children's books dealing with issues affecting our society today, such as war, death, divorce, and multicultural issues. Rudman includes annotations of hundreds of recommended books on these and other issues.

Rudman, M. K. (ed.). (1989). *Children's literature: Resource for the classroom.* Needham Heights, MA: Christopher-Gordon Publishers.

The chapters in this book were written by authorities involved in various aspects of children's literature. Evaluation, selection, censorship, bibliotherapy, and literature in the reading program are addressed, as well as the part television and family-school partnerships can play in helping children learn to read.

Rudman, M. K., & Pearce, A. M. (1988). *For love of reading: A parent's guide to encouraging young readers from infancy through age 5.* Mount Vernon, N.Y.: Consumers Union.

As the authors discuss all aspects of rearing young children, they describe books appropriate for various developmental levels and stages of emotional growth. A list of more than 800 books of interest to children by age level is followed by an annotated bibliography that indicates the chapter in which each book is discussed.

Saltman, Judith. (1987). *Modern Canadian children's books: Perspectives on Canadian culture.* Toronto: Oxford Univeristy Press.

This brief survey traces the historical developments in Canadian children's literature during the major growth years from 1975 to 1985, highlighting contemporary trends and discussing significant titles in each of the major genres. Bibliographic information accompanies each

chapter. Indexes by title, author, and illustrator are included.

Sims, R. (1982). *Shadow and substance: Afro-American experience in contemporary children's fiction.* Urbana, IL: NCTE.

Sims analyzed 150 books of realistic fiction about the Afro-American experience that were written for children and published in the United States between 1965 and 1979. Her well-written narrative puts into historical context societal changes as they were reflected in those books.

Strickland, D. S., & Morrow, L. M. (eds.) (1989). *Emerging literacy: Young children learn to read and write.* Newark, DE: IRA.

Contributors, who are well-known for their work with a variety of issues concerning how children become literate share practical ideas, based on theory and research, with teachers who work with young children.

Sutherland, Z., & Arbuthnot, M. H. (1991). *Children and books* (8th ed.). New York: HarperCollins.

Written from a librarian's point of view, this text uses a major-author approach, with the greatest portion of the book devoted to discussing books by genre. Bringing children and books together is treated in a separate section. Essays on areas and issues of current concern related to children's literature are included, as are annotated appendixes of book selection aids and adult references. The end-of-chapter lists of children's books are coded to indicate a particular religious or ethnic group.

Taylor, D., & Strickland, D. S. (1986). *Family storybook reading.* Portsmouth, NH: Heinemann.

This book aims to help parents establish their own family rituals as they share books with their children by describing what other families have done. Taylor and Strickland emphasize the connection between family storybook sharing and learning to read and write.

Trelease, J. (1989). *The new read-aloud handbook* (2nd rev. ed.). New York: Viking Penguin.

This bestseller of practical suggestions has helped Trelease become a spokesman for reading aloud.

He annotates 300 of his favorite read-alouds, giving the listening level of each. Many of the annotations include suggestions of other books by the same author.

Watson, D. J. (ed.). (1987). *Ideas and insights: Language arts in the elementary school.* Urbana, IL: NCTE.

The whole language activities described here have come from teachers everywhere. Bibliographies of children's books are organized by the type of literature and the age of the reader.

Weiss, J. S. (1983). *Prizewinning books for children: Themes and stereotypes in U.S. prizewinning prose fiction for children.* Lexington, MA: Lexington Books/D. C. Heath & Co.

After explaining her belief that children can learn to identify the explicit and implicit themes of the books they read, the author discusses 717 prize-winning fictional prose books by genre and then categorizes them by theme. Weiss notes when books have been criticized for the use of stereotypes. The appendix provides information about many types of awards, including some children's choice awards.

Wood, K. D., with Moss, A. (eds.) (1992). *Exploring literature in the classroom: Contents and methods.* Norwood, MA: Christopher Gordon Publishers.

Examining what to teach as well as how to teach, experts in their fields provide perspectives on a variety of literacy issues, including the place of today's basal readers in literature-based reading programs and the current status of multiethnic literature.

Books about the History of Children's Literature

Bingham, J., & Scholt, G. (1980). *Fifteen centuries of children's literature: An annotated chronology of British and American works in historical context.* Westport, CT: Greenwood.

Gillespie, M. C. (1970). *History and trends: Literature for children.* Dubuque, IA: Brown.

Marshall, M. R. (1982). *An introduction to the world of children's books: Books about the history of*

children's literature. Aldershot, England: Gower.

Meigs, C., Eaton, A. T., Nesbitt, E., & Vigeurs, R. H. (1969). *A critical history of children's books in English* (rev. ed.). New York: Macmillan.

Smith, E. S. (1980). In M. Hodges & S. Steinfirst (eds.), *The history of children's literature* (rev. ed.). Chicago: ALA.

Journal Articles

Altwerger, B., Edelsky, C., & Flores, B. M. (1987). Whole language: What's new? *The Reading Teacher, 41,* 144–154.

The authors explain that whole language is not a practice but a set of beliefs based on certain ideas that they list here. The authors clearly describe what whole language is and is not and provide definitions for terms frequently used.

Atwell, N. (1984). Writing and reading literature from the inside out. *Language Arts, 61,* 240–252.

Atwell describes the literate environment she and her students created in her eighth-grade classroom after she noticed contradictions between her beliefs about written language and the instruction she provided in reading.

Byrnes, D. A. (1988). Children and prejudice. *Social Education, 52,* 267–271.

Although most multicultural educational programs at the elementary school level aim to promote understanding of other cultures, Byrnes feels that teachers should also teach children about prejudice and discrimination. She recommends specific activities and strategies teachers can use to reduce children's prejudices.

Cohen, D. H. (1968). The effect of literature on vocabulary and reading achievement. *Elementary English, 45,* 209–213, 217.

This landmark study is often cited because it demonstrates that spending classroom time reading aloud to second-graders from low socioeconomic backgrounds results in significant increases in vocabulary, word knowledge, and reading comprehension.

DeFord, D. E. (1981). Literacy: Reading, writing, and other essentials. *Language Arts, 58,* 652–658.

DeFord studied three first-grade classrooms where different approaches to reading and writing were emphasized. Analysis of samples of these children's writing indicated that the writing of the children in the whole language classroom reflected familiarity with a greater variety of literary forms, such as stories, poetry, and newspaper reports. DeFord recommends that reading and writing be taught as interactive processes.

Durkin, D. (1961). Children who read before grade one. *The Reading Teacher, 14,* 163–166.

When Durkin looked for factors that might explain why the 49 children identified for this study had learned to read before they started first grade, she found that they all had been read to regularly at home, some since the age of 2. This was one of the first studies to recognize this important correlation.

Eldredge, J. L., & Butterfield, D. (1986). Alternatives to traditional reading instruction. *The Reading Teacher, 40,* 32–37.

Teachers who want to use children's literature to help children learn to read will find support in this research, which found more significant gains in achievement and attitudes toward reading in second-grade classrooms where literature was part of the reading instruction program than in those classrooms relying on basal instruction.

Goodman, K. S. (1986). Basal readers: A call for action. *Language Arts, 63,* 358–363.

Although basal readers dominate reading instruction in the United States, Goodman points to an ever-widening gap between the methods employed in basal readers and the latest theory and research in reading instruction. Perhaps partly because of recommendations such as Goodman's, today's basal reading programs have improved and now include more children's literature.

Goodman, K. S. (1988). Look what they've done to Judy Blume!: The 'basalization' of children's literature. *The New Advocate, 1,* 29–41.

Goodman suggests that if we accept the idea that children learn to read by reading, we should offer them authentic children's literature rather than adaptations that have been rewritten under the mistaken notion that they can be made easier to read by controlling vocabulary.

Hepler, S. (1988). A guide for the teacher guides: Doing it yourself. *The New Advocate, 1,* 186–195.

Hepler suggests ways to develop guides that will encourage a young reader to examine his or her own response to the reading of a book. These guidelines to developing questions and appropriate activities should help teachers evaluate commercial guides as well as create their own.

Holdaway, D. (1982). Shared book experience: Teaching reading using favorite books. *Theory into Practice, 21,* 293–300.

Holdaway explains the rationale and research behind what he called the "shared book experience," a form of natural literacy learning that has become widely used in classroom literature programs planned for young children, both in New Zealand and the United States.

Huck, C. S. (1982). I give you the end of a golden string. *Theory into Practice, 21,* 315–321.

Huck cites research that firmly supports her plea for making children's literature the central part of our programs for helping children learn to read. She also thoroughly describes the aesthetic aspects of developing in children a love for literature that will help them become lifelong readers.

Koeller, S. (1981). 25 years advocating children's literature in the reading program. *The Reading Teacher, 34,* 552–56.

Koeller reviewed 25 years of The Reading Teacher, looking for research reports and suggestions for classroom practices involving children's literature in the elementary reading program. She found that many of the ideas still being advocated when she wrote the article had been recommended frequently in the past.

Lamme, L. L., & Ledbetter, L. (1990). Libraries: The heart of whole language. *Language Arts, 67,* 735–741.

Focusing on the changed role of the school librarian in whole language schools, the authors describe some of the many ways in which teachers and librarians can collaborate to maximize the use of a school's library media resources for the benefit of everyone in the school.

Larrick, N. (1965). The all-white world of children's books. *Saturday Review of Literature, 11,* 63–65, 84–85.

This landmark article describes a study Larrick made of children's books published between 1962 and 1964 in which she found very little mention of people of color in the texts or illustrations. Articles reporting on the status of multicultural literature often cite this article, which described some of the negative stereotypes prevalent in the early 1960s. Many years later, publishers and editors told Larrick of the impact this article had, which resulted in an increased sensitivity to books by and about minorities.

Milz, V. (1980). First graders can write: Focus on communication. *Theory into Practice, 19,* 179–185.

Milz describes her first-grade classroom, which she has stocked with 2,000 books and magazines for her students' self-selection. Children are surrounded by print, and in this literate environment, Milz encourages the interactive use of listening, speaking, reading, and writing.

Rasinski, T. V., & Padak, N. D. (1990). Multicultural learning through children's literature. *Language Arts, 67,* 576–580.

Teachers who use children's literature as part of a multicultural curriculum are challenged to broaden their expectations of the role of that literature in their programs. These authors suggest ways we can encourage our students to engage in constructive action regarding multiethnic issues, including civil rights.

Rhodes, L. K. (1981). I can read! Predictable books as resources for reading and writing instruction. *The Reading Teacher, 34,* 511–518.

Rhodes explains the characteristics of predictable books and demonstrates how such books can be used as resources for reading and writing instruction with young children. The article includes a bibliography of predictable books, which Rhodes updated in 1988. (See Rhodes and Dudley-Marling, Readers and Writers with a Difference, *in the first section of this appendix.)*

Swibold, G. V. (1984). Textbooks need trade books: One librarian's case study. *Top of the News, 41,* 93–98.

Swibold, a school library media specialist, describes how she found trade books to use in conjunction with her school's fifth- and sixth-grade social studies texts. She points out that children's learning can be greatly enhanced when trade books are used in addition to social studies textbooks.

Tunnell, M. O., & Jacobs, J. S. (1989). Using "real" books: Research findings on literature based reading instruction. *The Reading Teacher, 42,* 470–477.

Tunnell and Jacobs looked at a number of studies that directly compared literature-based reading programs with basal instruction. They also looked at research reports on the reading growth of children in whole language classrooms where real literature was prevalent. Tunnell and Jacobs concluded that children's literature is a viable alternative approach to the teaching of reading.

Journals and Periodicals

Book Links: Connecting Books, Libraries, and Classrooms. A bimonthly magazine published by Booklist Publications, an imprint of the American Library Association, 50 E. Huron St., Chicago, IL 60611.

Started in 1991, Book Links *publishes articles with suggestions for exploring a particular theme through literature. Descriptions of books, strategies for stimulating classroom discussion about them, and activities for student involvement are among the offerings. A calendar of seasonal literary ideas is also included.*

Bookbird: International Periodical on Literature for Children and Young People. A joint publication of the International Board on Books for Young People (IBBY) and the International Institute for Children's Literature and Reading Research. Published four times a year by Forlaget ARNIS, Postboks 130, Toendervej 197, DK-6200 Aabenraa, Denmark. In the United States, order from EBSCO, P.O. Box 1943, Birmingham, AL 35201.

This English-language journal includes articles, author's and illustrator's portraits, reports and announcements, and reviews of children's books and professional literature of international interest. Authors are from the 50 member nations of IBBY.

CBC Features. Published biannually by the Children's Book Council, Inc., 568 Broadway, New York, NY 10012. Lifetime subscription for one fee; write for information to CBC Order Center, 350 Scotland Road, Orange, NJ 07050.

CBC Features is a 12-sided folder with brief articles and profiles of authors written by people well known in the field of children's literature. Issues often are themed, and each includes a listing of materials available from CBC member publishers, many of which are free.

Children's Literature in Education: An International Quarterly. Published by Human Sciences Press, Inc., 233 Spring Street, New York, NY 10013-1578.

The types of articles published in this journal include interviews with authors and illustrators, and articles by or about them; accounts of classroom practice involving literature or the reading process; critical evaluation of literature; and analysis or commentary on social issues as reflected in books.

The CLA Bulletin. Journal of the Children's Literature Assembly of the National Council of Teachers of English, published and sent to CLA members three times a year. NCTE members may join the Children's Literature Assembly by obtaining the name and address of the current Membership Chair of CLA. Write to NCTE, 1111 Kenyon Road, Urbana, IL 61801.

The CLA Bulletin solicits and publishes manuscripts regarding any aspect of children's literature, as well as reviews of children's books and professional resources. News and items of interest to members are also featured.

The Dragon Lode. The Journal of the Children's Literature and Reading Special Interest Group of the International Reading Association is published three times a year for members. IRA members may join this interest group by obtaining the name and address of its current Membership Chair from IRA, 800 Barksdale Road, P.O. Box 8139, Newark, DE 19714-8139.

The Dragon Lode publishes articles about children's literature and the teaching of it, classroom ideas, and book reviews of books published internationally as well as in the United States.

Interracial Books for Children Bulletin. Published eight times a year, sometimes less frequently because of double issues, by the Council on Interracial Books for Children, 1841 Broadway, New York, NY 10023.

Founded in 1966, CIBC is a nonprofit organization dedicated to promoting antiracist and antisexist children's literature and teaching materials. Book reviews appearing in the Bulletin are always written by members of the minority group depicted in the reviewed book.

JOYS, Journal of Youth Services in Libraries, previously titled *Top of the News.* Quarterly journal of the Association for Library Services to Children and the Young Adult Library Services Association, divisions of the American Library Association, 50 Huron St., Chicago, IL 60611.

JOYS' goal is to to provide news and information about both of the above named professional library associations and to inform librarians who work with children and/or young adults about current practices in both specialties. Teachers as well as librarians will find the thorough reviews of professional resources helpful.

Language Arts. Published monthly, September through April, by the National Council of Teachers of English for its members. For membership information, write NCTE, 1111 Kenyon Road, Urbana, IL 61801-1096.

Language Arts publishes themed issues on topics relating to the content and teaching of English and the language arts, with the contributed articles often being written by classroom teachers. Regular features include author profiles, annotations of children's books, reviews of professional resources, and commentary on trends in the field.

The New Advocate: For Those Involved with Young People and Their Literature. Published quarterly since 1988 by Christopher-Gordon Publishers, 480 Washington Street, Norwood, MA 02062.

The New Advocate contains articles on using children's literature in the classroom and often includes author or illustrator profiles. Reviews of children's books and literature resources for teachers appear in each issue. An annual themed fifth issue will appear each October, beginning in 1992 with an issue devoted to poetry.

The Reading Teacher. A journal of the International Reading Association, published monthly eight times during the school year. For information on joining the IRA and subscribing to its journals, write to IRA, 800 Barksdale Road, P.O. Box 8139, Newark, DE 19714-8139.

The Reading Teacher contains articles that reflect current theory, research, and practice regarding the teaching of reading. Regular columns deal with instructional issues, practical ideas for classroom use, and evaluation of children's trade books and professional resources.

The United States Board on Books for Young People, Inc. (USBBY) Newsletter. Published twice a year by the U.S. section of the International Board on Books for Young People (IBBY). To join USBBY and receive the newsletter, write for the address of the current USBBY Secretariat, c/o International Reading Association, P.O. Box 8139, Newark, DE 19714-8139.

This newsletter includes news and articles concerning national and international activities related to children's literature. It also includes reviews of international children's books.

The Web: Wonderfully Exciting Books. Published three times a year by Ohio State University, Room 220 Ramseyer Hall, 29 West Woodruff, Columbus, OH 43210.

Each issue includes a "web of possibilities" along with reviews of books on a related theme stressing ideas for using books in the classroom. Write to the above address for a list of the topics of back issues that are available for purchase.

Information on Authors and Illustrators

American writers for children, 1900–1960. (1983). J. Cech (ed.). (*Dictionary of Literary Biography, 22*). Detroit: Gale Research.

American writers for children since 1960: Fiction. (1986). G. Estes (ed.). (*Dictionary of Literary Biography, 52*). Detroit: Gale Research.

American writers for children since 1960: Poets, illustrators, and nonfiction authors. (1987). G. Estes (ed.). (*Dictionary of Literary Biography, 61*). Detroit: Gale Research.

These three volumes profile writers and illustrators whose work is primarily for children; they are written for the adult student of children's literature. The most recent volume of the Dictionary of Literary Biography *indexes the entire series.*

Children's literature review: Excerpts from reviews, criticism, and commentary on books for children and young people, 1–23. (1976–1991). Detroit: Gale Research.

This reference provides information about authors and illustrators, often in their own words, as well as excerpts from reviews of their work. Each volume contains a cumulative index to authors and titles, with the most recent volumes including a cumulative index of nationalities. Students writing reports on authors and their work are shown the correct way to credit the original sources for information obtained from this series.

Junior book of authors (1951), *More junior authors* (1963), and the *Third* through *Sixth book of jun-*

ior authors and illustrators. (1972–1989). S. H. Holtze. (ed.). New York: H. W. Wilson.

This reference includes biographical sketches of authors and illustrators written for young people; each book's index is cumulative. Most entries include a photograph, selected list of works, and sources for additional information.

Roginski, J. (1985). *Behind the covers: Interviews with authors and illustrators of books for children and young adults.* Englewood, CO: Libraries Unlimited.

This volume provides bibliographical information and interviews with 22 authors and illustrators of children's books. Behind the Covers II, covering additional authors and illustrators, was published in 1989.

Rollock, B. (1988). *Black authors and illustrators of children's books: A biographical dictionary.* New York: Garland Publishing.

This short work includes brief biographical information about 115 black authors and illustra-

tors who were included because they are making literary history in the world of children's books.

Something about the author autobiography series, 1–13. (1986–1992). Detroit: Gale Research.

Autobiographical information has been provided by authors and illustrators for this series. A cumulative index in each volume includes entries appearing in all of Gale Research's books on authors and illustrators.

Something about the author: Facts and pictures about authors and illustrations of books for young people, 1–65 (1971–1991). Detroit: Gale Research.

This series includes comprehensive information about authors and illustrators, written for young people. A cumulative index is included in the odd-number volumes after Volume 57. Volumes 50 (1988) and 54 (1989) also include a cumulative character index, featuring many well-known literary characters.

Book Selection Aids

Bibliographies: Annual Lists

"CCBC Choices."

This is an annual spring annotated booklist, published by and for the members of the Friends of the CCBC, Inc. (Cooperative Children's Book Center). Introductory information explains the book selection criteria and also provides statistics on how many books for children were published that year, how many of them were written or illustrated by minorities, and how many of them were published by small presses. For information about CCBC publications and/or membership in the Friends, send a self-addressed stamped envelope to Friends of the CCBC, P.O. Box 5288, Madison, WI 53705-0288.

"Children's Choices."

This yearly list of newly published books, chosen by young readers themselves, appears each

October in The Reading Teacher *as a project of the International Reading Association/Children's Book Council Joint Committee. Single copies are available for a self-addressed, 9" × 12" envelope, stamped with first-class postage for four ounces, from Children's Choices, International Reading Association, PO Box 8139, Newark, DE 19713-8139.*

"Notable Children's Books."

This annual American Library Association list is compiled during the ALA midwinter meeting by a committee of the Association for Library Service to Children (ALSC), which is organized each year for that purpose. The list, which is not annotated, appears in the March issue of School Library Journal *and also in the March 15 issue of* Booklist *as part of the news from the ALA midwinter meeting. Copies of this and other awards lists are available from ALA. Write for price list and/or catalog to ALA Graphics, American Li-*

brary Association, 50 E. Huron St., Chicago, IL 60611.

"Notable Children's Trade Books in the Field of Social Studies." (This list appears in the April/May issue of *Social Education*.)

"Outstanding Science Trade Books for Children." (This list appears in the March issue of *Science and Children*.)

Both of these annual lists are available from the Children's Book Council. Send for their current materials brochure, available for a first-class stamped, self-addressed, business-size envelope. CBC Order Center, 350 Scotland Road, Orange NJ 07050.

"Reference Book Roundup."

This list appears in the May issue of School Library Journal. *It includes children's books that were published in the previous calendar year and are recommended as worthy of inclusion in elementary and middle school library collections by the Reference Books Review Committee of* SLJ.

"Teacher's Choices."

This yearly list includes books recommended by teachers. It appears each November in The Reading Teacher, *along with an explanation of how they were chosen. It is another project of the International Reading Association. Single copies available for two-ounce postage on a 9" × 12" self-addressed envelope. The address is the same as for "Children's Choices."*

Bibliographies: Books and Indexes

Barstow, B., & Riggle, J. (1989). *Beyond picture books: A guide to first readers*. New York: R. R. Bowker.

This work annotates 1,610 recommended books, published between 1951 and 1989, intended for beginning readers of first- or second-grade children. They are indexed by subject, title, illustrator, readability, and series. Also included is a list of 200 titles that the authors consider outstanding.

Children's book review index. (1975–1991). Detroit: Gale Research.

This annual work indexes the reviews appearing in 200 periodicals. Although it contains no actual reviews, this work compiles those citations appearing in Book Review Index, *which locates reviews of books written for children and young adults. A five-volume master cumulation of book reviews that appeared from 1965 to 1984 is available. The entries are arranged by title under author, with separate indexes of titles and illustrators.*

Children's books in print. (Published annually). New York: R. R. Bowker.

This is an index of juvenile titles that are listed in publishers' catalogs as "in print," but it does not always include books from smaller publishing companies. Access is by title, author, or illustrator. Prices and ISBN (International Standard Book Number) numbers are given for library binding, trade, and/or paperback editions, thus indicating which are available. This work includes a separate listing of addresses of publishers.

The children's catalog (16th ed.). (1991). J. Yaakov (ed.). New York: H. W. Wilson.

Part 1 lists books and magazines recommended for preschool children through sixth-graders, as well as useful professional resources, in a classified catalog format arranged by Dewey Decimal System, fiction, story collections, and easy books. The descriptive entries often include quotes from book reviews. Part 2 helps the user locate entries through one alphabetical, comprehensive key that includes author, title, subject, and analytical listings. A new edition is published every five years with supplements being sent to subscribers annually. Wilson offers other similar print media catalogs, one for junior high and another for high school readers.

Dreyer, S. S. (1977, 1981, 1985, 1989). *The bookfinder: A guide to children's literature about the needs and problems of youth aged 2–15*. Circle Pines, MN: American Guidance Service.

Arranged so that users can locate books on a particular subject relating to children's needs and problems, Dreyer provides critical annotations for each of the suggested books. The third edition features a cumulative subject index of the first three volumes, covering books published through 1982. The fourth edition covers 731 additional books published from 1983 to 1986.

The elementary school library collection: A guide to books and other media (18th ed.). (1992). L. Lee (ed.). Williamsport, PA: Brodart.

In addition to books and periodicals, this work also recommends all kinds of nonprint media and resources for teachers and parents. A classified arrangement features entries in catalog card format that provide critically descriptive annotations as well as such information as priority for acquisition and estimates of reading level and interest level. The work is indexed by subject, title, author, and illustrator. A revised edition is issued biennially.

Gagnon, A., & Gagnon, A. (eds.). (1988). *Canadian books for young people: Livres Canadiens pour la jeunesse* (4th ed.). Toronto: University of Toronto Press.

This concise book includes brief annotations, with suggested reading levels, of the best Canadian books printed in English and French. The work includes reference works and magazines, and is indexed by title and author.

Gillespie, J. T., & Naden, C. J. (1990). *Best books for children: Preschool through grade 6* (4th ed.). New York: Bowker.

This comprehensive index consists of one-sentence annotations for more than 11,000 books, recommended by at least one reviewer, which were still in print in 1989. The user is directed to one of eight broad subject headings by an alphabetical list of major subjects. Author, illustrator, title, and subject/grade level indexes are included.

Horning, K. T. (ed.). (1991). *Alternative press publishers of children's books: A directory* (4th ed.). Madison, WI: Friends of the CCBC, Inc.

This directory lists names and addresses of small presses in the United States and Canada that publish one or more books for children and indicates the types of books published by each.

Lima, C. W., & Lima, J. A. (1989). *A to zoo: Subject access to children's picture books* (3rd ed.). New York: R. R. Bowker.

This index indicates the subject matter of 12,000 picture books for children with access through author, illustrator, and title, as well as 700 subjects. An introductory chapter provides information on the genesis of the English language picture book.

Adventuring with books: A booklist for pre-K–grade 6 (9th ed.). (1989). M. Jett-Simpson, (ed.). Urbana, IL: NCTE.

Books for you: A booklist for senior high students (10th ed.). (1988). R. F. Abrahamson & B. Carter (eds.). Urbana, IL: NCTE.

High interest-easy reading: A booklist for junior & senior high school students (6th ed.). (1990). W. G. McBride (ed.). Urbana, IL: NCTE.

Your reading: A booklist for junior high and middle school students (8th ed.). (1991). A. P. Nilsen (ed.). Urbana, IL: NCTE.

All of these books include annotated listings of fiction and nonfiction books recommended for children and young people in the grades specified in each title. The books are grouped by topics such as adventure, animals, friendship, mystery, fantasy and folkore, biography, and so on. Although all of these indexes are useful to teachers and other adults, too, the annotations in all except the first one are written for the student audience. These works are frequently updated by NCTE.

Pilla, M. L. (1990). *The best: High/low books for reluctant readers.* Englewood, CO: Libraries Unlimited.

This index contains brief annotations of 374 quality books that are of interest to reluctant readers. The work is indexed by title, subject, grade level, and reading level.

Richardson, S. K. (1991). *Magazines for children: A guide for parents, teachers, and librarians* (2nd ed.). Chicago, ALA.

Richardson provides detailed descriptive annotations of 112 magazines for children up to age 14, including evaluative comments that will help teachers and parents decide which ones to order.

Ryder, R. J., Graves, B. B., & Graves, M. F. (1989). *Easy reading: Book series and periodicals for less able readers* (2nd ed.). Newark, DE: IRA.

The authors provide evaluative information on 44 book series and 15 periodicals. An introductory chapter includes a useful overview, with references, on factors that influence the difficulty of reading materials.

Stoll, D. R. (ed.). (1990). *Magazines for children.* Newark, DE: IRA.

This brief work gives addresses and information about the purpose of 120 children's periodicals deemed worthwhile for children. Subject and age/grade indexes are included.

Subject guide to children's books in print. (Published annually). New York: R. R. Bowker.

This comprehensive reference provides a subject approach to children's books in print. Headings are based on the Sears list of subject headings with additional entries from the Library of Congress. A directory of publishers and distributors is included.

Sutherland, Z., Hearne, B., & Sutton, R. (1991). *The best in children's books: The University of Chicago guide to children's literature 1985–1990.* See also earlier volumes edited by Zena Sutherland (1973, 1980, 1986) covering, respectively, books published between 1966 to 1972, 1973 to 1978, 1979 to 1984. Chicago: University of Chicago Press.

Compiled from reviews of books originally designated as "recommended" in the Bulletin of the Center for Children's Books, *each volume annotates the best books published during the inclusive years. Annotations are arranged alphabetically by author's name with indication of probable grade level use. The books are indexed by title, developmental values, curricular use and subject matter, as well as reading level.*

Bibliographies: Special Topics

Adamson, L. G. (1987). *A reference guide to historical fiction for children and young adults.* New York: Greenwood Press.

This reference work provides plot summaries of historical fiction written by 80 award-winning authors since 1940. An appendix of setting dates and locales will aid in the selection of historical fiction appropriate for the study of a particular period in history. Another appendix will assist those searching for historical fiction appropriate for the study of a particular period in history. A third appendix lists the titles of the included works by reading level and gives the interest level of each.

Baskin, B. H., and Harris, K. H. (1977). *Notes from a different drummer: A guide to juvenile fiction portraying the handicapped.* New York: R. R. Bowker.

Baskin, B. H., & Harris, K. H. (1984). *More notes from a different drummer: A guide to juvenile fiction portraying the disabled.* New York: R. R. Bowker.

The earlier work includes plot descriptions and analyses of works of fiction published between 1940 and 1975 that portrays handicapped people. The later edition describes 348 books published between 1976 and 1981 dealing with disabled people. Each book includes information about the patterns and trends of dealing with the disabled in our society which may be reflected in the books written at a particular time.

Bernstein, J. E., & Rudman, M. K. (1989). *Books to help children cope with separation and loss* (3rd ed.). New York: R. R. Bowker.

This reference work summarizes, evaluates, and indicates reading and interest levels for 606 fiction and nonfiction loss titles published between 1983 and 1988. Introductory information discusses the use of books to help children deal with issues of loss. Titles are grouped by topics ranging from temporary situations, such as sibling interaction, moving, growing up, leaving home, and old age, to more tragic losses, including death, suicide, divorce, kidnapping, desertion,

*serious illness, abuse, and war and displace-
ment. The second edition, from 1983, remains
useful because it covers earlier titles in a similar fashion.*

The black experience in children's books. (1989).
New York: The New York Public Library.

*This periodically revised pamphlet briefly anno-
tates folklore, fiction, and nonfiction, written for
children from preschool to age 12, that portrays
black life. The titles are arranged geographical-
ly, with the majority of them being in the section
on the United States. The book is well indexed,
with an appendix listing which included authors are black.*

Friedberg, J. B., Mullins, J. B., & Sukiennik, A. W.
(1985). *Accept me as I am: Best books of juvenile nonfiction on impairments and disabilities.*
New York: R. R. Bowker.

*This useful book contains lengthy, perceptive
annotations of 350 works of nonfiction, many
of which are based on real-life stories of how
people have coped with physical challenges and
serious illness. The interest level and reading
difficulty for each work are given.*

Jenkins, E. C., & Austin, M. C. (1987). *Literature for
children about Asians and Asian Americans:
Analysis and annotated bibliography, with additional readings for adults.* New York: Greenwood Press.

*The annotations are arranged by country and
then by genre; introductory historical information is provided about each country. The copy is
computer generated.*

Kobrin, B. (1988). *Eyeopeners! How to choose and
use children's books about real people, places,
and things.* New York: Penguin Books.

*Kobrin shares her enthusiasm for 500 interest-
ing informational books that she has annotated
and organized for access through what she calls
her "Quick-Link Index." For information about
a subscription to Kobrin's newsletter, which provides information on current nonfiction books,
write to* The Kobrin Letter, *732 Greer Road, Palo
Alto, CA 94304.*

Kruse, G. M., & Horning, K. T. (1991). *Multicultural literature for children and young adults: A
selected listing of books 1980–1990 by and
about people of color* (3rd ed.). Madison, WI:
Wisconsin Department of Public Instruction.

*This reference annotates recently published
multicultural books recommended for their high
quality by the Children's Cooperative Book Center. The work includes information about the
selection process, a list by racial/national background of some authors and illustrators whose
works are included, a list of titles divided into
the ethnic/cultural groups depicted in those
books, and a brief bibliography of recommended adult resources.*

Miller-Lachman, L. (1991). *Our family, our friends,
our world: An annotated guide to significant
multicultural books for children and teenagers.*
New Providence, NJ: R. R. Bowker.

*This reference work provides critical evaluations
of approximately 1,000 fiction and nonfiction
books, published between 1970 and 1990, with
a multicultural and/or international focus. The
introduction provides an overview of the history of publishing books about minorities and explains the evaluation criteria used. When flawed
books are included, strengths and weaknesses
have been explained with the hope of helping
students and teachers become sensitive to the
issues raised. Presentation is by grade level within each chapter. A subject specialist has written
the background information about each particular minority group as well as the annotations
of the books about that group.*

Schon, I. (1978–1989). *Books in Spanish for children
and young adults: An annotated guide* (Series
I–V). Metuchen, NJ: Scarecrow Press.

*Each volume covers a three-year period. These
are selection guides for books in Spanish written by Hispanic authors for children, preschool
through high school. The list is comprehensive
and includes some negative reviews because not
all of the included books are recommended. The
entries are arranged by country and topic; most
of them originate in Latin America or Spain.*

Slapin, B., & Seale, D. (1991). *Through Indian eyes: The native experience in books for children* (Vol. 3). Philadelphia: New Society Publishers.

This is a reprint of volume 2 with some additions. The entries provide detailed, critical content analysis, from an American Indian perspective, of children's books dealing with Indian themes. Also included are essays by Indian writers and educators, and bibliographies of recommended books.

Stensland, A. L. (1979). *Literature by and about the American Indian: An annotated bibliography* (2nd ed.). Urbana, IL: NCTE.

The introductory material includes suggestions for avoiding stereotypes when teaching about Native Americans. Capsule biographies of 54 selected American Indian authors are included. The main body of the work consists of critical reviews, often based on a Native American viewpoint, of 800 books for children and young adults, many of which are familiar titles and still available.

Verrall, C., & McDowell, P. (1990). *Resource reading list 1990: Annotated bibliography of resources by and about native people.* Toronto, Ontario: Canadian Alliance in Solidarity with the Native Peoples.

This annotated bibliography of nonprint media and books for children and teenagers indicates the degree to which Native Peoples were involved in the creation of each listed item.

Review Journals

Appraisal: Science Books for Young People. Published quarterly by the Children's Science Book Review Committee, a nonprofit organization sponsored by the Science Education Department of Boston University School of Education and the New England Roundtable of Children's Librarians. Diane Holzheimer, Editor, 605 Commonwealth Avenue, Boston MA 02215.

This journal presents lengthy, thorough, critical reviews, one written by a children's librarian and one by a subject specialist for each science book considered. The reviews are arranged al-phabetically by author's name; ratings are given. A separate section contains reviews of books issued as part of a series.

Booklist. Published twice monthly September through June and monthly in July and August by American Library Association, 50 E. Huron St., Chicago, IL 60611.

Booklist *reviews current print and nonprint materials for children and adults that are worthy of consideration for purchase by small and medium-sized public libraries and school media centers. Inclusion in* Booklist *is a recommendation for library purchase. Reviews of children's books are presented by age and grade levels. Subject lists of good books in particular fields are often presented. Audiovisual media and reference books are reviewed in separate sections.*

The Bulletin of the Center for Children's Books. Published monthly except August by the University of Illinois Press, 54 E. Gregory Dr., Champaign, IL 61820.

This publication reviews current children's books, with adverse as well as favorable reviews, assigning a recommendation code to each. An age or grade level is given to each book, and annotations include information on curricular use, developmental values, and literary merit. Reviews are arranged alphabetically by the author's last name. An annual index by title, author, and illustrator is included in the July/August issue.

Children's Book News. Quarterly newsletter published by the Canadian Children's Book Center, 35 Spadina Road, Toronto, Ontario M5R 2S9.

This newsletter features articles and reviews; it lists all children's books published in Canada. Subscribers also recieve Our Choice: Your Annual Guide to Canada's Best Children's Books, *which contains brief reviews of the 300 best Canadian children's books of the year.*

The Horn Book Guide to Children's and Young Adult Books. Published twice a year in March and September by the Horn Book, Inc., 14 Beacon Street, Boston, MA 02108.

First published in 1990, The Horn Book Guide contains brief reviews of all hardcover children's trade books published in the United States during the previous six months. Fiction is organized by age, and nonfiction by Dewey Decimal System. Within each category, the reviews are arranged by ratings and then by the author's name. If a book was reviewed in The Horn Book, *information is provided so that the complete review may be consulted. Author, illustrator, and subject indexes are also included.*

The Horn Book Magazine. Published six times a year by the Horn Book, Inc., 14 Beacon Street, Boston, MA 02108.

The Horn Book *includes detailed reviews of children's books deemed the best in children's literature by the editorial staff. It provides information about reissues, paperbacks, and books in Spanish. It also contains articles about literature and interviews with authors. The Newbery and Caldecott acceptance speeches are featured in the July/August issue. An annual index appears in the November/December issue.*

School Library Journal: The Magazine of Children's, Young Adult, and School Librarians. A Cahners/R. R. Bowker Publication, published monthly. For subscription information, write to *School Library Journal,* P.O. Box 1978, Marion, OH 43305-1978.

This journal prints reviews, written by practicing librarians, of most children's books published. It includes both negative and positive reviews. It also includes news from the field and articles of interest to school librarians. An index appears each December; that issue also features a "Best Books" section. A twice yearly free supplement called Star Track: For Teachers and Other Adults Who Support Good Reading *compiles reviews of books considered outstanding in relation to others on the same subject or in the same genre. To be added to the mailing list for this supplement, write Attention: Circulation Department, 249 W. 17th St., New York, NY.*

Index

ABC books (*see* Alphabet books)
Abstract art style, 30
Academic value, 4–7
Accuracy of information, 155, 158
Adamson, L. G., 137–138, 145
Adoff, A., 171
Adventure, books about, 128–129
Aesthetic reading, 7
African-American literature, 178–179
Age levels, books for, 15–18
  ages 0 to 2, 15–16
  ages 2 to 4, 16
  ages 4 to 7, 16–17
  ages 7 to 9, 17
  ages 9 to 12, 17–18
Alexander, L., 257
Aliki, 257
"All the Colors of the Race" (Arnold Adoff), 171
Alliteration, definition of, 39
Alphabet books (ABC books), 16, 62, 63
Alternative families, stories about, 127–128
Amelia Frances Howard-Gibbon Award, 57
American Library Association, 187, 221
Anderson, R. C., 4, 5, 18, 19, 208, 231
Animal fantasy, 109–110
Animal stories (*see* Realistic animal stories)
Animated videos, definition of, 244
Applebee, A. N., 5, 18
Applied sciences (nonfiction), 160–161
Art appreciation, 6–7
Artistic media, 30–31
Artistic styles, 29–30
Asian-American literature, 179–180
Assisted reading, 241
Association of Jewish Libraries Awards, 180
Assonance, definition of, 39
Audiotapes, 162, 244
Authentic biographies, 161–162
Author, literature curriculum, 212
Autobiographies, 161
Award lists as source for selection, 9–11

Baby books, 15–16, 60
Backdrop setting, definition of, 25
Ballads, 45–46, 93
Barstow, B., 17, 18

Basal reading program, 207–209
Beast tales, 95
Beatty, P., 231
Behn, H., 46
Bibliographic sources, 10–11
Bibliotherapy, definition of, 123
Biennale of Illustrations Bratislava
  (BIB), 187
Big books, 255–256
Binding of book, 33
Biographies, 158, 161–163
Biography series, 162–163
Biological sciences (nonfiction), 160
Bjork, C., 257, 258
Board books, 60
  definition of, 16
Bodart, J., 239, 258
"Book, A," (Hannah More), 20
Book format, 31–33
Book reports, traditional, 253
Book selection, 7–9, 12, 21, 33–34, 218
Book titles, sources for, 9–11
Bookfairs, 225
Booktalks, 239–240
"Broken-Legg'd Man, The" (John Mackey
  Shaw), 44
Bromley, K. D., 221, 231
Browning, E., 232
"Buffalo Dusk" (Carl Sandburg), 137
Bulletin boards, 257
Butler, D., 5, 18
Butterfield, D., 5, 19

Caldecott Award, 57
Carlsen, G. R., 5, 19
Cartoons as art style, 30
Carus, M., 183, 186, 189
Censorship, 223–224
Chapbooks, 91
Chapter books, 17, 64, 153
  reading aloud, 235–237
Character development, definition of, 24
Character foil, definition of, 24
Characterization, definition of, 24
Characters in fiction, 23–25
Charles, D., 47

Charts, 257
Checklist for classroom environment, 229–230
Checklist for student involvement with literature, 227–228
Checklist for teaching activities, 230–231
Child development, 14–15
Children from other lands, stories about, 125
Children's backgrounds, 8, 12–14
Children's Book Council (CBC), 9
Children's Books in Print, 14
Children's Catalog, 14
Children's literature:
   definition of, 1
   genres, 34–35
Choral poetry, 243–244
Chronological plots, 21
Ciardi, J., 258
Cinquains, 44
Classroom library collection, 216–217
Classroom newspapers and newsletters, 256
Classroom reading environment, 213–216, 229–230
Cloth books, 60
Cohen, D., 5, 19
Collages, 254
Collected biography, 162
Color as a visual element, 28
Comenius, J. A., 57
Complete biography, 162
Composition as a visual element, 29
Computer games, 113
Concept books, 62–63
   definition of, 16
"Concrete Cat" (Dorthi Charles), 47
Concrete poetry, 47
Conferences between teacher and student, 246
Conflict within plot, 21
Consonance, definition of, 39
Contemporary realism, definition of, 121
Content area subjects, 6
Content of children's books, 2
Cooley, W. W., 5, 19
Coretta Scott King Award, 175
Cosgrove, M. S., 5, 19
Council on Interracial Books for Children, 176
Counting books, 16, 62, 63
Couplets, 44
Cover of book, 31
Creation stories, 93
Creative drama, 248–249

Cullinan, B., 5, 19
Culturally conscious books, 129, 174
Cumulative folktales, 94
Curiosity, nourishing, 152
Curriculum:
   developing, 213–231
   models in literacy, 205–210
   organization of, 211–213
   year–long, 217–220
Cycle format, definition of, 104

Damjan, M., 189
Davidson, J. L., 4, 19
de la Mare, W., 87
Diagrams, 257
Dialogue in historical fiction, 139
Dickinson, E., 36
Difficulty level (*see* Reading level)
Dioramas, 255
Discipline-based literature instruction, 211
Displays, 257
Divergent questions, 246–247
Doublespread, definition of, 32
Drawing pictures, 254
Dreyer, S. S., 19
Duggins, J., 5, 19
Durkin, D., 5, 19, 207, 231
Dust jacket, definition of, 31

Easy-to-read books, 17, 22, 64
Eaton, A. T., 157, 163
Edgar Allan Poe Award for Juvenile Mystery Novels, 124
Efferent reading, 7
Eldredge, J. L., 5, 19
Elleman, B., 104, 113, 130, 163
Emotional realism, definition of, 121
Endpapers, definition of, 31
Engineered books, 61
Epics, 93
Episodic plots, 22
Esbensen, B. J., 47, 258
Evaluating literature program, 227–231
Experiment books, 161
Expressionistic art style, 30
Extended families, stories about, 127

Fables, 95
Fact books, 153

Faction, definition of, 152
Factual realism, definition of, 121
Fader, D., 5, 19
Fairy tales, 94
Familiarity with books, 8 (*see also* Sources for
    book titles)
Family situations and realistic fiction,
    127–128
Fantasy (*see* Modern fantasy)
Fantasy story, definition of, 103 (*see also* Modern
    fantasy)
Farnan, N., 208, 231
Fears, books about, 128
Fiction, elements of, 21–27 (*see also* Historical
    fiction; Realistic fiction)
    characters, 23–25
    plot, 21–23
    setting, 25
    style, 26–27
    theme, 25–26
Fictionalized biography, 162
Field, R., 39
Fielding, L. G., 5, 19
Figurative language in poetry, 39–40
Finn, T., 5, 19
First-person narrator, 27
Flashback, 22–23
Flat character, definition of, 24
Fleischman, P., 250
Flood, J., 208, 231
Flyleaf, definition of, 31
Focus books, 218
Folk art style, 30
Folk song books, 61
Folktales, 16, 17, 25, 92, 94–95 (*see also* Modern
    folktales; Traditional literature)
Followup questions, 248
Foreign countries, books about, 129
Foreshadowing, 23
Format (*see* Book format)
Formula fiction, 130
Fox, C., 213, 231
Fox, P., 258
Framing a picture, 32
Free verse, 47
Free-choice writing, 13
Freedman, R., 158, 163
Freeman, Y., 6, 19
Friendships, books about, 128

Frontispiece, definition of, 31

Genres:
    of children's literature, 34–35
    literature curriculum, 212–213
Giblin, J. C., 158, 163
Goals, definition of, 217
Golden Age of Poetry for Children, 43
Golden Age poets, 41, 42
Goodman, K. S., 6, 19
Graphic arts response to literature, 253–257
Greenfeld, H., 258
Growing-up stories, 121, 128
Growth/maturity and realistic fiction, 128–129
Guest authors/illustrators, 226–227

Haiku, 46
Hans Christian Andersen Award, 183, 186
Haugen, T., 189
Haynes, C., 11, 19
Heterogeneous reading groups, 209
Hiebert, E. H., 4, 18, 208, 231
High fantasy (quest stories), 112
Hillegas, F., 19
Hispanic-American literature, 180
Historical fantasy, 111–112, 138
Historical fiction, 18, 25, 137–150
    definition and description, 137–138
    early books and trends, 140–141
    evaluation and selection, 139–140
    topics in, 137–145
    values of, 138–139
Holdaway, D., 241, 258
Hopkins, L. B., 258
Hoskisson, K., 241, 258
How-to books, 161
Hughes, L., 43
Humanities (nonfiction), 161
Humorous folktales, 94
Humorous stories, 130
Hyperbole, definition of, 40

Iconographic videos, definition of, 244
Illustrated dictionary, 16
Illustrations, 6, 27–29 (*see also* Picture books)
Illustrator, literature curriculum, 212
Impressionistic art style, 30
Infants and books, 15–16
Informational books (nonfiction), 17, 152, 153

Integral setting, definition of, 25
Integrated day curriculum model, 209–210
Interactive books, 60–61
    definition of, 16
Interactive classroom, 214, 215, 216
Interest inventories, 13–14
International Board on Books for Young People
    (IBBY), 183, 186
International literature, 34, 171, 181–189, 198–204
    definition and description, 181–182
    evaluation and selection, 182–184
    historical overview, 185–188
    values of, 182
    world regions, 188–189
International Reading Association (IRA), 183
International Youth Library (IYL), 186
Interpretation of literature, 7
Isaacson, R., 19

Jaggar, A., 5, 19
Jansen, M., 152, 163
Jewish-American literature, 180
Jingle, definition of, 37
Journal writing, 13
Judging literature, 21

Kate Greenaway Award, 57
Koch, K. 258
Kuskin, K., 103

Lapp, D., 208, 231
Larrick, N., 176, 189
Lawson, R., 258
Lear, E., 45
Legends, 93–94
Leinhardt, G., 5, 19
Lepman, J., 186, 189
Level of difficulty (*see* Reading level)
Library media center, 224–225
Lima, C. W., 19
Lima, J. A., 19
Limericks, 44–45
Limited omniscient point of view, definition of, 27
Line as a visual element, 28
"Listen!" (Walter de la Mare), 87
"Listening to grownups quarreling," (Ruth Whit-
    man), 120
Literacy (*see* Curriculum, models in literacy)
Literary canon, 220
Literary element, curriculum, 213

Literary folktales, 109
Literature across the curriculum, 210
    definition of, 6
Literature curriculum committees, 223
Literature journals, 252
Literature response groups, 245
Literature, traditional (*see* Traditional literature)
Literature-based reading, 206–207
Little people, worlds of, 111
"Long Trip" (Langston Hughes), 43
Lynch-Brown, C., 235, 258
Lyric poetry, definition of, 43

Magic tales, 94, 95
Making books, 255–256
Male and female characters, balancing, 33
Maps, 256–257
Marshall, M. R., 113, 121, 130
Martin, R., 156, 163
McCaslin, N., 248–249, 250–251, 258
McCord, D., 38–39, 258
McNeil, E., 5, 19
Meaning of poetry, 38
Mechanical books, 61
Meigs, C., 157, 163
Melting pot books, 174
Mental development of child, 15
Metaphor, definition of, 39
Mildred L. Batchelder Award, 183, 187
Minor characters, 24
Minorities (*see also* Multicultural literature):
    authors, 141, 174
    characters, 33–34
    groups, stories about, 125
Models for stories and poems, 252–253
Modern fantasy, 103–119
    definition and description, 103–104
    evaluation and selection, 105
    historical overview, 105–108
    types of, 108–113
    values of, 104–105
Modern folktales, 96, 109
More, Hannah, 20
Moss, J. F., 223, 231
Mother Goose books, 61
Multicultural literature, 33–34, 129, 171–181,
    189–198
    definition and description, 172
    evaluation and selection, 173–175
    historical overview, 175–178

types of, 178–181
values of, 172–173
Murals, 254
Murphy, S., 6, 19
"My Book Holds Many Stories" (Annette
    Wynne), 1
Mysteries, 129–130
Mystery fantasy, 111
Mystery Writers of America, 124
Myths, 93

Naming books, 63
Narrative poetry, definition of, 43, 44
National Council of Social Studies, 140
National Council of Teachers of English (NCTE), 6,
    19, 43, 183
National Council of Teachers of English (NCTE)
    Award, 41, 157, 158
National Jewish Book Awards, 180
Native-American literature, 181
Nesbitt, E., 157, 163
New realism books, 127
Nonfiction, 151–170
    definition and description, 152–153
    evaluation and selection, 154–157
    historical overview, 157–159
    types of, 159–163
    values of, 153–154
Nonfiction chapter books, 153
Notable Children's Trade Books in the Field of So-
    cial Studies, 10
Novels, 17–18
Nuclear families, stories about, 127
Nursery books, 61
Nursery rhyme books, 16, 61

Objectives, definition of, 217, 221
Ohio State University Reading Center, 221
Onomatopoeia, definition of, 39
Oral response to literature, 245–251
Orbis Pictus Award for Outstanding Nonfiction for
    Children, 157, 158–159
Organization of book, 26
"Outlandish Knight, The," 45–46
Outstanding Science Trade Books for Children, 9

Page layout, 32
Pages of book, 32–33
Paired reading, 241–242
Parables, 96

Parent involvement, 225–226
Partial biography, 162
Peer stories, 18, 128
Penny-dreadfuls, 3
Personal value, 3–4
Personification, definition of, 39–40, 155
Personified toys and objects, 110
Phonics instruction, 209
Photo essays, 158
Physical development of child, 14
Physical sciences, 160
Piaget, Jean, 15
Picture books, 54–86, 153
    definition and description, 54–55
    evaluation and selection, 56–57
    historical overview, 57–58, 59–60
    for older readers, 64
    reading aloud, 234–235
    types of, 58, 60–65
    values of, 55
"Picture Books" (Tom Robinson), 54
Picture storybooks, 63
    definition of, 16
Plot in fiction, 21–23
Poetic form, definition of, 44
Poetry, 36–53 (*see also* Choral poetry)
    definition and description, 36–37
    elements of, 38–40
    evaluation and selection, 41
    historical overview, 41–43
    preferences of children, 38
    reading aloud, 237
    types and forms, 43–47
    values of, 40
Point of view as author's style, 27
Pourquoi tales, 95
Preaching at readers, 25–26
Preferences of students, 234
Primitive art style, 30
Print styles of book, 32
Problem novel, definition of, 121–122
Progressive plots, 22
Promoting good books (*see* Book selection)
Prophetic fiction, 112
Prose and poetry, 37
Protagonist (as character), definition of, 24
Publishing history of book, 31–32
Purdy, S., 258

Quality of children's books, 2–3

Quatrains, 44
Quest stories, 112
"Question, The" (Karla Kuskin), 103
Questioning techniques, 246–248
"Questions at Night" (Louis Untermeyer), 151

Raskin, E., 258
Read-aloud programs, 18
Readers' theatre, 249–251
Reading ability, 4, 6
Reading aloud by teachers, 4, 9, 233–237
   book selection, 233–234
   effectiveness, 234–237
   preparing students, 234
Reading centers, 215–216
Reading interests, 12–14
Reading level, 8–9
Reading preferences, 11–12
"Reading" (Elizabeth Browning), 232
"Reading Rainbow," 239
Realism in literature (*see* Realistic fiction)
Realistic animal stories, 18, 125, 130
Realistic art style, 29
Realistic family stories, 124–125, 127–128
Realistic fiction, 120–136
   definition and description, 121–122
   evaluation and selection, 123–124
   historical overview, 124–127
   types of, 127–130
   values of, 122–123
Realistic tales, 95
Regional stories, 125
Religious stories, 95–96
Rereading same book, 17, 18, 20
Research in children's literature, 11
Responding to literature, 244–257
   graphic arts, 253–257
   oral, 245–251
   written, 251–253
Retold tale, definition of, 92–93
Rhyme and poetry, 37, 39
Rhythm of poetry, 38
Riechman, H. F., 231
Riggle, J., 17, 18
Rite-of-passage stories, 121, 128
Robinson, T., 54
Roller movies, 254–255
Rosenblatt, L., 7, 19, 20, 35, 245, 258

Round character, definition of, 24
Rudman, M., 175, 189

Sandburg, C., 137
Satire, 105–106
Sauer, M., 213, 231
Scheduling units and activities, 220
School bookstores, 225
Schoolwide curriculum in literature, 223–227
Science concept picture book, 153
Science fantasy, 112, 113
Science fiction, 18, 107, 112–113
Scieszka, J., 258
Scott O'Dell Award, 140, 141
Scott, J. A., 4, 18, 208, 231
Scripts for readers' theatre, 250
Secondary characters, 24
Selection of books (*see* Award lists as source for selection; Book selection)
Sense imagery in poetry, 40
Series romances, 130
Series stories, 130
Setting in fiction, 25
Sexuality and realistic fiction, 128
Shannon, P., 6, 19
Shape as a visual element, 28–29
Shared reading, 240–242
Shared–book experience, 240–241
Shaw, J. M., 44
Sherman, T. M., 241, 258
Sherrill, A., 5, 19
Shifting point of view, 27
Silent reading by students, 4, 9, 238–239
Simile, definition of, 39
Sims, R., 174, 189
Situational realism, definition of, 121
Size of book, 33
Smith, L. L., 241, 258
Social conscience books, 174
Social realism, definition of, 121
Social science concept picture book, 153
Social sciences (nonfiction), 160
Societal issues, focus on, 121–122, 123, 127
"Song of the Train" (David McCord), 38–39
Sound patterns in poetry, 39
Sources for book titles, 9–11
Spoken language, 206
Sports stories, 129–130
Sputnik, 157

Steig, W., 258
Stereotyping, 156, 173
Storytelling, 242–243, 251
Strange situations, 110–111
Strickland, D., 5, 19
Student-centered environment, 214
Studies on literature and reading, 5
Style of writing in fiction, 26–27
Styles of authors and illustrators, 3–4
Subject Guide to Children's Books in Print, 14, 19
Subject matter (*see* Content of children's books)
"Summer Morning, A" (Rachel Field), 39
Supernatural events, 111
Surrealistic art style, 30
Survival stories, 18, 128–129
Sustained silent reading (SSR) programs, 238
Sutherland, Z., 19
Symbolism, 27

Tall tales, 93–94
Teacher–centered classroom, 214
Teaching strategies, 232–257
    audiotapes, 244
    booktalks, 239–240
    choral poetry, 243–244
    reading aloud by teacher, 233–237
    shared reading, 240–242
    silent reading by students, 238–239
    storytelling, 242–243
    videotapes, 244
Teleology, definition of, 155
Tercets, 44
Textbook, definition of, 2
Texture as a visual element, 29
Thematic learning curriculum model, 209, 210
Theme or topic:
    in fiction, 25–26
    literature curriculum, 211–212
Time lines, 256
Time-warp fantasy, 111–112
Title of book, 31
Title page of book, 31
Toddlers and books, 16
Tomlinson, C. T., 235, 258
Toy books, 61
Trade book, definition of, 2
Traditional literature, 87–102
    definition and description, 87–88
    evaluation and selection, 90

historical overview, 91–92
types of, 92–96
values of, 88–89
Transactional view of reading (L. Rosenblatt), 7
Transitional books, 64–65
Transitional readers, definition of, 17
Translated books, 188
Truth in themes, 25
Tway, E., 19
Typeface, definition of, 32

Unit evaluation, 221, 223
Units of study, 218, 220–223
Untermeyer, L., 151, 163
Unusual characters, 110–111

Variant, definition of, 93
Verse, definition of, 37
Vicarious experiences, 3, 172
Videotapes, 162, 244
Viguers, R. H., 157, 163
Vinyl books, 60
Visual elements, 27–29

Waiting after questioning, 248
Watson, D., 19
Weaver, C., 19
Webbing, 220–221, 222
Weiss, H., 258
What Works: Research about Teaching and Learning, 6, 19
Whitman, R., 120
Whole language approach to literacy, 206
Wilkinson, I. A., 4, 18, 208, 231
Wilson, P. T., 5, 19
Winkel, L., 19
"Word, A" (Emily Dickinson), 36
Word books, 16
Wordless books, 63
Wrightson, P., 258
Writing ability, 6
Writing folders, 13
Written response to literature, 251–253
Wynne, Annette, 1

Yaakov, J., 19

Zigmond, N., 5, 19

This page constitutes a continuation of the copyright page.